D0989613

The Pillar New Testament Commentary

General Editor
D. A. CARSON

The Letter
to the
EPHESIANS

PETER T. O'BRIEN

WILLIAM B. EERDMANS PUBLISHING COMPANY
GRAND RAPIDS, MICHIGAN / CAMBRIDGE, U.K.

APOLLOS
LEICESTER, ENGLAND

First published 1999
in the United States of America by
Wm. B. Eerdmans Publishing Co.
2140 Oak Industrial Drive N.E., Grand Rapids, Michigan 49505
www.eerdmans.com
and in the U.K. by
APOLLOS
38 De Montfort Street, Leicester, England LE1 7GP

Printed in the United States of America

12 11 10 09 08 07   11 10 9 8 7 6 5

Library of Congress Cataloging-in-Publication Data

O'Brien, Peter Thomas.
The letter to the Ephesians / Peter T. O'Brien.
p.   cm.   — (The Pillar New Testament Commentary)
Includes bibliographical references and indexes.
ISBN 978-0-8028-3736-3 (cloth: alk. paper)
1. Bible. N.T. Ephesians Commentaries.
I. Title.   II. Series.
BS2695.3.O75   1999
227'.5077 — dc21   99-27734
CIP

British Library Cataloguing in Publication Data

A catalogue record for this book is available from the British Library.

Contents

Series Preface   viii
Author's Preface   x
Chief Abbreviations   xii
Select Bibliography   xv

INTRODUCTION   1

I. AUTHORSHIP   4
  A. The Impersonal Character of Ephesians   5
  B. Language and Style   5
  C. The Literary Relationship between Ephesians
     and Colossians   8
  D. The Theological Emphases of Ephesians   21
  E. The Picture of Paul   33
  F. Authorship and Pseudonymity   37
  G. Conclusions   45
II. DESTINATION OF THE LETTER   47
III. LIFE-SETTING, PURPOSE, AND PROVENANCE   49
  A. The Life-Setting of Ephesians   49
  B. The Purpose of the Letter   51
  C. The Provenance of Ephesians   57
IV. THE CENTRAL MESSAGE   58
V. CONTENTS AND GENRE   66
  A. Contents   66
  B. Genre   68

COMMENTARY ON EPHESIANS   83

I. PRESCRIPT, 1:1-2   83

II. THE NEW HUMANITY A DIVINE CREATION, 1:3–3:21   88

  A. Introductory Eulogy: Praise for God's Blessings
in Christ, 1:3-14   88

    1. Praise to God for Every Spiritual Blessing, 1:3   93

    2. Praise for Election and Adoption, 1:4-6   98

    3. Praise for Redemption and the Forgiveness of Sins, 1:7-8   105

    *4. Praise for the Mystery — God's Plan to Sum Up
All Things in Christ, 1:9-10*   108

    5. Praise for the Assurance of the Believers' Heritage, 1:11-14   115

  B. Thanksgiving, Intercession, and Praise to God for
Exalting Christ, 1:15-23   123

    1. Thanksgiving for the Readers' Faith and Love, 1:15-16a   127

    2. Intercession for Their Growth in Knowledge, 1:16b-19   128

    *3. God's Mighty Strength Shown in Raising and Exalting
Christ, 1:20-23*   138

  C. Saved by Grace: Raised and Exalted with Christ, 2:1-10   153

    1. Dead in Transgressions and Sins, 2:1-3   155

    *2. Because of His Mercy and Love God Made Us Alive
with Christ, 2:4-7*   164

    3. God's New Creation, 2:8-10   173

  D. The Inclusion of Gentiles in the One Body, 2:11-22   182

    1. The Gentiles' Former Plight and Now, 2:11-13   185

    *2. Through Christ We Have Access to the Father by
One Spirit, 2:14-18*   191

    3. The Gentiles' Membership of God's House, 2:19-22   210

  E. The Divine Mystery and Paul's Stewardship, 3:1-13   223

    1. Paul's Intercessory Prayer Begins, 3:1   225

    2. Paul's Stewardship of the Mystery, 3:2-7   226

    3. Making Known the Mystery in God's Purposes, 3:8-13   240

  F. Paul's Intercession for Power, Love, and Spiritual
Maturity, 3:14-21   252

    1. Prayer for Power, Love, and Maturity, 3:14-19   254

    *2. Doxology to God Who Can Do More Than All We
Ask or Imagine, 3:20-21*   266

III. THE NEW HUMANITY IN EARTHLY LIFE, 4:1–6:20 — 271

  A. Unity, Diversity, and Maturity within the Body
of Christ, 4:1-16 — 271

    1. The Unity of the Church as an Urgent Concern, 4:1-6 — 273

    2. Diversity in Unity That Leads to Maturity, 4:7-16 — 286

  B. Live according to the New Humanity, Not the Old,
4:17-24 — 317

  C. Specific Exhortations about the Old Life and the
New, 4:25–5:2 — 334

  D. From Darkness to Light, 5:3-14 — 357

    1. Abstain from Immorality and Greed, 5:3-7 — 358

    2. Once Darkness, But Now Light, 5:8-14 — 366

  E. Be Careful How You Live: Generally and within the
Christian Household, 5:15–6:9 — 378

    1. Be Careful, Then, How You Live, 5:15-21 — 379

    2. Relationships within the Christian Household, 5:22–6:9 — 405

      a. Wives and Husbands: Christ and the Church, 5:22-33 — 409

      b. Children and Parents, 6:1-4 — 439

      c. Slaves and Masters, 6:5-9 — 447

  F. Spiritual Warfare, 6:10-20 — 456

    1. Be Strong in the Lord, 6:10-13 — 460

    2. Stand Firm and Put On God's Armour, 6:14-17 — 472

    3. Watch and Pray, 6:18-20 — 483

IV. LETTER CLOSING, 6:21-24 — 490

INDEXES — **497**

  I. SUBJECTS — 497

  II. AUTHORS — 501

  III. SCRIPTURE REFERENCES — 508

  IV. EXTRABIBLICAL LITERATURE — 533

Series Preface

Commentaries have specific aims, and this series is no exception. Designed for serious pastors and teachers of the Bible, the Pillar commentaries seek above all to make clear the text of Scripture as we have it. The scholars writing these volumes interact with the most important informed contemporary debate, but avoid getting mired in undue technical detail. Their ideal is a blend of rigorous exegesis and exposition, with an eye alert both to biblical theology and the contemporary relevance of the Bible, without confusing the commentary and the sermon.

The rationale for this approach is that the vision of "objective scholarship" (a vain chimera) may actually be profane. God stands over against us; we do not stand in judgment of him. When God speaks to us through his Word, those who profess to know him must respond in an appropriate way, and that is certainly different from a stance in which the scholar projects an image of autonomous distance. Yet this is no surreptitious appeal for uncontrolled subjectivity. The writers of this series aim for an evenhanded openness to the text that is the best kind of "objectivity" of all.

If the text is God's Word, it is appropriate that we respond with reverence, a certain fear, a holy joy, a questing obedience. These values should be reflected in the way Christians write. With these values in place, the Pillar commentaries will be warmly welcomed not only by pastors, teachers, and students, but by general readers as well.

*   *   *   *   *

I am especially grateful for this commentary on Ephesians. Having already written major and exemplary commentaries on Philippians and

Colossians, Peter O'Brien is wonderfully equipped to write the present work. Widely respected for his careful and probing exegesis, Dr. O'Brien writes out of many years of experience as a missionary, preacher, college lecturer, vice-principal, and scholar. His wide reading and firm, thoughtful interaction with those with whom he disagrees make this volume useful to scholars as well as to pastors. But above all, his handling of the text of Scripture is fresh and penetrating, edifying as well as informing, profoundly centered on the gospel even while it wrestles engagingly with details. It is a privilege to recommend this commentary.

D. A. CARSON

Author's Preface

Ephesians was the first document of the New Testament I read as a teenager when I became a Christian and joined a study group in our church. I did not understand much about the letter at the time, but I remember being moved by some of the exhortations in the closing chapters. Since then Ephesians has fascinated me, though I have struggled with its long, complex sentences and its interlocking theological themes. It was a privilege, then, to be invited to prepare this volume for the Pillar New Testament Commentary series. It has enabled me over the last five years, in the midst of other responsibilities, to turn aside and wrestle with this majestic though challenging part of God's word. Ephesians, with its broad sweep of the divine purposes, its grand themes and emphasis on unity, truth, and love, along with its profound concerns that God's people should live as his new humanity in Christ, has proven to be both an encouragement and a searching challenge.

The completion of this volume also brings to fruition a desire to write a commentary on each of Paul's Prison Epistles—*Colossians, Philemon* (Word), *Philippians* (Eerdmans), and now *Ephesians*. I am conscious of how much I owe to those who have written on this letter before me. In particular, I am indebted to the earlier commentaries of F. F. Bruce (my teacher), Markus Barth, Rudolf Schnackenburg, Andrew Lincoln, and most recently Ernest Best, to mention only a few. Lincoln's commentary contains many exegetical and theological insights, and I have learned much from it. Even at those points where I differ from Andrew (and not least on the important question of the Pauline authorship of the letter), I have been grateful for the way he has laid out the issues. He has helped to clarify my thinking, and I hope his views have been represented fairly throughout the commentary. My thanks are also due to Harold Hoehner for his allowing me to use the manuscript of his forthcoming commentary on Ephesians.

Moore College is generous in its provision of study leave for its faculty members. This generosity has enabled me to complete the commentary, after pleasant and productive stays in the congenial surroundings of Trinity Evangelical Divinity School, Deerfield, Illinois, and later those at Tyndale House, Cambridge.

I am indebted to many, and wish to place my thanks on record. In particular, I value the personal friendship, encouragement, and wise scholarly advice of two princes among God's people, Don Carson, the General Editor of the Pillar series, and Peter Jensen, Principal of Moore College. Both have been a tower of strength in countless ways, and under God I owe them much. I am also grateful to Anne Macklin and Rob Maidment for their help in preparing the indexes for this volume.

Finally, my heartfelt thanks are due to my wife, Mary, to whom I dedicate this book. Her cheerful, loving support and persistent prayer have under God led to this work being brought to its conclusion. On top of that, her gracious example in our married life has helped me to understand more about the mystery of Christ loving his responsive church.

PETER O'BRIEN

Chief Abbreviations

I. MODERN WORKS

AnBib	*Analecta Biblica*
ANRW	*Aufstieg und Niedergang der römischen Welt*
ASV	American Standard Version
AV	Authorized Version (= KJV)
BAGD	W. Bauer, W. F. Arndt, F. W. Gingrich, and F. W. Danker, *Greek-English Lexicon of the New Testament* (2nd ed.)
BBR	*Bulletin for Biblical Research*
BDB	F. Brown, S. R. Driver, and C. A. Briggs, *Hebrew and English Lexicon of the Old Testament*
BDF	F. Blass, A. Debrunner, and R. W. Funk, *A Greek Grammar of the New Testament and Other Early Christian Literature*
Bib	*Biblica*
BibInt	*Biblical Interpretation*
BJRL	*Bulletin of the John Rylands University Library of Manchester*
BSac	*Bibliotheca Sacra*
CBQ	*Catholic Biblical Quarterly*
CTJ	*Calvin Theological Journal*
DPL	G. F. Hawthorne, R. P. Martin, and D. G. Reid (eds.), *Dictionary of Paul and His Letters*
EDNT	H. Balz and G. Schneider (eds.), *Exegetical Dictionary of the New Testament*
EvQ	*Evangelical Quarterly*
ExpTim	*Expository Times*
GNB	Good News Bible (= Today's English Version)
HTR	*Harvard Theological Review*

IB	*Interpreter's Bible*
Int	*Interpretation*
JB	Jerusalem Bible
JBL	*Journal of Biblical Literature*
JETS	*Journal of the Evangelical Theological Society*
JSNT	*Journal for the Study of the New Testament*
JSOT	*Journal for the Study of the Old Testament*
JTS	*Journal of Theological Studies*
KJV	King James Version (= AV)
LSJ	Liddell-Scott-Jones, *Greek English Lexicon*
LXX	Septuagint
MHT	J. H. Moulton, W. F. Howard, and N. Turner, *Grammar of New Testament Greek*
MM	J. H. Moulton and G. Milligan, *The Vocabulary of the Greek New Testament*
MT	Massoretic Text
NAB	New American Bible
NEB	New English Bible
Neot	*Neotestamentica*
NIDNTT	C. Brown (ed.), *The New International Dictionary of New Testament Theology*
NIV	New International Version
NJB	New Jerusalem Bible
NovT	*Novum Testamentum*
NRSV	New Revised Standard Version
NTS	*New Testament Studies*
PGM	*Papyri Graecae Magicae*
REB	Revised English Bible
ResQ	*Restoration Quarterly*
RevExp	*Review and Expositor*
RGG	*Religion in Geschichte und Gegenwart*
RSV	Revised Standard Version
RTR	*Reformed Theological Review*
SBL	Society of Biblical Literature
SE	*Studia Evangelica*
StrB	H. L. Strack and P. Billerbeck, *Kommentar zum Neuen Testament aus Talmud und Midrasch*
TDNT	G. Kittel and G. Friedrich (eds.), *Theological Dictionary of the New Testament*
TEV	Today's English Version
TLNT	C. Spicq, *Theological Lexicon of the New Testament*
TrinJ	*Trinity Journal*

TU	Texte und Untersuchungen zur Geschichte der altchrist-lichen Literatur
TynBul	*Tyndale Bulletin*
UBS	United Bible Societies Greek New Testament (4th ed.)
USQR	*Union Seminary Quarterly Review*
ZNW	*Zeitschrift für die neutestamentliche Wissenschaft*
ZTK	*Zeitschrift für Theologie und Kirche*

II. GENERAL ABBREVIATIONS

A.D.	*anno Domini,* in the year of our Lord
B.C.	before Christ
bk.	book
c.	*circa,* around
cf.	*confer,* compare
chap.	chapter
ed.	editor, edition, edited by
e.g.	*exempli gratia,* for example
esp.	especially
etc.	*et cetera,* and so forth
EVV	English versions
Gk.	Greek
i.e.	*id est,* that is
lit.	literally
MS (MSS)	manuscript(s)
n. (nn.)	footnote(s)
pt.	part
sc.	*scilicet,* namely
v. (vv.)	verse(s)
v.l.	*varia lectio,* variant reading
vol.	volume

Select Bibliography

Throughout this work I have referred to commentaries on Ephesians simply by author surname and page number.

I. COMMENTARIES ON EPHESIANS

Abbott, T. K., *A Critical and Exegetical Commentary on the Epistles to the Ephesians and to the Colossians* (Edinburgh: T & T Clark, 1897).

Barth, M., *Ephesians,* 2 vols. (Garden City: Doubleday, 1974).

Beare, F. W., 'The Epistle to the Ephesians', in *IB,* ed. G. A. Buttrick and others, vol. 10 (New York/Nashville: Abingdon, 1953), 597-749.

Best, E., *A Critical and Exegetical Commentary on Ephesians* (Edinburgh: T & T Clark, 1998).

Bratcher, R. G., and E. A. Nida, *A Translator's Handbook on Paul's Letter to the Ephesians* (London/New York: United Bible Societies, 1982).

Bruce, F. F., *The Epistle to the Ephesians* (London: Pickering & Inglis, 1961).

Bruce, F. F., *The Epistles to the Colossians, to Philemon, and to the Ephesians* (Grand Rapids: Eerdmans, 1984).

Caird, G. B., *Paul's Letters from Prison: Ephesians, Philippians, Colossians, Philemon, in the Revised Standard Version* (Oxford: Oxford University Press, 1976).

Calvin, J., *The Epistles of Paul the Apostle to the Galatians, Ephesians, Philippians and Colossians* (Edinburgh/Grand Rapids: Oliver & Boyd/Eerdmans, 1965).

Dahl, N. A., 'Bibelstudie über den Epheserbrief', in *Kurze Auslegung des Epheserbriefes,* ed. N. A. Dahl and others (Göttingen: Vandenhoeck & Ruprecht, 1965), 7-83.

Dibelius, M., and H. Greeven, *An die Kolosser, Epheser, An Philemon* (Tübingen: J. C. B. Mohr [Paul Siebeck], 1953).

Ernst, J., *Die Briefe an die Philipper, an Philemon, an die Kolosser, an die Epheser* (Regensburg: Pustet, 1974).

Foulkes, F., *The Letter of Paul to the Ephesians* (Leicester/Grand Rapids: Inter-Varsity/Eerdmans, 1989).

Gnilka, J., *Der Epheserbrief* (Freiburg/Basel/Vienna: Herder, 1971).

Hendriksen, W., *Ephesians* (Grand Rapids: Baker, 1967).

Hoehner, H. W., *Ephesians* (Grand Rapids: Baker, forthcoming).

Houlden, J. L., *Paul's Letters from Prison: Philippians, Colossians, Philemon, and Ephesians* (Philadelphia: Westminster Press, 1977).

Kitchen, M., *Ephesians* (London/New York: Routledge, 1994).

Lincoln, A. T., *Ephesians* (Dallas: Word, 1990).

Lindemann, A., *Der Epheserbrief* (Zürich: Theologischer Verlag, 1985).

Martin, R. P., *Ephesians, Colossians, and Philemon* (Atlanta: John Knox, 1991).

Masson, C., *L'Épître de Paul aux Éphésiens* (Neuchâtel: Delachaux & Niestlé, 1953).

Meyer, H. A. W., *Critical and Exegetical Handbook to the Epistle to the Ephesians and the Epistle to Philemon* (Edinburgh: T & T Clark, 1880).

Mitton, C. L., *Ephesians* (London: Oliphants, 1976).

Morris, L., *Expository Reflections on the Letter to the Ephesians* (Grand Rapids: Baker, 1994).

Mussner, F., *Der Brief an die Epheser* (Gütersloh/Würzburg: Mohn/Echter, 1982).

Patzia, A. G., *Ephesians, Colossians, Philemon* (Peabody: Hendrickson, 1990).

Pokorný, P., *Der Brief des Paulus an die Epheser* (Leipzig: Evangelische Verlagsanstalt, 1992).

Robinson, J. A., *St. Paul's Epistle to the Ephesians* (London: Macmillan, 1904).

Sampley, J. P., 'Ephesians', in *The Deutero-Pauline Letters: Ephesians, Colossians, 2 Thessalonians, 1-2 Timothy, Titus* (Minneapolis: Fortress Press, 1993).

Schlier, H., *Der Brief an die Epheser: Ein Kommentar* (Düsseldorf: Patmos, 1957).

Schnackenburg, R., *Ephesians: A Commentary* (Edinburgh: T & T Clark, 1991).

Simpson, E. K., and F. F. Bruce, *The Epistles of Paul to the Ephesians and the Colossians* (London/Grand Rapids: Marshall, Morgan & Scott/Eerdmans, 1957).

Snodgrass, K., *Ephesians: The NIV Application Commentary* (Grand Rapids: Zondervan, 1996).

Stott, J. R. W., *The Message of Ephesians: God's New Society* (Leicester: Inter-Varsity, 1979).

Turner, M., 'Ephesians', in *New Bible Commentary: 21st Century Edition*, ed. D. A. Carson, R. T. France, J. A. Motyer, and G. J. Wenham (Downers Grove/Leicester: Inter-Varsity, 1994), 1222-44.

Westcott, B. F., *Saint Paul's Epistle to the Ephesians* (London: Macmillan, 1906).

II. OTHER WORKS

Adai, J., *Der Heilige Geist als Gegenwart Gottes in den einzelnen Christen, in der Kirche und in der Welt: Studien zur Pneumatologie des Epheserbriefes* (Frankfurt: Lang, 1985).

Agrell, G., *Work, Toil and Sustenance* (Verbum: Hakan Ohlssons, 1976).

Allan, J. A., 'The "In Christ" Formula in Ephesians', *NTS* 5 (1958-59), 54-62.

Allen, T. G., 'Exaltation and Solidarity with Christ: Ephesians 1:20 and 2:6', *JSNT* 28 (1986), 103-20.

Allen, T. G., 'God the Namer: A Note on Ephesians 1:21b', *NTS* 32 (1986), 470-75.

Andersen, F. I., 'Yahweh, the Kind and Sensitive God', in *God Who Is Rich in Mercy: Essays Presented to Dr. D. B. Knox*, ed. P. T. O'Brien and D. G. Peterson (Homebush West, NSW: Lancer, 1986), 41-88.

Anderson, R. D., *Ancient Rhetorical Theory and Paul* (Kampen: Kok, 1996).

Arnold, C. E., *The Colossian Syncretism: The Interface between Christianity and Folk Belief at Colossae* (Tübingen/Grand Rapids: J. C. B. Mohr [Paul Siebeck]/Baker, 1995/1996).

Arnold, C. E., *Ephesians: Power and Magic: The Concept of Power in Ephesians in Light of Its Historical Setting* (Cambridge: Cambridge University Press, 1989).

Arnold, C. E., 'Jesus Christ: "Head" of the Church (Colossians and Ephesians)', in *Jesus of Nazareth: Lord and Christ: Essays on the Historical Jesus and New Testament Christology*, ed. J. B. Green and M. Turner (Grand Rapids/Carlisle: Eerdmans/Paternoster, 1994), 346-66.

Arnold, C. E., *Powers of Darkness* (Leicester: Inter-Varsity, 1992).

Arnold, C. E., *Three Crucial Questions about Spiritual Warfare* (Grand Rapids: Baker, 1997).

Aune, D. E., *The New Testament in Its Literary Environment* (Philadelphia: Westminster, 1987).

Aune, D. E., *Prophecy in Early Christianity and the Ancient Mediterranean World* (Grand Rapids: Eerdmans, 1983).

Balch, D. L., *Let Wives Be Submissive: The Domestic Code in 1 Peter* (Chico, CA: Scholars Press, 1981).

Balz, H. R., 'Anonymität und Pseudepigraphie im Urchristentum', *ZTK* 66 (1969), 403-36.

Banks, R. J., *Paul's Idea of Community* (Grand Rapids: Eerdmans, 1980).

Barclay, J. M. G., 'The Family as the Bearer of Religion in Judaism and Early Christianity', in *Constructing Early Christian Families: Family as Social Reality and Metaphor*, ed. H. Moxnes (London/New York: Routledge, 1997), 66-80.

Barnett, P., *The Second Epistle to the Corinthians* (Grand Rapids/Cambridge: Eerdmans, 1997).

Barrett, C. K., 'Pauline Controversies in the Post-Pauline Period', *NTS* 20 (1973-74), 229-45.

Barrett, C. K., *The Signs of an Apostle* (Philadelphia: Fortress, 1972).

Barth, M., *The Broken Wall: A Study of the Epistle to the Ephesians* (Chicago: Judson Press, 1959).

Barth, M., *The People of God* (Sheffield: JSOT, 1983).

Barton, S. C., 'Living as Families in the Light of the New Testament', *Int* 52 (1998), 130-44.

Bash, A., *Ambassadors for Christ: An Exploration of Ambassadorial Language in the New Testament* (Tübingen: J. C. B. Mohr [Paul Siebeck], 1997).

Batey, R. A., *New Testament Nuptial Imagery* (Leiden: Brill, 1971).

Bedale, S., 'The Meaning of κεφαλή in the Pauline Epistles', *JTS* 5 (1954), 211-15.

Benoit, P., 'Body, Head, and *Pleroma* in the Epistles of the Captivity', in *Jesus and the Gospels* (London: Darton, Longman & Todd, 1974), 59-78.

Best, E., 'Dead in Trespasses and Sins (Eph. 2:1)', in *Essays on Ephesians* (Edinburgh: T & T Clark, 1997), 69-85.

Best, E., *Ephesians* (Sheffield: Academic Press, 1993).

Best, E., 'Ephesians 1.1 Again', in *Essays on Ephesians* (Edinburgh: T & T Clark, 1997), 17-24.

Best, E., 'Ephesians 4:28: Thieves in the Church', in *Essays on Ephesians* (Edinburgh: T & T Clark, 1997), 179-88.

Best, E., 'Ephesians i.1', in *Essays on Ephesians* (Edinburgh: T & T Clark, 1997), 1-16.

Best, E., *Essays on Ephesians* (Edinburgh: T & T Clark, 1997).

Best, E., 'Fashions in Exegesis: Ephesians 1:3', in *Scripture: Meaning and Method, Essays Presented to Anthony Tyrrell Hanson,* ed. B. P. Thompson (Hull: Hull University Press, 1987), 79-91.

Best, E., 'The Haustafel in Ephesians (Eph. 5.22–6.9)', in *Essays on Ephesians* (Edinburgh: T & T Clark, 1997), 189-203.

Best, E., 'Ministry in Ephesians', in *Essays on Ephesians* (Edinburgh: T & T Clark, 1997), 157-77.

Best, E., *One Body in Christ* (London: SPCK, 1955).

Best, E., 'Paul's Apostolic Authority — ?', in *Essays on Ephesians* (Edinburgh: T & T Clark, 1997), 25-49.

Best, E., 'Recipients and Title of the Letter to the Ephesians: Why and When the Designation "Ephesians"?', in *ANRW*, ed. W. Haase and H. Temporini, pt. 2, vol. 25.4 (Berlin/New York: de Gruyter, 1987), 3247-79.

Best, E., 'Two Types of Existence', in *Essays on Ephesians* (Edinburgh: T & T Clark, 1997), 139-55.

Best, E., 'Who Used Whom?: The Relationship of Ephesians and Colossians', *NTS* 43 (1997), 72-96.

Betz, H. D., *Galatians: A Commentary on Paul's Letter to the Galatians* (Philadelphia: Fortress, 1979).

Bilezikian, G., *Beyond Sex Roles* (Grand Rapids: Baker, 1985).

Bilezikian, G., 'Hermeneutical Bungee-Jumping: Subordination in the Godhead', *JETS* 40 (1997), 57-68.

Bjerkelund, C. J., *Parakalô: Form, Funktion und Sinn der parakalô-Sätze in den paulinischen Briefe* (Oslo: Universitetsforlaget, 1967).

Blocher, H., *Original Sin: Illuminating the Riddle* (Leicester/Grand Rapids: Apollos/Eerdmans, 1997).

Bockmuehl, M. N. A., *Revelation and Mystery in Ancient Judaism and Pauline Christianity* (Tübingen: J. C. B. Mohr [Paul Siebeck], 1990).

Boer, M. C. de, 'Images of Paul in the Post-Apostolic Period', *CBQ* 42 (1980), 359-80.

Bradley, K. R., *Slaves and Masters in the Roman Empire: A Study in Social Control* (Oxford: Oxford University Press, 1987).

Breeze, M., 'Hortatory Discourse in Ephesians', *Journal of Translation and Textlinguistics* 5 (1992), 313-47.

Brown, R. E., *An Introduction to the New Testament* (New York: Doubleday, 1997).

Brown, R. E., *The Semitic Background of the Term "Mystery" in the New Testament* (Philadelphia: Fortress, 1968).

Bruce, F. F., *An Expanded Paraphrase of the Epistles of Paul* (Exeter: Paternoster, 1965).

Bruce, F. F., *Paul: Apostle of the Free Spirit* (Exeter/Grand Rapids: Paternoster/Eerdmans, 1977).

Bruce, F. F., 'St. Paul in Rome. 4. The Epistle to the Ephesians', *BJRL* 49 (1967), 303-22.

Caird, G. B., 'The Descent of the Spirit in Ephesians 4:7-11', *SE* 2 (1964), 535-45.

Campbell, R. A., *The Elders: Seniority within Earliest Christianity* (Edinburgh: T & T Clark, 1994).

Caragounis, C. C., *The Ephesian* Mysterion: *Meaning and Content* (Lund: Gleerup, 1977).

Carr, W., *Angels and Principalities: The Background, Meaning and Development of the Pauline Phrase* hai archai kai hai exousiai (Cambridge: Cambridge University Press, 1981).

Carson, D. A., *A Call to Spiritual Reformation: Priorities from Paul and His Prayers* (Grand Rapids: Baker, 1992).

Carson, D. A., D. J. Moo, and L. Morris, *An Introduction to the New Testament* (Grand Rapids: Zondervan, 1992).

Carson, D. A., *Showing the Spirit: A Theological Exposition of 1 Corinthians 12–14* (Grand Rapids: Baker, 1987).

Chadwick, H., 'Die Absicht des Epheserbriefes', *ZNW* 51 (1960), 145-53.

Chae, D. J.-S., *Paul as Apostle to the Gentiles: His Apostolic Self-Awareness and its Influence on the Soteriological Argument of Romans* (Carlisle: Paternoster, 1997).

Clark, K. W., 'The Meaning of Ἐνεργέω and Καταργέω in the New Testament', *JBL* 54 (1935), 93-101.

Clark, S. B., *Man and Woman in Christ: An Examination of the Roles of Men and Women in Light of Scripture and the Social Sciences* (Ann Arbor: Servant, 1980).

Clarke, A. D., '"Be Imitators of Me": Paul's Model of Leadership', *TynB* 49 (1998), 329-60.

Cotterell, P., and M. Turner, *Linguistics and Biblical Interpretation* (London: SPCK, 1989).

Coutts, J., 'The Relationship of Ephesians and Colossians', *NTS* 4 (1958), 201-7.

Craigie, P. C., *Psalms 1–50* (Waco, TX: Word, 1983).

Crouch, J. E., *The Origin and Intention of the Colossian Haustafel* (Göttingen: Vandenhoeck & Ruprecht, 1972).

Dahl, N. A., 'Cosmic Dimensions and Religious Knowledge', in *Jesus und Paulus: Festschrift für Werner Georg Kümmel zum 70. Geburtstag*, ed. E. E. Ellis and E. Grässer (Göttingen: Vandenhoeck & Ruprecht, 1975), 57-75.

Dahl, N. A., 'Form-Critical Observations on Early Christian Preaching', in *Jesus in the Memory of the Early Church* (Minneapolis: Augsburg, 1976), 30-36.

Dahl, N. A., 'Gentiles, Christians, and Israelites in the Epistle to the Ephesians', *HTR* 79 (1986), 31-39.

Daube, D., 'Participle and Imperative in 1 Peter', in *The First Epistle of St Peter*, ed. E. G. Selwyn (London: Macmillan, 1947), 467-88.

Dawes, G. W., *The Body in Question: Metaphor and Meaning in the Interpretation of Ephesians 5:21-33* (Leiden: Brill, 1998).

de la Potterie, I., 'Jésus et la verité d'après Eph 4,21', *AnBib* 18 (1963), 45-57.

Deichgräber, R., *Gotteshymnus und Christushymnus in der frühen Christenheit: Untersuchungen zu Form, Sprache und Stil der frühchristlichen Hymnen* (Göttingen: Vandenhoeck & Ruprecht, 1967).

Donelson, L. R., *Pseudepigraphy and Ethical Argument in the Pastoral Epistles* (Tübingen: J. C. B. Mohr [Paul Siebeck], 1986).

Doty, W. G., *Letters in Primitive Christianity* (Philadelphia: Fortress, 1973).

Duff, J., 'A Reconsideration of Pseudepigraphy in Early Christianity' (unpublished D.Phil. thesis, Oxford, 1998).

Dumbrell, W. J., *The Search for Order: Biblical Eschatology in Focus* (Grand Rapids: Baker, 1994).

Dunn, J. D. G., '"The Body of Christ" in Paul', in *Worship, Theology and Minis-*

try in the Early Church: Essays in Honor of Ralph P. Martin, ed. M. H. Wilkins and T. Paige (Sheffield: Academic Press, 1992), 146-62.

Dunn, J. D. G., *The Epistle to the Galatians* (London: Black, 1993).

Dunn, J. D. G., 'How New Was Paul's Gospel? The Problem of Continuity and Discontinuity', in *Gospel in Paul: Studies on Corinthians, Galatians and Romans for Richard N. Longenecker,* ed. L. A. Jervis and P. Richardson (Sheffield: Academic Press, 1994), 367-88.

Dunn, J. D. G., *Jesus and the Spirit* (London: SCM, 1975).

Dunn, J. D. G., *The Partings of the Ways: Between Christianity and Judaism and Their Significance for the Character of Christianity* (London/Philadelphia: SCM/TPI, 1991).

Dunn, J. D. G., 'The Problem of Pseudonymity', in *The Living Word* (London: SCM, 1987), 65-85.

Dunn, J. D. G., 'Pseudepigraphy', in *Dictionary of the Later New Testament and Its Developments,* ed. R. P. Martin and P. H. Davids (Downers Grove/Leicester: Inter-Varsity, 1997), 977-84.

Dunn, J. D. G., *The Theology of Paul the Apostle* (Grand Rapids/Cambridge: Eerdmans, 1998).

Ellis, E. E., 'Paul and His Co-Workers', in *Prophecy and Hermeneutic in Early Christianity: New Testament Essays* (Tübingen: J. C. B. Mohr [Paul Siebeck], 1978), 3-22.

Ellis, E. E., *Paul's Use of the Old Testament* (Grand Rapids: Eerdmans, 1981).

Ellis, E. E., 'Pseudonymity and Canonicity of New Testament Documents', in *Worship, Theology and Ministry in the Early Church: Essays in Honor of Ralph P. Martin,* ed. M. J. Wilkins and T. Paige (Sheffield: Academic Press, 1992), 212-24.

Engberg-Pedersen, T., 'Ephesians 5,12-13: ἐλέγχειν and Conversion in the New Testament', *ZNW* 80 (1989), 89-110.

Engelmann, H., D. Knibbe, and R. Merkelbach, *Die Inschriften von Ephesos* (Bonn: Rudolph Habelt, 1984).

Ernst, J., *Pleroma und Pleroma Christi: Geschichte und Deutung eines Begriffs der paulinischen antilegomena* (Regensburg: Pustet, 1970).

Faust, E., *Pax Christi et Pax Caesaris: Religionsgeschichtliche, traditionsgeschichtliche und sozialgeschichtliche Studien zum Epheserbrief* (Fribourg/Göttingen: Universitätsverlag/Vandenhoeck & Ruprecht, 1993).

Fee, G. D., *The First Epistle to the Corinthians* (Grand Rapids: Eerdmans, 1987).

Fee, G. D., *God's Empowering Presence: The Holy Spirit in the Letters of Paul* (Peabody, MA: Hendrickson, 1994).

Fischer, K. M., *Tendenz und Absicht des Epheserbriefes* (Göttingen: Vandenhoeck & Ruprecht, 1973).

Fitzmyer, J. A., '*Kephalē* in 1 Corinthians 11:3', *Int* 47 (1993), 52-59.

Fitzmyer, J. A., '"To Know Him and the Power of His Resurrection" (Phil

3.10)', in *Mélanges Bibliques en hommage au R. P. Béda Rigaux*, ed. A. Descamps and A. de Halleux (Gembloux: Duculot, 1970), 411-25.

Fitzmyer, J. A., 'The Use of Explicit Old Testament Quotations in Qumran Literature and in the New Testament', *NTS* 7 (1960-61), 297-333.

Fleckenstein, K.-H., *Ordnet euch einander unter in der Furcht Christi: Die Eheperikope in Eph 5,21-33: Geschichte der Interpretation, Analyse und Aktualisierung des Textes* (Würzburg: Echter, 1994).

Fong, B. W., 'Addressing the Issue of Racial Reconciliation according to the Principles of Eph 2:11-22', *JETS* 38 (1995), 565-80.

Forbes, C., *Prophecy and Inspired Speech in Early Christianity and Its Hellenistic Environment* (Tübingen: J. C. B. Mohr [Paul Siebeck], 1995).

Fredrickson, D. E., 'Παρρησία in the Pauline Epistles', in *Friendship, Flattery, and Frankness of Speech: Studies on Friendship in the New Testament World*, ed. J. T. Fitzgerald (Leiden: Brill, 1996), 163-83.

Fung, R. Y. K., 'Ministry in the New Testament', in *The Church in the Bible and the World*, ed. D. A. Carson (Exeter: Paternoster, 1987), 154-212, 318-42.

Fung, R. Y. K., 'The Nature of the Ministry according to Paul', *EvQ* 54 (1982), 129-46.

Gese, M., *Das Vermächtis des Apostels: Die Rezeption der paulinischen Theologie im Epheserbrief* (Tübingen: J. C. B. Mohr [Paul Siebeck], 1997).

Gnilka, J., 'Das Paulusbild im Kolosser- und Epheserbrief', in *Kontinuät und Einheit*, ed. P. G. Müller and W. Stenger (Freiburg/Basel/Vienna: Herder, 1981), 179-93.

Goodspeed, E. J., *The Meaning of Ephesians* (Chicago: University of Chicago Press, 1933).

Gordon, T. D., '"Equipping" Ministry in Ephesians 4?', *JETS* 37 (1994), 69-78.

Gosnell, P. W., 'Ephesians 5:18-20 and Mealtime Propriety', *TynBul* 44 (1993), 363-71.

Green, M., *I Believe in Satan's Downfall* (London/Grand Rapids: Hodder & Stoughton/Eerdmans, 1981).

Grudem, W., 'Does *kephalē* ('head') Mean "Source" or "Authority Over" in Greek Literature? A Survey of 2,336 Examples', *TrinJ* 6 (1985), 38-59.

Grudem, W., 'The Meaning of Κεφαλή ('Head'): A Response to Recent Studies', *TrinJ* 11 (1990), 3-72.

Grudem, W. A., *The Gift of Prophecy in 1 Corinthians* (Washington, DC: University Press of America, 1982).

Grudem, W. A., *The Gift of Prophecy in the New Testament and Today* (Westchester, IL: Crossway, 1988).

Gudorf, M. E., 'The Use of πάλη in Ephesians 6:12', *JBL* 117 (1998), 331-35.

Gundry, R. H., *Sōma in Biblical Theology, with Emphasis on Pauline Anthropology* (Cambridge: Cambridge University Press, 1976).

Guthrie, D., *New Testament Introduction* (Leicester: Apollos, 1990).

Haas, O., *Paulus der Missionar: Ziel, Grundsätze und Methoden der Missionstätigkeit des Apostels Paulus nach seinen eigenen Aussagen* (Münsterschwarzach: Vier Türme-Verlag, 1971).

Hanson, S., *The Unity of the Church in the New Testament: Colossians and Ephesians* (Uppsala: Almquist & Wiksells, 1946).

Harder, G., *Paulus und das Gebet* (Gütersloh: Bertelsmann, 1936).

Harris, M. J., *Colossians and Philemon* (Grand Rapids: Eerdmans, 1991).

Harris, M. J., *Jesus as God: The New Testament Use of* Theos *in Reference to Jesus* (Grand Rapids: Baker, 1992).

Harris, M. J., *Raised Immortal: Resurrection and Immortality in the New Testament* (London: Marshall, Morgan & Scott, 1983).

Harris, M. J., *Slave of Christ* (Leicester: Apollos, forthcoming).

Harris, W. H., 'The Ascent and Descent of Christ in Ephesians 4:9-10', *BSac* 151 (1994), 198-214.

Harris, W. H., *The Descent of Christ: Ephesians 4:7-11 and Traditional Hebrew Imagery* (Leiden: Brill, 1996).

Harris, W. H., '"The Heavenlies" Reconsidered: Οὐρανός and Ἐπουράνιος in Ephesians', *BSac* 148 (1991), 72-89.

Harrisville, R. A., 'The Concept of Newness in the New Testament', *JBL* 74 (1955), 69-79.

Hay, D. M., *Glory at the Right Hand: Psalm 110 in Early Christianity* (Nashville: Abingdon, 1973).

Hays, R. B., *Echoes of Scripture in the Letters of Paul* (New Haven: Yale University Press, 1989).

Hemphill, K. S., *Spiritual Gifts: Empowering the New Testament Church* (Nashville: Broadman, 1988).

Hendrix, H., 'On the Form and Ethos of Ephesians', *USQR* 42 (1988), 3-15.

Hengel, M., 'Hymns and Christology', in *Between Jesus and Paul* (London: SCM, 1983), 78-96.

Hengel, M., *The Pre-Christian Paul* (London/Philadelphia: SCM/TPI, 1991).

Hester, J. D., *Paul's Concept of Inheritance: A Contribution to the Understanding of Heilsgeschichte* (Edinburgh: Oliver and Boyd, 1961).

Hill, D., *Greek Words and Hebrew Meanings: Studies in the Semantics of Soteriological Terms* (Cambridge: Cambridge University Press, 1967).

Hill, D., *New Testament Prophecy* (London: Marshall, Morgan & Scott, 1979).

Hoch, C. B., *All Things New: The Significance of Newness for Biblical Theology* (Grand Rapids: Baker, 1995).

Hock, R. F., *The Social Context of Paul's Ministry* (Philadelphia: Fortress, 1980).

Holtzmann, H. J., *Kritik der Epheser- und Kolosserbriefe: Auf Grund einer Analyse ihres Verwandtschaftsverhältnisses* (Leipzig: Wilhelm Engelmann, 1872).

Horsley, G. H. R., ed., *New Documents Illustrating Early Christianity*, vol. 4: *A*

Review of the Greek Inscriptions and Papyri Published in 1979 (Sydney: Macquarie University, 1987).

Howard, G., 'The Head/Body Metaphors of Ephesians', *NTS* 20 (1974), 350-56.

Hui, A. W. D., 'The Concept of the Holy Spirit in Ephesians and Its Relation to the Pneumatologies of Luke and Paul' (unpublished Ph.D. thesis, Aberdeen, 1992).

Hurley, J. B., *Man and Woman in Biblical Perspective: A Study in Role Relationships and Authority* (Leicester: Inter-Varsity, 1981).

Jensen, J., 'Does *Porneia* Mean Fornication? A Critique of Bruce Malina', *NovT* 20 (1978), 161-84.

Judge, E. A., 'Contemporary Political Models for the Inter-Relations of the New Testament Churches', *RTR* 22 (1963), 65-76.

Kamlah, E., ''Υποτάσσεσθαι in den neutestamentlichen Haustafeln', in *Verborum Veritas: Festschrift für G. Stählin zum 70. Geburtstag*, ed. O. Bocher and K. Haacker (Wuppertal: Brockhaus, 1970), 237-43.

Käsemann, E., 'Epheserbrief', in *RGG*, ed. H. F. von Campenhausen, vol. 2 (Tübingen: J. C. B. Mohr [Paul Siebeck], 1958), 517-20.

Käsemann, E., 'Ephesians and Acts', in *Studies in Luke-Acts: Essays Presented in Honor of Paul Schubert*, ed. L. E. Keck and J. L. Martyn (Nashville: Abingdon, 1966), 288-97.

Keener, C. S., *Paul, Women and Wives: Marriage and Women's Ministry in the Letters of Paul* (Peabody, MA: Hendrickson, 1992).

Kennedy, G. A., *New Testament Interpretation through Rhetorical Criticism* (Chapel Hill: University of North Carolina Press, 1984).

Kern, P. H., *Rhetoric and Galatians: Assessing an Approach to Paul's Epistle* (Cambridge: Cambridge University Press, 1998).

Kim, S., *The Origin of Paul's Gospel* (Grand Rapids: Eerdmans, 1982).

Kirby, J. C., *Ephesians: Baptism and Pentecost* (London: SPCK, 1968).

Kitchen, M., 'The ἀνακεφαλαίωσις of All Things in Christ: Theology and Purpose in the Epistle to the Ephesians' (unpublished Ph.D. thesis, Manchester, 1988).

Kitchen, M., 'The Status of Law in the Letter to the Ephesians', in *Law and Religion: Essays on the Place of the Law in Israel and Early Christianity*, ed. B. Lindars (Cambridge: James Clarke, 1988), 141-47, 187.

Kittredge, C. B., *Community and Authority: The Rhetoric of Obedience in the Pauline Tradition* (Harrisburg, PA: TPI, 1998).

Klein, W. W., *The New Chosen People: A Corporate View of Election* (Grand Rapids: Zondervan, 1990).

Knight, G. W., 'Husbands and Wives as Analogues of Christ and the Church: Ephesians 5:21-33 and Colossians 3:18-19', in *Recovering Biblical Manhood and Womanhood: A Response to Evangelical Feminism*, ed. J. Piper and W. Grudem (Wheaton, IL: Crossway, 1991), 165-78.

Köstenberger, A. J., 'The Mystery of Christ and the Church: Head, Body, "One Flesh"', *TrinJ* 12 (1991), 79-94.

Köstenberger, A. J., 'What Does It Mean to Be Filled with the Spirit? A Biblical Investigation', *JETS* 40 (1997), 229-40.

Kroeger, C. C., 'The Classical Concept of *Head* as "Source"', in *Equal to Serve,* ed. G. G. Hull (London: Scripture Union, 1987), 267-83.

Kuhn, K. G., 'The Epistle to the Ephesians in the Light of the Qumran Texts', in *Paul and Qumran,* ed. J. Murphy-O'Connor (London: Chapman, 1968), 115-31.

Kümmel, W. G., *Introduction to the New Testament* (London/Nashville: SCM/Abingdon, 1975).

Larsson, E., *Christus als Vorbild: Eine Untersuchung zu den paulinischen Tauf- und Eikontexten* (Uppsala: Almquist & Wiksells, 1962).

Lemmer, H. R., 'A Multifarious Understanding of Eschatology in Ephesians: A Possible Solution to a Vexing Issue', *Hervormde Teologiese Studies* 46 (1990), 102-19.

Lemmer, H. R., 'Reciprocity between Eschatology and *Pneuma* in Ephesians 1:3-14', *Neot* 21 (1987), 159-82.

Lightfoot, J. B., *Saint Paul's Epistles to the Colossians and to Philemon* (London: Macmillan, 1890).

Lincoln, A. T., 'The Church and Israel in Ephesians 2', *CBQ* 49 (1987), 605-24.

Lincoln, A. T., 'Ephesians 2:8-10: A Summary of Paul's Gospel?', *CBQ* 45 (1983), 617-30.

Lincoln, A. T., *Paradise Now and Not Yet: Studies in the Role of the Heavenly Dimension in Paul's Thought with Special Reference to Eschatology* (Cambridge: Cambridge University Press, 1981).

Lincoln, A. T., 'A Re-Examination of "The Heavenlies" in Ephesians', *NTS* 19 (1972-73), 468-83.

Lincoln, A. T., '"Stand, Therefore . . .": Ephesians 6:10-20 as *Peroratio*', *BibInt* 3 (1995), 99-114.

Lincoln, A. T., 'The Use of the OT in Ephesians', *JSNT* 14 (1982), 16-57.

Lincoln, A. T., and A. J. M. Wedderburn, *The Theology of the Later Pauline Letters* (Cambridge: Cambridge University Press, 1993).

Lindars, B., *New Testament Apologetic* (London: SCM, 1961).

Lindemann, A., *Die Aufhebung der Zeit: Geschichtsverständnis und Eschatologie im Epheserbrief* (Gütersloh: Mohn, 1975).

Llewelyn, S. R., and R. A. Kearsley, eds., *New Documents Illustrating Early Christianity,* vol. 6: *A Review of the Greek Inscriptions and Papyri Published in 1980-81* (Sydney: Macquarie University, 1992).

Lohse, E., *Colossians and Philemon* (Philadelphia: Fortress, 1971).

Lona, H. E., *Die Eschatologie im Kolosser- und Epheserbrief* (Würzburg: Echter, 1984).

Longenecker, R. N., *Biblical Exegesis in the Apostolic Period* (Grand Rapids: Eerdmans, 1975; 2nd ed. 1999).

Longenecker, R. N., *Galatians* (Dallas: Word, 1990).

Longenecker, R. N., ed., *The Road from Damascus: The Impact of Paul's Conversion on His Life, Thought, and Ministry* (Grand Rapids/Cambridge: Eerdmans, 1997).

Louw, J. P., and E. A. Nida, *Greek-English Lexicon of the New Testament Based on Semantic Domains*, 2 vols. (New York: United Bible Societies, 1988, 1989).

Lövestam, E., *Spiritual Wakefulness in the New Testament* (Lund: Gleerup, 1963).

Luz, U., 'Rechtfertigung bei den Paulusschülern', in *Festschrift für Ernst Käsemann zum 70. Geburtstag*, ed. J. Friedrich, W. Pöhlmann, and P. Stuhlmacher (Tübingen: J. C. B. Mohr [Paul Siebeck], 1976), 365-83.

Luz, U., 'Überlegungen zum Epheserbrief und seiner Paraenese', in *Neues Testament und Ethik: Für R. Schnackenburg*, ed. H. Merklein (Freiburg/Basel/Vienna: Herder, 1989), 376-96.

Lyall, F., *Slaves, Citizens, Sons: Legal Metaphors in the Epistles* (Grand Rapids: Zondervan, 1984).

MacDonald, M. Y., *The Pauline Churches* (Cambridge: Cambridge University Press, 1988).

Mack, B. L., *Rhetoric and the New Testament* (Minneapolis: Fortress, 1990).

Mackay, J. A., *God's Order: The Ephesians Letter and This Present Time* (London: Nisbet, 1953).

Maclean, J. B., 'Eph 1:10 in Patristic Exegesis: Controlling the Meaning of a Volatile Tradition'. Paper presented at the Society of Biblical Literature, The Pauline Epistles Section, Chicago, 1994.

Malherbe, *Ancient Epistolary Theorists* (Atlanta: Scholars, 1988).

Malina, B., 'Does *Porneia* Mean Fornication?', *NovT* 14 (1972), 10-17.

Marrow, S. B., '*Parrhēsia* in the New Testament', *CBQ* 44 (1982), 431-46.

Marshall, I. H., 'An Assessment of Recent Developments', in *It Is Written: Scripture Citing Scripture*, ed. D. A. Carson and H. G. M. Williamson (Cambridge: Cambridge University Press, 1988), 1-21.

Marshall, I. H., 'Church and Temple in the New Testament', *TynBul* 40 (1989), 203-22.

Marshall, I. H., 'The Development of the Concept of Redemption in the New Testament', in *Reconciliation and Hope: New Testament Essays on Atonement and Eschatology, Presented to L. L. Morris on His 60th Birthday*, ed. R. J. Banks (Exeter: Paternoster, 1974), 153-69.

Marshall, I. H., 'Salvation, Grace and Works in the Later Writings of the Pauline Corpus', *NTS* 42 (1996), 339-58.

McKay, K. L., 'Aspect in Imperatival Constructions in New Testament Greek', *NovT* 27 (1985), 201-26.

McKay, K. L., *A New Syntax of the Verb in New Testament Greek: An Aspectual Approach* (New York: Lang, 1994).

McKelvey, R. J., *The New Temple: The Church in the New Testament* (Oxford: Oxford University Press, 1969).

Meade, D. G., *Pseudonymity and Canon: An Investigation in the Relationship of Authorship and Authority in Jewish and Earliest Christian Tradition* (Tübingen: J. C. B. Mohr [Paul Siebeck], 1986).

Merklein, H., *Christus und die Kirche: Die theologische Grundstruktur des Epheserbriefes nach 2,11-18* (Stuttgart: KBW Verlag, 1973).

Merklein, H., *Das kirchliche Amt nach dem Epheserbrief* (München: Kösel, 1973).

Merklein, H., 'Eph 4,1–5,20 als Rezeption von Kol 3,1-17', in *Kontinuität und Einheit: Für Franz Mussner*, ed. P. G. Müller and W. Stenger (Freiburg/Basel/Vienna: Herder, 1981), 194-210.

Merklein, H., 'Paulinische Theologie in der Rezeption des Kolosser- und Epheserbriefes', in *Paulus in den neutestamentlichen Spätschriften*, ed. K. Kertelge (Freiburg/Basel/Vienna: Herder, 1981), 25-69.

Metzger, B. M., *A Textual Commentary on the Greek New Testament* (Stuttgart: Deutsche Bibelgesellschaft, 1994).

Miletic, S. F., *"One Flesh": Eph. 5.22-24, 5.31: Marriage and the New Creation* (Rome: Pontifical Biblical Institute, 1988).

Mitton, C. L., *The Epistle to the Ephesians* (Oxford: Clarendon, 1951).

Moo, D. J., 'The Law of Christ as the Fulfillment of the Law of Moses: A Modified Lutheran View', in *The Law, the Gospel, and the Modern Christian: Five Views*, ed. W. Strickland and others (Grand Rapids: Zondervan, 1993), 319-76.

Moritz, T., *A Profound Mystery: The Use of the Old Testament in Ephesians* (Leiden: Brill, 1996).

Moritz, T., 'Reasons for Ephesians', *Evangel* 14 (1996), 8-14.

Moritz, T., '"Summing Up All Things": Religious Pluralism and Universalism in Ephesians', in *One God, One Lord*, ed. A. D. Clarke and B. W. Winter (Cambridge/Grand Rapids: Tyndale House/Baker, 1991/1992), 88-111.

Morris, L., *The Apostolic Preaching of the Cross* (London: Tyndale, 1965).

Motyer, J. A., *The Prophecy of Isaiah* (Leicester: Inter-Varsity, 1993).

Moule, C. F. D., *The Epistles of Paul the Apostle to the Colossians and to Philemon* (Cambridge: Cambridge University Press, 1953).

Moule, C. F. D., *An Idiom Book of New Testament Greek* (Cambridge: Cambridge University Press, 1959).

Moule, C. F. D., *The Origin of Christology* (Cambridge: Cambridge University Press, 1977).

Mouton, E., 'The Communicative Power of the Epistle to the Ephesians', in *Rhetoric, Scripture and Theology: Essays from the 1994 Pretoria Conference,* ed. S. E. Porter and T. H. Olbricht (Sheffield: Academic Press, 1996), 280-307.

Mouton, E., 'Reading Ephesians Ethically: Criteria towards a Renewed Identity Awareness?', *Neot* 28 (1994), 359-77.

Mussner, F., *Christus, das All und die Kirche: Studien zur Theologie des Epheserbriefes* (Trier: Paulinus, 1955).

Neufeld, T. Y., *Put On the Armour of God: The Divine Warrior from Isaiah to Ephesians* (Sheffield: Academic Press, 1997).

Newman, C. C., 'Election and Predestination in Ephesians 1:4-6a: An Exegetical-Theological Study of the Historical, Christological Realization of God's Purpose', *RevExp* 93 (1996), 237-47.

Norden, E., *Agnostos Theos: Untersuchungen zur Formengeschichte religiöser Rede* (Leipzig/Berlin: Teubner, 1913).

O'Brien, P. T., 'The Church as a Heavenly and Eschatological Entity', in *The Church in the Bible and the World,* ed. D. A. Carson (Exeter: Paternoster, 1987), 88-119, 307-11.

O'Brien, P. T., *Colossians, Philemon* (Waco, TX: Word, 1982).

O'Brien, P. T., 'Divine Analysis and Comprehensive Solution: Some Priorities from Ephesians', *RTR* 53 (1994), 130-42.

O'Brien, P. T., 'Ephesians I: An Unusual Introduction to a New Testament Letter', *NTS* 25 (1979), 504-16.

O'Brien, P. T., *The Epistle to the Philippians: A Commentary on the Greek Text* (Grand Rapids/Exeter: Eerdmans/Paternoster, 1991).

O'Brien, P. T., *Gospel and Mission in the Writings of Paul: An Exegetical and Theological Analysis* (Grand Rapids/Carlisle: Eerdmans/Paternoster, 1995).

O'Brien, P. T., *Introductory Thanksgivings in the Letters of Paul* (Leiden: Brill, 1977).

O'Brien, P. T., 'Principalities and Powers: Opponents of the Church', in *Biblical Interpretation and the Church: An International Study,* ed. D. A. Carson (Exeter: Paternoster, 1984), 110-50.

O'Brien, P. T., 'Romans 8:26, 27. A Revolutionary Approach to Prayer?', *RTR* 46 (1987), 65-73.

O'Brien, P. T., 'Thanksgiving and the Gospel in Paul', *NTS* 21 (1974-75), 144-55.

O'Brien, P. T., 'Thanksgiving within the Structure of Pauline Theology', in *Pauline Studies: Essays Presented to F. F. Bruce on His 70th Birthday,* ed. D. A. Hagner and M. J. Harris (Grand Rapids: Eerdmans, 1980), 50-66.

Ortlund, R. C., *Whoredom: God's Unfaithful Wife in Biblical Theology* (Leicester/Grand Rapids: Apollos/Eerdmans, 1996).

Page, S. H. T., *Powers of Evil: A Biblical Study of Satan and Demons* (Grand Rapids/Leicester: Baker/Apollos, 1995).

Patzia, A. G., 'The Deutero-Pauline Hypothesis: An Attempt at Clarification', *EvQ* 52 (1980), 27-42.

Perriman, A., '"His body, which is the church . . .": Coming to Terms with Metaphor', *EvQ* 62 (1990), 123-42.

Perriman, A., *Speaking of Women: Interpreting Paul* (Leicester: Apollos, 1998).

Peterson, D. G., *Engaging with God: A Biblical Theology of Worship* (Leicester/ Grand Rapids: Apollos/Eerdmans, 1992).

Peterson, D. G., *Possessed by God: A New Testament Theology of Sanctification and Holiness* (Leicester: Apollos, 1995).

Piper, J., and W. Grudem, eds. *Recovering Biblical Manhood and Womanhood: A Response to Evangelical Feminism* (Wheaton: Crossway, 1991).

Polhill, J. B., 'The Relationship between Ephesians and Colossians', *RevExp* 70 (1973), 439-50.

Pope, R. M., 'Studies in Pauline Vocabulary: Redeeming the Time', *ExpTim* 22 (1910-11), 552-54.

Porter, S. E., *Idioms of the Greek New Testament* (Sheffield: Academic Press, 1994).

Porter, S. E., ἴστε γινώσκοντες in Ephesians 5,5: Does Chiasm Solve the Problem?', *ZNW* 81 (1990), 270-76.

Porter, S. E., *Καταλλάσσω in Ancient Greek Literature, with Reference to the Pauline Writings* (Cordoba: Ediciones el Almendro, 1994).

Porter, S. E., 'Paul of Tarsus and His Letters', in *Handbook of Classical Rhetoric in the Hellenistic Period 330 B.C.–A.D. 400,* ed. S. E. Porter (Leiden: Brill, 1997), 533-85.

Porter, S. E., 'Pauline Authorship and the Pastoral Epistles: Implications for Canon', *BBR* 5 (1995), 105-23.

Porter, S. E., 'The Theoretical Justification for Application of Rhetorical Categories to Pauline Epistolary Literature', in *Rhetoric and the New Testament: Essays from the 1992 Heidelberg Conference,* ed. S. E. Porter and T. H. Olbricht (Sheffield: Academic Press, 1993), 100-122.

Porter, S. E., *Verbal Aspect in the Greek of the New Testament, with Reference to Tense and Mood* (New York: Lang, 1989).

Porter, S. E., and K. D. Clarke, 'Canonical-Critical Perspective and the Relationship of Colossians and Ephesians', *Bib* 78 (1997), 57-86.

Qualls, P., and J. D. W. Watts, 'Isaiah in Ephesians', *RevExp* 93 (1996), 249-59.

Rader, W. H., *The Church and Racial Hostility: A History of Interpretation of Ephesians 2,11-22* (Tübingen: J. C. B. Mohr [Paul Siebeck], 1978).

Rapske, B., *Paul in Roman Custody* (Grand Rapids/Carlisle: Eerdmans/Paternoster, 1994).

Reed, J. T., 'The Epistle', in *Handbook of Classical Rhetoric in the Hellenistic Period 330 B.C.–A.D. 400,* ed. S. E. Porter (Leiden: Brill, 1997), 171-93.

Reumann, J., 'OIKONOMIA — Terms in Paul in Comparison with Lucan *Heilsgeschichte*', *NTS* 13 (1966-67), 147-67.

Reynier, C., *Évangile et Mystère: les enjeux théologiques de l'Épître aux Éphésiens* (Paris: Cerf, 1992).

Ridderbos, H., *Paul: An Outline of His Theology* (Grand Rapids: Eerdmans, 1975).

Roberts, J. H., 'The Enigma of Ephesians: Rethinking Some Positions on the Basis of Schnackenburg and Arnold', *Neot* 27 (1993), 93-106.

Robertson, A. T., *A Grammar of the Greek New Testament in the Light of Historical Research* (New York: Hodder & Stoughton, 1919).

Roels, E. D., *God's Mission: The Epistle to the Ephesians in Mission Perspective* (Franeker: Wever, 1962).

Rogers, C., 'The Dionysian Background of Ephesians 5:18', *BSac* 136 (1979), 249-57.

Sampley, J. P., *'And the Two Shall Become One Flesh': A Study of Traditions in Eph 5:21-33* (Cambridge: Cambridge University Press, 1971).

Sanders, J. T., 'Hymnic Elements in Ephesians 1–3', *ZNW* 56 (1965), 214-32.

Sanders, J. T., 'The Transition from Opening Epistolary Thanksgiving to Body in the Letters of the Pauline Corpus', *JBL* 81 (1962), 348-62.

Sandnes, K. O., *Paul — One of the Prophets? A Contribution to the Apostle's Self-Understanding* (Tübingen: J. C. B. Mohr [Paul Siebeck], 1991).

Schenk, W., *Der Segen im Neuen Testament: Eine Begriffsanalytische Studie* (Berlin: Evangelische Verlagsanstalt, 1967).

Schlier, H., *Christus und die Kirche im Epheserbrief* (Tübingen: J. C. B. Mohr [Paul Siebeck], 1930).

Schmid, J., *Der Epheserbrief des Apostels Paulus: Seine Adresse, Sprache und literarischen Beziehungen* (Freiburg: Herder, 1928).

Schrage, W., 'Zur Ethik der neutestamentlichen Haustafeln', *NTS* 21 (1974-75), 1-22.

Schreiner, T. R., *The Law and Its Fulfillment: A Pauline Theology of Law* (Grand Rapids: Baker, 1993).

Schubert, P., *Form and Function of the Pauline Thanksgivings* (Berlin: Töpelmann, 1939).

Schütz, J. H., *Paul and the Anatomy of Apostolic Authority* (Cambridge: Cambridge University Press, 1975).

Schweizer, E., 'Dying and Rising with Christ', *NTS* 14 (1967), 1-14.

Scott, J. M., *Adoption as Sons of God: An Exegetical Investigation into the Background of ΥΙΟΘΕΣΙΑ in the Pauline Corpus* (Tübingen: J. C. B. Mohr [Paul Siebeck], 1992).

Silva, M., 'The Pauline Style as Lexical Choice: ΓΙΝΩΣΚΕΙΝ and Related Verbs', in *Pauline Studies: Essays Presented to F. F. Bruce on His 70th Birthday*, ed. D. A. Hagner and M. J. Harris (Grand Rapids: Eerdmans, 1980), 184-207.

Smillie, G. R., 'Ephesians 6:19-20: A Mystery for the Sake of Which the Apostle Is an Ambassador in Chains', *TrinJ* 18 (1997), 199-222.

Smith, D. C., 'The Ephesian Heresy and the Origin of the Epistle to the Ephesians', *Ohio Journal of Religious Studies* 5 (1977), 78-103.

Smith, G. V., 'Paul's Use of Psalm 68:18 in Ephesians 4:8', *JETS* 18 (1975), 181-89.

Spencer, F. S., *The Portrait of Philip in Acts: A Study of Roles and Relations* (Sheffield: Academic Press, 1992).

Speyer, W., *Die literarische Fälschung im heidnischen und christlichen Altertum: Ein Versuch ihrer Deutung* (München: Beck, 1971).

Stamps, D. L., 'Rhetorical Criticism of the New Testament: Ancient and Modern Evaluations of Argumentation', in *Approaches to New Testament Study*, ed. S. E. Porter and D. Tombs (Sheffield: Academic Press, 1995), 129-69.

Steinmetz, F.-J., *Protologische Heils-Zuversicht: Die Strukturen des soteriologischen und christologischen Denkens im Kolosser- und Epheserbrief* (Frankfurt: Knecht, 1969).

Stowers, S. K., *Letter Writing in Greco-Roman Antiquity* (Philadelphia: Westminster, 1986).

Strelan, R., *Paul, Artemis, and the Jews in Ephesus* (Berlin: de Gruyter, 1996).

Strickland, W., and others, eds., *The Law, The Gospel, and the Modern Christian* (Grand Rapids: Zondervan, 1993).

Stuhlmacher, P., '"He Is Our Peace" (Eph. 2:14): On the Exegesis and Significance of Eph. 2:14-18', in *Reconciliation, Law, & Righteousness: Essays in Biblical Theology* (Philadelphia: Fortress, 1986), 182-200.

Stuhlmacher, P., 'The Pauline Gospel', in *The Gospel and the Gospels*, ed. P. Stuhlmacher (Grand Rapids: Eerdmans, 1991), 149-72.

Stuhlmacher, P., 'The Theme: The Gospel and the Gospels', in *The Gospel and the Gospels*, ed. P. Stuhlmacher (Grand Rapids: Eerdmans, 1991), 1-25.

Tachau, P., *'Einst' und 'Jetzt' im Neuen Testament* (Göttingen: Vandenhoeck & Ruprecht, 1972).

Tannehill, R. C., *Dying and Rising with Christ: A Study in Pauline Theology* (Berlin: Töpelmann, 1967).

Taylor, R. A., 'The Use of Psalm 68:18 in Ephesians 4:8 in Light of Ancient Versions', *BSac* 148 (1991), 319-36.

Thomson, I. H., *Chiasmus in the Pauline Letters* (Sheffield: Academic Press, 1995).

Thrall, M. E., *Greek Particles in the New Testament: Linguistic and Exegetical Studies* (Leiden: Brill, 1962).

Towner, P. H., *1-2 Timothy and Titus* (Downers Grove/Leicester: Inter-Varsity, 1994).

Turner, M., 'Mission and Meaning in Terms of "Unity" in Ephesians', in *Mission and Meaning: Essays Presented to Peter Cotterell*, ed. A. Billington, T. Lane, and M. Turner (Carlisle: Paternoster, 1995), 138-66.

Turner, M., *Power from on High: The Spirit in Israel's Restoration and Witness in Luke-Acts* (Sheffield: Academic Press, 1996).

Turner, M., 'Spiritual Gifts Then and Now', *Vox Evangelica* 15 (1985), 7-64.

van der Horst, P. W., 'Is Wittiness UnChristian? A Note on εὐτραπελία in Eph. v.4', in *Miscellanea Neotestamentica*, ed. T. Baard, A. F. J. Klijn, and W. C. van Unnik, vol. 2 (Leiden: Brill, 1978), 163-77.

van der Horst, P. W., 'Observations on a Pauline Expression', *NTS* 19 (1972-73), 181-87.

van Roon, A., *The Authenticity of Ephesians* (Leiden: Brill, 1974).

van Unnik, W. C., 'The Christian's Freedom of Speech in the New Testament', in *Sparsa Collecta*, vol. 2 (Leiden: Brill, 1980), 269-89.

van Unnik, W. C., 'The Semitic Background of ΠΑΡΡΗΣΙΑ in the New Testament', in *Sparsa Collecta*, vol. 2 (Leiden: Brill, 1980), 290-306.

Verner, D. C., *The Household of God: The Social World of the Pastoral Epistles* (Chico, CA: Scholars Press, 1983).

Vielhauer, P., *Oikodomē: Aufsätze zum Neuen Testament* (München: Kaiser, 1979).

Volf, M., *After our Likeness: The Church as the Image of the Trinity* (Grand Rapids/Cambridge: Eerdmans, 1998).

Wallace, D. B., *Greek Grammar beyond the Basics: An Exegetical Syntax of the New Testament* (Grand Rapids: Zondervan, 1996).

Wallace, D. B., ''Οργίζεσθε in Ephesians 4:26: Command or Condition?', *Criswell Theological Review* 3 (1989), 353-72.

Wallace, D. B., 'The Semantic Range of the Article-Noun-*kai*-Noun Plural Construction in the New Testament', *Grace Theological Journal* 4 (1983), 59-84.

Wallis, I. G., *The Faith of Jesus Christ in Early Christian Traditions* (Cambridge: Cambridge University Press, 1995).

Warfield, B. B., *The Inspiration and Authority of the Bible* (Philadelphia: Presbyterian and Reformed, 1948).

Watts, R. E., *Isaiah's New Exodus and Mark* (Tübingen: J. C. B. Mohr [Paul Siebeck], 1997).

Webb, B. G., *The Message of Isaiah: On Eagles' Wings* (Leicester: Inter-Varsity, 1996).

Weber, B., '"Setzen" — "Wandeln" — "Stehen" im Epheserbrief', *NTS* 41 (1995), 478-80.

Weima, J. A. D., *Neglected Endings: The Significance of the Pauline Letter Closings* (Sheffield: Academic Press, 1994).

Weima, J. A. D., 'The Pauline Letter Closings: Analysis and Hermeneutical Significance', *BBR* 5 (1995), 177-98.

Weima, J. A. D., 'What Does Aristotle Have to Do with Paul? An Evaluation of Rhetorical Criticism', *CTJ* 32 (1997), 458-68.

Wessels, G. F., 'The Eschatology of Colossians and Ephesians', *Neot* 21 (1987), 183-202.

Westermann, C., *The Praise of God in the Psalms* (London: Epworth, 1966).

White, J. L., 'The Greek Documentary Letter Tradition Third Century B.C.E. to Third Century C.E.', *Semeia* 22 (1982), 92-100.

White, J. L., 'New Testament Epistolary Literature in the Framework of Ancient Epistolography', in *ANRW*, ed. W. Haase and H. Temporini, pt. 2, vol. 25.2 (Berlin/New York: de Gruyter, 1984), 1730-56.

White, L. M., 'Social Authority in the House Church Setting and Ephesians 4:1-16', *ResQ* 29 (1987), 209-28.

Wiedemann, T., *Greek and Roman Slavery* (London: Croom Helm, 1981).

Wiederkehr, D., *Die Theologie der Berufung in den Paulusbriefen* (Freiburg: Universitätsverlag, 1963).

Wilcox, M., *The Semitisms of Acts* (Oxford: Clarendon, 1965).

Wilcox, M., 'Text Form', in *It Is Written: Scripture Citing Scripture*, ed. D. A. Carson and H. G. M. Williamson (Cambridge: Cambridge University Press, 1988), 193-204.

Wild, R. A., '"Be Imitators of God": Discipleship in the Letter to the Ephesians', in *Discipleship in the New Testament*, ed. F. F. Segovia (Philadelphia: Fortress, 1985), 127-43.

Wild, R. A., 'The Warrior and the Prisoner: Some Reflections on Ephesians 6:10-20', *CBQ* 46 (1984), 284-98.

Wiles, G. P., *Paul's Intercessory Prayers: The Significance of the Intercessory Prayer Passages in the Letters of St. Paul* (Cambridge: Cambridge University Press, 1974).

Wilson, R. A., '"We" and "You" in the Epistle to the Ephesians', in *SE,* ed. F. L. Cross, vol. 2 (Berlin: Akademie-Verlag, 1964), 676-80.

Wink, W., *Engaging the Powers: Discernment and Resistance in a World of Domination* (Minneapolis: Fortress, 1992).

Wink, W., *Naming the Powers: The Language of Power in the New Testament* (Philadelphia: Fortress, 1984).

Wink, W., *Unmasking the Powers: The Invisible Forces That Determine Human Existence* (Philadelphia: Fortress, 1986).

Winter, B., 'Is Paul among the Sophists?', *RTR* 53 (1994), 28-38.

Witherington, B., *Women in the Earliest Churches* (Cambridge: Cambridge University Press, 1988).

Wolter, M., *Rechtfertigung und zukünftiges Heil: Untersuchungen zu Röm 5,1-11* (Berlin: de Gruyter, 1978).

Wright, J., 'Spirit and Wilderness: The Interplay of Two Motifs within the Hebrew Bible as a Background to Mark 1:2-13', in *Perspectives on Language and Text: Festschrift for F. I. Andersen*, ed. E. W. Conrad and E. G. Newing (Winona Lake, IN: Eisenbrauns, 1987), 269-98.

Yates, R., 'A Re-Examination of Ephesians 1:23', *ExpTim* 83 (1971-72), 146-51.

Zuntz, G., *The Text of the Epistles* (London: British Academy, 1954).

Introduction

The Letter to the Ephesians is one of the most significant documents ever written. Samuel Taylor Coleridge called it 'the divinest composition of man'. This letter was John Calvin's favourite, and J. Armitage Robinson later described it as 'the crown of St Paul's writings'.[1] F. F. Bruce regarded it as 'the quintessence of Paulinism' because it 'in large measure sums up the leading themes of the Pauline letters, and sets forth the cosmic implications of Paul's ministry as apostle to the Gentiles'.[2] Among the Pauline writings, Raymond Brown claimed, only Romans could match Ephesians 'as a candidate for exercising the most influence on Christian thought and spirituality'.[3]

Although relatively few commentaries on this letter have come down to us from the early church, this document, which was regarded as Pauline, has had an important impact on the lives of Christians from the time it was written, as is evidenced by the numerous quotations from it in early Christian literature.[4] It has had considerable influence on Christian liturgy and piety down the centuries; liturgical prayers and short readings have frequently been taken from Ephesians (cf. 2:4-6, 19-22; 4:11-13, 23-26).

---

1. Robinson, vii.
2. F. F. Bruce, *Paul: Apostle of the Free Spirit* (Exeter: Paternoster, 1977), 424. Bruce used the expression 'the quintessence of Paulinism', originally coined by A. S. Peake, in his lecture 'St. Paul in Rome. 4. The Epistle to the Ephesians', *BJRL* 49 (1967), 303.
3. R. E. Brown, *An Introduction to the New Testament* (New York/London: Doubleday, 1997), 620.
4. So Schnackenburg, 311, following the two volumes of *Biblia Patristica*. Snodgrass, 17, thinks that only the Psalms, the Gospel of John, and Romans have been as significant as Ephesians in shaping the life and thought of Christians, and all of these are much longer documents.

Whether it is because of its magnificent sweep of God's saving purposes from election before the foundation of the world to his summing up of all things in Christ, the place of the exalted Christ within those purposes and believers' relationship to him, God's victory in Christ over the powers, the grand presentation of the church, its language of worship and prayer, or the scope and depth of its ethical teaching, Ephesians has had a profound influence on the lives of many.[5]

But the letter has not only had a significant impact on the lives of men and women in the past. It also speaks with great power to our contemporary situation. To a world that seems to have lost all sense of direction, and a society that for all its great achievements is in a mess, the divine analysis of the human predicament along with God's gracious and comprehensive salvation, such as is found in Ephesians 2:1-7, ultimately provides the only hope for a world that stands under divine judgment. Klyne Snodgrass aptly remarks: 'The understanding of the gospel in Ephesians challenges and redefines the superficial understanding of the gospel prevalent in our day'.[6]

Ephesians repeatedly draws attention to the sharp contrasts between believers' former way of life and their new life in Christ, contrasts that are underscored by means of the *once–now* form (note especially chap. 2). This fundamental distinction between unbelievers and those in Christ is epitomized in 5:8: 'For once you were darkness, but now you are light in the Lord. Live as children of light'. This and similar portrayals of the readers' Christian existence are clearly intended to remind them of the privileged position into which they have now come, and to urge them to pattern their lives on the character of God and Christ (see on 4:32–5:2). This will also mean that their lifestyle should not conform to that of the surrounding society.

In an increasingly postmodern world, Ephesians is refreshing in its strong affirmations that *truth* is important, namely, the truth of God and his gospel, a truth that stands over against all sham and lack of reality. The letter, however, does not focus on truth at the expense of love. Quite the reverse. The love of God and of Christ is regarded as foundational throughout the letter, while believers, who are urged to *imitate God*, are to do this by living a life of love (5:1-2), words which summarize much of the exhortatory material in the second half (chaps. 4–6). In fact, it has been claimed that, apart from 1 Corinthians 13, Ephesians has more references per page to love, or at least believers living *in love*, than anywhere

---

5. Note the chapter 'The Influence of the Epistle throughout History', in Schnackenburg, 311-42.
6. Snodgrass, 18.

else in the Pauline letters. Furthermore, this concern for truth and love in relationship is tied in with unity. In the light of God's magnificent saving purposes (spelled out in chaps. 1–3) and his plan to bring all things together in unity in Christ, those who are recipients of 'every spiritual blessing in the heavenly places in Christ' (1:3) are urged to live a life worthy of the calling they have received (4:1). Central to this exhortation is the urgent and powerful admonition, 'Make every effort to keep the unity of the Spirit through the bond of peace' (4:3). The strong motivation for this appeal is presented through a series of seven acclamations (vv. 4-6) in which the readers are reminded of the fundamental unities on which the Christian faith and life are based.

Following its important theological affirmations in chapters 1–3, the exhortatory material of the second half of the letter (chaps. 4–6) is both considerable and highly significant (note the teaching on marriage in 5:21-33). But Ephesians does not provide us with lists of rules to follow; nor does it suggest slick and easy solutions to our fundamental needs before God and others. Instead, on the basis of our union with Christ, and thus our relationship with God, the letter urges us 'to change our inner being and character in a radical way'.[7] Every aspect of our lives is now to be lived with reference to our Lord. We are to give thanks always to God the Father for everything, in the name of our Lord Jesus Christ (5:20). In the light of God's revelation in the gospel, Christians are to grow in their understanding so as to know him better (1:17-19). We need divine empowering in order to understand the love of Christ which surpasses knowledge, because it is God's desire that we may be filled to all the measure of the fulness of God (3:19).

Ephesians makes some important theological affirmations about the people of God. It introduces a series of highly significant images describing the church, including terms such as body, building, temple, in Christ, bride, new humanity, family, and marriage. It comes as no surprise, then, to learn that many claim that this New Testament writing contains the 'highest ecclesiology of all'. The referents in view and the specific teaching that is presented through this wide-ranging imagery are considerable, while the entailments challenge much that is superficial, worldly, self-centred, and individualistic within our contemporary churches.

Yet for all this, Ephesians presents something of an enigma. We do not know to whom the letter was sent, from where it was dispatched, or exactly why it was sent. Further, the majority of contemporary scholars do not accept Paul as the author of Ephesians.

---

7. Snodgrass, 19.

I. AUTHORSHIP

In keeping with the convention of his time the author begins by announcing himself as the apostle Paul (Eph. 1:1; cf. 3:1). Further, the letter contains many personal notes: the writer has heard of the readers' faith and love (1:15); he gives thanks and prays for them (1:16); he calls himself 'the prisoner of Christ Jesus' (3:1; 4:1), and he asks for his readers' intercessions on his behalf (6:19-20). The 'man who claims to be Paul was known to the readers and was confident that his claim would not be overthrown'.[8] We should hold anyone who claims to be the author of any letter coming to us from antiquity to be just that unless there is very strong evidence to the contrary.[9]

This affirmation of the Pauline authorship of Ephesians was universally accepted in the early church, and was not challenged until the late eighteenth and early nineteenth centuries. The letter was referred to early and often, apparently from Clement of Rome (A.D. 95) on.[10] It is quoted by Ignatius, who shows familiarity with the armour of God (6:11-17), and by Polycarp, who cites Ephesians 4:26 along with Psalm 4:4 as Scripture. Irenaeus quotes Ephesians 5:30, with the introduction 'as blessed Paul declares in his epistle to the Ephesians'. In fact, Irenaeus attributed Ephesians to Paul on a number of occasions (*Adversus Haereses* 1.8.5; 5.2.3; 8.1; 14.3; 24.4). Marcion considered Ephesians to be a genuine letter of the apostle, though written to Laodicea (Tertullian, *Adversus Marcionem* 5.17), while it is listed as one of the Pauline letters in the Muratorian Canon (*c.* A.D. 180). In the third century it was regularly attributed to Paul by both the orthodox and their heretical opponents.

By the end of the eighteenth and the early nineteenth centuries the first challenges arose to the traditional view of Pauline authorship. The strong denial of F. C. Baur and his followers had considerable influence on the subsequent course of scholarship, so that today scholarly opinion is divided. A majority holds that the letter was not written by Paul. In spite of this, the case against Pauline authorship is not obvious, and those who argue for it still claim that the author has reflected on Paul's letters (especially Colossians) so intimately that they have become part and parcel of his thinking. But if Ephesians is so Pauline, should its authorship have been so seriously questioned?

---

8. D. A. Carson, D. J. Moo, and L. Morris, *An Introduction to the New Testament* (Grand Rapids: Zondervan, 1992), 306.

9. The onus of proof lies with those who deny the claim of authenticity.

10. Best, 15, disputes the conclusion that Clement knew Ephesians. He does concede, however, that there is 'a fair possibility that either Ignatius or Polycarp or both knew Ephesians' (17). Note his survey of the apostolic fathers on pp. 15-17.

The main arguments against Pauline authorship are as follows:

A. The Impersonal Character of Ephesians

The 'implied author' of the letter to the Ephesians is Paul (1:1; 3:1), who claims apostolic authority and describes himself as a suffering prisoner for Christ, the gospel, and the Gentiles (3:1, 13; 4:1; 6:19, 20). But he gives no details of his suffering or imprisonment in the letter. He appears to have only a general knowledge of his readers (1:13, 15, 16), and questions whether they had heard of his administration of God's grace in ministering to Gentiles (3:2); he also questions their reception of the instruction they had received (4:21). The lack of personal greetings to members of the church at Ephesus is surprising, given that he sends extended greetings to the Christians in Rome, a city he had not visited (Rom. 15–16). All this reinforces the picture of an author without any intimate connection with his readers.

According to the book of Acts Paul first arrived in Ephesus at the end of his second missionary journey (in the autumn of A.D. 52) and ministered in the synagogue for a short time before leaving for Jerusalem (Acts 18:18-21). He returned a year later on his third missionary journey and remained in Ephesus for a further two and a half years, leaving in the spring of A.D. 56 (19:1–20:1). A year later he visited the elders of the church of Ephesus in Miletus on his way to Jerusalem from Corinth (20:16-38). Given that Paul had spent considerable time with the Ephesians, how is it possible for him to speak of 'having heard' of their faith and love (1:15)? And why does he close his letter with so brief and impersonal a farewell?

A critical factor in this discussion is how we interpret Ephesians 1:1 (see the discussion below). If for the moment we anticipate our later conclusion that the words 'in Ephesus' were not part of the original reading, then the letter might still have been written by the apostle Paul as a general epistle, and sent to mainly Gentile believers in southwestern Asia Minor (see on 1:1).

B. Language and Style

Ephesians, it is claimed, shows significant differences of language and style from the generally accepted Pauline letters. Forty-one words are used only in Ephesians, and a further 84 are not found elsewhere in Paul's writings but appear in the rest of the New Testament. These statis-

5

tics are not particularly significant, however, in comparison with those of other New Testament writings. Galatians, for example, which is of similar length and has 35 hapax legomena, is almost universally regarded as Pauline. Perhaps it is more important that many of these unique terms appear in the apostolic fathers, giving the letter greater affinity with the postapostolic literature.[11] However, one wonders whether these early church fathers knew and used Ephesians, and therefore whether the influence has gone the other way.

Of particular significance are the combinations of words and phrases which are unique to Ephesians and which reflect this writer's distinctive mode of expression. These include 'spiritual blessing' (1:3), 'the foundation of the world' (1:4), 'the forgiveness of trespasses' (1:7), 'the mystery of his will' (1:9), 'the word of truth' (1:13), 'the Father of glory' (1:17), 'the desires of the flesh' (2:3), and 'to learn Christ' (4:20). Other stylistic features include Ephesians' use of 'in the heavenlies' (1:3, 20; 2:6; 3:10; 6:12) in relation to the heavenly realm (rather than 'in the heavens'), and the term 'devil' (4:27; 6:11), rather than Satan (Rom. 16:20; 1 Cor. 5:5; 7:5; 2 Cor. 2:11; 11:14; 12:7; 1 Thess. 2:18; 2 Thess. 2:9),[12] along with the introductory formula 'wherefore it says' to introduce quotations.[13] But 'the word of truth' is found elsewhere in Paul (Col. 1:5; cf. 2 Cor. 6:7; 2 Tim. 2:15), while similar language appears in the rest of the New Testament: 'the desires of the flesh' (2:3) is parallel to John 1:13, and 'the Father of glory' (1:17) is similar to 'the God of glory' (Acts 7:2; cf. Matt. 16:27; Rom. 6:4; Phil. 2:11; 4:20). Many of these expressions are unique within the Pauline corpus, although some have parallels in other parts of the New Testament. It needs to be borne in mind, however, that Paul uses distinctive vocabulary in each of his letters, not just in Ephesians.[14] This may be due to a range of factors bound up with the apostle's mood, his relationships with the readers, and the issues addressed — in short, the whole epistolary situation.

The style of Ephesians, which has been called 'pleonastic', is characterized by lengthy sentences that are extended by relative or causal clauses and participial constructions (e.g., 1:3-14, 15-23; 2:1-7; 3:1-13;

---

11. For example, terms such as ἄθεος ('without God'; 2:12), ἄσοφος ('unwise'), ἑνότης ('oneness, unity'), etc.

12. διάβολος ('devil') is a common word anyway, and appears 37 times in the New Testament.

13. For further details see Lincoln, lxv.

14. Even C. L. Mitton, *The Epistle to the Ephesians* (Oxford: Clarendon, 1951), 29, admits: 'Several of the undoubtedly genuine epistles have an even higher percentage of words which are not found in the other Pauline writings'; cited by H. W. Hoehner, *Ephesians* (Grand Rapids: Baker, forthcoming).

4:11-16; 6:14-20). K. G. Kuhn has pointed out that these loosely strung clauses also occur with frequency in the Qumran literature, especially in the Hymns of Thanksgiving, and he suggests that their presence in Ephesians may be due to a continuity of tradition.[15] Repeatedly in Ephesians synonymous words are linked by genitival constructions (note especially terms for power at 1:19; 3:7; 6:10), while on other occasions synonyms are placed side by side (e.g., 'wisdom and insight', 1:8; 'trespasses and sins', 2:1) for rhetorical effect. The simple repetition of keywords or cognates is another feature of Ephesians' rhetorical style, for example, the piling up of terms referring to God's choice or purpose (1:3-11), knowledge (1:17-18), or grace and mercy (2:4-8). Finally, there is a 'rhyming of thoughts' in 2:14-18 in relation to 'peace', 'unity', and the destruction of 'enmity'.[16]

These features[17] dominate the first half of the letter, where the author intentionally uses the lofty language of eulogy, praise, prayer, and doxology. Elsewhere he shows that he is capable of writing more direct, succinct, and lively discourse.[18] Furthermore, when compared with other Pauline literature the long sentences are not all that unusual, even if Ephesians does have a greater number of them. A. van Roon has pointed out that Paul chose to use long sentences in doxologies and prayers (Eph. 1:3-14, 15-23; 3:14-19; cf. Rom 8:38-39; 11:33-39; 1 Cor. 1:4-8; Phil. 1:3-8; 1 Thess. 1:2-5; 2 Thess. 1:3-10),[19] in statements where there is considerable doctrinal content (Eph. 2:1-7; 3:2-13; cf. Rom. 3:21-26; 1 Cor. 1:26-29; 2:6-9), and in exhortatory materials (Eph. 4:1-6, 11-16; 6:14-20; cf. 1 Cor 12:8-11; Phil. 1:27–2:11).[20] To suggest that he could not have written in this vein is really to question Paul's resourcefulness. These sentences are not out of character with his other letters. Perhaps in a more reflective mood, when there were no major or pressing pastoral problems, the apostle deliberately used exalted liturgical language (some of which may have been borrowed from early Christian worship) as he praised God for his glori-

---

15. K. G. Kuhn, 'The Epistle to the Ephesians in the Light of the Qumran Texts', in *Paul and Qumran*, ed. J. Murphy-O'Connor (London: Chapman, 1968), 116-20; note the discussion and interaction with this in P. T. O'Brien, 'Ephesians I: An Unusual Introduction to a New Testament Letter', *NTS* 25 (1979), 504-16, esp. 507-9.

16. A. van Roon, *The Authenticity of Ephesians* (Leiden: Brill, 1974), 135-58.

17. Note also the use of paronomasia and repetition of sounds for rhetorical effect (1:23), and the stringing together of prepositional phrases at 1:5, 6 and 4:12, for example (so Lincoln, xlv-xlvi).

18. Note the references to 'riches' (1:7, 18; 2:7; 3:8, 16) and the frequent recurrence of 'all'. Lincoln, xlvi, who argues against Pauline authorship, admits this point.

19. See further P. T. O'Brien, *Introductory Thanksgivings in the Letters of Paul* (Leiden: Brill, 1977).

20. A. van Roon, *Authenticity*, 105-11; cf. Hoehner.

ous plan of salvation (esp. in chaps. 1–3) and edified his predominantly Gentile readers.

Although there are some differences of language and style in Ephesians, they are not enough, in our judgment, to discount authenticity. If the letter was written by a disciple of the apostle, it is surprising that such an outstanding author, of the calibre of Paul himself, should be unknown in the first-century church.

C. The Literary Relationship between Ephesians and Colossians

That there is a literary relationship between Ephesians and Colossians is clearly evident. T. K. Abbott's synoptic chart shows the striking verse-by-verse similarities between the two letters.[21] This relationship between them is the most critical factor in the case against the Pauline authorship of Ephesians. Most scholars who regard Ephesians as pseudonymous contend that it depends heavily on Colossians as its primary literary source.[22] Andrew Lincoln, for example, believes that this is the main reason for rejecting Pauline authorship of the letter: 'Most decisive against Paul as the author of Ephesians is its dependence on Colossians and its use of other Pauline letters, particularly Romans'.[23]

Leslie Mitton's statistics show that of the 1,570 words in Colossians 34 percent are parallelled in Ephesians, while 26.5 percent of the 2,411 words in Ephesians are parallelled in Colossians. These figures do not reveal the extent of the similarity between the letters, and advocates of the dependence of Ephesians on Colossians claim that one must take into account that Colossians comes closest to the distinctive style of Ephesians, and that the overall structure and sequence of the letters are similar. Surprisingly, the most extensive point of contact is the commendation of Tychicus (Col. 4:7-8; Eph. 6:21-22). Here there is verbatim correspondence between 29 consecutive words (although 'and fellow servant' is omitted

21. Abbott, xxiii-xxiv.

22. So, e.g., C. L. Mitton, *Epistle*; Lindemann, 9-12; Schnackenburg, 30-33; and Lincoln, xlvii-lviii. A recent exception is Best, 20-25, and 'Who Used Whom? The Relationship of Ephesians and Colossians', *NTS* 43 (1997), 72-96, who claims that the literary relationships are most satisfactorily explained in terms of a 'two-way traffic' between the two letters. Significantly, Best contends that his research 'removes one main argument from those who believe the non-Pauline authorship of Ephesians can be firmly asserted on the basis of the use of Colossians by Ephesians' (25)!

23. A. T. Lincoln and A. J. M. Wedderburn, *The Theology of the Later Pauline Letters* (Cambridge: Cambridge University Press, 1993), 84; cf. Lincoln, xlvii-xlviii.

in Ephesians). Beyond this there are only three other places where the parallels extend to seven words, and two places where five words are parallel.[24] Clinton Arnold comments: 'This appears to be very slim evidence for the postulation of literary dependence'. He then adds pointedly: 'It seems especially odd that the longest passage reproduced in Ephesians is not from the theological argumentation or paraenesis of Colossians, but about the sending of Tychicus'.[25] One would have thought that had an imitator copied from Colossians there would have been far more verbal correspondence between the two epistles given that much of the content of the two letters is similar.

The statistical parallels mentioned above do not provide decisive evidence against Pauline authorship, so most advocates of the literary dependence of Ephesians on Colossians place more weight on the similar overall structure and sequence of the two letters with their same thematic material. Colossians, of all the other Pauline letters, comes closest to the distinctive style of Ephesians. As we have seen, both epistles contain long sentences, frequent relative clauses, genitive constructions, and prepositional phrases with 'in'.

The following chart, based on the work of J. Schmid and followed by others,[26] shows that Ephesians has much thematic material in common with Colossians, and that the main sections of the two letters follow the same sequence.

COMPARISON OF EPHESIANS AND COLOSSIANS

Col	Unique to Col	Parallel Material	Unique to Eph	Eph
1:1-2		Prologue		1:1-2
			Eulogy	1:3-14
1:3-14			Thanksgiving and Intercession	1:15-23
1:15-20	Supremacy of Christ in creation and reconciliation			

24. Cf. Eph. 1:1-2 and Col. 1:1-2, which is not particularly significant; Eph. 1:7 and Col. 1:14; Eph. 2:5 and Col. 2:13; Eph. 3:2 and Col. 1:25; Eph. 3:9 and Col. 1:26; Eph. 4:16 and Col. 2:19; Eph. 4:32 and Col. 3:13; Eph. 5:5-6 and Col. 3:5-6; Eph. 5:19-20 and Col. 3:16-17; Eph. 6:1-4 and Col. 3:20-21; Eph. 6:5-9 and Col. 3:22–4:1. Cf. Lincoln, xlix; and Snodgrass, 25.

25. C. E. Arnold, *DPL*, 242.

26. J. Schmid, *Der Epheserbrief des Apostels Paulus: Seine Adresse, Sprache und literarischen Beziehungen* (Freiburg: Herder, 1928), 412. Cf. also J. Ernst, *Die Briefe an die Philipper, an Philemon, an die Kolosser, an die Epheser* (Regensburg: Pustet, 1974), 254-55; Lincoln, xlix; and Hoehner.

		Reminder of readers' salvation	2:1-10
1:21-23		From alienation then to reconciliation now	(Also reconciliation of Jews and Gentiles into one body)	2:11-22
1:24–2:3		Paul as a suffering apostle and his ministry of the mystery		
2:4–3:4	Warning against false teaching and reminder of true teaching			
			Prayer for strengthening in love and doxology	3:14-21
		(Head-body of Christ — Col. 2:19 = Eph. 4:15, 16)	Exhortation to unity	4:1-16
3:5-17		Exhortations about the old and new humanity — sexual morality, anger, truth, love, thanksgiving, singing	(Light/darkness contrast — 5:8-14)	4:17–5:20
3:18–4:1		Household code	(Christ and the church — 5:22-32)	5:22–6:9
			Spiritual warfare	6:10-17
4:2-4		Exhortation to prayer and proclamation of the mystery		6:18-20
4:5-6	Conduct toward outsiders			
4:7-9		Commendation of Tychicus		6:21-22
4:10-17	Greetings			
4:18	(Autograph)	Benediction	(Peace and love)	6:23-24

1. Ephesians Drew Heavily on Colossians

All scholars recognize the close relationship between Ephesians and Colossians and the possibility that the author of one letter may have used the other. Some hold to the priority of Ephesians,[27] but most think

27. For example, J. Coutts, 'The Relationship of Ephesians and Colossians', *NTS* 4 (1958), 201-7. A. van Roon, *Authenticity,* 413-37, thinks that Colossians possibly borrowed from Ephesians, although he believes that both letters were dependent on an earlier text.

Colossians was written first.[28] Andrew Lincoln, one of the more recent advocates of the latter view, contends that the author of Ephesians drew heavily on Colossians. His arguments are as follows:[29]

a. Ephesians 'builds on the overall structure and thematic sequence of Colossians'.[30] Lincoln notes that in the first parts of the letters, the prologue, the thanksgiving period with its intercessory prayer report, the reminder of the readers' previous experience of alienation and their present reconciliation in Christ, along with the discussion of Paul's suffering as an apostle and his ministry of the mystery, are all parallel.[31] He recognizes that each letter treats these forms and subjects in a slightly different fashion, but even in those sections which appear to be distinctive there are counterparts found elsewhere in the other epistle (e.g., note the more developed counterpart of Col. 1:13-14 in Eph. 2:1-10). Even where the main topics of a section are distinctive, there are verbal parallels within it (cf. the use of Col. 1:23-28 by the author of Ephesians in 3:1-13, who then takes up in 3:14-21 material from Col. 1:29–3:10). Lincoln claims that in the second half of the letters 'the bulk of the paraenesis has parallel material in the same broad sequence'.[32] This includes exhortatory material about putting off the old humanity and putting on the new, both of which involve similar specific injunctions. Instruction about relationships within the Christian household follow, and the sequence of the injunctions in the Ephesian and Colossian codes is similar. Both letters conclude with a similar exhortation to prayer, a commendation of Tychicus, and a benediction. Once again Lincoln draws attention to the distinctive ways in which each letter treats similar material. He claims that it is inadequate to 'hold that the two letters simply reproduce common traditions', for even 'if there was some [such] use . . . , it looks far more likely that the primary explanation must be that the one letter served as the model for the other'.[33]

b. The close verbal links within parallel sections of the two letters all point to a one-way dependence of Ephesians on Colossians.[34] The greet-

---

28. For the more nuanced treatment of E. Best, see below.

29. Lincoln, xlviii-lvi, is heavily indebted to C. L. Mitton, *Epistle*, but he modifies the latter's work at significant points (e.g., liii-liv).

30. Lincoln, li.

31. Lincoln, xlviii-l.

32. Lincoln, l.

33. Lincoln, l; cf. H. Merklein, *Das kirchliche Amt nach dem Epheserbrief* (München: Kösel, 1973), 39. For a survey of the various solutions up to 1973, see J. B. Polhill, 'The Relationship between Ephesians and Colossians', *RevExp* 70 (1973), 439-50, and for a comprehensive listing of positions taken by scholars, see the forthcoming commentary of Hoehner.

34. Lincoln, li; cf. the synoptic arrangement of C. L. Mitton, *Epistle*, 279-315.

ings are similar, with the addressees being described only in these two letters of the Pauline corpus as 'saints' and 'faithful in Christ (Jesus)'. There are correspondences of keywords (e.g., redemption, reconciliation, body, flesh), particularly in Ephesians 3:1-13, which is based on Colossians 1:24-29 (e.g., affliction, ministry, mystery, riches, and power). In the second half of each letter there are terminological connections in relation to putting off the old humanity and putting on the new, along with lists of vices and virtues (Col. 3:5-17; Eph. 4:17–5:20),[35] and these show that Ephesians is dependent on the earlier epistle. Almost all the words of the Colossians household code (Col. 3:18–4:1) have been taken over in the same sequence in the Ephesians counterpart (Eph. 5:21–6:9); to this is then added the author's own more developed Christian interpretation. Finally, the verbal links are evident in the exhortations to prayer (Col. 4:2-4; Eph. 6:18-20) and in the letters' postscripts (Col. 4:7-8; Eph. 6:21-22).

c. The terminological connections between the two letters occur not only in the major parallel sections but also in quite different contexts.[36] The eulogy of Ephesians 1:3-14, which has no exact counterpart in Colossians, nevertheless contains many parallels with the earlier letter (cf. 'holy and blameless before him', Eph. 1:4 with Col. 1:22; 'in whom we have redemption', Eph. 1:6, 7 with Col. 1:13, 14, 20; 'in all wisdom and insight', Eph. 1:8 with Col. 1:9; 'all things . . . things in heaven and things on earth', Eph. 1:10 with Col. 1:20; 'having heard the word of truth, the gospel', Eph. 1:13 with Col. 1:5). The thanksgiving and intercessory prayer report of Ephesians have parallels with similar material (as well as other parts) in Colossians (cf. Eph. 1:18 with Col. 1:27; Eph. 1:19, 20 with Col. 2:12; etc.). Lincoln notes verbal links between the second intercessory prayer report and doxology of Ephesians 3:14-21 and Colossians 1:27–2:10, and thinks that there are clear parallels between Ephesians 4:1-16 and the Colossian paraenetic ('exhortatory') material (e.g., Col. 3:12-15; 2:19).

d. The author of Ephesians has picked up and used key terms and concepts already expressed in Colossians, or employed the same term but with different connotations in Colossians[37] so as to suit his own theological purposes. Either way his dependence on the former letter is evident, it is claimed. So, in the case of the word 'body',[38] Colossians has already reinterpreted the word from its original cosmic sense to mean the 'church' (Col. 1:18; 2:19), and Ephesians takes this reinterpretation for

---

35. Cf. also H. Merklein, 'Eph 4,1–5,20 als Rezeption von Kol 3,1-17', in *Kontinuität und Einheit: Für Franz Mussner,* ed. P. G. Müller and W. Stenger (Herder: Freiburg/Basel/Vienna, 1981), 194-210.

36. Lincoln, lii-liii.

37. Lincoln, liii-lv.

38. Gk. σῶμα.

granted (cf. 4:15-16). Here the author of Ephesians makes no change in meaning, but the priority of Colossians appears to be underlined.[39] The same point occurs in the case of the term,[40] which can refer to God's act of administering (Eph. 1:10; 3:9) or the office of administering, that is, the apostle's stewardship (Col. 1:25; Eph. 3:2). The term can be used differently in different contexts, but where there is the same context (as in Col. 1:25 and Eph. 3:2), Lincoln contends, 'the writer of Ephesians is dependent on the prior use in Colossians'.[41] An example of a changed connotation is the term 'mystery': in Colossians 1:27 it refers to Christ in the believer, but in Ephesians 3:6 the word is used of believing Jews and Gentiles united in Christ. Similarly, the use of the term 'fulness' in Colossians, according to Lincoln, is 'decisive for its force in Ephesians'. At the same time, 'there has been a development between the two letters, and it is one that corresponds to the shift in emphasis between their perspectives'.[42] In Colossians the focus is primarily christological, while in Ephesians it is primarily ecclesiological. These and similar examples will be taken up in the section on the theology of Ephesians (and in the commentary below), but the question remains as to whether these differences are best explained as coming from an imitator who knew Paul well or from the hand of the apostle himself.

e. Lincoln concludes his overview by declaring that Ephesians is dependent 'on a prior Colossians in terms of its overall structure and sequence, its themes, and its wording'. The author of Ephesians has, however, shown a 'free and creative dependence, not a slavish imitation or copying'. As one who has 'immersed himself in his source material to such an extent that it has become part of his way of thinking',[43] he frequently modifies the material of Colossians (and other material in the Pauline corpus)[44] through change of word order, omissions, additions, and conflations. For Lincoln, as we have noted, that author could not have been Paul.

---

39. H. Merklein, *Das kirchliche Amt,* 30-31; and Lincoln, liii.

40. Gk. οἰκονομία.

41. Lincoln, liv. But has not Lincoln already assumed his conclusion, namely, the priority of Colossians? Is he not rather defensive when in Ephesians there is a diverse usage of terms? And could not Paul be the author of such different uses in both letters anyway?

42. So Lincoln, liv. His treatment of the author of Ephesians' use of Colossians' terminology with different connotations (on liii-lv) is more moderate than that of C. L. Mitton (*Epistle,* 84, 90, 97), but open to the same question: Could not these changes have come from the hand of Paul himself rather than an imitator?

43. Lincoln, lv.

44. Lincoln, lviii, thinks that Ephesians makes use of other letters in the Pauline corpus, especially Romans, 'although Colossians is his primary model and source'.

2. Challenging the Consensus

There are, however, considerable difficulties with the approach of Mitton and Lincoln to the literary relationship of Ephesians and Colossians. In our judgment, their conclusions raise more problems than they solve. The following issues are taken up by way of question and critique. Although many of these were raised by earlier writers, for the sake of convenience we shall draw particular attention to the recent important work of Ernest Best, since he has significantly reopened the question of the literary relationship between the two letters.[45]

a. The influential study of H. J. Holtzmann in 1872 concluded that the evidence of some of the parallels between the two letters pointed more in the direction of the dependence of Colossians on Ephesians.[46] Mitton and Lincoln have argued that all the parallels between the letters point to a one-way dependence of Ephesians on Colossians. A. van Roon has brought this hypothesis into question, claiming to have found no sure indication of literary priority on the part of either letter. What evidence there was pointed towards the priority of Ephesians. Although van Roon's suggestion of a third document upon which both Colossians and Ephesians were dependent is very questionable, he has shown the difficulty of proving literary dependence on the available evidence.[47] Lincoln rejects van Roon's findings. But the problem of proving the consistent literary dependence of Ephesians on Colossians will not go away. After an extensive analysis, Best concludes: 'There is . . . insufficient evidence to enable us to come down

---

45. E. Best, 'Who Used Whom?', 72-96; cf. also his commentary, 20-25. Best makes a telling point in his recent article: 'The detailed discussion of the relationship between the two letters has now largely been given up and it has become an accepted tenet of scholarship that Colossians was written prior to Ephesians and the latter composed in its light'. He adds that 'the priority of Colossians is now the accepted position and is adopted in the many commentaries which reject the Pauline authorship of Ephesians; their writers . . . do not stop to argue grounds for Colossian priority but simply explain how and why the author of Ephesians has modified Colossians in using it; often they then use the supposed change to unearth the special point of view of Ephesians. The possibility of the use of Ephesians by Colossians is not even considered'. Even the way that the parallels between the letters are set out assumes the 'widespread acceptance of the priority of Colossians as if it was proven fact' ('Who Used Whom?', 73-74). By contrast, '[c]onservative scholars who accept the Pauline authorship of both letters are more even-handed in the way they set out the parallels, being under no pressure to make one letter depend on the other in the way which those who reject the Pauline authorship of Ephesians see dependence on Colossians as a crucial argument in their armoury' ('Who Used Whom?', 73-74).

46. H. J. Holtzmann, *Kritik der Epheser- und Kolosserbriefe: Auf Grund einer Analyse ihres Verwandtschaftsverhältnisses* (Leipzig: Wilhelm Engelmann, 1872).

47. A. van Roon, *Authenticity*, 413-37, esp. 426; cf. C. E. Arnold, *DPL*, 243.

firmly in favour of the priority of either letter, though there is a slight probability in favour of the use of Ephesians by A/Col [i.e., the author of Colossians]'.[48] In fact, he contends that his research 'removes one main argument from those who believe the non-Pauline authorship of Ephesians can be firmly asserted on the basis of the use of Colossians by Ephesians'![49]

b. The similarities in the overall structure and thematic sequence of the two letters are not surprising, especially if both epistles were written at approximately the same time to Christians in somewhat similar circumstances (e.g., in Asia Minor). This includes the introduction, the body of the letter with its related themes, including the readers' previous experience of separation from God and alienation, their present reconciliation in Christ, and the discussion of Paul's suffering and his ministry of the gospel. In the second half of the letters it is true that 'the bulk of the paraenesis has parallel material in the same broad sequence'.[50] At the same time, there are significant differences. Ephesians 1 contains an introductory *berakah* or eulogy of considerable length (vv. 3-14), an introductory thanksgiving report, and an intercessory prayer report conjoined to the latter (vv. 15-19). By inserting an introductory thanksgiving after the opening *berakah* the author has made this letter different not only from Colossians but also from *any other letter* in the Pauline corpus.[51] Would an imitator have taken such a risk?[52] In our judgment, the person most likely to have done this is Paul. Further, why is there no mention of the Colossians 'hymn' (1:15-20) in Ephesians or, for that matter, no reference to any polemic against the 'heretics' in Colossians 2?

48. E. Best, 'Who Used Whom?', 79; cf. also his commentary, 22-25.

49. Best, 25; cf. his further comment: 'There is a relationship with Colossians but it cannot be proved that AE [*sc.*, the author of Ephesians] used that letter; the customary argument that his use of it would imply he was not Paul cannot then be sustained'.

50. Lincoln, l.

51. P. T. O'Brien, 'An Unusual Introduction', 505, 512-13.

52. Some have concluded that the thanksgiving is superfluous and that the author, in attempting to imitate the usual Pauline form, did not wish to omit anything that was essential to a genuine Pauline letter; cf. P. Schubert, *Form and Function of the Pauline Thanksgivings* (Berlin: Töpelmann, 1939), 44; and J. C. Kirby, *Ephesians: Baptism and Pentecost* (London: SPCK, 1968), 131. Such an argument, however, is a two-edged sword. Two of the *Hauptbriefe* do not commence with introductory thanksgivings: Gal. 1 and 2 Cor. 1, which commences with an introductory eulogy about God's comfort (vv. 3-4). If our author followed the latter *berakah,* as F. W. Beare, 'The Epistle to the Ephesians', *IB,* ed. G. A. Buttrick and others, vol. 10 (New York/Nashville: Abingdon, 1953), 613, claims, why did he not omit the introductory thanksgiving? In fact, he has kept the careful Pauline distinction between using εὐχαριστέω ('I give thanks') for the expression of gratitude for God's work in the lives of the addressees and employing εὐλογητός ('blessed') for praise to God for blessings in which he himself participated (P. T. O'Brien, 'An Unusual Introduction', 512-13).

c. The close verbal links within parallel sections of the two letters do not necessarily point to a one-way dependence of Ephesians on Colossians. The issues are more nuanced than Mitton's and Lincoln's claims imply.

(1) Ephesians 1:1-2 may resemble Colossians 1:1-2 because both employ the normal epistolary Pauline formulae and not because either depends on the other.[53] The description of the two sets of addressees as 'saints' and 'faithful in Christ (Jesus)' is explicable if the same author wrote both letters at about the same time to Christians in similar circumstances.

(2) The correspondences of keywords such as redemption, reconciliation, body, and flesh are explicable if some of the subjects covered in the letters are the same, as is the case (on the particular relationship of Eph. 3:1-13 to Col. 1:24-29, see below).

(3) Further, the close verbal links between two exhortatory passages dealing with the motif of putting off the old man and putting on the new (Eph. 4:22-24 and Col. 3:8-12) do not necessarily show that Ephesians is dependent on the 'earlier' Colossians. Mitton argues for 'a very close interdependence, and yet the freest development and rearrangement of borrowed ideas'.[54] The theme of putting off the old and putting on the new man is found earlier in Paul (Rom. 13:14; Gal. 3:27; 1 Thess. 5:8), while there are significant differences here between Ephesians and Colossians. Different words for 'new' appear (though this may be insignificant). Colossians uses aorist participles in relation to a past happening and aorist imperatives in relation to what is yet to be done (3:8-10, 12), while Ephesians has only aorist infinitives (4:22-24) with rather different nuances. There is an intermediate reference to the process of renewal (Eph. 4:23) not found in Colossians. The mention of not lying in Ephesians 4:25 is fuller than that found in Colossians 3:9, and, rather than being part of the argument about putting off the old humanity and putting on the new, this text stands at the head of a new paragraph giving detailed exhortations about Christian conduct. The Ephesians admonition, which is a citation from Zechariah 8:16, has important thematic, structural, and theological connections with its Old Testament counterpart (see the exegesis of 4:25), and is not simply a reworking of the Colossians material as advocates of the literary dependence of Ephesians claim.

(4) To say that the author of Ephesians quotes the vice list of Colossians 3:5 (at Eph. 5:3, 5), but omits two of the five vices mentioned in the source, does not follow unless we are sure that he was using Colossians

---

53. E. Best, 'Who Used Whom?', 76.
54. C. L. Mitton, *Epistle*, 61; cf. the discussion of E. Best, 'Who Used Whom?', 84-85.

and that he did not know the vice list from some other source or have independent knowledge of it. Both 'authors' may have been dependent on earlier Pauline material (in 1 Cor. 5:10-11; 6:9-10),[55] or else Paul may have written both.

(5) The parallel sections in the two letters which use the household table can give us no certain knowledge about the dependence of one letter on the other, since both may have used the *Haustafel* (lit. 'house-table') directly. Further, the position of the table in Ephesians (5:21–6:9) does not necessarily show the author's dependence on Colossians (3:18–4:1).[56] Although each table is followed by similar passages (Eph. 6:18-20; Col. 4:2-4), there are significant differences. Colossians moves directly to prayer, while in Ephesians the prayer is separated from the table by the account of the struggle with the powers (6:10-17). The author of Ephesians apparently included the table and expanded it in order to advance his theme of the church, which he had already treated in 4:7-16. In 5:18-20 the theme of the church was brought to the forefront again, and the household code was intimately linked with it via the transition verse, that is, v. 21. It is as likely that the Ephesians table is dependent on tradition as it is on the Colossians table, given the significant differences.[57] The passage on slaves and masters cannot provide a convincing argument for the use of Colossians by the author of Ephesians: sometimes Ephesians may be seen to have greater Christian content (note the addition 'as to Christ', Eph. 6:5); on other occasions the emphasis goes the other way (the slave's fear is related to the Lord, not to the owner, Col. 3:22). The variations suggest that both letters may be using traditional material independently.

(6) Regarding Ephesians 6:21-22 and Colossians 4:7-8 where there is a very high degree of verbal agreement, it is possible to justify the use by either 'author' of the other letter.[58] Best concedes, however, that both epistles may have been written by the same person (who presumably could have referred to the earlier letter when sending his greetings), and this has recently been supported strongly by G. R. Smillie, who demonstrates that the differences in wording reflect the varying historical circumstances of Paul's two letters.[59]

---

55. E. Best, 'Who Used Whom?', 75-76.

56. As H. Merklein, 'Eph 4,1–5,20 als Rezeption von Kol 3,1-17', 194-210, claimed.

57. So Best, 'Who Used Whom?', 80; against H. Merklein, 'Eph 4,1–5,20 als Rezeption von Kol 3,1-17', 194-210.

58. E. Best, 'Who Used Whom?', 79.

59. G. R. Smillie, 'Ephesians 6:19-20: A Mystery for the Sake of Which the Apostle Is an Ambassador in Chains', *TrinJ* 18 (1997), 199-222. On the difficulty of the suggestion that the pseudonymous author of Ephesians adapted material from Col. 4:3, 4, see on Eph. 6:19.

(7) It is difficult to understand the author of Ephesians replacing the precise formulation of Colossians 3:16, 'teaching and admonishing', by the vague 'speaking' (Eph. 5:19), especially in the light of his strong preference for full and synonymous expressions.[60] In this instance, if there is literary dependence it seems to have gone the other way: the author of Colossians has used Ephesians, or else both epistles were written by the same person.

(8) H. Merklein argues that Ephesians 4:1–5:20 is a change and amplification of Colossians 3:1-17: the ethic of Colossians plays on the contrast between the earthly and the heavenly, but this has been transformed in Ephesians into a contrast between pagan preexistence and Christian existence. But the discussion of the church in Ephesians 4:7-16 picks up the theological argument of the first half of the letter and provides the background for the second half, with the tone being set up by 4:25 for what follows. 'The ecclesiology and ethic of Ephesians are thus consistent with one another and there is no need to have recourse to Colossians to explain the ethic of Ephesians'.[61]

d. We next turn to verbal links between the letters, which occur in quite different contexts.

(1) If these parallels have been drawn from traditional material as, for instance, phrases that may have been used in Christian worship (e.g., 'the God and Father of our Lord Jesus Christ'; Eph. 1:17; Col. 1:3), or expressions found in the Old Testament and Judaism (such as references to 'heaven and earth' to denote the totality of existence), then these examples should be ignored in decisions of 'priority and dependence between the two letters'.[62]

(2) The author of Ephesians is supposed to have conflated Colossians 1:14, 20 when writing Ephesians 1:17, and in 1:15-16 he has drawn from Colossians 1:9, 4. But Best rightly asks whether this is the way people use documents. They do not normally search the writings of others to find suitable words at diverse points to express their own ideas. 'The random nature of the way A/Eph is supposed to have drawn on references from Colossians suggests that if he did depend on it he did not have a copy of it in front of him as he wrote but had its words in his mind, and the same would be true of the way A/Col would have used Ephesians'.[63] Obviously, another possibility is that Paul was the author of both.

(3) There is further doubt as to whether the author of Ephesians

---

60. E. Best, 'Who Used Whom?', 82.
61. E. Best, 'Who Used Whom?', 83.
62. E. Best, 'Who Used Whom?', 76.
63. E. Best, 'Who Used Whom?', 76.

used Colossians 2:19 (at Eph. 4:15b-16), while the connections between the two letters (Eph. 1:4 with Col. 1:22; cf. Eph. 1:7 with Col. 1:14, 20 above; Eph. 1:8, 9 with Col. 3:16 and 1:27) are probably evidence of independent use of well-known ideas and phrases, rather than a reworking of Colossians by the author of Ephesians.[64]

(4) According to Best, the author of Ephesians cannot be dependent on Colossians 1:27 at 1:18, because of the grammatical and relational differences between the two passages. Furthermore, the fact that the author of Ephesians does not pick up the relation of Gentiles to the church from Colossians 1:27, even though it was one of his main themes, suggests that he has not used the earlier letter.[65]

e. The priority of Colossians is evident, according to Lincoln,[66] in the use made by the author of Ephesians of several key theological terms, such as 'body', 'administration', 'mystery', and 'fulness', which had already appeared with changed or nuanced meanings in the earlier epistle. There has been a development between the two letters, a change in perspective, for example, from Christology to ecclesiology, and the author of Ephesians has employed these terms, sometimes with different connotations, to suit his own theological purposes. However, to take one example, the instances of the term 'mystery', which turn up in Ephesians with several different nuances (cf. the use in 1:10 with 3:3, 4, 9), often reflect an emphasis on one aspect or more of the comprehensive use of the word. In other words, the question is one of continuity and emphasis rather than discontinuity and a variant theology.[67] It may be appropriate to speak of a change of perspective from Christ (Colossians) to the church (Ephesians), and this may go some distance to accounting for the different nuances of the term(s) held in common between the two letters.[68] But it is unnecessary to regard this as a development from Colossians that evidences the hand of a different author.[69]

f. Stanley Porter and K. D. Clarke have recently examined the literary relationship between Colossians and Ephesians from a canonical-critical perspective in connection with Paul's use of reconciliation language. In two undisputed letters (Rom. 5:10; 2 Cor. 5:18-20) the apostle uses the

---

64. E. Best, 'Who Used Whom?', 85-87.

65. E. Best, 'Who Used Whom?', 89.

66. Lincoln, liii-lv.

67. M. N. A. Bockmuehl, *Revelation and Mystery in Ancient Judaism and Pauline Christianity* (Tübingen: Mohr, 1990), 202; cf. C. C. Caragounis, *The Ephesian* Mysterion: *Meaning and Content* (Lund: Gleerup, 1977), 143: 'they are not different *mysteria*, but wider or narrower aspects of one and the same *mysterion* — God's *mysterion* in Christ'.

68. Bruce, 231.

69. See below under the section 'The Theological Emphases of Ephesians'.

verb 'reconcile', in the latter instance in a distinctive way to speak of God as the explicit primary agent in reconciliation, and this sets the tone for subsequent Pauline usage.[70] In Colossians 1:20, 22 and Ephesians 2:16 the first recorded instances of a new form of the verb in all extant ancient Greek writing appears.[71] If Colossians was the first letter of the two written, then Paul is 'the innovator who first apparently prefixed this verb form' (Col. 1:20).[72] This is more likely than that a faithful disciple of the apostle coined a new word for such a theologically significant term. In Ephesians 2:16, the new verb appears again, this time with a significantly different object of reconciliation from previous usage: Christ reconciles both *Jew and Gentile* in one body. Whereas previous objects of reconciliation were believers, the world, or all things, now the human sphere is divided along ethnic/salvation-historical lines: 'both' = Jews and Gentiles. Porter and Clarke conclude: 'In terms of authorship, it appears that the Pauline usage of reconciliation language points to authentic Pauline authorship of Colossians and Ephesians'.[73]

g. To conclude, the issue of the literary relationship between Ephesians and Colossians is far more nuanced than Mitton, Lincoln, and others have claimed. Lincoln concludes his overview of this relationship between the letters by declaring that Ephesians is dependent 'on a prior Colossians in terms of its overall structure and sequence, its themes, and its wording'.[74] For the majority of scholars this has now become the new consensus, one of the assured results of New Testament criticism. But Best is right in claiming that there is 'insufficient evidence to enable us to come down firmly in favour of the priority of either letter'.[75]

It is inappropriate, therefore, to conclude that Ephesians is non-Pauline *because of* the author's use of Colossians. Colossians may have been written prior to Ephesians, but, if so, it is probable that the two epistles were written within a short time of each other, perhaps no more than a

---

70. 2 Cor. 5:18-20 is 'apparently the first instance in ancient Greek literature in which the author has used the active voice form of the verb καταλλάσσω ['reconcile'] to speak of the offended party instigating reconciliation'; S. E. Porter and K. D. Clarke, 'Canonical-Critical Perspective and the Relationship of Colossians and Ephesians', *Bib* 78 (1997), 78.

71. That is, ἀποκαταλλάσσω ('reconcile').

72. E. Best, 'Who Used Whom?', 87.

73. S. E. Porter and K. D. Clarke, 'Canonical-Critical Perspective', 81. They add that 'the reconciliation language of Colossians and Ephesians, although it diverges in several significant ways, is sufficiently Pauline in its basic thrust to be consonant with Pauline usage. In some other ways it is radical and new, but to our way of thinking too radical to have been created by someone other than Paul'.

74. Lincoln, lv.

75. E. Best, 'Who Used Whom?', 79.

year or two apart. The view that Paul wrote both letters, as we shall endeavour to show, does greater justice to the evidence.

D. The Theological Emphases of Ephesians

Many scholars contend that there are significant theological differences between Ephesians and the generally recognized Pauline letters, and that these provide a telling criticism against the apostle's authorship of the epistle. It is not simply that there has been a development in Paul's thought or that the apostle needed to address a historical situation different from those to which the genuine letters were sent. Rather, there are too many divergences, and these indicate an entirely changed perspective which reveals a later stage of theological reflection.[76] So, for example, W. G. Kümmel states that 'the theology of Eph makes the Pauline composition of the letter completely impossible'.[77]

Unquestionably, Ephesians has its own special theological emphases, but it is particularly in the areas of Christology, soteriology, ecclesiology, and eschatology that doubts about the Pauline authorship of the letter have surfaced. We shall address each of these in turn:

1. An Emphasis on Christ's Exaltation
Rather Than His Death

The Letter to the Ephesians has a high Christology which appropriately has been described as a 'cosmic Christology'. Christ is portrayed in numerous ways as superior to 'all things'. In particular, his resurrection, exaltion, and cosmic lordship are emphatically underscored. By contrast, it is claimed that Paul's stress on Jesus' death and his theology of the cross have receded into the background. The cross is mentioned only at 2:16, and this is dependent on Colossians 1:20 anyway, while the death of Christ is touched upon only in traditional formulations such as 1:7; 5:2, 25. Likewise the believer's relationship to Christ is spoken of in terms of his or her being raised and seated with Christ (2:5, 6), not with reference to their dying with him.

Two observations about these claims need to be made. First, the stress on Christ's resurrection, exaltation, and enthronement in Ephesians is an emphasis of the New Testament as a whole, appearing in the

---

76. Schnackenburg, 26-28; and Lincoln, lxiii.

77. W. G. Kümmel, *Introduction to the New Testament* (London/Nashville: SCM/ Abingdon, 1975), 360.

sermons of Acts (by Peter: Acts 2:24-36; 3:15-16, 21, 26; and by Paul: 23:6; 24:14-15; 26:23), the generally acknowledged writings of Paul (Rom. 8:34; 1 Cor. 15:3-28; Phil. 2:9-11), as well as in other authors (Heb. 1:3, 13; 8:1; 10:12; 12:2; 1 Pet. 3:22; Rev. 3:21). Further, the prominence given to Christ's exaltation is central to the writer's intention of bringing home to his readers the significance of Christ's lordship over the spirit-powers.[78] The relationship of Christ to these principalities appears to have been a live issue for the Christian readers of this letter (see below). They were living in a sociocultural context where such powers were acknowledged and feared. The author takes up the traditional linking of Psalm 110:1 and Psalm 8:6 in order to emphasize Christ's lordship over the powers. Through Christ's resurrection and exaltation all his enemies have been decisively conquered (1:20, 21); God has now placed them under his feet (v. 22), and this has profound ramifications for the recipients of the letter. They have been united with him in his resurrection and exaltation, and in consequence his destiny has become theirs (2:5, 6). His supremacy over the principalities was good news indeed, for they needed no longer to fear them; instead, they were to appropriate the power of God as they engaged in their daily spiritual warfare (6:10-20). Hence the stress on their union with him is grounded in his resurrection and exaltation rather than in their being baptized into his death. The latter motif has not faded into the background, but it did not need to be mentioned in the light of the author's immediate purpose.

Secondly, the death of Christ is not neglected in this letter. In fact, '[a]s elsewhere in the NT Jesus' death is central to the understanding of salvation',[79] even if there is no fully amplified theology of the atonement. Traditional terminology for Christ's death, such as his 'blood' (1:7; 2:13), 'cross' (2:16), 'flesh' (= 'death' at 2:15), 'sacrifice' (5:2), and 'gave himself up' (5:25), all appear. Redemption and the forgiveness of sins have been won through his sacrificial death (1:7). Also, in what has been described as the theological centrepiece of Ephesians, namely 2:14-18, it is confidently asserted that both Jews and Gentiles have been reconciled to one another and to God through the cross. Gentiles who had previously been without God and without hope have now been brought near to God through the blood of Christ (2:13). It is through his death that the hostility which existed between these two elements of humanity has been put to death. Jesus has done away with the law, including its commandments and regulations, and effected a reconciliation that is both vertical and horizontal, bringing the two together in a sovereign act that was nothing

78. Note in particular the work of C. E. Arnold, 124-29, 145-58, etc.
79. Best, 51.

less than a new creation (2:14-16). This glorious reconciliation, which serves as the ground for the subsequent exhortations to unity throughout the letter (e.g., 4:1-3), is central to God's gracious plan of summing up all things in Christ, and it has been won through his mighty death on the cross. Furthermore, consistent with the 'conformity' pattern found elsewhere in the New Testament, including the 'genuine' Paul (see on 5:2; 4:32), Christ's saving activity, especially his sacrifice on the cross, is set forth as a paradigm of the lifestyle to which believers are to 'conform'. They are to 'live a life of love, just as Christ loved us and gave himself up for us as a fragrant offering and sacrifice to God' (5:1-2). Then, as a specific example of this, the model and ground for the husband's love for his wife are Christ's love for the church, a love which is further characterized in terms of his taking the initiative in handing himself over to death (5:25). Again Christ's death on the cross provides the model for the believer's godly attitudes and behaviour.

2. Salvation and Not Justification

Closely related to the preceding discussion are two related issues. First, there is no longer any treatment in Ephesians of justification by grace through faith over against the works of the law, which was so prominent in Galatians and Romans. Rather, Ephesians deals more broadly with the issue of salvation, and, in particular, 2:8-10 speaks of salvation by grace through faith, which is set over against works in general, that is, human effort.[80] Also, the Pauline distinction between present justification and future salvation has been dropped from Ephesians, and instead the stress is placed upon a completed salvation for believers. Secondly, it is also claimed that the Letter to the Ephesians contradicts Paul's teaching in Romans in relation to the 'law'. The 'historical' Paul is at pains to show that his gospel does not abolish the law (Rom. 3:31), but Ephesians states that this is precisely what Christ has done through his death (2:15), and the same verb meaning to 'nullify or abolish'[81] is used in both passages.

The following comments are pertinent to these areas of concern. First, although a wider discussion of the present experience of salvation in Ephesians is reserved for the forthcoming section on eschatology (see below), it is important to recognize that the author does not appear to be grappling with Judaizing opponents who were making an issue out of

---

80. See Lincoln, lxiii-lxiv; and his article 'Ephesians 2:8-10: A Summary of Paul's Gospel?' *CBQ* 45 (1983), 617-30.

81. Gk. καταργέω. Cf. BAGD, 417; Louw and Nida, §76.26.

obedience to the law.[82] Rather than use the judicial terminology of justification, the more general concept of salvation, particularly a salvation that was realized, apparently served his purposes better. It enabled him to stress the transfer of dominions experienced by believers, and to assure them that Christ's destiny had become theirs and that they no longer needed to fear the spiritual powers. Ephesians states that no one is saved by works (2:9), but it does not refer to 'works *of the law*', presumably because it was mainly, though not exclusively,[83] a Gentile audience that was being addressed (cf. 2:11; 3:1). The term 'law' appears only once in the letter, in a passage which reminds Gentiles of what God has done through Christ's death to allow them access to the God of Israel (2:15). 'You have been justified' would not have summarized the three compound verbs ('God made us alive *with*', 'he raised us up *with*', and 'he seated us *with*', vv. 5, 6) in the way 'you have been saved' accurately does. A major issue of concern for the readers appears to have been the fear of evil, supernatural powers, not a threat from Jewish legalists.[84]

Secondly, the 'historic' Paul's teaching on the place and function of the law is considerably nuanced, even in Romans and Galatians, and as a result contextual considerations are clearly important for understanding his meaning.[85] The law is not abrogated but upheld for unbelievers to show them that they are sinners and need to come to God by faith (Rom. 3:31). Yet the law is nullified[86] for believers, not only in Ephesians (2:15) but also in Romans (7:2, 6). Further, the apostle asserts that Christ is the culmination of the law 'so that there may be righteousness for everyone who believes' (Rom. 10:4). He is the one to whom the law has been pointing all along, and now that this goal has been reached, the regime of the law has ended.[87] Believers are no longer under the law (Gal. 3:25). Ephesians 2:15 (see the exegesis) is not at odds with Paul's teaching on the law in Romans and Galatians.

---

82. So Arnold, 149, to whom I am indebted in what follows; cf. Snodgrass, 24, who states: 'If the letter was written around A.D. 60, the problem of the Judaizers would not be at the fore'.

83. See 176-77.

84. For a critique by I. H. Marshall of the arguments of U. Luz that Eph. 2 represents a significant alteration to the Pauline teaching on justification, the righteousness of God, and works of the law, see on 2:8.

85. Note the important treatment of this theme by D. J. Moo, 'The Law of Christ as the Fulfillment of the Law of Moses: A Modified Lutheran View', in *The Law, the Gospel, and the Modern Christian,* ed. W. Strickland and others (Grand Rapids: Zondervan, 1993), 319-76.

86. Gk. καταργέω.

87. Note the full discussion by D. J. Moo, 'The Law of Christ', 358.

3. *The Ecclesiology of Ephesians*

The theme of the church is an important subject in Ephesians, and according to some it is the primary motif of the letter.[88] Many aspects of the epistle's ecclesiology are thought to be discontinuous with Paul and therefore reflect a later temporal setting, moving in the direction of, though not having quite reached, an 'early catholicism'.[89] The term 'church',[90] which originally meant 'an assembly or gathering' and was most frequently used by the apostle Paul for local assemblies of believers, has now come to be employed by Ephesians exclusively of the universal church. All nine references in the letter point to the Christian community in its totality.[91] There is now a concentration on a universal church which is one (4:4), holy (5:26, 27), catholic (1:22, 23), and apostolic (2:20), and which therefore represents a stage beyond the ministry of Paul. Christ is now seen as the 'head' of the church, whereas in the earlier Pauline letters (apart from Colossians) the head is one member among others. Instead of Christ being the foundation, as in 1 Corinthians (3:11), the apostles and prophets, who are increasingly venerated (witness the term 'holy' that is used of them, Eph. 3:5), are depicted theologically as the foundation of the universal church (2:20). This is different even from Colossians, where believers are 'rooted and built up in him [i.e., Christ]' (2:7). Finally, Ephesians differs notably, it is argued, from the earlier Pauline letters in the place given to the continuance of ethnic Israel. For the author of Ephesians the significance of Israel lies in the past.

There is no doubt that the Letter to the Ephesians presents a 'high' ecclesiology, and that a number of important images are employed to refer to the people of God, often in rather different ways from those of the earlier letters. These divergences may, however, be due to a number of factors which can plausibly be explained as occurring during the lifetime of the apostle. The following points need to be made:

First, while it is true that the term 'church' in Paul's earlier letters refers to individual congregations or churches that met in particular houses, in some instances within Colossians and Ephesians the word has *a wider reference than either a local congregation or a house-church.*[92] Most commenta-

88. According to H. Chadwick, 'Die Absicht des Epheserbriefes', *ZNW* 51 (1960), 146.

89. E. Käsemann, 'Ephesians and Acts', in *Studies in Luke-Acts: Essays Presented in Honor of Paul Schubert,* ed. L. E. Keck and J. L. Martyn (Nashville: Abingdon, 1966), 288-97, esp. 288.

90. Gk. ἐκκλησία.

91. Eph. 1:22; 3:10, 21; 5:23, 24, 25, 27, 29, 32. Lincoln, lxiv; and in *Theology,* 92, 93.

92. On this view, Colossians uses the term ἐκκλησία ('church, congregation') in three ways: (a) of a local assembly (Col. 4:16), (b) of a house-church (Col. 4:15; cf. Phlm. 2), and

tors interpret these as referring to the church universal, to which all believers belong, and which is scattered throughout the world (i.e., Col. 1:18, 24; Ephesians 1:22; 3:10, 21; 5:23-24, 27, 29, 32). We have already suggested, however, that there are difficulties with this view,[93] and that it is preferable to interpret them of a heavenly gathering centred on Christ. Paul has already mentioned in relation to the readers that God has 'made us alive with Christ . . . raised us up with him and seated us in the heavenly realms in Christ Jesus' (2:5-6). The same readers of this circular letter have been 'blessed . . . in the heavenly realms with every spiritual blessing in Christ' (1:3). Again reference is made to Christ's headship over the 'church', which is his body (1:22-23). If the term is to be understood here of a 'church' or gathering taking place in heaven, then this would mean that Christians participate in that assembly as they go about their ordinary daily tasks. They are already assembled around Christ, and this is another way of saying that they now enjoy fellowship with him.

The New Testament does not discuss the relationship between the local church and this heavenly gathering. The link is nowhere specifically spelled out. Certainly the local congregation was neither a *part* of the church of God nor *a* church of God, as is made plain in 1 Corinthians 1:2, where the apostle writes 'to *the church* of God which is at Corinth'. It would seem that local congregations, as well as house-groups that met in particular homes, were concrete, visible expressions of that new relationship which believers have with the Lord Jesus. Local gatherings, whether in a congregation or a house-church, were earthly manifestations of that heavenly gathering around the risen Christ.

Two observations may be made: first, the uses of 'church, congregation' within Ephesians (and Colossians) could easily be a natural and logical development from the earlier uses in Paul. Secondly, there appears to be a twofold nuance to many, if not all, the references to the term 'church' within the epistle. This suggestion needs to be tested further, but one example from Ephesians may suffice, namely, 3:10. Here the manifold wisdom of God is being made known to the spiritual authorities *through the church,* an unusual expression which means that this communication was neither by evangelism nor by social action. Instead, it signifies that the very existence of the church,[94] this new multiracial community in which Jews and Gentiles have been brought together in unity in the one body, is

(c) of a heavenly gathering centred in Christ (Col. 1:18, 24); P. T. O'Brien, *Colossians, Philemon* (Waco, TX: Word, 1982), 60-61.

93. P. T. O'Brien, 'Entity', 88-119, 307-11, and *DPL*, 125-26.

94. Most recent commentators are agreed that the very presence of the church, comprising Jews and Gentiles, who are reconciled to God and to one another, is what is in view.

itself the manifestation of God's richly diverse wisdom. But it is inadequate to view this entity as simply a heavenly gathering or, for that matter, the universal church. The context of Ephesians 3:10 strongly suggests that there should be a concrete and visible expression of this new relationship which Jewish and Gentile believers have with their Lord Jesus. Local congregations and house-churches are that concrete, visible expression. If occasionally the term 'church' refers to a heavenly meeting with Christ, and this is a metaphorical way of speaking about believers' ongoing fellowship with him, then it was appropriate that this new relationship with the ascended Lord should find particular, concrete expression in their regular coming together, that is, 'in church' (cf. Heb. 10:25).[95] In the light of these remarks, then, 'the church' here in 3:10 may be taken as speaking of this heavenly gathering that is assembled around Christ,[96] and, at the same time, of a local congregation of Christians, in which Jews and Gentiles are fellow members of the body of Christ, as a concrete expression of this heavenly entity (see the exegesis).

Secondly, the notion of Christ as 'head' of the church is a clear development over Paul's earlier presentation of the metaphor of the body of Christ,[97] but it is likely that the apostle's thinking developed in this direction, probably because of the needs of the Colossian church.[98] He seems to have reflected on it further for the benefit of the readers of Ephesians. To rule out the possibility that Paul himself has moved 'from the language of simile . . . to the real and interpersonal involvement'[99] expressed

95. In 1963 E. A. Judge, using contemporary political models, suggested that the *polis* ('city-state') denoted 'a visible assembly of persons to whom great theoretical significance might be attached. All the ideals of the *polis* were fulfilled completely and identically in each particular case where it was established'. If the parallel works, we should expect to find, Judge claimed, that 'everything that can be said about the *ekklesia,* can be said equally and fully of each *ekklesia'*. He added that the difficulty New Testament lexicographers have in allotting instances of the term ἐκκλησία to the two categories 'local church' and 'whole church' suggests 'that the categories are themselves false'; 'Contemporary Political Models for the Inter-Relations of the New Testament Churches', *RTR* 22 (1963), 65-76, esp. 74-75.

96. Cf. Gnilka, 174, who claims that the domain of the church, like that of the principalities and powers, is 'in the heavenlies'.

97. Where the head has no special position or honour (so 1 Cor. 12:21; cf. Rom. 12:4, 5).

98. F. F. Bruce, *Paul,* 421; cf. C. E. Arnold, 'Jesus Christ: "Head" of the Church (Colossians and Ephesians)', in *Jesus of Nazareth; Lord and Christ: Essays on the Historical Jesus and New Testament Christology,* ed. J. B. Green and M. Turner (Grand Rapids/Carlisle: Eerdmans/Paternoster, 1994), 346-66, who thinks that Ephesians combined the Old Testament view of 'head' as 'superior' or 'ruler' over the 'body' (understood along the lines of corporate personality) with contemporary Greek medical ideas.

99. F. F. Bruce, *Paul,* 421.

in Colossians and Ephesians is to raise serious doubts about his ability and versatility, as well as to assume that an author like Paul can only use terms with a mathematical precision.

Thirdly, the language of building on a foundation and of a temple indwelt by the Spirit has already been used by Paul in 1 Corinthians 3:9-17. There the apostle was the master builder who had laid the foundation, namely, Christ himself, on which he, Apollos, Cephas, and others were continuing to build. Here in Ephesians 2:20, however, the figure of the building is retained but the individual parts of it have changed. Paul alters the metaphors to make slightly different points: the foundation now consists of the apostles and prophets, and Christ Jesus is the cornerstone.[100] Though the imagery is changed, there is no contradiction: as the foundation, the apostles and prophets do not replace Christ. He is the *chief cornerstone,* an expression that draws attention to his special importance and function (cf. Col. 2:7).

Finally, Lincoln suggests that the church, as a new creation (Eph. 2:11-22), has replaced Israel within God's purposes, and for the author of Ephesians the significance of Israel lies in the past. However, Ephesians 2:11-22, as Lincoln himself has clearly shown,[101] is addressed specifically to believing Gentiles, drawing a contrast between their pre-Christian past in relation to Israel's privileges and their present status in Christ. The author wants to help his Gentile readers[102] appreciate the greatness of their salvation by setting it in the context of Israel's former privileges and their own spiritual deficiencies (vv. 11-12). They are 'no longer foreigners and aliens, but fellow-citizens with God's people and members of God's household' (v. 19). They have entered into the heritage of Israel, and have a place in God's saving history. Christ through his death has created a new humanity, *one new humanity,* and they have become members of this new community which transcends the division of Jew and Gentile. However, the distinction between the church and Israel, which is an important

---

100. In Eph. 2:20 it is the persons who are built upon the foundation who are in mind, whereas in 1 Cor. 3 it is the builders and the kind of materials they use that are particularly in view. To suggest that all the metaphors must mesh precisely, or that the differences are evidence of diversity of authorship, is to view the metaphors too inflexibly. See the exegesis of 2:20, and note the discussion of Snodgrass, 25-26.

101. Lincoln, 124-34, especially.

102. This is not to suggest that the congregation(s) consisted solely of Gentiles. The fact that Gentiles are particularly singled out in 2:11 and 3:1 suggests that Jewish Christians were also present. The fact, too, that Ephesians uses the Old Testament so frequently and explicitly (in contrast to Colossians) may indicate that there was a significant Jewish contingent among the readers; cf. T. Moritz, *A Profound Mystery: The Use of the Old Testament in Ephesians* (Leiden: Brill, 1996), 1-8, 29-31, 213-18; and his article 'Reasons for Ephesians', *Evangel* 14 (1996), 8-14.

issue elsewhere in Paul, especially in Romans where it looms large, is not addressed in Ephesians. This letter underscores the incorporation of believing Jews and Gentiles into God's plan, but does not elaborate on his purposes for Israel in relation to the church. Accordingly, it is inappropriate to speak of 'replacement' categories in relation to Israel or of the nation's significance lying in the past.[103]

In general terms, the high ecclesiology of Ephesians, which cannot ultimately be separated from its high Christology, is intimately bound up with the place of God's people within his saving purposes. Since this epistle presents the broad sweep of that saving plan, it is not surprising that his people, who are set forth as a pilot project and pattern of a reconciled universe, should figure prominently. At the same time, Ephesians continually relates ecclesiology to the initiating work of the Father, the reconciling work of the Son, and the applicatory work of the Holy Spirit. Ultimately, the ecclesiology of the letter makes no sense apart from the activity of the triune God (see, e.g., Eph. 4:4-6).

4. A Realized Eschatology

The fourth major argument against the Pauline authorship of Ephesians concerns the letter's eschatology. Colossians, many claim, evidences a realized eschatology that goes beyond the Paul of the major letters; Ephesians, however, represents an even later stage of theological reflection. Several features stand out: first, the parousia, which was a constant expectation in Paul's early ministry, is not mentioned because it has faded into the background. Salvation as a present fact is stressed much more strongly than in Paul,[104] and believers are viewed as already raised from death and seated in the heavenlies (2:5, 6; cf. 1:3, 20-21). Ephesians stresses more forcefully than Paul the present nature of the new life of believers; this emerges particularly in the household code of 5:21–6:9, which reflects a realized eschatology, or at least a very distant parousia. The future expectation does not disappear entirely from the letter, but it receives much less attention (cf. 1:18; 4:4). Ephesians does not echo Paul's

103. Lincoln is right, however, to speak of the church of Eph. 2:11-22 as a unity between believing Jews and believing Gentiles that is distinct from Israel, rather than a unity between Christians and Jews, or church and synagogue, as Barth asserts; cf. Lincoln, 'The Church and Israel in Ephesians 2', CBQ 49 (1987), 605-24; and his Theology, 159; against M. Barth, The People of God (Sheffield: JSOT, 1983). See also the recent examination of the issue by Best, 267-69.

104. Best, 53, 54, prefers to speak of a 'realised soteriology' rather than a 'realised eschatology', since the author shows little interest in eschatology as such, and uses few of its traditional terms.

sense of the transitoriness of the world (1 Cor. 7:31); there is no need to abstain from marriage. Instead, it is elevated in such a way that it is compared to the relationship of Christ and the church (5:21-33).

There is undoubtedly a clear, realized eschatological perspective running through Ephesians.[105] Also, the letter does lack some of the specific future eschatological terms found elsewhere in Paul, for example, 'the day of the Lord', 'parousia', and specific references to a future resurrection. A future eschatology, however, has not collapsed into an eschatology that is realized, with its emphasis on the presence of salvation.[106] The author explicitly refers to a future consummation at the beginning of the epistle; he looks forward to the 'summing up' of all things as a unity under the sovereign rule of Christ — an *anakephalaiōsis* that will occur 'when the times will have reached their fulfilment' (1:10). Believers await a day of redemption for which they have already been sealed by the Holy Spirit (4:30; 1:13). They look forward to an inheritance, for which they have already received a down payment, implying that there is something more to come (1:14, 18; 5:5). On the final day Christ will present to himself the now glorified church as his holy and purified possession (5:27). It will also be a day, however, when God's wrath will be poured out on the disobedient (5:6).

Nevertheless, the realized eschatological perspective of the letter needs to be given its full weight and, if possible, satisfactorily accounted for. The key passage for discerning the author's understanding of eschatology and salvation is 2:4-10.[107] Here the mighty work of God on behalf of believers is described by means of three compound verbs (prefixed by 'with') in the past tense: '[God] made us alive with [Christ]' (v. 5); 'he raised us up with [Christ]' (v. 6); and 'he seated us with [him]' (v. 6). The resulting status of believers is then summarized by the phrase 'you have been saved' (vv. 5, 8).[108] Clearly, 'the author has emphasized the present aspect of salvation to a degree unparalleled in Paul'.[109] How is this best

105. On the realized eschatology of Ephesians, see F.-J. Steinmetz, *Protologische Heils-Zuversicht: Die Strukturen des soteriologischen und christologischen Denkens im Kolosser- und Epheserbrief* (Frankfurt: Knecht, 1969), 37-49, passim; A. Lindemann, *Die Aufhebung der Zeit: Geschichtsverständnis und Eschatologie im Epheserbrief* (Gütersloh: Mohn, 1975); H. E. Lona, *Die Eschatologie im Kolosser- und Epheserbrief* (Würzburg: Echter, 1984); G. F. Wessels, 'The Eschatology of Colossians and Ephesians', *Neot* 21 (1987), 183-202; Arnold, 145-58; H. R. Lemmer, 'A Multifarious Understanding of Eschatology in Ephesians: A Possible Solution to a Vexing Issue', *Hervormde Teologiese Studies* 46 (1990), 102-19.

106. Cf. H. E. Lona, *Eschatologie*, 427-28.

107. Arnold, 147-50.

108. The three aorists are συνεζωοποίησεν, συνήγειρεν, and συνεκάθισεν, while the resulting status is summarized with ἐστε σεσῳσμένοι.

109. Arnold, 147.

explained? Clinton Arnold, following and developing the argument of H. E. Lona,[110] claims that because of the hostile role of the principalities and powers as presented in the larger context of Ephesians (2:1-2; 1:20-22), it is likely that 2:4-7 focusses particularly on the salvation of believers from the spiritual 'powers'. The author has taken up the language of 1:20-22 relating to the resurrection and exaltation of Christ and directly applied it to believers (2:4-6, 8). His destiny has become theirs, and of first importance within the flow of the argument is that they have been resurrected and exalted with Christ to a position of authority and power which is far superior to that of the evil principalities. Because of the presence of salvation the believer no longer lives under the tyranny of 'the prince of the power of the air' and his hosts.[111] Ephesians thus stresses the presence of salvation in history in order to strengthen Christians facing the increasing threats of their environment.

This present salvation, however, has not swallowed up the future expectation. The author of Ephesians employs the Old Testament and Jewish concept of the two ages, and speaks of 'the coming age' in relation to the rule of Christ (1:21), as well as the general expression 'the ages to come' to signify 'throughout time and eternity' when God will lavish his grace in full measure on believers, after having procured their salvation in the present age (2:5, 8). Further, although Ephesians emphasizes the spatial dimension (the heavenly and the earthly), this feature is not a replacement of the temporal. The author has employed it to underscore the transfer of dominions experienced by believers, and to demonstrate that there was a decisive break with the past when the readers turned to Christ.[112] Not only do the two ages overlap as a result of Christ's decisive intervention in history, so that the believer is involved in two spheres of influence simultaneously; the vertical dimension participates in the two-age structure as well. Ephesians, like Paul, 'can employ *both* spatial and temporal terms since they are bound together as both heaven and earth are involved in the two-age structure'.[113]

Given that believers have been blessed with Christ in the heavenlies (1:3) and 'already' experience salvation (2:4-7), why does the author of Ephesians devote half of his letter to exhortatory material and moral teaching? Why should the readers be warned against falling back into

110. Arnold, 147-50; H. E. Lona, *Eschatologie*, 428-48.

111. Arnold, 149.

112. Note the interaction of Arnold, 150-51, with the views of H. Conzelmann, H. Merklein, P. Tachau, and A. Lindemann, who hold that the spatial idea has replaced the time concept, and that a salvation-historical dimension has disappeared from Eph. 2.

113. Arnold, 153, following A. T. Lincoln, 'A Re-Examination of "The Heavenlies" in Ephesians', *NTS* 19 (1972-73), 468-83, esp. 479-81.

their pagan past (cf. 2:11-22 with 4:17-32; 5:8-14),[114] and urged to be careful how they live, to make the most of every opportunity, and to be filled by the Spirit (5:15-18)? Clearly, their lifestyle in the here and now is important: they are to behave in a manner that is consistent with the new humanity into which they have been incorporated, for this has been created to be like God in true righteousness and holiness (4:24). Accordingly, they are to have their eyes fixed on the final goal, for ultimately they are to be 'filled up to all the fulness of God' (3:19); they are all to 'reach unity in the faith and the knowledge of the Son of God', since God desires that they 'become mature, attaining to the whole measure of the fulness of Christ' (4:13). The future dimension for these Christian readers is clearly important in Ephesians as elsewhere in Paul.

Future eschatology features in several places of the household table (cf. 6:8), not least in the section addressed to husbands (5:25-28). Christ's love for the church is the model for them to follow in loving their wives (v. 25). He took the initiative in giving himself over to death in order to sanctify and purify the church, and his goal was 'to present her to himself in splendour, without spot or wrinkle . . . so that she might be holy and blameless', an expression which focusses on the eschatological radiance and brightness of God's presence on the final day (see on 5:27). The author sets before husbands and wives a high view of marriage which is patterned on Christ's relationship to the church and looks forward to the eschaton. This elevated view of marriage, however, is not at odds with Paul's sense of the transitoriness of the world, which is supposedly reflected in his admonition to abstain from marriage (as in 1 Cor. 7:29-31).[115] In 1 Corinthians 7 Paul did not forbid marriage; instead, he urged Christians, in the light of the present distress (whatever precisely this was), not to marry.[116] In Ephesians the author is not discussing a change

---

114. Best, 52-55, thinks that 'the already' dimension of salvation does not sit easily with the future in Ephesians. The letter 'contains two tendencies difficult to reconcile with each other'. He adds: 'It is impossible to eliminate from his letter the evidence supporting either view' (54)! But is not this similar to the 'already–not yet' tension appearing in the generally acknowledged letters of Paul?

115. Best, 34-35, believes that the most significant variation of Ephesians from the earlier Paulines lies in the ethical area, especially 'the restriction in Ephesians of the HT [i.e., household table] to households consisting entirely of believers' (35). He finds it 'very difficult to see Paul as either compiling such a code or, if he received it in the tradition, embodying in it what he writes'. For Best there is the added problem of Paul 'ignoring the relation of believers to the world in which they live', or being the author of a letter that 'lacks a missionary impulse'. Cf. 'The Haustafel in Ephesians (Eph. 5.22–6.9)', in *Essays*, 189-203. For a critique of this view, see the exegesis of 5:22–6:20 (below).

116. For a discussion as to the nature of 'the present distress', see G. D. Fee, *The First Epistle to the Corinthians* (Grand Rapids: Eerdmans, 1987), 334-42.

in status but addressing those who are married. The purposes of the two passages are different.

Finally, in the debate over the eschatology of Ephesians, the climactic paraenetic passage which urges believers to take up the armour of God in their ongoing spiritual warfare against the principalities and powers (6:10-20) has been largely neglected. If these powers are already subject to Christ (1:20-22), and by implication to believers in him, then why does the author advise his readers about the ongoing struggle with them? The paragraph presents a major difficulty to those who advocate a fully realized eschatology in Ephesians.[117] But this passage, to which the rest of the letter has been pointing (see on 6:10-20), integrates appropriately within the 'already–not yet' poles of Pauline eschatology. Christ's triumph over the powers has 'already' occurred (1:21). Because of believers' union with him in his resurrection and exaltation (2:5, 6), they no longer need to fear the powers. The fruits of Christ's victory have 'not yet' been fully realized. However, those in him possess all the resources needed to resist the influence and attacks of the devil and his hosts (cf. 6:10-20). Believers must be aware of the conflict and appropriate the divine power to withstand them. On the final day Christ's victory over the powers will be consummated.

In conclusion, the eschatology of Ephesians underscores the present aspect of salvation in an emphatic way. Specific future eschatological terms found elsewhere in Paul do not appear. But other references, which focus on the future, turn up at significant points in the letter, notably the 'summing up' (anakephalaiōsis) of all things at 1:10 (cf. also 1:13, 14, 18, 21; 2:7; 3:19; 4:12, 13, 30; 5:5, 6, 27; 6:8). We contend that this emphasis on 'the already' aspect of salvation has been occasioned by the needs of the readers, whom the author seeks to strengthen as he presents the grand sweep of God's purposes. Because of the many similarities with the genuine Pauline letters, we believe that this emphasis represents not a later stage of theological reflection but arises out of the pastoral and apostolic ministry of Paul.

E. The Picture of Paul

Paul is certainly the 'implied' author of Ephesians. But what picture of the apostle[118] is painted by the 'implied' author, and is it the same as that

---

117. As Arnold, 155-57, correctly observes.

118. See further H. Merklein, *Das kirchliche Amt*, 335-45; C. K. Barrett, 'Pauline Controversies in the Post-Pauline Period', *NTS* 20 (1973-74), 229-45; M. C. de Boer, 'Images of

derived from Paul's genuine letters? A range of scholars believes that the point of view presented by the 'implied' author of Ephesians is later than that of the apostle Paul. The main factors that lead to this negative conclusion are as follows:

Ephesians 3:1-13 is thought to look more like the estimate of Paul's apostleship by someone looking back rather than Paul referring to himself and his ministry. His recommendation of his own insights in 3:4 is supposed to be the device of a person who wishes to 'boost claims for the authority of the apostle's teachings for a later time'. Similarly, the place given to the other apostles in their reception of the special revelation about the Gentiles in the plan of God (together with the use of the adjective 'holy' to describe them, 3:5) suggests a postapostolic setting. The humility expressed in 3:8, 'the very least of all the saints', is said to be exaggerated, while the Paul who is supposed to be speaking in the letter is regarded as a revered figure, a dignitary. Missing from Ephesians is Paul's 'personal presence . . . with its passion, urgency, joy, and anger', along with the tensions and struggles of his ministry.[119]

Significantly, Ernest Best, who on balance thinks that the apostle did not write Ephesians, considers the picture of Paul presented in this epistle to be basically in harmony with the account the apostle gives of himself in his own letters. Certain characteristics, such as his unique place in God's plan, may have been stretched a little further. But Best concludes: 'it is easily conceivable that Paul could have developed his thinking in these ways'.[120] Further, Klyne Snodgrass has rightly pointed out that the material in 3:1-13, which many think provides the strongest arguments against the letter's authenticity, has also been taken as evidence of a convincing case in favour of Pauline authorship.[121]

Paul in the Post-Apostolic Period', *CBQ* 42 (1980), 359-80; H. Merklein, 'Paulinische Theologie in der Rezeption des Kolosser- und Epheserbriefes', in *Paulus in den neutestamentlichen Spätschriften*, ed. K. Kertelge (Freiburg/Basel/Vienna: Herder, 1981), 25-69; J. Gnilka, 'Das Paulusbild im Kolosser- und Epheserbrief', in *Kontinuät und Einheit*, ed. P. G. Müller and W. Stenger (Freiburg/Basel/Vienna: Herder, 1981), 179-93; M. Y. MacDonald, *The Pauline Churches* (Cambridge: Cambridge University Press, 1988), 123-36; U. Luz, 'Überlegungen zum Epheserbrief und seiner Päranese', *Neues Testament und Ethik: Für Rudolf Schnackenburg*, ed. H. Merklein (Freiburg/Basel/Vienna: Herder, 1989), 376-96; Lincoln, lxii-lxiii; Snodgrass, 25-27; and Best, 40-44.

119. Lincoln, lxiii.

120. See Best, 40-44, esp. 44, where detailed connections are made. He alleges that the only area where a definite difference appears is in the household table. His final, judicious comment is worth quoting in full: 'It is natural that there should be some differences in the picture of Paul in Ephesians and in the other letters simply because it is a short letter and cannot present as rounded a picture as the longer letters, and of course also the picture in any single letter is always less than the total picture' (44).

121. Snodgrass, 26. Note his treatment on 26-27, to which I am indebted.

We now turn to those expressions which have occasioned some difficulty. First, Paul's statements about his own apostolic role appear to be somewhat self-centred (3:3-7). This has led some to conclude that a pseudonymous writer has sought to claim Paul's authority and theology for himself. At the same time, his self-identification as 'less than the least of all God's people' (v. 8) has been regarded as 'theatrical . . . artificial exaggeration . . . forced and unnatural'.[122] The tension that is thought to exist (in the one paragraph!) between Paul's exaltation of his apostolic ministry (vv. 3-7) and his humility (v. 8) does, however, occur within his earlier letters.

On the one hand, Paul was conscious of the incredible privilege that had been given to him as the apostle to the Gentiles. His role as an accredited representative of Christ depended on the revelation of the Lord Jesus to him on the Damascus road (Gal. 1:15-17),[123] and according to 2 Corinthians 3:7–4:6 this glorious ministry, with its revelation in the gospel, was superior to the ministry of Moses. Paul had been 'called to be an apostle and set apart for the gospel of God' (Rom. 1:1). As one who had received 'grace and apostleship' his task was to bring about the obedience of faith among the Gentiles (Rom. 1:5; 15:18; 16:26), a role that held a significant place within the saving plan of God and had its warrant within the Old Testament Scriptures (notably Isaiah).[124] It is not surprising, then, that in Ephesians, where the broad sweep of God's saving purposes is so magnificently presented, particularly in relation to his 'mystery' (Eph. 1:9-10), Paul's ministry *to the Gentiles*, which is such an important motif of the letter, should be highlighted in relation to that same 'mystery' (in 3:2-9 the term appears four times).

On the other hand, his description of himself as 'less than the least of all God's people' (3:8) is evidence of neither hypocrisy, nor a groveling in self-deprecation on the part of the apostle, nor too exaggerated and artificial a self-denigration to be authentic to Paul. It is even less likely that a Paulinist, who is thought to have penned these words, would speak of his hero in this fashion![125] The 'historic' Paul knew that he was unworthy

122. C. L. Mitton, *Epistle*, 15, 36, 152.

123. P. T. O'Brien, *Gospel and Mission in the Writings of Paul: An Exegetical and Theological Analysis* (Grand Rapids/Carlisle: Baker/Paternoster, 1995), 2-12; see also R. N. Longenecker, ed., *The Road from Damascus: The Impact of Paul's Conversion on His Life, Thought, and Ministry* (Grand Rapids/Cambridge: Eerdmans, 1997).

124. On this facet of the subject, see D. J.-S. Chae, *Paul as Apostle to the Gentiles: His Apostolic Self-Awareness and Its Influence on the Soteriological Argument of Romans* (Carlisle: Paternoster, 1997), esp. 39-44; and P. T. O'Brien, *Gospel and Mission*, 58-60, 69-70.

125. F. F. Bruce, *Ephesians*, 63, interprets the description in 3:8 as 'the very hallmark of apostolic authenticity'. It is hard to imagine a disciple of Paul according him such a low place. See further on 3:8.

of this privileged ministry (1 Cor. 15:8-10); he had violently persecuted the church *of God* (the additional words draw attention to the enormity of the crime). The tone and attitude of the words in Ephesians 3:8 are close to these words in 1 Corinthians 15 as well as to his apostolic defence in 2 Corinthians 10–12.

Secondly, the phrase '*holy* apostles and prophets' (3:5) has no parallel elsewhere in Paul's letters, and has been taken as characteristic of a later author venerating people like the apostle. It might explain 2:20, 'built on the foundation of the apostles and prophets', as well (though note the discussion above). The adjective 'holy' is an awkward term since it is thought to venerate the apostles and prophets from the past, adding an aura to them. However, the term 'holy ones' (NIV 'saints') is a common way to refer to Christians, and speaks of those whom God has set apart. If this is its significance in 3:5, then it is describing the apostles and prophets as separated to God for their 'distinctive role as recipients of the central revelation'.[126]

Thirdly, and related to the preceding, Paul's recommendation of his own insights (3:4), and the place given to the other apostles in their reception of the special revelation about the Gentiles in the plan of God, has occasioned some difficulty. But the mention of different recipients is not a fundamental problem. The mystery was made known 'to all the nations' (Rom. 16:26) through the worldwide preaching of the gospel. It was disclosed to God's holy people, especially Gentiles (Col. 1:26), because they were the beneficiaries of God's saving work through his Son and thus of the revelation concerning it. The divine secret was revealed to 'the apostles and prophets', for they 'were the ministers through whom the truth of God was communicated to their fellow-believers'. The apostles 'represent the authority of primary witness to the Gospel facts, while prophets represent the living guidance of the Spirit by which the facts were apprehended in ever fuller meaning and scope'.[127] And it was disclosed to Paul by revelation on the Damascus road, for he, as the apostle to the Gentiles, held the primacy among those ministers (Gal. 1:11-12, 15-16; cf. Acts 26:12-18).

In sum, then, one wonders what a pseudonymous author would have gained by using this language in 3:1-13. Why refer to Paul's imprisonment and make so little of it? On the other hand, one can understand the apostle entreating his readers not to become discouraged because of his sufferings (cf. Phil. 1:12-14; Col. 1:24). He has written about the eternal purposes of God, the place of his Gentile readers within the divine plan, as well as his own role in relation to it. In view of so momentous a task

126. Turner, 1234.
127. Bruce, 315. Note his discussion on 3:5, and see our treatment below.

given to him in his calling, he urges his Christian readers not to become disheartened at his sufferings, which he undergoes on their behalf.

F. Authorship and Pseudonymity[128]

In the preceding discussion we examined a range of arguments raised by contemporary scholars against the Pauline authorship of Ephesians. In spite of the perceived difficulties with the traditional view, we contended that the case against it is anything but proven. In fact, the denial that Paul wrote the letter raises more problems than it solves.[129] The final issue which now needs to be addressed under this heading of the authorship of Ephesians (though it is a matter that affects other letters in the New Testament corpus, including Colossians, 2 Thessalonians, the Pastoral Epistles, and 2 Peter) is that of pseudonymity.

Contemporary scholars, who have claimed that Paul was not the author of Ephesians, have maintained that the writer of the letter used the literary device of pseudonymity.[130] This was a widespread and ac-

128. It is impossible to enter fully into the issue of pseudonymity on which so much has been written. A limited bibliography includes: H. R. Balz, 'Anonymität und Pseudepigraphie im Urchristentum', *ZTK* 66 (1969), 403-36; W. Speyer, *Die literarische Fälschung im heidnischen und christlichen Altertum: Ein Versuch ihrer Deutung* (München: Beck, 1971); A. G. Patzia, 'The Deutero-Pauline Hypothesis: An Attempt at Clarification', *EvQ* 52 (1980), 27-42; L. R. Donelson, *Pseudepigraphy and Ethical Argument in the Pastoral Epistles* (Tübingen: J. C. B. Mohr [Paul Siebeck], 1986); J. D. G. Dunn, 'The Problem of Pseudonymity', in *The Living Word* (London: SCM, 1987), 65-85; D. G. Meade, *Pseudonymity and Canon: An Investigation in the Relationship of Authorship and Authority in Jewish and Earliest Christian Tradition* (Tübingen: J. C. B. Mohr [Paul Siebeck], 1987); E. E. Ellis, 'Pseudonymity and Canonicity of New Testament Documents', in *Worship, Theology and Ministry in the Early Church: Essays in Honor of Ralph P. Martin*, ed. M. J. Wilkins and T. Paige (Sheffield: Academic Press, 1992), 212-24; S. E. Porter, 'Pauline Authorship and the Pastorals', *BBR* 5 (1995), 105-23; J. D. G. Dunn, 'Pseudepigraphy', in *Dictionary of the Later New Testament and Its Developments*, ed. R. P. Martin and P. H. Davids (Downers Grove/Leicester: Inter-Varsity, 1997), 977-84; J. Duff, 'A Reconsideration of Pseudepigraphy in Early Christianity' (unpublished D.Phil. thesis, Oxford, 1998).

129. A. G. Patzia, 'The Deutero-Pauline Hypothesis', 42, at the conclusion of his sympathetic survey, acknowledges the need to ask 'whether the type of reconstruction suggested by the proponents of the deutero-Pauline hypothesis is any less problematic than existing theories which try to make sense out of the difficulties surrounding the life of the apostle and his literary activity'.

130. Pseudonymity is to be distinguished from anonymous authorship, the use of a pen name, and plagiarism (cf. Best, 10-11). As far as the New Testament is concerned, all four Gospels, Acts, Hebrews, and the Johannine Epistles are formally anonymous. The issue of pseudonymity arises only in relation to those books which have explicit

cepted literary convention in the Jewish and Graeco-Roman worlds in which an author chose to write under the name of an eminent predecessor of a previous generation, already known and respected by the readers. In the case of Ephesians, the author, who may have been a coworker or associate of Paul, perhaps even one of the members of a Pauline 'school', was aware of the apostle's thinking, and consciously worked with the heritage of his thought in order to preserve it and pass it on in a form that was adapted for his or her own time. Ephesians is an attempt by the author to present a timely reaffirmation of the essentials of Paul's teaching to a later generation. According to Mitton, the letter, 'with its reiterated affirmations, pleas and exhortations, is entirely appropriate to the special needs of the second generation, and may even be said to become "illumined" if it is interpreted and addressed to them'.[131]

Some advocates of the pseudonymity theory reject the charge that this constitutes forgery, fraud, or fiction — all of which carry emotive and negative overtones. Instead, it is claimed that the phenomenon of pseudonymity, which was a device probably as old as literature itself, must not be judged by modern standards with their 'intellectual propriety, plagiarism and copyright laws'.[132] There is, however, significant difference of opinion as to whether it was the intention of pseudonymous authors to deceive their readers. Some pseudepigrapha in the ancient world were clearly intended to deceive.[133] Several recent writers believe that the New Testament pseudepigrapha were composed and promoted as obvious fiction, so that 'almost certainly the final readers were not in fact deceived'.[134] But the notion of transparent fiction has generally been rejected, and others believe that the situation was much more ambiguous. In relation to the Pastoral Epistles, L. R. Donelson, for example, states candidly:

> In the interest of deception [the author of the Pastorals] fabricated all the personal notes, all the . . . commonplaces in the letters. . . . [He employs] any device that . . . might seem necessary to accomplish his deception.[135]

---

claims to authorship, such as the Pauline and Petrine Letters, together with the Epistles of James and Jude.

131. C. L. Mitton, *The Epistle*, 242. More recently, Dunn claims that pseudonymity was 'a means of affirming the continuity of God's purpose between the circumstances of the named author and the circumstances of the actual author'; J. D. G. Dunn, 'The Problem', 68.

132. A. G. Patzia, 'The Deutero-Pauline Hypothesis', 31.

133. L. R. Donelson, *Pseudepigraphy*, 11; cf. Lincoln, lxxi.

134. J. D. G. Dunn, 'Problem', 84.

135. L. R. Donelson, *Pseudepigraphy*, 24, 55; cited by E. E. Ellis, 'Pseudonymity and Canonicity', 221.

But D. R. Meade thinks that if a document had its origin in a 'school', 'then within the school the work would most likely have been openly known and acknowledged to be pseudonymous (though no less authoritative)'.[136]

Lincoln holds that Ephesians specifically 'was intended for the churches of the Pauline mission in Asia Minor in the generation after the apostle's death' and that 'its writer was in fact a member of a Pauline "school"'.[137] If the letter was sent after Paul's death, then these churches would have known of his martyrdom and recognized Ephesians to be the work of one of their trusted teachers who wrote his letter in harmony with the Pauline tradition. Lincoln adds:

> Therefore both writer and original readers would have been knowing participants in this particular mode of communication, in which the writer wishes to present his teaching not simply as his own but as in the apostolic tradition which has Paul as its source.[138]

On the question of the letter's authority and inspiration, recent advocates maintain that the pseudonymity of Ephesians does not in any way detract from its canonicity, or from the validity and authority of its message. Whether it was written by Paul or by one of his followers, Ephesians stands within the canon. As such, it is as authoritative and foundational for the teaching and life of the people of God as the Gospels or Paul's Letter to the Romans.[139] Meade comments: 'the discovery of pseudonymous origins or anonymous redaction in no way prejudices either the inspiration or canonicity of the work. Attribution, in the context of canon, must be primarily regarded as a statement (or assertion) of authoritative tradition'.[140]

Pseudonymous literature existed and was widespread in the ancient world — Graeco-Roman, Jewish, and Christian. The evidence for this fact is the comments of ancient authors regarding writings known to have false authorship, and other materials, especially of a literary type, which were shown to be pseudonymous.[141]

---

136. D. R. Meade, *Pseudonymity and Canon*, 198.
137. Lincoln, lxxii.
138. Lincoln, lxxii.
139. Lincoln, lxxiii.
140. D. R. Meade, *Pseudonymity and Canon*, 215-16.
141. L. R. Donelson, *Pseudepigraphy*, 9-23, 23-42, who is followed by S. E. Porter, 'Pauline Authorship', 113-14. On the widespread use of false authorship for purposes of fraud and deception in pagan, Jewish, and Christian circles of the Graeco-Roman world, see W. Speyer, *Die literarische Fälschung*, 5-10, etc.; and note E. E. Ellis, 'Pseudonymity and Canonicity', 217.

In relation to this widespread phenomenon of pseudepigrapha, two important points need to be made. First, the question we are addressing is not whether pseudonymous writings existed in the ancient world. They did, and these included letters (even if there were relatively few).[142] Rather, the issue is whether pseudonymous writings exist *in the New Testament*.[143] Lincoln cites a number of noncanonical Jewish and Christian documents as examples of pseudonymous literature,[144] as if this demonstrates the presence of pseudonymity within the New Testament, and shows that Ephesians was part of an ongoing pseudepigraphical tradition. But this is to assume one's conclusion. It may be argued more credibly that these documents, which are noncanonical, confirm the fact that they were found to be pseudonymous and did not get into the canon.[145] We shall return to this issue below.

Secondly, the way these pseudonymous writings were handled is significant. The general pattern was that if a work was known to be pseudonymous it was excluded from the canon of authoritative writings. Referring to both Christian and non-Christian documents, Donelson observes: 'No one ever seems to have accepted a document as religiously and philosophically prescriptive which was known to be forged. I do not know a single example'.[146] So in Judaism there were many examples of pseudepigrapha, such as *The Book of Enoch* and *The Testaments of the Twelve Patriarchs,* but these were composed centuries after the deaths of those mentioned in the works, and they were not considered canonical by the Jews.

---

142. Among Jews and Christians pseudepigraphic letters were rare. Only two pseudonymous letters have come down to us from Jewish sources, namely, the *Epistle of Jeremy* and the *Letter of Aristeas,* neither of which is really a letter. The former, which uses Jeremiah's name to denounce idolatry and was written somewhere between the early fourth and late second century B.C., is a short sermon or hortatory address rather than a letter. The *Letter of Aristeas* is an account of the translation of the Old Testament into Greek, and was composed sometime between the third century B.C. and the first century A.D. Neither of these works was considered genuine and hence canonical either by the rabbis or the Christian church in the first century A.D.

143. See, e.g., S. E. Porter, 'Pauline Authorship', 113-14.

144. Lincoln, lxx-lxxi.

145. So S. E. Porter, 'Pauline Authorship', 115-16.

146. L. R. Donelson, *Pseudepigraphy,* 11. He adds that by contrast there are 'innumerable examples of the opposite. Both Greeks and Romans show great concern to maintain the authenticity of their collections of writings from the past, but the sheer number of the pseudepigrapha made the task difficult'. Note also J. Duff's comment: 'It simply cannot be maintained that in the pagan culture surrounding the early Christians there was no sense of literary property, or no concern over authenticity' ('Pseudepigraphy', 276). Note also his conclusions in relation to first-century Judaism and early Christianity (277-79).

40

Early Christian leaders took this approach towards pseudepigrapha, particularly those written in the name of an apostle. For example, the *Epistle to the Laodiceans* was clearly a spurious letter that was ascribed to Paul, presumably to fill the vacuum created by the loss of the letter mentioned in Colossians 4:16. It is one of a small number of letters circulating among Christians that was pseudonymous. It is a poor compilation of Pauline passages and phrases, mainly from the Letter to the Philippians. The author had a high regard for Paul, but there is no doubt that, although the letter was orthodox, it was rejected by the Christian church. The Muratorian Canon (c. A.D. 170-200) refers to it and a letter to the Alexandrians as 'both forged in Paul's name'.[147]

In another instance, some Asian elders deposed a colleague for being the author of an Acts of Paul, which included a pseudepigraphic writing, *3 Corinthians,* and even though his motive was out of 'love for Paul', they condemned him for presuming to write in the name of an apostle. Serapion, Bishop of Antioch, first thought that the *Gospel of Peter* could be genuine. But after investigating it further, he concluded it was not. Serapion enunciated the following principle to the church of Rhossus in Cilicia:

> For we, brothers, receive both Peter and the other apostles as Christ. But pseudepigrapha in their name we reject, as men of experience, knowing that we did not receive such [from the tradition].[148]

Other apostolic pseudepigrapha that brought no doctrinal objections were also excluded from the church's canon.[149] Following Horst Balz, Earle Ellis comments: 'The exclusion of such documents presupposes . . . that the "apostles of Jesus Christ" had a normative authority and that writings in their names were regarded as deceptive and fraudulent'.[150]

At this juncture we need to examine the important contribution of D. G. Meade to the issue of pseudonymity. He seeks to show that this literary device, practised in New Testament times, has its basis within

147. Muratorian Canon, 64-65.

148. Eusebius, *Ecclesiastical History* 6.12.3; cf. 3.25.4-7; cited by E. E. Ellis, 'Pseudonymity and Canonicity', 218; cf. S. E. Porter, 'Pauline Authorship', 115, who quotes the example of Bishop Salonius, who rejected Salvian's pamphlet written to the church in Timothy's name.

149. For example, the *Apocalypse of Peter,* the *Epistle of the Apostles,* the *Correspondence of Paul and Seneca;* cf. the *Gospel of Thomas;* for details and further references see E. E. Ellis, 'Pseudonymity and Canonicity', 218; and Hoehner.

150. E. E. Ellis, 'Pseudonymity and Canonicity', 218; cf. H. R. Balz, 'Anonymität und Pseudepigraphie', 420.

the Old Testament and Jewish writings where traditions were supplemented, interpreted, and expanded in the names of earlier authors. This occurred within three major traditions of the Old Testament: the prophetic, the wisdom, and the apocalyptic. Under the first heading, he proposes that Second Isaiah (chaps. 40–55) which was written in the light of the Babylonian exile in the sixth century B.C., and Third Isaiah (chaps. 56–66), which appeared in the era of post-exilic Jerusalem between the fourth and second centuries B.C., were added to First Isaiah (chaps. 1–39) for the purpose of making his message contemporary.[151] Meade further applies this principle of continuity between revelation and tradition to the Wisdom literature, Daniel, and 1 Enoch.[152] But Meade's proposals have been subjected to searching criticism. Of the three Old Testament traditions, the prophetic is the only one that is relevant for discussing the New Testament, but even this type of literature is different.[153] Strictly speaking, Isaiah is anonymous and therefore comparable with the Gospels. The process of literary production is different, for in Isaiah the tradition is supposed to have expanded and compiled so that the document grows. This is not what is thought to be happening with the Pauline letters, and certainly not in relation to Ephesians. The issue of the latter's pseudonymity is not about a document growing with the addition of new material. Also, his Old Testament model in which Second and Third Isaiah supposedly contemporize First Isaiah centuries later does not fit the Pauline literature, for the so-called imitators of Paul rarely contemporize the apostle's teaching a century later. Further, Meade's hypothesis is based on critical Old Testament presuppositions proposed during the last two centuries for which there is no historical evidence in the Jewish or Christian communities.[154] Finally, Meade admits that one cannot use this tool to discover the pseudonymous origins of a given piece of literature, such as Ephesians. His proposal can only 'explain the possible development of the tradition once it has been shown that the material is pseudonymous'.[155] In other words, it does not solve the problem being considered in relation to Ephesians (or the other Pauline and Petrine letters).

We now turn to the New Testament and the question of whether there were pseudonymous writings within it. First, the early Christians knew how to pass on the teachings of an authority figure without using

---

151. D. R. Meade, *Pseudonymity and Canon*, 17-43.

152. D. R. Meade, *Pseudonymity and Canon*, 44-102.

153. D. Guthrie, *New Testament Introduction* (Leicester: Apollos, 1990), 1027; and S. E. Porter, 'Pauline Authorship', 117.

154. Hoehner.

155. Note the incisive criticisms of S. E. Porter, 'Pauline Authorship', 117-18.

the literary device of pseudonymity. Mark introduces his work as 'the beginning of the gospel of Jesus Christ' (Mark 1:1), while in Acts Luke narrates apostolic teaching in the third person. They deceived no one, while by contrast 'the pseudo-Pauline and pseudo-Petrine authors [noted above] did not merely create a title but engaged in an elaborate and complex deception to transmit their own ideas under apostolic color'.[156]

Secondly, the author of 2 Thessalonians was aware of forgeries as he wrote his letter and warns his readers accordingly: 'we ask you, brothers, not to become easily unsettled or alarmed by some prophecy, report or letter supposed to have come from us, saying that the day of the Lord has already come' (2:1-2). If that author was not Paul, but a later writer engaging in pseudonymity (as many New Testament critics assume), then he is condemning forgery while at the same time engaging in it himself! On the other hand, if 2 Thessalonians was written by the apostle, then he is warning his readers of the existence of pseudonymous letters, making it clear that he did not agree with the practice (at least when someone was writing a letter in his name!), and giving them 'a token whereby they might know which writings come from him and which make a false claim' (2 Thess. 3:17).[157]

Thirdly, on the view that Ephesians was not written by the apostle, the pseudonymous author has not only carefully imitated the introductions and to some extent the conclusions of the apostle's letters;[158] he has also fabricated situations in Paul's lifetime, including references to his imprisonment (Eph. 3:1; 4:1) as an ambassador (6:20), his sending a brief letter by which the readers will be able to grasp Paul's understanding of the mystery of Christ (3:3-4), and an affirmation that he has sent Tychicus to the readers 'that you may know our circumstances' (6:21-22)! But perhaps the most unconvincing argument and serious weakness to the theory of pseudonymity in relation to the supposed situations in Paul's lifetime is the request that the readers pray specifically for Paul's needs (6:19-20), when, on the later date, the author (and perhaps the readers too) know that the apostle is already dead! Either Paul seeks prayer for himself, or someone seeks to mislead the readers into thinking he does (see on 6:19-20). And if it is the latter, how does this fit with the notions of honesty and integrity in prayer that is offered to a righteous, holy God? Finally, given the strong emphasis in Ephesians on the need for truthful-

---

156. E. E. Ellis, 'Pseudonymity and Canonicity', 220.

157. D. A. Carson, D. J. Moo, and L. Morris, *Introduction*, 367. See also J. Duff, 'Pseudepigraphy', 215-22.

158. Cf. Eph. 1:1 with 2 Cor. 1:1; and Eph. 6:23-24 with 1 Cor. 16:23-24; 2 Cor. 13:11, 14; Gal. 6:18; E. E. Ellis, 'Pseudonymity and Canonicity', 220.

ness (4:15, 24, 25; 5:9; 6:14; cf. 1:13; 4:21),[159] is the author being hypocritical when he condemns deceit at 4:25: 'Putting away falsehood, let each one speak truth with his neighbour'?

We conclude that although pseudonymity was a widely practised literary convention in the ancient world among Greeks, Romans, Jews, and Christians, there is no certain evidence that any document which was known to be fraudulent was accepted as religiously and philosophically prescriptive. Further, the widespread phenomenon of pseudonymous writings does not demonstrate their presence within the New Testament, or show that Ephesians, for example, was part of an ongoing pseudepigraphical tradition.[160] In fact, the reverse is true. The early Christians knew how to pass on the teachings of an authority figure without using the literary device of pseudonymity, and they 'appear to have had no great urge to attach apostolic names to the writings they valued'.[161] More than half of the books of the New Testament do not bear the names of their authors. Why was this strong tradition of anonymity discarded by authors in favour of other people's names (rather than their own), if the theory of pseudonymous authorship is correct? There is no evidence 'that any member of the New Testament church accepted the idea that a pious believer could write something in the name of an apostle and expect the writing to be accepted'. Rather, the evidence that we do have 'is that every time such a writing could be identified with any certainty, it was rejected'.[162]

Meade's attempt to show that pseudonymity as a literary device practised in New Testament times had its basis in the Old Testament and Jewish writings must be judged to have failed. He argues that the development of an ongoing tradition found in Judaism and early Christianity is independent of the kind of literature in which it is found. But Meade provides no evidence to show that Christians wrote letters purporting to come from a person other than the actual author, and then successfully managed to have those letters accepted for what they really were.

Finally, some have claimed that the pseudonymity of Ephesians

159. Best, 12, after drawing attention to some of the references to 'truth' in Ephesians, adds: 'The need for truthfulness is absolute but the perception of what is truth varies from age to age and from culture to culture; it is wrong then to judge the first century by our standards of truth'. In general terms this may be correct, but is Best in danger of driving too sharp a wedge between the concepts of truth in the first century and our day?

160. The conclusion of J. Duff, 'Pseudepigraphy', 272, is that 'there is no positive evidence at all within first and second-century Christian texts that pseudonymity was seen simply as a literary technique accepted by Christians, in which an attribution of authorship was seen as reasonable though strictly speaking false'.

161. D. A. Carson, D. J. Moo, and L. Morris, *Introduction*, 368.

162. D. A. Carson, D. J. Moo, and L. Morris, *Introduction*, 371.

does not in any way detract from its canonicity, or from the validity and authority of its message. Whether it was written by Paul or by one of his followers, Ephesians stands within the canon. It is therefore authoritative, and to be treated as foundational for the life and teaching of God's people, just like the Gospels or Paul's Letter to the Romans.[163] We agree with these sentiments about the need for God's people to regard Ephesians as both authoritative and foundational, and for Christians to take it seriously both publicly and privately. However, there appears to be some confusion in the argument here. The claim is made that because Ephesians is in the canon it is therefore authoritative. But for the early church the argument went the other way: Ephesians was recognized as apostolic and authoritative, and as a result it was accepted into the canon. Its placement in the canon did not give the letter authority; rather, its authority as an apostolic writing preceded its acknowledgement and inclusion within the canon. Given the early church's uniform response of refusing to include within the canon writings known to be or subsequently discovered to be pseudonymous,[164] it is questionable whether we can treat a document as both pseudonymous and canonical.[165] It is one or the other, but not both. Moreover, for all that is said about the letter standing within the Pauline tradition and reflecting the apostle's theology, both scholarly and popular treatments of themes in Ephesians are often relegated to a secondary place, while some Pauline theologies consistently emphasize the differences between the 'historic' Paul and the Paul of Ephesians, especially in the areas of Christology, ecclesiology, and eschatology. Practitioners often fail to expound Pauline theology in relation to God's purposes of summing up all things in Christ (Eph. 1:9-10), and do not come to grips with, for example, the relationship between the apostle's teaching on Israel in Romans 9–11 and the one new humanity in God's purposes in Ephesians 2:14-18. The latter is normally relegated to a secondary position, while the teaching on marriage in Ephesians 5:21-33 is regarded as being significantly different from that of the 'genuine' Paul.

G. Conclusions

The Letter to the Ephesians is distinctive among the epistles attributed to Paul. The early and consistent attestation to its apostolic authorship is

---

163. Lincoln, lxxiii; cf. D. R. Meade, *Pseudonymity and Canon*, 215-16.

164. Hebrews is not an exception to this, since it nowhere claims to have been written by Paul, even though the early church initially took it as such.

165. Cf. E. E. Ellis, 'Pseudonymity and Canonicity', 224.

highly significant, not only because Christians of the first centuries were closer than we are to the situation when it was written, but also because they were careful in weighing and evaluating their founding documents. This uniform testimony to its apostolic authorship should not be easily dismissed.

But the range of differences between Ephesians and the generally accepted Pauline letters has caused many scholars, as we have seen, to conclude that the epistle was not written by the apostle Paul. In the preceding evaluation we have addressed a series of questions dealing with matters such as the 'impersonal character' of Ephesians, its language and style, the literary relationship between this epistle and Colossians, its theological emphases, the picture of Paul presented in it, and the vexed question of apostolic authorship and pseudonymity. On the whole my arguments have been more negative than I would have wished, but this has been because I have tried to evaluate fairly a critical consensus that has developed regarding the pseudonymity of Ephesians, approximating 'an assured result of New Testament criticism'. If detailed arguments have been presented in 'the case for the prosecution', then it has been necessary to provide an extensive 'case for the defence'. Of course, it has been claimed with some justice that if so many defences have had to be produced again and again, 'doubts must begin to be raised about the tenability of the position defended'.[166] But not all the presumed difficulties raised against the apostolic authorship of Ephesians have been of equal weight or value.

Further, there is a number of hard-core problems for the advocates of pseudonymity that will not easily go away — including the early and consistent testimony to apostolic authorship, the expressions in Ephesians that seem to have been used by the author of Colossians, the evidence against pseudonymity in relation to the New Testament letters, the restrictions placed on Paul's ability and versatility as a writer and theologian, the changed epistolary situation envisaged in Ephesians, and so on. Is it being unfair, then, to suggest that the problems created by pseudonymity are greater than the ones solved by it?[167]

In our judgment the traditional view has the most evidence in its fa-

---

166. Lincoln, lxix.

167. J. H. Roberts, 'The Enigma of Ephesians: Rethinking Some Positions on the Basis of Schnackenburg and Arnold', *Neot* 27 (1993), 93-106, esp. 94, complains that the wide consensus against Pauline authorship has meant that 'scholars no longer seem to argue the case from all perspectives'; instead, they list only the arguments in favour of the consensus point of view, and this has now 'attained the status of dogma. It now only needs to be confirmed. Variant opinions are regarded as aberrations that need not be taken seriously'!

vour. 'It is not unreasonable to think of Paul re-expressing, developing and modifying his own thoughts for a different readership facing a different set of circumstances'.[168] The onus of proof is upon those who must establish that Paul was incapable of this versatility. We agree that 'the best explanation . . . seems to be that the same man wrote Colossians and Ephesians a little later, with many of the same thoughts running through his head and with a more general application of the ideas he had so recently expressed'.[169]

II. DESTINATION OF THE LETTER[170]

Traditionally Paul's letter has been understood to have been written to believers in Ephesus: the city is mentioned in the superscription 'To the Ephesians', and in the prescript, 'to the saints who are in Ephesus' (1:1). However, the words 'in Ephesus' are absent from some of the best manuscripts (note the discussion of the textual problem at 1:1). Also, the impersonal tone of the letter and its more general contents cast further doubt on the authenticity of the words 'in Ephesus'. Accordingly, these features have suggested to many that Ephesians was some form of circular letter.

E. J. Goodspeed suggested that Ephesians was a general letter written toward the end of the first century as an introduction to the collected letters of Paul. This was effected by some follower of the apostle who, having first collected the Pauline epistles, wrote this letter in the style of his master as a way of introducing his readers to some of Paul's thinking.[171] Although this theory was widely accepted for a time, it is almost universally rejected today because of its inherent difficulties.[172]

Clinton Arnold, who has recently argued in favour of the original text of Ephesians 1:1 including the words 'in Ephesus',[173] adopts a circular letter hypothesis. He claims that we need not assume that the letter was written to one church in the city. The wording of the address, 'to the

---

168. C. E. Arnold, *DPL*, 243.

169. D. A. Carson, D. J. Moo, and L. Morris, *Introduction*, 308.

170. See further the discussions, together with bibliographical details, by Lincoln, lxxiii-lxxxiii; D. A. Carson, D. J. Moo, and L. Morris, *Introduction*, 305-16, esp. 309-11; C. E. Arnold, *DPL*, 238-49, esp. 243-46; R. E. Brown, *Introduction*, 620-37, esp. 626-27; and Best, 1-6; also his *Essays*, 1-24.

171. E. J. Goodspeed, *The Meaning of Ephesians* (Chicago: University of Chicago Press, 1933).

172. Note the evaluation by Best, 65-66; cf. D. A. Carson, D. J. Moo, and L. Morris, *Introduction*, 311.

173. C. E. Arnold, *DPL*, 244-45. Note his text-critical evaluation of 1:1.

saints in Ephesus who are faithful in Christ Jesus', omits any reference to the term 'church', which might suggest one congregation.[174] In other contexts, this omission may not be particularly significant (since 'church' does not appear in all of Paul's greetings), but it does allow the possibility here (as well as in the greeting to the Roman Christians: Rom. 1:7) that the author was addressing Christians who were members of house-churches scattered throughout the city and its environs, and perhaps even further afield (e.g., in the Lycus valley). One needs to bear in mind that at this stage the population of Ephesus was probably at least a quarter of a million people; we need not suppose (since the text does not demand it) that all the Christians in the city were 'jammed' into one megachurch! For the author to state that he has 'heard' of their faith and love (1:15) does not necessarily imply that he does not know them. It could easily refer to his hearing of the progress they had made since he had been with them five or so years earlier, as well as the faith of many who had been converted since he left the city. The possibility of the letter being read by a wide range of Christians in western Asia Minor, centred in Ephesus, makes sense of his question about their hearing of God's grace given to him to minister to Gentiles (3:2; cf. 4:21). The absence of personal greetings is not particularly significant, according to Arnold, since Paul sends no extended greetings in other letters to churches he knew well (about whose authorship there is no doubt, e.g., 1 and 2 Corinthians, Galatians, and Philippians). Finally, the fact that he prays for his readers (1:16) and asks them to intercede for him so that he may proclaim the mystery of the gospel boldly and clearly (6:19-20) suggests that the letter is not wholly impersonal.[175]

In contrast to Arnold, we contend that the textual tradition which omits the words 'in Ephesus' was the original (see on 1:1). At the same time, the evidence of the great mass of manuscripts, in which no other place name appears, and the improbabilities of all the other views suggest that the letter, in some form or other, was sent to Ephesus. But the impersonal features and other general characteristics of the letter should not be underestimated. Paul has evangelized the Ephesians and come to know them well over a three-year period (Acts 19:8, 10; 20:31). It is unlikely that he is now addressing the one Ephesian congregation where he

---

174. Note especially the address in 1 Corinthians 1:2, τῇ ἐκκλησίᾳ τοῦ θεοῦ τῇ οὔσῃ ἐν Κορίνθῳ, ἡγιασμένοις ἐν Χριστῷ Ἰησοῦ, κλητοῖς ἁγίοις ('to the church of God in Corinth, to those sanctified in Christ Jesus and called to be holy'). Later in this letter Paul can refer to ἡ ἐκκλησία ὅλη ('the whole church') meeting together (14:23), while at the same time he recognizes that individual house-churches will also come together (16:19). On the significance of this relationship see P. T. O'Brien, 'Entity', 88-119, 307-11.

175. So, among others, Hoehner.

had ministered for this lengthy period (Acts 20:31). Even if that church now contains new converts, and Paul has only 'heard' about the significant Christian progress of those whom he already knew (cf. Eph. 1:15), one would expect him to mention his warm relationships with them if his epistle were addressed only to them. The mention of Tychicus, who will provide the readers with further information about Paul's welfare and circumstances (Eph. 6:21-22; cf. Col. 4:7-9), pegs the letter to the geographical situation of Asia Minor. It appears to have been written for churches in this province, perhaps in and around Ephesus, or on the road to Colossae. Beyond this, we have no certain knowledge of who the intended recipients of the letter were. The overwhelming manuscript evidence in favour of Ephesus suggests that most of the extant copies (apart from those which have no geographical place name) may have been made from one that was sent to Ephesus. On this view, however, a specific knowledge of the ancient city of Ephesus, in spite of the increasing amount of information available to us, especially through the inscriptions, does not assist us a great deal in interpreting the letter.[176]

III. LIFE-SETTING, PURPOSE, AND PROVENANCE

A. The Life-Setting of Ephesians

Of all the letters in the Pauline corpus, Ephesians is the one that appears to be the most general and least situational. No particular problem appears to be addressed in the epistle, and it does not have the same sense of urgency or response to a crisis as do Paul's other letters.

The following may be gleaned about the readers from the epistle.[177] First, they are men and women whom God has blessed with every spiritual blessing in the heavenly places in Christ (Eph. 1:3). In particular, God had chosen them in his Son before the foundation of the world, and predestined them to be adopted as his sons and daughters in Christ before the foundation of the world (1:4, 5). For their part, they had heard the word of truth, the gospel of salvation, and appropriated it for themselves (1:13).

The readers, along with other Christians, are described by a host of designations used of God's people in the Old Testament and in the New.

---

176. Cf. Snodgrass, 21.
177. For details see Lincoln, lxxv-lxxvii, who, however, draws different conclusions about the setting and purpose of Ephesians. Cf. Best, 83-93.

They are 'saints' (1:1, 15, 18; 3:18; 5:3; 6:18) who believe (1:1, 13, 15; 2:18; 3:12) and love our Lord Jesus Christ (6:24). The readers are spoken of as 'children of light' (5:8) who are God's work of new creation (2:10). They have experienced the grace of God (1:6, 8; 2:5, 8), and the love of God and Christ (2:4; 5:2, 25). They understand in a personal way the blessings of redemption (1:7), the forgiveness of sins (1:7; 4:32), life (2:5), salvation (1:13; 2:5, 8), and reconciliation (2:14-18). Having been sealed with the Holy Spirit until the day of redemption (1:13; 4:30), they know what it means to have access to the Father through Christ by the same Spirit (2:18). Along with others who have been incorporated into Christ, they have been united with him in his resurrection and exaltation, so that now his destiny has become theirs (2:5-6).

A number of the images and metaphors used of these Christian readers are corporate and describe them in terms of their belonging to a wider community of men and women in Christ. As 'saints' they are also 'fellow citizens with God's holy people' (lit. 'holy ones'; 2:19; cf. 3:18; 6:18); they are 'brothers and sisters' who have been adopted as sons and daughters into God's family and are members of his household (cf. 6:23; 1:5; 5:1; 2:19). They belong to the church, which is related to the exalted Christ (1:22; 3:10, 21; 5:23, 25, 27, 29, 32), and are members of his body (1:23; 2:16; 3:6; 4:4, 16; 5:23). These Christian men and women are members of God's temple, which is built on the foundation of the apostles and prophets, and which has Christ Jesus as the chief cornerstone (2:19-22). Of particular importance in Ephesians is the fact that the readers belong to one new humanity which was created in Christ out of Jews and Gentiles (2:14-16; 3:6) who have been reconciled to God and to one another. This new creation of God is characterized by its unity in diversity and maturity (4:1-16).

These designations are true of all Christians, and therefore do not mark the readers as being different from other believers. To this extent the descriptions in Ephesians are general. More specifically, however, the particular focus of the letter is towards Gentile Christians, even though both Jewish and Gentile Christian believers are in view (cf. 1:11-14). So Gentile Christians are explicitly addressed in 2:11 and 3:1, while their past is described in terms of their being separated from Israel as the people of God (with the result that they had been without God and without hope, 2:12), a characterization that was applicable only to former Gentiles. Further, they are urged not to return to their previous Gentile lifestyle (4:17; cf. 2:1-3). When the apostle speaks about his imprisonment and ministry, he explicitly relates it to 'you Gentiles' (3:1), and he urges them not to be discouraged on account of his sufferings, which are 'for you' (3:13).

As far as the more concrete historical circumstances are concerned, the apostle assumes that his readers know of him (1:1; 3:1; 6:21, 22), particularly of his special ministry of proclaiming the mystery of the gospel to Gentiles (3:2, 3, 7, 8), as well as his suffering and imprisonment (3:13; 4:1), and even perhaps of his detention in Rome where he was awaiting his appearance before the supreme tribunal in which he might have opportunity to bear witness before Caesar himself (see on 6:20). Finally, the readers will receive a visit from Tychicus, who will tell them all about the apostle's personal circumstances so that they may learn how he is and be encouraged by Tychicus's news (6:21-22).

B. The Purpose of the Letter[178]

1. Some Previous Suggestions

This information gleaned from the text of Ephesians about the 'implied readers' is not particularly specific. Given that there has been considerable difference of scholarly opinion about the authorship, destination, audience, and date of composition of the letter, it is not surprising that there is no unanimity as to the purpose(s) for which it was written! Most of Paul's letters are occasional, penned to meet specific pastoral and theological needs. But it is not easy to find any particular occasion that called forth this letter. The companion epistle to the Colossians was written (probably) to counter a heresy that had begun to make inroads into the congregation, but there is no false teaching against which Ephesians is aimed (see below).

Because of its general nature, some scholars question whether Ephesians should be regarded as a letter at all. Instead, it has been suggested that it is a theological tract, a wisdom discourse, an early Christian hymn, a baptismal or eucharistic liturgy, or a sermon written by a disciple of Paul (see above, where we concluded that Ephesians is a genuine letter, written for a broad readership). But we must be careful not to specify a concrete situation or particular problem to which a letter has been sent, if the evidence is otherwise. There is no reason, in principle, why a letter could not be general in nature and written for the purpose of instructing and edifying Christians over a wide area or in a range of congregations. In the case of Ephesians, its solemnity and the broad sweep of

---

178. For recent surveys of the purpose(s) for which Ephesians was written, together with further bibliographical details, see D. A. Carson, D. J. Moo, and L. Morris, *Introduction*, 309-12; C. E. Arnold, *DPL*, 245-46, 248-49; R. E. Brown, *Introduction*, 620-37; Best, 63-75, and Hoehner.

God's majestic saving purposes set forth in the first half of the epistle, together with the wide-ranging exhortatory material of chapters 4–6, suggest that Paul could have had such purposes in mind.

Before turning to this issue more specifically, however, we shall note briefly some of the scholarly suggestions that have been made regarding the purpose of Ephesians.

a. Some interpreters have emphasized a baptismal setting for the letter: Ephesians is either a homily or a reminder to young Gentile Christians of the implications of their faith and baptism, in which they are exhorted to live up to their calling,[179] or it is a renewal of baptismal vows associated with the Feast of Pentecost.[180] But it is surprising that in a letter supposedly devoted to baptism there should be only one reference to the term, and this in a context concerned with unity, not baptism (4:5).[181]

b. Ephesians has been interpreted as a polemical letter directed against various kinds of false teaching. It has been claimed, for example, that the epistle was intended to refute an increasing Gnosticism of a Jewish kind.[182] But current New Testament scholars have increasingly rejected understanding Ephesians against a Gnostic backdrop. Ernest Best can claim that the author of Ephesians was 'neither motivated by gnosis nor did he set out to counteract its influence among his readers'.[183] K. M. Fischer[184] discerns in the letter a twofold polemical thrust: there was a crisis in which the unity of Jewish and Gentile Christians was threatened. Against this the author wrote to remind Gentile believers, who have been boasting of their position within the church, that Jewish Christians also have a right to be there. But there is no evidence in the letter (including 2:11-22) of a polemic to suggest that Gentile Christians despised fellow

179. N. A. Dahl, 'Gentiles, Christians, and Israelites in the Epistle to the Ephesians', *HTR* 79 (1986), 31-39, esp. 38; cf. also U. Luz, 'Überlegungen zum Epheserbrief', 376-96.

180. J. C. Kirby, *Ephesians,* 145-61; note the interaction of Best, 71-72.

181. Note the criticisms of C. C. Caragounis, *Mysterion,* 46; and Arnold, 135-36.

182. Scholars such as R. Bultmann, H. Schlier, E. Käsemann, W. Schmithals, and E. Norden have understood Ephesians against the backdrop of Gnosticism, while P. Pokorný, *Der Brief des Paulus an die Epheser* (Leipzig: Evangelische Verlagsanstalt, 1992), 443-46, believes that the author sought to refute a number of Gnostic tendencies.

183. Best, 88-89. He adds; 'An examination of Ephesians does not reveal any positive evidence that AE [= 'the author of Ephesians'] was consciously opposing gnosticism'; note his careful analysis, 87-89; also Arnold, 7-13.

184. K. M. Fischer, *Tendenz und Absicht des Epheserbriefes* (Göttingen: Vandenhoeck & Ruprecht, 1973), 21-39, 79-94. Along similar lines, R. P. Martin, *Ephesians, Colossians, and Philemon* (Atlanta: John Knox, 1991), 5, proposed that Gentile Christians thought they were independent of Israel, and so were intolerant of Jewish believers. They also misunderstood Paul's teaching and adopted an easygoing moral code.

Jewish believers.[185] At the same time, Fischer sees a crisis in ecclesiastical development with a new order of episcopacy being promoted within Gentile Christian congregations in Asia Minor. But this reconstruction is highly speculative, given the letter's silence about bishops, presbyters, and deacons. On a rather more positive note, H. Chadwick,[186] building on the insight of J. A. Robinson that Ephesians emphasizes that God's purpose for the human race is its unity in Christ, suggests that the letter was written to show the authority and antiquity of the Christian message in the face of the apparently late arrival of the church on the scene of history. Further, because of the unity of the church the non-Pauline congregations needed to be united with the Pauline churches and Jewish Christians. However, it is very doubtful that Ephesians reads like such an extended polemic. The concern of the letter is not with the past as such but with God's dealings with Israel, so that the readers might appreciate their present privileges in contrast to their past alienation and separation from the promises of God.[187] The real difficulty with each of these interpretations is that, for all their differences, they understand the main purpose of Ephesians in polemical terms. But there appear to be no signs in the letter itself that its purpose was to combat opponents or refute different kinds of false teaching.

c. A number of recent interpreters have suggested that the readers of Ephesians were in a state of spiritual crisis and that the letter was written to deal with it. The nature of the spiritual crises varies. Lindemann, for example, proposes that the readers faced a situation of persecution during the reign of the Emperor Domitian (A.D. 96), and that they needed strengthening and encouragement.[188] This is suggested by the battle imagery of Ephesians 6:10-20. But the exhortation to take up the whole armour of God does not necessarily presuppose a specific situation of persecution. The imagery of 'the evil day' and 'the burning arrows of the evil one' does not require external persecution for it to make sense; rather, the paragraph is referring to the spiritual warfare of every believer against evil supernatural powers under the control of the devil (see on 6:10-20).[189]

d. A recent influential proposal regarding the nature of the spiritual crisis the readers were facing and which Ephesians was written to deal

185. Best, 68. Lincoln, lxxx, rightly observes that this is 'to misinterpret the letter's treatment of the themes of unity and the Church's relationship to Israel and to misconstrue the force of its rhetoric'.
186. H. Chadwick, 'Die Absicht', 145-53.
187. Cf. Lincoln, lxxx; and Best, 69-70.
188. A. Lindemann, *Die Aufhebung*, 14-15.
189. Note Schnackenburg, 33-34; and Lincoln, lxxx-lxxxi.

with is that of Arnold,[190] who seeks to explain the strong emphasis in the epistle on the cosmic spiritual powers. He claims that Ephesians was a pastoral letter addressed to a group of churches in western Asia Minor. Many Gentile members of these congregations had been converts from a Hellenistic religious environment which included the mystery religions, magic, and astrology, and some had previously been steeped in the worship of the goddess Artemis, whose cult was centred in Ephesus. Some of these believers, whose fear of evil spirits and cosmic powers was of great concern, had probably been tempted to syncretize their past magical beliefs and practices with their new-found faith. Perhaps, too, there had been false teaching about the role of Christianity in relation to these evil powers. These new believers lacked a personal acquaintance with Paul, but needed positive grounding in the apostolic gospel. Because of their pagan past they had to be admonished to cultivate a lifestyle consistent with their new-found salvation in Christ.[191] According to Arnold, Paul emphasizes God's mighty power by which he raised Christ from the dead and brought all things, including every power and authority, under the rule of Christ (Eph. 1:19-22). Because of their being identified with Christ in his resurrection and exaltation, believers have been made to sit with him in the heavenly realms (2:6). His destiny has become theirs, and now God's power by which they live their lives is more than sufficient to protect them against those principalities which once enslaved them and which seek to reassert their control over them. It is not necessary to resort to pagan ritual or practices in order to appropriate this divine strength. Instead, by faith and through prayer they are to don the whole armour of God in order to resist the evil one and his minions in their daily spiritual warfare (6:10-20).

Arnold's proposal (unlike those of many earlier interpreters) gives considerable attention to the place of the 'powers' in Ephesians, where they are mentioned more often per page than in any other Pauline letter.[192] Further, he has helped us to understand the function and significance of 6:10-20 within the flow of the letter,[193] and plausibly suggests

---

190. Arnold, 123-24, 167-72, and in *DPL*, 246. Arnold builds on the work of H. E. Lona, *Die Eschatologie*, 428-48.

191. C. E. Arnold, *DPL*, 246. Note also his recent work on first-century syncretism in western Asia Minor, particularly in relation to Colossae: C. E. Arnold, *The Colossian Syncretism: The Interface between Christianity and Folk Belief at Colossae* (Tübingen/Grand Rapids: J. C. B. Mohr [Paul Siebeck]/Baker, 1995/1996).

192. Cf. Rom. 8:38; 1 Cor. 2:6-8; 10:19-21; 15:24-26; Gal. 4:3, 9; Phil. 2:10, as well as the references in the companion Letter to the Colossians: Col. 1:16; 2:15; cf. 2:8, 20. For details see the exegesis on Eph. 1:21, etc.

193. Arnold, 103-22.

why there is correspondingly greater mention of the power of God in this epistle than elsewhere in Paul.[194] His proposed life-setting for Ephesus and its environs need not be limited to this city, however, since the cosmic and supernatural were important factors in the general milieu of readers in Asia Minor, a milieu that was not simply economic, political, scientific, or artistic. But Arnold himself admits that, even if his proposed life-setting for Ephesians explains the prominence of the power-motif, it 'is not sufficient to give a full account of the reasons Ephesians was written, or . . . to explain all of the theological peculiarities of the epistle'.[195] The place of major themes in both halves of the epistle, as well as the key motif of cosmic reconciliation in Christ (together with the function of the key passage, 1:9-10), is not sufficiently accounted for by his otherwise creative and fresh approach. Further, his use of sources primarily from Egypt, and mostly from the third and fourth centuries A.D., has been questioned,[196] while it has been argued that there is no evidence that the Ephesians considered Artemis evil and demonic.[197]

e. Lincoln[198] thinks that Ephesians deals with broad Christian principles, and he warns of the danger of attempting to find a specific setting for the letter or of concluding that there is one specific purpose for its being written. His analysis of the rhetorical situation indicates that the letter has a broad, universal appeal. Ephesians has a number of general purposes which would help and encourage Christians 'in a variety of settings'. These purposes include providing believers who

> were in need of inner strength, further knowledge of their salvation, greater appreciation of their identity as believers and as members of the Church, increased concern for the Church's unity, and more consistent living in such areas as speech, sexuality, and household relationships.[199]

Lincoln views Ephesians as belonging to a post-Pauline situation, but, having stated his caution about nailing it down to a specific context,

194. These positive gains from Arnold's work do not seem to have been properly appreciated by Lincoln, lxxxi, or Best, 73.

195. Arnold, 168.

196. Though note Arnold's more recent work, *The Colossian Syncretism*, which draws upon fresh evidence.

197. So R. Strelan, *Paul, Artemis, and the Jews in Ephesus* (Berlin: de Gruyter, 1996), 83-86. But should one expect to discover this in the extrabiblical material? Did Christians regard the worship of Artemis as demonic? And, if so, in what sense?

198. Lincoln, lxxxi-lxxxiii.

199. Lincoln, lxxxi.

he then proceeds to reconstruct the historical situation addressed.[200] Although the evidence is not certain, Ephesians seems to be linked with western Asia Minor. The author was a disciple of Paul who wrote to second-generation Pauline Christians whose hopes of the second coming of Jesus were fading and who needed to understand who they were in Christ. They were exhorted to pursue a distinctive Christian lifestyle in the world, in contrast to their former way of life as Gentiles, through the enabling power of Christ and his Spirit.[201]

Lincoln's warning against attributing a specific setting or particular purpose to the letter seems justified,[202] whether one thinks Paul was the author of Ephesians or not.[203] The considerable differences between commentators and students of Ephesians show that there is no agreement about the purpose of the letter, even if there is considerable unanimity among them about significant themes within it.[204]

2. A Way Forward?

This interaction with the previous scholarly literature regarding the purpose of Ephesians provides the context from which to suggest a possible way forward for understanding why Paul wrote the letter. On the negative side, it is clear that Ephesians was not sent to deal with some particular false teaching in a specific congregation. The general contents and relative lack of personal details prevent us from coming to this conclusion.

Instead, as a general letter it was probably sent to a number of predominantly Gentile churches (perhaps in the area Tychicus was passing through). We agree with Max Turner[205] that 'Ephesians makes dominant a theme which was already important in Colossians, that is, cosmic rec-

200. He poses the question: 'But what then can be said about *the actual setting and recipients* of the letter?' (emphasis added); Lincoln, lxxxi. Note the response of Hoehner.

201. Lincoln, lxxxiii-lxxxvii.

202. Even if his practice of finding an actual setting and recipients of the letter is inconsistent. Presumably if Paul were the author of the letter, on Lincoln's criterion it would be appropriate to come to similar conclusions to those of Arnold, but Lincoln rejects these because it 'links the setting too closely to Ephesus itself' (Lincoln, lxxxi)!

203. A point which Snodgrass, 22, concedes.

204. Hoehner recognizes this, and focusses on the major themes of unity and love. Regarding the latter, he contends that it has a dominant place in the letter. Accordingly, it is 'reasonable to conclude that the purpose of Ephesians is to promote a love for one another which has the love of God and Christ as its basis'. This provides the basis for unity.

205. Turner, 1223. I had come to similar conclusions regarding the purpose of Ephesians prior to reading the expansive article of M. Turner, 'Mission and Meaning in Terms of "Unity" in Ephesians', in *Mission and Meaning: Essays Presented to Peter Cotterell*, ed. A. Billington, T. Lane, and M. Turner (Carlisle: Paternoster, 1995), 138-66, which supports and undergirds many of the arguments in his brief commentary.

onciliation in Christ' (cf. Eph. 1:9-10, 20-23; 2:10-22, and 3:6 with Col. 1:19-20). Having addressed a specific problem in Colossians, Paul has remodeled his letter for a more general Christian readership. He writes Ephesians to his mainly Gentile Christian readers, for whom he has apostolic responsibilities, with the intention of informing, strengthening, and encouraging them by assuring them of their place within the gracious, saving purpose of God, and urging them to bring their lives into conformity with this divine plan of summing up all things in Christ (1:10). Paul wants to 'ground, shape and challenge' his readers in their faith. In other words, the main purpose of his letter is *identity formation*.[206] Our comments below regarding the central message, contents, and genre of the letter will help to fill out this assertion in more detail.

C. The Provenance of Ephesians

In the light of our foregoing discussion, we conclude that Ephesians was written by the apostle Paul during his imprisonment in Rome, around A.D. 61-62. The connections between this letter and Colossians, notably the personal details concerning Paul's coworker, Tychicus (see the discussion above), suggest that Ephesians was written from the same place as Colossians. It is just possible that both epistles were written from an imprisonment in Ephesus itself, which would date the letter about A.D. 55, or from Caesarea in about A.D. 58. But an imprisonment in Rome, around A.D. 61-62, is more likely. I have already presented the case for this in relation to Colossians,[207] and, although certainty is not attainable, from the evidence available it does not seem necessary to change this view. The apostle wrote the Letter to Philemon on the occasion of his returning Onesimus to his Christian master. Onesimus was entrusted to the care of Tychicus, Paul's coworker (Col. 4:7-9), who took both the personal letter and the epistle which Paul wrote to the whole church at Colossae, warning the congregation of the false teaching that was on the horizon.

Turner plausibly suggests that on their journey Tychicus and Onesimus would have sailed to Ephesus and then struck east along the main Roman road to the Euphrates in order to reach Colossae in the Lycus valley. Tychicus may well have taken Ephesians with him, either as a circular letter for the churches in the whole Roman province of Asia (including the

---

206. Snodgrass, 23 (original emphasis), following J. P. Sampley, 'Ephesians', in *The Deutero-Pauline Letters: Ephesians, Colossians, 2 Thessalonians, 1-2 Timothy, Titus* (Minneapolis: Fortress, 1993), 23.

207. P. T. O'Brien, *Colossians, Philemon*, xlix-liv.

seven mentioned in Rev. 1–3), or, if Turner is right, 'it was written for the churches along or near the road Tychicus would have taken from Ephesus to Colosse, including Magnesia, Tralles, Hierapolis and Laodicea'.[208]

IV. THE CENTRAL MESSAGE

Cosmic reconciliation and unity in Christ are the central message of Paul's Letter to the Ephesians. This emerges initially from Ephesians 1:9-10, where it is proclaimed that God has made known to us the mystery of his will, the content of which is 'that he might sum up all things in Christ'. This text provides the key for unlocking the glorious riches of the letter, 'draws together into a unity' many of its major themes, and enables us to gain an integrated picture of the letter as a whole. We note the following points:

1. Ephesians 1:9 and 10 appear within Paul's long sentence of vv. 3-14, in which the God and Father of our Lord Jesus Christ is praised for blessing us with every spiritual blessing in the heavenly places in Christ. This opening paragraph, which celebrates the accomplishment of God's gracious purposes in Christ, provides a sweep from eternity to eternity, and the climactic note is struck with the mention of the mystery and its content (vv. 9-10). Syntactically and structurally, the explication of the mystery in terms of the 'summing up' is the 'high point' of the eulogy, or, as T. Moritz puts it, the 'pivotal statement' of the passage (see the exegesis of 1:9-10).[209] The immediately following words of the eulogy (vv. 11-14) stress that the magnificent blessings already described are for both Jewish and Gentile believers. Once the high point of this *berakah* has been reached, the author turns to explain who is included within the sphere of these salvation blessings. The 'bringing all things together in unity', which points forward to eternity, is the climax of Paul's statements.

2. As we have pointed out in the exegesis of 1:9 and 10, the increasing consensus among modern scholars is that the verb used here derives from a noun meaning the 'main point', 'sum', or 'summary' (cf. Acts 22:28; Heb. 8:1) rather than the term 'head', and that its basic meaning is 'to bring something to a main point', or 'to sum up'.[210] In connection with Christ's eschatological relationship to a multitude of entities (including

208. Turner, 1222.
209. C. C. Caragounis, *Mysterion,* 143; T. Moritz, '"Summing Up All Things"; Religious Pluralism and Universalism in Ephesians', in *One God, One Lord,* ed. B. W. Winter and A. D. Clarke (Cambridge/Grand Rapids: Tyndale House/Baker, 1991/1992), 96.
210. See the details below.

personal beings), the text suggests that God's 'summing up' of these entities in Christ is his act of bringing all things together in (and under) Christ, that is, his unifying of them in some way in Christ.

3. As throughout the rest of the eulogy, the divine purpose is said to be 'in Christ', and this point is emphatically reiterated in the concluding words of v. 10, 'in him'. Although this expression might be understood as instrumental, suggesting that the Messiah is the means (or instrument) through whom God sums up the universe, it is better to take the phrase as referring to him as the sphere, in line with the earlier instances of this phrase within the paragraph (vv. 3-7, 9). Christ is the one *in whom* God chooses to sum up the cosmos, the one in whom he restores harmony to the universe. He is the focal point — not simply the means, the instrument, or the functionary through whom all this occurs. The previous examples of 'in Christ' and its equivalents within the eulogy focussed on the Son as God's chosen one in whom believers have been blessed. Now in vv. 9 and 10 the stress is placed on the one in whom God's overarching purposes for the *whole* of the created order are included. The emphasis is now on a universe that is centred and reunited in Christ.[211] The mystery which God has graciously made known refers to the summing up and bringing together of the fragmented and alienated elements of the universe in Christ as the focal point. All things are to be summed up in God's anointed one and presented as a coherent totality in him.

4. Regarding the timing of bringing all things together in Christ, the text indicates that the content of the mystery *has been* revealed: God has lavished his grace upon us in all wisdom and insight by making known[212] to us the mystery of his will. This, however, is not to assert that the actual outworking of God's saving purposes has taken place or been consummated.[213] The apocalyptic expression, 'when the times will have reached their fulfilment', looks forward to the time of the consummation of God's purposes. The aorist infinitive 'to bring all things together' does not point to the past, but signifies purpose: the summing up of all things is the goal to be achieved. Yet the implementation of the divine plan is already under way. The letter makes it quite plain that significant steps have already been taken to set in motion the achievement of this goal: in

---

211. Lincoln, 34.

212. See on 1:9 for a discussion of the precise relationship between the aorist participle γνωρίσας ('made known') and the principal verb ἐπερίσσευσεν ('he lavished'). We contend that the participle following the main verb describes coincident action: 'he lavished his grace on us in all wisdom and insight in that he made known to us the mystery of his will'.

213. An architect's plan for a building which is submitted well in advance of the actual construction of the building may be a helpful analogy.

particular, it is through Jesus' saving work that the revelation of the mystery's content has come about (1:7-9), while God's placing all things under his feet and appointing him to be head over everything for the church (1:22) is an important step towards the fulfilment of this goal. But the summing up awaits the consummation, which will occur at the end.

5. Of special importance for our task of determining how Ephesians 1:9-10 provides the key for unlocking the treasures of the epistle are the grammatical objects of the verb 'to bring together in unity'. The divine intention is to sum up as a whole 'all things' in Christ. This is amplified by the following parallel statement, 'things in heaven and things on earth'. At first glance, these additional words seem to be simply a rhetorical flourish. After all, is it not just a typical way, in biblical terms, of speaking of the whole or totality to refer to 'things in heaven' and 'things on earth'? In particular, the opening words of the Bible, 'In the beginning God created the heavens and the earth' (Gen. 1:1), signify that God made everything.

But on closer examination it is evident that the two phrases 'things in heaven' and 'things on earth' represent two important strands running throughout the epistle which signify two separate spheres or domains. It is well known that Ephesians has distinctive things to say about 'the heavenlies' (1:3, 10, 20; 2:6; 3:10; 6:12; cf. 3:15; 4:10; 6:9), as well as about 'the things on earth' (1:10; 3:15; 4:9; 6:3). A proper understanding of God's intention of summing up everything in Christ has to do with each of these two spheres and what is represented by them, as well as with the bond between the two. The *anakephalaiōsis* in Christ has to do with both realms. At the same time there is an inseparable connection between them, so that we may speak of both heaven and earth being summed up as a totality in him.[214]

In his stimulating monograph dealing with the mystery in Ephesians, Chrys Caragounis[215] claims that as Paul proceeds to amplify and explain the meaning of the *anakephalaiōsis* throughout the letter, he concentrates on the two main representatives of these spheres, namely, the *powers* representing 'the things in heaven', and the *church* (particularly in relation to Jews and Gentiles in the body of Christ) representing 'the things on earth'. Caragounis further suggests that the two obstacles which need to be overcome before the divine purposes of bringing everything back into unity in Christ can be fulfilled are (a) the rebellion of the powers, and (b) the alienation of the Jews from the Gentiles (2:11-22, as well as the estrangement of both from God, 2:16). Much of the rest of

214. A. T. Lincoln, in *Theology*, 96-97.
215. C. C. Caragounis, *Mysterion*, 144-46, cf. 96.

Ephesians is given over to explicating, with reference to each of these two spheres, the steps in the process that God has taken in order to 'bring all things into unity in Christ'.

Before turning to each, we recognize that both Ephesians and the companion Letter to the Colossians presuppose that the unity and harmony of the cosmos have suffered a considerable dislocation, even a rupture, requiring reconciliation or restoration to harmony. At Colossians 1:20-22 the apostle speaks of a reconciliation of 'all things' to God that has already been effected by the death of Christ, and the particular focus is the reconciliation of human beings to him. The later reference in Colossians to the conquest of the principalities (2:15) is to be understood in the light of God's mighty reconciliation and pacification (1:20). Ephesians 2:1-3 particularly draws attention to the desperate plight of men and women outside of Christ, and their situation is described in terms of death, condemnation, and bondage to evil, determining influences. Apart from God's mighty and gracious intervention to save, there could be no hope for rebel sinners in the midst of this profound need (2:4-7).

a. In Ephesians, God is shown to be in controversy with the powers which represent 'the things in heaven'. They are presented as rebellious towards him, but also as influencing humanity in the same direction (2:2-3). He has, however, won the decisive victory over the powers by raising Christ from the dead and exalting him to a position of unparalleled honour and universal authority (1:19-22). Not only are they made subordinate to the exalted Christ; they are also placed under his feet and reduced to a mere footstool (1:22). In 4:8 Paul applies the imagery drawn from Psalm 68 to Christ's ascension. Vv. 8-10, where there is a link between heaven and earth,[216] provide supplementary evidence to 1:19-22 in establishing Christ's supremacy over the powers of evil. They are the 'captives' whom Paul had in mind when he applied Psalm 68:18 to Christ's ascension. The text 'underlines the cosmic supremacy of Christ in a fresh way',[217] and this would have brought strengthening and encouragement to the readers in their spiritual warfare with the hosts of darkness. The tension between the 'already' and the 'not yet' continues for the Christian in relation to the powers, because believers are engaged in an ongoing spiritual struggle (6:10-20). Christ has won a decisive victory at the cross; Satan and his hosts continue to exist in order to make war on the saints, even though their time is short and their ultimate overthrow fixed by God (Rev. 20:3). The powers hold their own in the fight against Christians, who are exhorted to stand firm and successfully resist them (vv. 11,

216. So A. T. Lincoln, in *Theology*, 97.
217. Arnold, 56-58, esp. 58; cf. D. G. Reid, *DPL*, 754.

13, 14). By donning God's own armour in their warfare against these unseen enemies believers are to resist temptation and to take the offensive by fearlessly proclaiming the gospel.

b. If the bringing of all things into unity in Christ means the subjugation of the powers to the exalted Christ so that they are reduced to being a mere footstool, then it signifies something very different when applied to the people of God, namely, the church, which represents 'the things on earth'. According to the first words of the eulogy (1:3-14), the readers, through their incorporation into Christ, have been linked with the heavenly realm and already enjoy the blessings of that sphere, even though they are still dwelling on earth (1:3).

But it was not always so, as the apostle makes plain in chapters 2 and 3, where he concentrates on the process leading to the final summing up. Both Jewish and Gentile believers, before their incorporation into Christ, were in the same dreadful predicament as the rest of humanity were — and are (2:1-3).[218] But God in his marvelous grace has saved them. This he has done by making them alive, freeing them from condemnation, and delivering them from the dreadful bondage in which they once lived (2:4-7). In a series of highly significant statements, Paul points out that Christ's destiny has become their destiny (cf. 1:20-21 with 2:5-6). Not only did God raise Christ. He also raised up those who are united with him. Believers have also been seated with him in the heavenly realms (2:6), so that they now participate in his supremacy over the powers and in his restoration of harmony to the cosmos. The eschatological tension remains. But God's purpose of summing up all things in Christ has been achieved in principle, and the powers of darkness have been defeated. Because the decisive victory has been won by God through Christ, the readers are encouraged to stand firm and resist the principalities and powers in God's own armour (6:10-20).

In 2:11-18 the language of reconciliation and unity is taken up directly. Paul's Gentile readers were once without God and without hope, but they have now been incorporated along with Jews into the one new humanity, the body of Christ. Christ's bringing together Jew and Gentile in himself as the 'one new person' is a highly significant step towards the fulfilment of God's eternal plan, that is, the consummation of the mystery (1:9-10). Christ's creating one new person in himself, his bringing together Jew and Gentile is the effecting of a reconciliation between two hostile elements here 'on earth'. Christ has achieved it by his death on the cross. It may thus be spoken of as 'realized eschatology'. By his death

218. Note the discussion of M. Turner, 'Mission', 143-45, which leads to similar conclusions.

Christ has done away with the law, in order not only to make Jew and Gentile into 'one new person' (v. 15b), but also to reconcile them both in one body to God.

We turn finally to the key passage which focusses on the grand design of God's salvation-historical plan, namely, Ephesians 3:9-10. Significantly, this passage spans the two spheres, earth and heaven, as well as the two entities, the reconciled people of God and the powers. These verses are intimately related to and provide significant comment on the consummation of the mystery, the summing up of all things in Christ (1:9-10). The terms employed in 3:9 for the disclosure of the mystery, namely, 'make known', 'administration', and 'mystery', were all used in the earlier paradigmatic passage. There God's summing up of all things involves bringing all things together in (and under) Christ so that these divine purposes might be fulfilled. Now with the reconciliation of Jews and Gentiles in the body of Christ and the creation of the two entities in one new humanity (2:13-16; 3:3-6), together with the disclosure of this as tangible evidence of the manifold wisdom of God, one significant difficulty to everything being summed up in Christ is being overcome. The consummation of God's cosmic plan is drawing nearer every day, and this reconciliation of the formerly disparate elements of the people of God is a token that his final purpose in Christ is about to reach its conclusion.

Furthermore, the very existence of the church (made up of these formerly irreconcilable elements, Jews and Gentiles) is a reminder that the authority of the powers has been decisively broken, and that their final defeat is imminent. Accordingly, the removal of the second obstacle, that is, the final overthrow of the principalities and powers 'in the heavenly realms', moves inexorably to its climax. Perhaps, as F. F. Bruce suggests, the church appears as 'God's pilot scheme for the reconciled universe of the future'. The uniting of 'Jews and Gentiles in Christ was . . . God's masterpiece of reconciliation, and gave promise of a time when not Jews and Gentiles only, but all the mutually hostile elements in creation, would be united in that same Christ'.[219] The church is not only the pattern but also the means God is using to show that his purposes are moving triumphantly to their climax.

6. This emphasis in Ephesians 1–3 on the broad sweep of God's saving purposes, together with his intention to bring all things together into

---

219. F. F. Bruce, *Ephesians,* 321-22, 262. He adds that there is probably a further implication that the church is to be God's agency for bringing about this ultimate reconciliation. (Cf. A. T. Lincoln, *Paradise Now and Not Yet: Studies in the Role of the Heavenly Dimension in Paul's Thought with Special Reference to Eschatology* [Cambridge: Cambridge University Press, 1981], 155.) If this is so, then Paul himself is indirectly God's 'instrument for the universal reconciliation of the future'.

unity in Christ, provides the theological basis for the long paraenesis of chapters 4–6, which is fundamentally an exhortation to unity.[220] The second half of the letter begins with a call to the readers to live in accordance with their calling (v. 1); the particular focus, then, is unity, for Paul immediately issues a compelling appeal for them urgently and zealously to maintain the unity of the Spirit (v. 3). This exhortation is an essential element in living according to their calling (v. 1), it is dependent on a life characterized by the graces of Christ (v. 2), and it is motivated by the fundamental unities of the Christian faith (vv. 4-6).

The believers' unity is described rather surprisingly. It is the unity of the Spirit, that is, a unity which God's Spirit creates, and is not the readers' own achievement. It already exists, hence the admonition to 'maintain' it. Believers certainly do not create it, but are responsible to keep it. God has inaugurated this unity in Christ, through the events described in Ephesians 2:11-22 — particularly through the death of his Son — and as a result of this work of reconciliation believers, Jew and Gentile together, have access to God 'in one Spirit' (2:18).

This gives us a clue as to why it is so important to maintain the unity of the Spirit. God has done the impossible. He has brought together the absolutely irreconcilable, that is, Jew and Gentile, and united them in one body, the Lord Jesus Christ. This, as we have seen, is evidence of his master plan (3:10). How disastrous, then, it would be if believers did not eagerly maintain the unity of the Spirit. This would be to behave as though they were not reconciled to God or to one another. It would be tantamount to saying that Jesus' work of reconciliation had had no real effects in their lives. Such behaviour would be completely inconsistent with being God's masterpiece of reconciliation and ultimately with his purposes of summing up everything as a totality in Christ.

7. The following paragraphs set forth other aspects of this unity and living in the light of the new creation humanity as it is revealed in Jesus. So in 4:7-16, for example, the diversity of Christ's gifts of grace, given to various members of his people, is meant to contribute to the unity and maturity of the whole body. Also, since the first half of the letter has spelled out the reconciliation that has been effected between Jews and Gentiles in the body of Christ, 4:17–5:2 describes first what it means to live according to the new humanity in contrast to the old (vv. 17-24), and this is followed with specific exhortations about the old life and the new, culminating in the exhortation to be imitators of God (5:1). Significantly, Paul's exhortations are directed against those sins, such as anger and falsehood (4:25-26), which cause dissension and alienation within the

---

220. Note the insightful discussion of M. Turner, 'Mission', 148-57.

body, that is, they are sins which work against the body's unity. In 5:3-14, the contrast is now drawn between the believing community and outsiders and cast in terms of the readers' move from darkness to light. This paraenesis of vv. 15-20 is now set in terms of wise living over against that of folly. Wise living involves being filled by the Spirit (5:18), and this is amplified in terms of general Christian living (5:18-21) and relationships within the believing household (5:22–6:9). The household table in Ephesians, particularly the section dealing with relationships between husbands and wives (5:22-33), has been described as 'idealistic' because it is strangely silent about 'mixed' marriages or the day-to-day problems faced by husbands and wives living in an alienated world. But Paul, who was undoubtedly aware of the problems of mixed marriages (cf. 1 Cor. 7), has chosen to focus his attention on the ideal of Christian marriage and its relationship to the union of Christ and his church. Marriage between Christians serves as an example of the kind of unity the apostle has in mind between the 'head' (both the husband and Christ) and his 'body' (5:25-27). Such a marriage bears living witness to the meaning of 'the two becoming one', and reproduces in miniature the beauty shared between the Bridegroom and the Bride. Within the wider context of the letter as a whole, the union between Christian husband and wife, which is part of the unity between Christ and the church, is thus a pledge of God's purposes for the unity of the cosmos.

8. The exhortations of Ephesians 4–6 clarify further the kind of unity[221] Paul sees as being at the centre of God's saving plan to bring all things into unity in Christ. This orientation towards unity is not just a matter of pragmatism.

> [A]s the predominating 'once–now' contrast of the letter indicates, it goes to the heart of the gospel itself; such unity in love is the distinguishing mark of the new humanity over against the alienated world that is doomed to pass away. For this reason, truly to 'comprehend' the incomprehensible love of Christ is already to be filled with that fullness of God that will eventually reunite all things at the End (3:18-19).[222]

---

221. For a detailed contribution to the issue of unity in Ephesians see A. G. Patzia, *Ephesians, Colossians, Philemon* (Peabody, MA: Hendrickson, 1990), 133-39.

222. M. Turner, 'Mission', 157.

V. CONTENTS AND GENRE

A. The Contents

The Letter to the Ephesians falls into two distinct though related halves: chapters 1–3 and 4–6.[223] The first has been loosely called 'theological' or 'doctrinal', while the second has been referred to as 'ethical', although neither of these descriptions fully reflects the content of each half or the interplay between them.

Chapters 1–3 comprise an extended benediction and prayer (1:3–3:21) which provide the framework for celebrating God's accomplishment of his eternal purpose in Christ.[224] This first half begins with an introductory *berakah* or eulogy in which God is praised for bestowing on his people 'in Christ' all the privileges of salvation — beginning with election in him, adoption (v. 5), redemption, and the forgiveness of sins (v. 7), and pointing toward the consummation of all things in Christ (1:3-14). This is followed by a thanksgiving paragraph (1:15-23) in which Paul reports his thanks to God for the readers (vv. 15-16a), as well as his intercessions for them. He prays that they might grow in their knowledge of God and his power, and ultimately comprehend what he has already done for them in Christ (cf. vv. 3-14). The mention of God's almighty power (v. 19) leads on to a declaration that the supreme demonstration of this power took place in God's raising Christ from the dead and exalting him to a position of authority in the heavenly realms above all hostile spiritual powers (vv. 20-23). Paul's initial intercession leads on to a reminder of the greatness of the salvation which God has won for them. This intercession is picked up in chapter 3 with a further petition that the readers may understand and experience God's power, love, and fulness (vv. 1, 14-19), after which the first half of the letter is then rounded out with a doxology (3:20-21). The reminder of God's great salvation is expressed by means of a twofold contrast between their past and present situation in Christ: first, in relation to the change from spiritual death to new life in Christ (2:1-10) and, secondly, in terms of the change from their being Gentiles who were separated from God's people Israel and her privileges to their becoming part of God's new humanity in Christ with access to the Father and a place in his household and holy temple (2:11-22). Through Christ's peacemaking work, Gentiles and Jews have been reconciled to God and to one another in the one new humanity. Ephe-

---

223. This is apart from the prescript (Eph. 1:1-2) and the personal notes and greeting at the conclusion (Eph. 6:21-24), which give the document the form of a letter.

224. Bruce, 241; cf. Lincoln, xxxvi-xxxvii.

sians 3:1-13, though syntactically a digression within Paul's intercessory prayer (3:1, 14-19; cf. 1:17-19), reminds the readers of his distinctive ministry for them as Gentiles (hence his imprisonment and willingness to suffer for them, vv. 1, 13), and its place within the divine mystery. Through the gospel Gentile believers participate in the promises of God in Christ Jesus. The place of the mystery within God's eternal plan and the role which the church has in the divine purposes for the cosmos are presented. Flowing out of his ministry for them is Paul's intercession for his readers, which develops from his earlier prayer and is a petition for power, love, and maturity (3:14-19). The paragraph and first half of the letter conclude with a single-sentence doxology in which God is praised as the one 'who can do far more abundantly than all we ask or think' (vv. 20-21).

The second half of Ephesians (chaps. 4–6) is characterized by a lengthy paraclesis ('admonition') which extends from 4:1 to 6:9 at least (and probably to 6:20), in other words, almost to the end of the letter. In the first three chapters the apostle has unfolded for his readers the eternal plan of God with its goal of summing up all things in Christ. Now his direct appeal in chapter 4 is based on the foundation of their being reconciled in Christ and made part of God's new humanity. Indeed, the content of his many appeals is regularly informed by what has been written in the earlier part of the letter.[225] From the first ethical admonition in v. 1, which is signalled by the clause 'I urge you . . .' (cf. 1 Thess. 4:1; Rom. 12:1), which follows a fairly fixed pattern and marks a transition to a new section, there is a preponderance of ethical material. The apostle uses a favourite term, 'walk', to describe Christian behaviour throughout, and this keyword appears within five major sections of chapters 4–6 (4:1, 17; 5:2, 8, 15). Maintaining the unity of the church, which is on the road to maturity, through the diverse ministries which the ascended Christ has poured out upon his people is the key admonition of this first exhortatory section (4:1-16). These verses set the stage for what follows in 4:17–6:20. In 4:17-24 the apostle deliberately picks up the language of walking, and contrasts the readers' lifestyle in Christ with that of outsiders (v. 17). Having made a clear distinction between the way of life which characterized 'the old humanity' and that which marked out 'the new' (vv. 17-24), Paul now lays out specific, concrete exhortations (4:25–5:2) which flow directly from the paraenesis of these verses. The movement of thought is from the lofty heights of learning Christ and the new creation to 'the

225. Caird, 71, thinks that Ephesians is 'unique among the letters of Paul in that the wealth of general ethical instruction which follows in the next three chapters is subordinated to the main theme of the first three'.

nitty-gritty of Christian behaviour'. Paul has been concerned that God's people might show unity in love in practical ways. So he urges them to be kind, compassionate to one another, and forgiving each other, and concludes by laying before them the motivation and example of God's love in Christ and Christ's voluntary offering of himself (4:32–5:2). In 5:3-14, the contrast is once again drawn between believers and sinful outsiders (as in 4:17-21), and is presented in terms of the imagery of light and darkness (vv. 8-14). However, believers, who are exhorted to '*Live* as children of light', are encouraged to think that the light, which is Christ, will have a positive effect on the surrounding darkness (v. 14). In the following section of the letter (5:15–6:9), the apostle urges his readers to be careful how they *walk* (this key verb appears for the last time). Wise *living*, understanding the Lord's will (v. 17), and being filled by the Spirit (v. 18) all tie in together. The apostle amplifies what this involves, and sees the results in terms of Christian lives characterized by singing (v. 19), thanksgiving (v. 20), and a glad submission within ordered relationships (v. 21) in the Christian household: wives and husbands (5:22-33), children and parents (6:1-4), slaves and masters (6:5-9). Paul's exhortatory material is brought to a conclusion, and the letter to a climax, in the call to believers to be strong in the Lord and to put on God's mighty armour as they engage in a spiritual warfare with the powers of evil (6:10-20).

B. Genre[226]

1. Ephesians as an Epistle

Having looked at the contents of Ephesians, we now turn to consider the literary genre of this work. Considerable attention has been paid in recent years to the genres of the New Testament writings, but few definite conclusions have been reached in relation to Ephesians. Other writings of the New Testament have been placed into known literary categories and discussed in terms of ancient rhetoric, and this includes most of the New Testament letters, but little has been done on Ephesians.[227] In 1990 An-

---

226. Recent literature on this subject is vast. A limited number of works have been referred to in the following discussion. For further bibliographical details, see E. Mouton, 'The Communicative Power of the Epistle to the Ephesians', in *Rhetoric, Scripture and Theology: Essays from the 1994 Pretoria Conference*, ed. S. E. Porter and T. H. Olbricht (Sheffield: Academic Press, 1996), 280-307; J. T. Reed, 'The Epistle', in *Handbook of Classical Rhetoric in the Hellenistic Period 330 B.C.–A.D. 400*, ed. S. E. Porter (Leiden: Brill, 1997), 171-93.

227. Note the discussion by Best, 59-63, esp. 59. As examples he refers to the important works of G. A. Kennedy, *New Testament Intrepretation through Rhetorical Criticism*

drew Lincoln claimed that 'Ephesians resists clear-cut classification in terms of ancient epistolary and rhetorical categories',[228] and apart from his and a few others' attempts to observe the rhetorical movement of thought throughout the letter, little has been done since then, in spite of the unabated flow of literature, especially on rhetoric.[229]

Like the other Pauline letters, Ephesians follows the normal pattern of epistolary address and closing greetings, but as with each of the others there is some variation. Ephesians begins with the usual prescript with its mention of writer and addressees and its Christian greetings (1:1-2). This is expanded by a description of the relationship to God in Christ, so that Paul calls himself 'an apostle of Christ Jesus by the will of God', and the epithets describing the recipients are 'the saints . . . , the faithful in Christ Jesus' (v. 1). The usual Hellenistic greeting is replaced by 'grace to you and peace from God our Father and the Lord Jesus Christ', which is typical of Paul's other greetings.[230] As we have already seen, the address is general rather than directed to a specific group (see above). Normally after his greetings Paul begins his letters with an introductory thanksgiving paragraph in which he expresses his gratitude to God for his Christian readers (1 Cor. 1:4-9; Phil. 1:3-11; Col. 1:3-14; 1 Thess. 1:2–3:13; 2 Thess. 1:2-12; 2:13-14; Phlm. 4-7) and then intercedes for them.[231] In Ephesians, however, an extended *berakah* or eulogy[232] immediately follows the greeting, after which an introductory thanksgiving with its thanksgiving and petitionary prayer reports are included.

The ending of Ephesians is similar to others of Paul's letters, and its closing features are parallelled in Hellenistic literature, except that the apostle omits the customary health wish[233] and the word of farewell. Included is a reference to Tychicus, an apostolic representative (using the same wording as Col. 4:7-8), along with a wish of peace and a grace-benediction (6:21-24). But in Ephesians Paul associates no colleagues or fel-

---

(Chapel Hill: University of North Carolina Press, 1984), 156, who mentions that the author must have been 'someone of considerable rhetorical skill'; S. K. Stowers, *Letter Writing in Greco-Roman Antiquity* (Philadelphia: Westminster, 1986); and D. E. Aune, *The New Testament in Its Literary Environment* (Philadelphia: Westminster, 1987).

228. Lincoln, xxxvii.

229. Exceptions to this are E. Mouton, 'The Communicative Power', 280-307, and C. B. Kittredge, *Community and Authority: The Rhetoric of Obedience in the Pauline Tradition* (Harrisburg, PA: TPI, 1998), 111-49. Note the discussion below.

230. Instead of χαίρειν ('greeting'), χάρις ('grace') appears. See on 1:2.

231. P. T. O'Brien, *Introductory Thanksgivings*.

232. P. T. O'Brien, 'Ephesians I', 504-16. These eulogies resemble some Old Testament examples of blessings (Ps. 41:13; 72:18-19; 106:48).

233. See J. A. D. Weima, *Neglected Endings: The Significance of the Pauline Letter Closings* (Sheffield: Academic Press, 1994), 34-39.

low-Christians with him in the salutation, nor does he name any as recipients of his greetings at the end.

Although the opening and closing of the letter reveal Hellenistic influences, the body of Ephesians, like many of its contemporary counterparts,[234] is more difficult to classify. Indeed, the question has been asked whether Ephesians has a letter body at all.[235] Generally, there are difficulties in determining where the body of Paul's letters begins and ends,[236] and this is true of Ephesians. Nevertheless, it does contain a number of features that are characteristic of the Pauline letter body. It has its own formal opening with an introductory eulogy praising God (1:3-14) and a thanksgiving paragraph with an intercessory prayer (vv. 15-19). Ephesians also contains transitional formulae (cf. 4:1), and commends Tychicus whom Paul is sending to his readers (6:21-22). As with other Pauline letters, Ephesians contains a considerable amount of instruction, a long paraenetic section with exhortatory material, as well as various types of prayer material. The letter makes significant use of the Old Testament. Although there are only four explicit quotations, many allusions turn up, as is evidenced by Paul's dependence on the phraseology of the Old Testament, along with terms and concepts (including references to the temple, redemption, God's election, hope, mercy, promise, wisdom, Father, and the helmet of salvation, to name only a few). These 'show how deeply steeped the author was in the OT and how the language of the OT influenced his own composition'.[237] Ephesians also employs early Christian traditional material (cf. possibly 4:4-6; 5:14, etc.), including a household code (5:21–6:9) through which he addresses relationships within the Christian household: wives–husbands; children–parents; slaves–masters.

While most scholars recognize that Ephesians as a whole falls into two main halves, there is difference of opinion as to where precisely the body of the letter begins. Are the introductory eulogy, thanksgiving, and intercessory prayer (1:3-19 [or 23]) to be classified as part of the introduction, with the body commencing at 2:1, or does the body proper begin with the eulogy (1:3-14), thanksgiving, and intercessory prayer (1:15-19)? On balance, we prefer the latter view. First, the material in Ephesians after the eulogy and thanksgiving period (1:3-19 [or 23]) does not contain

---

234. Cf. J. L. White, 'The Greek Documentary Letter Tradition Third Century B.C.E. to Third Century C.E.', *Semeia* 22 (1982), 92-100; and J. T. Reed, 'The Epistle', 186-92.

235. 'Epistolary prescripts and postscripts could be used to frame almost any kind of composition' (D. E. Aune, *Literary Environment*, 170).

236. W. Doty, *Letters in Primitive Christianity* (Philadelphia: Fortress, 1973), 34; and D. E. Aune, *Literary Environment*, 183.

237. C. E. Arnold, *DPL*, 239.

any disclosure formula, formula of request, or the like, which might signal the conclusion of the thanksgiving and the transition to the body of the letter. Neither vv. 22-23 nor the beginning of chapter 2 suggests a fresh unit, since both continue the train of thought begun in the preceding intercessory prayer report about God's power being displayed on behalf of believers (v. 19). They have now experienced the same power of God which was effective in Christ's resurrection and exaltation. To separate 2:1-10 and vv. 11-21 from the preceding is thus inappropriate. Likewise, the resumption of the intercessory prayer of 3:1, the 'digression' on Paul's apostleship in relation to the mystery (3:2-13), and the conclusion of the intercessory prayer (3:14-19) together with its climactic doxology (3:20-21) ought not to be separated from chapters 1 and 2 (see the exegesis). The result is that 1:3–3:21 hang together as a unit, as many scholars have seen. Secondly, the structure of 1 Thessalonians provides a good parallel to Ephesians, as several recent writers have recognized.[238] This letter, too, has no main body since the thanksgiving period of 1:2–3:13 itself constitutes the body.[239] Further, the request formula of 1 Thessalonians 4:1 ('I urge [you]') provides the transition to the exhortatory material of the letter, and this is precisely the function of the same formula in Ephesians 4:1 (see the exegesis). In both letters it introduces the second major part of the body. We therefore agree with Lincoln that 1:3–3:21 'functions as the equivalent to the first part of the body'. The opening clause of 4:1 ('I urge . . .') serves to make the transition to the exhortatory material, and this is equivalent to the body's second major part.[240] In spite of the formal parallel with 1 Thessalonians it is better not to describe 1:3–3:21 as an 'Extended Thanksgiving'.[241] The term 'thanksgiving' has already been used of the prayer report (1:15-16) and of the prayer of thanks itself. Rather, it is preferable to designate the first half of the letter in relation to its content.[242]

The second part of the letter body is the paraenesis (4:1–6:20), which begins with the words, 'I exhort you'.[243] Having offered his prayer for the

---

238. C. J. Bjerkelund, *Parakalô: Form, Funktion und Sinn der parakalô-Sätze in den paulinischen Briefe* (Oslo: Universitetsforlaget, 1967), 184-85; and W. G. Kümmel, *Introduction*, 351-52.

239. P. Schubert, *Form*, 16-27; and P. T. O'Brien, *Introductory Thanksgivings*, 141-46.

240. Lincoln, xxxix; cf. Hoehner.

241. As Lincoln, xliii, does.

242. Along similar lines Best, 63, thinks that it is wrong to describe 1:3–3:21 as the prayer section, simply because there are prayers within it or it comes at the beginning of the letter. He adds: '2.1–3.13 is not a prayer and should not be forced into that category to accord with a doubtful classification of genre'. It is better to describe it, as Bruce, 247, does, in relation to its content, namely, as 'The New Humanity a Divine Creation'.

243. C. J. Bjerkelund, *Parakalô*, 15-19, 179-87.

Christian readers to be strengthened with Christ's love (3:14-19), Paul's exhortatory material further emphasizes the need for them to demonstrate love in all their relationships. Chapter 4:1-16 sets the stage for the exhortatory material that follows in 4:17–6:20, and serves as the introductory framework for the rest of the paraenesis. What follows consists of a series of paragraphs which spell out in detail how local congregations and Christian households should heed the exhortation of 4:1-3. The key verb 'walk' or 'live' is a catchword in each section of the paraenesis from 4:1 on (cf. 4:17; 5:2, 8, 15), as Paul depicts the contrast between the readers' lifestyle in Christ and that of outsiders. The final paragraph of the paraenesis, in which the readers are urged to be strong in the Lord and to put on God's mighty armour as they engage in a spiritual warfare with the powers of evil (6:10-20), occupies a highly significant place in the epistle. It not only concludes the paraenetic material begun in 4:1, but it also serves as the climax of the letter as a whole and brings it to its conclusion.

Accordingly, Ephesians evidences many characteristics of a Hellenistic letter, not only in relation to its opening and closing, but also with reference to its body. It is unnecessary to conclude that Ephesians is another type of writing dressed up as a letter,[244] whether a theological tractate[245] or a 'wisdom discourse'[246] with Christ personified as wisdom. The long paraenesis of 4:1–6:20 militates against its being either a theological tract or a discourse on wisdom.[247] Nor should we regard Ephesians as 'an epistolary decree in which the author recites the universal benefactions of God and Christ and proceeds to stipulate the appropriate honors, understood as the moral obligations of the beneficiaries'.[248]

Lincoln claims that because Ephesians does not address specific issues and lacks personal greetings which are typical of other Pauline let-

244. Schnackenburg, 23, comments: 'The epistolary pattern is not an assumed cloak but a literary form deliberately chosen by the author because it was probably in keeping with the objective or aim of his writing'.

245. E. Käsemann, 'Epheserbrief', in *RGG* 2:518. Note the comments of Lincoln, xxxviii.

246. Schlier, 21-22.

247. Schnackenburg, 23; and Hoehner.

248. H. Hendrix, 'On the Form and Ethos of Ephesians', *USQR* 42 (1988), 3-15, esp. 9. He suggests that this may explain some of the peculiar features of Ephesians, notably its long sentences and the exhortations in chaps. 4–6. Best, 62, suggests that, while the honorific decrees engraved on Graeco-Roman monuments might explain 1:3-14, it is 'difficult to accept them as models for the remainder of the letter'. Regarding the moral instruction in Ephesians, this sort of material formed a normal part of earlier Jewish and Christian teaching. For other criticisms in relation to Ephesians as a letter, see Hoehner. See also above on 'The Purpose of the Letter', 51-56.

ters, it is best understood as the 'written equivalent of a sermon or homily'.[249] This suggestion is plausible, but it should not be based on the absence from Ephesians of specific issues or personal greetings. Furthermore, if Ephesians is regarded as a written sermon or homily, then what are we to make of Romans, Galatians, and several other Pauline letters, which were obviously read aloud like a homily to a Christian audience?

Picking up the notion of a written equivalent of a sermon, the liturgical forms of Ephesians, especially its opening sequence of eulogy, thanksgiving, intercession, and doxology, would have enabled the letter, as it was read, to fit appropriately into a liturgical setting. Accordingly, Ephesians has been described as 'a liturgical homily'.[250] But there is 'no clear-cut evidence from this period of any fixed forms for either early Christian or Jewish synagogue homilies'.[251]

2. Ephesians and Rhetoric

a. Rhetoric and the Pauline epistles. The suggestion that most of Ephesians is equivalent to a sermon naturally leads on to the question whether a rhetorical analysis of the letter is appropriate, perhaps even the best way of interpreting the document. Before examining this specific issue, however, it is necessary to set it in the wider context of rhetoric and the Pauline letters, a subject to which a considerable amount of scholarly attention has been devoted in recent times.[252]

Rhetorical criticism is 'the application of the ancient Greco-Roman rules for speech to the written text of the New Testament, especially to the letters of Paul'.[253] It has become one of the major forms of Pauline study,[254] with scholars focussing their attention on two out of five fea-

---

249. Lincoln, xxxix.

250. Cf. Gnilka, 33.

251. Lincoln, xxxix-xl.

252. Note the significant articles by S. E. Porter, 'Paul of Tarsus and His Letters', in *Handbook of Classical Rhetoric in the Hellenistic Period 330 B.C.-A.D. 400*, ed. S. E. Porter (Leiden: Brill, 1997), 533-85, and J. T. Reed, 'The Epistle', in *Handbook of Classical Rhetoric*, 171-93. Porter's article draws together much of his earlier work on rhetorical criticism of the New Testament letters, spells out 'the current state of play', and critically analyzes the principles and results of its practitioners.

253. J. A. D. Weima, 'Rhetorical Criticism', 458-59.

254. Porter observes that the scholars who utilize the categories of ancient rhetoric follow one of two closely related models: one represented by Kennedy which 'approaches the letters as essentially speeches, with the epistolary openings and closings treated almost as incidental features', the other represented by Betz, who follows the rhetorical handbook tradition and 'wishes to assert the epistolary integrity of the letter but with full consideration of the rhetorical features as well'; S. E. Porter, 'Paul of Tarsus',

tures in composing a speech: (1) the genre or species of rhetoric, and (2) the arrangement or structure of the parts of the oration.[255] Accordingly, many recent commentaries apply these Graeco-Roman rules for speech directly to the interpretation of Paul's letters, in the following ways: (1) They classify a particular letter according to the three major types of speech: judicial (or forensic) rhetoric, which belongs to a courtroom setting and where the audience functions as a judge, giving a verdict on some past event; deliberative (or persuasive) rhetoric, which belongs to a public assembly where an audience must make a decision about some future course of action; or epideictic (or demonstrative) rhetoric, which belongs to the public arena (often at ceremonial occasions), and where the orator seeks to persuade his hearers to adopt or reaffirm some point of view in the present, and so to praise or blame some person or quality. (2) These commentaries also divide the Pauline letter into the four rhetorical parts of an ancient discourse:[256] the exordium, or introduction, which establishes rapport between the speaker and the audience and foreshadows major topic(s) of the speech; the narratio, which sets forth the proposition and states the facts of the case; the probatio, which presents the various arguments in support of the proposition; and the peroratio, or conclusion, which summarizes the major points of the argument and seeks to gain support for the proposition or the speaker.[257]

In spite of the rapidly increasing acceptance of Graeco-Roman rules for speech and the direct application of them for the interpretation of Paul's letters, serious questions have been raised about the legitimacy of this enterprise. After a careful evaluation of some nineteen rhetorical analyses of seven Pauline letters (including six on Galatians), produced by New Testament scholars between 1977 and 1995, Stanley Porter[258] makes the follow-

---

540; G. A. Kennedy's major work is *New Testament Interpretation through Rhetorical Criticism*, while H. D. Betz's is *Galatians: A Commentary on Paul's Letter to the Galatians* (Philadelphia: Fortress, 1979).

255. Surprisingly, relatively little attention has been given to the question of *style*, i.e., the choice of proper words and figures of speech in order to heighten the argument or achieve clarity. The other two 'canons', *memory* and *delivery*, are not relevant to the study of written documents such as Paul's letters.

256. Our reference is to 'ancient rhetoric', in which the biblical text is analyzed according to categories drawn from the ancient rhetorical handbooks, and which dominates most of the rhetorical studies being practised in New Testament studies. This is distinct from a modern-based rhetorical criticism ('new rhetoric'), which is more a philosophically based approach in which the biblical text is analyzed according to contemporary rhetorical categories and concentrates on the structure, premises, and techniques of argumentation (cf. J. A. D. Weima, 'Rhetorical Criticism', 459).

257. J. A. D. Weima, 'Rhetorical Criticism', 460; cf. G. A. Kennedy, *Rhetorical Criticism*, 19.

258. S. E. Porter, 'Paul of Tarsus', 541-61.

ing observations: first, the dissimilarity in the findings among the commentators results from differences in the analyses, both as to the genre of rhetoric and the arrangement of the rhetorical parts. Secondly, there is 'a wide divergence in the categories' used, including Aristotelian and a mix of Greek and Roman categories, which is not evidenced in the ancient rhetorical handbooks themselves. Thirdly, the amount and kind of Pauline material placed within each rhetorical category vary significantly. Fourthly, and most seriously, a consistent difficulty that surfaces in these analyses is 'the relationship of [the] rhetorical and epistolary structures'. Porter points out, as he has done in earlier evaluations of this issue, that 'the Pauline writings are first and foremost letters, no matter what other category of analysis [exists] into which they may fit'.[259]

These findings raise once again the broader issue of principle, namely, 'the theoretical justification for the application of rhetorical categories to the Pauline epistolary literature'.[260] The following points are relevant to this issue:

First, it is generally assumed by those who advocate a rhetorical analysis of Paul's letters that the apostle had been trained in formal rhetoric or that its use was so pervasive in the ancient world that he inductively appropriated these rules for speech, and employed them when he wrote his letters. So, in relation to Galatians, Richard Longenecker states: 'The forms of classical rhetoric were "in the air," and Paul seems to have used them almost unconsciously for his purposes'.[261] But this assumption is far from certain, and there is no concrete evidence that Paul knew or was ever trained in ancient rhetoric. Tarsus, the place of Paul's birth, was known as a centre of learning, particularly in the areas of philosophy and rhetoric. However, it is probable that he was brought up in Jerusalem rather than Tarsus (cf. Acts 22:3),[262] in which case he would not have received formal rhetorical training in the city of his birth. There is difference of opinion as to whether he could have received some form of rhetorical training in Jerusalem, but this seems unlikely.[263] Although some

259. S. E. Porter, 'Paul of Tarsus', 561.

260. S. E. Porter, 'Paul of Tarsus', 562-67. The issue was first raised in an essay with this title, 'The Theoretical Justification for Application of Rhetorical Categories to Pauline Epistolary Literature', in *Rhetoric and the New Testament: Essays from the 1992 Heidelberg Conference*, ed. S. E. Porter and T. H. Olbricht (Sheffield: Academic Press, 1993), 100-122.

261. R. N. Longenecker, *Galatians* (Dallas: Word, 1990), cxiii.

262. There is some uncertainty as to whether 'this city' where Paul was brought up is a reference to Tarsus or Jerusalem. Most scholars now favour the latter; cf. M. Hengel, *The Pre-Christian Paul* (London/Philadelphia: SCM/TPI, 1991), 18-39.

263. M. Hengel, *The Pre-Christian Paul*, 58, thinks that Paul received his basic training in speech to facilitate public speaking in the synagogue, but this 'did not correspond

have argued that Paul's vocabulary indicates that he had a formal knowledge of rhetoric, his use of a number of words associated with it only establishes an intelligent use of the Hellenistic Greek of the day, not that he was formally trained in rhetoric.[264]

The direct evidence from the New Testament of Paul as an orator is slight. 2 Corinthians 10:10, 'his bodily presence is weak and his speech of no account', suggests that the Corinthians did not like Paul's unprofessional manner of speech and poor public presentation, even if they acknowledged the power of his letters (they were 'weighty and forceful'). The Corinthians criticized him as being an 'amateur' or 'unskilled'[265] in public speaking — an accusation he was prepared to acknowledge (2 Cor. 11:6); he did not present the kind of physical presence expected of a rhetorician (2 Cor. 10:1). Paul's statement that he came to Corinth 'not with eloquence or superior wisdom. . . . For I determined to know nothing among you except Jesus Christ and him crucified' (1 Cor. 2:1-2) has been understood to mean that he deliberately chose not to present the gospel in the sort of professional, rhetorical manner that the Corinthians wanted.[266] The evidence of Acts, particularly his reported speeches in 14:15-17 and 17:22-31, does not provide any direct access to his rhetorical ability. Paul's own testimony suggests that his capability as an orator was not great. More significantly, he chose not to make use of ancient rhetoric in his preaching of the gospel.

Secondly, there is the fundamental problem of mixing the genre of a speech (oral discourse) with that of a letter (written discourse). Although letters and rhetorical speeches were two of the most important forms of communication in the ancient world, they served rather different purposes, with speeches being primarily for the law courts and public arena, while letters were intended to bridge the spatial distance separating people.[267] If one takes seriously the fact that Paul wrote let-

---

to the Attic-style school rhetoric of the time' and was 'not orientated on classical literary models'; cf. J. A. D. Weima, 'Rhetorical Criticism', 465; and R. D. Anderson, *Ancient Rhetorical Theory and Paul* (Kampen: Kok Pharos, 1996).

264. S. E. Porter, 'Paul of Tarsus', 536. Among others, Porter lists ἀλληγορεῖν (Gal. 4:24), βεβαίωσις (Gal. 5:8), and παράκλησις (1 Cor. 14:5).

265. Gk. ἰδιώτης.

266. B. Winter, 'Is Paul among the Sophists?', *RTR* 53 (1994), 28-38, esp. 35, concludes: 'Paul, as a matter of principle, did not "display his speeches rhetorically or according to the received form of the sophists" (On Rhetoric 2.139, II). He renounced the use of oratory in preaching as inappropriate, for it was designed to draw attention to the messenger and his rhetorical abilities, and not the content of his message'; cited by J. A. D. Weima, 'Rhetorical Criticism', 466. Others have taken Paul's statement in 1 Cor. 2:1-2 simply as a disclaimer that he had any formal rhetorical training.

267. J. T. Reed, 'The Epistle', 171.

ters, then we would expect that the most important source for under-standing these writings would be the epistolary handbooks of the day, not the rules for oral discourse, the rhetorical handbooks. Rhetorical an-alysts such as G. A. Kennedy, H. D. Betz, and others hold, even if im-plicitly, that the application of categories of classical rhetoric (particu-larly those related to the genre and the arrangement or structure of the oration) to ancient letters was something with which the ancients them-selves would have been familiar, and something that Paul himself in-tended to use.[268] Several factors, however, militate against this funda-mental assumption. The epistolary handbooks, which are concerned with developing a theory of letter writing, provide no justification for the application of rhetorical principles to letters. In relation to two rele-vant handbooks, *Epistolary Types* (*c.* first century B.C.) and *Epistolary Styles* (*c.* A.D. 400-600), D. L. Stamps comments: 'neither specifically re-lates letter writing to the five traditional aspects of rhetorical practice: invention, arrangement, style, memory and delivery, or to the three tra-ditional species of rhetoric: judicial, deliberative and epideictic'.[269] Fur-ther, even in the ancient rhetorical handbooks the same picture emerges. They contain very few references to letters, and where they do, they normally comment on the subject of *style*. They state virtually nothing about the rhetorical topics of *invention,* the arguments or proofs to be used in a speech, or *arrangement,* the structuring of the various ele-ments of the argument so that it will be most persuasive. Yet these are the very areas where New Testament scholars have spent the most en-ergy applying the rules of ancient rhetoric to Paul's letters![270] Porter agrees that 'the handbooks themselves are a logical place to look for a defense of an established relationship between epistolary and rhetorical forms'. But he adds that when 'such support is sought, however, it is *conspicuously missing'*.[271] It is not until the fourth century A.D. (Julius Victor) that letter writing is discussed in a rhetorical handbook, and even here the comments are confined to style. The upshot of all this is that there is little theoretical justification for the sort of rhetorical analy-

268. S. E. Porter, 'Paul of Tarsus', 565-66.

269. D. L. Stamps, 'Rhetorical Criticism of the New Testament: Ancient and Mod-ern Evaluations of Argumentation', in *Approaches to New Testament Study,* ed. S. E. Porter and D. Tombs (Sheffield: Academic Press, 1995), 129-69, esp. 144-45; cf. J. A. D. Weima, 'Rhetorical Criticism', 463. J. T. Reed, 'The Epistle', 179, suggests that one of the reasons 'epistolary theorists do not prescribe rhetorical arrangements to epistolary structures is because letters had their own long-established, structural conventions'.

270. Note the strong criticisms of S. E. Porter, 'Paul of Tarsus', 5; and J. A. D. Weima, 'Rhetorical Criticism', 463.

271. S. E. Porter, 'Paul of Tarsus', 566 (emphasis added). See also A. J. Malherbe, *Ancient Epistolary Theorists* (Atlanta: Scholars, 1988), 2, 3, whom Porter cites in support.

sis, that is, of species and arrangement,[272] found in many commentaries on the rhetoric of Paul's letters.

Thirdly, this is not to suggest, however, that there could not be any functional correspondence between parts of a letter and those of an oration. For example, a letter opening had a number of formal features, such as the greeting and thanksgiving, the functions of which were to establish and maintain contact between the sender and the recipients, and to open up some of the main themes of the letter. Also, the thanksgiving often set the tone for what was to follow in the body of the letter. Similarly, the function of the exordium of a speech was to introduce the speaker to the audience and provide the right kind of environment for communication. It might also indicate the subject to be addressed. Likewise, the body of a letter develops the main idea(s) or content of the epistle, and in functional terms this might be equivalent to parts of an oration such as the *propositio,* which states the major issue at hand, or the *probatio* with its important function of proving the case.[273] It has also been suggested that some epistolary types may be functionally parallel with several of the rhetorical species (e.g., the deliberative and epideictic types of rhetoric). But this does not suggest that an author patterned the letter on the rhetorical handbooks. Instead, as J. T. Reed claims, these similarities may point to the way differing groups within a society sought to 'persuade others', or simply to bear testimony to the fact that 'argumentation is universal as well as particular'.[274]

Fourthly, the area in which ancient letter writers and epistolary theorists do appear to show more signs of rhetorical influence is that of style.[275] Under this rubric questions of grammar, syntax, and choice of words are to be included. But the issues of clarity, figures of speech, metaphors, citations, and the like were also discussed in the epistolary handbooks. The two features of epistolary style that particularly parallel the rhetorical discussions are *clarity* and *appropriateness* for the situation. Yet even in the discussions about these features it was recognized that there was a fundamental difference between the epistolary and the rhetorical styles that was the result of 'spatial separation'.[276] In what has been described as the 'ornamentation' level of style, Paul displays a number of standard features. These include extended metaphors (Gal. 4:21-31), synecdoche (2 Cor. 3:15), hyperbole (Gal. 1:8), litotes (Rom. 1:16), ana-

272. Either as an indicator of what Paul actually did, or in terms of helping us interpret his letters.

273. S. E. Porter, 'Paul of Tarsus', 569-70; cf. J. T. Reed, 'The Epistle', 180-81.

274. J. T. Reed, 'The Epistle', 174, 191.

275. Note J. T. Reed, 'The Epistle', 182-86; and S. E. Porter, 'Paul of Tarsus', 576-84.

276. J. T. Reed, 'The Epistle', 185.

phora (Rom. 3:22-25), as well as many other categories. Porter concludes: 'it is here that Paul is arguably closest to the utilization of ancient rhetorical technique and the interpreter is justified in analysing Paul's letters from an ancient rhetorical standpoint'.[277] This is not to suggest that the apostle used a handbook with such a listing in it, or that he was necessarily aware of the technical name for each of them. Rather, they are convenient labels for describing the sorts of stylistic features found in ancient writing, including Paul's.

Finally, the evidence of the early church, especially the fathers, many of whom had received rhetorical training, shows that they did not interpret Paul's letters from the perspective of rhetorical theory. After a careful examination of early Christian writers, both the Greek (including Origen, Basil, and Chrysostom) and Latin fathers (including Tertullian, Cyprian, Gregory of Nazianus, and Augustine), P. H. Kern concludes:

> the earliest Christians found in Paul no rhetorician or high-born orator but a humble author of weighty letters . . . for the early church, the text [*sc.*, of the epistles] was powerful enough so as not to need 'the subtle and complicated outward expressions of verbal debate'. . . . Paul's eloquence apart from rhetoric freed the fathers to develop alternative modes of discourse.[278]

To sum up. The rhetorical analyses of the Pauline letters over the past two decades or so by New Testament scholars have demonstrated considerable diversity from one another, and have often been inconsistent with the conventions of ancient rhetoric. More seriously, however, those which have concentrated on the *genre* of rhetoric and the *arrangement* of the oratorical parts have no real theoretical basis for their enterprise. Certainly early Christian writers did not think that the epistles were actually orations. Paul was involved in 'the art of persuasion' both as a preacher of the gospel and a writer of letters. He employs in his letters a variety of literary or so-called rhetorical stylistic devices (see above). But his letters were not informed by Graeco-Roman rhetoric, and previous ages did not commonly use classical rhetoric to understand them or the rest of the New Testament.[279] Paul's letters, then, ought not to

---

277. S. E. Porter, 'Paul of Tarsus', 578.

278. P. H. Kern, *Rhetoric and Galatians: Assessing an Approach to Paul's Epistle* (Cambridge: Cambridge University Press, 1998), 167-203, esp. 203, where he cites Florescu.

279. P. H. Kern, *Rhetoric and Galatians*, 203. He adds that it is 'not until the Reformation era that we find Pauline texts treated with the help of rhetoric in any significant way, and even then it is *with the awareness that external categories are being forced on to the text'* (emphasis added).

be interpreted 'through the grid of the ancient rhetorical rules', and the notion that 'this method better than any other holds the hermeneutical key that will unlock the true meaning of the apostle's writings' is seriously flawed.[280]

Instead, given that Paul does seek to persuade his readers in his letters, it is more appropriate that attention be directed to the apostle's own internal method of argument, in which there may be functional counterparts with ancient oratory that reflect a universal method of argumentation, rather than that alien categories be imposed on his epistles.

b. Rhetoric and Ephesians. It has already been pointed out that, although the seven generally accepted Pauline letters have been the subject of intensive rhetorical analysis by New Testament scholars over the past two decades, little research has been done on the Letter to the Ephesians. The major exception to this is the work of Andrew Lincoln.

Applying rhetorical categories to Ephesians, Lincoln suggests that the two major halves of the book utilize two elements of rhetoric.[281] The first half is epideictic discourse in which the writer seeks to establish a community of values with his readers. The opening thanksgiving and prayer of Ephesians 1–3 are 'an effective rhetorical strategy'. By giving thanks and praying for the readers they are 'affirmed, . . . their sympathies are gained, and . . . a common relationship to God and to Christ and common values grounded in this relationship are consolidated'.[282] This kind of rhetoric avoids confrontation. Paul prays for them, and underscores the relationship which they have with God and with their fellow-Christians, Jewish and Gentile believers who have become part of the one new humanity in Christ. The second half of Ephesians is primarily deliberative rhetoric in which the writer seeks to persuade the readers to take certain actions. It may involve a call to preserve what is already held, as part of their common values, or it may necessitate their adjusting their behaviour. So in chapters 4–6 Paul exhorts them to change their behaviour in the light of their new relationship to Christ and fellow-believers. Lincoln finally provides a brief rhetorical outline of Ephesians which includes an *Exordium* or introduction (1:1-23), a *Narratio* of the grounds for

---

280. J. A. D. Weima, 'Rhetorical Criticism', 468.

281. Lincoln, xli. His student, R. R. Jeal, 'The Relationship between Theology and Ethics in the Letter to the Ephesians' (unpublished Ph.D. thesis, University of Sheffield, 1990), believes that chaps. 1–3 and 4–6 of Ephesians are difficult to reconcile to each other. 'Epistolary analysis does not lead to an explanation of how the two sections can be integrated'. He thinks that Ephesians is a document that can be described as a 'sermon', and is 'a combination of epideictic and deliberative rhetorical genres that does not address a specific issue or controversy' (author's abstract).

282. Lincoln, xlii.

thanksgiving (2:1–3:21), an *Exhortatio* (4:1–6:9), and a *Peroratio* (6:10-20), the final section of the speech that sought to sum up the main themes and arouse the audience to action, in this case to stand firm in the spiritual battle.

Several comments are in order. First, Lincoln faces a similar tension to that of other rhetorical analysts (see Porter's evaluation above). His rhetorical structure appears to be an alternative to his epistolary analysis, no doubt because Lincoln thinks that Ephesians is a letter; at the same time he regards it, or at least the bulk of it, as a sermon. Secondly, the categories or genres into which Lincoln divides Ephesians, namely, epideictic and deliberative rhetoric, work within certain limits,[283] but these do not fit Ephesians.[284] Deliberative rhetoric, for example, is restricted to the speaker seeking to persuade a member of the general assembly on topics which Aristotle identifies as 'ways and means, war and peace, the defence of the country, imports and exports, and legislation'. The addition of religious rituals is set within a political context. Likewise, Cicero thinks of it in terms of the concerns of the state. Further, epideictic discourse is paid little attention in the handbooks.[285] Finally, Lincoln's comments at the end of each section of his commentary in which he sought to determine: (1) the function of each paragraph within the flow of the letter's argument, and therefore (2) how the author sought to persuade his readers, make considerable sense. But it is unnecessary to appeal to classical rhetorical categories in order to support his approach.[286]

In the light of these conclusions about a rhetorical analysis of the Pauline letters generally, any study of Ephesians should be focussed on the apostle's own method of argument within the letter itself. Categories

---

283. P. H. Kern, *Rhetoric and Galatians*, 125-29.

284. P. H. Kern, *Rhetoric and Galatians*, 126. The same questions might be raised in relation to C. B. Kittredge, *Community and Authority*, 145-49, who, unlike Lincoln, concludes that the whole of Ephesians is best characterized as deliberative rhetoric. She claims that the author of Ephesians 'seeks to move the audience toward a notion of unity constructed as a hierarchy in which inferior is linked to superior by the expectation of obedience' (148).

285. Note P. H. Kern's discussion in *Rhetoric and Galatians*, 126-29.

286. E. Mouton's recent articles, 'Reading Ephesians Ethically: Criteria towards a Renewed Identity Awareness?' *Neot* 28 (1994), 359-77; and 'The Communicative Power', 280-307, show an awareness of 'the unnuanced application of formal ancient rhetorical categories to the New Testament' (280). In his handling of Ephesians he is aware that there are 'universal communicative and persuasive practices at play in the everyday use of all human language' (283). Whether in his application Mouton has wholly escaped the dangers Porter and Reed have drawn to our attention is a moot point, but he is right in concluding that 'the Ephesians author encourages his readers to think of themselves in terms of the new position they ought to assume — as fellow citizens with God's people and members of God's household, as one in Christ, as a new humanity' (303).

of genre and arrangement should not be imposed from the world of oratory onto his letters if we want to determine how the apostle sought to persuade his readers.[287]

287. Accordingly, within this commentary we have sought, at the end of each section, to determine how each paragraph functions within the overall argument.

Ephesians 1

I. PRESCRIPT, 1:1-2

> *[1]Paul, an apostle of Christ Jesus by the will of God, To the saints in Ephesus, the faithful in Christ Jesus: [2]Grace and peace to you from God our Father and the Lord Jesus Christ.*

The prologue of Ephesians follows the regular Pauline pattern with its three elements: the name of the sender, the recipients, and a greeting. Although the structures of Paul's greetings are consistent with the letters of the period, he adapts his description of himself and his credentials to the circumstances of each letter, employs various phrases to describe his Christian readers, and pours theological content into his greetings — all of which are creative variations of the opening formulae. Here in Ephesians the name of 'Christ' is mentioned in relation to all three elements of the prescript. As in Romans (and the Pastorals) Paul's name appears alone: in his other letters one or more colleagues are associated with him.

1 'Paul' immediately identifies himself as the author of the letter with the name he used in the Hellenistic-Roman world, in place of his Jewish name 'Saul'. He then adds the self-designation, 'an apostle of Christ Jesus by the will of God',[1] which is the same as in Colossians 1:1 and 2 Corinthians 1:1 (cf. 1 Cor. 1:1). He establishes his credentials at the outset, and in so doing draws attention to the official character of his writing. The term 'apostle' is used in the New Testament of: (a) the

---

1. On the subject of 'apostle', see P. W. Barnett, 'Apostle', in *DPL*, 45-51; C. K. Barrett, *The Signs of an Apostle* (Philadelphia: Fortress, 1972); E. Best, 'Paul's Apostolic Authority — ?', in *Essays on Ephesians* (Edinburgh: T & T Clark, 1997), 25-49.

Twelve who were called and named by Jesus (Matt. 10:2-4; Mark 3:16-19; Luke 6:13-16; Acts 1:13). They were with the Lord Jesus during his earthly ministry and witnessed his resurrection (Acts 1:22-23; 4:33). (b) Those in addition to the Twelve whom Paul recognized, and who included Barnabas (1 Cor. 9:5-7; cf. Acts 14:4, 14), James the Lord's brother (1 Cor. 15:7; Gal. 1:19), and Apollos (1 Cor. 4:6, 9), along with others. (c) The term is also used by Paul on occasion in a nontechnical sense to signify a 'messenger' of the churches (2 Cor. 8:22-23; Phil. 2:25). However, the overwhelming number of instances in his letters are to 'apostles' in a technical sense who were called and sent by Christ. Paul often refers to himself as an apostle (1 Cor. 1:1; 2 Cor. 1:1; Col. 1:1; 1 Tim. 1:1; 2 Tim. 1:1; Tit. 1:1). It was 'through Jesus Christ' that Paul had received his apostleship (Rom. 1:5; cf. Gal. 1:1), since Jesus had 'called' him to be an apostle and 'separated' him for the gospel of God (Rom. 1:1; 1 Cor. 1:1). The goal of this ministry was to bring about the obedience of faith among the Gentiles (Rom. 1:5; 11:13; cf. Eph. 3:1-13, on which see further).

To speak of himself as an apostle *of Christ Jesus* not only signifies that he belongs to Christ, but also that he is a messenger who is fully authorized[2] and sent by him. As an apostle he has the authority to proclaim the gospel in both oral and written form, as well as to establish and build up churches (see on 2:20 and 4:11). He has been called to this ministry 'through the will of God',[3] an expression that appears four times in the space of a few verses (vv. 1, 5, 9, 11; see below), and has particularly to do with God's saving plan or some aspect of it. Paul's calling to be an apostle to the Gentiles fits within that gracious divine plan (cf. 3:1-13). He had not appointed himself to this position; God chose him. Hence the words *by the will of God* have overtones of God's unmerited grace, and emphasize that there was no personal merit on Paul's part either in becoming an apostle or continuing as one.

The second element in the prescript refers to the recipients of the letter. Their identity involves a well-known textual problem.[4] Although the

2. For a summary of the suggestions regarding the origin of the concept of an apostle, see P. W. Barnett, *DPL*, 45-46 and 50-51 (for further literature). Best, 97, rightly comments: 'Whether or not the Christian use of apostle derives from Hebrew *shaliach*, Paul viewed himself as the representative or ambassador of Christ'.

3. The preposition διά ('through') signifies the efficient cause or agency by which Paul received his apostleship; so BAGD, 180; C. F. D. Moule, *An Idiom Book of New Testament Greek* (Cambridge: Cambridge University Press, 1959), 57; and D. B. Wallace, *Greek Grammar beyond the Basics: An Exegetical Syntax of the New Testament* (Grand Rapids: Zondervan, 1996), 434.

4. For a full discussion see particularly the works of E. Best, 'Recipients and Title of the Letter to the Ephesians: Why and When the Designation "Ephesians"?', in *ANRW*, 3247-79; 'Ephesians 1.1', in *Essays on Ephesians* (Edinburgh: T & T Clark, 1997), 1-16; 'Ephesians 1:1 Again', in *Essays*, 17-24; note also Best's commentary, 98-101; cf. Lincoln, 1-4.

NIV reads: *To the saints in Ephesus, the faithful in Christ Jesus,* the weight of textual evidence indicates that the phrase 'in Ephesus' was probably not part of the original wording.[5] This is consistent with the internal evidence of the letter (see the Introduction) where little in the contents suggests that it was written to a church where Paul has ministered for the best part of three years. There is no mention of 'individuals or groups among the people addressed; there are no allusions to features or problems in the local situation'.[6] The only personal reference, apart from Paul himself, is to Tychicus, whom the apostle is sending to the readers so that he might inform them of his personal circumstances (6:21-22).

The difficulty, however, is that the manuscripts which omit 'in Ephesus' put nothing in its place.[7] This omission results in an awkward grammatical construction: 'to the saints who are also believers in Christ Jesus' is not a natural form of address. Convinced that 'in Ephesus' was not original, that some indication of place was required by the construction, and that the epistle had the appearance of a circular letter, F. F. Bruce conjectures that a space was left after the verb 'are' for Tychicus to insert the appropriate geographical name for each place to which he delivered a copy of the letter.[8] Bruce admits that such a practice was difficult to attest for the first century, but still finds the arguments in favour of it convincing.[9] However, while this practice is understandable in an age of photocopiers, it makes less sense at a time when every copy had to be made by hand. If the whole had to be handwritten, there seems to be little reason for omitting

---

5. The manuscript evidence is as follows: ἐν Ἐφέσῳ ('in Ephesus') is omitted by 𝔓[46] ℵ B 424[c] 1739 Basil, Origen, apparently Marcion (who called the letter 'the epistle to the Laodiceans'), and Tertullian: τοῖς ἁγίοις τοῖς οὖσιν καὶ πιστοῖς ('to the saints who are also believers in Christ Jesus'). 𝔓[46] differs slightly from the others in that it omits τοῖς ('those who') before οὖσιν ('are'). The vast majority of the manuscripts read τοῖς ἁγίοις τοῖς οὖσιν ἐν Ἐφέσῳ καὶ πιστοῖς ('to the saints in Ephesus, the faithful in Christ Jesus'). However, the combination of 𝔓[46] (which dates from the beginning of the third century and is the earliest manuscript we have of this letter), ℵ, and B is strong external evidence for the omission of the place name as being original.

6. Bruce, 250.

7. Although the letter was listed in Marcion's canon as 'To the Laodiceans', this destination has not found its way into any manuscripts. Ephesus is the *only* place name found in them.

8. Bruce, 250.

9. Bruce cites G. Zuntz, *The Text of the Epistles* (London: British Academy, 1954), 228, who pointed out that multiple copies of royal letters, which were identical in wording, were sent out to various addresses in the Hellenistic period. These were based on a master-copy that left the address blank. W. G. Kümmel, *Introduction,* 355, however, asserts that the 'supposition of a letter with a gap in the prescript or a subsequent insertion of the address is without parallel in antiquity'; quoted by D. A. Carson, D. J. Moo, and L. Morris, *Introduction,* 310.

the two words of the address. Furthermore, it is surprising that no copy of this circular letter survived other than that addressed to Ephesus. Even those manuscripts that lack the words 'in Ephesus' do not have another geographical place name. A further suggestion is that there were originally two place names in the prescript, Hierapolis and Laodicea.[10] But again there is no manuscript evidence in support of this.

Several other emendations have been proposed,[11] but none is fully convincing. No satisfactory solution to this textual difficulty has been advanced. Clinton Arnold and Harold Hoehner claim that the majority of the manuscripts which include the words 'in Ephesus' represent the original reading, and that Paul intended his letter to be sent (albeit as a circular) to Ephesus.[12] But the lack of personal details tells against this. If the letter were for Ephesus, we would have expected more of the warmth evidenced in Philippians than the general tone it has. We conclude that Ephesians was a general epistle sent to mainly Gentile believers in southwestern Asia Minor, and that it was linked with Ephesus at an early

10. So A. van Roon, *Authenticity*, 80-85; and Lincoln, 3-4. It is argued that this has the advantage of explaining the presence of the awkward καί ('and') in the text. As is well known, Marcion thought that this letter was really meant for the Laodiceans. But there is no reference to Laodicea in any extant manuscript. Further, if it is claimed that this is the letter referred to in Col. 4:16, then, given the similarities between Colossians and Ephesians, one wonders why it was necessary to exchange the letters. Further, if Ephesians was written later than Colossians, then Col. 4:16 refers to another writing.

11. A. van Roon, *Authenticity*, 80-85, supposes that there were originally two place names in τοῖς ἁγίοις τοῖς οὖσιν ἐν . . . καὶ ἐν . . . πιστοῖς ἐν Χριστῷ Ἰησοῦ. The two place names were left out, but the καί remained, so creating the B text. Van Roon thinks that the two names were Hierapolis and Laodicea (cf. also Lincoln, 3-4). But this now requires two scribal blunders and is very doubtful.

12. Arnold contends that we are left with no satisfactory explanation of Eph. 1:1 if the original text omitted the words ἐν Ἐφέσῳ ('in Ephesus'). He therefore rejects the textual tradition as represented by 𝔓⁴⁶ ℵ B 424ᶜ 1739 Basil, Origen, apparently Marcion (who called the letter 'the epistle to the Laodiceans'), and Tertullian, and prefers the alternative tradition. In favour of this conclusion he argues: (1) there is still strong manuscript support for the inclusion of the words ἐν Ἐφέσῳ ('in Ephesus'). (2) An Ephesian destination was the unanimous tradition of the early church, and is the only reading specifically mentioned in all the extant versions. (3) At an early date, because 'the letter was of general, not local, application' (so B. M. Metzger, *A Textual Commentary on the Greek New Testament* [Stuttgart: Deutsche Bibelgesellschaft, 1994], 505), churches universalized the address by omitting the prescript in copies initially made for their own teaching purposes. (4) When the apostle states that he has 'heard' of the Ephesians' 'faith and love' (1:15), it could refer to the progress that has been made by Christians since he had left them, as well as the faith of new converts. (5) The absence of personal greetings is not particularly significant since he sends no extended greetings in other letters (about whose authorship there is no doubt) to churches he knew well (e.g., 1 and 2 Corinthians, Galatians, and Philippians); see Arnold, 5-6; and his article in *DPL*, 244-45; and Hoehner on 1:1.

stage, perhaps because of its being a strategic church or because it was one of the several cities to which the letter was sent.

The identification of the readers as 'saints' (lit. 'holy ones') is Paul's regular description of Christians (cf. 1 Cor. 1:1, 2; 2 Cor. 1:1; Rom. 1:1; Phil. 1:1). The antecedents of the term are to be found in the Old Testament. Israel was God's holy people (Exod. 19:6), chosen by him and appointed to his service. Since the one who had brought them into a covenant relationship was holy, Israel herself was to be a holy nation (Lev. 11:44; 19:2, etc.). Christians are 'saints', not in the sense that they are very pious people, but because of the new relationship they have been brought into by God. It is not because of their own doing or good works but on account of what Christ has done. They are set apart for him and his service; as the people of his own possession they are the elect community of the end time whose lives are to be characterized by godly behaviour. Paul will expand on the implications of this term at 1:4, where holiness is the intended result of God's election, and at 5:26, 27, where it is viewed as the effect of Christ's death on behalf of his church. The second description of the addressees, *faithful in Christ Jesus*,[13] points not so much to their being trustworthy or reliable[14] as to their being 'believers' (cf. 2 Cor. 6:15, where the word stands in contrast to 'unbelievers'; 1 Tim. 4:10, 12; 5:16; 6:2; Tit. 1:6). *In Christ Jesus* speaks of the one in whom they have been brought together into a living fellowship (on the significance of being 'in Christ' see on 1:3; 2:5, 6), rather than the person in whom they believed. The latter is of course true, but it is not the particular point Paul is making here. At the outset, then, Paul describes his readers first in terms of their being marked out by God to be his holy people, but also in terms of their believing response to the gospel, a response which is ultimately due to God's gracious initiative as well (cf. 2:8).[15]

2 Grace and peace to you from God our Father and the Lord Jesus Christ, which is the third element of the Pauline prescript, remains basically unchanged throughout the apostle's letters (Rom. 1:7; 1 Cor. 1:3; 2 Cor. 1:2; Phil. 1:2; 2 Thess. 1:2; Phlm. 3). Instead of the standard Hellenistic greeting *chairein,* he employs the similar-sounding but theologically more profound *charis* ('grace'), together with the Greek rendering of the Jewish greeting for 'peace'. A close parallel to this is the combination 'mercy and peace' in some Jewish salutations (cf. *2 Apoc. Bar.* 78:2). Here in Ephesians these two wide-ranging blessings are said to flow from the twin source of *God our Father and the Lord Jesus Christ.* Right at the outset

13. πιστοῖς ἐν Χριστῷ Ἰησοῦ ('faithful in Christ Jesus') is to be taken as in apposition to 'saints' and referring to the same group of people.

14. A meaning which the word πιστός can have, and is used by Paul to speak of the reliability of his coworkers (Col. 1:7; 4:7, 9).

15. So, rightly, Lincoln, 6.

of the letter, Paul's thought is theocentric, emphasizing God's activity in Christ. And the close linking of Christ with God in such expressions bears witness to his exalted place in Paul's thought. As the risen and exalted one Christ has been seated at the right hand of God in the heavenly realms, far above all rule and authority, power and dominion (1:20-21). God and Christ are entirely at one in securing and bestowing salvation.

Paul's readers have already experienced, in some measure, God's grace and peace in the Lord Jesus Christ. The apostle recognizes this, and in his salutation he expresses his desire that these twin blessings may be understood and experienced in greater measure, especially through the letter itself, for these two major themes are taken up again and again throughout Ephesians.[16]

II. THE NEW HUMANITY A DIVINE CREATION, 1:3–3:21

A. Introductory Eulogy: Praise for God's Blessings in Christ, 1:3-14

> [3]*Praise be to the God and Father of our Lord Jesus Christ, who has blessed us in the heavenly realms with every spiritual blessing in Christ.* [4]*For he chose us in him before the creation of the world to be holy and blameless in his sight. In love* [5]*he predestined us to be adopted as his sons through Jesus Christ, in accordance with his pleasure and will —* [6]*to the praise of his glorious grace, which he has freely given us in the One he loves.* [7]*In him we have redemption through his blood, the forgiveness of sins, in accordance with the riches of God's grace* [8]*that he lavished on us with all wisdom and understanding.* [9]*And he made known to us the mystery of his will according to his good pleasure, which he purposed in Christ,* [10]*to be put into effect when the times will have reached their fulfillment — to bring all things in heaven and on earth together under one head, even Christ.* [11]*In him we were also chosen, having been predestined according to the plan of him who works out everything in conformity with the purpose of his will,* [12]*in order that we, who were the first to hope in Christ, might be for the praise of his glory.* [13]*And you also were included in Christ when you heard the word of truth, the gospel of your salvation. Having believed, you were marked in him with a seal, the promised Holy Spirit,* [14]*who is a deposit guaranteeing our inheritance until the redemption of those who are God's possession — to the praise of his glory.*

16. χάρις ('grace') turns up at 1:6, 7; 2:5, 7, 8; 3:2, 7, 8; 4:7, 29; 6:23; and εἰρήνη ('peace') in 2:14, 15, 17; 4:3; 6:15.

After his greeting Paul usually begins his letters with an introductory thanksgiving which focusses on God's work in the lives of his readers (Rom. 1:8; 1 Cor. 1:4; Phil. 1:3; Col. 1:3, etc.). Here in Ephesians, however, the opening paragraph is an outburst of *praise* to *the God and Father of our Lord Jesus Christ* (cf. 2 Cor. 1:3-4; 1 Pet. 1:3-5) in the typical Old Testament and Jewish style of an extended eulogy or *berakah* ('Blessed be God, who has . . .').[17] The ground for giving praise is expressed by the participial clause, *who has blessed us in the heavenly realms with every spiritual blessing in Christ* (v. 3). These wide-ranging blessings, which are said to be 'in Christ', are then amplified through the 'even as' clause of v. 4 and the following words. Ideas come tumbling out as Paul refers to election (v. 4), adoption (v. 5), God's will (v. 5), his grace (v. 6), redemption (v. 7), wisdom (v. 8), the mystery (v. 9), and the consummation of all things (v. 10), before mention is made of Christ as the one in whom Jewish and Gentile believers ('we' and 'you') are incorporated (vv. 11-14). The eulogy extends from v. 3 to v. 14, and like that of 2 Corinthians 1 it includes the writer within the sphere of blessing ('who has blessed *us*', v. 3). But the introductory thanksgiving has not been replaced by the eulogy (1:3-14); instead, it follows the *berakah* in vv. 15-16.

The earliest and simplest form of a *berakah* or eulogy, an example of 'declarative praise', to use Westermann's term, was a single sentence in which an individual responded joyfully to God's deliverance or provision (Gen. 14:20; 24:27).[18] Later it came to be associated with the cult and Israel's worship (1 Kings 8:15, 56). Finally, in a developed and liturgically fuller form the *berakah* provided the doxological conclusions to the books of the Psalter (Ps. 41:13; 72:19-20, etc.). It remained dominant in rabbinic Judaism (cf. the Eighteen Benedictions of the synagogue service) and the Qumran literature (1QH 5:20; 11:15). Along with its roots in the Old Testament (and Judaism), the specifically Christian dimension of the eulogy appears, first, in the way in which the God of Israel is described: he is praised as the *Father of our Lord Jesus Christ* (v. 3).[19] Two other major eulogies in the New Testament begin in this manner, namely, 2 Corinthians 1:3 and 1 Peter 1:3. Secondly, the thoroughly Christian dimension of this

---

17. There appears to be no precedent outside the New Testament for a blessing introducing a letter. (The letter of Hiram to Solomon in 2 Chron. 2:11, 12 contains a blessing, but it was independent prior to the letter, as 1 Kings 5:21 shows.) The form of the *berakah* in 2 Cor. 1:3-4 approximates the earlier, simpler type, while the longer *berakoth* of Eph. 1:3-14 and 1 Pet. 1:3-5 conform more to the later eulogies.

18. Cf. 'Blessed be God, who has not rejected my prayer' (Ps. 66:20). Note C. Westermann, *The Praise of God in the Psalms* (London: Epworth, 1966), 87-89.

19. On the subject of 'blessing' in relation to the εὐλογ- word group (and further bibliography), see P. T. O'Brien, *DPL*, 68-71.

eulogy is evident in the constant repetition of the phrase 'in Christ' (or 'in him', 'in whom'). All that God has done for his people, and for which he is praised, has been effected in and through Christ.

Ephesians 1:3-14 is one long sentence (of 202 words) marked by an accumulation of relative clauses and phrases whose relation to one another is often difficult to determine.[20] It has occasioned different, indeed contradictory, comments from scholars, from E. Norden's oft-quoted caustic comment, 'the most monstrous sentence conglomeration that I have ever found in the Greek language', to the appreciation of C. Masson: 'one is struck by the fulness of its words, of its liturgical majesty and its perceptible rhythm from beginning to end'![21] In fact, the Letter to the Ephesians contains eight lengthy sentences (1:3-14, 15-23; 2:1-7; 3:2-13, 14-19; 4:1-6, 11-16; 6:14-20), three of which are items of praise and prayer (1:3-14, 15-23; 3:14-19). It is not unusual in reported prayers and worship to have long sentences of exalted language. Many of the stylistic features are the result of Semitic influence, and some have their closest parallels in the Qumran literature.[22]

Although there have been many efforts to determine the form and structure of the paragraph,[23] no general agreement has been reached. J. T. Sanders' verdict, 'every attempt to provide a strophic structure for Eph 1.3-14 has failed',[24] still holds true, even after further attempts have been made since he wrote. This is not to suggest, however, that there is no plan to the pericope. The eulogy has been carefully constructed, as can be seen

20. On the extent of the eulogy, see Best, 106-7. The passage contains an accumulation of relative clauses (vv. 6, 7, 8, 9, 11, 13, 14), participial (vv. 3, 5, 9, 13) and infinitival (vv. 4, 10, 12) constructions, a large collection of prepositional expressions (including fifteen instances of ἐν, most of which are ἐν Χριστῷ ['in Christ'] or its equivalent), and examples of synonymous words linked together with the genitive case, as well as other genitival constructions.

21. E. Norden, *Agnostos Theos: Untersuchungen zur Formengeschichte religiöser Rede* (Leipzig/Berlin: Teubner, 1913), 253; and C. Masson, *L'Épître de Paul aux Éphésiens* (Neuchâtel: Delachaux & Niestlé, 1953), 149.

22. Noted particularly by R. Deichgräber, *Gotteshymnus und Christushymnus in der frühen Christenheit: Untersuchungen zu Form, Sprache und Stil der frühchristlichen Hymnen* (Göttingen: Vandenhoeck & Ruprecht, 1967), 72-75; and K. G. Kuhn, 'The Epistle to the Ephesians', 116, who observed: 'Semitic syntactical occurrences appear four times more frequently in the Epistle to the Ephesians than in all the remaining letters of the *corpus Paulinum*'. This statement had particular reference to conditional sentences. There are, however, in Eph. 1:3-14 no instances of parataxis or asyndeton.

23. Hoehner interacts with at least eighteen in his recent survey. Cf. also Best, 107-8. There have also been a number of attempts, without success, to find an original hymn in 1:3-14.

24. J. T. Sanders, 'Hymnic Elements in Ephesians 1–3', *ZNW* 56 (1965), 214-32, esp. 227.

from v. 3, where 'bless' appears three times.[25] There are recurring phrases, such as 'according to the good pleasure of his will' (vv. 5, 9, 11) and 'to the praise of his glory' (vv. 6, 12, 14), which appears after the work of Father, Son, and Spirit (in this order). The prepositions 'in' (especially the phrase 'in Christ' and its equivalents) and 'according to' are frequently used. Three important participles — 'having blessed' (v. 3), 'having predestined' (v. 5), and 'having made known' (v. 9) — represent significant steps in the movement of the paragraph. There is a further progression within the passage, from the declaration of praise to God (v. 3) to a description of his great purpose and its outworking (vv. 4-10), which are the grounds for such exultation, on to its application to the lives of the readers, who are Jewish and Gentile believers (vv. 11-14).

The increasing consensus among many recent scholars is that the eulogy is an ad hoc composition of the author in exalted liturgical language that contains Old Testament and traditional Christian material.[26] The abundance of descriptive words for God's purpose in a long sentence is entirely fitting within the scope of a eulogy.

The divine saving purposes from eternity to eternity which are celebrated in Ephesians 1:3-14 are clearly set forth as the work of the triune God.[27] First, the origin and source of 'every spiritual blessing' which believers enjoy is 'the God and Father of our Lord Jesus Christ' (v. 3), who is also 'our Father' (v. 2). His initiative is seen at every point: it is he who has 'blessed us' (v. 3), 'chosen us' (v. 4), 'destined us to be his sons and daughters' (v. 5), 'lavished his grace upon us' (vv. 6, 8), made known to us his plan and purposes for the world (vv. 9-10), and accomplishes all things in accordance with his will (v. 11). There is also significant mention of God's love, grace, will, purpose, and plan. God the Father, who has set his love and grace upon us, is working out his eternal plan. Secondly, the sphere within which the divine blessing is given and received is God the Son, the Lord Jesus Christ. In the first fourteen verses of this letter the name or title 'Christ' (or its equivalent or a personal pronoun) occurs no fewer than fifteen times. The phrase 'in Christ', 'in whom', or 'in him' appears eleven times. It is in Christ, that is, because of our incorporation in him, that God has blessed us. It is in him that both Jewish believers, who have become God's people (vv. 11-12), and Gentile Christians, who have been sealed as belonging to God (vv. 13-14), now belong to the redeemed

25. Εὐλογητός ('blessed'), ὁ εὐλογήσας ('who has blessed'), and εὐλογία ('blessing').

26. Lincoln, 14, comments: 'The nature and amount of the traditional material are not such as to warrant the proposal . . . that a preformed eulogy lies behind the passage.'

27. This has been recognized by many scholars, including Stott, 33-36; Lincoln, 43; and G. D. Fee, *God's Empowering Presence: The Holy Spirit in the Letters of Paul* (Peabody: Hendrickson, 1994), 665.

humanity. In Christ it is God's intention to bring everything back into unity under his rule (1:9, 10). Thirdly, the Spirit's presence is in view at both the beginning and ending of the paragraph. He stamps his character on every blessing (they are 'spiritual', v. 3), and he marks God's ownership and serves as the guarantee of the fulfilment of his purposes (v. 14).

Within this framework of the triune God's activity, however, there is a threefold emphasis in the eulogy. The theocentric thrust is dominant throughout the passage. God is the origin and source of salvation as well as its goal. As we have seen, his initiative is evident throughout the eulogy. His gracious electing plan shapes past, present, and future. The ultimate goal is that God himself may be glorified — hence the refrain 'to the praise of his glory' (vv. 6, 12, 14). There is an important christological dimension to the paragraph as well. Christ, who is the mediator and 'sphere' of divine blessing, has the Father's glory as his goal. Finally, there is a stress on believers as undeserving beneficiaries of God's gracious saving work. Again and again Paul speaks of 'us' and 'we' as the people of God who have been 'blessed with every spiritual blessing in Christ' (v. 3; cf. vv. 4, 5, 6, 7, 8, 9, 11, 12, 14). In vv. 4-14 the same people are in view. Paul includes himself along with his readers within the first person plurals. At the same time, the apostle has all of God's people in mind, both corporately and individually (see below). 'God as the origin and goal of salvation, Christ as its mediator, and believers as its recipients — these themes give the passage a threefold theocentric, christological, and ecclesiological focus'.[28]

God is blessed for revealing that his gracious plan in history is all-embracing. The paragraph, which celebrates the accomplishment of his gracious purposes in Christ and provides a sweep from eternity to eternity, strikes its climactic note with the mention of the mystery and its content (vv. 9, 10). Syntactically and structurally, the exposition of the mystery in terms of the *anakephalaiōsis* ('summing up') is the 'high point' of the eulogy, or, as T. Moritz puts it, the 'pivotal statement' of the passage.[29] The *anakephalaiōsis* ('summing up'), which points forward to eternity, is the summit of Paul's statements. Then, the following words of the eulogy (vv. 11-14) stress that the magnificent blessings already described are for both Jewish and Gentile believers. Once the high point of this eulogy has been reached, the author turns to explain who is included within the sphere of these salvation blessings.

The eulogy functions in a number of important ways. First, as Paul begins his general letter to Christians in Asia Minor, he meditates on

---

28. Lincoln, 43.
29. C. C. Caragounis, *Mysterion*, 143; T. Moritz, 'Summing Up All Things', 96.

God's gracious purposes in Christ, and praise to God wells up within him. His desire is that this adoration might overflow to his readers, so that they will be stimulated to respond as he does and give glory to God for all the gracious blessings to them. He wishes to 'evoke a cognitive and emotional response in the readers by reminding them in a fresh way of their redemption in Christ and their experience of salvation'.[30] Secondly, the eulogy functions like an introductory thanksgiving paragraph:[31] it strikes the keynote of the letter, introducing and prefiguring many of its key ideas. Some of these are expounded and enlarged upon in the body of the epistle itself (e.g., the heavenlies, v. 3; the mystery, vv. 9, 10; and the Spirit, v. 13; cf. v. 3). Others are elaborated by way of contrast (1:3 with 2:3; 1:13 with 2:3), while some themes provide the theological basis for the writer's moral appeal as he exhorts his readers in 4:1–6:20 (cf. 1:13 with 4:30; 5:18).[32] The paragraph, then, has an introductory function within the author's didactic and exhortatory goals, the details of which will become clear as the letter unfolds.

1. Praise to God for Every Spiritual Blessing, 1:3[33]

3 The opening words are an outburst of *praise* to *the God and Father of our Lord Jesus Christ* (cf. 2 Cor. 1:3-4; 1 Pet. 1:3-5) in the typical Old Testament and Jewish style of an extended blessing or *berakah* ('Blessed be God, who has . . .'). The apostle begins by blessing God for showering us with every spiritual blessing. This word of praise stands as the 'topic' sentence and title of the whole paragraph.[34]

Within the New Testament 'blessed' always refers to God,[35] who is praised as creator (Rom. 1:25), as the Father of our Lord Jesus Christ

---

30. Arnold, 70, following Schnackenburg, 47-49, 67-69.

31. Cf. P. T. O'Brien, *Introductory Thanksgivings*.

32. For further details, see P. T. O'Brien, 'An Unusual Introduction', 510-12.

33. For a history of interpretation of this verse, see E. Best, 'Fashions in Exegesis: Ephesians 1:3', in *Scripture: Meaning and Method, Essays Presented to Anthony Tyrrell Hanson*, ed. B. P. Thompson (Hull: Hull University Press, 1987), 79-91.

34. G. D. Fee, *God's Empowering Presence*, 666, considers these opening words to be a kind of 'subtitle' for the whole letter. I. H. Thomson, *Chiasmus in the Pauline Letters* (Sheffield: Academic Press, 1995), 52, 53, etc., believes that v. 3 constitutes an introduction to what he regards as a chiasmus in vv. 3-10.

35. When εὐλογητός ('blessed') renders the Hebrew *bārûk* ('blessed, praised'). In addition to the five instances in Paul, εὐλογητός ('blessed') occurs at Mark 14:61; Luke 1:68; and 1 Pet. 1:3. On three occasions in the apostle's letters, but nowhere else in the New Testament, short interjections of praise (with εὐλογητός, 'blessed') appear (Rom. 1:25; 9:5; 2 Cor. 11:31). When men and women are called 'blessed' (as in the Gospels) εὐλογημένος is used.

(2 Cor. 1:3; 11:31; and Eph. 1:3), and as the one who is over all, the Messiah (Rom. 9:5). While it has been claimed that the term signifies that God is 'worthy of praise' (rather than that he is actually *praised*), so that the 'eulogy expresses a delicate prompting to ponder what God has done and to ascribe to Him the glory which is His due',[36] here Paul *actually ascribes* praise to God[37] (cf. 2 Cor. 1:3) for his mighty salvation.[38] Gratitude and thanksgiving once more well up within the apostle as he recalls God's marvellous salvation plan in Jesus Christ. At the same time the whole paragraph, which is a paean of praise, is intended to instruct the readers and cause them in turn to respond by magnifying and glorifying God, who is worthy of their adoration. Paul's eulogies do not express a wish; they describe a fact ('Blessed *is* God'),[39] as he proclaims that God is the source of blessing.

The distinctively Christian feature of this eulogy appears in the words *the God and Father of our Lord Jesus Christ*. The person to whom this praise is ascribed is the One, who in the Old Testament was praised as the God of Israel (1 Kings 1:48; 2 Chron. 2:12; Ps. 72:8), the God of Shem (Gen. 9:26), God Most High (Gen. 14:20), and Lord (Ps. 31:21), and who is now known to Paul as *the God and Father of our Lord Jesus Christ*. Although this form appears to have become fixed for Christian eulogies (cf. 2 Cor. 1:3; 1 Pet. 1:3), the point about the Father's being the God of Jesus Christ is given a particular nuance in Ephesians 1:17. It is solely through God's beloved Son (1:5-6; 4:13) that believers have gained access to the Father (2:18), which they enjoy with freedom and confidence (3:12). For Gentile Christians who had formerly believed in many other gods, this was good news indeed.

In the typical Old Testament *berakoth* the name of God is followed by a relative pronoun and a participial clause which gives the reasons for praising God: 'Blessed be the LORD, the God of Israel, who alone does wondrous things' (Ps. 72:18). The same construction is followed in the

---

36. C. C. Caragounis, *Mysterion*, 80.

37. As with most Old Testament *berakoth* or eulogies, the predicate in Eph. 1:3 ('the God and Father') is in the third person (cf. 'Blessed be the Lord, the God of Israel', Ps. 41:13); in many of the later Jewish blessings the address is in the second person: 'Blessed are you, O Lord our God, King of the universe, who brings forth bread from the earth' (Mishnah *Berakot* 6.1).

38. However, the line between God being worthy of praise and actually praised is a fine one: praise is offered to one who is worthy of it, and because he is worthy of honour he is praised.

39. The missing copula after εὐλογητός, 'blessed', should be understood as indicative (ἐστίν, 'is'); cf. Rom. 1:25; 2 Cor. 11:31; 1 Pet. 4:11; this also accords well with the preference of the LXX translators. Cf. BDF §128(5), Schnackenburg, 50, and most other commentators.

New Testament eulogies (2 Cor. 1:3; 1 Pet. 1:3), and here the ground for blessing God is similarly expressed by a participial clause: *'who has blessed*[40] *us'*. As we have noted, there is a deliberate play on words, for three terms from the same stem are compactly woven together in this short verse: *'Blessed* be God, who has *blessed* us with every spiritual *blessing'*. The same verb is used for men and women blessing God and for his blessing them, although in a different sense. In the former case *blessed* denotes the ascription of praise to God, while in the latter the verb describes God's providing his benefits. The cognate noun 'blessing', which modifies the second use of the verb, completes the trio.

With every spiritual blessing is the first of three phrases commencing with the preposition 'in' or 'with', which modifies the verb *blessed*. These expressions describe in different ways the content of God's blessings, the meaning of which is elaborated in the rest of the eulogy. Everything that Christians have received through God's saving act in Christ is comprehensively summarized in the expression *every spiritual blessing*. Here the adjective *spiritual* means 'pertaining to or belonging to the Spirit', and thus 'spiritual blessings' signify those which 'properly pertain to the life of the Spirit'.[41] The adjective does not primarily point to a contrast with what is material (e.g., Deut. 28:1-14), secular, or worldly. Nor do Paul's words suggest simply the spiritual gifts listed in 1 Corinthians 12:3-11. The nature of these gracious gifts is made plain in the following words of the eulogy (vv. 4-14), and include election to holiness, adoption as God's sons and daughters, redemption and forgiveness, a knowledge of God's gracious plan to sum up all things in Christ, the gift of the Spirit, and the hope of glory. Although each gracious gift of God is mediated to *us* by the Spirit, and his activity is assumed throughout the paragraph, the apos-

40. The aorist participle εὐλογήσας ('blessed') has been taken as referring to a definite event in the past, either the sending of God's Son (Abbott) or the time when believers were incorporated into Christ and received blessing (at their baptism, according to Schlier and J. Adai). But while it is theologically correct to state that the readers were blessed by God when they were united with Christ, it is quite another thing to suggest that the aorist participle, as such, specifically draws attention to the time note. The other saving acts of God, including his choice and predestination (vv. 4-5), his gracious work in Jesus Christ's act of salvation (v. 6), and his revelation of the mystery (v. 9), are all reported by means of aorists, and it is doubtful whether the times are specifically in view. For example, the expression could be rendered 'who blesses us', referring to the panoply of his blessings perceived as a glorious whole.

41. So G. D. Fee, *God's Empowering Presence*, 666-67; and H. R. Lemmer, 'Reciprocity between Eschatology and *Pneuma* in Ephesians 1:3-14', *Neot* 21 (1987), 159-82, esp. 168-69. Cf. Louw and Nida §12.21, 'pertaining to being derived from or being about the Spirit — "spiritual, from the Spirit"'; and BAGD, 678-79. Best, 114, comments: 'The whole blessing is said to be spiritual because it belongs to the sphere of the Spirit'.

tle's language does not state explicitly that the Spirit himself is the blessing.[42] The following verses, which explain the content of *every spiritual blessing,* do not make this identification and, had the apostle chosen to make it, there was a much simpler way in Greek, as Galatians 3:14 shows.[43] The first unambiguous mention of the Spirit occurs in vv. 13-14, where he is received as 'the guarantee of our inheritance'. All the gifts between vv. 3 and 14 are understood as elements of this one blessing and are therefore grounds for giving praise.[44]

The recipients of these gracious gifts of God are 'us'. In almost every verse of the paragraph[45] the apostle speaks of 'us' (or 'we') as the people of God who have received his mighty salvation. There is a stress in the paragraph on those who are the beneficiaries of God's gracious saving work. Since the content of every spiritual blessing is unpackaged in vv. 4-14, the 'us' and 'we' must refer to those already mentioned here in v. 3. Clearly, Paul includes himself[46] and his readers within this sphere of blessing. But the flow of the paragraph and the nature of the divine gifts being described show that the apostle has all of God's people in mind, viewed both corporately and individually.[47]

These blessings are enjoyed *in the heavenly realms.* This expression, which is exclusive to Ephesians (1:3, 20; 2:6; 3:10; 6:12),[48] is used consis-

---

42. A view which has been strongly put in some recent German scholarship, notably by W. Schenk, *Der Segen im Neuen Testament: Eine Begriffsanalytische Studie* (Berlin: Evangelische Verlagsanstalt, 1967), 50, and in more detail by J. Adai, *Der Heilige Geist als Gegenwart Gottes in den einzelnen Christen, in der Kirche und in der Welt: Studien zur Pneumatologie des Epheserbriefes* (Frankfurt/Bern/New York: Peter Lang, 1985), 53-60. They regard the phrase *every spiritual blessing* as denoting 'the totality of spiritual blessing'. The πᾶς means 'total' or 'whole' rather than 'every, every kind', while 'spiritual' focusses on the essence of the blessing. Only the Spirit himself qualifies as the totality of God's blessing to believers, it is argued.

43. The expression 'the promise of the Spirit' (ἡ ἐπαγγελία τοῦ πνεύματος) means 'the promise which is the Spirit', and this appears to be identified with 'the blessing (εὐλογία) of Abraham'.

44. Schnackenburg, 50.

45. Verse 3; cf. vv. 4, 5, 6, 7, 8, 9, 11, 12, 14.

46. Paul's introductory thanksgivings focus on God's work in the lives of others, but his eulogies praise God for blessings in which he himself participates. The formula from a Jewish background was apparently more apt when Paul himself came within the circle of blessing; see P. T. O'Brien, *DPL,* 68.

47. For the view that the language (particularly that relating to election) concerns only the people of God corporately, see on v. 4.

48. ἐπουράνιος ('heavenly'), which is synonymous with οὐράνιος, occurs fourteen times in the New Testament in various contexts, five of which are in Ephesians within the set phrase ἐν τοῖς ἐπουρανίοις ('in the heavenly realms'): Matt. 18:35; John 3:12; 1 Cor. 15:40 (twice), 48, 49; Phil. 2:10; 2 Tim. 4:18; Heb. 3:1; 6:4; 8:5; 9:23; 11:16; 12:22, in addition to the Ephesians references. The expression ἐν τοῖς ἐπουρανίοις is probably neuter plural, signify-

tently in a local sense. Surprisingly, however, the phrase is employed for both the sphere of God or Christ (1:3, 20; 2:6) and the location of the evil 'principalities and powers' (3:10; 6:12). Behind the expression, which stands within an Old Testament and Jewish rather than a Gnostic tradition, is the notion of several 'heavens' (cf. 4:10). Christ has ascended above all the heavens (4:10) and sits at God's right hand in the heavenly places 'far above all rule and authority'. The principalities and powers are located in the lower heavens, in the realm of the air (cf. 2:2), in the darkness of this world (6:12). However, *in the heavenly realms* is not describing some celestial topography, for the sense conveyed by the local imagery is metaphorical rather than literal. *In the heavenly realms* is bound up with the divine saving events and is to be understood within a Pauline eschatological perspective. In line with the Jewish two-age structure heaven is seen from the perspective of the age to come, which has now been inaugurated by the death and resurrection of the Lord Jesus Christ. At the same time, it is still part of this present evil age until the final consummation, for hostile powers are currently active in the heavenly realms (cf. 3:10; 6:12). The blessings of salvation which believers have received from God link them with *the heavenly realms.* These gracious gifts are not simply future benefits but are a present reality for us, since they have already been won for us by God's saving action in Christ. As the following verses make plain, these blessings are integrally related to the whole course of salvation history and have been applied to believers by the Spirit.

The blessings of the heavenly realms which believers receive are *in Christ.* This third phrase which modifies the verb *blessed* signifies that God's gracious gifts come not only through the agency of Christ but also because the recipients are incorporated in him who is himself in the heavenly realm.[49] The phrase *in Christ,* together with its variants 'in him' and

---

ing 'in the heavenly places' or 'in the heavenly realms' rather than 'among the heavenly beings'. For a full discussion see C. C. Caragounis, *Mysterion,* 146-52; A. T. Lincoln, 'A Re-Examination', 468-83; W. H. Harris, '"The Heavenlies" Reconsidered: Οὐρανός and Ἐπουράνιος in Ephesians', *BSac* 148 (1991), 72-89, esp. 73-74; and Best, 115-19.

49. ἐν Χριστῷ ('in Christ') and its equivalents are used in a variety of ways in Ephesians so that the precise force must be derived from each context. Often its use is instrumental, signifying 'through Christ's agency'. But J. A. Allan's claim, 'The "In Christ" Formula in Ephesians', *NTS* 5 (1958-59), 54-62, esp. 59, that the phrase has an instrumental force 'predominantly, if not exclusively' — and thus is further evidence of the non-Pauline authorship of Ephesians — fails to take account of the references where ἐν Χριστῷ has a local sense and involves the notion of incorporation into Christ; cf. 2:6, where the words 'God raised us up with Christ and seated us with him in the heavenly realms in Christ Jesus (ἐν Χριστῷ Ἰησοῦ)' are a deliberate echo of 1:20; what is said of Christ can now be stated of believers since they are included in him. 'Christ is the "place" in whom believ-

'in whom', occurs eleven times in the paragraph. It is 'in Christ' that God has chosen us in eternity (vv. 3-4). The Father has bestowed his grace upon us 'in the Beloved', so that we now have redemption and the forgiveness of sins 'in him' (v. 7). In Christ the first Jewish believers were chosen to become God's people (vv. 11-12), while Gentile believers were also included 'in him' and were sealed as belonging to him by the Holy Spirit (vv. 13-14). Significantly, it is 'in Christ' that God has set forth his plan to unite all things 'in him' or under his headship (vv. 9-10). This constantly repeated formula has an essential function in the eulogy, which surveys the whole of God's redemptive plan: it is 'in Christ' alone that God has blessed men and women from eternity to eternity.

2. Praise for Election and Adoption, 1:4-6

4 The sweeping blessings of v. 3, which are said to be 'in Christ', are now amplified through the 'just as' clause of v. 4 and the following verses. Paul elaborates throughout the rest of the *berakah* what is involved in their being blessed with every spiritual blessing in Christ as he moves on to speak of their election before the foundation of the world, predestination to sonship, redemption through Christ's sacrificial death, the forgiveness of sins, and so on — blessings which relate to the past, the present, and the future. At the same time the clause introduces a causal nuance (hence the NIV's *for*):[50] God has so richly blessed us *because* he has chosen us in Christ, predestined us for adoption, and so on.

The great theme of divine election is the first to be introduced as Paul's mind reaches back before creation, before time began, into eternity in which only God himself existed. Election is one of a variety of motifs found in this magnificent paragraph that describe different facets of God's gracious, saving purposes: note the language of predestination (vv. 5, 11), good pleasure (vv. 5, 9), will (vv. 5, 9, 11), mystery (v. 9), purpose (v. 9; cf. v. 11), appointment (v. 11), and plan (v. 11).

In the Old Testament God chose Abraham so as to bless him and to

---

ers are and in whom salvation is', E. Best, *One Body in Christ* (London: SPCK, 1955), 8. Cf. C. C. Caragounis, *Mysterion*, 152-57, who thinks of Christ as the 'sphere' in which the divine decisions are made and put into effect. He is not only the 'place' in which the believer has been set by God's electing plan; he is also the one in whom the believer will have his future existence. The idea of the incorporation of many into a representative head (using the preposition ἐν) appears in the LXX in relation to Abraham (Gen. 12:30) and Isaac (Gen. 21:12), as well as in Paul with reference to Adam (1 Cor. 15:22); cf. C. F. D. Moule, *The Origin of Christology* (Cambridge: Cambridge University Press, 1977), 54-62; and Lincoln, 21. For bibliographical details see M. A. Seifrid, 'In Christ', in *DPL*, 433-36.

50. Note this use of καθώς ('just as') in Paul's introductory thanksgivings (1 Cor. 1:6; Phil. 1:7).

bring blessing to the nations of the earth through him (Gen. 12:1-3). Subsequently, the Lord chose Israel to be his treasured possession from among all the peoples. Her election was due solely to God's gracious decision; it had nothing to do with Israel's choice or righteous behaviour (Deut. 7:6-8; 14:2). It was because the Lord loved her and kept the oath he had sworn to her forefathers that he chose her for himself. Here in Ephesians, the object of God's choice is *us,* that is, believers, who now belong to the people of God and *praise the God and Father of our Lord Jesus Christ.* There is clearly a corporate dimension to God's election. It was God's intention to create for himself a people perfectly conformed to the likeness of his Son (Rom. 8:29-30). It is inappropriate, however, to suggest that election in Christ is primarily corporate rather than personal and individual.[51] We have already seen that throughout the paragraph the recipients of 'every spiritual blessing' are mentioned again and again (vv. 3, 4, 5, 6, 7, 8, 9, 11, 12, 14) — in what has been called an 'ecclesiological focus'. The same group of people is clearly in view. Some of the divine gifts, for example, redemption and the forgiveness of sins in Christ (v. 7), together with the sealing of the Holy Spirit following belief in the gospel of salvation (vv. 13, 14), must be understood as coming to believers personally and individually (without thereby denying the corporate element). The plurals ('we', 'us') are common, not corporate. God has chosen a people for himself in Christ, and this includes members of that people. Further, to suggest that election in Christ is 'not related primarily to individual salvation but to God's purpose'[52] introduces an unnecessary 'either-or'. Predestination is to a relationship with God the Father through his Son, described in v. 5 under the imagery of adoption. This is in line with God's *purpose* according to v. 4, and since it is his intention that they should 'be holy and blameless in his sight' on the last day (see below), it has to do with final salvation.

God's choice of his people 'in Christ' is the new element in election. He is the Chosen One par excellence (Luke 9:35; 23:35).[53] The statement, however, does not mean that because Christians are *conscious* of being 'in

51. Note the emphases of Snodgrass, 49, and Best, 119-20, together with the treatments of W. W. Klein, *The New Chosen People: A Corporate View of Election* (Grand Rapids: Zondervan, 1990), 179-80; and C. C. Newman, 'Election and Predestination in Ephesians 1:4-6a: An Exegetical-Theological Study of the Historical, Christological Realization of God's Purpose', *RevExp* 93 (1996), 237-47, esp. 239.

52. As Best, 119, states.

53. However, against the view of Barth, 107-9 (cf. K. Barth), that God has chosen Christ, the object of God's choice here in Eph. 1:4 is ἡμᾶς ('us'), who are in Christ, not Χριστόν. The point made in Gal. 3 is slightly different: Christ is the seed of Abraham (v. 16). In him the blessing of Abraham has come to Gentiles (v. 14), so that they too, because they are Christ's, are Abraham's offspring.

Christ' they know themselves to be elect (even though this may be true on other grounds). Rather, it is objective, signifying that *in him* the people of God are chosen. If all things were created 'in him' (Col. 1:16), then it is no less true to say that earlier still it was *in him* that our election took place. 'He is [the] foundation, origin, and executor: all that is involved in election and its fruits depends on him'.[54] Election is always and only in Christ.

That choice in Christ was made in eternity, before time and creation, as the phrase *before the creation of the world*[55] makes plain.[56] The language of election before the foundation of the world occurs a number of times in the Pauline letters, not least in the context of thanksgiving (1 Thess. 1:4; 2:13; cf. Rom. 8:29; 2 Tim. 1:9), as part of an expression of gratitude for God's amazing grace. To say that election took place before creation indicates that God's choice was due to his own free decision and love, which were not dependent on temporal circumstances or human merit. The reasons for his election were rooted in the depths of his gracious, sovereign nature. To affirm this is to give to Christians the assurance that God's purposes for them are of the highest good, and the appropriate response from those who are chosen in Christ from all eternity is to praise him who has so richly blessed us.

The goal for which God chose his people in Christ is that we should *be holy and blameless* before him *in love*. Election does bring privilege, but it also carries with it responsibility. The divine purpose in our election was not simply to repair the damage done by sin but also to fulfil God's original intention for humankind, namely, to create for himself a people perfectly conformed to the likeness of his Son (Rom. 8:29-30). Again we see that God's election arose entirely from his grace, for if his intention was that we should *be holy and blameless in his sight*, then when he chose us we must have been unholy and blameworthy, and therefore deserving of judgment rather than adoption.[57]

Holy and blameless in his sight echoes the language of Colossians 1:22, where the purpose of Christ's reconciling work is the presentation of his people 'holy, blameless and irreproachable in his presence'. The two ad-

---

54. Bruce, 254-55.

55. The same phrase occurs at John 17:24; 1 Pet. 1:20 (cf. also Matt. 13:35; 25:34; Luke 11:50; Heb. 4:3; 9:26; Rev. 13:8; 17:8). καταβολή is the act of laying or putting down a foundation (cf. Heb. 6:1); cf. Louw and Nida §42.37.

56. God's election of believers *in Christ* before creation presupposes Christ's preexistence (cf. Col. 1:15-16). It does not imply the preexistence of God's people since it is not the church as such but the choice of them which precedes the foundation of the world. See the discussion in Lincoln, 23-24.

57. Stott, 36.

jectives *holy and blameless*[58] were used to describe the unblemished animals set apart for God as Old Testament sacrifices (Exod. 29:37-38; cf. Heb. 9:14; 1 Pet. 1:19). But already within the Old Testament this language was employed to describe ethical purity (e.g., Ps. 15[LXX 14]:2; 18:23 [17:24]). Both terms have lost any cultic overtones in Colossians 1:22 and Ephesians 1:4 (cf. Eph. 5:27; Phil. 2:15; Jude 24), referring instead to ethical holiness and freedom from moral blemish. In Paul's petitions of Philippians 1:9-10 and 1 Thessalonians 3:12-13 he intercedes for the same Christian graces of love in the present and holiness and blamelessness at the parousia. At 1 Corinthians 1:8 the irreproachability of the Corinthians is envisaged as occurring 'on the day of our Lord Jesus Christ'. Here the holiness and blamelessness are viewed as being 'before him'. Since the whole expression is dealing with the goal of election, that is, their full perfection in Christ, it is likely that the day of the Lord Jesus is in view. God chose his people in Christ with the ultimate goal that they would be holy and blameless before him when they appear in his presence. But this is not to suggest that there is consequently no concern for holiness and blamelessness in the here and now. 'The "holiness without which no one will see the Lord" (Heb. 12:14) is progressively wrought within the lives of believers on earth by the Spirit, and will be consummated in glory at the *parousia,* the time of the "redemption" anticipated in Eph. 1:14; 4:30'.[59] And the clear implication for believers is that even now they should live according to the divine intention.

It is not certain whether the words 'in love' should be attached to what precedes (as it is in the UBS Greek text) or to what follows (as in the NIV; cf. RSV). If it is the former, then it adds a specific quality to holiness and blamelessness: the purpose of God is that his people should be marked by holiness and blamelessness, coupled with love. If it is to the latter, then 'in love' expresses God's attitude to his people when he foreordained them for adoption into his family. On balance it is preferable to attach 'in love' to what precedes so that it is viewed as part of the goal election is intended to achieve, namely, 'a life before God which is holy and blameless and lived in love'.[60]

---

58. Gk. ἁγίους καὶ ἀμώμους; both terms turn up at Eph. 5:27 with a similar perspective.

59. Bruce, 255.

60. Lincoln, 17. The reasons adduced in favour of taking ἐν ἀγάπῃ ('in love') with what precedes are: (1) Elsewhere in the letter human associations predominate when the term "love" is used: 1:15; 4:2, 15, 16; 5:2, 25, 28, 33; 6:23, 24. Contrast, however, 2:4; 3:17, 19. It might plausibly be argued that in the latter half of Ephesians where there is paraenetic material we would expect the examples to refer to the love of Christians. (2) On most occasions where the expression ἐν ἀγάπῃ ('in love') turns up in Ephesians (4:2, 15, 16; 5:2; contrast 3:17), it refers to the love of believers. (3) When ἀγάπη ('love') ap-

5 If God has chosen his people in Christ from before the foundation of the world, then he has predestined them for adoption into his family as sons and daughters through Jesus Christ. Here the thought of v. 4 is developed in relation to the divine goal of adoption for those who are elect.[61] Believers praise God the Father because his purpose in choosing them was to bring them into a personal relationship with himself as his children.

The verb 'foreordain, predestine',[62] which appears six times in the New Testament, is used exclusively of God (Rom. 8:29, 30; 1 Cor. 2:7; Eph. 1:5, in relation to sonship; cf. 1:11; Acts 4:28) and serves to emphasize his sole initiative and authority in our salvation. Predestination is for a God-designed purpose, in this instance, 'adoption'.[63] This was understood in Graeco-Roman law as referring to the adoption as sons of those who were not so by birth. It signified entry to a privileged position. Paul applies this term from the Graeco-Roman world to the special relationship which believers have with God. This reference to adoption must also be understood against the background of Israel's relationship with the Lord as his 'firstborn son' (Exod. 4:22; Isa. 1:2), a relationship which was established at the Exodus: 'When Israel was a child I loved him, and out of Egypt I called my son' (Hos. 11:1). Paul asserts that adoption as sons was one of

---

pears in Paul's introductory thanksgivings, whether in intercession or thanksgiving, it refers to human love (Phil. 1:9-10; Col. 1:4, 8; 1 Thess. 3:12-13). Conversely, the divine love is nowhere connected with predestination or election, even if the notion is theologically acceptable. (4) Although structural arguments need to be used with caution, it has been claimed that if ἐν ἀγάπῃ concludes the line, then it fits the pattern of the rest of the eulogy where each section ends with a prepositional phrase with ἐν. Throughout this paragraph the verb in each clause precedes the phrase which qualifies it (Caird, 35). An objection levelled by C. C. Caragounis, *Mysterion*, 84, against this interpretation is that ἐν ἀγάπῃ ('in love') occurs after κατενώπιον αὐτοῦ ('before him'). His further semantic criticisms (85-86) of taking ἐν ἀγάπῃ ('in love') with what precedes are unconvincing. See Hoehner.

61. Exegetes differ on the relationship of the finite verb *chose* (ἐξελέξατο) to the participle *predestined* (προορίσας). (1) The participial expression is repeating the same truth of v. 4 in different words (Stott, 36; Best, 122-23). (2) It expresses the means by which the choice was made: 'He chose us . . . by predestining us' (Bratcher and Nida, 13; cf. D. B. Wallace, *Greek Grammar*, 629). (3) A fresh start is made with a new aspect being developed, in this case, the *goal* of predestination (Gnilka, 72, among others). (4) The participial clause is causal, giving the reason for the election: 'because of having predestined us, he chose us' (Hoehner).

62. Προορίζω, which according to BAGD, 709 (cf. Louw and Nida §30.84), means to 'decide upon beforehand', and with reference to God, to 'predestine'.

63. Gk. υἱοθεσία. For a detailed study, see J. M. Scott, *Adoption as Sons of God: An Exegetical Investigation into the Background of ΥΙΟΘΕΣΙΑ in the Pauline Corpus* (Tübingen: J. C. B. Mohr [Paul Siebeck], 1992), 3-117; and *DPL*, 15-18; cf. also F. Lyall, *Slaves, Citizens, Sons: Legal Metaphors in the Epistles* (Grand Rapids: Zondervan, 1984), 67-99.

the particular privileges belonging to Israel (Rom. 9:4). Now it belongs to Christians (cf. Rom. 9:26; 2 Cor. 6:18). The fulfilment of the divine purpose is the (final) 'adoption' confidently expected by those 'who have the first fruits of the Spirit' (Rom. 8:23). But because of 'the first fruits of the Spirit' the enjoyment of the new relationship with God as heavenly Father is ours already (Rom. 8:15-16). Ephesians 1:5 indicates that before time began God chose to adopt men and women into a personal and intimate relationship with himself.[64] Being adopted into his family as sons (and daughters) is an incredible privilege, because those now able to call upon him as Father were at one time 'sons of disobedience' and 'children of wrath' (2:2, 3). This personal relationship is made possible only *through Jesus Christ*, a highly significant expression which points to his agency.[65] It is only through the work of God's *Son*, the Beloved, that believers can be adopted as *sons* (cf. Eph. 4:13; Rom. 8:29; Gal. 3:26; 4:4, 5).

The basis or standard of God's action in foreordaining us to be his children is spelled out in the compound phrase *in accordance with his pleasure and will*. This is one of many synonymous expressions used for emphasis in Ephesians and which can be parallelled in the Qumran literature (cf. CD 3:15). Even so, a distinction between the terms *pleasure* and *will* is preserved. *Pleasure*,[66] which is used of the passionate concern of Paul's heart (Rom. 10:1) and the generous motives that prompted Christians in Rome to proclaim Christ (Phil. 1:15), signifies not simply the purpose of God but also the delight that he takes in his plans. It has warm and personal connotations, and draws attention to God's willingness and joy to do good. *Will* signifies that which is purposed, or intended,[67] and stresses his active resolve, his redemptive purpose (cf. the proximity of the terms in 1:9). The preposition 'according to' *(kata)* indicates the norm or standard, showing that his choosing many to come into a special relationship with himself was in keeping with what he delighted to do and with his saving plan. 'He enjoys imparting his riches to many children'.[68] Consequently, as men and women break out in praise (vv. 3, 6, 12, 14), their pleasure in God is a response to his delight in doing good to them.

---

64. The εἰς αὐτόν ('for him') continues the theocentric focus of v. 4 and may be paraphrased: '[God predestined us] for his own sons'. The christological emphasis comes out in the preceding words, 'through Jesus Christ'. Cf. Schnackenburg, 55.

65. At Eph. 2:18 it is 'through him [Christ]' that both Jew and Gentile have access by one Spirit to the Father. Elsewhere in the letter διά ('through') is used with reference to the will of God (1:1), the blood of Christ (1:7), faith (2:8; 3:12, 17), the cross (2:16), the gospel (3:6), the church (3:10), and the Spirit (3:16).

66. Gk. εὐδοκία.

67. Gk. θέλημα. Louw and Nida §30.59.

68. Barth, 81.

6 It was God's intention that his free and glad choice of men and women to be his sons and daughters might redound *to the praise of his glorious grace*. This compound phrase is similar to those of vv. 12 and 14, although in the present context the emphasis is on God's *grace*, rather than his glory, as the object of praise. (The additional relative clause which focusses on God's gracious pouring out of his love in the Beloved underscores this stress on divine grace.) Grace is a key theme in Ephesians: it is through grace that we are saved (2:5, 8), the forgiveness of our trespasses is in accordance with the riches of divine grace (1:7), while Paul's receiving the gospel, his calling to minister to the Gentiles, and his ability to fulfil his missionary task from beginning to end were due solely to the grace of God (see on 3:2, 7-8).

In this full phrase which focusses on the divine purpose that believers should praise God for his grace, the noun 'glory' (in the genitive case) is used adjectivally to assert that this grace is truly *glorious*. 'Glory' is used often in the Bible to describe the manifestation of God's presence with his people; it refers to his saving presence. Glory is frequently described in terms of a brilliant light (Exod. 16:10; 1 Kings 8:10-11; Ezek. 10:3-4). To say, then, that God's grace is truly *glorious* means that it reflects his glory, his revealed character, and is therefore worthy of our praise. If God's choice of men and women to be his sons and daughters arises from his grace, then the final goal of this divine predestination is that it might resound to the praise of that glorious grace.

The refrain, *to the praise of his glorious grace*, which is repeated in vv. 12 and 14, would suggest that a stage has now been completed. We are driven on, however, by the relative clause, which makes a further important statement about God's glorious grace and prepares us for its manifestation in history (vv. 7-9).[69] This clause[70] stresses that it is in the Beloved, Jesus Christ, that God has poured out all his grace upon us. The verb rendered *freely given* is cognate with the noun *grace*,[71] and emphasizes the abundance of God's gift of salvation as well as implying his generous attitude as the giver. In this paragraph grace and salvation are virtually synonymous.

The expression 'in the Beloved' continues the notion that all of God's blessings come to us 'in Christ' (vv. 3, 4; cf. 5). 'Beloved' marks out Christ as the supreme object of the Father's love; at Colossians 1:13

---

69. Best, 127.

70. The relative ἧς ('which') has been attracted to the antecedent χάριτος ('grace') in the genitive case; cf. BDF §294(2).

71. χαριτόω means to 'bestow favor upon, favor highly' and within the New Testament (cf. Luke 1:28) and early Christian literature is only used with reference to the divine χάρις (BAGD, 879; cf. Louw and Nida §88.66).

he is called 'the Son of his love'. This designation may have been a messianic title among Jews of the first century A.D., although there is no certain evidence for this pre-Christian usage. It became a messianic title among early Christians (Ignatius, *Letter to the Smyrnaeans; Barnabas* 3:6; 4:3, 8), having been used in the Old Testament of Israel as God's beloved people (Deut. 33:12; Isa. 5:1, 7; Jer. 11:15; 12:7).[72] At his baptism and transfiguration Jesus is named by the Father as his 'beloved Son' (Mark 1:11; 9:7 and parallels; cf. 12:6; Luke 20:13). Elsewhere in Paul's letters this description of Israel as 'the beloved' is applied to believers in the context of their election (1 Thess. 1:4; 2 Thess. 2:13; Rom. 9:25; Col. 3:12): they have been chosen in Christ the Beloved, and are dearly loved by God. The term "Beloved" here in v. 6 shows that God's election of believers to be his sons and daughters is intimately related to their being in Christ the Chosen One (cf. v. 5), and that the bounty which he lavishes on them 'consists in their being caught up into the love which subsists between the Father and the Son'[73] (cf. John 3:35; 5:20; 17:23, 26).

3. Praise for Redemption and the Forgiveness of Sins, 1:7-8

7-8 Having blessed God for his election and adoption of men and women 'in Christ', Paul next praises him for his redemption and the forgiveness of our trespasses 'in the Beloved'. This stage in God's saving purposes occurs on the plane of history. Those who praise God for his glorious grace freely given in Christ can rejoice in a deliverance from their trespasses through his sacrificial death on the cross.

Redemption, which connotes liberation from imprisonment and bondage, is not simply the object of our hope (though it does have this significance at the conclusion of the eulogy, v. 14; cf. Eph. 4:30; Rom. 8:23). Here it is an existing reality, a present possession (note the verb *we have*),[74] as elsewhere in the Pauline writings (Rom. 3:24; 1 Cor. 1:30; Col. 1:14), and is 'bound up strictly with the person of Jesus'.[75] It is 'in the Beloved' that we have this deliverance, for God made him to be our redemption (1 Cor. 1:30). The Pauline concept of redemption has its antecedents in the Old Testament, where it describes the release of slaves (Exod. 21:8; cf. Lev. 25:48) and more particularly God's mighty deliver-

---

72. ἠγαπημένος ('beloved') appears in the LXX for the 'pet name' *Jerushurun* at Deut. 32:15; 33:5, 26; Isa. 44:2.

73. Caird, 36.

74. The present tense, ἔχομεν ('we have'), stands in contrast to the surrounding aorists.

75. F. Büchsel, *TDNT* 4:354.

ance of his people from the bondage of Egypt (Deut. 7:8; 9:26; 13:5; 1 Chron. 17:21, etc.). On occasion, there is specific mention of the ransom price paid in order to effect such redemption.[76] Paul asserts that believers have been bought with a price (1 Cor. 6:20; 7:23), and that Christ redeemed us from the curse of the law by becoming a curse for us (Gal. 3:13; cf. 4:5). In Ephesians 1:7 the redemption which we have in the Beloved has been procured *through his blood.* This abbreviated expression is pregnant with meaning, and signifies that Christ's violent death on the cross as a sacrifice is the *means* by which our deliverance has been won (cf. Rom. 3:25).[77] It was obtained at very great cost.

The *redemption* in view is equated with, or at least in apposition to, *the forgiveness of sins,*[78] for it involved a rescue from God's just judgment on our trespasses. As a result we now have free access to our heavenly Father, knowing that we have been redeemed and forgiven. Redemption, forgiveness, and Christ's sacrifice are occasionally linked in the New Testament, forming an early Christian triad that may have been used for liturgical and catechetical purposes (cf. Rom. 3:24-25; Tit. 2:14; Rev. 1:5). The 'forgiveness of *sins*' (lit. 'trespasses')[79] does not occur frequently in Paul's writings. Normally he refers to 'sin' in the singular, as a power which entered the world through Adam's action (Rom. 5:12) and since then has tyrannized men and women until that power was broken by Christ's death on the cross (Rom. 8:3, etc.). However, 'forgiveness of sins' is implicit in the great Pauline themes of justification (cf. Rom. 4:5-8) and reconciliation, so too much should not be made of this 'omission'. 'Forgiveness of sins' is mentioned with reference to John's baptism (Mark 1:4), while in the Acts of the Apostles it is repeat-

76. L. Morris, *The Apostolic Preaching of the Cross* (London: Tyndale, 1965), claims that the terminology of redemption *invariably* conveys the idea of release on payment of a price or ransom. He states: 'When the New Testament speaks of redemption, . . . it means that Christ has paid the price of our redemption' (58). *Linguistically* this has been challenged by D. Hill, *Greek Words and Hebrew Meanings: Studies in the Semantics of Soteriological Terms* (Cambridge: Cambridge University Press, 1967), 73-74 (cf. Lincoln, 27-28), and qualified by I. H. Marshall, 'The Development of the Concept of Redemption in the New Testament', in *Reconciliation and Hope: New Testament Essays on Atonement and Eschatology, Presented to L. L. Morris on His 60th Birthday*, ed. R. J. Banks (Exeter: Paternoster, 1974), 153-54. Marshall acknowledges that Christ's death is the 'price' paid for our redemption; however, it is not expressly in view on every occasion that redemption language is mentioned.

77. J. Behm, *TDNT* 1:174: 'The interest of the NT is not in the material blood of Christ, but in His shed blood as the life violently taken from Him. Like the cross, the "blood of Christ" is simply another and even more graphic phrase for the death of Christ in its soteriological significance'. Cf. L. Morris, *Preaching*, 112-28.

78. Cf. D. B. Wallace, *Greek Grammar*, 199.

79. On the relationship of 'trespasses' and 'sins', see on 2:1.

edly cited as the content of salvation (Acts 2:38; 5:31; 10:43; 13:38; 26:18). Because men and women apart from Christ are 'dead in trespasses and sins' (Eph. 2:1), divine forgiveness is essential to the restoration of a relationship with the Father.

Significantly, the references to our sin and to the divine redemption and forgiveness are framed by important statements about the grace which God has lavished on us (vv. 6b, 7c-8a).[80] The decisive rescue from divine judgment on our trespasses is wholly in keeping with *the riches of God's grace that he lavished on us.* Moreover, these riches of divine grace are the ultimate cause of our redemption, for the preposition which speaks of the norm that governs something (= 'in accordance with') at the same time provides the reason (= 'because') for that deliverance.[81] This statement about the abundance of divine grace has been intensified by means of the noun 'riches'[82] — in Colossians and Ephesians the 'wealth of God' is a prominent idea pointing to the lavish bestowal of his blessings in Christ (Col. 1:27; 2:2-3; Eph. 1:18; 3:8, 16) — and the verb 'lavish',[83] which, with their connotations of wealth and extravagance, make it crystal clear that the readers' redemption is all of grace. Words are hardly adequate to describe the inexhaustible nature of God's giving (cf. Eph. 2:7; Rom. 5:15, 20).

Although some interpreters have taken the expression 'with all wisdom and insight' as qualifying what follows, namely, 'he made known' (v. 9), and referring to God's own wisdom and insight (cf. NRSV, TEV),[84] on balance it is better to link them with the preceding relative clause, *that he lavished on us* (cf. NEB, NIV, JB), and to understand them of God's gifts of grace. Similar spiritual gifts are sought for the readers in the prayer of 1:17, while in the parallel passage of Colossians 1:9 Paul prays that the believers might be filled 'with all spiritual wisdom and understanding'. The phrase then gives a good rhythmic flow and allows this unit of the text (v. 8) to end as the previous one (v. 6), that is, with a relative clause and prepositional phrase which foreshadow the theme of the following unit.[85] The generous bestowal of God's grace is accompanied by[86] other

80. Schnackenburg, 56, states: 'The expression "according to the riches of his grace" is nothing other than a resumption and intensification of the thought in v. 6'.

81. Gk. κατά. BAGD, 407.

82. Gk. πλοῦτος.

83. Gk. περισσεύω.

84. Best, 132-33, makes a good case for this interpretation.

85. Schnackenburg, 48; cf. Lincoln, 17, 29; C. C. Caragounis, *Mysterion,* 93; and recently Hoehner.

86. Note Bruce, 260, who claims that the ἐν is comitative, signifying 'along with [all wisdom and insight]'.

spiritual gifts, namely, all wisdom and insight, which are mentioned because of their relevance to what follows.

The themes of wisdom, understanding (note the parallel Col. 1:9),
and insight were frequently found in various combinations in the LXX.[87]
In the writings of the Qumran community 'knowledge', 'insight', and
'wisdom' were understood as gifts of God which he had imparted by his
Spirit (1QS 4:3-4; 1QSb 5:25) to the faithful members of the community.
Here the second term, 'insight', consistent with the author's style of
heaping up synonymous terms, probably reinforces the more general
term 'wisdom' and forms one idea with it.[88] God's lavish grace has bestowed on us not only redemption, but along with this all the necessary
wisdom and insight by which we should live wisely (cf. 5:15), particularly in the light of his saving plan in Christ (which is developed in what
follows).

4. Praise for the Mystery — God's Plan to Sum Up All Things in Christ, 1:9-10

9 God intended that we should understand his saving purposes.
He therefore lavished his grace upon us 'in all wisdom and insight' by
making *known*[89] *to us the mystery of his will*,[90] the content of which is the
summing up of all things in Christ (see v. 10b). Although v. 9 is syntactically dependent upon and explains the meaning of God's grace poured
upon us (v. 8), with these words about the divine mystery there is a significant development in the eulogy, leading to its climax. God's saving
purposes, planned from eternity, had as their final goal the uniting of all

---

87. The respective terms are σοφία ('wisdom') and φρόνησις ('insight'). See Exod.
31:3; 35:31, 35; Deut. 34:9; 1 Chron. 22:12; Prov. 1:2; 3:19; 8:1; Jer. 10:12; Dan. 2:21, etc.

88. At Colossae Paul's expression 'all wisdom' (Col. 1:9, 28; 3:16) was to be understood against the syncretistic, religious background of Asia Minor. The false teaching
making inroads into that community had only 'the appearance of wisdom' (Col. 2:23),
but in Christ all the treasures of wisdom and knowledge were stored up (2:3).

89. The precise relationship between the aorist participle γνωρίσας ('made known')
and the principal verb ἐπερίσσευσεν ('he lavished') is disputed (cf. vv. 4, 5). C. C.
Caragounis, *Mysterion*, 93, considers the participle independent, carrying on the argument to the next stage. But others, including many earlier commentators and more recently S. E. Porter, *Verbal Aspect*, 384; and D. B. Wallace, *Greek Grammar*, 625, rightly think
that the participle following the main verb describes coincident action: 'he lavished his
grace on us in all wisdom and insight in that he made known to us the mystery of his
will'.

90. According to C. C. Caragounis, *Mysterion*, 93-94, the genitive 'of his will' (τοῦ
θελήματος αὐτοῦ) is one of apposition, and rendered, 'he made known to us the mystery,
namely, what he willed'.

things in heaven and earth in Christ, the details of which are spelled out in what follows.

'Making known a mystery' refers to the disclosure of a previously hidden secret. In Paul's world 'mystery' was employed in the ancient pagan cults, philosophy, secular usage, and Gnosticism. Recent biblical scholarship, however, has focussed attention on the Old Testament and Judaism, particularly the wisdom literature and apocalyptic material, as the proper background for understanding Paul's and other New Testament writers' use of 'mystery' language. In apocalyptic writings it normally referred to an event that will be revealed at the end of history (4 Ezra 14:5), although God's seers may know of it because he has revealed to them 'the things that must come to pass' (LXX Dan. 2:28-29). 'Mystery' translates the Aramaic equivalent, frequently found in the book of Daniel (2:18, 19, 27, etc.), and this provides several parallels with its use in Ephesians: it connotes God's purpose, which is a unified plan with eschatological and cosmic dimensions.[91]

'Mystery', which appears twenty-one times in Paul's letters (out of a total of twenty-seven New Testament occurrences), is used in a variety of ways, though the apostle normally employs the term with reference to the revelation of what was previously hidden but has now been disclosed by God (Rom. 16:25-26; 1 Cor. 2:10; Col. 1:26-27; Eph. 3:3, 5). The 'mystery of God' (1 Cor. 2:1 *v.l.*; cf. v. 7) focusses on salvation through the cross of Jesus Christ. It cannot be understood through human wisdom but comes to be known as God reveals it by his Spirit to those who love him (v. 10). The plural 'mysteries' can draw attention to the essential elements of the one mystery (1 Cor. 4:1), or anything that transcends human power of comprehending (13:2; cf. 14:2). In Romans 16:25 there is a correlation between the disclosure of the mystery and Paul's preaching of Jesus Christ. The connection between the mystery and the salvation of *Gentiles* is a feature that is developed in Colossians and Ephesians, while in Romans 11:25 an element of new teaching may be in view where the 'mystery' points to the salvation of *Jews*.

In Colossians 'mystery' refers to the heart of Paul's message and has to do with the fulfilment of God's plan of salvation in Christ here and now (1:26-27). This 'open secret' is characterized by 'riches' (for in it the wealth of God has been lavished in a wonderful way) and 'glory', which

---

91. The Aramaic *rāz* ('mystery, secret'). C. C. Caragounis, *Mysterion*, 134-35. On 'mystery' in Paul, see G. Bornkamm, *TDNT* 4:802-28; R. E. Brown, *The Semitic Background of the Term "Mystery" in the New Testament* (Philadelphia: Fortress, 1968); and M. N. A. Bockmuehl, *Revelation*.

suggests that it shares in the character of God himself. Its content is 'Christ in you [Colossians], the hope of glory' (cf. 2:2; 4:3).

The notion in Colossians of the mystery being the eschatological fulfilment of God's plan of salvation in Christ is similar to the usage in Ephesians: 1:9; 3:3, 4, 9; 5:32; and 6:19. Different aspects of this one mystery are unfolded within Ephesians. This key motif refers to the all-inclusive purpose of God which has as its ultimate goal the uniting of all things in heaven and earth in Christ. At the same time, there is a more limited dimension to the mystery which focusses on Gentiles, along with Jews, being incorporated into the body of Christ and thus participating in the divine salvation. Paul's making the gospel known to Gentiles plays a key role in achieving this purpose of incorporating them into Christ, and ultimately fulfilling the goal of the mystery itself. It is, therefore, inappropriate to claim that the content of the mystery in Ephesians is defined *solely* in terms of God's acceptance of the Gentiles and their union with Jews on an equal footing in Christ (Eph. 3:3-4). Christ is the starting point for a true understanding of the mystery in this letter, as elsewhere in Paul. There are not a number of 'mysteries' with limited applications, but one supreme 'mystery' with a number of applications.[92]

The words '[he made known] *to us*' show that there is not only a salvation-historical dimension to the mystery but also a personal one. The recipients of this disclosure are the Christian community,[93] who are thus able to praise God for his great kindness lavished on them.[94] They are not some group of initiates but those who have received the word of God, for it is in the effective preaching and teaching of the gospel that the revelation of the mystery takes place (cf. 1 Cor. 2:1, 7; 4:1; Eph. 3:8, 9; 6:19). Later in the eulogy (vv. 11-14; cf. 3:2-13) Paul will explain how both Jews and Gentiles are included within the sphere of these blessings related to the mystery. As God's choice of believers to be adopted as his sons and daughters was *in accordance with his pleasure and will* (v. 5), so, too, his making known the mystery of his salvation plan was wholly in line with his sovereign and eternal purpose which he had previously determined

---

92. C. C. Caragounis, *Mysterion*, 143.

93. At Qumran 'mystery' can refer to an event which has already been realized in the community; cf. 1QS 11:5-8.

94. Precisely how God has *made known* the mystery of his will is not yet spelled out. It becomes clearer in the course of the letter: God had revealed it to his holy apostles and prophets by the Spirit (Eph. 3:5) and granted Paul special insight (3:3). The apostle proclaimed the unsearchable riches of Christ to the Gentiles and made plain to everyone the administration of this mystery (vv. 8-9). The verb γνωρίζω ('make known') is an established one in the vocabulary of revelation and is used by Paul at 3:3, 5, 10; 6:19 (cf. v. 21; Rom. 9:23; 16:26; 1 Cor. 12:3; 15:1; 2 Cor. 8:1; Gal. 1:11; Col. 1:27).

in Christ. 'God's carefully designed strategy to make known the mystery, like the mystery itself, has always had its focus in Christ'.[95]

10 The content of the mystery, which is now specified at this high point of the eulogy,[96] is impressively formulated in the explanatory infinitive clause of v. 10b: it is 'to sum up all things in Christ, things in heaven and on earth'. The increasing consensus among modern scholars is that the unusual verb used here derives from a word meaning the 'main point', 'sum', or 'summary' (cf. Acts 22:28; Heb. 8:1) rather than 'head', and that its basic meaning is 'to bring something to a main point', or 'to sum up'.[97] In connection with Christ's eschatological relationship to a multitude of entities (including personal beings), the text suggests that God's 'summing up' of these entities in Christ is his act of 'bringing all things together in (and under) Christ, i.e. his unifying of them in some way in Christ'.[98]

Throughout the rest of the eulogy God's grand purpose is said to be 'in Christ'; the same holds true for the finale, the summing up, as the concluding words of v. 10, 'in him', emphatically reiterate. Although this expression might be understood as instrumental, suggesting that the *Messiah*[99] is the means (or instrument) through whom God sums up the universe, it is better to take the phrase as referring to him as the sphere, in line with the earlier instances of this phrase within the paragraph (vv. 3-7, 9). Christ is the one *in whom* God chooses to sum up the cosmos, the one

---

95. Lincoln, 31.

96. Syntactically and structurally, the explication of the mystery in terms of the *anakephalaiōsis* ('summing up') is the 'high point' of the eulogy, or, as T. Moritz puts it, the 'pivotal statement' of the passage; T. Moritz, 'Summing Up All Things', 96. The RSV, NEB, and NIV represent this by beginning a new sentence.

97. ἀνακεφαλαιόω is thought to come from κεφάλαιον ('main point, summary') rather than κεφαλή ('head'). This suggestion appears to fit the only other New Testament use at Rom. 13:9, where the commandments of the second table of the Decalogue are summarized in the command to love one's neighbour, but this basic meaning is also appropriate in view of its usage for speech or letter conclusions throughout ancient Greek rhetoric down to Roman times (cf. Ps. 71:20 Theodotion). Whether the verb ἀνακεφαλαιώσασθαι ('to sum up') was chosen because it contains an echo of the term κεφαλή ('head') is doubtful; cf. G. W. Dawes, *The Body in Question: Metaphor and Meaning in the Interpretation of Ephesians 5:21-33* (Leiden/Boston/Köln: Brill, 1998), 142-44, esp. 143.

98. M. Turner, 'Mission', 139, following Lincoln, 33. Recent research based on evidence from the *Thesaurus Linguae Graecae* also supports the meaning 'sum up'; so J. B. Maclean, 'Eph 1:10 in Patristic Exegesis: Controlling the Meaning of a Volatile Tradition', SBL Paper in the 'Pauline Epistles Section' read on November 20, 1994, in Chicago. See also M. Kitchen, 'The ἀνακεφαλαίωσις of All Things in Christ: Theology and Purpose in the Epistle to the Ephesians' (unpublished Ph.D. thesis, Manchester, 1988), and his *Ephesians* (London/New York: Routledge, 1994), 35-42.

99. The Greek ἐν τῷ Χριστῷ might signify this.

in whom he restores harmony to the universe. He is the focal point, not simply the means, the instrument, or the functionary through whom all this occurs. The previous examples of 'in Christ' and its equivalents within the *berakah* focussed on the Son as God's chosen one in whom believers have been blessed. Now in vv. 9 and 10 the stress is placed on the one in whom God's overarching purposes for the *whole* of the created order are included. The emphasis is now on a universe that is centred and reunited in Christ.[100] The mystery which God has graciously made known refers to the summing up and bringing together of the fragmented and alienated elements of the universe ('all things') in Christ as the focal point.

The divine intention to sum up 'all things' as a whole in Christ is amplified by the following parallel statement, 'things in heaven and things on earth'. At first glance, these additional words seem to be simply a rhetorical flourish. After all, is it not just a typical way, in biblical terms, of speaking of the whole or totality by referring to 'things in heaven' and 'on earth'? In particular, the opening words of the Bible, 'In the beginning God created the heavens and the earth' (Gen. 1:1), signify that God made *everything.* But on closer examination it is evident that the two phrases, 'things in heaven' and 'things on earth', are not simply a rhetorical flourish to describe some cosmic reality. They represent two important strands running throughout the epistle which signify two separate spheres or domains. Ephesians has distinctive things to say about 'the heavenlies' (1:3, 10, 20; 2:6; 3:10; 6:12; cf. 3:15; 4:10; 6:9) as well as about 'the things on earth' (1:10; 3:15; 4:9; 6:3). A proper understanding of God's intention of summing up everything in Christ has to do with each of these two spheres and what is represented by them, as well as with the bond between the two. The *anakephalaiōsis* in Christ has to do with each realm. At the same time there is an inseparable connection between them, so that we may speak of both heaven and earth being summed up as a totality in him.[101]

In his monograph dealing with the mystery in Ephesians, Chrys Caragounis[102] claims that as Paul proceeds to amplify and explain throughout the letter the meaning of bringing all things together, he concentrates on the two main representatives of these spheres, namely, the *powers* representing 'the things in heaven', and the *church* (particularly the unity of Jews and Gentiles in the body of Christ) representing 'the things on earth'. He further suggests that the two obstacles which

---

100. Lincoln, 34.
101. A. T. Lincoln, in *Theology,* 96-97.
102. C. C. Caragounis, *Mysterion,* 144-46, cf. 96.

need to be overcome before the divine purposes of bringing everything back into unity in Christ can be fulfilled are: (a) the rebellion of the powers, and (b) the alienation of Jews from Gentiles (2:11-22, as well as the estrangement of both from God, 2:16). Much of the rest of Ephesians is given over to explaining, with reference to each of these two spheres, the steps in the process that God has taken in order to achieve this supreme goal.

As to the timing of the *anakephalaiōsis*, the summing up of all things together in Christ, the text indicates that while the content of the mystery has been revealed (v. 9), the outworking of God's saving purposes has not been completed.[103] The apocalyptic expression *when the times will have reached their fulfilment* looks forward to the occasion when this will take place. The important word employed here,[104] which in the Greek world was regularly used of God's ordering and administration of the universe, has an active sense of his 'ordering, arranging or implementing' the mystery, his secret purpose.[105] The term refers to 'the manner in which the purpose of God is being worked out in human history',[106] rather than the content of that purpose or saving plan (a technical meaning it has in the second century). 'The fulness of times' in apocalyptic literature indicated 'a sequence of periods of time under God's direction' (cf. LXX Dan. 2:21; 4:37; also 1QS 4:18; 1QM 14:14), while the term 'fulness' suggests that this sequence of time will come to its appointed climax or full measure.[107] Accordingly, the expression may be rendered 'for implementing in the fulness of times'.[108] According to Galatians 4:4, 'when the fulness of time had come', that is, when the time was ripe for his coming, God sent his Son into the world. When the time is ripe for 'the consummation of his purpose, in his

103. An architect's plan for a building which is submitted well in advance of the actual construction of the building may be a helpful analogy. God has revealed his perfect plan, and in Christ he has taken decisive steps to bring it to completion. We still await its consummation.

104. Gk. οἰκονομία.

105. H. Kuhli, *EDNT* 2:500; against BAGD, 559-60; see the discussion of οἰκονομία at 3:2.

106. Robinson, 145. οἰκονομία can designate (1) the act of ordering, arranging, or administering (Eph. 1:10; 3:9), (2) that which is administered, the salvation plan itself, and (3) the office or task of the administrator (e.g., Paul: 1 Cor. 4:1; 9:17; Eph. 3:2; Col. 1:25). Many instances of the οἰκονομία terminology in Paul occur in close proximity to the word 'mystery', suggesting that the latter was important for understanding the meaning of οἰκονομία.

107. Lincoln, 32. The term πλήρωμα ('fulness') is not used here in a technical theological sense. See further on 1:23.

108. The genitive τοῦ πληρώματος τῶν καιρῶν ('of the fulness of times') is one of definition (so Robinson, 145).

providential overruling of the course of the world, that consummation will be realized'.[109]

The aorist infinitive 'to bring all things into unity' points not to the past, but signifies purpose: the summing up of all things is the goal to be achieved.[110] This is not to suggest that the implementation of the divine plan is not already under way. Indeed, the letter makes it quite plain that significant steps have already been taken to set in motion the achievement of this goal: in particular, it is through Jesus' saving work that the revelation of the mystery's content has come about (1:7-9), while God's placing all things under his feet and appointing him to be *head* over everything for the church (1:22) is an important step towards the fulfilment of this goal. But the summing up awaits the consummation which will occur at the end.

Both Ephesians and the companion Letter to the Colossians presuppose that the unity and harmony of the cosmos have suffered a considerable dislocation, even a rupture, requiring reconciliation or restoration to harmony. At Colossians 1:20-22 the apostle speaks of a reconciliation of 'all things' to God that has *already been effected* by the death of Christ, and the particular focus is the reconciliation of human beings to him. The later reference in Colossians to the conquest of the principalities (2:15) is to be understood in the light of God's mighty reconciliation and pacification (1:20). Ephesians 2:1-3 particularly draws attention to the desperate plight of men and women outside of Christ, and their situation is described in terms of death, condemnation, and bondage to evil, determining influences. Apart from God's mighty and gracious intervention to save, there could be no hope for rebel sinners in the midst of this profound need (2:4-7). Unlike Colossians, where the reconciliation has already been effected through Christ's death, Ephesians points to the summing up of the universe in Christ as the final goal of God's plan which has *not yet* been realized. The

109. Bruce, 262. According to M. Turner, 'Mission', 142, 'the fulness of the times' includes, if not principally denotes, 'the times which follow the end of "this evil age"' (1:21; cf. 2:2; 5:16; 6:13). That fulness may commence with the Christ-event (so M. Barth, Schnackenburg, and Lincoln), but 'the author can hardly be suspected of believing the cosmic . . . [summing up] has been completed'. A. Lindemann, *Die Aufhebung,* 95-96, rejects any reference to the climax of history in this phrase. He thinks that all temporal categories have been suspended in Christ, and one cannot therefore make a distinction between history and eschatology. But as Lincoln, 32, rightly comments: 'This is to ignore completely the apocalyptic background of the terminology of this verse, its context in early Christian eschatology, and the continuity between Ephesians and Paul's gospel'. Note also the treatment of Arnold, 145-58.

110. Against A. Lindemann, *Die Aufhebung,* 96-99, who eliminates any future connotations from the term and argues that the 'summing up' has already occurred. He claims that the aorist infinitive points to the past!

content of the mystery has already been disclosed (1:9), and as a result of his Son's exaltation God has already placed all things under Christ's feet and appointed him to be Head over everything (vv. 20-22).

5. Praise for the Assurance of the Believers' Heritage, 1:11-14

Verses 11-14 continue the long sentence which began at v. 3, and their connection with the preceding (v. 10) is made by means of the relative pronoun 'in *whom*', which again focusses on Christ as the one in whom believers are incorporated. For the sake of clarity, however, translations and commentaries commence a new paragraph at v. 11, which stresses that God's blessings belong to Jewish and Gentile believers alike (see the discussion below). The structure of vv. 11-14 shows that both groups participate in God's grace. There is a movement from *we* (vv. 11-12; which includes Paul and his fellow Jewish believers) to *you also* (v. 13; a reference to Gentile readers) and on to *our* inheritance (v. 14; in which both groups share equally). This anticipates the motif of the reconciliation of Jews and Gentiles in Ephesians 2:14-18, a reconciliation with God and with one another which has been effected through Christ's death on the cross.

11-12 The Christ who is at the centre of God's plan to sum up all things in heaven and on earth is also the one in whom we were claimed by God as his portion. The unusual verb which appears means to 'appoint or choose by lot'; in the passive voice (used here) it can signify to 'be appointed by lot'. It has been taken more generally to mean 'we were destined or chosen' (a nuance it has in the papyri; cf. RSV), and is thus synonymous with terms of election in vv. 4 and 5. But doubts have been raised about this translation; hence the NEB renders the passive as 'we have been given our share in the heritage', that is, 'we were assigned our portion' by God, thereby referring to the inheritance we received from him (cf. AV). But the rendering 'we were claimed by God as his portion' brings out the passive voice more accurately[111] and is at the same time more in keeping with Old Testament precedent. In the Song of Moses (Deut. 32:8-9) the nations of the world are assigned to 'the sons of God', that is, to various angelic beings, but the Lord retains Israel as his personal possession:

> For the LORD's portion is his people,
> Jacob his allotted inheritance.
> (Cf. Ps. 33:12; Deut. 4:20; 9:29; 1 Kings 8:51; Ps. 106:40, etc.).

111. Note Robinson's well-reasoned conclusion: 'the meaning must be *"we have been chosen as God's portion"'* (146).

Now men and women *in Christ* are God's chosen people, having been claimed by him as his inheritance.[112] But who are the *we* that have become God's portion? At first glance the clause appears simply to be describing all Christians, that is, the same recipients of all the other blessings in Christ mentioned in the eulogy of vv. 3-10. However, at v. 11 the *we* is restricted, for in the following verse the same people[113] are spoken of as those who 'first hoped in Christ' (v. 12). The reference is to Paul and his fellow Jewish believers.[114] The Gentile readers of the letter are not included in this designation, but are explicitly mentioned, in some sense by way of contrast, in the *you* of v. 13.

Against this distinction it has been claimed that everything asserted in vv. 11-12 applies to believers in general:[115] their predestination by God, their appointment for the praise of his glory, and the fact that they have *already* hoped in Christ are regarded as equally appropriate to Jewish and Gentile believers. This case, however, is unconvincing for the following reasons: (a) Although it is correct to say that both Jews and Gentiles have been predestined and appointed for the praise of God's glory (cf. vv. 4, 5), this particular point is not being made in vv. 11 and 12. Instead, it is being asserted that within the wider purposes of God's saving plan, it was those of Jewish origin, the more immediate heirs of 'the covenants of promise', who accepted the Lord Jesus Christ first (perhaps including the original disciples of Jesus together with others like Paul), that have been chosen for this goal of *the praise of his glory*. They represent the people of God, the believing remnant of Israel, who have been claimed by God as his portion. This interpretation fits exactly with the Song of Moses (Deut. 32:8-9) already cited, and the other Old Testament texts, where the Lord's *portion* is his people, Jacob/Israel. Jews who accepted the Lord Jesus Christ first are the remnant in whom these Old Testament promises have been fulfilled. (b) The significance of the change to the second person plu-

---

112. Bruce, 263. According to Col. 1:12 the believers at Colossae have been fitted by God for a share in an eternal inheritance of God's holy people, an inheritance that belongs to a higher plane and a more lasting order than any earthly Canaan. It could not be ravaged by war, famine, or the like since it belongs to the realm of light in the age to come.

113. There is no break between vv. 11 and 12: the 'we' of ἐκληρώθημεν ('we have been chosen', v. 11) is the same as ἡμᾶς . . . τοὺς προηλπικότας ('we who first hoped', v. 12).

114. Ernst, 278; Caird, 40-41; Bruce, 264; G. D. Fee, *God's Empowering Presence*, 669; and I. H. Thomson, *Chiasmus*, 77-79. T. Moritz, 'Summing Up All Things', 97, contends that this interpretation fits in with the salvation-historical priority of the Jews.

115. Lincoln, 9, 36-38. As a variation on this, R. A. Wilson, '"We" and "You" in the Epistle to the Ephesians', *SE* 2, ed. F. L. Cross (Berlin: Akademie-Verlag, 1964), 676-80, thinks that 'we' in Ephesians always refers to all believers. 'What is said of "us", then, is applicable to all Christians; what is said of "you" to new converts, or to the newly baptized' (677).

ral ('you') at v. 13 is not adequately explained on the alternate view. (c) The rendering of the verb by '[we] who have *already* hoped [in Christ]' is, in my judgment, less than satisfactory (see below). (d) It may be questioned as to whether the theological significance of the Jew-Gentile question in the letter and its relation to the mystery have been taken sufficiently into account. One should not be surprised at its anticipation in vv. 3-14.[116] Many of the important theological themes of the letter are prefigured in the introductory eulogy.[117] (e) Finally, the return to the first person plural 'we', speaking of all Christians in v. 14, does not tell 'overwhelmingly against such a proposal', as Lincoln contends. Having mentioned that Jewish Christians were claimed by God as his portion and that believing Gentiles, too, were sealed with the Holy Spirit of promise (the very point made in the Cornelius incident of Acts 10 and 11), it is entirely appropriate for Paul to assert that *the promised Holy Spirit* is the guarantee of *our* inheritance, that is, of Jew and Gentile alike (see below). The same kind of argument has been understood of Paul's words to the Galatians in 3:13 and 14.

Although God's salvation-historical plan is under his providential ordering, within this wider purpose Jewish Christians being claimed by him as his portion is emphatically shown to be part and parcel of his sovereign will. Paul picks up his earlier language of predestination[118] and the divine will (v. 5) and applies it now to those who 'first hoped in Christ' being chosen as the Lord's personal possession. Further, as the apostle praises God for this, he reinforces the notion of a special place for them within the divine plan by means of two additional phrases beginning with 'according to' and two synonymous nouns meaning 'plan' and 'decisive resolve'. The one who has acted in this gracious way towards the believing heirs of 'the covenants of promise' is the one who mightily works out *everything*, that is, the sum total of his design, according to his will. His unconditional freedom is stressed, so that whatever he has planned and decided to do will certainly come to pass.

In v. 5 the adoption of believers as God's sons and daughters, which was the purpose of their predestination, redounds to *the praise of his glori-*

---

116. Ernst, 278, aptly comments: 'If one considers the general theme of Ephesians to be "the one church from Jews and Gentiles", then the appearance of the accented "we" (v 11) and "you" (v 13) makes clear sense. Not only to the first called Christians from among the Jews, but also to those from heathenism belongs the gospel of salvation in Jesus Christ'.

117. See P. T. O'Brien, 'Ephesians I', 504-16, where this point is made more fully.

118. The aorist participle προορισθέντες ('having been foreordained', v. 11) is coincidental with the main verb ἐκληρώθημεν ('we were claimed as God's portion', v. 11); cf. S. E. Porter, *Verbal Aspect*, 384.

ous grace. Here also *the praise of his glory* is the object for which those who 'first hoped in Christ'[119] were chosen as the Lord's portion. The outworking of God's gracious purposes for Jews (and Gentiles; cf. v. 14) is for his own glory, and that goal is fulfilled, partially at least, as he is honoured 'in the presence of human beings and angelic powers when men and women, redeemed from sin, live in accordance with his will and display the family likeness which stamps them as his children'.[120]

13 The Lord's heritage or personal possession, however, is not limited to Jewish believers, for Gentile Christians, who are now addressed specifically as *you also*, were sealed with the Holy Spirit of promise and made his own when they heard the message of truth and received it. Within God's eternal purpose in Christ Gentile believers were incorporated into the one people of God. Their share in God's heritage was as complete as those of Jewish birth who first hoped in Christ. Thus, in the new community of the redeemed there are no first- or second-class citizens!

The opening words of v. 13, 'in him you also', are incomplete. Part of the verb 'to be' may be added to make sense of the ellipsis; cf. the NIV rendering: *you* [Gentiles] *also were included in Christ.* The phrase 'in him' is resumed in the second half of the verse,[121] with reference to the main statement, '[in Christ] you were sealed', indicating that it was *in him* that the seal of the same Holy Spirit, promised to Israel, was received by the Gentiles when they believed.

Like Jewish believers before them, Gentiles heard the gospel and realized that the salvation of which it spoke was for them too. The apostolic announcement which they heard is called *the word of truth, the gospel of your salvation.* This language, which is very similar to that of Colossians 1:5, was part and parcel of the early Christian mission terminology employed by Paul and other evangelists; cf. 'hearing the word' (cf. Rom. 10:14-17; Acts 2:37; 13:7, 44; 19:10), the apostolic gospel as truth (cf. Gal. 2:5, 14; 5:7; 2 Cor. 4:2), as 'the word of the Lord' (1 Thess. 1:8; 2 Thess. 3:1), 'the word of God' (1 Thess. 2:13), 'the word of Christ' (Col. 3:16), and 'the word of life' (Phil. 2:16). This *word of truth* is to be understood against an Old Testament back-

---

119. προελπίζω occurs only here in the New Testament. The prefix προ- can stress the notion of 'ahead of time' or 'beforehand', and thus the compound verb refers either to those who hoped before Christ's coming or, as we have taken it, to Jewish believers, the firstfruits of God's people in the age inaugurated by Christ's death and resurrection. Lincoln, 37, consistent with his view discussed above, understands the prefix as reinforcing the notion already present in the verb. He renders the verb 'we have *already* hoped'. See BAGD, 705; and Louw and Nida §25.60.

120. Bruce, 264.

121. A. T. Robertson, *A Grammar of the Greek New Testament in the Light of Historical Research* (New York: Hodder & Stoughton, 1919), 540.

ground where God's word, spoken and revealed to men and women, partakes of his character and is utterly reliable. So the Psalmist prays, 'take not the word of truth . . . out of my mouth' (Ps. 119:43). In Colossians, where the gospel is called 'the word of truth' (1:5), a contrast with the false teaching of the heretics seems to be intended. Here in Ephesians, the *word of truth* reveals the truth of God, particularly as it is related to his saving purposes and humankind's place within them. The appositional expression, *the gospel*[122] *of your salvation* (cf. Rom. 1:16), with its emphatic personal pronoun *your* reminds the readers of their conversion, and draws attention to what this powerful message has accomplished for them: it has effected 'a rescue operation, a deliverance from spiritual death, from God's wrath, from bondage to evil powers, sin and the flesh'[123] (cf. Eph. 2:1-3; according to 2:5, 8 the readers have been saved through Christ; 5:23).

When the Gentiles believed the gospel, they were sealed with the Holy Spirit of promise.[124] The aorist participle 'believed' is best interpreted in this context as being coincident with the main verb 'you were sealed'. The participle does not here express antecedent action,[125] as though the Gentiles believed and then *subsequently* were sealed with the Holy Spirit. Rather, the believing and being sealed were two sides of the one event. A similar conjunction with the same verb form is found in Acts 19:2, where Paul asks a group of 'disciples' at Ephesus if they received the Holy Spirit when they believed.[126] Here in Ephesians he is called 'the Holy Spirit of promise', which might be a Semitism meaning the Holy Spirit promised in the Old Testament Scriptures[127] and poured out by the

---

122. On the important theme of the 'gospel', see P. Stuhlmacher, 'The Theme: The Gospel and the Gospels', in *The Gospel and the Gospels*, ed. P. Stuhlmacher (Grand Rapids: Eerdmans, 1991), 1-25, esp. 19-23; and his 'The Pauline Gospel', in *The Gospel and the Gospels*, 149-72; and P. T. O'Brien, *Gospel and Mission*, 77-81.

123. Lincoln, 39.

124. J. Adai, *Geist*, 68, consistent with his presentation, claims that the sealing with the Holy Spirit is the high point of the whole eulogy, not only of v. 13. He adds that receiving the Holy Spirit is not simply an aspect of, but also the goal of becoming a Christian.

125. S. E. Porter, *Verbal Aspect*, 383-85, observes that when the aorist participle precedes the main verb, as here, there is a tendency towards antecedent action. He does indicate, however, that there are exceptions, and this appears to be one of them. Cf. Hoehner.

126. Again πιστεύσαντες ('having believed') is to be construed as a coincident aorist participle; cf. J. D. G. Dunn, *Baptism in the Holy Spirit* (London: SCM, 1970), 158-59; Bruce, 265; and Lincoln, 39. G. D. Fee, *God's Empowering Presence*, 670, considers the aorist participle antecedent to the main verb, but he understands this as a logical precedence. He adds that 'the two verbs have nothing to do with separate and distinct experiences of faith'. There is nothing on either grammatical or contextual grounds 'that would cause one to think that Paul intends to refer here to two distinct experiences'.

127. Cf. Gal. 3:14, where the Spirit is the fulfilment of the promise given to Abraham *for the Gentiles*.

exalted Jesus at Pentecost (note Acts 2:33, which speaks of 'the promise of [= which is] the Holy Spirit'). When Gentiles received the Spirit the Old Testament promise was fulfilled, and as in Galatians 3:14 so here the Spirit is to be understood as the content of the promise. On the other hand, the expression has been taken to signify that the Holy Spirit brings the promise of glory yet to come (cf. Eph. 4:30).

In speaking of the Holy Spirit as a *seal* the notions of ownership and protection are in view. Cattle, and even slaves, were branded with a seal by their masters to indicate to whom they belonged. Owners thus guarded their property against theft; in this sense the seal was a protecting sign or a guarantee. In the Old Testament God set a sign on his chosen ones to distinguish them as his own possession and to keep them from destruction (Ezek. 9:4-6). The figure of sealing is used by Paul in relation to the Spirit at 2 Corinthians 1:22: 'God has made them his inviolable possession; the pledge of this is the Spirit of God in the heart'.[128] By giving Gentile believers the Spirit, God 'seals' or stamps them as his own now, and he will be protect them through the trials and testings of this life (cf. 6:10-18) until he takes final possession of them (cf. v. 14) on 'the day of redemption' (4:30).[129]

Although many have claimed that the imagery of sealing by the Holy Spirit corresponds to the experience of baptism, there is no direct reference to baptism in Ephesians 1:13; 4:30 (or 2 Cor. 1:22).[130] In fact, the only specific mention of baptism in Ephesians is at 4:5, in a context which is concerned with unity, not baptism! The sealing is a reference to the actual reception of the Spirit by the readers. The Pauline connection between hearing the gospel, believing, and receiving the Spirit is made, and these are important elements of conversion-initiation.

14 The Holy Spirit by whom the Gentiles were sealed when they believed the gospel is now called the *deposit*[131] *guaranteeing our inheritance.* Behind this translation lies the word that signifies a 'down pay-

128. G. Fitzer, *TDNT* 7:949.

129. Cf. G. D. Fee, *God's Empowering Presence,* 669.

130. G. Fitzer, *TDNT* 7:949. Cf. J. D. G. Dunn, *Baptism,* 160. Arnold, 135, who claims that 'any hint of baptism is extraneous to the context' of Eph. 1:13, argues that the notion of Ephesians being a 'baptismal homily' should be viewed with skepticism. There is only one explicit reference to the term (4:5), 'not for the sake of baptism itself but as one of a number of points that constitute the Christian faith' (see the Introduction).

131. On the textual question whether Paul wrote (or dictated) ὅ ('which'), in agreement with its antecedent πνεῦμα ('Spirit'), or the masculine ὅς ('who'), by attraction to its predicate noun ἀρραβών ('deposit'), see B. M. Metzger, *A Textual Commentary on the Greek New Testament* (Stuttgart: Deutsche Bibelgesellschaft, 1994), 601-2. Either way, the sense is the same and the personhood of the Spirit is not at issue.

ment' or 'pledge',[132] and which in the New Testament is used only in the Pauline writings and always with reference to the Spirit of God. Originally of Semitic origin, this word in Hellenistic Greek became the ordinary commercial term for a down payment or first instalment.[133] According to 2 Corinthians 1:22 the Corinthians received the 'down payment' of the Spirit to guarantee the consummation of their future salvation. Their longing for the heavenly dwelling (2 Cor. 5:1-5) results from the certainty that they have been provided with an advance instalment of the Spirit (cf. Rom. 8:23). Here in v. 14 the Spirit received is the *deposit guaranteeing our inheritance:* in giving him to us God is not simply promising us our final inheritance but actually providing us with a foretaste of it, even if it 'is only a *small fraction* of the future endowment'.[134]

The term 'inheritance'[135] quite fittingly continues the notion of v. 11 (cf. v. 18), 'we were claimed by God as his portion'. There the apostle was speaking of Jewish Christians, who first hoped in Christ, as having been claimed by God as his personal possession, *his* inheritance. Here in the expression *'our* inheritance' the reference is to both Jews and Gentiles[136] who have a sure and certain hope of inheriting the glory of the life to come (cf. v. 18), promised in the gospel. Because of the ministry of the Spirit to their hearts and lives, they can begin to enjoy this everlasting possession *now.* The Spirit received is the first instalment and guarantee of the inheritance in the age to come that awaits God's sons and daughters (v. 5).

The expression which immediately follows, (lit.) 'for the redemption of the possession', has been understood along two main lines. First, some think that the phrase speaks of the way in which believers have received the Spirit as a down-payment or foretaste (v. 14a) of the inheritance which will become *their* possession fully on the future day of redemption (Eph. 4:30). The term rendered 'possession' is taken as a noun of agency pointing

132. Gk. ἀρραβών.

133. The Hebrew word *'ērābôn* appears three times in Gen. 38:17-20 of Judah's personal property handed over to Tamar as a 'pledge'. Cf. BAGD, 109: As a *first instalment* it 'pays a part of the purchase price in advance, and so secures a legal claim to the article in question, or makes a contract valid'; and A. Sand, *EDNT* 1:157-58. The modern Greek form of the word means 'an engagement ring'.

134. Lightfoot, 324.

135. κληρονομία ('inheritance') is cognate with the verb ἐκληρώθημεν (v. 11). On the subject of inheritance generally in Paul, see J. D. Hester, *Paul's Concept of Inheritance: A Contribution to the Understanding of Heilsgeschichte* (Edinburgh: Oliver and Boyd, 1961); and J. H. Friedrich, *EDNT* 2:298-99 (together with the literature cited).

136. G. D. Fee, *God's Empowering Presence,* 669, rightly observes that 'with a subtle shift of pronouns Paul moves from "our" (= Jews) having obtained the inheritance, to "your" (= Gentiles) having been sealed by the "promised Holy Spirit," to the Spirit as God's down payment on "our" (= Jew and Gentile together) final inheritance'.

to believers 'possessing' their inheritance. It is claimed that at 1 Thessalonians 5:9 and 2 Thessalonians 2:14 the word denotes Christians' acquisition of final salvation or glory, and it is to be understood along similar lines here. So the phrase is regarded as temporal and is rendered 'until the redemption, the acquisition (of our inheritance)'.[137]

The second line of interpretation, which is more likely, takes the expression as referring to believers as God's possession rather than their possessing the promised inheritance.[138] Elsewhere in the New Testament *redemption* is always an act of God. Here, too, he is the agent of redemption and the one who possesses his people. He has made them his own; they are his treasured possession. In the Old Testament God's people Israel are called by Yahweh 'my own possession from among all peoples' (Exod. 19:5; cf. Deut. 14:2; 26:18, and especially Mal. 3:17, '"They will be mine", says the LORD Almighty, "in the day when I make up my treasured possession"'). This term occurs in the same sense in 1 Peter 2:9, where believers are called 'a chosen race, a royal priesthood, a holy nation, a people for [God's own] *possession*'. The whole phrase '*for* the redemption of the possession' does not have a purely temporal sense; instead, it indicates the goal of the action described in the main verb, 'you were sealed'.[139] When God sealed and guaranteed Gentile believers with his Holy Spirit, he had in view their full and final redemption as his prized possession. Redemption, which is a present 'spiritual blessing' at 1:7, here signifies the final deliverance (cf. 4:30), when God takes full and complete possession of those who are already his.

That the language used in the Old Testament of Israel as the Lord's treasured possession should now be applied to Gentile believers was good news indeed. As those who had previously been 'separated from Christ, strangers to the covenants of promise, without hope and without God in the world' (2:12), they now have a sure place within the community of God's own people. They fully share 'present blessing and future hope with their fellow-believers of Jewish stock'.[140]

The praise of God's glory was the object for which those 'who first hoped in Christ' were chosen (v. 12). Now as a climactic parallel to what has preceded, God's *final* aim in sealing Gentile believers with the Holy

---

137. So recently Schnackenburg, 45, 67, who is one of a number taking this line.

138. See, e.g., I. H. Marshall, in *Reconciliation,* 161-62; Bruce, 266-67; and Lincoln, 41-42.

139. 'For the redemption of the possession' has been grammatically related to the guarantee in the preceding phrase rather than the main verb 'you were sealed' (cf. NAB, 'the first payment against the full redemption of a people God has made his own'). The difference in meaning, however, is not great.

140. Bruce, 267.

Spirit is joyfully presented as *to the praise of his glory.* Gentile Christians ('you also') have been assigned the same ultimate destination predicated of Jewish believers (v. 12), for the glory of *God* is the final aim of the whole unfolding of salvation. There may be an echo here, as F. F. Bruce suggests, of Old Testament language, especially Isaiah 43:20-21, where God speaks of 'my chosen people, the people whom I formed for myself that they might declare my praise'.[141] And he is to be praised not only for what he has already done, but also for the prospect of his completing redemption and taking possession of his people.

The eulogy of vv. 3-14 began with an outburst of praise as Paul blessed God for all the blessings he had showered on his people in the Lord Jesus Christ. The note of praise has been sustained throughout by means of the recurring refrain 'to the praise of his glory' (vv. 6, 12, 14). The recipients of these wide-ranging blessings of salvation, along with Paul, have been stimulated by this recital of God's mighty acts in his Son to express their gratitude and praise.

The theocentric character of the passage, its christological focus, particularly God's intention to bring all things together in Christ, its emphasis on divine grace, and God's calling of a people to himself are all key issues for the letter as a whole. The eulogy of vv. 3-14 has provided the keynote of the epistle, opened up many of its main ideas that recur in the body of the letter, set the style and tone, and provided an introduction for Paul's didactic and exhortatory goals.

B. Thanksgiving, Intercession, and Praise to God for Exalting Christ, 1:15-23

> [15]*For this reason, ever since I heard about your faith in the Lord Jesus and your love for all the saints,* [16]*I have not stopped giving thanks for you, remembering you in my prayers.* [17]*I keep asking that the God of our Lord Jesus Christ, the glorious Father, may give you the Spirit of wisdom and revelation, so that you may know him better.* [18]*I pray also that the eyes of your heart may be enlightened in order that you may know the hope to which he has called you, the riches of his glorious inheritance in the saints,* [19]*and his incomparably great power for us who believe. That power is like the working of his mighty strength,* [20]*which he exerted in Christ when he raised him from the dead and seated him at his right hand in the heavenly realms,* [21]*far above all rule and authority, power and dominion, and every title that can be given, not only in the present age but also in the one to*

---

141. Bruce, 267.

come. ²²And God placed all things under his feet and appointed him to be head over everything for the church, ²³which is his body, the fullness of him who fills everything in every way.

At the conclusion of his magnificent eulogy, Paul includes an introductory thanksgiving paragraph in which he gives thanks to God for his readers (vv. 15-16a), and then intercedes for them (vv. 16b-19). In the following verses (vv. 20-23), which are a continuation of the same sentence, God is praised for exercising his mighty power in raising Christ from the dead and exalting him to be head over all things for the church. The introductory eulogy or *berakah* of Ephesians 1 has not replaced the thanksgiving structure; instead it is followed by one.[142]

The thanksgiving of Ephesians, which follows hard upon the eulogy (vv. 13-14), is short. For although most of the structural elements are present,[143] the grounds for Paul's thanksgiving are brief. Many of the elements that would have featured in the latter paragraph have already appeared in the eulogy (see above). But this does not mean that the expression of gratitude to God is superfluous. Paul has kept his normal distinction of using the form of a eulogy in relation to salvation blessings in which he himself participated (vv. 3-14, esp. vv. 11, 12) and the thanksgiving terminology to express his gratitude for God's work in the lives of his addressees. He now turns to the latter in this thanksgiving.

This paragraph (especially vv. 15-19) is linked with the eulogy of vv. 3-14. The opening words *For this reason* (v. 15) point back to the whole paragraph, and especially to vv. 13-14 where the eulogy is applied to the

---

142. This form of introductory thanksgiving is also found in Hellenistic Judaism (cf. 2 Macc. 1:10-13). Paul adopts this Hellenistic epistolary *model*, frequently using it at the beginning of his letters as he expresses his gratitude to God, the Father of Jesus Christ, for what he has effected in the lives of his predominantly Gentile readers. However, while the *structure* of the Pauline thanksgiving periods is Hellenistic, there are good grounds for believing that the *contents* (apart from their specifically Christian elements such as the gospel, etc.) show the influence of Old Testament and Jewish thought.

143. Two basic forms of introductory thanksgiving can be distinguished in the Pauline corpus: after the verb of thanksgiving εὐχαριστέω ('I give thanks') (a) the more detailed type contains up to seven basic elements, concluding with a ἵνα-clause (or its equivalent) which spells out the content of the apostle's intercession for the readers: Phil. 1:3-11; Col. 1:3-14; Phlm. 4-6. (b) The second type, simpler in form, also commences with the giving of thanks to God, but concludes with a ὅτι-clause which notes the reason for this expression of gratitude: 1 Cor. 1:4-9; cf. Rom. 1:8-10. Eph. 1:15-19 falls within the first category; instead of containing the personal object ('God') of the verb of thanksgiving, the full title ('the God of our Lord Jesus Christ, the glorious Father') in v. 17 makes clear to whom the thanksgiving has been addressed. (For a detailed discussion of these two main types as well as the mixed structures, see P. Schubert, *Form and Function,* 10-39; and P. T. O'Brien, *Introductory Thanksgivings,* 6-15.)

recipients, that is, to Gentiles who are now in Christ on an equal footing with Jews. The causal expression, *ever since I heard,* like its equivalent in the Colossian letter (Col. 1:4), indicates that the writer had received news of the addressees' faith. There may also be a reference to *believed* of v. 13, and this may point to a further reason for the brevity of the thanksgiving report. If the suggestion that Ephesians is a circular letter is correct, then we can understand why this report would be brief. In the eulogy Paul has already made reference to gospel and missionary terminology as well as to the sealing of the Gentile readers by the Holy Spirit. There is no need to repeat them in the thanksgiving report.

Paul's intercession in vv. 17-19 is linked with his thanksgiving prayer. Several ideas contained in the paragraph pick up themes and ideas of the eulogy.[144] The intercession is a prayer for the realization of the blessings of the eulogy in the lives of the readers. The style of vv. 17-19 is almost liturgical, while the emphatic stress on wisdom and knowledge, which is closely tied in with a true grasp of the mystery, is understandable if Paul desires that the addressees might comprehend the tremendous themes mentioned in vv. 3-14. Like the spiritual blessings enunciated in the *berakah,* such wisdom is given by God alone (vv. 17, 18). If the intercessory prayer of vv. 17-19 looks back to some of the motifs of the eulogy, then it also points forward to the prayer of chapter 3:14-19. Basically it is a petition that those who have been so richly blessed by God may learn about hope, glory, and power.

The language of the intercession passes almost imperceptibly into elevated language in praise of God for his exaltation of Christ to be head over the universe for the church (vv. 20-23).[145] If these verses provide the eschatological climax to the thanksgiving paragraph (although in one sense the whole of 1:3–3:21 can be viewed as the introductory thanksgiving),[146] then

144. Note that the address, 'the God of our Lord Jesus Christ, the Father of glory' (v. 17), is not unlike the words of v. 3, while 'glory' is found in the request of v. 18. The 'Spirit of wisdom and revelation in the knowledge of him' (v. 17) is an echo of 'he has made known to us in all wisdom and insight the mystery of his will' (v. 9), while the terms 'riches', 'wisdom', 'inheritance', 'hope', and their synonyms also reappear. Note, too, the repeated themes of 'faith' and God's 'glory'.

145. These verses have sometimes been regarded as an early Christian hymn, or at least based on one. There are several phrases which appear to be parallelled in catechetical or liturgical material, but this is different from saying that they are a hymn or formal statement of belief, or adapted from either. To try to reconstruct a hymn in vv. 20-23 is problematic. Note the discussions of R. Deichgräber, *Gotteshymnus und Christushymnus,* 161-65; T. G. Allen, 'Exaltation and Solidarity with Christ: Ephesians 1:20 and 2:6', *JSNT* 28 (1986), 103-20; and Best, 157.

146. J. T. Sanders, 'The Transition from Opening Epistolary Thanksgiving to Body in the Letters of the Pauline Corpus', *JBL* 81 (1962), 348-62; and Lincoln, 50.

the emphasis falls upon the present rule of Christ and thus on an eschatology that is realized. This would certainly be in keeping with the dominant emphasis on the 'already' aspect of chapters 1–3.

The paragraph as a whole with its long sentence containing a thanksgiving (vv. 15-16a), an intercession (vv. 16b-19), and confessional material in praise of God who has raised and exalted Christ (vv. 20-23), presents God's purposes for his people on a broad canvas.[147] Like the preceding eulogy (vv. 3-14), the pattern of thought encompasses past, present, and future, as Paul describes the work of the triune God on behalf of his people. Regarding the past, mention is made of God's raising Christ and exalting him to the place of highest honour, and of his calling believers to himself. In the present there is a focus on the privileges that God's people have, not least his power that is available to them, and on Christ's present cosmic rule along with the church's relation to him. As to the future, there is mention of the hope to which Christians have been called and of the age to come. The Father is addressed in the intercession (v. 17), for he is at work on behalf of his people. Christ is the focus of the Father's activity — in his raising Christ, exalting him, placing all things under his feet, and appointing him to be head over everything for the church. The Spirit is the agent of revelation 'who interprets God's activity and enables believers to appropriate what has been accomplished for them'.[148] Again, as in the eulogy, there is a theological, christological, and ecclesiological focus. Paul prays that his readers might know more of the hope to which God has called them, the rich inheritance which he possesses in them, and the mighty power by which he energizes them. These are all aspects of the mighty salvation which has been won for them in Christ (vv. 18-19). The place of the church in the purposes of God is particularly underscored in this passage: it begins with thanksgiving and prayer for believers, which in turn leads to a statement of God's purposes for them in Christ. The role of the church in a cosmic context concludes the paragraph: Christ's rule over all things is for the benefit of his people.

Clearly the apostle wants his readers to appropriate more fully 'every spiritual blessing' that has graciously been given to them in Christ. Paul wishes them to understand the place which they as God's people have in the divine purposes. What has been done in Christ is for their benefit: God's power in him is available for those who believe (v. 19), and Christ's rule over the universe is for their benefit (v. 22). There are profound implications arising from all of this. But for the moment let them grasp the wonder of God's majestic purposes in his Son.

147. Note the insightful treatment of Lincoln, 81-82.
148. Lincoln, 81.

1. Thanksgiving for the Readers' Faith and Love, 1:15-16a

15-16a Immediately following the introductory *berakah* or eulogy, Paul reports his thanksgiving (vv. 15-16a) and intercession for his readers (vv. 16b-19). He mentions his unceasing gratitude to God for the good news he has received about them, and assures them that he constantly intercedes for them.[149] In the eulogy Paul had praised God for blessings which he and his fellow-Christians received; now in his thanksgiving he expresses his gratitude for the divine work in the lives of his readers.

The thanksgiving is linked syntactically with the eulogy: *For this reason* probably refers to the whole of the eulogy, but especially to vv. 13 and 14, where mention was made of the Gentile readers ('and you') being drawn into the sphere of God's saving purposes. Paul, 'for his part' ('I also'), has painted the broad sweep of God's magnificent plan; now he turns to offer thanks to God for what he has heard about the readers.

Although this thanksgiving is rather short, the parallelism with Colossians 1:3 and 4 is striking: Paul has 'heard[150] about [the readers'] faith in the Lord Jesus and [their] love for all the saints'. In both letters the Christians' love and faith are clear evidence that God has been mightily at work in their midst.[151] In Ephesians, however, there is strong manuscript evidence to suggest that 'your love' should be omitted as an editorial addition to the text under the influence of Colossians 1:4. If the shorter reading is correct, then the addressees' 'faith' would have to include the notion of their fidelity, since it was being exercised not only 'in the Lord Jesus' but also towards all their fellow-believers. But on balance the longer reading is to be preferred.[152]

Accordingly, the basis for the apostle's expression of gratitude is the

---

149. See P. T. O'Brien, 'Thanksgiving within the Structure of Pauline Theology', in *Pauline Studies: Essays Presented to F. F. Bruce on His 70th Birthday,* ed. D. A. Hagner and M. J. Harris (Grand Rapids: Eerdmans, 1980), 50-66.

150. This is expressed by means of a causal participial clause: ἀκούσας ('heard', Eph. 1:15; cf. ἀκούσαντες, 'heard', Col. 1:4). The statement that news had reached the apostle does not, of itself, tell against the Pauline authorship of Ephesians as a circular letter, or of a letter sent *to Ephesus* (against Lincoln, 54). Paul may have been receiving occasional reports about those already known to him and, if Ephesians was a circular letter, then he may have been personally unacquainted with other members of congregations in western Asia Minor. (See the Introduction with its discussion of the authorship and destination of the letter.)

151. On the relationship, in the introductory thanksgivings, between Christian graces evidenced in the lives of his converts and the prior work of God through the gospel, see P. T. O'Brien, 'Thanksgiving and the Gospel in Paul', *NTS* 21 (1974-75), 144-55.

152. It is possible that the word dropped out at an early stage through haplography. For a detailed discussion see Lincoln, 46-47; cf. B. M. Metzger, *Textual Commentary,* 602.

first two elements of the familiar Christian triad, faith–love–hope (1 Thess. 1:3; 2 Thess. 1:3; cf. Rom. 5:1-5; Gal. 5:5-6; Eph. 4:2-5). Their *faith* is 'in the Lord Jesus', an expression which denotes not the object to which their faith is directed, but the sphere in which it lives and acts (cf. 1:1, where the readers are addressed as *the faithful in Christ Jesus*). The readers' *love* has been shown to *all the saints*. If the term *the saints* is a reference to the Jerusalem church or to Jewish Christians (a significance it sometimes has), then these Gentile readers' *love* is proof of the breaking down of the ancestral barriers between Jew and Gentile (which is central to the argument of Ephesians).[153] However, without denying that these ancient barriers were being removed, here the readers' practical expression of care and concern has been directed to *all*[154] God's holy people, which signifies Christians generally, Jews and Gentiles alike, in the environs of Ephesus and beyond. This is consistent with later references in Ephesians to 'all the saints' (3:18; 6:18; cf. 6:24) and Paul's use of the phrase in other introductory thanksgivings (cf. Col. 1:4; Phlm. 5). It is through *love* that Christians serve one another, and according to the reports reaching Paul, these predominantly Gentile believers knew something of this service. The third member of the triad, hope, does not appear in the thanksgiving; it has already been mentioned in the *berakah* (v. 12) and will become an important element of Paul's intercessory prayer for his readers (v. 18).

As in most of his other thanksgiving reports (1 Cor. 1:4; Phil. 1:4; Col. 1:3; 1 Thess. 1:2; 2 Thess. 1:3; 2:13; Phlm. 4), so here Paul assures his readers of his *constant* thanksgiving to God for them. To say, *I have not stopped giving thanks for you*, is not a claim to uninterrupted prayer or unceasing thanksgiving. To speak of prayer by this and similar terms (e.g., 'continually', 'at all times', 'day and night') was part and parcel of the style of ancient letters, both Jewish and pagan (see on 6:18). Paul means that he regularly gave thanks for them in his times of prayer: morning, noon, and evening (the customary three hours each day), and whenever else he prayed. Here the temporal note, *I have not stopped* [*giving thanks*], is further explained by the phrase *in my prayers*. Even as he writes his letter thanksgiving to God once more wells up within him.

2. Intercession for Their Growth in Knowledge, 1:16b-19

16b We have seen that the introductory thanksgiving is quite brief. There was no need to make further reference to the gospel, missionary terminology, or the readers' sealing with the Holy Spirit, for these

---

153. Cf. Caird, 43.
154. The πάντας accentuates the breadth of the love.

had already been mentioned in the eulogy. Instead, Paul moves on directly to his intercessory prayer report. Having offered thanksgiving to God for his readers, he matches it with regular petitionary prayer for them. The expression *remembering* (lit. 'making mention'), which is equivalent to 'making petition', is one of several used by Paul in his introductory paragraphs to signify petitionary, especially intercessory, prayer.[155] And as with his thanksgivings, so he offers intercessions for those who come within the sphere of his apostolic responsibilities.

The apostle regards the mutual intercession of himself and his converts as of paramount importance. He recognizes that the Christian growth of his readers, as well as the furtherance of his own ministry of the gospel, is wholly dependent upon the living God, who gives generously to his children when they call upon him in prayer. As a result, Paul constantly offers petitions for his converts and others for whom he has pastoral and apostolic responsibilities. Petitionary prayer is an essential weapon in his apostolic armoury. Paul knows that he is engaged in a deadly spiritual warfare and needs to make use of the whole armour of God; he heeds his own advice to 'Pray at all times in the Spirit, with all prayer and supplication' (Eph. 6:18). At the same time, he urges his readers to support him in their petitions (6:19, 20).

17 Verses 17-19 spell out the content (note the introductory 'that')[156] of Paul's regular intercession for his readers. His prayer, which echoes several themes in the eulogy, is that they may comprehend what God has already done for them in Christ and which is set forth in vv. 3-14. He has already blessed them in Christ with every spiritual blessing; Paul now prays that he will open their eyes so that they will fully grasp the implications of all these privileges. Unlike many contemporary Christians, the apostle does not pray for fresh spiritual blessings, as though he is unaware of the fact that God has graciously given them every spiritual priv-

155. μνείαν ποίουμαι ('make mention'): Rom. 1:9; 1 Thess. 1:2; Phlm. 4; cf. 2 Tim. 1:3; δέησιν ποίουμαι ('make petition'): Phil. 1:4; προσεύχομαι ('pray'): Phil. 1:9; Col. 1:3, 9; 2 Thess. 1:11; δέομαι ('ask, request'): Rom. 1:10; 1 Thess. 3:10. For further references, see G. P. Wiles, *Paul's Intercessory Prayers: The Significance of the Intercessory Prayer Passages in the Letters of St. Paul* (Cambridge: Cambridge University Press, 1974). Unfortunately he provides no detailed analysis of the prayers in Ephesians or Colossians, since he judges the letters to be non-Pauline. Note also on 6:18.

156. There has been considerable discussion among earlier writers as to whether the ἵνα ('that')-clause here and elsewhere (which follows verbs of praying, interceding, thanking, etc.) expresses the content of the relevant prayer or its purpose. Our slight preference is for the former (cf. Best, 161), on the grounds that verbs of asking, speaking, requesting, etc., when followed by a ἵνα ('that')-clause, spell out the content. However, there is a fine line between the two, since the content of what is requested may also indicate the purpose of the request.

ilege in Christ. On the other hand, Paul does not want his readers to become complacent. He does not assume that because everything is theirs in Christ they do not need to grow in their understanding or experience of these Christian blessings. Hence his intercession for them. John Stott puts it aptly: 'What Paul does in Eph. 1, and therefore encourages us to copy, is both to keep praising God that in Christ all spiritual blessings are ours and to keep praying that we may know the fullness of what he has given us'.[157]

The apostle's rich intercessory prayer is directed to *the God of our Lord Jesus Christ*, who is also called 'the Father of glory'. This full title,[158] which has a liturgical ring to it, is a variation on the opening address of the eulogy (v. 3), with the notion of the divine fatherhood being expanded and emphasized. The first predicate, *the God of our Lord Jesus Christ*, seems specifically intended to recall the similar address in the *berakah*. The one to whom Paul's petition is directed is the God who has *already* blessed us in the Lord Jesus Christ (v. 3); any prayer, then, for the realization of these blessings in the lives of the readers can be offered to him with full confidence. Since the apostle's usual designation is 'the God and Father of our Lord Jesus Christ' (v. 3), the second title 'the Father of glory' breaks the sequence and is specifically emphasized. This suggestion finds support in the closely related prayer of Ephesians 3:14-19, where God is humbly addressed as 'Father' and then identified as the one 'from whom every family in heaven and on earth derives its name' (vv. 14-15). What is the significance of this stress on God in his character as 'Father of glory'?

Recent study of the titles for God (or Christ) in the New Testament confessions and prayers has shown that these have often been chosen because of their particular appropriateness to the content of the prayer, word of praise, or confession. So, for example, in his introductory eulogy of 2 Corinthians 1, Paul, who praises God for the consolation and comfort he has received, calls him 'the Father of compassion and the God of all comfort' (2 Cor. 1:3; cf. Rom. 15:5 with v. 4). Other examples could be added. The titles for God in petitionary prayers often highlight some aspect of his character or saving activity that is especially appropriate to the content of the request. It is as if the prayer address is asserting: God's

---

157. Stott, 51-52.

158. The titles by which God is addressed in the two intercessory prayers of Ephesians are significantly fuller than their counterparts in the other Pauline introductory thanksgiving paragraphs, and in each case there is a strong emphasis on God as Father: here at 1:17 'the God of our Lord Jesus Christ' is named 'the Father of glory', while at 3:14-15, which picks up the earlier petition, Paul asserts that he bows his knees to 'the Father, from whom his whole family in heaven and on earth derives its name'.

grace, power, and glory are unlimited; he is more than adequate to meet our needs. Here in Ephesians 1 the title 'Father of glory' has special reference to the petition of vv. 17-19 (see below). Accordingly, the full wording of the address in Ephesians 1:17 points in two directions: the first, *the God of our Lord Jesus Christ*, looks back with confident assurance to the eulogy, while the second, the predicate 'the Father of glory', focusses on the petitionary prayer with its request for knowledge and wisdom, hope, glory, and power.

'Father of glory' displays Semitic influence, the unmistakable influence of the Old Testament. Although this exact expression is unique, in the earlier Testament and Judaism God was called 'the God of glory' (Ps. 29:3; cf. Acts 7:2), 'the King of glory' (Ps. 24:7, 10; cf. 1QM 12:8; 19:1), and later 'the Lord of glory' (1 Enoch 22:14; 25:3, 7, etc.).[159] The title 'Lord of glory' is also applied to Christ (1 Cor. 2:8; Jas. 2:1). Here in Ephesians 1:17 'of glory' is an adjectival genitive, indicating that God is *the glorious Father*. At the same time, consistent with similar predicates (e.g., 'the Father of compassion', 2 Cor. 1:3), the genitive is one of origin, meaning that the Father is the *source* of all true glory. Both ideas, which are present here, are not fully caught by the English rendering *the glorious Father*. Glory also speaks of the splendour and brightness of the divine presence.

Further, in Paul 'glory' and 'power' are often used synonymously; for example, the resurrection of Christ is attributed to the power of God (1 Cor. 6:14), and it is also regarded as a manifestation of his glory (Rom. 6:4). As the Father of glory God is the source of all glory and power. He is omnipotent and is, therefore, perfectly qualified to answer the apostle's wide-ranging petition out of his boundless resources. Thus, Paul intercedes with confidence to 'the Father of glory' to enlighten the spiritual eyesight of his readers (note the connection between God's glory and the light of knowledge in 2 Cor. 4:4, 6) so that they might know more fully about the hope of his calling, the riches of his glorious inheritance, and the surpassing greatness of his power.

God has already been praised for having lavished his grace upon us with all wisdom and understanding by making known to us the mystery of his will (vv. 8-9). Now the apostle takes up this language and asks that his readers may be given *the Spirit of wisdom and revelation, so that you may know him* [i.e., God] *better*. A similar petition was offered on behalf of the Colossians: that 'God may fill you with the knowledge of his will in all spiritual wisdom and understanding' (1:9). The phrase 'the spirit of wisdom and revelation' could be a reference to the be-

---

159. On the notion of the glory of the Lord filling the whole earth, see Num. 14:21; Ps. 72:19; Isa. 6:3; 66:18-19.

liever's own spirit (RSV, NAB) to which God's Spirit imparts understanding of divine realities. However, since the 'revelation' word-group always describes a disclosure given by God, Christ, or the Holy Spirit, or is the result of events brought about by them,[160] it is more likely that our phrase is speaking of the Holy Spirit; hence the NIV rendering *the Spirit of wisdom and revelation*. 'Spirit of wisdom' turns up several times in the Old Testament (but not the expression 'Spirit of revelation'), the most notable reference being Isaiah 11:2, where the Spirit is said to rest on the Messiah. 'Wisdom' has to do with a knowledge of God's will (Col. 1:9), that is, his saving purposes, and this necessarily involves walking worthily of the Lord (1:10). Often wisdom relates to an understanding of God's activity in Christ, which in Ephesians is specifically bound up with the mystery (Eph. 1:8-9). The Spirit's activity in revealing to believers the wisdom of God is most clearly enunciated by Paul in 1 Corinthians 2:6-16.

In Ephesians[161] the motif of 'revelation' has specially to do with making known the mystery or various aspects of it. So at 3:5 God's open secret is revealed by the Spirit to his holy apostles and prophets, while at 3:3 the revelation is to Paul himself. Here in the intercession of vv. 17-19, the apostle's prayer to God is that the Spirit, who had been given to the readers at their conversion (cf. v. 13),[162] might impart wisdom and revelation to them so that they might understand more fully God's saving plan and live in the light of it. The mystery had already been made known in Christ (vv. 9-10), but the readers needed to grasp its full significance, not least of all their own place within it. And as the Spirit worked in their midst, giving them insights and revealing God's purposes in Christ, so they would grow in the knowledge of God.[163]

Paul's view of knowledge is largely determined by the Old Testament. To know God means to be in a close personal relationship with him

160. Matt. 11:25, 27; 16:17; Rom. 2:5; 8:19; 1 Cor. 1:7; 2:10; Gal. 1:12, 16; Eph. 3:5.

161. The noun ἀποκάλυψις ('revelation'; cf. 3:3), the cognate verb ἀποκαλύπτω ('reveal'; 3:5), and the synonymous γνωρίζω ('make known'; 1:9; 3:3, 5, 10; 6:19) all occur in connection with various aspects of the mystery.

162. G. D. Fee, *God's Empowering Presence*, 676 n. 55, comments that 'the prayer is not for some further Spirit reception, but for the indwelling Spirit whom they have already received to give them further wisdom and revelation'. He later adds that the term 'revelation' (instead of 'insight', used in Col. 1:9) is particularly appropriate in this prayer, since it is 'through the Spirit's revelation that his readers will be able also to *understand their place in the people of God*' (692; emphasis added).

163. ἐν ἐπιγνώσει αὐτοῦ means 'consisting in the knowledge of him', i.e., God, rather than Christ. The growth in knowledge comes about through the Spirit's activity of revealing and giving insight. Some take the phrase 'in the knowledge of him' to signify the *goal* of the wisdom and revelation being imparted (cf. Bruce, 269).

because he has made himself known. There is an obedient and grateful acknowledgement of his deeds on behalf of his people. The knowledge of God begins with a fear of him, is linked with his demands, and often is described as knowing his will. In the Old Testament, as well as in the writings of Paul, knowledge is not a fixed quantum but rather something that develops in the life of people as they are obedient.

'Knowledge'[164] appears in the intercessory prayers of Paul's four Captivity Epistles (Phil. 1:9; Col. 1:9-10; Phlm. 6, in addition to Eph. 1:17), yet it does not turn up in prayer requests outside these letters. Knowledge is closely connected with *'the knowledge of Christ and conformity to his likeness,* which, in turn, is the substance of *God's self-revelation'*.[165] Paul's use of this term here (cf. Col. 2:2; 3:10) and its cognate noun[166] (Eph. 3:19; cf. Col. 2:3) may stand over against the faulty notions of wisdom and knowledge circulating in Asia Minor. His prayer, then, is for the true knowledge of God. What this means is explained in the rest of the prayer in vv. 18-19.

18 Paul continues with his request for the readers' spiritual understanding, for he wants them to know (1) the hope to which God has called them, (2) the rich inheritance which he possesses in them, and (3) the mighty power by which he energizes them. These are all aspects of the mighty salvation which has been won for them in Christ.

Using an Old Testament expression ('the eyes of your heart', Pss. 13:3[LXX 12:4]; 19:8[18:9]), he prays that they may have spiritual insight[167] so as to grasp the truth of God's purposes. At 2 Corinthians 4:6 similar language is employed to indicate that God has shone in his people's hearts to give 'the illumination[168] of the glorious knowledge of God in the face of Christ'. The corollary to the knowledge of God himself is an understanding of his ways and his purposes.[169] Once Paul's readers were

---

164. Gk. ἐπίγνωσις.

165. C. F. D. Moule, *The Epistles of Paul the Apostle to the Colossians and to Philemon* (Cambridge: Cambridge University Press, 1962), 161 (his italics).

166. Gk. γνῶσις ('knowledge').

167. The participial clause 'the eyes of your heart having been enlightened' is awkward syntactically, although the general sense is plain. πεφωτισμένους τοὺς ὀφθαλμοὺς τῆς καρδίας [ὑμῶν] has been taken as the second direct object of δώη ('give', v. 17). Accordingly, the petition is that God might give (1) the Spirit of wisdom and revelation, and (2) eyes of the heart that have been enlightened. It is preferable, however, to connect the clause with ὑμῖν ('you') and to explain the accusative case (instead of the dative) as being influenced by the accusative and infinitive construction which immediately follows. Cf. Meyer, 72; Robinson, 149; and Lincoln, 47.

168. φωτισμός ('illumination') is formed from the verb φωτίζω ('enlighten, illuminate') used here.

169. Bruce, 270.

'darkened in their understanding' (Eph. 4:18) and could themselves be described as 'darkness' (5:8). With their conversion, however, a decisive transformation has occurred: they have been enlightened by the Spirit of God. Paul now prays that they may see with the eyes of their heart. Here *heart* is employed in its customary Old Testament sense to describe the seat of the physical, spiritual, and mental life of a person. It denotes the centre and source of both physical life (Ps. 101:5; 103:15; Acts 14:17) and the whole inner life with its feelings or emotions (Rom. 1:24; 9:2; 2 Cor. 2:4, etc.), volition (2 Cor. 9:7), and, as here, its thinking (Eph. 1:18; 2 Cor. 4:6). The word *enlightened* was employed in the Mystery religions as a technical term for the rite of initiation, while in later Christian tradition it described the picture of light or enlightening as the mystery of baptism (Justin). But there is no identification of enlightenment with baptism here or elsewhere in Ephesians.

The purpose of this spiritual insight is that Paul's readers may *know* three things:[170]

(1) *The hope to which he has called you.* Not 'the hope of *your* calling', which might be interpreted in a narrow or individualistic sense, but 'the hope of *his* [i.e., God's] calling',[171] which is to be understood comprehensively in relation to his calling within his saving purposes (see on 4:4). God's calling finds its origin in the choice of his people in Christ before the world's foundation (1:4) and becomes effective in their lives, as it did in the case of the readers,[172] through the preaching of the gospel (Rom. 8:30). Paul prays that his readers might grasp more fully the hope into which God has brought them by his call (cf. Eph. 4:4), that hope which is held out in the gospel (Col. 1:5).

Paul uses both the noun 'hope' and its cognate verb 'to hope' to denote the act of hoping as well as the objective content of the hope, that which is hoped for. Hope in Paul is oriented to what is unseen in the future, the content of which is defined in various ways: salvation (1

---

170. The purpose (signified by εἰς τό with the infinitive εἰδέναι ὑμᾶς, 'that you might know') of the enlightenment of the heart is presented by the three clauses introduced by τίς, τίς, and τί (each of which may be rendered by 'what'), and further aspects of the salvation mentioned in the eulogy (vv. 3-14) are set forth; cf. Best, 166. There does not appear to be any particular significance in Paul using the verb οἶδα ('know') rather than γινώσκω ('know'); see M. Silva, 'The Pauline Style as Lexical Choice: ΓΙΝΩΣΚΕΙΝ and Related Verbs', in *Pauline Studies: Essays Presented to F. F. Bruce on His 70th Birthday*, ed. D. A. Hagner and M. J. Harris (Grand Rapids: Eerdmans, 1980), 184-207, esp. 202, 207.

171. Greek: ἡ ἐλπὶς τῆς κλήσεως αὐτοῦ.

172. In this sense the clause looks back to the past when the readers were called by God into a relationship with himself. The hope itself points to the future. Cf. D. Wiederkehr, *Die Theologie der Berufung in den Paulusbriefen* (Freiburg: Universitätsverlag, 1963), 199-210, esp. 205.

Thess. 5:8), righteousness (Gal. 5:5), resurrection in an incorruptible body (1 Cor. 15:52-55), eternal life (Tit. 1:2; 3:7), and God's glory (Rom. 5:2). On occasion, both noun and cognate verb can denote the act or disposition of hoping, as in the introductory eulogy (Eph. 1:12; cf. Rom. 4:18; 5:5; 12:12; 1 Cor. 13:7), though Romans 8:24-25 shows that the terms could be employed by the apostle in both ways within the one context. In Colossians (cf. 1:5, 23, 27, and the related ideas of 3:1-4), as here in Ephesians 1:18, the concrete meaning is to the fore: the noun denotes 'the content of hope', 'that which is hoped for'.[173] This hope to which God has called them is linked with 'the summing up of all things in Christ', which is the final purpose of God's saving activity in his Son (1:10). Hope is what these Gentile readers did not have before they believed (2:12). Elsewhere Paul describes the hope to which God has called believers as that of sharing in the glory of God (Rom. 5:2), the expectation of appearing with Christ in glory when he is revealed (Col. 3:4).

(2) *The glorious wealth of his inheritance in the saints.* On the basis of v. 14, with its statement about 'our inheritance', and the parallel in Colossians 1:12, which speaks of the Father 'who has qualified us to share in the inheritance of the saints in light', some scholars hold that the reference here is to the inheritance which God will give to us.[174] But the text speaks of '*his* [sc., God's] inheritance', and it is better to understand this of the portion which belongs to him, namely, his own people,[175] rather than the inheritance which he bestows. According to v. 11, men and women who first hoped *in Christ* are his chosen people and have been claimed by him as his portion or inheritance. Gentile believers, too, have been sealed and guaranteed by God's Holy Spirit with their full and final redemption as his prized possession in view (v. 14). God has made them his own; they are his treasured possession, and he will redeem them completely on the final day.

In the compound genitive phrase 'the wealth of the glory of his inheritance', the abstract 'glory' may be understood attributively as 'glorious inheritance', while 'the wealth of the glory' is probably a genitive construction indicating degree. Accordingly, the whole phrase is ren-

---

173. Described as 'the hope into which God has brought them by his call' (A. T. Lincoln, in *Theology*, 118).

174. For example, Meyer, 74, who interprets the inheritance as the messianic salvation; Schnackenburg, 75; and Stott, 56-57.

175. So C. C. Caragounis, *Mysterion*, 66; Bruce, 270-71; Arnold, 88; and Lincoln, 59-60. In the Old Testament God's inheritance is often a synonym for his people, Israel; see, e.g., Deut. 4:20; 9:26, 29; 2 Sam. 21:3; 1 Kings 8:51, 53; Ps. 28:9; 33:12; 78:62, 71; 106:5, 40; Isa. 19:25; 47:6; 63:17; Jer. 10:16; 51:19, etc.

dered 'the very glorious inheritance':[176] God's people, comprising both Jews and Gentiles,[177] are his inheritance, his own possession, in whom he will display to the universe the untold riches of his glory.

'That God should set such a high value on a community of sinners, rescued from perdition and still bearing too many traces of their former state, might well seem incredible were it not made clear that he sees them in Christ, as from the beginning he chose them in Christ'.[178] As a consequence, then, Paul prays that his readers might appreciate the extraordinary value which God places on them. He views them as in his beloved Son and estimates them accordingly. And this is true of all who are 'in Christ'. Let us, therefore, as Christians realize that God purposes 'to accomplish his gracious plan through [us] . . . as the first fruits of the reconciled universe of the future'.[179] May we live consistently with this high calling (cf. Eph. 4:1) and accept with gratitude and true humility the grace and glory that he has lavished on us.

19 Paul has prayed that his readers might know the hope to which God has called them and how greatly prized they are as his treasured possession. In his third and climactic request, which is specially emphasized by its connection with vv. 20-23, the focus of his prayer is upon the amazing power of God working on behalf of believers. Paul's petition is that the readers might understand and experience (3) *his* [God's] *incomparably great power for us who believe, according to the operation of his mighty strength.* The resources in Christ available to believers who live in the overlap of the ages are enormous. Of particular significance is God's almighty power, which will enable them to engage in an ongoing spiritual warfare (cf. 6:10-12) and finally to share in the divine glory. God wants them to obtain their full salvation, and he has provided the means for them to do so.

---

176. Cf. C. C. Caragounis, *Mysterion,* 67; and Bruce, 270. Other options are 'the wealth of his glorious inheritance' and 'his rich and glorious inheritance'. Bratcher and Nida, 33, acknowledge that one cannot be certain how the phrase should be rendered. They claim, quite correctly, that it is 'the rhetorical effect of the total phrase that matters', rather than the separate meaning of each word. Beare speaks of this phrase as 'a redundant fullness of expression which does not make for clarity'.

177. While the term ἅγιοι ('holy ones', saints') can be used to designate angels (Deut. 33:2-3; Ps. 89:6, 8; Dan. 8:13; cf. 1QS 11:7-8), and some understand Eph. 1:18 to be a reference to heavenly beings (cf. Schlier, 84; Gnilka, 91; and Schnackenburg, 75), the phrase 'among the saints' (ἐν τοῖς ἁγίοις) speaks of the community of believers, Jew and Gentile alike. This fits with the notion of the inheritance being God's, with the emphasis of the eulogy on God's people as his possession, the other references to 'saints' in Ephesians (1:1, 15; 2:19; 3:8), and the focus in the letter on God's people within his purposes (cf. 3:21; 5:27); so rightly Lincoln, 60.

178. Bruce, 270.

179. Bruce, 271.

The notion of God's power, which features prominently in Colossians and Ephesians,[180] is introduced in a remarkably emphatic way. Reference is made first of all to its 'exceeding greatness'.[181] Then, after using the regular term for 'power', Paul employs an additional phrase with three synonymous terms to underscore the basis or standard of this exceptional might: 'according to the *operation* of the *strength* of his *might*'. The preposition 'according to' is found elsewhere in Paul's petitions and thanksgivings (cf. Eph. 3:16; Phil. 4:19) as well as in other contexts[182] where God's power, grace, or glory is seen as the source of blessing to the recipient. In prayer contexts the supply corresponds to the riches of the divine attribute and is more than adequate for the needs. Although slightly different nuances have been suggested for the power synonyms used here,[183] it is their similarity which is underscored. Paul has piled up equivalents because he wants to convince his readers that God's power working on behalf of believers is incomparable and able to bring them to final salvation.

This petition contains a significant change from the second person to the first: the mighty power of God is exercised 'for *us* who believe' rather than simply 'for *you*', the readers.[184] By using the first person Paul includes himself and other Christians.[185] God's might is effective for *all* who believe. The apostle and other Christians came within the sphere of blessing in the eulogy of vv. 3-14. Since his intercession of vv. 17-19 is a

---

180. Eph. 3:7, 16, 20; 6:10; Col. 1:11; 29; 2:12. Note the exegesis at the relevant points of Ephesians.

181. By using the adjectival participle of the verb ὑπερβάλλω (to 'go beyond, surpass, outdo'; cf. Eph. 2:7; 3:19) combined with the adjective μέγεθος ('greatness, size'). This combination brings out in a most emphatic way the greatness of the power towards those who believe. Both words appear in the magical papyri and a number of inscriptions from Ephesus. Cf. *PGM* XII.284. (G. H. R. Horsley, *New Documents* 4 [1987], 107.) Other terms for power, sometimes strung together for effect, were common in the Greek versions of Jewish material and in the magical papyri. For details and a discussion of this passage, particularly in relation to the power terms used, see Arnold, 72-75. Cf. K. W. Clark, 'The Meaning of Ἐνεργέω and Καταργέω in the New Testament', *JBL* 54 (1935), 93-101; and Best, 168-70.

182. Note especially Phil. 3:21, where the transformation of believers' weak, mortal bodies into the likeness of Christ's glorified body is 'in accordance with' or 'appropriate to' (κατά) his *power* of universal subjection.

183. With δύναμις meaning 'power' or the 'ability' to accomplish something, ἐνέργεια denoting the operation or realization of δύναμις, κράτος the power to overcome obstacles, and ἰσχύς the exercise of power.

184. The textual evidence for ὑμᾶς ('you') is limited almost entirely to the Western text. The first person is surprising in an intercession and probably led to this variant; so Best, 168.

185. It is not merely a stylistic change (against Lincoln, 61).

prayer for the effective realization of these blessings in the lives of all the recipients, it is entirely appropriate that the circle be widened here. Furthermore, the two earlier petitions caught up the readers into the broader sweep of God's purposes: they were to realize 'the hope of *his* [i.e., God's] calling' and 'the glorious wealth of *his* inheritance'. Quite consistently, then, in the third request God's tremendous power is seen to be exercised on behalf of all believers, including Paul himself.

At the same time, this prayer with its ringing note of confidence would have proven to be especially comforting to recipients of this circular letter if, as Clinton Arnold has claimed, some were converted out of a background of magic, the Artemis cult, or astrological beliefs. He believes Ephesians was 'written to a group of churches in western Asia Minor which needed help in developing a Christian perspective on the "powers" and encouragement in their ongoing struggles with these pernicious spirit-forces', and has shown that several of the particularly rare terms in this petition appear in the magical papyri and inscriptions from Ephesus.[186] He claims that believers in these young Christian congregations 'lived in a milieu characterized by flourishing magical practices, the renowned Artemis cult, and a variety of other Phrygian mysteries and astrological beliefs'.[187] The common feature in the midst of this religious diversity was that people had an extraordinary fear of hostile spiritual powers. Paul's prayer presupposes and emphasizes the supremacy of God's power, which was shown particularly in Christ's resurrection and exaltation to a position of authority over all things. In the light of this superior power of God, who works all things in accordance with the purpose of his will, there is no longer any reason for the readers to fear tyrannical evil powers.

Although these words effectively conclude Paul's intercession, a closely related prayer is begun in Ephesians 3:1 and, after a long parenthesis, completed in 3:14-19. Further, the buildup of power terms in v. 19 anticipates both the latter prayer and the doxology of 3:20-21.

3. God's Mighty Strength Shown in Raising and Exalting Christ, 1:20-23

The third request for an increased knowledge of God's almighty power (v. 19) leads on to a declaration that the supreme demonstration of this power took place in God's raising Christ from the dead and exalting him to a position of authority in the heavenly realms above all hostile spiri-

---

186. Arnold, 167.
187. Arnold, 167, and passim.

138

tual powers. In these verses, which are a continuation of the preceding sentence and round out the introductory thanksgiving of vv. 15-19, God is praised for exercising his mighty power in raising Christ from the dead and exalting him (vv. 20-21) to be head over all things for the church (vv. 22-23).

20 This verse is linked[188] with what precedes by means of an adjectival clause, *which he exerted in Christ,* that qualifies 'the *exertion* of his mighty strength' (v. 19). It affirms that the decisive demonstration of God's power available to believers occurred in the resurrection and exaltation of Christ, as well as in the subjection of the powers to him and his being given as head over everything to the church. The whole paragraph (vv. 20-23),[189] then, prepares the way for the significant affirmation about the raising and enthronement of believers with their Lord in 2:4-7.

The verb 'exert', already used in v. 11, is cognate with the noun that appears in v. 19 and describes God's powerful operation in Christ. His mighty strength was *exerted* first in Jesus' resurrection.[190] Elsewhere in Paul's letters, notably at Colossians 2:12 where the same noun appears, God's power is said to have been at work in the resurrection of Christ (cf. 1 Cor. 6:14; Rom. 1:4; Phil. 3:10). His power is life-giving. By it he raised Jesus from the dead, and now it functions as the source of the risen Jesus' life. Christ's resurrection from the dead is determinative for the believer's life, and later the apostle will discuss the relevance of this life-giving power to those who have been raised and seated with Christ (cf. 1:20 with 2:5, 6). J. A. Fitzmyer appropriately remarks that this resurrection power

emanates from the Father, raises Jesus from the dead at the resurrection, endows him with a new vitality, and finally proceeds from him as the life-giving, vitalizing force of the 'new creation' and of the new life that Christians in union with Christ experience and live.[191]

188. The connection is made syntactically through the relative pronoun ἥν ('which'), which is dependent on ἐνέργειαν ('mighty working') and linguistically through the cognate verb ἐνήργησεν ('wrought mightily'), as well as by the continuation of the theme of power.

189. For a discussion whether these verses are an early Christian hymn, see Lincoln, 50-52; and Best, 157, together with the literature cited.

190. The finite verb ἐνήργησεν ('he wrought') governs the two participles ἐγείρας ('raised') and καθίσας ('seated') of v. 20, and the two finite verbs ὑπέταξεν ('subjected') and ἔδωκεν ('gave') of v. 22. These describe the way in which God's power was exerted in Christ: (1) in relation to Christ's resurrection, (2) in terms of his enthronement, (3) with reference to the subjection of the powers to him, and (4) in terms of Christ's being given to be head of the church. Cf. W. H. Harris, '"The Heavenlies"', 76; and Best, 170.

191. J. A. Fitzmyer, '"To Know Him and the Power of His Resurrection" (Phil 3.10)', in *Mélanges Bibliques en hommage au R. P. Béda Rigaux,* ed. A. Descamps and A. de Halleux (Gembloux: Duculot, 1970), 420.

Furthermore, this power guarantees the future resurrection of believers (1 Cor. 6:14; 15:43; Phil. 3:21).

In describing what God has achieved in Christ no mention is made here of Jesus' death on the cross. Some scholars have regarded this omission as serious and have drawn the conclusion that an early Christian hymn had to be modified drastically before it was included within the paragraph. But apart from the question whether a hymn has been used here, the focus of attention is upon the supreme demonstration of God's power — hence the reference to Jesus' resurrection and exaltation, not his death. If the emphasis had been on the love of God, then Paul may well have written about the cross of Christ as the supreme display of that love (Eph. 5:1-2; cf. Rom. 5:8).

God's mighty strength was also *exerted* in the exaltation of Christ (vv. 20b-23).[192] These verses allude to two different Psalm passages (110:1; 8:6), both of which were used in early Christian preaching.[193] Christ's exaltation was God's mighty act of raising him 'on high to a position of unparalleled honour and universal authority'.[194] His ascension to the right hand of God was an essential and regular element in the early apostolic preaching, finding echoes throughout the New Testament.[195] To grasp the meaning of these verses we must go back to the messianic interpretation of Psalm 110:1: 'The LORD says to my Lord: "Sit at my right hand, till I make your enemies your footstool"'. Jesus claimed these words for himself when he was brought before the Sanhedrin in Jerusalem (Matt. 26:64; Mark 12:36; Luke 20:41-44). After his resurrection and ascension the apostolic announcement was that his enthronement had taken place.[196] Though intimately related to

192. The verb used is καθίσας, from καθίζω meaning to 'cause to sit down, seat' (at Heb. 1:3; 8:1; 10:12; 12:2 it signifies to 'sit'). Cf. Louw and Nida §87.36.

193. For a discussion on the use of Pss. 8 and 110 together in this context, see A. T. Lincoln, 'The Use of the OT in Ephesians', *JSNT* 14 (1982), 16-57, esp. 40-42; M. Gese, *Das Vermächtis des Apostels: Die Rezeption der paulinischen Theologie im Epheserbrief* (Tübingen: J. C. B. Mohr [Paul Siebeck], 1997), 190-93; and T. Moritz, *A Profound Mystery*, 9-22, who questions whether Ps. 8 was used as widely in the New Testament as has often been claimed. He thinks that the author of Ephesians has drawn the two Psalm passages together in a creative way, conscious of the Old Testament contexts of each and aware of 'the intertextual relationship between Ps 8 and the biblical creation accounts' (22).

194. M. J. Harris, *Raised Immortal: Resurrection and Immortality in the New Testament* (London: Marshall, Morgan & Scott, 1983), 85.

195. Acts 2:33-35; 5:31; 7:55-56; Rom. 8:34; Col. 3:1; Heb. 1:3, 13; 8:1; 10:12; 12:2; 1 Pet. 3:22; Rev. 3:21.

196. D. M. Hay, *Glory at the Right Hand: Psalm 110 in Early Christianity* (Nashville: Abingdon, 1973), 15, claims that some thirty-three quotations of or allusions to Psalm 110 (vv. 1 and 4) are scattered throughout the New Testament, occurring in a range of contexts that point to Jesus or Christians being seated at the right hand of God (Rom. 8:34; Eph. 1:20; 2:6; Col. 3:1; Mark 14:62, etc.), where affirmations are made about the subjec-

his resurrection, which is the vindication of his messiahship and sonship, Christ's exaltation is distinguished from his resurrection in several New Testament texts, since it is related to the inauguration of his lordship.[197] 'The Resurrection proclaims "He lives — and that for ever"; the Exaltation proclaims "He reigns — and that for ever"'.[198]

The Son's being seated by the Father points to the completion of his God-given task; his earthly mission was accomplished. And where he sat down, that is, at God's *right hand,* is as significant as the fact that he sat down. To be at someone's *right hand* is to be in the position of special honour and privilege (1 Kings 2:19). In the Old Testament the Lord's right hand is the position of favour (Ps. 80:18; Jer. 22:24), victory (Ps. 20:6; 44:3; Isa. 41:10), and power (Exod. 15:6; Ps. 89:13; Isa. 48:13). For Christ, then, to be seated at God's right hand meant sharing the Father's throne (Rev. 3:21). Although Ephesians will later assert that God has seated believers with Christ in the heavenly realms (2:6), significantly there is no mention of their being placed at 'his right hand'. Christ's exalted status cannot be shared. 'Angels stand or fall in worship (1 Kings 22:19; Rev. 4:10) in God's presence; the exalted Son sits'.[199]

So the power with which God works in the lives of believers is the same might by which he raised Christ from death to share his throne.[200] And God's throne is *in the heavenly realms,* the sphere in which Christ's people have been blessed with 'every spiritual blessing in him' (v. 3). With Christ's exaltation to heaven the centre of reference has shifted from earth to heaven, where he is now (cf. 6:9). His presence there is determinative for believers' ongoing existence (cf. Eph. 2:5-6; Col. 3:1-4).

21 Because of his enthronement at the right hand of God, Christ now possesses the full authority of the Father. His position is superior to every imaginable hostile power. Although the residence of the 'principalities and powers' is in the heavenly realm (Eph. 3:10; 6:12), God's throne to which Christ has been exalted is 'high above'[201] all these. The whole hi-

---

tion of the powers to Christ (1 Cor. 15:25; Eph. 1:20; Heb. 10:12-13; Rev. 3:21), and where statements are made in connection with Jesus' intercession and priestly office (Rom. 8:34; cf. Heb. 7:25).

197. Rom. 8:34; Eph. 1:20; 2:6; Col. 3:1; cf. Acts 2:32-33; 1 Pet. 3:21-22.

198. M. J. Harris, *Raised Immortal,* 85. He adds that Christ's 'resurrection has its corollary in his exaltation, for whenever the New Testament describes the present state of Christ he is portrayed not merely as an inhabitant of heaven but as an enthroned monarch'.

199. M. J. Harris, *Raised Immortal,* 79.

200. Bruce, 273. Cf. M. Gese, *Das Vermächtis,* 226-28.

201. ὑπεράνω ('high above'; cf. Eph. 4:10) may be intended here to contrast Christ's position with that of the powers, which in the magical papyri were thought to dwell 'above' (cf. *PGM* IV.569; XII.256). This adverb occurs in *T. Levi* 3:4 to denote the dwelling place of God. Cf. Arnold, 78, 196, though note the caveats of Hoehner.

erarchy of authorities, including death, is subject to the risen and exalted Lord.

Various designations of authority are specified in order to stress Christ's supremacy: *all rule and authority, power and dominion.* Whatever levels of power there are in the universe, all are subordinate to him. Consistent with the use of Psalm 110 elsewhere in the New Testament, Paul identifies the 'enemies' of the Psalm with the invisible 'powers' which have been subjected to Christ. He first characterizes them as 'rule' and 'authority', and adds the inclusive 'all' to denote the whole group. Mention of this pair of spiritual forces (which appears in Col. 1:16; 2:10, 15) anticipates the important references in Ephesians 3:10 and 6:12.[202] The third expression, 'power', which is used for an angelic power (cf. 1 Cor. 15:24; Rom. 8:38; cf. 1 Pet. 3:22), has its roots in the Old Testament, where it often turns up in the expression 'the LORD of *hosts*' (LXX). Yahweh is presented as King and Lord, surrounded by angelic armies. The same word 'powers' refers to 'the *hosts* of heaven' (LXX 2 Kings 17:16; 21:3, 5; 23:4-5), which Israel was prohibited from worshipping (Deut. 4:19). In later Judaism and the syncretistic magical papyri this personalized sense of 'power' was widely known. Paul's fourth term in the list of subjected 'enemies' is 'dominion'. Along with the previous three it denotes 'a special class of angelic powers'.[203]

Finally, to emphasize the comprehensive scope of Christ's supremacy Paul asserts that he has been enthroned *far above . . . every title that can be given, not only in the present age but also in the one to come.* Every conceivable power is encompassed within the mighty reign of the Lord Jesus Christ. In the so-called 'hymn' of Philippians 2:6-11 God exalted the humiliated Jesus and gave him 'the name which is above every name' — his own personal name 'Lord' — together with all the honours and authority that this name involved. It was the Father's intention that universal acclamation and homage should be accorded to the one whose position outranked all others. Here in Ephesians 1:21 the preceding list of four designations was not intended to be exhaustive,[204] so the apostle makes it plain that Christ is *far*

202. Paul uses ἀρχαί to denote 'powers' at Rom. 8:38, and ἐξουσίαι ('authorities') at 1 Cor. 15:24 (cf. 1 Pet. 3:22 with its list of subjected powers). Ephesians reflects a Jewish view of the spirit-world, with all four terms used here being listed in *2 Enoch* 20–22. By the time of the first century, Judaism was intensely interested in the spirit realm, and this resulted in elaborate demonologies with long lists of names and categories. It was believed that God had delegated authority over the nations to angelic beings, so that what happened to them in heaven affected the nations on earth (cf. Dan. 10:13, 20).

203. BAGD, 461; and Arnold, 54.

204. S. H. T. Page, *Powers of Evil: A Biblical Study of Satan and Demons* (Grand Rapids/Leicester: Baker/Apollos, 1995), 241-54, esp. 245. He adds that the expression 'and every title that can be given' implies that the preceding designations were 'used

above every name that is given. The context suggests that the powers were given their names by God, thus pointing to their inferiority to him. If God gave them their names and sent Christ, then Christ's superiority to them is all the more certain. This comprehensive statement specifies that regardless of designation or title, every ruling power in heaven or on earth is inferior to Christ, who is at the right hand of God.[205]

Christ's rule is supreme over every name of renown whether belonging to *the present age* or *the one to come,* whether in the present or in the future. The distinction between 'this age' and 'the coming age' is drawn from Jewish apocalyptic. With the first coming of the Lord Jesus the new age has already broken in upon the present, so that the two ages now overlap. The age to come has been inaugurated but not yet consummated, and it is in this future sense that Paul refers to it here. Ephesians emphasizes 'realized' eschatology, what God has already achieved in Christ. The focus on Christ's exaltation to heaven and the saving benefits that have already been won for believers is consistent with this prominence. But the letter's realized eschatology has not dissolved all futurist eschatology (cf. 1:14; 2:7; 4:30; 5:5, 27; 6:8, 13). Nor is it necessary to claim that temporal categories are of no significance. The victory of Christ's exaltation above every name in this age continues into the coming age. Christ's supremacy was achieved in this age, in the very conditions of humanity's bondage, and under his control even the powers will find their proper place in the new order. In spite of their defeat the world-rulers of this darkness (Eph. 6:12) exercise considerable control over individuals and nations in the present. But in the coming age their control will be a thing of the past. Paul thus goes out of his way to show his readers that they need not fear the future.

The 'principalities and powers' featured prominently in the syncretistic teaching at Colossae. The proponents of the deceptive 'philosophy' there stood in judgment of others (Col. 2:16, 18) and believed that it was necessary to placate these supernatural spiritual forces, who controlled the lines of communication between God and humanity by keeping strict legal ordinances, particularly in the areas of food, drink, and holy days (2:16, 21). This teaching advanced beyond Epaphras's elementary gospel of the cross, the argument ran, and enabled the 'mature' who engaged in these ascetic practices to gain spiritual entrance into heaven and to join in

---

rather loosely and probably did not have well-defined referents'. This is confirmed by a variety of combinations in which the words appear elsewhere in the New Testament. It is therefore 'unwise to attempt to reconstruct a hierarchy of the powers on the basis of the vocabulary used to refer to them'.

205. Cf. T. G. Allen, 'God the Namer: A Note on Ephesians 1:21b', *NTS* 32 (1986), 470-75.

the 'angelic worship of God' as part of their present existence (2:18). In answer, Paul asserts that even the cosmic powers and principalities were created in Christ (1:16). All are subject to him as Creator. Further, the hostile powers were vanquished through that same Lord. None needs to be placated. They derive their existence from him and owe their obedience to him through whom they have been conquered (2:10, 15).

This background in Colossae has its echoes in Ephesians, which contains more about the powers than any other New Testament letter and provides the most detailed response to these spiritual authorities.[206] Consistent with prevailing Jewish and Hellenistic beliefs Ephesians recognizes the reality of evil spirit-beings. Many of the apostle's terms were used of the powers by both Jewish and Hellenistic groups. Against W. Carr, who argues that the references in Ephesians are to the pure angelic host surrounding the throne of God and that the notion of a multitude of demonic powers developed only in the second century, Paul speaks of the powers and authorities as evil forces (6:12; cf. 2:2);[207] the combination of allusions to Psalms 110:1 and 8:6 shows that they are 'enemies' who are put under Christ's feet.

Further, against Walter Wink the powers are not to be demythologized or collapsed into human rulers or political structures which oppress people. Paul believes that the powers are spiritual agencies *in the heavenly realms* which stand behind earthly and human institutions (cf. 6:12). All things are subject to Christ's present rule (1:22, 23), and this includes specifically the principalities and authorities over whom Christ is exalted in the heavenly realm. There seems to be no doubt that such spiritual powers can and do work through earthly structures; but to identify them with the structures is reductionistic.[208]

22 The all-embracing dominion of Christ is further emphasized[209] in a fresh way as Paul now quotes Psalm 8:6: God has *placed all things under his feet*. Christ has not only been given a position of authority, seated at the right hand of the Father; he is now able to exercise that authority in

206. Some reference to the 'powers' is made in Eph. 1:10, 21; 2:2; 3:10, 15; 4:8, 27; 6:11, 12, and 16 by a diverse collection of terms.

207. For a critique of W. Carr's view (*Angels and Principalities: The Background, Meaning and Development of the Pauline Phrase* hai archai kai hai exousiai [Cambridge: Cambridge University Press, 1981], 93-111), see P. T. O'Brien, 'Principalities and Powers: Opponents of the Church', in D. A. Carson, ed., *Biblical Interpretation and the Church* (Exeter: Paternoster, 1984), 110-50, esp. 125-28, 133-36; and Arnold, 47-51.

208. Cf. Stott, 267-75; and P. T. O'Brien, 'Principalities and Powers', 141-43. For an assessment of W. Wink, *Naming the Powers: The Language of Power in the New Testament* (Philadelphia: Fortress, 1984), see Arnold, 47-51, and Lincoln, 64.

209. The last two main statements of vv. 20-23 are expressed through finite verbs (v. 22), not participles as in v. 20 (see above). The thought continues to be God's action in relation to Christ.

the subjection of everything under his feet. The powers are not simply inferior to Christ; they are also subject[210] to him.

This clause continues the description begun in v. 20 as to how God's mighty power was demonstrated in Christ. The Psalmist recalls the language of Genesis 1:26-28 as he wonders in adoration at the honour which the Creator has bestowed on human beings by giving them dominion over the works of his hands. In the New Testament the words of the psalm are applied to Christ as the last Adam (1 Cor. 15:27; Heb. 2:6-9). The 'everything' of the psalm, which refers to that part of creation below humankind in the hierarchy, now designates the whole universe, heaven and earth (cf. 1:10, 23), and especially the spiritual powers which are subject to Christ. Although the complete fulfilment of these words will occur only when death is destroyed and God is all in all (1 Cor. 15:27; Heb. 2:8), Christ's present enthronement at God's right hand is 'assurance enough that this blessed consummation will come without fail'.[211] Elsewhere in Paul's letters Christ's rule over the universe is understood as having already occurred (Phil. 3:21; Col. 2:15).

The notion of Christ's supremacy over the universe has been developed at some length (vv. 20-22a). Paul thus ties this in closely with an assertion about God's purpose for Christ in relation to the church. Already in v. 19 the greatness of God's power, which was effective in the resurrection of Christ, is 'towards us who believe'. Now, in line with this, Christ's dominion over the cosmos is for the benefit of believers: God 'gave him to be head over everything to the church'.[212] These last three clauses of chapter 1, namely, vv. 22b-23, are some of the most difficult in the letter to interpret.

Although the verb 'gave' has been understood in an Old Testament sense of 'appointed' or *installed* (NIV), the usage elsewhere in Ephesians[213] suggests that the verb should be taken here in its regular sense of 'gave'.[214] This underscores God's grace towards the church, which is an emphasis found elsewhere in Ephesians. 'Head over all things' denotes Christ's supremacy over the creation,[215] including the principalities and powers. These are specifically named in the parallel passage, 'Christ . . . is the Head

210. On the verb ὑποτάσσω ('place under, subordinate') see on 5:21.

211. F. F. Bruce, *Ephesians*, 43.

212. The emphasis falls on τῇ ἐκκλησίᾳ ('to the church), the last words in the clause, which are then further accented in what follows (cf. Lincoln, 67).

213. Where δίδωμι ('give') appears with an indirect object in the dative case: 1:17; 3:2, 7, 8, 16; 4:7, 8, 11, 27, 29; 6:19; cf. Col. 1:25.

214. However, the RSV, NEB, NIV, and NRSV render the word 'appointed'.

215. Rather than 'supreme head', as F. Mussner, *Christus, das All und die Kirche: Studien zur Theologie des Epheserbriefes* (Trier: Paulinus, 1955), 30-31; BAGD, 839; and Bruce, 272, 274, take it. On this view, ὑπὲρ πάντα is a modal attribute to κεφαλήν ('the Head which surpasses all things'). Note Best's criticisms of this view, 182.

over every power and authority' (Col. 2:10), and about which Paul is particularly concerned in Ephesians. The 'all things' in the psalm quotation is taken up in the second half of the verse: since all things have been put under his feet by God, then he is 'head over all things'. The terms 'head' and 'feet', 'over' and 'under', are obviously complementary. 'Head'[216] appears frequently in the LXX to render the Hebrew term 'ruler' or 'leader' (Deut. 28:13; Judg. 10:18; 11:11; 2 Sam. 22:44; Isa. 7:8, 9); the notion of authority is connected with that of priority in the Hebrew term. The idea of Christ as head is *not derived* from the image of the church as his body.[217] Paul develops it quite independently (cf. 1 Cor. 11:3); the motifs of head and body can be quite separate (1 Cor. 12:12-27; cf. v. 21). Here Christ's headship has to do with his relation to the cosmos; then body is introduced (v. 23) as a description of the church to which Christ is given. The term 'head' expresses his ruling authority. The rendering 'source' is inappropriate, indeed inexplicable, in the light of the words 'over everything'.[218]

The term 'church', which in Paul frequently refers to a local congregation of Christians in a particular place (1 Thess. 1:1; 2 Thess. 1:1, 4; 2:14; Gal. 1:2, etc.), or a gathering that met in a home, namely, a 'house church' (Rom. 16:5; Col. 4:15; Phlm. 2, etc.), can on occasion have a wider reference.[219] While most commentators interpret these terms as instances of the church universal to which all believers belong and which is scattered throughout the world, there are serious difficulties with this view[220] and it is better to understand the term metaphorically of *a heavenly gathering*

216. According to Louw and Nida §87.51 κεφαλή is used figuratively of 'one who is of supreme or pre-eminent status, in view of authority to order or command', and comes to signify 'one who is the head of, one who is superior to, one who is supreme over'. For a discussion of κεφαλή in 5:21-33, particularly in relation to the meanings 'head' or 'source', see the exegesis below (for bibliographical details, see Best, 189; and Hoehner). Note the recent treatment of, and interaction with recent scholarship by, G. W. Dawes, *The Body*, 122-49, esp. 139-42, in relation to Eph. 1:22.

217. 'Christ is head not because the church is his body, but because all things have been subjected under his feet'; G. Howard, 'The Head/Body Metaphors of Ephesians', *NTS* 20 (1974), 353.

218. C. E. Arnold, 'Jesus Christ', 365; cf. Best, 196; and G. W. Dawes, *The Body*, 139, who remarks that the 'first thing that emerges from the context is that . . . the word κεφαλή must have the sense of "authority"'. He thinks that this is clear from the allusion to Ps. 8.

219. Col. 1:18, 24; Eph. 1:22; 3:10, 21; 5:23-24, 27, 29, 32.

220. First, the term ἐκκλησία can no longer have its usual meaning of 'gathering' or 'assembly', since it is difficult to envisage how the worldwide church could assemble, and so the word must be translated in some other way to denote an organization or society. Secondly, the contexts of passages such as Col. 1:15-20, which move on a heavenly plane, suggest that it is not an earthly phenomenon that is being spoken of, but a supernatural and heavenly one. See further R. Banks, *Paul's Idea of Community* (Grand Rapids: Eerdmans, 1980), 44-47; P. T. O'Brien, 'Entity', 88-119, 307-11, and *DPL*, 123-31.

around Christ in which believers already participate (cf. Heb. 12:22-24). The readers of the letter have already been 'blessed . . . in the heavenly realms with every spiritual blessing in Christ' (1:3), and God has made them alive with him, raised them up with him, and seated them in the heavenly realms in Christ (2:5-6). To speak of 'church' as a gathering taking place in heaven where believers are already assembled around Christ is a metaphorical way of saying that they now enjoy fellowship with him. It is a figurative manner of speaking about Christians being personally related to Christ as they are related to one another. And Paul's point in the immediate passage is that Christ's headship over the universe is for the benefit of his people who gather around him in fellowship.

However, the dimension of the local congregation is also in view. The New Testament does not discuss the relationship between the local church and this heavenly gathering. Although the link is nowhere specifically spelled out, it seems that local congregations, as well as house-groups that meet in particular homes, are concrete, visible expressions of that new relationship which believers have with the Lord Jesus. Local gatherings, whether in a congregation or a house-church, are earthly manifestations of that heavenly gathering around the risen Christ (cf. Heb. 10:25). Therefore, here as elsewhere in Ephesians (e.g., 3:10), the apostle also has in mind local congregations of Christians, in which Jews and Gentiles are fellow-members of the body of Christ and concrete expressions of this heavenly entity.[221]

23 *Head* has been used of Christ who rules over all things and has been given to the church. As such the head is distinct from the body. But with the appositional statement, *the church, which is his body,* head and body are juxtaposed. They are similarly coordinated in Colossians 1:18 (cf. 2:19) — which some see as the source of this conception in Ephesians — and are brought closely together later in Ephesians (cf. 4:15; 5:23).

Considerable difference of scholarly opinion exists as to the origin of Paul's coordination of head and body. It has been traced to several different sources, including the notion of the universe as a cosmic body, Gnostic thought about the Primal Man–Redeemer who constitutes one huge body, rabbinic speculation on the body of Adam, contemporary political ideas, the Christian eucharist, a physiological model in which the head controls the brain, which directs the nervous system of the rest of the body, as well as the Old Testament concept of corporate personality.[222]

It is probably best to understand this coordination of head and body

---

221. Cf. M. Volf, *After Our Likeness: The Church as the Image of the Trinity* (Grand Rapids/Cambridge: Eerdmans, 1998).

222. For a full discussion see Lincoln, 67-72. On the theme of 'body' in Paul, see R. H. Gundry, Sōma *in Biblical Theology, with Emphasis on Pauline Anthropology* (Cambridge: Cambridge University Press, 1976); and G. W. Dawes, *The Body.*

as a natural development from Paul's earlier letters, where the body terminology and its constituent parts refer to the mutual relations and obligations of church members (Rom. 12:4-5; 1 Cor. 12:12-27). In Colossians and Ephesians there is an advance in the line of thought so that the relationship which the church, as the body of Christ, bears to Christ as head of the body is treated.[223] The Pauline concept of 'the body of Christ' may have come from Paul's encounter with the exalted Christ on the Damascus road, where the risen Christ identified himself with his followers: 'Saul, Saul, why do you persecute *me?*' (Acts 9:4; 22:7; 26:14). Further, the idea of the body of Christ can partly be explained in terms of the Old Testament concept of corporate personality where the movement between the one and the many can be expressed by the one term and yet have overtones of solidarity. For Paul, Christ as the last Adam and second man is representative of the new humanity (Rom. 5:12-21; 1 Cor. 15:22, 45-49), so that one is either 'in Adam' or 'in Christ'.

This still leaves the difficulty of how to interpret 'head' in relation to the body. Perhaps if Old Testament notions of 'head' are combined with Greek medical ideas regarding the function of the head in relation to the body and its members, then the head is to be understood as 'inspiring, ruling, guiding, combining, sustaining power, the mainspring of its activity, the centre of its unity, and the seat of its life'.[224] Instead of separating Christ from his body, the head is shown to be 'the cohesive and enabling factor for the body'. Accordingly, 'Ephesians (and Colossians) highlights the personal presence of a powerful one who strengthens the individual through the concept of Christ as "head"'.[225] This interpretation provides the best explanation for Ephesians 4:16 and Colossians 2:19 ('from it [the head] the whole body grows') and is also consistent with the thought of the head 'nourishing' the body (Eph. 5:19).[226]

---

223. F. F. Bruce, *Paul*, 421, points out that the 'advance from the language of simile in 1 Corinthians and Romans to the real and interpersonal involvement expressed in the language of Colossians and Ephesians may have been stimulated by Paul's consideration of the issues involved in the Colossian heresy'. For a range of views in relation to this advance, see P. Benoit, 'Body, Head, and *Pleroma* in the Epistles of the Captivity', in *Jesus and the Gospels,* vol. 2 (London: Darton, Longman & Todd, 1974), 59-78; A. Perriman, '"His body, which is the church . . .": Coming to Terms with Metaphor', *EvQ* 62 (1990), 123-42; and J. D. G. Dunn, '"The Body of Christ" in Paul', in *Worship, Theology and Ministry in the Early Church: Essays in Honor of Ralph P. Martin,* ed. M. H. Wilkins and T. Paige (Sheffield: Academic Press, 1992), 146-62.

224. Lightfoot, 227. This view has been taken up and developed by Barth, 190, who has examined the evidence of the medical parallels, as well as by Arnold, 80-82, and his 'Jesus Christ', 346-66.

225. Arnold, 82.

226. See the exegesis of Eph. 4:16; 5:19.

The final clause of v. 23, rendered by the NIV as *the fulness of him who fills everything in every way,* is one of the most complex in Ephesians.[227] It has led to a considerable variety of interpretations and a spate of different translations. The following significant issues need to be addressed:

(1) How is the key term 'fulness' to be interpreted in this context? 'Fulness' occurs four times in Ephesians (1:10, 23; 3:19; 4:13) and twice in Colossians (1:19; 2:9), while appearing six times elsewhere in the Pauline corpus (Rom. 11:12, 25; 13:10; 15:29; 1 Cor. 10:26; Gal. 4:4). Earlier references in Paul show that the term does not have a technical significance,[228] but in Ephesians and Colossians (except for Eph. 1:10) it is related to God or Christ.

The term probably reflects the influence of the Old Testament rather than Valentinian Gnosticism or Stoicism, and denotes the revelation of the divine presence. The noun is found in the Old Testament in stereotyped expressions such as the sea and its fulness,[229] but it is not specifically employed in the LXX to denote the divine power and glory. The cognate verb and adjective ('full'), however, frequently appear with these notions (Ezek. 44:4, 'the house of the LORD is *full* of his glory'; cf. 43:5; Isa. 6:1; Jer. 23:24; Hag. 2:7), and Paul seems to have taken up the noun to express the Old Testament idea of the divine presence and manifestation, the 'Shekinah' of later Judaism.[230] If 'fulness' denotes something like the divine power, essence, and glory, then the references to 'the fulness of God' (Eph. 3:19) and 'the fulness of Christ' (Eph. 4:13; cf. Col. 1:19; 2:9) are appropriately explained. According to Colossians 1:19 Christ is the person in whom God in all his fulness was pleased to take up his residence. All the attributes and activities of God — his spirit, word, wisdom, and glory — are perfectly displayed in Christ. In him all the fulness of deity dwells bodily (Col. 2:9).

(2) What, then, is the antecedent of 'fulness'? The notions of the divine presence and manifestation might suggest that this key term in Ephesians 1:23 is a description of Christ (the antecedent would be 'him' in v. 22b) as the 'fulness' of God who fills all in all (cf. Col. 1:19; 2:9), and a

---

227. Gk. τὸ πλήρωμα τοῦ τὰ πάντα ἐν πᾶσιν πληρουμένου. In addition to the detailed treatments in the commentaries, see R. Yates, 'A Re-Examination of Ephesians 1:23', *ExpTim* 83 (1971-72), 146-51; and G. W. Dawes, *The Body,* 237-48, who concludes that there is ambiguity in the clause, which 'reflects the ambiguity about the relationship of Christ and the Church' (237)!

228. Rom. 11:12, 25; 13:10; 15:29; 1 Cor. 10:26; Gal. 4:4.

229. 1 Chron. 16:32; Ps. 96:11; 98:7; cf. the earth and everything in it (Ps. 24:1; Jer. 8:16; 47:2; Ezek. 12:19; 19:7; 30:12), and the world with all it contains (Ps. 50:12; 89:11).

230. Note the discussion of πλήρωμα ('fulness') in Arnold, 83-85; Lincoln, 72-76; and Best 183-89.

number of commentators have taken the expression this way. But it is better on syntactical and contextual grounds to regard 'body' as in apposition to 'fulness' and to take it as a reference to the church.[231]

(3) Does 'fulness' have an active or a passive significance? In other words, does it mean 'that which fills' or 'that which is filled'? The answer to this question turns, in part, on how the present participle of the cognate verb is to be understood (see below). But, given the conclusion reached above that the antecedent of 'fulness' is 'body', the passive force is more probable: it is the church which is filled or completed by Christ rather than that which fills or completes him. The latter notion is entirely foreign to the thought of Ephesians and Colossians — indeed, to the rest of the New Testament. Elsewhere Christ is depicted as actively filling believers. Like Colossians 2:10, Ephesians 4:13 refers to believers attaining to the fulness of Christ, while the apostle's prayer in Ephesians is that the readers may be filled with all the fulness of God (3:19).[232]

(4) What is the meaning of the final words, rendered by the NIV as *him who fills everything in every way?*[233] In particular, how is the present participle to be understood: is it passive, middle, or middle with an active significance? The participle might be treated as being in the passive voice, thus signifying that the church is the fulness of Christ, who 'is being filled' (by God, or by the church). In favour of this interpretation is that the verb occurs only here in the New Testament, and elsewhere it rarely has an active sense. According to Colossians, however, Christ *already* is the fulness of God. The whole fulness of deity dwells in him bodily now (Col. 1:19; 2:9), and it is improper to speak of filling him with God's presence. On the other hand, it would be strange to speak of the

231. Syntactically πλήρωμα ('fulness') is more naturally read as in apposition to σῶμα ('body'), which immediately precedes it, than with αὐτόν ('him'), which is twelve words earlier. The clause 'which is his body', on the latter view, becomes unhinged from the context and is merely an aside. Furthermore, the emphasis of vv. 22b and 23a is on the church in God's purposes. Given the drift of Paul's argument, it is natural to expect that this final clause would relate to the church. Finally, taking πλήρωμα ('fulness') as a reference to the 'body' is consistent with Eph. 3:19, where Paul prays that the readers may be filled with all the fulness of God. Cf. Col. 2:10, where, after mentioning that Christ is the fulness of God (v. 9), Paul speaks of the Colossians' having been filled in their union with him. Barth, 158, aptly comments: 'Eph 1:23 contains, in the form of appositions, two definitions of the Church: she is Christ's body and she is his fullness'.

232. Note the detailed discussion and interaction with other viewpoints by Lincoln, 73-76. The conclusion of J. Ernst, *Pleroma und Pleroma Christi: Geschichte und Deutung eines Begriffs der paulinischen antilegomena* (Regensburg: Pustet, 1970), 120, that the use of πλήρωμα ('fulness') is deliberately ambiguous (cf. also G. W. Dawes, *The Body*, 248), so that it involves both the church's being filled by Christ and the church's completing him is unlikely in the light of the theological context.

233. τοῦ τὰ πάντα ἐν πᾶσιν πληρουμένου.

church as already the 'fulness' but Christ as still being filled. Furthermore, the fact that only Christ (Eph. 4:10) and the Spirit (5:18) are seen elsewhere in Ephesians to be the active powers of filling suggests that the same role is attributed to Christ here. This is corroborated by Colossians 2:10, where the church is the recipient of the divine filling. Since the middle voice can have an active meaning in Koine Greek, it is preferable, with many writers, to treat the participle as having this significance here[234] (= 'him who fills').

(5) How, then, do we account for this equation of 'body' and 'fulness'? The flow of the argument in the immediate context is designed to assure the readers that they share in God's power and glory. His people are his inheritance in whom he will display to the universe the untold riches of his glory (v. 18). His incomparably great power is 'for us' (v. 19), while the body is empowered and directed by our head, Christ. Here in v. 23 Paul asserts that we, as Christ's body, *already* share in the divine 'fulness'. We may agree with J. B. Lightfoot: 'All the Divine graces which reside in Him are imparted to her [the church]; His "fullness" is communicated to her, and thus she may be said to be His pleroma'.[235] Later in the letter the apostle will pray that his readers 'might be filled with all the *fulness* of God' (3:19). Thus, the two sides of Pauline eschatology are precisely balanced, the 'already' and the 'not yet'. In the immediate context, however, where the apostle's concern is to assure the readers of the wealth of their resources in Christ, the stress is on the 'already'.

(6) Christ is the one who completely fills 'everything',[236] that is, the whole of creation, the earthly and the heavenly, comprising all of humanity as well as the entire angelic realm, especially the rebellious powers. The nature of this filling is not to be explained in a physical or spatial sense: Christ pervades all things with his sovereign rule, directing all things to their appointed end (cf. Heb. 1:3), and this entails his functioning as the powerful ruler over against the principalities (1:21) and giving grace and strength to his people, the church (4:13, 15-16).

To sum up. The conclusions of our exegesis of v. 23, albeit tentative,

---

234. So BDF §316(1), BAGD, 671, and a number of commentators. The participle πληρουμένου has been understood to be a true middle in which 'the action is done for the benefit of something vitally concerned with the subject' (G. E. Howard, 'The Head/Body Metaphors', 351), thereby stressing that Christ fills all things for himself. But there seems to be no good reason for such an emphasis, given that God is the subject of the main clause in v. 22b.

235. J. B. Lightfoot, cited by Arnold, 84.

236. τὰ πάντα ἐν πᾶσιν has been taken adverbally to signify that the church is the fulness of Christ, who is being *totally* filled by God, but it is preferable to understand τὰ πάντα ('everything') in its natural sense as the object of the clause and meaning the whole of creation, with ἐν πᾶσιν signifying 'in all respects' (BAGD, 633).

may be rendered as follows: '[the church, which is Christ's body], the fulness of him [i.e., Christ] who fills all things in every way'. God has given Christ as head over all things for the church. His supremacy over the cosmos is seen to be for the benefit of his people. As in Colossians (1:18, 24), so here in Ephesians 1:22-23 the church is said to be Christ's body. This is not stated of the cosmos, for even though he rules 'all things' as Lord, it is only the church that has the 'particular relationship with him which is indicated by the metaphor of the body'.[237] The final clause of v. 23 makes the additional point that the church is Christ's *fulness*. In Colossians, the term 'fulness' was applied to Christ; here in Ephesians its referent is the church. As head over all things Christ exercises his sovereign rule by 'filling' the universe. But only the church is his body, and he rules it, that is, he fills it in a special way with his Spirit, grace, and gifts: it is his fulness.[238] By speaking of the church as Christ's 'body' and 'fulness,' he emphatically underlines its significance within God's purposes. Its glorious place in the divine plan, however, provides no grounds for boasting, arrogance, or the display of a 'superior air', for the church is wholly dependent on Christ. In itself, it is nothing. Its privileged position comes from its relationship to the One who as head graciously fills it with his presence.

Paul's lengthy paragraph, which follows the magnificent eulogy (vv. 3-14), reports his thanks to God for the readers (vv. 15-16a) and his intercession for the realization of the blessings of the eulogy in their lives (vv. 16b-19), and employs confessional material in which God is praised for exercising his mighty power in raising Christ from the dead and exalting him to be head over all things for the church (vv. 20-23). Once again, there is a theological, christological, and ecclesiological focus in the passage. Paul wants his readers to understand and appreciate the divine salvation, and in particular the place which they as God's people have in the divine purposes. What has been done in Christ is for their benefit: God's power in him is available for those who believe (v. 19), and Christ's rule over the universe is for their benefit (v. 22). Let these predominantly Gentile Christians in Asia Minor, probably living under the pressures of the surrounding syncretistic environment with its truth claims and pagan lifestyle, take heart from what God has graciously and *powerfully* done in his Son on their behalf.

---

237. G. W. Dawes, *The Body*, 157.
238. Lincoln, 80.

Ephesians 2

C. Saved by Grace: Raised and Exalted with Christ, 2:1-10

[1]As for you, you were dead in your transgressions and sins, [2]in which you used to live when you followed the ways of this world and of the ruler of the kingdom of the air, the spirit who is now at work in those who are disobedient. [3]All of us also lived among them at one time, gratifying the cravings of our sinful nature and following its desires and thoughts. Like the rest, we were by nature objects of wrath. [4]But because of his great love for us, God, who is rich in mercy, [5]made us alive with Christ even when we were dead in transgressions — it is by grace you have been saved. [6]And God raised us up with Christ and seated us with him in the heavenly realms in Christ Jesus, [7]in order that in the coming ages he might show the incomparable riches of his grace, expressed in his kindness to us in Christ Jesus. [8]For it is by grace you have been saved, through faith — and this not from yourselves, it is the gift of God — [9]not by works, so that no one can boast. [10]For we are God's workmanship, created in Christ Jesus to do good works, which God prepared in advance for us to do.

Paul has prayed that his Christian readers might know the greatness of God's power towards them (1:17-19), and then praised God for exercising that same mighty power in raising Christ from the dead and exalting him to be head over all things for the church (vv. 20-23). He now reminds them of the mighty change that had been effected in their lives: they were spiritually dead (2:1-3), but out of his great kindness and mercy God has raised and exalted them with Christ (vv. 4-7).

There is some difference of opinion as to where Ephesians 2 fits into the structure of the letter. Those who regard the opening of the epistle as extending from 1:1-23 hold that the body of Ephesians commences at 2:1, where Paul begins to delineate the programmatic themes which he will develop further throughout the letter. Although the issue is finely balanced, our preference is to regard the letter body as commencing with the introductory eulogy of 1:3-14 (see the Introduction), and to understand 2:1-22 (which comprises two parallel sections, 2:1-10 and 2:11-22) as continuing and applying to the readers the major theme on which Paul is now launched, namely, the power of God's actions in Christ. The first half of Paul's reminder (vv. 1-10) presents the readers' past in terms of death, sinfulness, and bondage to evil forces and the flesh, while the second (vv. 11-22) depicts them as separated from the covenant promises to Israel and from God, and, in contrast, describes the present in terms of belonging to the new people of God (comprising Jews and Gentiles in the one new humanity) and being reconciled to God.

In this new stage of the argument the apostle goes out of his way to stress the close relationship between Christ (1:20-21) and believers (2:5-7). The connections and correlation are not simply literary devices.[1] Paul's readers have experienced the same power of God which was effective in Christ's resurrection and exaltation. God has made them alive with Christ (2:5). Believers have been raised from the dead with him (2:5, 6; cf. 1:19), they have been seated with him in the heavenly realms (2:6; cf. 1:20), and 'the coming age(s)' has particular reference to both (1:21; 2:7). Christ's destiny has become theirs.[2]

The paragraph consists of two sentences in the original: vv. 1-7 and vv. 8-10. The subject of the sentence ('God') and the main verb ('made alive') are not mentioned until vv. 4 and 5. Accordingly, the first sentence (vv. 1-7) falls into two parts, the anacoluthon of vv. 1-3 and the contrasting statement of vv. 4-7. This syntactical division of the paragraph reflects a threefold division in relation to its content: (a) vv. 1-3 describe the sinful condition of the readers' past and of the rest of humanity, (b) vv. 4-7 speak of the great love and mercy of God, who made the readers alive with Christ, and (c) vv. 8-10 summarize the nature of this salvation which God has effected. The sections are linked by means of repetitions: 'dead through trespasses' (vv. 1, 5) connects vv. 1-3 with vv. 4-7, while 'by grace you have been saved' (vv. 5, 8) links the middle section (vv. 4-7) with the summarizing conclusion (vv. 8-10). The verb 'live/walk' speaks of the pre-Christian way of life in v. 2 and of Christian living at v. 10, and thus it

---

1. T. G. Allen, 'Exaltation and Solidarity', 103-4. He adds: 'the correlations show the author's conviction that what God, who is the principal actor in both passages, has accomplished in Christ, he has also accomplished for believers'.

2. Schnackenburg, 87.

functions as an *inclusio* or envelope to bind the paragraph together as a unit.

One of the striking features of Ephesians 2 is the number of vivid contrasts between believers' previous condition outside of Christ and their current privileged experience of salvation. Those who were 'dead in trespasses and sins' (v. 1) have now been 'made alive' (v. 5). Following 'the ways of this world' and being under the lordship of the 'ruler of the kingdom of the air' (v. 2) stands in stark contrast to being in a relationship to Christ and seated with him in the heavenly realms (vv. 5, 6). God's wrath (v. 3) is balanced with his mercy, love, grace, and kindness (vv. 4, 5, 7), while the readers' former condition as children of wrath (v. 3) is parallelled with being saved by grace (vv. 5, 8).[3] (Note also the contrast in vv. 11-13.)

From a rhetorical perspective it has been argued that this pericope and the following one (2:11-22) function as the *narratio* ('statement of facts'), which states what has been done in the past so as to persuade the audience to ground their thinking and action upon it. But we have seriously questioned the application of rhetorical-critical principles to both the genre and the structure of Paul's letters (see the Introduction, 73-82). A number of the points Lincoln makes about the persuasive strategies in 2:1-10 seem to be valid, but there is no need to support our interpretation by using rhetorical analysis. There is a 'dramatic contrast in this passage between the readers' past and their present, a contrast addressed directly to the readers and appealing to both their minds and emotions, [as] the writer impresses on them how much they owe to what God has done in Christ'.[4] But this is evident from an exegesis of the text itself, not by appeal to external categories imposed on the material.

1. Dead in Transgressions and Sins, 2:1-3[5]

Following his introductory eulogy and prayer, Paul now concentrates on his readers in a special way. He describes their pre-Christian past (vv. 1-2) in terms of their being dead in trespasses and sins. Before God had made them alive with Christ they were deeply affected by evil, determining influences. These included their environment (*the ways of this world*, v. 2), an inner inclination towards evil (*the cravings of our sinful nature*, v. 3), and a supernaturally powerful opponent (*the ruler of the kingdom of the air, the*

---

3. On the 'once–now' contrast, see below, 157-58, 185, 190, 210.

4. So Lincoln, 91.

5. See P. T. O'Brien, 'Divine Analysis and Comprehensive Solution: Some Priorities from Ephesians', *RTR* 53 (1994), 130-42.

spirit who is now at work in those who are disobedient, v. 2). Like the rest of humanity outside of Christ they were out of fellowship with God, for they were *by nature objects of wrath* (v. 3).

1 The introductory 'and', which some earlier commentators took closely with 'you', indicates a new stage in the argument.[6] At the same time it signals a continuity of theme between 2:1-10 and the preceding paragraph. Those whom Paul addresses directly with an emphatic *you* are in the first place his Gentile readers in Asia Minor.[7] His mention of them in this way anticipates the specific reference to them as *Gentiles* in v. 11.

But he quickly goes on to write (v. 3a), *all of us also lived* in the same way (so adding himself and his fellow Jews), and then concludes with a reference to 'the rest of mankind' (v. 3b).[8] The spiritual state of the readers when they were outside of Christ, as well as of the rest of humanity, is death. The apostle's description is not that of 'some particularly decadent tribe or degraded segment of society, or even of the extremely corrupt paganism of his own day'. Rather, it is 'the biblical diagnosis of fallen man in fallen society everywhere'.[9]

Paul says that they were *dead in . . . transgressions and sins*. He uses the terms for death literally to denote physical death in Romans 14:9 and being united with Christ in his death in Colossians 2:20, while here he employs the adjective 'dead' figuratively to describe the state of being lost or under the dominion of death (*were* renders the present participle 'being'). It is sometimes called spiritual death and denotes a state of alienation or separation

---

6. See Acts 1:15; 2:1; 6:7; 15:1; Rom. 13:11; 1 Cor. 2:1; 3:1 for similar uses.

7. Lincoln, 91-92, concedes that the readers are 'primarily Gentile Christians (cf. 2:11)', but claims that this cannot be deduced from either the force of the καί ('and') or the use of the second person plural over against the first person plural. However, there has been a long history of interpretation which understands these and earlier second person plurals (see on 1:13-14, etc.) as referring to Gentile Christians. (Several recent interpreters who have rejected this view have, interestingly enough, also rejected Pauline authorship, e.g., Gnilka and Schnackenburg, in addition to Lincoln.) The mention of Gentiles as 'you' in 1:13-14 can be regarded as a typical Pauline anticipation of a motif developed more fully later in the letter (2:11-22; note esp. 3:6; cf. G. D. Fee, *God's Empowering Presence*, 669), while the parallels between 2:1-10 and 2:11-22, which Lincoln clearly recognizes, only serve to strengthen the case for the traditional interpretation. The *you* in v. 1 is specifically amplified as *you . . . Gentiles* in v. 11.

8. The participial clause καὶ ὑμᾶς ὄντας νεκρούς ('and you being dead') with which v. 1 begins demands a finite verb such as 'he brought you to life'. But the sentence is left incomplete as Paul expands not only on his readers' condition of spiritual death (vv. 1-2) but also on the condition of all humanity (v. 3). In v. 4 he starts a new sentence, picks up the participial clause in v. 5 (καὶ ὄντας ἡμᾶς νεκρούς), and then introduces the main verb, συνεζωοποίησεν ('he made us alive together').

9. Stott, 71.

from God.[10] This wretched and culpable condition has been caused by their transgressions and sins[11] (the datives are probably causal; cf. Rom. 11:20). At the same time the words characterize their previous existence outside of Christ as being spiritual death, hence 'dead *in* your trespasses and sins'. The plural *transgressions*[12] draws attention to individual acts of sin, while the addition of the synonym *sins* helps to form one concept (a hendiadys) which gives a comprehensive account of human evil. It conveys the idea of the fulness and variety of the readers' sinful past. As a result, they had no hope, were far from God (cf. 2:12), and were alienated from his life (4:18).

2 It was in these transgressions and sins[13] that the readers formerly lived their lives.[14] Twice in these verses the temporal adverb 'once' appears (vv. 2, 3) as Paul, by means of a short rhetorical form often employed in primitive Christian proclamation, draws a sharp contrast between the readers' pre-Christian past and their present standing in Christ (cf. Col. 1:22-23): 'you were once . . . but now you are . . .'. This schema appears almost exclusively in the epistolary literature of the New Testament (though see Acts 17:30), and is found in doctrinal, exhortatory, or personal contexts (Gal. 1:23; cf. 1 Tim. 1:13; Phlm. 11). It is frequently employed by Paul,[15] but

---

10. Against Meyer, 92, the description is not proleptic, 'liable to eternal death', but points to the present condition of those apart from Christ as being without spiritual life.

11. See the discussion of sin and its relationship to death in E. Best, 'Dead in Trespasses and Sins (Eph. 2:1)', in *Essays*, 69-85.

12. παράπτωμα, 'transgression, sin', usually refers to 'what a person has done in transgressing the will and law of God by some false step or failure' (Louw and Nida §88.297; cf. BAGD, 621). The word is used both of Adam's transgression (Rom. 5:16-20), and of Israel's (Rom. 11:11-12), where it carries the idea of rebellion against God. Note Rom. 4:25; Matt. 6:15. The ὑμῶν ('your [transgressions and sins]') at the end of the clause balances the ὑμᾶς ('you [were dead]') at the beginning.

13. The relative pronoun ἐν αἷς ('in which') agrees in gender with the nearer antecedent ἁμαρτίαις ('sins').

14. περιπατέω (lit. 'walk') is a Hebraism common in the Old Testament (translating *hālak*) which denotes ethical conduct or a way of living. Here it has to do with the behaviour of the readers before they became Christians. Paul often characterizes the life and conduct of the Christian by this verb 'walk' (Gal. 5:16; cf. v. 25; Rom. 6:4; 8:4; 14:15; 2 Cor. 4:2; Eph. 2:10; 4:1; 5:2, 15; Phil. 3:17, etc.). The Hebrew equivalent is found frequently in the Qumran texts to describe the activity of those who walk in 'the ways of darkness' (1QS 3:21), or of those who, showing themselves to be true sons of light, walk before God in an upright manner (1QS 1:8). The latter walk according to God's will (1QS 5:10; 9:24), refusing to please themselves (contrast CD 3:12). Cf. R. Bergmeier, *EDNT* 3:75-76.

15. Rom. 5:8-11; 7:5-6; 11:30-32; 1 Cor. 6:9-11; Gal. 1:23; 4:3-7, 8-10; Col. 2:13; 3:7. Note the treatment of this form in P. Tachau, *'Einst' und 'Jetzt' im Neuen Testament* (Göttingen: Vandenhoeck & Ruprecht, 1972), 12, 52-85. Although the 'once–now' contrast was used in Greek rhetoric as a stylistic device, the New Testament usage is far more than rhetorical and involves the substantial element of the contrast between the pre-Christian past and the Christian present (P. Tachau, *'Einst' und 'Jetzt'*, 94).

it is used by other New Testament authors as well.[16] The wonder of the salvation that has been experienced is contrasted with the lost situation from which God has freed them. The past condition is mentioned by terms relating either to sin (Rom. 5:8-11; 7:5; Eph. 2:1), ethical practices, alienation from God and his people (Col. 1:21; Eph. 2:3), or bondage to evil, supernatural forces (Eph. 2:2).

The gravity of their previous condition, however, serves to magnify the wonder of God's mercy. The past is recalled not because the emphasis falls upon it, but in order to draw attention to God's mighty action in Christ. In Ephesians 2:4, although there is no explicit use of 'now', the positive side of the contrast is strongly accented: '*But* God who is rich in mercy' has acted decisively on behalf of those who were objects of wrath; he has made them alive with Christ, raised them up, and seated them with him in the heavenly places (vv. 5-6). The break between the past and the present has already occurred. Vv. 8-10 underscore the contrast by repeating the clause 'by grace you have been saved' (v. 8) and indicating the purpose of 'walking' in good works (v. 10), which is the converse of 'walking in trespasses and sins', with which the passage began (v. 2).

The readers' former lifestyle, which characterizes all who are outside of Christ, was not true freedom but evidence of a fearful bondage to forces over which they had no control. Three compelling influences directed their lives: the world (v. 2), the devil (v. 2), and the flesh (v. 3). The first two of these evil influences are depicted by coordinated phrases, each of which is introduced by the preposition 'according to': (1) 'according to the age of this world', and (2) 'in accordance with the ruler of the realm of the air'.

In (1) the keyword[17] *aiōn* usually means 'age' or 'time span'. However, the term was well known in Hellenism as a personal deity, and it appears numerous times in the magical papyri with this sense. It was a popular expression for personal powers in the Nag Hammadi texts and other Gnostic documents. If it refers here to a deity 'Aion', as many commentators suppose, then it would have been readily intelligible to Gentile readers.[18]

But the context requires that this term be understood in the Jewish sense of a period of time. Paul has already used the word at 1:21 when referring to the typical Jewish two-age schema, and several verses later

16. 1 Pet. 2:10, 25; cf. Heb. 12:26.
17. Gk. αἰών.
18. Barth, Bruce, Gnilka, Nock, Sasse, Schnackenburg, and Schlier, e.g., take this line.

(v. 7) he employs it in a temporal sense.[19] The whole phrase 'according to the age of this world' signifies the world existing in that particular span of time. In these three references a contrast is being developed between the marks of the old age and the new age which is dawning in Christ Jesus. 'According to the manner of this world-age' is a way of speaking about both the spatial and temporal aspects of fallen human existence. The previous lifestyle of the readers has been dominated by this present evil age (cf. Gal. 1:4) and this world, rather than being focussed on heaven and the life of the age to come.[20] Their behaviour has been determined by the powerful influence of society's attitudes, habits, and preferences, which were alien to God and his standards.[21] Hence the NIV's rendering: *when you followed the ways of this world*.

(2) Those outside of Christ are not only subject to the pervasive bondage of the present evil age; they are also inspired and empowered by personal evil forces. Paul depicts the second hostile influence as a powerful supernatural being who rules over this host of evil spirits: *the ruler of the kingdom of the air*. Ephesians, as we have seen, contains more about the principalities and powers than any other New Testament letter and provides the most detailed response to these spiritual authorities (see on 1:21). Further, it draws special attention to the ultimate authority of evil lying behind them, namely, the devil (4:27; 6:11) or evil one (6:16), who is here called the 'ruler, or prince', a term used in the Old Testament for a national, local, or tribal leader,[22] and refers to him as the chief or leader among these powers of darkness. In the Gospels he is called the 'ruler of the demons' (Matt. 9:34; 12:24; Mark 3:22; Luke 11:15) and the 'prince of this world' (John 12:31; 14:30; 16:11). He is the god of this age (cf. 2 Cor. 4:4), a personal centre of the power of evil.

---

19. It would have been confusing to his readers for Paul to have switched from a temporal force of αἰών at 1:21 to a personal reference in 2:2 and back to a temporal sense at v. 7 without giving some clear indication of an intended change in meaning. Further, this would be the only clear use of αἰών in a personalized sense in the whole of the Pauline corpus. But understood as 'the *age* of this world' the phrase is another example of the piling up of synonyms in genitive constructions which is characteristic of Ephesians. Cf. Arnold, 59-61; and S. H. T. Page, *Powers,* 185.

20. Lincoln, 95.

21. Stott, 73, gives the following contemporary explanation: 'Both words "age" and "world" express a whole social value-system which is alien to God. It permeates, indeed dominates, non-Christian society and holds people in captivity. Wherever human beings are being dehumanized — by political oppression or bureaucratic tyranny, by an outlook that is secular (repudiating God), amoral (repudiating absolutes) or materialistic (glorifying the consumer market), by poverty, hunger or unemployment or racial discrimination, or by any form of injustice — there we can detect the sub-human values of "this age" and "this world"'.

22. Gk. ἄρχων. Gen. 12:15; Num. 2:3, 5, 7; Judg. 8:3; Ezek. 9:27.

This evil ruler is in control of *the kingdom of the air.* Here, as in Colossians 1:13,[23] the word rendered *kingdom* denotes the 'realm' or 'sphere' of the devil's influence rather than his personal authority. That realm is further defined as the 'air'.[24] According to the ancient world-view, the air formed the intermediate sphere between earth and heaven. It was the dwelling place of evil spirits (as the magical papyri[25] and the literature of Judaism[26] attest), not an atmosphere of opinion with ideas, attitudes, and the like, which is a more recent Western understanding. The 'kingdom of the air', then, is another way of indicating the 'heavenly realm', which, according to Ephesians 6:12, is the abode of those principalities and powers, the 'world-rulers of this darkness' and 'spiritual forces of wickedness', against which the people of Christ wage war. The hostile powers inhabit the heavenly realms (cf. Eph. 3:10; 6:12), a notion that has its antecedents in the Old Testament and Jewish thought.[27] If there is any distinction between the expressions the *kingdom of the air* and the 'heavenly realm', it is that the former indicates 'the lower reaches of that realm and therefore emphasizes the proximity of this evil power and his influence over the world'.[28]

The devil is further characterized as the spirit[29] who exercises effective and compelling power over the lives of men and women: *the spirit who is now at work in those who are disobedient.* His manner of operation is

23. Where ἐξουσία is rendered 'the *tyranny* [of darkness]'.

24. Gk. ἀήρ.

25. *PGM* I.97-194; IV.2699. See Arnold, 60, who suggests that *PGM* CI.39 may provide the closest parallel to Ephesians 2:2: 'And again I conjure you by the one who is in charge of the air (κατὰ τοῦ ἔχοντος τὸν ἀέρα)'. On ἀήρ see BAGD, 20, and H. Merklein, *EDNT* 1:34, together with the literature cited.

26. Note *T. Benjamin* 3:4: 'For the person who fears God and loves his neighbour cannot be plagued by the spirit of the air [ἀερίου πνεύματος] of Beliar since he is sheltered by the fear of God'. Cf. Arnold, 60, 191.

27. Job 1:6; Dan. 10:13, 21; 2 Macc. 5:2; cf. Philo, *De Somniis* 1.134-35, 141; note *De Gigantibus* 6, where God's angels are said to be 'souls that fly in the air'.

28. Lincoln, 96; cf. Schnackenburg, 91.

29. The genitive τοῦ πνεύματος ('of the spirit') has been taken: (1) as in apposition to the immediate antecedent, τοῦ ἀέρος ('of the air'), so providing an explanation of the air as the spiritual atmosphere controlling the disobedient (Caird, 51; Schlier, 104; cf. S. H. T. Page, *Powers,* 185), or (2) as parallel to τῆς ἐξουσίας ('of the realm') and governed by τὸν ἄρχοντα ('the ruler'), signifying that the ruler of the kingdom of the air is the ruler of the spirit that is now at work in the disobedient (Lincoln, 96). But to speak of 'the ruler of the spirit which now operates' is rather unusual if not awkward, and it is better (3) to regard the genitive τοῦ πνεύματος ('of the spirit') as one of apposition (cf. BDF §167) to τὸν ἄρχοντα ('the ruler'), or as attracted to the preceding genitive phrase (cf. Gnilka, 115; Arnold, 61; and G. D. Fee, *God's Empowering Presence,* 679; note, however, D. B. Wallace, *Greek Grammar,* 104). Accordingly, this phrase is independent of and parallel with the preceding one. This spirit is clearly the devil, the ruler of all spiritual forces.

described by means of a dynamic power term which, together with its cognate noun,[30] always denotes supernatural power in the New Testament. It has already been used in Ephesians of God, who mightily works out everything according to his will (1:11) and who has exerted his mighty strength in Jesus' resurrection and exaltation (1:20). Here the word designates the spirit's evil supernatural activity whereby he exercises a powerful, compelling influence over the lives of men and women. Indeed, so effective is his *present* evil working that Paul can refer to his victims as 'sons of disobedience', that is, men and women whose lives are characterized by disobedience. They are rebels against the authority of God who prefer to answer the promptings of the archenemy.[31] Such men and women have not responded in gratitude or praise to the evidences of God's eternal power and divinity which he has provided in creation (Rom. 1:19-21; cf. 2:8). They reject the gospel (cf. 2 Thess. 2:8) and disregard his will. This is not to suggest, as some contemporary Christians do, that those who live in disobedience to God are necessarily 'possessed' by an evil spirit. *All* who are outside of Christ live in a kingdom called 'the tyranny of darkness' (cf. Col. 1:13) in which the evil one holds sway. But not all 'sons of disobedience' are demon-possessed.

Although the ruler of this world has been defeated by Christ at the cross (Col. 2:14-15; cf. Heb. 2:14-15; Eph. 1:20-22), he does not surrender without a struggle and he continues to make his powerful influence felt. He is effectively at work in those who have not personally benefitted from God's deliverance in Christ, while he still poses a threat to believers (Rom. 8:38-39; Eph. 4:27), who must steadfastly resist him by God's power (Eph. 6:10-20; cf. 1 Pet. 5:8-9).

3 Having reminded his Gentile Christian readers of their former pagan existence, Paul now asserts that prior to their conversion he and other Jewish believers had been in a similar desperate state, for *all of us also* were included among the disobedient.[32] We Jews too, he states, had followed a lifestyle that was in conformity with 'the desires of the flesh'. Paul's point is similar to the argument of Romans 1:18–3:20, where it is clear that Jews were no better off than Gentiles. Both alike were 'under sin' (3:9).

---

30. Gk. ἐνεργέω (to 'function, work') and ἐνέργεια ('work, practice'), with possible focus upon the energy or force involved (Louw and Nida §42.3).

31. C. E. Arnold, *Powers of Darkness* (Leicester: Inter-Varsity, 1992), 125, notes that 'Paul emphasizes here the work of the evil spirit in people as opposed to institutions'. On the issue of the 'demonic' in relation to structures, see P. T. O'Brien, 'Principalities and Powers', 141-43.

32. The ἐν οἷς ('among whom') refers to the immediate antecedent 'those who are disobedient', not to the transgressions and sins of v. 1 (so most commentators, against Robinson, 155).

In turning to the role of the 'flesh' Paul now describes the nature of the pre-Christian life from a different perspective. According to vv. 1 and 2 men and women outside of Christ have been deeply affected by evil, determining influences — the environment ('the age of this world') and a supernaturally powerful opponent ('the prince of the power of the air, the spirit that is now at work among those who are disobedient'). Here the description of the former life is in terms of our fallen, self-centred human nature. In this context 'flesh' does not stand for a person's physical existence,[33] but humanity in its sinfulness and rebellion against God. It is the sphere in which a person is unable to please him (Rom. 8:8). The 'passions of the flesh' (cf. Gal. 5:16, 24) in which those outside of Christ had once *lived* are not to be thought of simply as sexual or carnal appetites. They include anger, envy, rage, dissensions, and selfish ambition as well (Gal. 5:20). *Following its desires and thoughts:* Paul adds that our conduct was once in keeping with the desires of this unregenerate outlook; it dominated our lives, and we carried out its dictates.[34] Even our thoughts[35] were corrupt, and they controlled our actions.[36]

Not only were Paul and his fellow Jews dead and enslaved; they also stood condemned: *we were by nature objects* [lit. children] *of wrath. By nature* can only mean 'by birth' at Galatians 2:15, and this is its significance here. The expression 'children of wrath' is a Hebraism, like 'sons of disobedience' (v. 2), and means worthy to receive divine judgment.[37] Paul and his fellow Jews were deserving of and liable to wrath just as much as the Gentiles were. This dreadful predicament has been inherited, according to Paul, from the one man through whom 'sin came into the world . . .

33. Note the other uses of 'flesh' in Ephesians: 2:11, 14; 5:29, 31; 6:5, 12.

34. Cf. Bruce, 284. Meyer, 101, suggested that the participial clause 'doing the will of the flesh' specifies 'the way and manner of this walk'.

35. διάνοια ('thought, understanding, disposition') usually appears in the singular. The bad connotation is not implied in the plural (cf. LXX Num. 15:39) but arises from the context. Note BAGD, 187, and M. Lattke, *EDNT* 1:309-10.

36. There is some difficulty in determining the precise relationship of τῆς σαρκός ('of the flesh') to τῶν διανοιῶν ('of our thoughts'). Some take the full expression τὰ θελήματα τῆς σαρκὸς καὶ τῶν διανοιῶν to mean 'the desires of our body and minds', with σάρξ signifying 'body' and διάνοιαι 'minds' (so, e.g., Bratcher and Nida, 42-43). The difficulty with this is that σάρξ has two different meanings in the one verse, 'flesh' as 'unregenerate human nature' and as 'body'. Lincoln, 83, 98, regards τῶν διανοιῶν ('thoughts') as a separate category from τὰ θελήματα τῆς σαρκός ('the wishes of the flesh') but in some sense parallel to it. He concedes that this may be moving away from Pauline usage. Perhaps it is best, with Bruce, 284, to take τῶν διανοιῶν ('of our thoughts') as in apposition to or explicative of τῆς σαρκός ('of the flesh'), and recognize that here the desires of the flesh are not different from those of the minds. Cf. Meyer, 101.

37. Note the expression 'a son of death' (2 Sam. 12:5), which means that 'he deserves to die'.

and so death spread to all because all sinned' (Rom. 5:12). If the result of one man's trespass led to condemnation for all human beings (v. 18), because all humanity was encapsulated in that one man, then this is to say that all are inherently *(by nature)* subject to condemnation.[38] The same point is made here: *like the rest* signifies that the whole of humanity outside of Christ lies in this sinful condition with its consequences (cf. Rom. 1:18–3:20).

The 'wrath' in view is God's holy anger against sin and the judgment that results (cf. Eph. 5:6; Col. 3:5, 6). It is neither an impersonal process of cause and effect, nor God's vindictive anger, nor unbridled and unrighteous revenge, nor an outburst of passion. Wrath describes neither some autonomous entity alongside God, nor some principle of retribution that is not to be associated closely with his personality. Furthermore, the wrath of God does not stand over against his love and mercy. Wrath and love are not mutually exclusive, as the following verse makes abundantly clear: *But because of his great love for us, God, who is rich in mercy* (v. 4). He is a holy God, and therefore he does not stand idly by when people act unrighteously, transgress his law, show disdain to him as their creator, or spurn his kindness and mercy. He acts in a righteous manner, punishing sin in the present and especially on the final day. Yet God also acquits the guilty, and only the person who understands something of the greatness of his wrath will be mastered by the greatness of his mercy. The converse is also true: only the person who has experienced the greatness of God's mercy can understand something of how great his wrath must be.[39]

In his profound analysis of the human condition the apostle has described the character of the pre-Christian life from three different perspectives — the world (v. 2), the devil (v. 2), and the flesh (v. 3). This analysis is consistent with the teaching of James (cf. Jas. 3:15) and John (1 John 2:15-17; 3:7-10). 'The source of evil tendencies is both internal and external to people as well as supernatural. Individuals possess an internal inclination toward evil, and their environment . . . also strongly influences them'.[40] As a result men and women cannot respond to life's decisions neutrally. They are deeply affected by evil, determining influences. These influences may be described in terms of the environment ('the age of this world'), a supernaturally powerful opponent ('the prince of the power of the air, the spirit that is now at work among those who are disobedient'),

---

38. Bruce, 284-85. For an insightful theological treatment of Adam's sin, see now H. Blocher, *Original Sin: Illuminating the Riddle* (Leicester: Apollos, 1997), esp. 63-81.

39. G. Stählin, *TDNT* 5:425.

40. C. E. Arnold, *Powers*, 125.

and an inner inclination towards evil ('the flesh'). Arnold's comment on this state of affairs is worth quoting in full:

> Paul's teaching suggests that the explanation for our behavior is not to be found exclusively in human nature or in terms of the world's influence. Similarly, an exclusively demonic explanation for deviant behavior is unduly myopic. Rather, we should explain behavior on the basis of human nature, environment and the demonic — all three simultaneously. One part may play a leading role, but all three parts need to be considered.[41]

In Ephesians there is considerable emphasis on the spirit 'powers'. This has apparently been occasioned by an epistolary situation in which many of the readers were keenly aware of demonic 'powers' being at work and needed (further) instruction about the place of these 'powers' in relation to Christ and the believer. But the Pauline conception of the 'flesh' has not been replaced in Ephesians by another explanation for sin. The influence of the world and the flesh is coordinated with the influence of the evil 'powers'. Paul regards the three influences as complementary, leading individuals into sin, transgression, and disobedience.[42]

2. Because of His Mercy and Love God Made Us Alive with Christ, 2:4-7

4 The magnificent change which God has effected is jubilantly sounded forth. His gracious initiative and sovereign action stand in wonderful contrast with the hopeless condition of fallen humanity which has been described in vv. 1-3. Men and women outside of Christ were the objects of divine wrath, *but God* had mercy on them. We were dead, *but* he has made us alive with Christ. We were in bondage to evil powers, *but God* has seated us with Christ in the heavenly realms. A completely new situation has arisen because he has taken every necessary step to reverse our condition in sin.

What prompted God to act so freely and mercifully on our behalf? Using four groups of words, the apostle shows that the origins of God's saving initiative are to be found in his *mercy* (v. 4), his *great love* (v. 4), his *rich grace* (vv. 5, 7, and 8), and his *kindness* to us in Christ Jesus (v. 7). The whole paragraph emphasizes that he acted on our behalf simply because of his own gracious and merciful character. Our experience of salvation was totally unmerited, since we were dead in our trespasses, subject to

41. C. E. Arnold, *Powers,* 125-26.
42. Arnold, 62.

the entanglements of the world, the devil, and the flesh, and thus destined for divine judgment.

Up to this point in the paragraph no subject or main verb has been mentioned.[43] Now the subject *God* is introduced, while the main verb *made alive* appears in v. 5. However, before God's saving intervention is described two participial clauses intervene. The first, '[God] being rich in mercy', draws attention to the circumstance or reason why he brought us to life with Christ, while the second, 'we being dead in our trespasses', reiterates the point made about spiritual death in v. 1, though now with reference to Jews and Gentiles alike.

God, who is rich in mercy. In the Old Testament God is frequently characterized in this way: he 'abounds in mercy' (Exod. 34:6; Ps. 103:8; Jonah 4:2), indeed, he delights in it (Mic. 7:8). 'Mercy' often represents the Hebrew term *ḥeseḏ*, which has been taken to refer to Yahweh's steadfast covenant loyalty and love, especially when Israel was unfaithful. F. I. Andersen has shown, however, that this is 'an expression of love and generosity which is unexpected'.[44] It does not fall within the domain of duty and obligation, though the promise to show mercy[45] leads to a commitment on Yahweh's part to his people. In the Old Testament his mercy is often spontaneous. It is shown to a recipient in a desperate, helpless situation, and it is regularly associated with his love, grace, and compassion (note especially Exod. 20:5-6; 34:6-7; Num. 14:18-19; Deut. 7:9-10), features which are explicitly found in the context of Ephesians 2.[46]

Paul speaks elsewhere of the free mercy of God in relation to the wide-scale rejection of the gospel by Israel (Rom. 9:15, 16, 18), as well as in terms of God's ultimate plan of salvation for both Israel and the Gentiles (Rom. 11:30-32).[47] According to Ephesians 2 the one who is *rich*

43. By means of this feature (anacoluthon) v. 1 is elaborated by vv. 2 and 3; at the same time the contrast appearing in v. 4 is more strongly set forth. 'The new position of believers is a result *only* of the nature and activity of God' (Best, 213, emphasis added).

44. F. I. Andersen, 'Yahweh, the Kind and Sensitive God', in *God, Who Is Rich in Mercy: Essays Presented to Dr. D. B. Knox*, ed. P. T. O'Brien and D. G. Peterson (Homebush West, NSW: Lancer, 1986), 41-88, esp. 44.

45. Lit. 'to do *ḥeseḏ*'.

46. The noun ἔλεος, 'mercy, compassion, pity' (BAGD, 250; cf. Louw and Nida §88.76), and its cognates appear over seventy times in the New Testament. In the Synoptic Gospels the divine mercy is singularly demonstrated in Jesus' ministry as he heals the sick (Mark 10:47, 48 and parallels; Luke 17:13), drives out demons (Matt. 15:22; 17:15; Mark 5:19), and proclaims God's unmerited forgiveness (Matt. 18:33). Mercy is to be shown to others by those who themselves have received God's mercy (Matt. 5:7; 18:33). See also F. Staudinger, *EDNT* 1:429-31.

47. Paul himself had received mercy from the Lord (1 Cor. 7:25), enabling him to become an apostle (2 Cor. 4:1; cf. 1 Tim. 1:13, 16). In these references the mercy of God is

in mercy has lavished it on Gentiles as well as Jews (here the *us* is inclusive).

God's love is conjoined with his mercy as another motivation[48] for the divine initiative in saving his people. That love is emphatically underscored by the adjective *great* and the cognate expression 'the great *love* with which he *loved* us'.[49] As Paul has stressed the riches of God's mercy, so he now asserts the greatness of his love. God's love for his people in Christ is a particular thrust of Romans (cf. 5:5, 8; 8:39). And as in Romans 5:8, so here God's love is focussed on the love of Christ, which led to his giving himself up as a sacrifice on behalf of his people (Eph. 5:2, 25).

5 Paul returns to the line of thought begun in v. 1 as he picks up the opening words of the paragraph. However, he makes two changes. First, he omits from the phrase *in your transgressions and sins* the noun *sins,* which had been used synonymously with *transgressions* to form one concept. This omission does not really alter the sense. The second change, from *you* to *we,* is more significant. It indicates, in the light of v. 2, that Jews along with Gentiles are now included among those who were spiritually dead: *when we were dead in transgressions.* The introductory 'and', which is also picked up from v. 1, connects the two participial clauses, and these together set out in full perspective what God has done: it was out of his great love *and* when we were dead in our trespasses that he made us alive with Christ.[50]

Only now is the main verb which governs the paragraph, (God) *made us alive,* introduced, and it is the first of three verbs compounded with the preposition 'with' which point to the union between Christ and his followers (cf. 1:20). Speaking of the mighty salvation that has already been won, Paul maintains that believers have been made alive together with Christ, raised up with him, and made to sit with him in the heavenly places.[51] What God has accomplished in Christ he has also accomplished

---

tied in with salvation or Paul's calling to be an apostle. At Phil. 2:27, as in the Synoptic examples, the divine mercy is shown to an individual in desperate physical need: it is the sovereign merciful act of God himself by which Epaphroditus is restored to health.

48. The preposition διά with the accusative case of words denoting emotion signifies motivation and here should be rendered 'out of [his great love]' (so BAGD, 181; Lincoln, 100; cf. Matt. 27:18; Luke 1:78; John 7:13; Phil. 1:15).

49. Note Eph. 1:6, 19, 20; 4:1 for a similar use of cognate nouns and verbs.

50. It is just possible that the introductory καί ('and') intensifies the participial clause, thus indicating that *even* when we were in this wretched condition of death God acted so graciously for us. The ὄντας stresses the condition of sinners as 'being' that of death; cf. Schnackenburg, 94.

51. Greek: συνεζωοποίησεν ('he made alive with'), συνήγειρεν ('he raised up with'), and συνεκάθισεν ('he seated with'). On the subject of our dying and rising 'with Christ', see R. C. Tannehill, *Dying and Rising with Christ: A Study in Pauline Theology* (Berlin:

for believers. There is a correlation in both thought and vocabulary between 1:20-21 and 2:1-7, particularly between 1:20 and 2:6 (see also below); the parallelism clearly goes beyond the bounds of coincidence. And the relationship with Christ that is in view affects believers' destinies, for it involves their sharing in his destiny.

At the very time when we were spiritually dead *God made us alive with Christ.*[52] The verb to 'make alive, give life to' was used as a simple synonym for the verb to 'raise'[53] when speaking of the eschatological raising from the dead (cf. 1 Cor. 15:22 with Rom. 8:11). Only in Colossians 2:13 and Ephesians 2:5 is the compound verb 'make alive, together with', to be found. Paul's readers have come to life with Christ, who was dead and rose again; their new life, then, is a sharing in the new life which he received when he rose from the dead. It is only in union with him that death is vanquished and new life, an integral part of God's new creation, received. Because the believer's previous condition has been spoken of as a state of death (vv. 1, 5), there is no direct reference to Christ's death or to the believer's participation in it. Instead, the sharp contrast between our former condition outside of Christ and being made alive with him is presented.

Because of the clear allusion here in vv. 5 and 6 to the historic event of Christ's resurrection (1:20) and the explicit association of believers with that event, it is best to understand Paul's focus as upon Christ's own resurrection, not the appropriation of it by the believer at baptism.[54] Unlike Colossians 2:12-13, the context of Ephesians 2:1-10 contains no hint of baptism.

The notion of believers being made alive with Christ is developed in v. 6, where God's action is described more precisely in terms of their being raised up and seated with Christ. Since the spiritual death depicted in 2:1-3 included a fearful bondage (to the world, the devil, and the flesh), and divine condemnation, the rescue act by which we are made alive implies the forgiveness of sins and liberation from these tyrannical forces. In Colossians 2:13 being made alive with Christ is closely associated with the forgiveness of sins and deliverance from principalities and powers (vv. 13-15).

Töpelmann, 1967); E. Schweizer, 'Dying and Rising with Christ', *NTS* 14 (1967), 1-14; and M. A. Seifrid, *DPL*, 433-36.

52. The 'making alive with' does not refer, as A. Lindemann (*Die Aufhebung,* 119) claims, to the union of Christians with one another — whether Gentile and Jewish Christians, or all Christians in general — but to being made alive with Christ. This presupposes the reading τῷ Χριστῷ ('with Christ') rather than ἐν τῷ Χριστῷ ('in Christ'). Cf. Schnackenburg, 94-95.

53. ζωοποιέω was used synonymously with ἐγείρω.

54. Or the sealing of the Spirit, as Barth, 232-38, argues.

In a parenthesis which anticipates the fuller discussion of v. 8, Paul addresses his (mainly Gentile) readers and, using salvation language, proclaims what has been done for them. He draws attention to a mighty rescue which arose out of God's gracious initiative, which had already been accomplished in Christ, and which has abiding consequences for them: *it is by grace*[55] *you have been saved*. This joyful acclamation,[56] in effect, provides a summary of what God has already done in making them alive together with Christ, raising them up with him, and making them sit with him in the heavenly places.

Grace[57] is the theological concept that most clearly expresses Paul's understanding of Christ's work of salvation (cf. Rom. 3:23-24). The apostle's message is the 'gospel of the grace of God' (Acts 20:24); it stands opposed to any idea of work or merit — indeed, the idea of gift (free and unearned) is at the heart of this word (cf. Eph. 2:8-10). Grace, 'favour towards men contrary to their desert', is attributed to God in his relations with sinful human beings (Rom. 3:21-26; 4:4; 5:15, etc.) and to Christ (Rom. 5:15; 1 Cor. 16:23), inasmuch as the gracious attitude of God to sinners is also that of Christ (2 Cor. 8:9; cf. Rom. 5:8); and it is the work of Jesus, especially his death, that manifested God's grace (Rom. 3:24; 5:2; Eph. 1:6-7). It is the basis of the whole work of salvation.

Grace is a key theme in Ephesians. According to the introductory eulogy (Eph. 1:3-14) God lavished his grace on us in the Beloved (vv. 6-8), particularly by delivering us from judgment on our trespasses. The riches of divine grace are the ultimate cause of our redemption (v. 7) and provide the reason for that deliverance. Paul's receiving the gospel, his calling to minister to the Gentiles, and his ability to fulfil his missionary task from beginning to end were due solely to the grace of God (3:2, 7-8). The significance of this grace is amplified and further explained, not least by a number of contrasts, in the immediate context of 2:7-9. In particular, it is to be noted that although Paul's readers have experienced the reality of God's grace in the present, according to v. 7 it is his intention to lavish the full abundance of his grace upon believers in the coming age.

---

55. The dative χάριτι is a dative of cause and is best translated 'by grace' rather than 'because of grace', since the latter might be taken 'as indicating only God's motive, but not the basis of our salvation' (so D. B. Wallace, *Greek Grammar,* 167-68).

56. That those who were dead in sin should be granted a share in Christ's resurrection life is such a magnificent demonstration of divine grace that 'it calls for an immediate tribute to that grace' (Bruce, 286).

57. For further details on 'grace' in Paul see K. Berger, *EDNT* 3:457-60, and A. B. Luter, *DPL,* 372-74.

In Paul's letters the 'salvation' word-group[58] is used only in connection with humankind's relations with God. The terms often have an eschatological orientation, so that negatively they refer to a deliverance from God's wrath at the final judgment (Rom. 5:9-10; 1 Cor. 3:15; 5:5; 1 Thess. 1:10; 5:9) and positively to the reinstatement in that glory of God which was lost through sin (Rom. 8:18-30; 2 Thess. 2:13-14).[59] Here in Ephesians 2:5 (cf. v. 8), however, salvation has already been accomplished and experienced. The verb to 'save'[60] includes God's acts of making us alive, raising us up, and seating us with Christ. It describes a rescue from death, wrath, and bondage and a transfer into the new dominion with its manifold blessings. The periphrastic perfect construction draws attention to the resulting state of salvation.[61]

However, this emphasis in Ephesians on the past and present aspects of salvation should not surprise us.[62] In the eulogy of 1:3-14 God has been praised for the blessings of salvation *already* granted to believers. Elsewhere in Paul salvation has a present[63] dimension to it as well as a past. At Romans 8:24 the apostle states: 'we were saved'.[64] But this is immediately qualified with the words 'in hope', a phrase which points to the future when believers will experience fully all that salvation means. Finally, the aorists and realized eschatology of Ephesians 2:5 and 6 are balanced by the future dimension of v. 7 (cf. 1:21),[65] thus confirming that a future eschatology has not been entirely displaced by this stress on the presence of salvation.[66]

58. For example, σῴζω (to 'save') and σωτηρία ('salvation').

59. Cf. also Rom. 13:11; Phil. 1:28; 2:12; 1 Thess. 5:8.

60. The question has been raised why Paul, if he was the author of Ephesians, has used salvation language rather than the more usual 'justification' terminology. In response we note: first, it is doubtful whether the expression 'you have been justified' accurately summarizes the three surrounding verbs, each of which begins with συν- ('with'). Secondly, the threat to the readers appears not to have been from Jewish legalists who made an issue out of obedience to the law. The term 'law' appears only once (Eph. 2:15), while at 2:9, where Paul asserts that no one is saved by works, he makes no reference to 'works *of the law*', an expression which might have been expected had he been engaged with Judaizing opponents. Thirdly, the salvation language, together with the dying and rising with Christ terminology, suggests a transfer of dominions, and this was particularly apt for readers living in fear of demonic influence. Note the discussion in Arnold, 149.

61. So S. E. Porter, *Verbal Aspect*, 468, renders ἐστὲ σεσῳσμένοι as 'you are in a state of salvation'; cf. D. B. Wallace, *Greek Grammar*, 575. The passive voice and the emphatic reference to *grace* underscore the point that it comes as a gift of God.

62. Against A. Lindemann, *Aufhebung*, 137, who considers the thought to be 'totally un-Pauline'.

63. 1 Cor. 1:18; 15:2; 2 Cor. 2:15; 6:2; Phil. 2:12.

64. The aorist ἐσώθημεν is used.

65. Lincoln, 105.

66. Note the conclusion of H. E. Lona, *Die Eschatologie*, 427-28, and Arnold's discussion, 145-49.

6 The thought of believers being made alive with Christ is developed in v. 6, where God's action is more precisely described in terms of their being raised up and seated with Christ.[67] In conscious dependence on the christological statement of 1:20, Paul uses two compound verbs commencing with the prefix 'with', 'raised *with*' *(synēgeiren)* and 'seated *with*' *(synekathisen)*, and these, qualified by the prepositional phrase *in Christ Jesus* (signifying 'in our union with Christ'),[68] indicate that what God did for Christ he did at the same time for believers. The inclusive nature of Christ's resurrection and exaltation is thus underscored; it is not simply a case of believers accompanying Christ on a journey over the same terrain.[69]

Here, as in Colossians 2:12; 3:1, the resurrection of believers with Christ has *already* taken place. It is sometimes suggested that this notion is at variance with the 'genuine' Pauline letters, where the resurrection of believers remains a hope for the future (cf. Rom. 6:5-8; 2 Cor. 4:14; Phil. 3:11). But while the concept of the believer's participation in the risen life of Christ finds clearer expression in Colossians and Ephesians than elsewhere, this is not to suggest that it is absent from the earlier epistles, or that someone else is responsible for the phraseology, so giving clearer expression to the apostle's central thought than Paul himself could give! The earlier epistles presume the *present* experience of the resurrection life in Christ. Whether we regard the future tenses of Romans 6:5 and 8 as logical futures or real ones, it is clear that in vv. 11 and 13, where Paul bids his readers to present themselves as alive to God, he believes that they as Christians enjoy a new sort of life here and now. How can believers be expected to 'walk in newness of life' (Rom. 6:4) or to behave as those 'who have been brought from death to life' (v. 13; cf. v. 9) if they are still dead and buried with no hope of resurrection before the last trumpet? The variations in terminology are less significant for the question of the authorship of Ephesians (and Colos-

---

67. The statement 'God made us alive (συνεζωοποίησεν) with Christ' is further explained through the following two verbs: 'that is (καί), he has raised us (συνήγειρεν) with him and made us to sit (συνεκάθισεν) with him' (so Schnackenburg, 88, 95; cf. A. Lindemann, *Die Aufhebung*, 121. Against Stott, 80-81, who claims: 'These verbs ["made alive", "raised", and "made to sit"] refer to the three successive historical events in the saving career of Jesus, which are normally called the resurrection, the ascension and the session').

68. Rather than 'through the agency of Christ Jesus', which is the way J. A. Allan, 'The "in Christ" Formula', 58, and Gnilka, 120, take it. Note T. G. Allen, 'Exaltation and Solidarity', 116.

69. T. G. Allen, 'Exaltation and Solidarity', 105; cf. B. Weber, '"Setzen" — "Wandeln" — "Stehen" im Epheserbrief', *NTS* 41 (1995), 478-80.

sians) than for their distinctive emphases in response to the different situations of the letters.[70]

Elsewhere in Paul the language of dying and rising with Christ (e.g., Rom. 6:3-4; Col. 2:11-12, 20; 3:1, 3) focusses particularly on being joined with Christ in the events of redemptive history. For men and women to have died and been raised with him means to be transferred from the old dominion to the new. The same point is made in Ephesians 2:6 with its focus on God's having raised believers in Christ Jesus. The additional element in Ephesians, which goes beyond anything mentioned elsewhere in Paul, is that God has seated them with Christ in the heavenly realms.[71] This fresh point, however, is simply making explicit what was implied in Colossians 3:1-3, where believers are said to share Christ's risen life in the heavenly realm, and on the basis of which they are exhorted to seek the things above.[72] Not only do the readers participate in Christ's resurrection life; they also share in his exaltation and consequent victory over the powers. The formulation in Ephesians 2:6 is parallel to the expression of 1:20, except that significantly Paul does not add 'at his right hand'. Christ's exalted status in the heavenly realm is not shared since his relationship to the Father is unique.

This emphasis on realized eschatology with its explicit mention of believers being seated with Christ in the heavenly realms makes good sense in the light of the hostile role of the 'powers', presented in the wider context of Ephesians (cf. 1:21; 2:1-2; 3:10; 6:10-20). According to 1:19-22 Paul praises God's incomparably great power by which he raised and exalted Christ to a position 'far above' every level of the powers. Now this exalted Christology is applied directly to the readers of the letter. Because they have been identified with Christ in his resurrection and exaltation, they, too, have a position of superiority and authority over the evil powers. They no longer live under the authority and coercion of the 'ruler of the kingdom of the air' (2:2). The implications are clear: since they have been transferred from the old dominion to the new reign of Christ, they do not have to succumb to the evil one's designs.[73] The power of God which raised Jesus from the dead is now available to them as they live in this world (cf. 2:10; 4:1, 17; 5:2, 8, 15),

---

70. Cf. P. T. O'Brien, *Colossians, Philemon,* 26, 119-21, 168-72.

71. Note W. H. Harris, '"The Heavenlies"', 77-78.

72. The idea of a present experience of heaven appears elsewhere in Paul (cf. Gal. 4:26; 1 Cor. 15:47-49; 2 Cor. 12:2-3; Phil. 3:20); cf. A. T. Lincoln, 'Summary', 621-22.

73. Arnold, 148, observes with reference to being 'co-seated' with Christ that 'there is no other theological construct which could so effectively and vividly communicate to the readers their access to the authority and power of the risen Lord' (cf. 148-50). Note also the treatment in his *Powers,* 114-15.

take their stand against the devil's schemes, and struggle against the spiritual forces of evil in the heavenly realms (6:11-12). Finally, the fact that believers conduct their lives in the world and have not yet experienced salvation in all its fulness but look forward to God's lavishing the full abundance of his grace upon them in the coming age (2:7) shows that the eschatology of Ephesians is not wholly realized but has a future dimension to it as well.

7 God's further purpose in lavishing his mercy on sinners, raising and exalting them in Christ Jesus, was that they should serve as a demonstration of his extraordinary grace for all eternity.[74] The flow of thought begun in vv. 4 and 5, with its focus on God's mercy in making us alive with Christ, is brought to its conclusion and climax with this final clause.[75] Already in the introductory eulogy of 1:3-14 the ultimate goal of salvation was seen to be the glory of God (vv. 6, 12, 14). His free and glad choice of men and women to be his sons and daughters was intended to redound 'to the praise of his glorious *grace*' (v. 6). Now a similar thought is expressed: God acted to save sinners so that they might serve to display the surpassing wealth of his grace.

Having already spoken of the divine mercy and love (v. 4), the apostle goes out of his way to underscore the extravagance of God's grace (cf. vv. 5, 8). The adjective 'surpassing, extraordinary'[76] is combined with the noun 'wealth' to show how incomparably rich God's grace is. Next, Paul refers to the divine goodness:[77] the 'surpassing wealth of God's grace' is displayed 'in his kindness *to us* in Christ Jesus'. This is an amazing statement, given that the recipients of this generosity had been enemies of God and liable to his wrath (v. 3). But they are now in *Christ Jesus*, and God views them as he views his beloved Son. In raising and exalting Christ God demonstrated 'the *surpassing* greatness of his power' (1:19-20); in raising and exalting us he has also displayed 'the *surpassing* riches of his grace'.

74. Bruce, 288.

75. The ἵνα ('that')-clause of purpose is not connected simply with the preceding clause about our being seated with Christ Jesus in heaven (καὶ συνεκάθισεν κτλ.), but serves as a conclusion to vv. 4-7 and spells out the goal of God's whole act of salvation. Cf. Schnackenburg, 96.

76. In Greek the adjectival participle of the verb ὑπερβάλλω meaning to 'be surpassing, extraordinary' is used, and this is rendered by an adjective in English. According to Louw and Nida §78.33, 'both ὑπερβάλλον and πλοῦτος serve as expressions of degree; ὑπερβάλλον indicates an implied comparison, while πλοῦτος suggests not only a high degree of something, but also value'. An appropriate rendering is 'his very, very great grace'. See also G. Delling, *TDNT* 8:520-22.

77. χρηστότης denotes 'goodness, kindness, generosity' (cf. Rom. 2:4; 11:22; Tit. 3:4; see BAGD, 886).

The setting for this manifestation of God's grace is spelled out by means of the temporal[78] phrase 'in the ages to come'. Many have taken this expression to be equivalent to 'the coming age' of Ephesians 1:21, which reflects the traditional division of time into two ages. But this is unlikely. The plural 'ages' is not simply a stylistic variation of the singular, but a more general conception, implying 'one age supervening upon another like successive waves of the sea, as far into the future as thought can reach'. In the light of this meaning it may thus be claimed: 'Throughout time and in eternity the church, this society of pardoned rebels, is designed by God to be the masterpiece of his goodness'.[79]

The apostle's thought in vv. 4-7 has gone full circle: he began by speaking of God's mercy and love as the motivation for his initiative in saving his people (v. 4); Paul then drew the readers' attention to the mighty rescue which arose out of God's gracious action (v. 5), and he concludes by declaring that God's lavishing his mercy on rebels is to serve as a demonstration of his grace for all succeeding ages. What God has done for those in Christ is a reality, but only in the coming ages will it be fully seen for what it is. In the light of God's gracious saving work, believers point men and women from themselves to the one to whom they owe their salvation.

3. God's New Creation, 2:8-10

Paul has just shown that what has happened to believers has been due to the amazingly rich grace of God, the demonstration of which will continue in the ages to come so that all who see it will marvel and praise God. Already in the preceding sentence Paul had interrupted the flow of his thought to assert that the salvation which God had provided for the readers was grounded in his grace. This salvation which met the dreadful needs of the human predicament involved delivery from death, wrath, and slavery, described in vv. 1-3.[80] Now in these final verses of the pericope he elaborates on the nature of this salvation, using several key theological terms: grace and faith are significant elements in the believer's union with Christ, while the apostle rejects the notion that their 'change in status from spiritual death to life and exaltation with Christ is

---

78. Although some have understood αἰῶνες ('ages') as a reference to personal powers (cf. 3:10), this interpretation has considerable difficulties (as H. E. Lona, *Die Eschatologie*, 365-66, has shown). The more natural sense is the temporal one, '[in] the ages [to come]'.

79. Bruce, 288, who adds: 'When he brings into being the reconciled universe of the future, the church will provide the pattern after which it will be modelled'.

80. P. T. O'Brien, 'Divine Analysis', 139-40.

due to any human effort. He concludes by stating that salvation is a call to a life of good works'.[81]

We come to a short paragraph that has often been called the heart of Paul's gospel 'because [it] capture[s] and summarize[s] the essence of some of the great thoughts that he develops in Romans and Galatians'.[82]

8 Paul has rightly focussed on the amazingly rich grace of God, for by it[83] salvation[84] has been secured for Gentile men and women. The great cry, *by grace you have been saved,* which had interrupted the flow of thought in v. 5, is now taken up in a renewed form and amplified, especially in relation to faith and works. The additional phrase 'by faith'[85] is the inseparable companion of 'by grace', and together the two expressions stand in stark contrast to any suggestion of human merit.

'Faith' is usually understood here to denote the human response by which God's salvation is received. If God's grace is the ground of salvation, then faith is the means by which it is appropriated. And faith itself cannot be a meritorious work; it is the response which receives what has already been done for us in Christ. The further point is then made that what is asserted here about salvation is elsewhere declared in relation to justification,[86] namely, it is freely given by God's grace (Rom. 3:24) and

81. Patzia, 183.

82. Patzia, 183; cf. Lincoln, 'Summary', 617-30.

83. The definite article τῇ ('the') in the expression τῇ γὰρ χάριτί ἐστε σεσῳσμένοι ('it is by this grace that you have been saved') is the article of renewed mention and points back to the 'grace' already referred to in vv. 5 and 7, namely, the grace which operates in Christ Jesus and will be exhibited in the coming ages (Best, 225). The γάρ ('for') shows that Paul was fully justified in speaking of '*the surpassing riches* of God's grace'. Cf. Meyer, 113; Abbott, 51.

84. On the significance of the periphrastic perfect construction see on v. 5.

85. διὰ πίστεως ('through faith'). The synonymous expression ἐκ πίστεως ('by faith') appears more frequently in Paul, but he uses the two phrases interchangeably (Gal. 2:16; Rom. 3:25-26, 30).

86. U. Luz, 'Rechtfertigung bei den Paulusschülern', in *Festschrift für Ernst Käsemann zum 70. Geburtstag,* ed. J. Friedrich, W. Pöhlmann, and P. Stuhlmacher (Tübingen: J. C. B. Mohr [Paul Siebeck], 1976), 365-83, has argued forcefully that the absence of the decisive Pauline keywords 'justify' and 'righteousness of God', their replacement by the notion of salvation, and the un-Pauline character of the keywords 'save' and 'good works' here in Eph. 2 are symptomatic of an alteration (albeit, unintentional) to Pauline teaching by the author. However, I. H. Marshall, 'Salvation, Grace and Works in the Later Writings of the Pauline Corpus', *NTS* 42 (1996), 339-58, esp. 342-48, has pointed out that when Paul writes about the gospel salvation terminology is quite normal (esp. Rom. 1:16; 10:9-10; 1 Thess. 2:16; 1 Cor. 15:2). Marshall thinks that instead of drawing a contrast between justification and salvation it is better to see both as having present and future elements. 'There does not appear to be any significant difference between the Hauptbriefe and Ephesians so far as the basic structure of salvation is concerned' (345).

received not on the grounds of legal works but through faith (Gal. 2:16; cf. Phil. 3:9).

Consistent with this view, some insist that 'through faith' here implies that Jesus Christ is the one to whom faith is directed, since he is explicitly its object in Galatians 2:16 ('faith in Jesus Christ'; cf. Rom. 3:22, 26; Phil. 3:9). However, if in the full expression the genitive 'of Jesus Christ' is regarded as subjective,[87] then the phrase denotes 'the faith [or faithfulness] of Jesus Christ'. The shorter expression in Ephesians 2:8 could signify the same thing. On this interpretation Paul is asserting that God's gracious salvation comes about through Christ's faithfulness, that is, his unflinching obedience to the Father's will.[88] Accordingly, the following words (vv. 8b, 9) stand out even more sharply.

In order to stress that salvation is by God's grace alone and through faith, Paul adds two balancing negatives: first, *and this not from yourselves, it is the gift of God* (v. 8b), and, secondly, *not by works, so that no one can boast* (v. 9). In the first clause, which emphasizes the divine initiative and activity, some have taken *this* to refer specifically to 'faith', which immediately precedes.[89] The point being made, then, is that the response of faith does not come from any human source but is God's gift. This interpretation is grammatically possible,[90] assuming that the term denotes 'faith' and not Christ's 'faithfulness', and it is consistent with Pauline teaching elsewhere (cf. Phil. 1:29). However, the context demands that *this* be understood of salvation by grace as a whole, including the faith (or faithfulness) through which it is received.[91]

God's magnificent rescue from death, wrath, and bondage is all of grace. It neither originates in[92] nor is effected by the readers. Instead, it is

---

87. Note the discussion of Phil. 3:9 in P. T. O'Brien, *The Epistle to the Philippians: A Commentary on the Greek Text* (Grand Rapids: Eerdmans, 1991), 398-400. For a recent advocacy of this interpretation in relation to 'faith' in Ephesians, see I. G. Wallis, *The Faith of Jesus Christ in Early Christian Traditions* (Cambridge: Cambridge University Press, 1995), 128-34.

88. Which Barth describes as 'the obedience and love of Christ toward God and man' (note his discussion, 224-25 and 347). Cf. Rom. 3:22, 26; Gal. 2:15, 16, 20; 3:22, 26; Eph. 3:12; Phil. 3:9.

89. Cf. Caird, 53. Early commentators who adopted this view include Augustine, C. Hodge, and E. K. Simpson.

90. The pronoun τοῦτο ('this'), which is an adverbial accusative ('and at that, and especially'; BDF §290[5]), is neuter, while πίστις ('faith, faithfulness') is feminine. Robinson, 157, agrees that 'the difference of gender is not fatal to such a view', but he concludes on contextual grounds that the wider reference to 'salvation by grace' is demanded.

91. So most recent commentators (cf. also Calvin). If πίστις refers to Christ's faithfulness, then a further reason is given for taking the demonstrative pronoun 'this' as referring to salvation as a whole.

92. The preposition ἐκ denotes 'origin, source, cause'; BAGD, 234-35.

God's own gift, a point which Paul goes out of his way to emphasize by changing the normal word order and contrasting 'God's' with 'yours'.[93] The particular word for gift,[94] though common enough, does not appear elsewhere in the Pauline corpus. Other words with a similar meaning are used to speak of God's gift of righteousness and life in Christ (Rom. 5:15-17; 6:23).

9 The second balancing clause, which stresses that salvation is by grace alone through faith/faithfulness, is *not by works, so that no one can boast*. If salvation is not because of human initiative (v. 8), then neither is it a reward for good deeds. And since there is no room for human merit, there can be no grounds for human boasting.

In conflict with the agitators for whom the law/gospel antithesis was prominent, Paul frequently uses the phrase 'works of the law'. This disputed expression denotes not 'legalism' but works which are commanded by the Mosaic law, that is, actions performed in obedience to it, possibly including practices required by Judaism such as circumcision, food laws, or sabbath keeping.[95] Accordingly, the apostle pronounces that no one is justified 'by works of the law' (Rom. 3:20; Gal. 2:16 [3 times]). Justification does not come via this route, since a person is counted righteous 'apart from works of the law' (Rom. 3:28). Indeed, 'works of the law' cannot confer the Spirit or work miracles (Gal. 3:2, 5), and all who rely on such works are under a curse (Gal. 3:10).

In Romans 3 and 4 the simple expression 'works', which denotes deeds that are performed, is used synonymously with the full phrase 'works of the law'. There is a direct connection between the full expression in Romans 3:20 and 28 and 'works' in 4:1-5, which states that Abraham was not justified either by his 'works' (v. 2) or by his working (vv. 4-5). What is said about 'works of the law' is asserted by the apostle in relation to 'works': so justification does not come 'by works' (Rom. 4:2; cf. 9:32). It is 'apart from works' (4:6), while election, too, is not 'by works' (Rom. 9:12; 11:6).

Ephesians is a letter written to predominantly Gentile readers in which 'works *of the law*' are not primarily in view;[96] 'works' now stand

---

93. θεοῦ ('of God') is placed first to contrast with ὑμῶν ('yours'). Literally the clause reads '*God's* is the gift'.

94. Gk. δῶρον.

95. For a brief discussion of this disputed phrase, together with bibliographical details (to 1993), see T. R. Schreiner, 'Works of the Law', *DPL*, 975-79; note further details in Hoehner.

96. The only reference to νόμος ('law') occurs in a context which reminds Gentile readers that God has, in the past, allowed them access to him as the God of Israel (Eph. 2:15; note, however, the reference to the fifth commandment in Eph. 6:2; cf. Lincoln, 112; Arnold, 149).

for human effort in general, a nuance found elsewhere in Paul. 'This inclusive reference to human activities does not exclude but includes the practices required by Judaism'.[97] In Romans 9:11-12 'works', which are *defined* as 'doing anything good or evil', are ruled out as a way of obtaining salvation. Salvation is not based on human performance or on any effort to win God's approval. And if it is 'by grace, it is no longer on the basis of works; otherwise grace would no longer be grace' (Rom. 11:6). Indeed, in the light of what has already been said about the desperate plight of men and women outside of Christ, dead in trespasses and sins, subject to wrath, and living in terrible bondage (Eph. 2:1-3), it was impossible for the readers to turn to their previous behaviour as the basis for achieving salvation. Their former life and works had caused the very predicament from which they needed to be delivered.

The divine intention[98] in providing salvation apart from any human effort or achievement is to exclude all human boasting. 'Boasting' is a characteristically Pauline theme,[99] which frequently occurs in polemical contexts.[100] The apostle's references to it need to be understood against the contemporary backgrounds of the professional practices of the sophists, among others, and of the Jews, whose basic attitude was one of self-confidence before God, convinced that their membership in the covenant people and keeping of the law would bring honour to themselves. As Paul attacks the doctrine of justification by works, so he opposes all boasting based on self-trust. According to Romans 3:21-26 justification is grounded in the redemption that is in Christ Jesus, and it comes as a gift from God. Every attempt to affirm oneself before God by boasting in one's own achievements is excluded, according to Romans 3:27. To boast is tantamount to putting one's confidence in the flesh, and this the apostle decisively rejects (cf. Phil. 3:3; Gal. 6:13). Men and women are in no po-

---

97. I. H. Marshall, 'Salvation', 345-46, following F. Mussner, *Der Brief an die Epheser* (Gütersloh/Würzburg: Mohn/Echter, 1982), 67.

98. Expressed by the ἵνα ('that')-clause.

99. καυχάομαι ('I boast') and its cognates. Of the thirty-seven occurrences of this verb in the New Testament thirty-five are in Paul. For details see R. Bultmann, *TDNT* 3: 645-54, and J. Zmijewski, *EDNT* 2:276-79.

100. In the Old Testament there are many proverbs against self-glorying or boasting (1 Kings 20:11; Prov. 25:14; 27:1). It is not simply a casual fault, but the basic attitude of the foolish and ungodly person (Ps. 52:1[LXX 51:3]; 94:4[93:3]), for in it one sees the person who stands on his own feet and does not depend on God. On the other hand, opposed to self-confident boasting there is a true boasting that consists in humbling oneself before God (Jer. 9:23-24), who is the praise of Israel (Deut. 10:21). Such boasting is related to 'confidence, joy and thanksgiving, and the paradox is that the one who glories thus looks away from himself, so that his glorying is a confession of God'; R. Bultmann, *TDNT* 3:647.

sition to claim even the slightest credit for their acceptance with God (note Paul's argument in Rom. 4:1-8). But in the gospel of reconciliation by which justification comes through Christ's death, men and women are now able to '*boast* in the Lord' (Rom. 5:9-11; 1 Cor. 1:31; Phil. 3:3). Here in Ephesians the apostle makes it plain that salvation by grace destroys all human boasting. Men and women have nothing which they can bring as their own to the living God.

10 God's salvation has already been described in terms of a resurrection from the dead, a liberation from slavery, and a rescue from condemnation. Now it is spoken of as a new creation, and a further reason (*for;* cf. v. 8) is given why this salvation is not of human origin and therefore cannot be the basis for human boasting. It is *God's* workmanship from first to last; believers *have been created*[101] in Christ Jesus for good works. These 'good works' cannot be the ground of our salvation or the subject of our boasting since they are the *goal* of the new creation. They are the fruit of salvation, not its basis or cause. So once again in this magnificent paragraph the apostle makes clear that we are wholly dependent on God's gracious, sovereign activity for our salvation.

The term rendered *workmanship,* which often appears in the LXX to denote creation as God's work,[102] has the same nuance of the physical creation in its only other New Testament occurrence (Rom. 1:20). But here in Ephesians 2:10, which stresses what believers are because of God,[103] the cluster of creation terms, including this word and *created,* along with *good works,* is applied directly to the *new* creation. This new entity transcends natural distinctions: God's purpose was to create one new humanity out of Jews and Gentiles (Eph. 2:15). In this new realm neither circumcision nor uncircumcision counts for anything (Gal. 6:15).

The following participle defines 'what God has made': we have been *created*[104] *in Christ Jesus* for the purpose of *good works*. The prepositional phrase *in Christ Jesus* may be taken simply as instrumental, signify-

---

101. Note the passive κτισθέντες ('created'), which implies God's activity.

102. Gk. ποίημα ('what is made, work, creation'): LXX Ps. 91:4; 142:5.

103. Note the emphatic placement of αὐτοῦ ('his') at the beginning of the principal clause: '*His* work are we'. In Paul's petition of 1:19 reference was made to God's incomparably great power at work in believers. Now at 2:10 they themselves are said to be the product of his mighty work.

104. The same verb κτίζω ('make, create' something which has not existed before; Louw and Nida §42.35) is used with reference to God creating the 'one new man' at 2:15, and of the 'new person' being made in his likeness at 4:24. Cf. 3:9, which speaks of him having created 'all things', both old creation and new.

ing 'through God's activity in Christ';[105] but it may also indicate 'in our union with Christ Jesus', and in the light of the surrounding context (esp. vv. 6, 7) the latter nuance is probably correct. Christ Jesus is the 'sphere' of God's new creation, just as divine election (1:4) is in him. At the same time it is theologically correct to state that the new creation has been inaugurated by God through him. As a consequence it may be unnecessary to choose between these alternatives. God has created us anew in Christ and through Christ.

This new creation has already begun in history in the lives of men and women. Believers *are* God's workmanship. We have *already* been created in Christ Jesus for good works. The new heaven and the new earth, spoken of in Isaiah 65:17; 66:22, have already come into existence in this new order that is created in God's Son (cf. 2 Cor. 5:17).[106] But, as we have already seen in Ephesians, there is an interplay between the 'already' and the 'not yet', not simply a one-sided emphasis on the former, as so many exegetes claim. The stress may fall on what has already been achieved in Christ Jesus. But the future dimension is not omitted; here the divine intention in this new creation, which will be consummated on the final day with the summing up of all things in Christ (1:9-10), is that we should perform the good works God has prepared for us to walk in.

The short but highly significant phrase '*for* good works' signifies purpose,[107] and points forward to the climax of the sentence, as it spells out God's intention for the new creation. The two following clauses, 'which [*sc.,* works] God prepared beforehand' and 'in order that we might walk *in them*', are grammatically and logically dependent on this purpose phrase, while the mention of the believers' *walk* in these activities forms an *inclusio*, at least by way of contrast, with the *walk* in trespasses and sins (v. 1) and in the lusts of the flesh (v. 2)[108] that characterized the unconverted Gentile and Jewish world. This *inclusio* or envelope draws attention to a movement from the negative to the positive, from the lifestyle of Jews and Gentiles outside of Christ to a walking in the deeds that God has prepared beforehand, now that his gracious salvation has come.

The positive mention of *good* works after the preceding devaluation of works (v. 9) has surprised a number of writers, who thought this re-

---

105. As Lincoln, 114, puts it.
106. Bruce, 290.
107. The preposition ἐπί with the dative case can denote purpose, goal, or result: BAGD, 287; BDF §235(4); cf. S. E. Porter, *Idioms of the Greek New Testament* (Sheffield: Academic Press, 1994), 161.
108. περιπατέω ('walk') occurs at vv. 1 and 10, the synonymous ἀναστρέφω ('conduct oneself, live') at v. 2.

flected a view that was 'scarcely Pauline', and which emanated from a disciple of Paul who had fallen back into the thought world of Jewish Christianity, or who had contracted Paul's teaching of justification in a moralistic direction![109] But such comments indicate a failure to understand Paul's statement within the flow of his argument and the place of good works in the Christian life. As *good* works they stand in sharp contrast to the works of v. 9, which were anything but this! Good works are God's design for his new creation and flow from his gracious salvation as its consequence or fruit.[110]

The New Testament generally and the apostle in particular consistently urge those who have experienced God's gracious redemption to lead holy and godly lives. A 'true and lively' faith is to work itself out in love (Gal. 5:6). God's people are urged to do good under all circumstances (1 Thess. 5:15; Gal. 6:10; 2 Cor. 5:10; Rom. 13:3).[111] In the companion letter to the Colossians Paul prayed that his readers might 'bear fruit in every good work' (Col. 1:10; cf. 2 Cor. 9:8; 2 Thess. 2:17) as they were filled with a knowledge of his will and purpose for their lives. The phrase 'good works' occurs often enough in the Pastoral Epistles.[112] In Titus 3:8 the context is similar to that of Ephesians: God saves men and women through his great mercy, not because of righteous things they have done (v. 5). Having trusted in God, they are now to be 'careful to devote themselves to doing what is good' (lit. 'good works')'. In Ephesians 2:10 *good works* is a general and comprehensive expression for godly behaviour. It is not further defined, but its implications will be taken up and amplified in the exhortatory sections of the letter (in 4:17–6:20). Put simply, it is God's will that those who belong to the new creation should be characterized by a lifestyle which ultimately reflects his own character and action.[113]

The concluding statement of this stunning paragraph about God's gracious salvation underscores the importance and divine origin of these good works: 'which God prepared in advance so that we might live in them'. In order to overcome the difficulty that such actions cannot be said

---

109. Note A. Lindemann's survey of the discussion in *Aufhebung*, 138.

110. They are 'neither meritorious nor the prerequisite for redemption'; so J. Baumgarten, *EDNT* 1:6.

111. Note Jesus' words to disciples of the kingdom who are both salt and light: 'let your light so shine before men, that they see your *good works* and praise your Father in heaven' (Matt. 5:16).

112. 1 Tim. 2:10; 5:10, 25; 6:18; Tit. 2:7, 14; 3:8; cf. Acts 9:36; Heb. 10:24. Note the similar expression 'every good work' in 2 Tim. 2:21; 3:17; Tit. 1:16; 3:1.

113. It is tempting to see a connection between God's 'good work' of Phil. 1:6 (together with the references to his works in the Old Testament) and the 'good works' he has prepared for believers here.

to exist prior to their being done — even God cannot prepare works ahead of time, it is argued, since they do not exist until they are performed, and the performance is a human action, not God's — it has been suggested that the clause 'which God prepared in advance' should be rendered 'the good deeds, for which God has designed us' (NEB). But the verb means to 'prepare beforehand'[114] and should not be weakened to signify simply 'intend or design', while it is the good works themselves that have already been prepared.[115] The only other use of this verb at Romans 9:23 presents a strongly predestinarian thrust, and it is likely that the prefix 'before' suggests that God's preparation precedes the foundation of the world. Already in the *berakah* he is praised for having chosen believers before the world's creation *to be holy and blameless in his sight* (1:4; cf. vv. 5, 11, 12). Believers are God's work, and the good deeds which he has purposed for us to walk in, which are achieved only through his enabling power, can be thought of as already prepared in his mind and counsel from before eternity.[116] His plan from of old was not simply to introduce his sons and daughters into a relationship with himself through his Son, but to bring us fully to glory (cf. Heb. 2:10), and this included the intermediate steps by which we were to reach our final goal (cf. 2 Thess. 2:13-14). These embrace the good deeds he has marked out for us beforehand. Thus, once again the apostle stresses the absolute priority of divine grace.

At the same time those who are part of God's new creation are expected to *live*[117] in godly ways. There are important ethical consequences of our being God's new creation, created in Christ Jesus. The divine intention, forcefully expressed by the purpose clause, is that we should walk in good deeds. We have a responsibility to live in the world so as to please him. There was a time when we walked in disobedience and sin, *followed the ways of this world,* were in terrible bondage to the devil, and were destined for wrath. But now because of God's mighty salvation in which a glorious change has been effected, we are expected, through the agency of his Holy Spirit, to demonstrate a changed life-style. Our attitudes and behaviour are to show all the hallmarks of the new creation. And when we walk in these ways which are according to his purpose, it is he himself who is powerfully working in our lives (Phil. 2:12, 13).

---

114. Gk. προετοιμάζω; BAGD, 705. In both Rom. 9:23 and Eph. 2:10 the preparation beforehand has the final goal in view, either glory or good works; cf. W. Radl, *EDNT* 2:67.

115. The οἷς ('which') is probably an attraction of the relative to the dative case of ἔργοις ('works'; instead of ἅ), rather than a dative of reference (against the NEB; cf. Abbott, 54-55).

116. Lincoln, 115.

117. With the catchword 'walk' (περιπατέω) there is a deliberate link with 2:2; 4:1, 17 (twice); 5:2, 8, 15. Six of these references are in the paraenesis of chaps. 4 and 5.

D. The Inclusion of Gentiles in the One Body, 2:11-22

> [11]*Therefore, remember that formerly you who are Gentiles by birth and called "uncircumcised" by those who call themselves "the circumcision" (that done in the body by the hands of men) —* [12]*remember that at that time you were separate from Christ, excluded from citizenship in Israel and foreigners to the covenants of the promise, without hope and without God in the world.* [13]*But now in Christ Jesus you who once were far away have been brought near through the blood of Christ.* [14]*For he himself is our peace, who has made the two one and has destroyed the barrier, the dividing wall of hostility,* [15]*by abolishing in his flesh the law with its commandments and regulations. His purpose was to create in himself one new man out of the two, thus making peace,* [16]*and in this one body to reconcile both of them to God through the cross, by which he put to death their hostility.* [17]*He came and preached peace to you who were far away and peace to those who were near.* [18]*For through him we both have access to the Father by one Spirit.* [19]*Consequently, you are no longer foreigners and aliens, but fellow citizens with God's people and members of God's household,* [20]*built on the foundation of the apostles and prophets, with Christ Jesus himself as the chief cornerstone.* [21]*In him the whole building is joined together and rises to become a holy temple in the Lord.* [22]*And in him you too are being built together to become a dwelling in which God lives by his Spirit.*

This paragraph provides one of the most wonderful descriptions of peace and reconciliation within the Pauline letters.[118] Here both the horizontal and vertical dimensions to this central salvation blessing are treated within the framework of God's saving plan. Further, the centrepiece of this comprehensive reconciliation, and the fundamental theological undergirding of the whole letter,[119] is to be found in vv. 14-18, where believers 'come near' to God and to one another (Gentiles and Jews) through the saving death of the Lord Jesus Christ.

We suggested earlier that the high point of the eulogy (1:3-14), which celebrates the accomplishment of God's gracious purposes in Christ and provides a sweep from eternity to eternity, was the mystery

---

118. For a recent detailed bibliography on the vast (and increasing) volume of literature on 2:11-22, see Best, 233-34.

119. Cf. Barth, 275; and Snodgrass, 123. Turner, 1230, thinks that in formal terms vv. 11-22 are a digression. But in another sense they are the 'theological heart of the letter for the truths contained in them undergird and explain Paul's eulogy and prayer, and reinforce their message'. He adds: 'If Ephesians is the crown of Paul's theological writing, 2:11-22 is perhaps the central jewel; but like a beautifully cut gem it has a depth and subtlety that is not easily summarized'.

and its content, that is, God's intention to bring *all things* together in unity in Christ (vv. 9-10). Two obstacles need to be overcome before the divine purposes would reach their fulfilment — the subjection of the powers (representing 'the things in heaven'), and the church, particularly the relationship of Jews and Gentiles (representing 'the things on earth'). The second of these areas is now specifically addressed in 2:11-22, and the passage reaches a crescendo in the concluding verses (19-22), where the consequences of Christ's mighty reconciling work are drawn out in a series of images depicting the privileges of God's people which transcend the old Jew-Gentile divisions: Gentiles who were formerly without God and without hope are now *fellow citizens with God's people, members of* his household, so that together they have become *a holy temple in the Lord* and *a dwelling in which God lives by his Spirit.* It is for reasons such as these that the paragraph has been regarded as 'perhaps the most significant ecclesiological text in the New Testament'.[120]

Within the context of Ephesians as a whole, 2:11-22 stands parallel to the preceding paragraph. In 2:1-10 Paul has reminded his Gentile Christian readers of the dramatic change that God had effected in raising them from death to new life in Christ. Here in the latter passage the 'once–now' schema appears again (vv. 11-13, 19), this time, however, providing a contrast in more specific terms: the readers' past is expressed in relation to Israel's previous privileged position in the saving plan of God, while the present is cast in terms of their being brought near to God 'through the blood of Christ' and to one another (Gentile and Jewish believers) in him. Both vv. 1-10 and 11-22 follow directly from 1:15-23, where Paul prayed that his readers might have a greater appreciation of the power of God that had been exercised on their behalf. The dramatic change, underscored in both paragraphs by the 'once–now' schema which is more than a rhetorical device, is testimony to the fact that God had been mightily at work in their lives.

Recent attempts, through 'a mirror reading' of vv. 11-22, to find some particular epistolary or rhetorical setting where there were problems between Jewish and Gentile Christians have not been convincing.[121] The failure of recent writers to come up with plausible suggestions simply underscores the point already made, that Ephesians is probably a circular letter written to several congregations in Paul's Gentile mission where his predominantly Gentile readers are helped to appreciate the greatness of their salvation. It has a history, and they have entered into the heritage of Israel. The use of the Old Testament Scriptures in this key

120. Snodgrass, 123.
121. Note particularly Lincoln's critiques, 132-33.

paragraph, both explicitly (cf. vv. 13, 17) and by way of allusion or echo (cf. vv. 19-22), underscores the note of continuity between Gentile Christians and the promises of God to Israel (cf. Gen. 12:1-3; Isa. 49:5, 6). But, if anything, there is a greater emphasis in this paragraph on the element of discontinuity: the new community of which these Gentiles have become a part is not simply a development out of Israel. It is a new creation (v. 15), not some kind of amalgam made out of the best elements of Israel and the Gentiles. The resulting new humanity transcends the two old entities, even though unbelieving Israel and disobedient Gentiles continue to exist.[122] The privileges Gentiles enjoy are based upon but transcend the blessings promised to Israel (vv. 19-22).

Although writers such as Kirby, Bailey, Giavini, and Thomson have discerned a circular or chiastic pattern in the paragraph, in part because of the clear parallels between vv. 11-13 and 19-22, it is preferable to regard the repetition of words and ideas in the passage as evidence of parallel features rather than a deliberate chiasmus.[123]

The paragraph (vv. 11-22) falls into three fairly easily defined sections: first, vv. 11-13 describe the pre-Christian past of Paul's Gentile readers in relation to Israel (vv. 11, 12) and their present privileged position of being *in Christ* (v. 13). Secondly, vv. 14-18 provide the centrepiece and explain how this coming near was made possible through Christ's reconciling death. Thirdly, by means of the 'once–now' contrast, vv. 19-22 apply the truths of vv. 14-18 to the readers' new privileged position in Christ. Using building and household images, Paul states that they are members of God's new community which transcends the division of Jew and Gentile.

The apostle begins a new section of the letter and reminds his readers of their past as unconverted Gentiles[124] who had formerly stood outside the covenant promises to Israel. At the same time this paragraph is linked with and parallel to the preceding one (2:1-10) by means of the 'once–now' schema which is dominant throughout (vv. 11-13, 19). The contrast between the past and the present, which has been viewed in the earlier passage in terms of living in disobedience, sin, and bondage over

122. There are both continuous and discontinuous elements within the paragraph, with an emphasis on the latter. This does not justify, on the one hand, our using 'replacement categories' (cf. N. T. Wright) or, on the other hand, our failing to recognize that Christ has created a new entity (cf. J. D. G. Dunn; see on v. 15).

123. As Best, 236, notes, one gains the impression that 'too much is being forced into a preordained scheme'. This is not to deny, however, the helpful exegetical insights throughout the chapter of, e.g., I. H. Thomson, *Chiasmus,* 84-115, who builds on the work of K. E. Bailey.

124. The earlier mention of *you* (1:13-14; 2:1, etc.) anticipated this specific reference to 'you Gentiles' here in 2:11-22 (cf 3:6). See on 115-17, 156.

against salvation, new life, and being seated with Christ (2:1-10), is now set forth in salvation-historical categories, particularly in terms of the readers' pre-Christian past in relation to Israel's special position within God's saving purposes. Once again the gravity of their previous situation serves to magnify the wonder of God's grace. As with vv. 1-10, the past is recalled, not because the emphasis falls upon it, but in order to draw attention to Christ's mighty work on their behalf (vv. 14-18), to encourage an attitude of profound thankfulness to God, and to urge the readers to accept all that is involved in being God's new creation in Christ.

1. The Gentiles' Former Plight and Now, 2:11-13

11 *Therefore,* in the light of the change God has effected (2:1-10) and the wholly unmerited blessings he has imparted to them (cf. 1:3-14), the apostle's Gentile readers are to *remember*[125] their pre-Christian past from another standpoint. The exhortation to *remember,* which stands like a rubric over vv. 11, 12 (the NIV repeats the verb in v. 12), does not mean that they have actually forgotten what they were, only that Paul wants to call these matters to their attention so that they will have a greater understanding and appreciation of the past and the mighty reversal Christ has effected on their behalf. The privileges which they now enjoy would be appreciated all the more if they reflected carefully upon the spiritual condition from which they had been rescued.[126]

Using a number of terms found in the companion letter to the Colossians (2:11, 13) to describe the previous state of alienation of the Colossian Christians (though now with a slightly different twist),[127] Paul addresses his readers as those who had once been 'Gentiles in the flesh'

---

125. This summons to remember is akin to the appeal of Deuteronomy to the Israelites to recall their slavery in Egypt (Deut. 5:15; 15:15; 16:12; 24:18, 22). This was not simply a recalling of certain facts or situations, nor was it just a mental activity. It involved an evaluation of what had happened, and an acting upon it as a result. A. Lindemann, *Die Aufhebung,* 146-47, makes the valid point that the statement of 2:11-12 is not to be viewed as a description of an 'objective' empirically recognized past which the readers themselves are now to be reminded of 'subjectively' in their own consciousness. They cannot 'remember' being once Gentiles in the flesh, when they were heathen in the eyes of Jews. Schnackenburg, 102-3, calls this use of theology and address ('you') in the exposition an *anamnēsis* (from the verb 'remember'). It is 'not intended to bring any new instruction but simply to remind the readers of the knowledge' they had already received in order to make them more aware of it and to encourage them to respond appropriately. He claims that this type of 'theological anamnesis permeates the whole document but is especially pronounced in 2.11–3.21'.

126. Bruce, 292.

127. 'Circumcision, uncircumcision, flesh, made with[out] hands'. In Colossians, however, the circumcision language is used metaphorically.

(RSV; rendered by the NIV as *Gentiles by birth*). This description arises from a Jewish standpoint since neither Romans nor Greeks would call themselves 'Gentiles'.[128] 'In the flesh' refers to a real physical difference, but in the light of Christ's work this difference is no longer of ultimate significance.

The Jewish portrait continues with the words *called "uncircumcised" by those who call themselves "the circumcision"*. Although they were not the only ones who practised circumcision,[129] the Jewish custom was sufficiently distinctive in the first century for them to be called the 'circumcision', while they dismissed the rest of the world as the 'uncircumcision'. For Jews circumcision, which had been given by God to Abraham (Gen. 17), was the physical sign of their covenant with the Lord, the God of all the earth. It pointed to the particular and exclusive relationship which Israel had with the God of the covenant. The uncircumcision of Gentiles was evidence of their estrangement from God, which in Jewish eyes could only be dealt with if a Gentile became a proselyte to the Jewish faith.

Paul had once taken pride in the fact that he 'was circumcised on the eighth day' (Phil. 3:5). He may well have been an ardent proselytizer before his conversion (cf. Gal. 5:11). Since becoming a Christian, however, he knew that circumcision was religiously irrelevant (Gal. 5:6; 1 Cor. 7:19). His description here in Ephesians of the Gentiles' former position, where he employs Jewish language to refer to their 'outside' status, is significantly qualified, indicating that he was clearly not happy with this way of putting things: theirs was a circumcision 'so-called', and it was 'in the flesh' — external, that and nothing more. But perhaps the most critical comment of all is that this circumcision was 'made with hands',[130] an

---

128. The definite article in τὰ ἔθνη ἐν σαρκί has the effect of assigning these Gentiles to a class in their own or someone else's eyes (cf. Gal. 6:1). It was Jews who called non-Jews 'the Gentiles'. The barrier was of Jewish making (Caird, 55; cf. Meyer, 119). (On the omission of the article before ἐν σαρκί see BDF §272.)

129. ἀκροβυστία ('uncircumcision') and περιτομή ('circumcision') are abstract nouns used as collective nouns. Bruce, 292, notes that in earlier Old Testament times other Semitic groups and the Egyptians practised circumcision, whereas the Philistines notoriously did not (1 Sam. 31:4; 2 Sam. 1:20).

130. The adjective χειροποίητος ('made with hands') was employed in the LXX to denote idols (Lev. 26:1; Isa. 2:18), an idol's sanctuary (Isa. 16:12), false gods (Isa. 11:9), or images (Lev. 26:30). It therefore described the gods as made with human hands and standing over against the living God. In all of its New Testament occurrences χειροποίητος ('made with hands') is used to set forth the contrast between what is constructed by human beings and the work of God (E. Lohse, *TDNT* 9:436; cf. Mark 14:58; Acts 7:48; 17:24; Heb. 9:11, 24). So to speak of something 'not made with hands' (ἀχειροποίητος) is to assert that God himself has created it: e.g., the temple that Jesus would erect in three days (Mark

expression which drives home the point that it was merely human and stood in contrast to the work of God. It belongs to the old order of Judaism with its external and material features, in contrast to the new spiritual order that was inaugurated with the coming of Christ. In the Old Testament Moses and the prophets had spoken of the true circumcision or cleansing of the heart for which God looked from his people (Deut. 10:16; 30:6; Jer. 4:4). The circumcision *done in the body by the hands of men* is not the real circumcision. That true circumcision was 'not made with hands'; it is the 'circumcision of Christ' (Col. 2:11), which is now available to Gentiles and Jews in the new order established in the gospel of the Lord Jesus (cf. Rom. 2:28, 29; Phil. 3:2, 3).

12 After this rather lengthy description of his Gentile readers Paul returns to his main point of urging them to *remember*[131] the inadequacies of their pre-Christian past so that they might appreciate more fully the many spiritual blessings (1:3) of their present status in Christ. The temporal note *at that time* picks up the *formerly* of v. 11 and points back to the time before the readers had been converted. It is not a salvation-historical expression that signifies 'throughout the whole period BC'.[132] Because they are now in Christ Jesus they are able to understand in retrospect the serious predicament of their pre-Christian situation.

Five deficiencies of these Gentile Christian readers are listed, and all of them have to do with their being outside God's people, Israel, and his saving purposes. By describing their spiritual predicament in these terms the apostle makes plain that the privileges given to Israel were substantial indeed. A similar point about the divine blessings bestowed on Israel, though for a somewhat different purpose, is made by the apostle in Romans 9. Not only were the Jews 'entrusted with the very words of God' (Rom. 3:2), but also theirs is 'the adoption as sons, . . . the divine glory, the covenants, the receiving of the law, the temple worship and the promises. Theirs are the patriarchs, and from them is traced the human ancestry of Christ' (Rom. 9:4, 5). From all of these privileges Paul's Gentile readers had been excluded.

The first of these former disadvantages, '[at that time] *you were separate from Christ*', has sometimes been taken as a designation of *all* unbe-

---

14:58), the heavenly house that will be given to believers at death (2 Cor. 5:1), and that circumcision which stood in contrast to Jewish circumcision and was truly the work of God, namely, Christ's death (Col. 2:11). Note P. T. O'Brien, *Colossians, Philemon*, 115-18.

131. The ὅτι ('that')-clause of v. 12 resumes the sequence of thought of v. 11 and, like the similar clause there, is the direct object of μνημονεύετε ('remember'). Cf. Best, 240.

132. As Stott, 95, one of several taking this line, puts it. Instead, τῷ καιρῷ ἐκείνῳ ('at that time') is resumptive of ποτέ ('once') in v. 11, and is antithetic to νυνὶ δέ ('but now') of v. 13.

lievers, Jews and Gentiles alike,[133] while the specifically Gentile predicament occurs in what follows: 'you [Gentiles] were separated from the commonwealth of Israel and aliens to the covenants of promise . . .'. *Separate from Christ* is the overarching programmatic expression which refers to all human existence outside the realm of salvation, while the specifics of this in relation to needy Gentiles are then amplified and explained by the following four expressions.[134]

A more natural reading of the Greek, however, is to take *separate from Christ* as signifying the first of the Gentiles' former disadvantages: '[remember that] you were, at that time, apart from Christ, separated from the commonwealth of Israel . . .'.[135] The five disadvantages that constitute the Gentile predicament are simply listed one after the other. Further, the first interpretation is driven to its conclusions by a misunderstanding of the term 'Christ'. Paul conceives of Christ as the Messiah, who belongs to Israel. The Messiah is first and foremost the king of Israel through whom God's saving purposes are being worked out. This is specifically asserted in Romans 9:4 and 5, while in the immediate context of Ephesians 2 there is a subtle shift in Paul's language from v. 12 to v. 13 which supports this interpretation: Gentiles had no part in 'Christ', but now they are 'in Christ *Jesus*' — the Messiah of Israel whom they have come to know is Christ *Jesus* (v. 13). Unbelieving Jews were separated from Jesus, but not from the messianic hope because they had been entrusted with the very oracles of God (Rom. 3:2), and these oracles spoke of this Messiah.

In the past these Gentiles had also been 'separated from the commonwealth of Israel'. The word rendered 'separated'[136] signifies in its only other New Testament occurrences an alienation or estrangement from God (Col. 1:21; Eph. 4:18), that is, from the one with whom they had been in a relationship previously. Further, these two references draw attention to the addressees' culpability. But the context here in Ephesians 2

---

133. χωρὶς Χριστοῦ ('apart from Christ') has been taken adverbially in connection with the temporal phrase, and rendered: '[remember that] you were, at that time when you were apart from Christ, separated from . . .'. On this view 'apart from Christ' is understood as 'the existence by which all men are defined, Gentiles as well as Jews'; so A. Lindemann, *Aufhebung,* 148.

134. H. Merklein, *Christus und die Kirche: Die theologische Grundstruktur des Epheserbriefes nach 2,11-18* (Stuttgart: KBW Verlag, 1973), 17, 18.

135. It is thus interpreted predicatively. There is nothing grammatical or syntactical to suggest that the four expressions, 'separated from the commonwealth of Israel', 'aliens of the covenants of promise', 'having no hope', and 'without God in the world', are explanatory, epexegetical, or consecutive. So Caird, 55, Lincoln, 136; note also the NRSV and NIV.

136. Gk. ἀπηλλοτριωμένοι.

does not imply the existence of an earlier fellowship with Israel from which these Gentiles withdrew, or that their present condition came about through the breakup of an original union (as the RSV 'alienated' might imply).[137] Paul simply states the fact of the separation; he does not assign responsibility for it. The term rendered *citizenship* is more likely to signify here 'commonwealth'.[138] Being separated from the chosen people of Israel was a serious disadvantage since it meant being outside the sphere of God's election and isolated from any covenant relationship with him. Hence Paul's readers were *foreigners* to the covenants of promise. The covenants with the patriarchs had held out the promise of great blessing to 'all nations of the earth', but it was not until the coming of Christ and the open proclamation of the gospel that believing Gentiles could be 'blessed along with Abraham, the man of faith' (Gal. 3:9). Here the plural *covenants* suggests a series of covenants with Abraham (Gen. 15:7-21; 17:1-21), Isaac (Gen. 26:2-5), Jacob (Gen. 28:13-15), Israel (Exod. 24:1-8), and David (2 Sam. 7),[139] while the genitive 'of the promise' probably refers to the foundation promise[140] made by God to Abraham. The Gentiles' exclusion from the community of God's people meant that they had no share in the covenants which promised the messianic salvation (note especially Rom. 9:4).

The litany of their serious disadvantages continues as Paul's description moves to a tragic climax. Before they were converted they had been *without hope.* This is not to suggest that Gentiles had no hopes or aspirations for the future because their golden age was past, although the absence of any hope in the face of death is amply attested in the literature and epigraphy of the day. Rather, Paul's *evaluative* comment indicates that his readers were outside the sphere of God's people and his covenant

---

137. Cf. Best, 242: 'There is no implication that they once belonged'.

138. Gk. πολιτεία. So BAGD, 686; Lincoln, 137; and D. B. Wallace, *Greek Grammar,* 108.

139. Hoehner thinks that the covenant with Abraham (Gen. 12:1-4; 13:14-18; 15:1-21; 17:1-21) and the other covenants of promise which enhance it, namely, the Davidic (2 Sam. 7:12-17; 23:5; Ps. 89:3, 27-37, 49; 132:11-12) and new covenants (Jer. 31:31-34; 32:38-40; Ezek. 36:23-36), all of which are specific and unconditional, are in view in this context. But within the flow of Eph. 2 it is appropriate, even necessary, to include the covenant with Israel (Gentiles were separated from Israel), since Paul's distinction between the Abrahamic covenant as one of promise and the Sinai covenant as one of law is not in view here (cf. Gal. 3:16-22).

140. Bruce, 292, takes the genitive τῆς ἐπαγγελίας ('of the promise') as epexegetic of διαθηκῶν ('covenants') and renders the phrase 'the covenants (which embodied) the promise'; note the similar force τῆς ἐπαγγελίας ('of promise') has in τῷ πνεύματι τῆς ἐπαγγελίας ('the Spirit of promise', Eph. 1:13). Schnackenburg, 110, refers to it as a 'modal genitive', with the singular pointing to a specific promise.

promises. Thus, they did not share the hope of Israel in the promised messianic salvation (or of the resurrection: 1 Thess. 4:5, 13). Only the presence of Christ among the Gentiles could produce that hope (cf. Col. 1:27).

Finally, their being *without God*[141] *in the world* signifies that they had no relationship with the true God, the God of Israel. Like many other Gentiles they may have had a pantheon of deities to whom they were devoted (cf. 1 Cor. 8:5, 6; Gal. 4:8; 1 Thess. 4:5), but Paul's comment is not a description of those who did not believe in a deity or deities, or were impious. Rather, like the previous statement, it is an evaluation, this time of those who, in contrast to Israel which had a relationship with the true God, were God-forsaken.

13 *But now in Christ Jesus* a dramatic change has occurred. In contrast to their former position as deprived Gentiles who were separated from Israel and her God, Paul's readers have now been *brought near* (NIV, NRSV) to him through the sacrificial death of Christ. The first part of the 'once–now' contrast was mentioned in vv. 11 and 12, and summarized here in v. 13 in terms of their being 'far off'. Now, however, a dramatic reversal has occurred. This mighty change parallels the divine reversal of vv. 1-10 (also described by means of the 'once–now' schema: *But . . . God*, v. 4), where God out of his great love and mercy made those who were dead in their trespasses and sins alive in Christ Jesus.

The words *in Christ Jesus* are not to be interpreted predicatively, meaning '[But now] you *are* in Christ Jesus'. Instead, they are connected with 'you have come near'.[142] It was not that the readers were in Christ prior to their approach; rather, their being in Christ was the immediate consequence of this coming near. They were brought near to God in him, and the means by which this approach occurred is spelled out in the concluding phrase — it was through Christ's sacrificial death. And, as noted above, Gentiles who had had no part in 'Christ', the Messiah through whom God's saving purposes were being worked out, had come to know Christ *Jesus*. The Christ in whom they had been incorporated was none other than the historic person, Jesus.

Paul employs common biblical imagery to express the contrast in their situation. The metaphors of *near* and *far* originated in Isaiah

141. The term ἄθεος occurs nowhere else in the New Testament or LXX. In Greek literature it signifies one who has never heard of the gods, who disdains or denies God or the gods, or who is forsaken by them (cf. BAGD, 20; Lincoln, 138).

142. The words ἐν Χριστῷ Ἰησοῦ ὑμεῖς ('in Christ Jesus you') are not to be supplemented by εἰσίν ('are') or ὄντες ('being'), but are joined with ἐγενήθητε ἐγγύς ('you came or were brought near'). So Meyer, 125, who rightly observes that the readers' 'being in Christ Jesus' was not prior to their coming near but its immediate consequence.

57:19,[143] and this dominates the description in vv. 17 and 18 where the wording of Isaiah is followed. However, it has been suggested that in v. 13 the apostle is using the language in a way that more closely resembles its special use in Judaism, where 'to bring near' a non-Israelite meant to make him or her a proselyte, so joining them to the people of Israel (cf. *Mekilta* on Exod. 18:5). In drawing near to the congregation of Israel that person 'came near' to God, who was 'near' his people. In the light of Paul's description of the relation between Gentiles and Israel in vv. 11 and 12, it is likely that he has formulated his statement about the change that has occurred in traditional proselyte language. The claim of v. 13, 'once you were far off',[144] summarizes their previous deficiencies mentioned in vv. 11 and 12.

But, as many[145] have recognized, this language undergoes a transformation. First, it is applied to Gentiles, not simply to proselytes coming into Judaism. Secondly, they do not become members of the commonwealth of Israel, but of a newly created community which transcends Israel and its privileges and where Gentiles, along with Jews, are on an equal footing. They are 'in Christ Jesus' and members together of his one body (cf. 2:19-22; 3:6). Further, their coming near means access to God himself, and this reconciliation has been brought about through Christ's sacrificial death (see on 1:7). There are no prerequisites such as fulfilling the Torah for entry into this privileged relationship.

2. Through Christ We Have Access to the Father by One Spirit, 2:14-18

These verses form the centrepiece of 2:11-22 and explain how the readers' coming near was made possible through Christ's death. It is an important section, for it shows just how deep the division was between Jews and Gentiles before Christ's coming, and what he has done to bring these two entities into one new humanity.[146] In contrast to the 'you' style of vv. 11-13 and 19-22, Paul here employs the 'we' style (vv. 14, 18) and, by means of a concentrated theological argument, takes us to the heart of his under-

---

143. Although this expression ἐγγὺς γίνομαι ('come near') occurs only here in the New Testament. In the Old Testament the Gentile nations are said to be 'far off' (Deut. 28:49; 29:22; 1 Kings 8:41; Isa. 5:26; Jer. 5:15), while Israel is regarded as 'near' (cf. Ps. 148:14).

144. The notion of Gentiles being 'far off' is implied in the apostolic message of Acts 2:39 ('the promise is to you and to your children and to all that are far off') and expressed in the Lord's commission to Paul: 'I will send you far off to the Gentiles' (Acts 22:21). Cf. Bruce, 295.

145. Note, e.g., Lincoln, 138-39.

146. Hoehner.

standing of reconciliation. Because vv. 14-18 apparently stand as a unit, most scholars identify them as a hymnic fragment.[147]

From the opening words *he himself* (v. 14) it is clear that Christ, rather than God who has been the major actor in the preceding paragraphs (1:3-14, 15-23; 2:1-10), is the central figure. The emphasis is now placed on Christ's reconciling work, and this stress continues throughout vv. 14-18. He is the subject of the finite verbs and participles which focus on reconciliation and the removal of alienation. This short but highly significant paragraph is closely tied in with the issues of vv. 11-13 (note the introductory *for*) and is rounded out by an *inclusio* or envelope in which the 'we' and 'our' now refer inclusively to both Jew and Gentile believers: Christ is *'our* peace' (v. 14), and it is through him that 'we both have access to the Father' (v. 18).

The structure of the paragraph is rather elaborate. The opening statement, 'he himself is our peace', forms a title to the section and equates Christ with peace. This is followed by three participles whose subject is Christ ('made', v. 14; 'destroyed', v. 14; and 'abolished', v. 15) and which form 'a series of positive and negative statements regarding either making into one or destroying enmity in its various forms'.[148] The participles lead on to two purpose clauses ('to create', v. 15, and 'to reconcile', v. 16). Vv. 17 and 18 are a new sentence which refers to Christ's proclamation of peace to both Gentile and Jew (v. 17), together with the ground ('for') of this announcement (v. 18). This may be expressed in the following pattern:

> He himself is our peace
>   who *made* both one
>   and *destroyed* the barrier, the fence that separated them,
>   having *abolished* in his flesh the hostility,
>   the law of commandments consisting in regulations,

147. The formal characteristics of the passage, including the unique words, the use of participles, the intensely christological content, the parallelism of the lines, and the 'we' style which interrupts the 'you' style (of vv. 13, 19-22), lead most scholars to conclude that it is hymnic (e.g., Lincoln, Martin, and Barth). This identification of vv. 14-18 as a hymnic fragment has been disputed, however, by Stuhlmacher (cf. Schnackenburg), who regards it as a Christian midrash on Isaiah 57:19 (plus the other two Isaiah passages), and Best. For detailed discussions (with bibliographies), see Lincoln, 126-29; I. H. Thomson, *Chiasmus*, 84-115, esp. 84-86; T. Moritz, *A Profound Mystery*, 25-29; and Best, 247-50.

148. S. E. Porter, Καταλλάσσω *in Ancient Greek Literature, with Reference to the Pauline Writings* (Cordoba: Ediciones el Almendro, 1994), 171. He also draws attention to the use of instrumental statements which indicate the means by which these actions have been effected: 'in his flesh' (v. 14), 'in him' (v. 15), 'in one body', 'through the cross', and 'in him' (v. 16). Note the discussion below.

> to create in himself one new humanity out of the two,
>> so making peace,
> and to reconcile both to God,
>> having put to death the hostility.
> And he came and preached peace to you who were far away,
>> and peace to those who were near;
> For through him we both together have access in one Spirit to the
> Father.

14-15 Paul begins with an important affirmation about Christ which confirms and explains how the readers' coming near was made possible through his death (v. 13): *For he himself*[149] *is our peace*. These opening words stand like a title to the whole passage and introduce the vital theme of 'peace' (vv. 14-18).[150] As he explains the wonder of Christ's reconciling work within this short, concentrated section, Paul employs the term 'peace' four times (vv. 14, 15, 17 [twice]), as well as the related motifs of reconciliation (v. 16), making the two into one (v. 14), creating one new humanity (v. 15), and gaining access to the Father in one Spirit (v. 18). Furthermore, the antonym of peace, 'enmity', is pressed into service to specify the nature of the hostility that has been destroyed and 'killed' by Christ in his peacemaking work. Is it any wonder that Ephesians 2:14-18 is regarded as the *locus classicus* on peace in the Pauline letters (cf. Rom. 5:1-11)?

The term 'peace' in both Old and New Testaments came to denote well-being in the widest sense, including salvation, the source and giver of which is God alone. 'Peace' was used for harmony among people (Acts 7:26; Gal. 5:22; Eph. 4:3; Jas. 3:18) and especially for the messianic salvation (Luke 1:79; 2:14; 19:42). The term could describe the content and goal of all Christian preaching, the message itself being called 'the gospel of peace' (Eph. 6:15; cf. Acts 10:36; Eph. 2:17). The biblical concept of peace has to do with wholeness, particularly with reference to personal relationships. Peace describes an order established by the God of peace (1 Cor. 14:33; cf. Rom. 15:33; 16:20; Phil. 4:9). Christ himself is the mediator of that peace (Rom. 5:1; Col. 1:20). He gives peace to believers (2 Thess. 3:16); indeed, he himself is that peace.[151]

---

149. All of the references to the intensive personal pronoun αὐτός ('he') in Ephesians focus emphatically on Christ: 2:14; 4:10, 11; 5:23, 27.

150. S. E. Porter, 'Peace, Reconciliation', *DPL*, 698-99; and his Καταλλάσσω, 169-71, 185-89.

151. Christ not only brings peace and reconciliation; he is this peace or, to put it another way, peace is a person, Jesus Christ (in Col. 3:16 'the peace of Christ' designates the peace which he both embodies and brings; cf. John 14:27).

This identification of Christ with peace is at first surprising. We usually think of him as making peace (v. 15) or proclaiming it, rather than being it.[152] While peace may have been personified in the Graeco-Roman world in relation to the *Pax Romana* ('the peace of Rome'), the origin of Paul's description of peace as personal is the well-known Old Testament messianic title, 'the Prince of Peace' (Isa. 9:6; cf. Mic. 5:5, 'he will be their peace'). In his programmatic statement, Paul uses the all-inclusive *our*, indicating that Christ is the embodiment of peace[153] for both Jewish and Gentile Christians, including himself. The focus of attention, in the first instance, is not on peace with God as such, although vv. 16-18 will show that this 'vertical' peace is foundational to the restoration of relationships between Jews and Gentiles.

What is meant by the programmatic statement, *he himself is our peace,* is developed by means of three relative clauses,[154] the subject of which is Christ and which speak of making two into one or destroying enmity. He is the central figure who effects reconciliation and removes hostility in its various forms. The first relative clause, 'who *made* both one', refers to the resulting unity of Jewish and Gentile believers.[155] Somewhat surprisingly, the nouns *two* and *one* are neuter, denoting entities. In the light of vv. 11-13 one might have expected masculine plurals to indicate the two groups of people previously mentioned, namely, Gentiles and Jews. But the neuter can be used for persons or groups of persons (cf. 1 Cor. 1:27, 28; Gal. 3:22; John 6:37, 39; 17:2; 1 John 5:4),[156] and there is no doubt in this context that Paul has these two groups in mind.[157] They have been brought into a mutual relationship and a unity which surpasses what they once were (cf. vv. 15, 16, 18). 'In accomplishing this, Christ has transcended one of the fundamental divisions of the first-century world'.[158] If Jews spoke of humanity

152. Best, 251.

153. Christ is identified with the blessings of salvation elsewhere in Paul: he is God's 'wisdom' for us (which is then amplified in terms of our righteousness, holiness, and redemption: 1 Cor. 1:30), our 'hope' (Col. 1:27; cf. 1 Tim. 1:1), and our 'life' (Col. 3:4).

154. Expressed by means of three participles: ὁ ποιήσας . . . λύσας . . . καταργήσας ('who made . . . destroyed . . . abolished').

155. 'The two groups are not strictly Jews and Gentiles; it is Christians from both these groups who are made into the one new group. Jews and Gentiles as such still exist as independent groups' (Best, 253).

156. BDF §138(1) comment: 'The neuter is sometimes used with reference to persons if it is not the individuals but a general quality that is to be emphasized'. Cf. P. Stuhlmacher, '"He Is Our Peace" (Eph. 2:14). On the Exegesis and Significance of Eph. 2:14-18', in *Reconciliation, Law, and Righteousness: Essays in Biblical Theology* (Philadelphia: Fortress, 1986), 185.

157. G. W. Dawes, *The Body,* 171.

158. Lincoln, 141.

being divided into Jews and Gentiles, then Paul makes a threefold division: Jews, Greeks (i.e., Gentiles), and the church of God (1 Cor. 10:32). Later Christians were to speak of themselves as a 'third race' or 'new race' — neither Jewish nor Gentile.[159]

The way in which Christ made the two one is next described in two parallel clauses (vv. 14b-15a): he 'has broken down the dividing wall, the fence, that separated them, having abolished in his flesh the hostility, the law of commandments consisting in regulations'. Paul uses an unusual metaphor to explain how Christ has made Jews and Gentiles into a new unity which transcends the old distinctions. The first phrase should be rendered 'the dividing wall which is the fence',[160] and what this means is elucidated in the clauses which follow.

What is the origin of this metaphor of the dividing wall? (a) Schlier[161] maintains that the analogy was provided by Gnostic notions of a barrier between the world below and the upper world of the 'fulness'.[162] But apart from the later dating of the relevant Gnostic material, the barrier between Jews and Gentiles was vertical, not horizontal. The notion of a cosmic wall has on the whole, therefore, been rejected.

(b) Some have understood the barrier as a reference to the temple balustrade separating the court of the Gentiles from the inner courts and the sanctuary in the Jerusalem temple. Attached to this barrier at intervals were notices in Greek and Latin warning Gentiles not to proceed further on pain of death (Josephus, *Jewish War* 5.194). Such a reference would powerfully symbolize the separation of Gentiles from Israel, and Paul's declaration later in the chapter that Gentiles, along with Jews, have become a holy temple in the Lord (vv. 20-22) would be all the more pointed. But whether the Gentile readers of this letter, living in Asia Minor, would have recognized such an allusion is questionable. Furthermore, this temple wall, as 'part of a microcosmic representation of Israel's view of the world (cf. Mishnah *Kelim* 1:6-9) . . . , was a Torah-inspired spatial representation of the distinction between Israel and the nations'.[163] The literal barrier in the temple which prohibited Gentiles from entering the inner courts where Israel worshipped was simply the outward expression of the Mosaic commandments.

159. Cf. Clement, *Stromateis* 6.5.41.6; *Epistle to Diognetus* 1.

160. μεσότοιχον means 'a wall or fence which separates one area from another', so a 'dividing wall' (Louw and Nida §7.62). Most commentators rightly conclude that τοῦ φραγμοῦ ('of the fence') is a genitive of apposition, 'the dividing wall which consisted in the fence', or 'the intervening wall that separates' (Louw and Nida §34.39).

161. H. Schlier, *Christus und die Kirche im Epheserbrief* (Tübingen: Mohr, 1930), 27-37.

162. Gk. πλήρωμα.

163. D. G. Reid, 'Triumph', *DPL*, 951-54, esp. 951.

(c) The real barrier was, in fact, the Mosaic law itself with its detailed holiness code. And since it is best to understand 'having broken down the dividing wall, the fence' as parallelled by 'having abolished . . . the hostility, the law . . .', then the most natural reference to the fence is the law.[164] Certainly, the 'oral' law was understood in Judaism as a 'fence' around the law (Mishnah *'Abot* 1:1), but even the law itself provided a fence around Israel.[165] It separated Jews from Gentiles both religiously and sociologically, and caused deep-seated hostility. The enmity which was caused by the Jews' separateness was often accompanied by a sense of superiority on their part.[166]

But Christ has abolished this hostility *in his flesh,* that is, 'by his death' (note the fuller expression in Col. 1:22, 'in the body of his flesh, through death'). Through the perfect offering of himself once for all upon the cross (cf. Eph. 2:13, 16) Christ has done away with what separated the Jew from the Gentile — 'the law of commandments consisting in regulations'.

These words of v. 15a are some of the most difficult to interpret in this tightly packed and theologically significant paragraph (vv. 14-18). They are without parallel elsewhere in the New Testament, although the heaping up of the synonymous expressions 'law', 'commandments', and 'ordinances' is characteristic of the style of Ephesians. The following issues are addressed as we seek to determine what is meant by the clause:

(1) The significance of the verb often rendered 'abolished' in the EVV. This word can mean to 'make ineffective, or powerless, nullify',[167] and it is employed figuratively with reference to nullifying the faithful-

---

164. The relationship between the clauses is not entirely clear. While it is grammatically possible for τὴν ἔχθραν ('the hostility') to be construed as the second object of λύσας ('broken down'), in apposition with τὸ μεσότοιχον ('wall'), it would be awkward to have the two objects of λύσας ('broken down') separated by the participle. It is better, therefore, to regard τὴν ἔχθραν ('the hostility') as the first object of καταργήσας ('has abolished'), with τὸν νόμον κτλ. the second object, explaining the content of 'the enmity'. Fortunately the sense is not greatly affected by the construction, though the balance of the clauses is maintained in this interpretation. So Robinson, 161; Bruce, 298; and Schnackenburg, 113, among others.

165. Note the oft-quoted second-century-B.C. *Epistle of Aristeas,* 139: 'Our lawgiver . . . fenced us about with impenetrable palisades and with walls of iron to the end that we should mingle in no way with any of the other nations . . .'.

166. Bruce, 298.

167. The verb is καταργέω. Cf. BAGD, 417. In 2 Cor. 3:6-15 it appears four times (vv. 7, 11, 13, 14) in relation to the old covenant or its glory being 'set aside' in Christ. See the discussion of καταργέω by H. Hübner, *EDNT* 2:267-68, who notes that apart from 1 Cor. 13:11 a 'striking aspect of Paul's theological use is that the grammatical or logical subj. of καταργέω is God or Christ'. He points out that Eph. 2:15 (along with 2 Thess. 2:8; 2 Tim. 1:10; and Heb. 2:14) stands in continuity with this.

ness of God (Rom. 3:3), of making God's promise ineffective (Gal. 3:17), or of nullifying the things that exist (1 Cor. 1:28). Here in Ephesians 2:15 the verb signifies that Christ by his death made the law of no effect. He nullified it, so that it is no longer binding. He 'abolished' the enmity by nullifying the law.

(2) The expression 'the law of commandments in ordinances'. The 'law' that has been 'abolished' is the Mosaic law, the Torah. The genitive 'of the commandments' indicates the contents of the law, while the phrase 'in ordinances, decrees'[168] suggests the essential form in which the commands are given.[169] The three nouns convey 'a sense of the oppressiveness of all the law's commandments'.[170]

(3) Because of the difficulty many have had with the notion that Christ dealt with the negative effects of the law (such as its dividing Jew from Gentile) by doing away with the law itself, the qualifiers to the word 'law' have been interpreted so as to focus on one element of it (the ceremonial rather than the moral), the wrongful use of the law, or simply one aspect of it. So, for example, H. Schlier[171] understands 'law' in the sense

---

168. Bruce, 299, renders ἐν δόγμασιν by 'ordinances and all' (following the analogy of ₊Col. 2:14, though the Greek is slightly different). The phrase could be translated 'consisting of ordinances' or 'contained in ordinances'. The term 'regulation' (δόγμα) is employed in a variety of ways in the New Testament to denote a 'decree' of Caesar Augustus concerning the enrolment (Luke 2:1; cf. Acts 17:7) and the 'decisions' (plural δόγματα) of the Jerusalem council (Acts 16:4). The only other instance of the term in the Pauline corpus is Col. 2:14, where the plural 'decrees' (δόγματα) refers to ascetic regulations rather than to the law (cf. the cognate δογματίζεσθαι ['conform to rules and regulations'] in v. 20). In Hellenistic Judaism the commandments of God were called δόγματα (3 Macc. 1:3; 4 Macc. 10:2; and for further references in Josephus and Philo cf. G. Kittel, *TDNT* 2:230-32). C. J. Roetzel, 'Jewish Christian–Gentile Christian Relations: A Discussion of Eph. 2,15a', *ZNW* 74 (1983), 81-89, esp. 84, following the variant reading of 𝔓⁴⁶ and vg^ms, takes the phrase as a later addition to the text. It was added to counter the idea that the coming of Christ had made the commandments obsolete for 'spiritual' Christians. But this is unlikely; note the criticisms of M. Kitchen, 'The Status of Law in the Letter to the Ephesians', in *Law and Religion: Essays on the Place of the Law in Israel and Early Christianity*, ed. B. Lindars (Cambridge: James Clarke & Co., 1988), 141-47, 187, esp. 145-47; Best, 260; and Hoehner.

169. So Meyer, 130-31. Bruce, 299 (following Robinson, 161), states that in speaking of the law here, 'it is as a code of manifold precepts, expressed in definite ordinances, that he declares it to have been annulled'. S. E. Porter, *Idioms,* 157, suggests that it denotes sphere: 'the law of commandments in [the sphere of its] ordinances', although he concedes that an instrumental sense ('by') is possible. Several EVV apparently understand the ἐν to be equivalent to σύν ('with') or καί ('and'), hence RSV 'the law of commandments and ordinances', NRSV 'the law with its commandments and ordinances', NEB 'the law with its rules and regulations', and NIV 'the law with its commandments and regulations'.

170. Lincoln, 142. Meyer, 130, suggests that 'the *dictatorial* character of the legal institute (as a whole, not merely partially . . .) is exhibited'.

171. Schlier, 125-26.

of legalism. Accordingly, it is the wrongful (i.e., legalistic or casuistic) use of the law that has been abolished by Christ's death, not the law as such. Markus Barth[172] holds that it was the law in its divisiveness rather than the law itself which had been annulled. But while the context demands a close link between the law and its divisiveness, to suggest that only one aspect of the law has been abolished seems to miss the plain statement of this clause. Thomas Schreiner, for his part, argues that here Paul 'sums up the commanding focus of the law'. He 'specifically defines the law in terms of its requirements'.[173] Ephesians 2:15 and 1 Corinthians 7:19, where circumcision is excluded from the commandments, show that Paul has in mind a reduced law. This focus on the moral dimensions of the law is not totally surprising, since early Judaism did the same. The moral law received the prominence, while the cultic law receded into the background. 'To the extent that Jewish literature stresses the moral law, it serves as a forerunner to Paul's teaching that the moral law must be fulfilled'.[174] Bruce takes a somewhat similar line. It is not the law 'as a revelation of the character and will of God' but 'as a written code, threatening death instead of imparting life' that has been done away with in Christ. So when 'the law in that sense is done away with, the barrier between Jews and Gentiles is removed; Jewish particularism and Gentile exclusion are things of the past'.[175]

(4) The claim which these writers make is that vv. 14 and 15 are not dealing with the Mosaic law as a whole but with the ceremonial requirements of the law which have ended. The undergirding moral law of God still stands.[176] But while we do not wish to deny that the moral law of God still stands (Paul elsewhere asserts that he is 'not free from God's

172. Barth, 287-91.

173. T. R. Schreiner, *The Law*, 39. He adds that to 'underline this point he describes the "law of the commandments" as consisting of decrees', with ἐν δόγμασιν probably being appositional.

174. T. R. Schreiner, *The Law*, 155-56.

175. Bruce, 298-99. Cf. E. Faust, *Pax Christi et Pax Caesaris: Religionsgeschichtliche, traditionsgeschichtliche und sozialgeschichtliche Studien zum Epheserbrief* (Fribourg/Göttingen: Universitätsverlag/Vandenhoeck & Ruprecht, 1993), 117-21, who understands the ritual law to be a dividing wall and principle of enmity.

176. So W. Kaiser, in a joint volume entitled *The Law, the Gospel, and the Modern Christian: Five Views*, ed. W. Strickland and others (Grand Rapids: Zondervan, 1993), 397. Kaiser adds that 'the law is not a monolithic unity'. Eph. 2:15 is not dealing with the Mosaic law as a whole but with the ceremonial requirements of the law. Note also G. L. Bahnsen, who argues that the description in Eph. 2:14 and 15 does 'not accurately apply to moral laws of the Old Testament' (104). For a rebuttal of this view and a treatment of the wider exegetical and theological issues involved in Christ's abrogation of the law, see especially the article by D. J. Moo in that volume, 'The Law of Christ as the Fulfillment of the Law of Moses: A Modified Lutheran View', 319-76.

law' but is in fact 'under the law of Christ', 1 Cor. 9:21), or that the law ceases to exist, or has no more relevance for the Christian, a wider reference to the Mosaic law is most probable in this context. The apostle may well be alluding to the Jewish teaching about the *Torah* as a whole. The text suggests that it is the law itself which Christ has nullified.[177] It has been 'rendered powerless', and thus 'ceases to stand as an immediate authority for God's people'.[178] Admittedly, Ephesians 2 is not all that Paul says about the law, and it is not without significance that having made this assertion in v. 15, he can later draw on one of those commandments (6:2) in support of his paraenesis. Paul, like James, 'reapplies' several Mosaic commands within the law (Gal. 5:14; Eph. 6:2; cf. Jas. 2:8-12). Significantly, nine of the ten commandments are taken up into the law of Christ.[179] But the Mosaic law, which is firmly tied to the Sinai covenant, is 'not a *direct* and *immediate* guid[e] to the new covenant believer'.[180]

(5) Perhaps it may help to say that what is abolished is the 'law-covenant', that is, the law as a whole conceived as a covenant. It is then replaced by a new covenant for Jews *and* Gentiles. The relationship between the stipulations of the old covenant and those of the new covenant still needs to be worked out. But because the old *Torah* as such, that is, the law-covenant, has gone, it can no longer serve as the great barrier between Jew and Gentile.[181]

The apostle now moves from the negative to the positive, from the removal of the enmity between Jew and Gentile to the creation of a new and undivided humanity. The purpose of Christ's removing this hostility by abolishing the law was twofold: (1) *to create in himself one new man out of the two* (v. 15b), and (2) *in this one body to reconcile both of them to God* (v. 16a).[182] Once the divisive law by which Jews and Gentiles had been alienated from one another was set aside, there was nothing to keep the two elements of humanity apart. Christ brought them together in a sovereign act that was nothing less than a new creation. Paul has already spoken of God's salvation in terms of a new creation (2:10). Believers are his workmanship who have already been *created* in Christ Je-

177. Notice that it is νόμον ('law') which is the direct object of the verb and which Christ has rendered powerless.

178. D. J. Moo, 'The Law of Christ', 367.

179. The only exception is the sabbath commandment, which Heb. 3–4 suggests is fulfilled in the new age as a whole.

180. D. J. Moo, 'The Law of Christ', 375 (original emphasis).

181. I owe this suggestion to Dr. D. A. Carson, who mentioned it in a private communication.

182. For a critique of Markus Barth's view that the church has been incorporated into historical Israel, see on v. 16.

sus for good works, and these are part of God's intention for that new creation. Here in v. 15 the same creation language[183] is employed for this new creation, but now the focus of attention (as throughout vv. 14-18) is on Christ's mighty work: he is the creator of a new humanity through his death.

This new humanity, or 'one new person' (cf. Eph. 4:24),[184] is a corporate entity; the expression used stands for the people of Christ (Jews and Gentiles alike) whom he has created in himself.[185] They have been united in him, the inclusive representative of the new order,[186] as members of his body (note the 'full-grown man' of Eph. 4:13). According to Colossians 3:11 the barriers that divided people from one another — racial, religious, cultural, and social — are abolished in Christ, who is all and in all (cf. Gal. 3:28; 6:15). Here in Ephesians 2, Jews and Gentiles who had been deeply divided and at enmity with one another are created in one new person. Nothing less than a new creation, an entirely new entity, was needed to transcend the deep rift between the two. It was effected through Christ's death, and the result is not an amalgam of the best elements of the two, but a 'new person' who transcends them both. The new humanity is not achieved by transforming Gentiles into Jews,[187] or vice versa. And by this new creation Christ truly 'makes peace'.[188] These words explain, in part, the heading to the section: *he himself is our peace* (v. 14). The *peace* in view in v. 15 is that between Jews and Gentiles, which is the opposite of *hostility*. Theologically, its basis is peace with God, and to this the apostle now turns.

Christ's bringing together Jew and Gentile in himself as the 'one new person' is a highly significant step towards the fulfilment of God's eternal plan, that is, the consummation of the mystery (1:9-10). God's ul-

---

183. Gk. κτίζω.

184. Gk. εἰς ἕνα καινὸν ἄνθρωπον.

185. Schnackenburg, 115, comments: 'Christ does not perform the role of a builder who constructs a new, unified building from separate parts and as it were sets it up on view; he builds this new entity in his own person, it is he himself in a new dimension'.

186. God wished to create one new humanity out of Jew and Gentile. For the centrality of this to Paul's theology see 1 Cor. 12:13; Gal. 3:28; Col. 3:11.

187. Against J. D. G. Dunn, *The Partings of the Ways: Between Christianity and Judaism and Their Significance for the Character of Christianity* (London/Philadelphia: SCM/TPI, 1991), 149, who fails to point out, in the context of Eph. 2, that Christ has created a new entity.

188. M. Barth, *Israel and the Church*, 95, claims that since faith is not mentioned in this context, all Jews and Gentiles are united by Christ, and this new entity is not limited to 'Jewish- and Gentile-born *Christians* only'. He states that every Jew is included, 'be he a faithful observer of the law or a rebellious trespasser, a Pharisee or a Sadducee, orthodox or secularized' (Barth, 255). See below, 203-4.

timate purpose is to bring together everything in Christ as the focal point. The object of this summing up is 'all things' (1:10), an expression which is amplified and explained by means of the parallel phrases 'things in heaven' and 'things on earth'. Christ's creating of one new person in himself has particular reference to the latter domain, namely, 'things on earth'. His bringing together Jew and Gentile is the achieving of a reconciliation between two hostile elements here 'on earth'. This work has, in principle, already been effected. Christ has achieved it by his death on the cross. It may thus be spoken of as 'realized eschatology'. But there is still a future dimension, for the new relationship between Jew and Gentile has yet to be consummated. Later Paul will contend that the very presence of Jews and Gentiles in the church, here and now, is magnificent evidence to the 'rulers and authorities in the heavenly realms' of the manifold wisdom of God (3:10).

16 In the preceding verses Paul's focus has been on the horizontal dimension, namely, Christ's removal of the enmity between Jew and Gentile. Now the vertical dimension is explicitly coupled with this, as the issue of reconciliation with God is introduced. By his death Christ has done away with the law, in order not only to make Jew and Gentile into 'one new person' (v. 15b), but also to reconcile them both in one body to God.

Although the notion of reconciliation turns up in Paul's major letters (Rom. 5:10, 11; 11:15; 2 Cor. 5:18-20), here an unusual compound verb meaning to 'reconcile' appears (cf. Col. 1:20, 22).[189] Generally the ground of reconciliation lies in God's gracious initiating activity (at Rom. 5:8 the basis is the love of God, while Col. 1:20 points to the divine good pleasure; cf. 2 Cor. 5:18). In Ephesians 2:16 several distinctive features stand out: first, it is Christ, rather than God, who does the reconciling. This stress on Christ's action, as noted above, is consistent with the emphasis in vv. 14-18 on his being the central figure. God is the one with whom those at enmity are reconciled. The two groups now rightly related are Jews and Gentiles *(both of them)*, and this has occurred *in one body*, which

189. The earliest attested usage of ἀποκαταλλάσσω ('reconcile'), an emphatically prefixed form of the verb καταλλάσσω ('reconcile'), is in Col. 1:20-22 and Eph. 2:16. Although καταλλάσσω ('reconcile') was available to the apostle (cf. 1 Cor. 7:11; Rom. 5:10; 2 Cor. 5:18, 19, 20), perhaps in the light of his 'discussion of the work of Christ it was felt that a particular intensification of the action was called for'. See S. E. Porter, *Idioms*, 140, 141, and for a treatment of reconciliation in these two letters as well as further bibliographical details, see both his article, 'Peace, Reconciliation', *DPL*, 697-99, and his book Καταλλάσσω, 169-71, 185-89 (cf. also Lincoln, 145; Best, 264). S. E. Porter and K. D. Clarke, 'Canonical-Critical Perspective', 77-81, have recently suggested that the use of the emphatically prefixed form (ἀποκαταλλάσσω, 'reconcile') points to the Pauline authorship of both Colossians and Ephesians (see the Introduction).

is a reference to the church[190] rather than the physical crucified body of Christ (or indeed to both).[191] The qualifying adjective 'one' makes this clear (cf. vv. 14, 15). Also, throughout Ephesians the 'body' of Christ designates the church (1:23; 4:4, 12, 16; 5:23, 30).[192] Here *one body* denotes the same as the 'one new person' of v. 15, to which the 'one Spirit' of v. 18 corresponds.

It has been argued that because the reconciliation between Jews and Gentiles is mentioned *before* the reconciliation of both with God, there is a significant change of perspective in Ephesians over against Paul's view. Through Jesus' death on the cross, it is claimed, 'the Church is first created as [the] realm of salvation; reconciliation is given through it'. This 'primacy of ecclesiology over soteriology' is characteristic of the author of Ephesians.[193] But this contention arises out of a failure to understand the flow of the writer's argument in the paragraph. His concern from v. 11 onwards has been to remind his Gentile readers ('you') of their pre-Christian past in relation to Israel (vv. 11, 12) and their present privileged position of being *in Christ* (v. 13). His intention was that they might have a greater understanding and appreciation of the past and of the mighty reversal Christ had won for them so that they would accept all that is involved in being God's new creation. The readers' separation from Israel, the people of God, and all the covenant privileges was the 'presenting problem' of vv. 11-13, and it was natural that the writer should address this issue first. But the horizontal dimension is not dropped from v. 16, since the two groups are reconciled *in one body*. Thus, the wording should not be pressed to mean that the church of Jew and Gentile was created first, and only then was it reconciled to God at the cross. Indeed, how could reconciliation between Jew and Gentile occur apart from reconciliation with God?[194]

This reconciliation of Jews and Gentiles in *one body* is parallel to Christ's creating 'in himself one new person' (v. 15b). The reconciliation

190. '[P]rovided that we think of the church not as an ecclesiastical organization but as the new humanity of v. 15' (so rightly Caird, 59).

191. Which is how P. Stuhlmacher, '"He Is Our Peace"', 190, understands the phrase.

192. Among recent writers who take this line note Schnackenburg, 117; and R. Y. K. Fung, 'Body of Christ', *DPL*, 80.

193. So H. Merkel, *EDNT* 2:263, following H. Merklein, *Christus*, 62-68.

194. Schnackenburg, 116, speaks of the '*two internally connected aspects of Christ's one peace-bringing work*. While by his death on the Cross he reconciled with God the two groups who were previously estranged, he reconciled them to one another' (our emphasis). At the conclusion of his important study Arnold, 163, 164, contends that 'Ephesians still maintains the Pauline primacy of Christology. Specifically, *ecclesiology is a function of Christology* in Ephesians' (his emphasis). Cf. Lincoln, 144; Turner, 1231.

of *both* with God introduces a new element, and the presupposition is that not only Gentiles but *also Israel* were alienated from God because of sin. From the context of vv. 11-13 it is clear that the Gentile readers' separation from Israel's Messiah and their exclusion from the community of God's people signified an alienation from the covenants which promised the messianic salvation, and from God himself. But even the elect nation Israel, which was the recipient and custodian of God's gracious covenant promises, had not as a whole appropriated these promises for itself. Vv. 1-3 refer *first* to Paul's Gentile readers being dead in trespasses and sins before coming to faith (vv. 1, 2), and *then* to Jewish believers (including the apostle himself) being in a similar desperate plight prior to their conversion (v. 3), so that they, too, *were by nature objects of wrath* and therefore like the rest of humanity. In a fundamental sense Israel, too, was alienated from God. Both 'Jews and Gentiles alike [were] under sin' (Rom. 3:9),[195] and both needed to be reconciled to God. It might be added that the law which separated Gentiles from Israel and so from Israel's God can be seen to have separated Israel herself from God.[196] Jews and Gentiles alike, for all their differences, were at enmity with one another and alienated from God; hence the desperate need for this twofold reconciliation, which Paul triumphantly affirms has been effected through the death of Christ.

In the light of this fact that Jews and Gentiles alike were under sin, and both needed to be reconciled to God since they were objects of his wrath, the view of Markus Barth that the church has been incorporated into historical Israel is incorrect. Barth thinks that because faith is not mentioned in the present context of Ephesians 2, all Jews (whether Christians or not) and Gentiles are united in Christ; there is no limitation to 'Jewish- and Gentile-born *Christians* only'.[197] Accordingly, there is no need to preach the message of salvation to Jews,[198] which includes a 'faithful observer of the law or rebellious trespasser, a Pharisee or a Sadducee, orthodox or secularized'.[199] But the flow of the letter as a whole, as well as the immediate context, assumes that it is believing Jews and be-

---

195. Although Lincoln, 145, 146, finally reaches this theological conclusion, his initial difficulties would have been reduced considerably if he had interpreted vv. 1-3 of Gentiles and of Jews (see on 1:11-14 and 2:1-3).

196. Note the same point in Paul's major letters: Gal. 3:10-22; 2 Cor. 3:7-11; Rom. 3:19, 20; possibly 7:7-25; 9:30–10:4.

197. M. Barth, *Israel and the Church*, 95; see also 74-75. Cf. also his *The People of God* (Sheffield: JSOT Press, 1983), 45-72.

198. M. Barth, *Israel and the Church*, 108-15 (cited by Hoehner).

199. Barth, 255; cf. also his *The Broken Wall: A Study of the Epistle to the Ephesians* (Chicago: Judson, 1959), 122, 128.

lieving Gentiles that make up this new entity. Paul gives thanks to God for the readers' faith (1:15). It is both Jews and Gentiles who are in need of God's saving grace that are God's workmanship, created in Christ Jesus (note the 'we' of 2:10, which includes Jewish and Gentile Christians). Only those in Christ, both near and far, have been brought near by his sacrificial death, and he has come and preached peace to both groups. The union of which vv. 14-17 speaks is not a union of Jews and Gentiles but of redeemed Jews and Gentiles who are in Christ.[200]

Thus, once again in this theologically important paragraph Christ's sacrificial death is set forth as the ground of reconciliation: v. 13 states that those who were far off have been brought near 'through the blood of Christ'; v. 15 speaks of Christ's abolishing the enmity 'in his flesh', that is, his death; and now the centrality of Christ's cross is reaffirmed, this time as the basis of that reconciliation by which Jews and Gentiles in one body are brought into fellowship with God (note the significance of Christ's death at 1:7; 5:2, 25).

The imagery of the cross has apparently suggested the language of death to the apostle, so he speaks of Christ *killing* the enmity. 'Christ in his death was slain, but the slain was a slayer too'.[201] This final clause is akin to the participial clause 'abolishing . . . the enmity in his flesh' (vv. 14, 15), and parallels the words at the end of v. 15, *thus making peace*. The words rendered *by which* refer to the cross as the immediate antecedent and indicate that Christ killed the enmity by means of his death. However, in the light of the number of times 'he', 'him', and 'his' turn up in vv. 14-16 with reference to Christ,[202] it may be better to understand the phrase of Christ himself (= 'by whom'), although it is his death which is particularly in view (cf. v. 15, 'in his flesh'). The fundamental point is the same either way.[203]

But what is the *hostility* that has been put to death? For many it is 'the enmity' of v. 14, that hostility between Jew and Gentile, occasioned by the law of Moses, which Christ abolished in his flesh (vv. 14, 15). In favour of this, it is argued that the expression 'the hostility' is identical, while the aorist participle 'killed' 'involves a backward reference to Christ's action preceding the reconciliation in one body and to God'.[204] But several factors

---

200. A. T. Lincoln, 'The Church', 605-24; B. W. Fong, 'Addressing the Issue of Racial Reconciliation according to the Principles of Eph 2:11-22', *JETS* 38 (1995), 565-80; and Hoehner. Cf. Best, 268-69.

201. Robinson, 65.

202. Beginning with 'he (αὐτός) is our peace' (v. 14). Note also 'in his (αὐτοῦ) flesh' (v. 14) and the same phrase, 'in him' (ἐν αὐτῷ) (v. 15).

203. Cf. S. E. Porter, Καταλλάσσω, 187.

204. So Lincoln, 146, following Meyer, 136. The aorist participle is ἀποκτείνας ('killed').

militate against this: first, the flow of Paul's argument suggests that a two-fold enmity is in view. Here in v. 16 the vertical dimension has been introduced along with the horizontal, which up to this point has been the focus of attention. A fresh stage in the argument has been reached. Furthermore, Lincoln understands the participle 'killed' as describing an action antecedent to Christ's reconciliation of the two in one body to God. But recent aspectual study of the aorist participle in Paul has suggested that when the participle follows the main verb there is a 'definite tendency toward coincidental action'.[205] If this is correct, and it is consistent with the flow of thought here, then it was *in his reconciliation* of both Jew and Gentile in one body to God that Christ *killed* the enmity. The same event is described from two perspectives, first in positive terms (reconciliation), then in negative categories (removal of the enmity). Paul is speaking of a twofold alienation, the rift between Jews and Gentiles and the hostility between both of them and God,[206] that has been removed.

Christ has abolished the law as a divisive instrument separating humanity from God and Jews from Gentiles. He has created a single new humanity that transcends the former deep divisions and made peace between them. He has reconciled both Jew and Gentile in this one body to God, killing the hostility. This does not mean, however, that the whole human race has been united and reconciled. There is a further stage in Christ's work which the apostle now mentions.

17 Having dwelt at length on Christ's work of reconciliation, Paul now turns to his proclamation of peace to both Gentile and Jew. The One who is 'our peace' and who made peace through his cross now announces that peace to those who were *far* off and those who were *near*. This terminology, *far* and *near*, which the apostle employed in v. 13 in a way that closely resembled its special use for proselytes in Judaism, ultimately derives from Isaiah 57:19. This text is now cited in a modified form and along with 52:7 is interpreted christologically in the light of Christ's peacemaking work for both Gentiles and Jews.

The opening words, (lit.) 'and having come he preached peace', are a notorious crux: When did Christ *come* and *proclaim* peace? Is the reference to his incarnation, his ministry, his cross and resurrection, his post-resurrection appearances, or his proclamation as the exalted Christ through the apostles by the Spirit?

---

205. Note S. E. Porter, *Verbal Aspect,* 383-84. (See the discussion on 1:13.)

206. Stott, 102, rightly points out that there is 'a certain mutuality' in the hostility between human beings and God. 'It is not just that our attitude to him has been one of rebellion; it is also that his "wrath" has been upon us for our sin (v. 3). And only "through the cross" have both hostilities been brought to an end'.

(1) Several recent scholars claim that the expression *He came and preached peace* points specifically to Christ's death. Vv. 14-16, it is argued, prepare the way for the christological interpretation of Isaiah 52:7 and 57:19 here in v. 17, and these opening words are best understood as a recapitulation and summary of the earlier verses. The expression *and preached peace* echoes Isaiah 52:7, while the rest of the verse approximately follows 57:19. *He came* is not to be taken of an advent following Christ's death. Instead, it 'provides a transition which summarizes this preparatory material'.[207] His work on the cross, then, *is* his proclamation of peace with God to both the Gentile readers and Jews. The verb 'preached',[208] it is argued, is not a technical term for Christian gospel preaching (as in Eph. 3:8), but is to be understood in the sense of Isaiah 52:7, where it describes the messenger's proclamation of Yahweh's victory over the world. In our text the verb has to do with the announcement of a new reality, mentioned in vv. 14-16, which has been effected through Christ's death. So, then, the 'preaching of peace occurs in the redemptive death of Jesus Christ on the cross'.[209] On this interpretation there is no need to look further for any other advent, either before or after the cross, to explain the meaning of the expression.

But there are difficulties with this approach. While the participle rendered 'he came' could be used by way of recapitulation and transition, a serious weakness concerns the interpretation of the verb 'preached'. Not only do this verb and its cognate noun 'gospel' in Paul regularly designate the gospel message and its proclamation,[210] but also the appeal to Isaiah 52:7 in order to show that the content of the announcement concerns Yahweh's sovereignty and thus is different from any notion of 'gospel' is mistaken. In the Old Testament context the herald of good tidings who proclaims the message of salvation announces to Zion, 'Your God reigns'. This is not some general proclamation about Yahweh's sovereignty over the world, but is specifically tied to his returning to Zion (v. 8), comforting and redeeming his people (vv. 8, 9), and sending his Ser-

---

207. Lincoln, 148. According to H. Merklein, *Christus*, 58, the word 'came' refers to 'nothing other than Christ as the one who came from God and is characterized as the eschatological messenger'.

208. Gk. εὐαγγελίζομαι.

209. D. C. Smith, 'The Ephesian Heresy and the Origin of the Epistle to the Ephesians', *Ohio Journal of Religious Studies* 5 (1977), 85, who adds that 'the apostolic message, which is a preaching of this redemptive death, is therefore the logical extension of Christ's preaching of peace through the cross'. According to Smith, the 'reason εὐαγγελίζομαι is used to describe this event is because of the reference to Isa. 52:7'. Cf. H. Merklein, *Christus*, 58, and note the discussion of E. Faust, *Pax Christi*, 165-66.

210. For a detailed examination of εὐαγγελίζομαι ('preach the gospel') and εὐαγγέλιον ('gospel'), see P. T. O'Brien, *Gospel and Mission*, 62-65, 77-81.

vant to suffer on their behalf (52:13–53:12). In other words, it is *gospel* which the herald announces. Christ's 'making peace', which was achieved on the cross, is not identical with his 'proclaiming peace', any more than God's act of reconciling the world to himself in his Son is to be identified with his commitment of the message of reconciliation to his ambassadors (2 Cor. 5:18-20). The two are closely related but not identical; the former is the basis of the latter. Accordingly, we contend that Paul's flow of thought from vv. 14-16 to v. 17 is different from what this 'recapitulation' view argues.

(2) The second main line of interpretation, which has some variations within it, regards Christ's coming and preaching peace as pointing to an advent following his death.[211] His post-resurrection appearances in which the first word he spoke to the apostles was, 'Peace be with you' (John 14:27), could be in view. Others understand the reference to the proclamation of the exalted Christ speaking by his Spirit in his messengers, the apostles, and this we think is the most likely meaning.[212] Schnackenburg, who takes a mediating position, regards the reference to the 'coming' as serving simply as an introduction to Christ's preaching, where the emphasis falls. At most the author is thinking of the apostolic preaching (cf. 3:8; 4:11) in which Jesus remains the preacher.[213] What does come out clearly is that Christ himself is the evangelist, the herald of good tidings from Isaiah, and his announcement, which is based on his death on the cross, is a royal proclamation that hostilities are at an end.

As he combines Isaiah 52:7 with 57:19 in his creative christological interpretation,[214] Paul brings out several important emphases. First, originally Isaiah 57:19 was applied to God's blessing on *Jews* in the land ('to those near') and *Jews* of the dispersion ('to those far'). Although later Jewish interpretations of the text referred to other divisions within Israel, for example, between repentant sinners and the righteous, or even proselytes and native-born Jews (cf. *Numbers Rabbah* 8), here Paul, as he had done earlier in the paragraph (v. 13), understands the Old Testament text to have reached a new level of fulfilment: Christ brings his messianic 'peace' to *Gentile* readers and to Jews. Secondly, the twofold reference to

---

211. C. L. Mitton and K. M. Fischer, however, understand the expression as referring to the proclamation of the earthly Jesus, while P. Stuhlmacher, among others (cf. T. Moritz, *A Profound Mystery*, 50, 53), takes it as a general reference to the whole of Christ's work.

212. K. O. Sandnes, *Paul — One of the Prophets? A Contribution to the Apostle's Self-Understanding* (Tübingen: J. C. B. Mohr [Paul Siebeck], 1991), 229.

213. Schnackenburg, 118.

214. On the use of Isa. 57:19 in Eph. 2:17, see A. T. Lincoln, 'The Use', 25-30; his commentary, 146-48; and T. Moritz, *A Profound Mystery*, 42-55.

peace in the Old Testament text ('peace upon peace to those who are far off and to those who are near', LXX Isa. 57:19) is divided so that in Ephesians 2:17 *peace* is emphatically proclaimed to each group: 'peace to you who were far off' *and* peace 'to those who were near'. The effect of this change is to underscore the vertical dimension to the *peace* Christ proclaims. This is not to suggest that the context of Isaiah 57:19 is otherwise: vv. 16 and 17 make it plain that a broken relationship with God because of human sins and divine wrath was clearly in view.[215] That relationship was restored by the one who says, 'Peace, peace . . . I will heal them'. By his change Paul has chosen to focus on this dimension, which appropriately follows on from v. 16, where reconciliation *with God* comes clearly into view. Furthermore, it is reinforced in v. 18, which states that through Christ the two groups together now have access 'to the Father'. Finally, the original text in Isaiah made no reference to 'you'. The symmetry has been 'broken' by the apostle, who by his insertion keeps his Gentile Christian readers clearly in view. To them, of all people, Christ is the *evangelist* who triumphantly proclaims peace and reconciliation with the God from whom they had once been alienated.

18 The ground for the previous declaration that Christ has announced reconciliation and the end of alienation to those who were far off and those who were near is now presented:[216] *For through him we both have access to the Father by one Spirit.* Since both Gentiles, particularly Paul's readers (*you*, v. 17), and Jews now have access to the Father, it follows that the same message of peace has been proclaimed by Christ to them both.

This statement is parallel with v. 16, where Paul had emphasized that through the cross Christ has reconciled both of them in one body to God.[217] Yet v. 18 does not simply repeat what was asserted in the earlier sentence. There attention was drawn to Christ's work of reconciling both Jew and Gentile in one body to God; here the focus is on their continuing

---

215. Cf. M. Wolter, *Rechtfertigung und zukünftiges Heil: Untersuchungen zu Röm 5,1-11* (Berlin: de Gruyter, 1978), 72.

216. So Lincoln, 149; and G. D. Fee, *God's Empowering Presence,* 682, among others. Best, 273, on the other hand, thinks that v. 18 summarizes and explains what has gone before, while some hold that it indicates result: 'Christ preached peace to Jews and Gentiles with the result that we both have access to the Father' (so Hoehner).

217. The parallels may be laid out as follows:

Verse 16	Verse 18
'[that] he might reconcile to God'	'we have access to the Father'
'them both'	'we both'
'in one body'	'in one Spirit'
'through the cross'	'through him'.

relationship with the Father which is the result of Christ's act of reconciliation.

Paul's language is similar to that of Romans 5:1 and 2, where peace with God and having access to grace are linked. The keyword 'access'[218] appears in both passages, as well as in Ephesians 3:12. Although in classical Greek the term conjured up the scene in an oriental court where subjects were granted an audience with the king or emperor and presented to him,[219] it is more likely that Paul's imagery derives from an Old Testament cultic context of bringing offerings in order to come into God's presence (cf. Lev. 1:3; 3:3; 4:14). This word with its cultic associations pointed to a free entry into the sanctuary as the place of God's presence. The Old Testament did envisage Gentiles gaining access to God in order to pray and worship in the temple (1 Kings 8:41-43; cf. Isa. 56:6-8; Zech. 8:20-23). But here Paul does not simply assert that Gentiles now enjoy the privileges of Jews. The old categories have been transcended. Their approach is through Christ and 'is not confined to a specific locality such as a temple'.[220] Furthermore, if Gordon Fee is right in suggesting that 'we both' means not simply 'we both *alike* have access' but 'we both *together* have access', then there is an added nuance. It is not simply that individual Gentiles and Jews have unhindered entry into the presence of God, wonderful as this is. In addition, both of them as *one new humanity* can come into his presence. 'Jew and Gentile stand together as one people in God's presence with old distinctions no longer having significance'.[221] The implications of this in relation to the rulers and authorities in the heavenly realms will be addressed in 3:10.

The one to whom Jewish and Gentile believers have this free and unhindered access is known as 'Father'. In Christ both have become members of his family; they are able to address him as 'Abba! Father!' (the name by

---

218. While προσαγωγή was employed by classical writers in a transitive sense of an 'introduction or bringing near', the intransitive sense of 'access' is preferable in the three New Testament contexts (Rom. 5:2; Eph. 2:18; 3:12). 'Access' is something Gentile and Jewish believers now possess (ἔχομεν).

219. Cf. Xenophon, *Cyropaedia* 1.3.8; 7.5.45.

220. Lincoln, 149. In Hebrews there is a similar idea of the contrast between the old covenant, in which only the high priest had the right to enter the holy of holies on the Day of Atonement, and the new covenant in which all believers can draw near to the throne of grace (4:16; 7:25; 10:22; 12:22).

221. G. D. Fee, *God's Empowering Presence,* 683, correctly argues that this is the emphasis in the two occurrences of 'both' in vv. 14 and 16. Less certain, however, is Fee's identification of the phrase 'in one Spirit' as locative here (in contrast to the other uses in Ephesians: 2:22; 3:5; 5:18; 6:18), although he does concede that the locative sense does merge with the instrumental (684, 685).

which Jesus addressed him; cf. Gal. 4:6; Rom. 8:15, 16), for in this family he makes 'no distinction between those children who are Jewish by birth and those who are Gentile'.[222] Their becoming his children is an amazing change, given that both had been spiritually dead, in a fearful bondage and subject to divine wrath (2:1-3). 'In one Spirit' corresponds to 'in one body' (v. 16 — the two are brought together in 4:4), and again stresses the oneness of Jew and Gentile in the church. The one Spirit lives and works in the one body.[223] Finally, in this passage also Paul speaks of salvation in trinitarian terms: Christ's peacemaking work has provided access to the Father for both Jews and Gentiles through the one Spirit.

3. The Gentiles' Membership of God's House, 2:19-22

19 The consequences[224] for these Gentile readers (*you*) of Christ's mighty reconciling work (vv. 14-18) are now drawn out in terms which transcend the old Jew-Gentile divisions and which describe their new position as *fellow citizens with God's people and members of God's household*. The contrast schema[225] of vv. 11-13 is restated as Paul employs citizenship and household images for the church. Once his Gentile readers had been foreigners and aliens in relation to God's people, Israel. Now their status has dramatically changed. They now have a privileged place in God's new community.

It is difficult to draw any sharp distinction between the terms 'foreigners' and 'aliens'.[226] The former was used at v. 12 to speak of their being *foreigners* to the covenants of promise. Elsewhere in the New Testament when used as a noun it signifies a 'foreigner or stranger'.[227] The

---

222. Bruce, 301.

223. G. D. Fee, *God's Empowering Presence*, 684, somewhat doubtfully, takes the point further: 'They are both in the one body because they are also both in the one Spirit. . . . What has made one body possible is the death of Christ; what makes the one body a reality is their common, lavish experience of the Spirit of God'.

224. ἄρα οὖν ('as a result, consequently') draws the inference from vv. 14-18 and provides the transition to the next paragraph. It is an 'emphatically inferential connective'; so M. E. Thrall, *Greek Particles in the New Testament: Linguistic and Exegetical Studies* (Leiden: Brill, 1962), 10-11. Cf. BDF §451(2b); and BAGD, 104. In the New Testament the combination is found only in Paul (Rom. 5:18; 7:3, 25; 8:12; 9:16, 18; 14:12, 19; Gal. 6:10; Eph. 2:19; 1 Thess. 5:6; 2 Thess. 2:15).

225. Note the contrast οὐκέτι ἐστέ . . . ἀλλὰ ἐστέ (including the emphatic repetition of the verb after ἀλλά): 'you *are* no longer . . . but you *are*'.

226. Gk. ξένοι καὶ πάροικοι.

227. As an adjective ξένος ('unknown, unfamiliar') is employed literally in Acts 17:18; Heb. 13:9, and figuratively at Eph. 2:12. As a noun ('stranger, foreigner') it occurs at Matt. 25:35, 38, 43-44; 27:7; Acts 17:21; Eph. 2:19; Heb. 11:13.

second designation, rendered 'alien', describes one who lived in a place that was not his home.[228] The two words were often used synonymously in the LXX. If there is any distinction, the former describes a person from another tribe or country, while the latter has in view the stranger who lives in the land as a resident alien. Here in Ephesians the two nouns together focus on the former 'outsider' status of Paul's Gentile readers.

But Christ's work has changed all that. Now they belong in a way they never did before. They are neither homeless nor even second-class citizens in someone else's homeland.[229] Instead,[230] they have become 'fellow citizens[231] with the saints'. Although Paul does not develop the metaphor, he appears to be alluding to citizenship in God's kingdom. According to Philippians 3:20, believers are attached to a heavenly commonwealth (cf. 1:27), that is, a heavenly kingdom. They belong to a heavenly city, the Jerusalem that is above (Gal. 4:26). Already in Ephesians mention has been made of their participation in the heavenly realm (Eph. 2:6). Here Paul's Gentile readers are fellow-citizens with 'the saints', a designation that refers not to Jews, although it may point to Jewish Christians. If this is the case, then in becoming full members of the believing community these Gentile Christians have become fellow-citizens with those who had 'first hoped in Christ' (Eph. 1:12).[232] But the term probably has all believers in view, since this is what 'saints' designates elsewhere throughout the letter (see on 1:18).[233] These Gentile Christians now have a homeland or commonwealth. They 'belong' as fellow-citizens with the rest of believers in that heavenly commonwealth ruled by God.

The imagery now changes from the political realm to that of an intimate family:[234] you are *members of God's household*. In Christ Gentiles are

228. The term πάροικος appears in Acts 7:6, 29 and 1 Pet. 2:11, as well as in Eph. 2:19.

229. Lincoln, 150.

230. ἀλλά ('but, in contrast') functions as a strong adversative here.

231. συμπολίτης is 'a fellow member of a socio-political unit — "fellow citizen"': 'you are fellow citizens with God's people', or 'you join with God's people as fellow citizens together with them' (Louw and Nida §11.72).

232. Bruce, 302, 303. Cf. Caird, 60. ἅγιοι ('saints') refers to Jewish Christians elsewhere in Paul (Rom. 15:25, 26, 31; 1 Cor. 16:1; 2 Cor. 8:4; 9:1, 12).

233. On the basis of: (1) the Old Testament description of angels as 'holy ones' (Job 15:15; Ps. 89:5, 6); (2) the strong parallels in the Qumran literature (1QS 11:7, 8, etc.); and (3) the conjunction of believers with angels in the heavenly realm elsewhere in the New Testament (notably Heb. 12:22), a number of continental scholars have understood ἅγιοι here of 'angels'. For an evaluation of the evidence see Lincoln, 150-51; cf. the lengthy treatment of Hoehner.

234. In fact, this is one of six household terms derived from the οἶκος root appearing in vv. 19-22: πάροικοι ('aliens, outsiders'), οἰκεῖοι ('members of the household'), ἐποικοδομηθέντες ('built on'), οἰκοδομή ('building'), συνοικοδομεῖσθε ('built together'), and κατοικητήριον ('dwelling place').

not only fellow-citizens with Jewish believers under God's rule; they are also children together in God's own family. The apostle has just written of the new and glorious access *to the Father* which Gentiles along with Jews enjoy through Christ (v. 18). He has already drawn attention to the blessings of both being adopted into God's family as sons and daughters (1:5). Later he will speak of God's archetypal fatherhood (3:14, 15) and about the 'one God and Father of us all' (4:6). Here, however, the emphasis is on Gentiles being at home in God's family.

The household terminology which appears in the Pauline corpus sheds light on the relations which God's people have with one other and with their heavenly Father. In the Pastorals the notion of the household is applied to the church in order to encourage appropriate and responsible behaviour (1 Tim. 3:15; 2 Tim. 2:20, 21). Here in Ephesians 2 Paul makes a slightly different point. In the Roman world of the day to be a 'member of a household meant refuge and protection, at least as much as the master was able to provide. It also meant identity and gave the security that comes with a sense of belonging'.[235] It is this assurance that the apostle wishes to engender among his Gentile readers here in v. 19 when he tells them that they are members of God's household (cf. Gal. 6:10).

20 Once more the apostle's imagery changes. The readers are not only intimate members of God's household. They also have a privileged position in his building and temple, the place where he dwells. The transition here from one metaphor to another is natural, for the term 'house' can mean 'household' or 'temple'.[236] As a result, the picture of the household combines easily with other metaphors of the new community in Christ.

In vv. 20-22 Paul elaborates on his vision of the new temple more fully than anywhere else. As he develops the image he speaks of both 'the foundation and cornerstone of the building, the structure as a whole and its individual stones, its cohesion and growth, its present function and (at least implicitly) its future destiny'.[237] R. J. McKelvey claims that Paul's language and ideas in vv. 11-19 have prepared the way for this presentation of the new community of God's people as the temple. The terms 'far' and 'near', which have been used to describe the status of Gentiles (vv. 13, 17), were Old Testament designations for Jews in their relationship to the Jerusalem temple (Isa. 57:19; Dan. 9:7), while the peace between Jew

235. Note the treatment of P. H. Towner, 'Households and Household Codes', *DPL*, 417-19, esp. 418.
236. So Caird, 60, 61, who rightly notes the play on the word 'house' (οἶκος) in 2 Sam. 7:5-11 to denote both a building and a dynasty.
237. Stott, 106.

and Gentile (Eph. 2:14, 17) 'recalls the eschatological peace which it was believed would prevail when Israel and the nations were united in one cult at Zion' (Isa. 2:4; Mic. 4:3). Further, the notion of Jews and Gentiles having common access to God (Eph. 2:18) seems to belong to the same complex of ideas. As the apostle to the Gentiles (3:1-6), Paul saw 'the inclusion of non-Jews in the church as the fulfilment of the great promises that in the eschatological age the nations would be graciously accepted by Yahweh in his house'.[238]

These Gentile believers are integral parts of the new building: God[239] has already set them as living stones on *the foundation of the apostles and prophets*. This presumably occurred when they were incorporated into Christ. The language of building on a foundation and of a temple indwelt by the Spirit has already been used by Paul in 1 Corinthians 3:9-17. There the apostle is the master builder who laid the foundation — Christ himself — on which he, Apollos, Cephas, and others continue to build. Here, however, the figure of the building is retained but the individual parts of it have changed. Paul alters the metaphors to make slightly different points:[240] the foundation now consists of the apostles and prophets, and Christ Jesus is the cornerstone, a term that draws attention to his special function and importance.

The *foundation of the apostles and prophets* is an unusual expression. Earlier interpreters, apparently in the interests of harmonizing the phrase with 1 Corinthians 3:11, understood it to mean 'the foundation laid by the apostles and prophets'.[241] But this confuses the imagery and does not fit with the qualifying phrase, 'Christ Jesus himself being the chief cornerstone'. It is more natural, with most interpreters, to understand the foundation as 'consisting of the apostles and prophets'.[242]

---

238. R. J. McKelvey, *The New Temple: The Church in the New Testament* (Oxford: Oxford University Press, 1969), 111-12 (see 108-20 for his treatment of vv. 20-22). Note also O. Michel, 'ναός', *TDNT* 4:880-90; 'οἶκος', *TDNT* 5:119-59; and I. H. Marshall, 'Church and Temple in the New Testament', *TynBul* 40 (1989), 203-22.

239. The participle ἐποικοδομηθέντες ('built') is probably a 'divine passive', indicating that God is the builder (cf. Best, 279).

240. In Eph. 2:20 it is the persons who are built upon the foundation who are in mind, whereas in 1 Cor. 3 it is the builders and the kind of materials they use that are particularly in view. To suggest that all the metaphors must mesh precisely, or that the differences are evidence of diversity of authorship, is pedantic.

241. τῶν ἀποστόλων καὶ προφητῶν ('of the apostles and prophets') was taken as a genitive of source (cf. Meyer, 142, and note the NEB; subsequently changed in the REB and GNB). More recently this has been advocated by K. O. Sandnes, *Paul*, 229.

242. The genitive is one of apposition (so, e.g., A. T. Robertson, *Grammar*, 498; Schnackenburg, 122-23; Bruce, 304; Lincoln, 153; and Best, 280; cf. D. B. Wallace, *Greek Grammar*, 100).

Apostles, as we have seen,[243] were those specially commissioned and sent by the Lord Jesus Christ. This includes the Twelve and Paul himself, together with one or two others (1 Cor. 15:7; Gal. 1:19; 2:7-9; cf. Rom. 16:7; 1 Cor. 9:6). They provided the essential link with their master, and their role was a foundational one. Although Paul on occasion uses the term 'apostle' in a nontechnical sense to signify a 'messenger' of the churches (cf. 2 Cor. 8:22-23; Phil. 2:25), the overwhelming number of references in his letters are to 'apostles' in a technical sense who were called and sent by Christ. They received the revelation of God through the Spirit to understand the mystery of Christ, and their task was to proclaim his gospel to Jews and, in the case of Paul especially, to Gentiles (Eph. 3:1-9; cf. 1 Cor. 2:6-16). This they did both verbally and in their writings (Rom. 16:25-26; 1 Cor. 2:13; Eph. 3:3-4). 'God has appointed apostles *first* in the church' (1 Cor. 12:28). Here in Ephesians 2:20 it is the circle of the Twelve plus Paul that are in view as the foundation on which these Gentiles have been built.

The *prophets* are New Testament prophets, not Old Testament ones.[244] Some have claimed that, because the one definite article is used to cover the two words 'apostles' and 'prophets',[245] we should understand the joint expression as referring to the same group of people, namely, 'the apostles who prophesy'. Wayne Grudem, for example, argues this point on syntactical and exegetical grounds, and asserts that Ephesians 2:20 (cf. 3:5) is speaking of only one group which is the foundation of the new building, namely, *apostles* who prophesy.[246] His exegesis is part of a wider treatment of New Testament prophecy,[247] in which he claims that the authority status of prophecy in Paul is considerably less than in the Old Testament. The legitimate heirs and successors of the Old

243. See on 1:1 (together with the relevant literature).

244. First, the word order ('apostles and prophets') is against their being identified as Old Testament prophets, as indeed are the other references to προφηταί in the letter (3:5; 4:11). The parallel and proximate expression at 3:5, 'his holy apostles and prophets', which seems to refer to the same group as in 2:20, cannot be Old Testament prophets since the mystery has been revealed to them *now,* that is, in the new age (cf. K. O. Sandnes, *Paul,* 233: 'The salvation-historical νῦν ['now'] definitely forbids us interpret them as OT prophets'). Also at 4:11 the ascended Christ is said to have given apostles, prophets, evangelists, and others *after* his ascension.

245. The Greek is ἐπὶ τῷ θεμελίῳ τῶν ἀποστόλων καὶ προφητῶν.

246. W. A. Grudem, *The Gift of Prophecy in 1 Corinthians* (Washington, DC: University Press of America, 1982), 82-105. Note also his *The Gift of Prophecy in the New Testament and Today* (Westchester, IL: Crossway, 1988). Cf. also D. Hill, *New Testament Prophecy* (London: Marshall, Morgan & Scott, 1979), 139.

247. Which takes us beyond the confines of this commentary, even though the issues are important theologically.

Testament prophets were not the New Testament prophets but the apostles. Paul places the authority of Christian prophets under his own (1 Cor. 14:37-38). Indeed, prophecy as a whole in his writings has a much lower profile than the writing prophets had in the Old Testament. So, for example, the Thessalonians are urged not to treat prophecies with contempt (1 Thess. 5:20), while in 1 Corinthians 14 Paul has to advance the cause of prophecy above that of tongues. Serious constraints are placed on the gift (1 Cor. 14:29, 30, 36), which make it clear that it stands 'considerably tamed'.[248] The view that it is 'apostles who prophesy' that are the foundation on which Paul's Gentile readers have been built is consistent with this lower profile attributed to prophecy. Prophets as prophets are not part of that foundation.

There are, however, exegetical difficulties with Grudem's interpretation, even if a number of points he is making about prophecy in general are valid. First, it is questionable syntactically as to whether 'apostles who prophesy' is an appropriate rendering of the Greek. A good case has been mounted for taking the expression, with the one definite article and two nouns, to refer to apostles *and* prophets.[249] Of particular importance is Paul's distinguishing apostles from prophets in Ephesians 4:11, where he views them as two separate groups.[250] The range of phenomena covered by the prophesy word-group in the New Testament, let alone the first-century world, was considerable.[251] For example, according to Acts 2, speaking in other tongues (vv. 4, 6) falls under the heading of 'prophesying' (vv. 17, 18). The broad semantic range of the terminology, which could include a number of speaking activities, in theory at least allows the possibility of different kinds of prophecy within the letters of Paul. Grudem's contrast between Old Testament prophecy and New Testament prophets, which drives his exegesis of this text, is an oversimplification. The Old Testament records the existence of 'schools' of the prophets, but

248. Cf. D. A. Carson, *Showing the Spirit: A Theological Exposition of 1 Corinthians 12–14* (Grand Rapids: Baker, 1987), 98. Note his discussion, 91-100, where, however, he expresses reservations about Grudem's position.

249. Note the discussion of D. B. Wallace, 'The Semantic Range of the Article-Noun-*kai*-Noun Plural Construction in the New Testament', *Grace Theological Journal* 4 (1983), 59-84 (cf. also his *Greek Grammar*, 284-86, and those listed by him).

250. 'He gave the apostles, the prophets' (τοὺς μὲν ἀποστόλους, τοὺς δὲ προφήτας; see the exegesis of 4:11). On the general subject of prophecy see D. E. Aune, *Prophecy in Early Christianity and the Ancient Mediterranean World* (Grand Rapids: Eerdmans, 1983); on prophecy in Paul note C. M. Robeck, 'Prophecy, Prophesying', *DPL*, 755-62, and the further literature cited.

251. Cf. D. E. Aune, *Prophecy*; and C. Forbes, *Prophecy and Inspired Speech in Early Christianity and Its Hellenistic Environment* (Tübingen: J. C. B. Mohr [Paul Siebeck], 1995), 188-250.

this is not to suggest that everyone in a particular 'school' enjoyed the status of an Isaiah or an Ezekiel. 'There is no single, stereotypical Old Testament prophecy and a different stereotypical New Testament prophecy'.[252]

On balance, then, we believe that *both* apostles and prophets are in view here (cf. 3:5). If the prophecy word-group in 1 Corinthians 12–14 can refer to prophecies which needed to be weighed carefully (cf. 1 Cor. 14:29), the presupposition being that they might be 'mixed in quality, and the wheat must be separated from the chaff',[253] then in Ephesians 2:20 (and 3:5) prophets are linked with apostles and enjoy a role with them not found elsewhere in the Pauline letters. The semantic range of the word group allows for this possibility. Together with the apostles, prophets were the first authoritative recipients and proclaimers of God's revelation in Christ. If the single article before the two nouns 'apostles' and 'prophets' does not indicate an identity, then it may focus on a certain unity. 'The apostles and Christian prophets are both seen as those to whom God made known the revelation of the gospel',[254] and who were the first proclaimers of it. To assert, then, that these Gentile believers are built upon the apostles and prophets is to state that their membership in God's people rests on the normative teaching that arises from divine revelation.[255] They have the right foundation. None may question their membership in God's new community.

Even more significant is the fact that the readers have been built on Christ, for he alone (note the emphatic *himself*) is the *chief cornerstone*. Since he is the foundation, the apostles and prophets do not replace him. Indeed, the genitive absolute construction at the end of the verse serves to distinguish Christ from the apostles and prophets, as well as those built on the foundation; the clause draws attention to his standing and special function.[256] Current New Testament scholarship is divided as to whether the unusual word used here[257] refers to the foundation stone (i.e., cornerstone) of the building or the crowning stone at the top of the edifice. In favour of the latter, it has been claimed that, apart from evidence outside the New Testament, the exalted place accorded to Christ

---

252. So D. A. Carson, *Showing the Spirit*, 94.

253. M. Turner, 'Spiritual Gifts Then and Now', *Vox Evangelica* 15 (1985), 7-64, esp. 16.

254. K. O. Sandnes, *Paul*, 235-36.

255. As R. J. McKelvey, *The New Temple*, 113, has put it, 'the bedrock of historic Christianity'.

256. ὄντος ἀκρογωνιαίου αὐτοῦ Χριστοῦ Ἰησοῦ ('with Christ Jesus himself as the chief cornerstone').

257. Gk. ἀκρογωνιαῖος.

elsewhere in Ephesians (cf. 1:20-23; 2:6; 4:8-10) and his special position in relationship to the rest of the structure point to his being the crowning stone of the building.[258] However, much of the extrabiblical material in favour of this interpretation is quite late, while the imagery of the *cornerstone* makes better sense in the immediate context, especially the relation of Christ to the apostles, and the picture of a growing and unfinished building. The preeminence, both in dignity and in time, accorded to Christ in the letter is enhanced, rather than diminished, by understanding this imagery of the cornerstone (see below).[259]

Important for the exegetical decision is Isaiah 28:16. Against Joachim Jeremias, who claimed that the Old Testament passage was not in view here, and Andrew Lincoln,[260] who pitted the LXX usage of Isaiah 28:16 and the christological imagery of 1 Corinthians 3:11 over against the author of Ephesians' perspective elsewhere, Ephesians 2:20 is to be understood in the light of this Old Testament text. The latter is the sole passage in the LXX where the term appears,[261] and it, like our text, juxtaposes the term 'foundation'. There is no doubt that the original Hebrew, as well as the LXX which strengthens the point considerably, had in view the *cornerstone* at the base of the building.[262] The expression 'I am laying . . . for a foundation . . . a cornerstone, of a sure foundation' reflected current building practice in which the laying of the cornerstone marked the beginning of the foundation (cf. Jer. 51:26; Job 38:6). The builder could then use it to determine the 'lie' or line of the building.

Paul seems, therefore, to be making the following points: Christ is the vital cornerstone on whom the building is constructed. The foundation and position of all the other stones in the superstructure were determined by him. He is 'the one from which the rest of the foundation is built outwards along the line of the proposed walls'. Accordingly, the

---

258. Note Lincoln's summary of the arguments (154-55). Evidence from Ps. 118:22 in Symmachus; LXX 2 Kings 25:17; Hippolytus, Tertullian, and the *Testament of Solomon* (second or third century A.D.) has been adduced in favour of the meaning, 'top stone of the edifice'.

259. Best, 286, who thinks one cannot be certain whether the cornerstone or capstone is meant, nevertheless concludes from the context that the author 'wishes to allot to Christ a place in the building different from that of the apostles and prophets and more important than that of either of them'.

260. Lincoln, 155.

261. The word is unknown in classical Greek literature.

262. R. J. McKelvey, *The New Temple*, 201, remarks: 'The juxtaposition of ἀκρογωνιαῖος and θεμέλιον and the duplicated εἰς τὰ θεμέλια show beyond all doubt that it is the base of the building that is in mind'. The Jews of Qumran as well as the rabbis believed the same (201-2). Note, too, the detailed arguments of H. Merklein, *Das kirchliche Amt*, 144-52.

temple is built out and up from the revelation given in Christ, with the apostles and prophets elaborating and explaining the mystery, which had been made known to them by the Holy Spirit (3:4-11, esp. v. 5). 'But all is built on Christ, supported by Christ, and the lie or shape of the continuing building is determined by Christ, the cornerstone'.[263]

21-22 The lengthy paragraph of vv. 11-22 concludes with two parallel relative clauses (vv. 21, 22),[264] each of which commences with the words 'in whom' — obviously a reference to Christ Jesus as the cornerstone. These parallel sentences expand on his significance for the unity of the building and its growth into a *holy temple* in the Lord (v. 21), and draw attention to the place Paul's Gentile readers have in this *dwelling* of God (v. 22). Only in v. 22 does the line of thought reach its conclusion and round out the paragraph which began by speaking of the readers' separation from Christ and his covenant people (vv. 11, 12). The central role played by Christ in the present construction of the building, that is, the new community, corresponds to his role as mediator in bringing peace ('in him', v. 16) and common access to the Father ('through him', v. 18). Here his indispensable position in relation to the unity and growth of the church is underscored: he is mentioned at the beginning of the verse, 'in whom', while the concluding phrase 'in the Lord' refers to Christ once more (rather than God). This building functions only in relation to him.

21 In spite of the difficulties of the Greek text form,[265] it is best to render the subject of the clause, with most EVV, as 'all the building' or *the whole building*. The apostle is not speaking about 'every building',[266] that

263. Turner, 1232-33. Cf. Schnackenburg, 124.

264. Both vv. 21 and 22 begin with ἐν ᾧ ('in whom'), which refers back to 'Jesus Christ' in v. 20. The two verbs συναρμολογουμένη ('being joined together', v. 21) and συνοικοδομεῖσθε ('you are built together', v. 22) are parallel, with the latter drawing specific attention to the readers' place in God's dwelling place, while the goal of the building process εἰς ναὸν ἅγιον ('into a holy temple', v. 21) is synonymous with εἰς κατοικητήριον τοῦ θεοῦ ('into a dwelling place of God', v. 22). Finally, the qualifying phrase ἐν κυρίῳ ('in the Lord', v. 21) is matched by ἐν πνεύματι ('in/by the Spirit', v. 22).

265. The more difficult reading is the anarthrous πᾶσα οἰκοδομή, even though it has stronger MS support (א* B D F G and the majority text) than the variant πᾶσα ἡ οἰκοδομή (א¹ A C P and a few minuscules). The former might have been thought to mean 'every building', so that the article was probably added in later MSS to signify 'the whole building'. But πᾶσα οἰκοδομή should be taken as a Hebraism (meaning 'every building') which has influenced the Koine usage (cf. Matt. 2:3; 3:15; Acts 2:36; Rom. 11:26; cf. BDF §275[4] and others).

266. Those who opt for this rendering of the expression πᾶσα οἰκοδομή believe that this 'sacred temple in the Lord' is like the Jewish temple, in which many buildings, rooms, and parts made up the 'whole temple'. Mitton, 115, prefers 'every structure' grammatically, gives it a metaphorical rather than a literal meaning, and takes the 'parts' as being the local congregations which make up the one universal or catholic church. Cf. Meyer, 146, 147.

is, every local congregation, being joined together as parts that make up one universal or catholic church. This does not make good sense in the immediate context. Nor is he using *building* in the sense of 'edification' or 'upbuilding'[267] as a process (a nuance found later in 4:12, 16, 29). Rather, 'all the building' is the entire construction — cornerstone, foundation, and superstructure — which forms a complete whole.

There is a mixture of building and organic images in the statement that the whole structure is 'being joined together' and is 'growing' into *a holy temple in the Lord*. The cornerstone unites the building 'because it is organically as well as structurally bound to it'. So to speak of the building being *joined together* refers not simply to the union of one stone with another, but also to the union of the whole structure with (and in) the cornerstone.[268] Both verbs, which occur together again in 4:15, 16, focus on the idea of continuous progress. There, in a similar mixing of metaphors, the body is 'joined together' and 'built up' from Christ the head.

The joining together of the elements that make up the total structure of this new divine community is an ongoing activity. The building is still under construction (cf. 1 Cor. 3:6, 7; 2 Cor. 9:10), which is another way of saying that the new community of God is growing and progressing to its ultimate goal of holiness, an objective that is not simply personal or individual but in the present context must be corporate as well.[269] On the other hand, to say that the building is under construction and growing into a holy temple in the Lord is not to imply that the divine indwelling associated with the temple will only be realized on the final day when the building is complete. God already dwells in his temple even though it is still growing. The character of the new building is derived from God who inhabits it, that is, it is *holy*.

In Paul's earlier letters the figure of the 'temple of God'[270] was used metaphorically to denote the local congregation at Corinth (1 Cor. 3:16-17), as well as the local church and other Christians including Paul (*'we are the temple of the living God'*, 2 Cor. 6:16) among whom God dwells by his Spirit. Here in Ephesians 2:21 the 'holy temple in the Lord' is not 'the universal church', as most claim. Rather, this dwelling place of God is a *heavenly* entity. Believers, because of their union with their risen and ascended Lord, are already seated with Christ in the heavenly realm (2:4-

267. Robinson, 70, 165, emphasizes the process of building and takes the phrase to mean 'all that is builded', i.e., what building is being done, not the finished product but the building in process. On the different nuances of οἰκοδομή see BAGD, 558, 559.

268. R. J. McKelvey, *The New Temple*, 116.

269. This point is made by the two verbs prefixed by συν-: συναρμολογουμένη ('is joined *together*') and συνοικοδομεῖσθε ('are being built *together*').

270. Gk. ναὸς ἅγιος.

6). As 'fellow citizens with the saints' (2:19; cf. Phil. 3:20), these Gentile readers are members of the heavenly city.[271] Through Christ's reconciling work they have access to 'the Father' (2:18), who is in heaven. According to Old Testament prophecy the temple at Jerusalem was to be the place where all nations at the end time would come to worship and pray to the living God (Isa. 66:18-20; cf. Isa. 2:1-5; Mic. 4:1-5).[272] The temple imagery here is to be understood in fulfilment of these promises. Now through Christ Gentiles have been brought near to God, and along with Jews they have become the new temple, the place where God's presence dwells.

To speak of the heavenly character of this *holy temple* is not to deny an existence to its members (or 'stones') on earth, any more than it is to imply that because Paul speaks of the Colossians as having been raised with Christ and that their life is hidden with him in God (Col. 3:1-4), they do not have corporate and common responsibilities here 'below'! The full and wide-ranging exhortations of Colossians 3:5–4:6 spell out some of the entailments of that heavenly existence. The apostle will assert here in the parallel statement of Ephesians 2:22 that membership of this holy temple signifies being indwelt by God's Spirit here and now, while the exhortatory material of Ephesians 4–6 directs the readers to their responsibilities as members of that heavenly community.[273]

22 In the second of the parallel clauses (cf. v. 21) the argument moves to its climax as attention is now focussed on the place these Gentile readers have in this *dwelling* of God (v. 22). Paul addresses them directly *(you also)* and tells them that in their union with Christ they too, along with Jewish Christians, are being built as living stones (cf. 1 Pet. 2:5) into this heavenly temple, the place where God lives by his Spirit.

What a magnificent change has occurred in the readers' situation. In contrast to what they once were — separated from the Messiah, outside the covenant community, without God and without hope (vv. 11, 12) —

271. 'To say believers are *already* citizens of that temple city is to say they *now* (in union with Christ) participate in that heavenly city, and that it shall finally be revealed and displace all that we know of as reality in this age' (M. Turner, 'Mission', 145, original emphasis; cf. P. T. O'Brien, 'Entity', 88-105).

272. It is the heavenly temple which much of Judaism expected in the Jerusalem of the age to come. Already certain parts of Judaism had come to think that God's *people* would constitute that holy dwelling place of God. At Qumran the connections between the elect on earth and the inhabitants of heaven were essential parts of the temple imagery (1QS 11:7, 8). Cf. Lincoln, 156, 157.

273. Accordingly, Gordon Fee's recently expressed concern, *God's Empowering Presence,* 689, that to interpret this passage of the universal church (which he calls 'a nebulous entity') without relating it to the local church, has real point. If we regard the temple as a heavenly entity rather than 'the universal church', Fee's concerns are more than adequately met.

now they are being built into the dwelling place of God himself. As if to underscore this dramatic change Paul uses an *inclusio, you,* at the beginning and end of the paragraph (vv. 11, 19), and the contrasting categories of 'in the flesh' (v. 11) and 'in the Spirit' (v. 19).

The two expressions *a holy temple in the Lord* (v. 21) and 'a dwelling place of God in the Spirit' (v. 22) are parallel descriptions of the same thing.[274] The latter term, 'dwelling place'[275] *(katoikētērion),* was significantly used in the Old Testament of God's dwelling in the temple at Jerusalem (1 Kings 8:13) and of his heavenly dwelling place (1 Kings 8:39, 43, 49). Here in Ephesians 2 the temple is God's heavenly abode, the place of his dwelling. Yet that temple is his people in whom he lives by his Spirit. Believers on earth, recipients of this circular letter, are linked with the heavenly realm in and through the Spirit of the risen Lord.

Just as Ephesians 2:1-10 had reminded these Gentile Christian readers of the great change that had been brought about in their situation, so here too their privileged position as members of God's new community should encourage an attitude of profound thankfulness to God and a willingness on their part to accept the entailments of their new creation in Christ. They have been reminded that in consequence of Christ's reconciling them to God and to Jewish believers in the one new humanity, they have become intimate members of God's household, and have a privileged position in his building and temple where God dwells by his Spirit. The apostle's exposition in vv. 11-22 regarding the privileged position into which these Gentile Christians have now entered through Christ's peace-making work (vv. 14-18) serves as a preparation for what follows in Ephesians 3. In his lengthy parenthesis which immediately follows (3:1-13), Paul describes his special, God-given role in receiving and making known the mystery of their and other Gentile believers' inclusion in the people of God. Further, Paul's intercessory prayer (vv. 14-19) that they might be strengthened inwardly through God's Spirit in order that they might know more fully the love of Christ and be filled to all the fulness of God is ultimately that they might be empowered to fulfil their role in the divine purposes.

---

274. H. Merklein, *Das kirchliche Amt,* 155, 156; and R. J. McKelvey, *The New Temple,* 116.

275. Gk. κατοικητήριον (cf. Louw and Nida, §85.70).

Ephesians 3

E. The Divine Mystery and Paul's Stewardship, 3:1-13

> ¹*For this reason I, Paul, the prisoner of Christ Jesus for the sake of you Gentiles — ²Surely you have heard about the administration of God's grace that was given to me for you, ³that is, the mystery made known to me by revelation, as I have already written briefly. ⁴In reading this, then, you will be able to understand my insight into the mystery of Christ, ⁵which was not made known to men in other generations as it has now been revealed by the Spirit to God's holy apostles and prophets. ⁶This mystery is that through the gospel the Gentiles are heirs together with Israel, members together of one body, and sharers together in the promise in Christ Jesus. ⁷I became a servant of this gospel by the gift of God's grace given me through the working of his power. ⁸Although I am less than the least of all God's people, this grace was given me: to preach to the Gentiles the unsearchable riches of Christ, ⁹and to make plain to everyone the administration of this mystery, which for ages past was kept hidden in God, who created all things. ¹⁰His intent was that now, through the church, the manifold wisdom of God should be made known to the rulers and authorities in the heavenly realms, ¹¹according to his eternal purpose which he accomplished in Christ Jesus our Lord. ¹²In him and through faith in him we may approach God with freedom and confidence. ¹³I ask you, therefore, not to be discouraged because of my sufferings for you, which are your glory.*

Paul begins his intercessory prayer with the words *for this reason* (v. 1), but breaks off almost immediately in order to give an account of his distinctive ministry to Gentiles and its place within the divine mystery that has been revealed to him. His prayer is not resumed until v. 14 when the opening words *for this reason* are repeated, and he spells out the content of his petition (vv. 14-19). The paragraph, then, is syntactically a digression within an intercessory prayer.

At the same time vv. 1-13 have many important thematic connections with the preceding paragraph, which deals with the incorporation of Paul's Gentile readers into Christ and his new community (2:11-22, esp. vv. 19-22). Indeed, the apostle's ministry to Gentiles was possible only because of Christ's work of reconciliation which had created the one new humanity and reconciled both Jews and Gentiles to God (2:15, 16). So v. 1 expressly addresses the readers as *you Gentiles* (cf. 2:11), while at v. 5 mention is made of the *holy apostles and prophets* (cf. 2:20). Three expressions commencing with the prefix 'together with' describe the present status of Gentile Christians (v. 6; cf. 2:19) and their participation in the promise in Christ Jesus (v. 6; cf. 2:12). Finally, this paragraph also mentions the freedom of access to the Father which is now available to Gentile Christians (v. 12; cf. 2:18). Thus, this new section reinforces ideas which were developed earlier, but now they are treated in relation to Paul as a proclaimer of the mystery to Gentiles. V. 13 returns to the statement made at the beginning (v. 1) about Paul enduring suffering (as a captive of Jesus Christ) for the sake of the readers, and leads on to the intercessory prayer of vv. 14-19. Since they now have a place within God's plan of salvation and are privileged to be part of his new temple, Paul prays that they may be empowered to love like the Lord Jesus Christ despite all opposition (the details of which are spelled out in chaps. 4–6).

A number of the important motifs in 3:1-13 have close parallels with Colossians 1:24–28.[1] These parallels in Ephesians follow the same sequence as in Colossians. So the introduction of Paul (Col. 1:23; Eph. 3:1), his suffering (Col. 1:24; Eph. 3:1, cf. v. 13), the grace or commission given to him (Col. 1:25; Eph. 3:2), the revelation of the mystery (Col. 1:26; Eph. 3:5), its content (Col. 1:27; Eph. 3:6), and the proclamation of that mystery to Gentiles (Col. 1:28; Eph. 3:8) are highly significant themes that are central to both passages. At the same time there are slightly different emphases, which are due in part to the different epistolary contexts of each letter and Paul's purposes in writing. In Colossians his call as a missionary to the Gentiles is not as specific as in Ephesians (3:8), where he is identified as a prisoner of Christ Jesus for the sake of the Gentiles, to whom his preaching of the unsearchable riches of Christ is directed. On the other hand, nothing is said

---

1. For a detailed analysis see H. Merklein, *Das kirchliche Amt*, 160-71. It is unnecessary, however, to conclude with Merklein and others, on the basis of these parallels, that Ephesians was not written by Paul (see the discussion of 'The Picture of Paul' in the Introduction, 33-37).

in Ephesians about Paul's filling up what was lacking in the afflictions of Christ (Col. 1:24). Further, the goal of the apostle's preaching is expressed in somewhat different terms: at Colossae Paul's public proclamation of Christ as Lord, which involved intensive teaching and admonition, had as its goal 'that we may present everyone perfect in Christ' (1:28), while in Ephesians his task is 'to bring to the Gentiles the good news of Christ's un-fathomable wealth' (v. 8) and, as a second integral element, *to make plain to everyone the administration of this mystery* (v. 9). Finally, the statements in Colossians about the 'mystery' are more brief (1:25-27) than the extended and nuanced treatment of this important motif in Ephesians 3:4-8.

The digression, which immediately follows the intercession that breaks off at v. 1, consists of three sentences, two longer ones (vv. 2-7, 8-12) and a short final sentence (v. 13). Vv. 2-7, which speak of God's grace embodied in the gospel, focus on the mystery that has now been revealed and in which the Gentiles participate. Vv. 8-12 refer to Paul's making known the mystery within God's eternal plan and the role of the church in God's purposes for the cosmos. It therefore recalls the earlier reference to the mystery at 1:9-10. The contents of vv. 2-12 account for and explain Paul's conduct in v. 1. The final words of the paragraph (v. 13) refer to the notion of his sufferings, which are the point of departure at v. 1 and neatly round out the period.[2] This parenthesis is intended to strengthen the bond between writer and readers. Paul presents himself as the one who is about to pray once more for them. He refers also to his bondage to Christ for the sake of them as Gentiles (v. 1). God had appointed him to enlighten them about the mystery, and as a result he undergoes suffering for them (vv. 1, 13). At the same time Paul enlarges upon their new status as Gentile believers who are sharers together with Jews in the promise in Christ Jesus (v. 6). The paragraph thus confirms and explains the words, 'a prisoner of Christ Jesus for the sake of you Gentiles' (v. 1) and leads on to the prayer of vv. 14-19 in which the one who intercedes for them is their apostle who undergoes tribulation on their behalf.[3]

1. Paul's Intercessory Prayer Begins, 3:1

1 Paul briefly begins his intercessory prayer. The verse com-mences with the unusual causal connective *for this reason* (cf. v. 14; Tit. 1:5) which provides the link with 2:11-22, especially vv. 19-22, which summa-rize and draw out the consequences of vv. 11-18. Accordingly, the apostle is about to pray for his Gentile readers who have now become part of the

2. See C. C. Caragounis, *Mysterion*, 72-74.
3. Note the analysis of C. C. Caragounis, *Mysterion*, 55-56.

new temple in which God dwells by his Spirit. But almost immediately the prayer is broken off. The sentence is incomplete, with an emphatic reference to *I, Paul* and the mention of his being *the prisoner of Christ Jesus for the sake of you Gentiles*. These serve as the basis for the account of the apostle's distinctive ministry that follows.

The expression *I, Paul* indicates a special emphasis on the few occasions it turns up in the apostle's letters.[4] Here, as in Colossians 1:23, it stresses his calling to proclaim the gospel to Gentiles, and it is in this role par excellence that he will pray again for his readers. To this emphatic self-reference is added 'the prisoner of Christ Jesus', language that he employs in relation to his literal imprisonment when writing to Philemon (vv. 1, 9) and Timothy (2 Tim. 1:8). His physical captivity arose out of his bondage to Christ (cf. Phil. 1:12-17), but the particular point he makes here is that it is *for the sake of you Gentiles*, since it was directly in consequence of his Gentile mission that he was now in prison. His proclamation of the law-free gospel to Gentiles led directly to his arrest and detention in Jerusalem, Caesarea, and Rome (cf. Acts 21:17-36 with Rom. 15:14-32). And as he now addresses his readers explicitly, *you Gentiles* (cf. 2:11-22), he digresses in order to strengthen the bond between them and himself by confirming and explaining his place within the administration of God's mystery for Gentiles.

2. Paul's Stewardship of the Mystery, 3:2-7

It is surprising how often in the context of his ministry to Gentiles Paul speaks of the marvellous grace of God given to him (cf. Gal. 1:15-16). In this paragraph he goes out of his way to underscore that grace in a most emphatic way: he uses not only the terms 'grace' (vv. 2, 7, and 8) and 'gift' (v. 7), but also the verb 'give' on three occasions (vv. 2, 7, and 8) when, strictly speaking, it was redundant. In addition to this, the whole passage focusses on the divine kindness to Paul and the Gentiles, who are recipients of 'the boundless riches of Christ' (v. 8).

2 The words with which the digression begins, *Surely you have heard*,[5] imply that some of those addressed were not personally ac-

---

4. At 1 Thess. 2:18, in a context where he has used first person plurals of himself and his colleagues, Paul introduces a personal statement with the words, 'I, Paul' (ἐγὼ Παῦλος). Twice he begins 'a solemn entreaty or warning' with the expression (2 Cor. 10:1; Gal. 5:2), and once when he formally undertakes to 'pay a debt' (Phlm. 19); cf. Bruce, 309.

5. The statement introduced by the construction εἴ γε, which turns up only five times in the New Testament (2 Cor. 5:3; Gal. 3:4; Eph. 3:2; 4:21; Col. 1:23), makes explicit an underlying assumption of the preceding assertion. Here it does not express doubt ('if, indeed, you have heard') but implies confidence or certainty: 'you must surely have heard'. Cf. M. E. Thrall, *Particles*, 87, 88, 90.

quainted with Paul. This is quite understandable if Ephesians was a circular letter written to congregations in Asia Minor not known to the apostle and his colleagues personally. To his friends at Ephesus he would probably have written 'you know'.[6] The content of what the readers should have heard is 'the stewardship of God's grace' given to Paul in relation to the Gentiles.

The meaning of the term rendered 'stewardship' is disputed here and could refer to Paul's activity as a steward, his office given him by God's grace, the administration of the grace given to him, God's plan and his administration of it, or some combination of these senses.[7] The word is employed in the Pauline letters to denote either: (1) Paul's administration of his apostolic office (1 Cor. 9:17; cf. 4:1, where he describes himself as one of the stewards of God's mysteries), or (2) God's administration of the world and salvation (Eph. 1:10; 3:9; cf. 3:2).[8] In the earlier references Paul is a steward (1 Cor. 4:1), having been entrusted with a commission (1 Cor. 9:17); he is not able to withdraw from this solemn responsibility, but must fulfil it obediently. He is a steward of the mysteries of God (1 Cor. 4:1), and it is naturally expected that he be found trustworthy (4:2; cf. Luke 16:2). In the later Pauline texts the emphasis is upon God's administration.[9] Most examples of this terminology in Paul occur in close proximity to the word 'mystery' (the only exception being 1 Cor. 9:17), suggesting that the latter was important for understanding the meaning of 'administration'.

Colossians 1:25 is a key verse in relation to the term: it stands between the earlier and later references in the Pauline corpus. In the context of Colossians the word appears to have the twofold sense of God's plan which is administered by him and, since the apostle speaks of it as 'given to me', his assignment or activity. So Colossians 1:25 may be paraphrased: 'I am a minister according to the plan of God, the execution of which has been conferred upon me in that which concerns you'.[10] In Ephesians 1:10 and 3:9 it clearly has to do with God's gospel-plan or mystery, together with its divine administration. Ephesians 3:2 is like Colossians 1:25: it mentions particularly the role given to Paul, and this

6. Bruce, 311.

7. J. Reumann, 'OIKONOMIA — Terms in Paul in Comparison with Lucan *Heilsgeschichte*', *NTS* 13 (1966-67), 165.

8. O. Michel, *TDNT* 5:151-53; J. Reumann, 'OIKONOMIA — Terms', 147-67.

9. This need not necessarily imply that the earlier epistles come from a time when Paul had no notion of a divine plan of salvation; so rightly J. Reumann, 'OIKONOMIA — Terms', 155-66.

10. J. Reumann, 'OIKONOMIA — Terms', 163; cf. P. T. O'Brien, *Colossians, Philemon*, 81.

obviously has to do with his making the mystery known. On this view it does not mean God's salvation plan pure and simple, but the carrying out or administration of the mystery.[11]

When in 3:2 Paul speaks of 'the stewardship of God's grace' he is thinking not so much of the grace of apostleship[12] (which is mentioned in v. 7 and developed in vv. 8-12) as of 'the grace of God[13] embodied and proclaimed in the gospel'.[14] To make this gospel known is Paul's special privilege. Obviously, the two are closely related, but as in Galatians 1 he deals first with the revelation of the gospel (vv. 11-12) and then his commission to preach it (vv. 15-17), so here in Ephesians 3 Paul focusses first on God's revelation to him of the mystery regarding the Gentiles' part in salvation (vv. 2-7) before spelling out the means by which this goal is achieved,[15] namely, by his enlightening them about this mystery (vv. 8-12). Divine grace was given not simply for Paul's personal enhancement. Instead, it was for the sake of the Gentiles, as the following words *for you* show.

3 As he explains and amplifies the meaning of v. 2 in the words which follow, Paul indicates that he received the stewardship of God's grace when the *mystery* was revealed to him. On the key motif of the *mystery*, see on 1:9-10. There it referred to God's all-inclusive purpose which has as its ultimate goal the uniting of all things in heaven and earth in Christ. Here, a more limited dimension to the mystery focusses on Gentiles, along with Jews, being incorporated into the body of Christ and thus participating in the divine salvation.

The *revelation* granted to Paul occurred on the Damascus road when

11. The term οἰκονομία is closely focussed on God's activity at 1:10; 3:9, but on Paul's apostleship in 3:2. But this should not be regarded as unusual. So rightly Lincoln, 174. Cf. Schlier, 63, 147-48, 155; J. Reumann, 'OIKONOMIA — Terms', 165; and S. Kim, *The Origin of Paul's Gospel* (Grand Rapids: Eerdmans, 1982), 21. C. C. Caragounis, *Mysterion*, 97, claims that the sense needed in 3:2 'is one that brings forward the connection of the author with the οἰκονομία'. For a different approach see Mitton, 120; and H. Merklein, *Das kirchliche Amt*, 174.

12. As Schlier, 148, interprets it. Cf. H. Merklein, *Das kirchliche Amt*, 174; and S. Kim, *Origin*, 21-22.

13. Syntactically, it was τῆς χάριτος τοῦ θεοῦ ('the grace of God') rather than τὴν οἰκονομίαν ('the stewardship') that was given to Paul. C. C. Caragounis, *Mysterion*, 98, claims that οἰκονομία ('the stewardship') is in close conjunction with χάρις ('the grace') and that both were given to the apostle.

14. Bruce, 311; and Best, 313. Note Stott, 115-16, who refers to the two closely related privileges given to Paul. (The grace of God embodied in the gospel is called 'the good news of God's grace' in Acts 20:24.) On this view τῆς χάριτος is an objective genitive (so most commentators) or a genitive of content (J. Reumann, 'OIKONOMIA — Terms', 165).

15. C. C. Caragounis, *Mysterion*, 74.

'God . . . was pleased to reveal his Son in me' (Gal. 1:12, 15-16).[16] The divine initiative is signalled here by means of the passive 'was made known', while the phrase 'according to revelation', which is placed first in the clause for emphasis, provides a standard for evaluation and refers to the ground or basis on which Paul became acquainted with the 'mystery' (cf. Rom. 16:25).[17] The event itself, Paul as the recipient of the revelation, and especially the ground on which he became acquainted with the mystery were all features which he wishes to draw to the attention of his readers.

About this revelation of the mystery Paul asserts: *as I have already written briefly.* This presumably refers to some document to which the readers had access. Colossians 1:25-27 might be in view, for there the apostle has a 'brief' statement about his stewardship and the unfolding to the Gentiles of the contents of the mystery, compared with the fuller statement in Ephesians 3:2-13. We do not know, however, whether these readers had access to the Letter to the Colossians. So it is most likely that Paul has in mind Ephesians 1:9-10 and 2:11-22, especially vv. 14-16 with its reference to the creation in Christ of 'one new man'.

4 What he has written earlier, then, will be the yardstick by which the readers can discern his *insight into the mystery of Christ.* The opening phrase, 'in accordance with which', points to what was written in chapters 1 and 2 (see above), with the preposition indicating the standard by which their judgment can be made.[18] The reference to *reading* probably has in view the public reading of the letter in the congregation. As a result of this Paul wants them to grasp the significance of God's 'open secret', which has been disclosed in Christ. Spiritual *insight* into or understanding of God's will and the mystery was a quality which Paul desired for all Christians. He had prayed to this end for the Colossians (1:9; cf. 2:2), and had interceded for his Ephesian readers along similar lines (cf. Eph. 1:17). In the present context it is the apostle himself who has re-

---

16. Caird, 63-64, claims that 'by revelation' refers not to the Damascus road Christophany but to a 'later experience of prophetic inspiration . . . particularly through the inspired reinterpretation of the Old Testament scriptures'. Although we are not persuaded by Caird's suggestion of a 'later experience of prophetic inspiration', it is likely that Paul, having understood the mystery through the 'revelation of Jesus Christ' on the Damascus road, would have naturally turned to the Scriptures and meditated upon those texts which spoke of God's mystery.

17. κατά with the accusative can 'refer to the thing which is the ground or basis of something, and hence the item provides a standard for evaluation', S. E. Porter, *Idioms,* 163; cf. BAGD, 407; and Lincoln, 175; against C. C. Caragounis, *Mysterion,* 99. On the view that the phrase signifies the mode of the disclosure, see Abbott, 79; H. Merklein, *Das kirchliche Amt,* 198; and M. N. A. Bockmuehl, *Revelation,* 201.

18. Gk. πρός. So Meyer, 157; and cf. BAGD, 710 (Gal. 2:14; 2 Cor. 5:10; Luke 12:47).

ceived this *insight into the mystery,* but he earnestly desires that they, too, will grasp it by reflecting on what he has already written to them.

In v. 3 the 'mystery' was left undefined, although the term had already appeared at 1:9, namely, 'the mystery of his [i.e., God's] will'. Now Paul[19] speaks of his insight into[20] 'the mystery *of Christ',* an expression which signifies either the mystery which is equated with Christ[21] or, more probably, that which consists in Christ — it is 'the mystery which is disclosed in him'.[22] According to the latter, it is in Christ that the unseen God is fully revealed.

It has been shown that the 'mystery' in Ephesians 3 stands for the 'gospel' in Galatians 1:12, 15-16.[23] Ephesians 3:3 states that the mystery was made known to Paul 'according to revelation', while in Galatians 1:12 he claims that he received the gospel 'through a revelation of Jesus Christ'. As the content of the gospel in Galatians 1 is Jesus Christ, so in Ephesians 3:4 the content of the mystery is Christ. Although it has been argued that the further statement of the mystery at 3:6 indicates a shift of emphasis to a salvation-historical and ecclesiological dimension, there is no contradiction between the christological gospel of Galatians 1 and the ecclesiological mystery of Ephesians 3. According to the former God revealed his Son in Paul in order that he might preach him as the content of the gospel among the Gentiles. It was the law-free gospel which Paul proclaimed, and because it was law-free it was applicable to Gentiles as well

---

19. It is mistaken to argue that v. 4 could only have come from an admiring pupil of Paul, rather than from the apostle himself, since the wording is incompatible with 'apostolic dignity' or might suggest he was courting favour. But the words could have been written without any suggestion of arrogance. Paul is not 'boast[ing] of his understanding' (as Lincoln, 176, suggests). 'He is claiming that the teaching he has just put before his readers is based on divine revelation, and he now invites them to judge for themselves the validity of his claim' (so, correctly, Caird, 64). The argument against Paul writing these words is, in fact, a two-edged sword: would another person who had merely assumed the name of Paul put into the mouth of the apostle such a 'self-display' of his understanding? Further, the alternative scenario suggested by Lincoln, 176, 177, Schnackenburg, 132, and others raises more problems than it solves.

20. The expression σύνεσις (συνίημι) ἐν ('insight into), which is not classical, is probably drawn from the Greek Old Testament, especially Daniel, where it is used of the understanding of dreams and visions, and by implication associated with revelations (1:4, 17; 9:13, 23; 10:1, 11); cf. Best, 303. Not surprisingly it appears in similar contexts in Qumran: 1QH 12:20; 1QS 9:18 (note K. G. Kuhn, 'The Epistle', 118-19).

21. With τοῦ Χριστοῦ ('of Christ') being taken as a genitive of apposition; cf. Col. 1:27.

22. On this view, the τοῦ Χριστοῦ ('of Christ') is epexegetic, with the genitive being one of definition (cf. Bruce, 313).

23. By H. Merklein, *Das kirchliche Amt,* 193-209, esp. 208-9. Note the careful evaluation of this by S. Kim, *Origin,* 23-24.

as to Jews. Gentiles, formerly kept apart from Jews by the barrier of the law, were now able to benefit from God's saving act in Christ and to be incorporated in him along with Jews. Ephesians 3 emphasizes this aspect of the 'secret' that has been revealed.

5 Before the content of this mystery is elaborated, attention is drawn to its eschatological character by means of a 'once–now' contrast (v. 5), the so-called 'revelation-schema'.[24] This verse with its antithetic parallelism contains three contrasting elements which may be set out as follows:

The mystery	(1) 'in other generations'	(2) 'was not made known	(3) 'to men'	(v. 5a)
	(1) 'as now'	(2) 'it has been revealed *by the Spirit*'	(3) 'to his holy apostles and prophets'.	(v. 5b)

The 'mystery of Christ' had not been made known to human beings in earlier generations.[25] It was wholly inaccessible to human understanding until the time when God[26] chose to reveal it. In essence the same point is affirmed in the concluding doxology of Romans (16:25-27), where Paul's gospel is said to be 'the revelation of the mystery which was kept secret for long ages', and in Colossians 1:25-27, where 'the word of God' which the apostle is to complete is 'the mystery that has been kept hidden for ages and generations'.

This is not to suggest, however, that Paul's gospel is an innovation.[27] Quite the reverse. The apostle insists elsewhere that it was prom-

24. Note also Rom. 16:25-27; 1 Cor. 2:6-10; 1 Tim. 3:16; 2 Tim. 1:9-11; Tit. 1:2-3; 1 Pet. 1:20. N. A. Dahl, 'Form-Critical Observations on Early Christian Preaching', in *Jesus in the Memory of the Early Church* (Minneapolis: Augsburg, 1976), 30-36, esp. 32-33. Cf. P. Tachau, *'Einst' und 'Jetzt'*; and H. Merklein, *Das kirchliche Amt,* 164-70, 181-87.

25. ἑτέραις γενεαῖς ('other generations') is a way of indicating the past and contrasting it with the present (Schlier, 149; C. C. Caragounis, *Mysterion,* 101; cf. A. T. Robertson, *Grammar,* 523; and BDF §200[4]), which is here portrayed by νῦν ('now'). For a discussion of the 'once–now' contrast here, see H. Merklein, *Das kirchliche Amt,* 181-87 (against F. J. Steinmetz, *Protologische Heils-Zuversicht,* 51-67, esp. 66, who argues that the contrast here is not basically temporal but theological).

26. The two passive verbs, οὐκ ἐγνωρίσθη ('was not made known') and ἀπεκαλύφθη ('has been revealed') emphasize that it is God alone who unfolds the mystery of Christ. On a possible distinction in meaning between γνωρίζω and ἀποκαλύπτω, see Schnackenburg, 133.

27. Note the important discussion of J. D. G. Dunn, 'How New Was Paul's Gospel? The Problem of Continuity and Discontinuity', in *Gospel in Paul: Studies on Corinthians, Galatians and Romans for Richard N. Longenecker,* ed. L. A. Jervis and P. Richardson (Sheffield: Academic Press, 1994), 367-88.

ised beforehand through the prophets in the holy scriptures (Rom. 1:2), that it was witnessed to by the law and the prophets (3:21) — in fact, that the gospel was preached beforehand to Abraham (Gal. 3:8). Furthermore, evidence of God's intention to bless Gentiles through this gospel may be found in the law, the prophets, and the writings,[28] passages which Paul takes up in Romans 15:8-12 to show that Christ came not only for Jews and their descendants but also for Gentiles, who would 'glorify God for his mercy', and to set forth the Old Testament basis for his Gentile mission.[29]

In what sense, then, could it be said that this 'mystery' was a new revelation if the prophets of the Old Testament had already looked forward to the saving purpose of God in which Gentiles along with Israelites would be embraced within its scope? The *manner* in which that purpose would come to fruition — by incorporation of both Jews and Gentiles into the body of Christ — was not made known. *This* had remained a mystery until the time of its fulfilment, and Paul, as the apostle to the Gentiles and first steward of this mystery, has the privilege of unfolding its wonder to his readers.

So now[30] there has been a dramatic turn of events. What was previously hidden has now been disclosed by God. This revelation has occurred in the immediate present, according to Ephesians 1:9, after the death and resurrection of the Lord Jesus. Again the parallel passages in Romans 16 and Colossians 1 affirm the same truth in slightly different wording. In the former what had previously been kept secret was '*now* disclosed and through the prophetic writings . . . made known to all the nations' (Rom. 16:26), while in the latter the previously hidden mystery was '*now* made manifest to his saints'.

Here in Ephesians 3:5 the recipients of this revelation are unusually described: the mystery has been revealed by the Spirit[31] 'to his holy apostles and prophets'. This expression is clearly connected with the earlier

28. From the law: Deut. 32:43; from the prophets: Isa. 11:10; from the writings: Ps. 18:49; 117:1 (Bruce, 314).

29. Bruce, 314.

30. ὡς νῦν should not be read comparatively, 'in the same degree as' or 'not so clearly as' (as C. C. Caragounis, *Mysterion*, 102-3, argues in detail; cf. Caird, 64). Instead, the contrast is definite, as in v. 9, indicating that 'the adoption of the Gentiles into God's people through the Messiah is a novel fact' (Barth, 334; cf. Schlier, 150; Schnackenburg, 133; and Best, 307; cf. M. N. A. Bockmuehl, *Revelation*, 201: 'The point is not one of degrees of revelation').

31. Against a number of interpreters who regard ἐν πνεύματι as modifying 'prophets' only, the phrase qualifies the verb and indicates that the revelation to *both* apostles *and* prophets occurred through or by the Spirit; cf. G. D. Fee, *God's Empowering Presence*, 692.

statement about the foundational role of the apostles and prophets in the church (2:20). The syntax suggests that both 'his' and 'holy' qualify only 'apostles', but not both nouns.[32] Accordingly, it is the apostles who are especially in view, which is perhaps not surprising given that the context is specifically Paul's discussion of his *apostolic* commission. Although 'his' may refer to Christ as the explicit antecedent in v. 4, it is preferable to understand the reference to God since he is the implied subject of the passive verb *revealed* (cf. Col. 1:26), hence the NIV's *God's holy apostles and prophets*.

The adjective *holy* has caused some difficulty, for this is thought to reflect a later 'early Catholic' limitation of the term 'saints' which Paul had employed for all Christians. But 'saints' appears frequently in the broader sense throughout Ephesians.[33] Furthermore, 'holy' as an adjective has a different nuance from its use as a substantive in the plural when it denotes the people of God in general, the 'saints'. By calling them *holy* Paul is not specially venerating apostles at the expense of other believers, for in v. 8 he speaks of himself as the least of all the *saints*. The language of Colossians 1:26-27, where the mystery is said to have been revealed to the saints, is close to the wording of Ephesians. It is quite possible that Paul has employed the earlier expression here (retaining the word 'holy') but has changed the focus, because he is discussing his apostolic commission to Gentiles. So 'holy' describes the 'apostles' as separated to God for their 'distinctive role as recipients of the central revelation'.[34]

This distinct expression, then, which is said to be at odds with other references to the recipients of the mystery, need not lead to the conclusion that the section vv. 2-7, if not the whole letter, comes from the hand of someone other than Paul.[35] The notion that the mystery was revealed to different recipients should cause no difficulty. It had been made known 'to all the nations' (Rom. 16:26) through the worldwide preaching of the gospel; it was disclosed to God's holy people, especially Gentiles (Col.

32. The αὐτοῦ ('his') divides the two nouns 'apostles' and 'prophets,' rather than coming after both, and because of this ἁγίοις ('holy') appears to qualify only ἀποστόλοις ('apostles'). Note the discussion by H. Merklein, *Das kirchliche Amt*, 187-88; Schnackenburg, 133-34; and Lincoln, 178-79.

33. Eph. 1:1, 4, 15, 18; 2:19; 3:8, 18; 4:12; 5:3; 6:18. See the Introduction, 36.

34. Turner, 1234. Note the discussions of Snodgrass, 26-27; and K. O. *Sandnes*, 231-36.

35. While acknowledging the problem of this expression in relation to Pauline authorship of the letter, G. D. Fee, *God's Empowering Presence*, 692 n. 113, adds: 'it is equally difficult to understand how a pseudepigrapher could have made such a gaffe and then write in v. 8 that Paul is the least of all the saints'. And, it is 'especially difficult to understand why someone writing in Paul's name, who has caught all the subtleties of his thought and language, would not have written, "to *us* apostles and prophets"'.

1:26), because they were the beneficiaries of God's saving work through his Son and thus of the revelation concerning it. The divine secret was revealed to 'the apostles and prophets,'[36] for they 'were the ministers through whom the truth of God was communicated to their fellow-believers'. The apostles 'represent the authority of primary witness to the Gospel facts, while prophets represent the living guidance of the Spirit by which the facts were apprehended in ever fuller meaning and scope'.[37] And it was disclosed to Paul by revelation on the Damascus road, for he, as the apostle to the Gentiles, held the primacy among those ministers (Gal. 1:11-12, 15-16; cf. Acts 26:12-18).

6 The content of God's 'open secret' (v. 4) is now spelled out.[38] For a heightened effect and in order to describe it more precisely Paul assembles three parallel, composite adjectives,[39] each beginning with the prefix 'with', to declare that Gentiles are 'fellow-heirs *with, one body with,* and joint partakers of the promise *with* [those of Jewish birth] in Christ Jesus through the gospel'.[40]

First, 'fellow-heirs' of the same blessing.[41] God promised Abraham that he would bless his descendants and that through him all the families of the earth would find blessing (Gen. 12:2-3). Now the divine plan has been revealed that through the gospel all the families of the earth should not only be blessed in Abraham's offspring, but also be counted among his children. They, too, share 'the faith of Abraham', who is 'the father of us all' (Rom. 4:16). They are fellow-heirs because they are heirs of God

---

36. In order to get round the difficulty of these particular recipients Caird, 65, claims: 'The *apostles and prophets* are not being distinguished from other members of the church, whether by personal sanctity or by ordination to sacred office, but from men of *other generations*'. He adds that 'ἅγιος is a word which applies equally to all Christians, and applies to them solely because they belong to Christ. In the present context, therefore, it comes very near to meaning "Christian"'. But this harmonization is both unnecessary and unconvincing.

37. Bruce, 314-15, esp. 315. Note the good discussion of G. D. Fee, *God's Empowering Presence*, 691-92.

38. Most scholars consider the infinitive εἶναι (lit. 'to be') to be epexegetical, explaining what is meant by the mystery.

39. The apostle uses three compounds with συν- ('with') in Eph. 2:19-22 to emphasize the unity of Gentile converts with the rest of the Christian community: συμπολῖται ('fellow-citizens'), v. 19; συναρμολογουμένη ('joined together'), v. 21; and συνοικοδομεῖσθε ('built together'), v. 22.

40. The three Greek terms are συγκληρονόμα, σύσσωμα, and συμμέτοχα. On the meaning of each see the following notes.

41. συγκληρονόμα signifies one who receives a possession together with someone else, hence 'one who also receives, receiver, fellow heir'; so Louw and Nida §57.134. They add that there is no 'implication of being an "heir" to anyone who has died'. The 'focus is upon receiving an unearned gift'.

and fellow-heirs with Christ (Rom. 8:17).[42] Earlier in Ephesians the notion of 'inheritance' pointed to the certain hope of participating in the future glory, the enjoyment of which has already begun through the Spirit who is the guarantee of that future possession (cf. 1:14; 5:5).

Secondly, 'fellow-members of the same body'. By means of a compound term found nowhere else in the New Testament, Paul states as an important element of the mystery that Gentile Christians have been incorporated into the same body as Jewish believers and are therefore fellow-members of the body of Christ.[43] Catching up ideas from 2:16, 19-22[44] which speak of Christ's purpose of creating in himself one new humanity and reconciling both Jew and Gentile in one body to God through the cross, Paul apparently coins a new word to 'express [this] revolutionary . . . concept [of] the inclusion of Gentiles in the people of God on the same footing as Jews'.[45]

The third privilege bestowed on the Gentiles, which Barth suggests may be the climax in the series,[46] is that they are *sharers together*[47] *in the promise*. The term 'promise' harks back to two earlier passages in Ephesians which speak of 'the covenants of promise' from which Gentiles had been excluded before being brought near to God through the death of Christ (2:12), and (lit.) 'the Holy Spirit of promise' by whom they were sealed when they believed. Accordingly, it has been claimed that this privilege of Gentiles being 'joint partakers of the promise' is not a duplication of the first blessing 'joint heirs', but a reference to the substance of the promise, that is, the Holy Spirit himself (cf. 1:13). 'Because his presence manifests God's presence among his people, the Spirit is indeed the epitome of God's promise'.[48] This suggestion fits neatly with what we

42. See the exposition of Bruce, 315-16.

43. σύσσωμα is 'surely designed to express an emphatic relation to the σῶμα τοῦ Χριστοῦ', E. Schweizer, *TDNT* 7:1080. Louw and Nida §11.9 think that the term signifies 'a person who is a member of a group, with emphasis upon his coordinate relation to other members of the group', hence a 'co-member'.

44. Rightly observed by E. Schweizer, *TDNT* 7:1080, and H. Merklein, *Das kirchliche Amt*, 205.

45. Bruce, 316.

46. Barth, 338.

47. συμμέτοχα means 'one who shares in a possession or a relationship', hence a 'sharer, partner' (Louw and Nida §57.8).

48. Barth, 338. Several recent writers have interpreted this third blessing as the *promised* Holy Spirit; see, e.g., Schlier, 151; and N. A. Dahl, 'Bibelstudie über den Epheserbrief', *Kurze Auslegung des Epheserbriefes*, ed. N. A. Dahl and others (Göttingen: Vandenhoeck & Ruprecht, 1965), 7-83, esp. 42-43. Bruce, 316, understands Paul's statement along the lines of the apostle's earlier exposition in Gal. 3:6-29 (which includes a reference to 'the promise of the Spirit', v. 14; cf. vv. 2, 5), but the focus of Galatians is upon the Gentiles being Abraham's offspring and thus 'heirs according to the promise'.

have observed elsewhere,[49] namely, that significant themes of the epistle which have been anticipated in the introductory *berakah* of 1:3-14 are explained and applied throughout the body of the letter. Thus, the mention of *Gentiles* (note the emphatic 'you' in 1:13) being sealed with the promised Holy Spirit has been taken up and applied not only in an exhortatory context of 4:30 ('Do not grieve the Holy Spirit of God, by whom you were sealed for the day of redemption'), but also in this didactic passage with its exposition of the mystery of Christ. Furthermore, this suggestion is consistent with the parallel passage (2:16-18), where both Jews and Gentiles have access through Christ *in one Spirit* to the Father (v. 18).

Each of these marvellous blessings in which Gentiles participate is said to be *in Christ Jesus* and *through the gospel* (v. 6). The former phrase qualifies all three nouns ('fellow-heirs', 'members together', and 'joint partakers'), not simply the last. It is not to be understood instrumentally as 'through Christ';[50] rather, it signifies that Christ Jesus is the *sphere* in which this incorporation of Gentiles occurs. It is in Christ, that is, Israel's Messiah, and in him alone, that Gentiles inherit the promises made to Abraham. Further, all this occurs through the instrumentality of the gospel. It declares the basis on which Gentiles, along with Jews, become sons and daughters of God, are made fellow-members of the body of Christ, and receive the promised Holy Spirit.[51] That basis is Christ's death and resurrection, which are part of the apostolic announcement. As the gospel is proclaimed, Gentile men and women, who hear its message and appropriate it for themselves, are united with the Lord Jesus in his death and resurrection. Thus, the gospel not only declares what is God's gracious plan, announcing the content of the mystery of Christ; it is also the instrument[52] by which God achieves his purposes of bringing Gentiles to faith and incorporating them into his Son. It is through the active proclamation of the gospel that God draws men and women to himself (cf. 2 Thess. 2:14).

To sum up. The mystery or open secret of Christ is 'the complete union of Jews and Gentiles with each other through the union of both with Christ. It is this double union, with Christ and with each other, which is the substance of the "mystery"'.[53]

---

49. P. T. O'Brien, 'Ephesians I', 510-12.

50. Which is signified instead by the preposition διά in the following phrase '*through* the gospel'.

51. Mitton, 123. 'The gospel is the proclamation of all the privileges which Christ has made available to men, and also the offer here and now of these privileges to those who respond in true faith'.

52. Cf. R. E. Brown, *Mystery,* 58.

53. Stott, 117.

Because this description of the mystery's content is unusual, it has often been argued that the term in Ephesians 3 has an entirely different sense from Paul's earlier uses, including that in Colossians 1:26-27.[54] But the apostle sometimes employed the term 'mystery' of one particular element in his message (cf. the similar use of 'gospel' to refer to one important component). So, for example, 'mystery' denotes the transformation of believers into spiritual bodies on the last day (1 Cor. 15:51) and Israel's final restoration after her temporary rejection (Rom. 11:25).[55] To speak of the whole by means of a part is entirely appropriate and certainly not inconsistent with the more general uses. Indeed, it has been claimed that the more comprehensive notion of the mystery is already present in Ephesians 3 (namely, at vv. 8, 10), apart from the instance in 1:9-10. Further, the differences between Colossians 1:27 and Ephesians 3:4, 6 are slight: in both passages the mystery is focussed on Christ, while in the former the term has to do with Christ as preached among the nations together with his indwelling with his people, whether Jews or Gentiles. Seyoon Kim, among others, has noted that mystery describes not simply God's eschatological act in Christ, but that saving act which includes Gentiles as recipients of its benefits.[56] In both Colossians 1:26-27 and Ephesians 3:3-6 mystery has christological and salvation-historical or ecclesiological aspects to it. The difference in the two epistles is one of emphasis, with Colossians 1 stressing the former and Ephesians 3 the latter.[57]

7 In what is a transitional verse Paul returns to the primary thought of the paragraph (vv. 2-7), namely, his stewardship of the mystery in the context of divine grace, and he prepares the way for his statement about the commission for him to preach the unsearchable riches of Christ to the Gentiles (v. 8). The repeated references to divine grace in v. 7 pick up this important theme of v. 2 ('the grace of God given to me') and function as an *inclusio*, thereby bracketing the paragraph (vv. 2-7),[58] as well as preparing the way for the further statement in v. 8. This rhetorical device underscores the point that everything Paul has said in this passage, about the revelation to him of the mystery, the incorporation of Gentiles into the body of Christ, and his commission, arises from and can only be understood within the context of God's overflowing grace.

---

54. Note especially Mitton, 89.
55. Noted by Bruce, 313.
56. S. Kim, *Origin*, 22-23.
57. So S. Kim, *Origin*, 23; following C. F. D. Moule, *Colossians*, 82-83; Bruce, 86; and H. Merklein, *Das kirchliche Amt*, 209.
58. So C. Reynier, *Évangile et Mystère: les enjeux théologiques de l'Épître aux Éphésiens* (Paris: Cerf, 1992), 61-68.

Having spoken of the revelation of the mystery *to him*, the apostle now turns his attention to the preaching of the mystery *through him*. The saving purposes of God involved not only a revealing of the gospel mystery to Paul, but also the pressing of him into the service of that gospel.[59] He became its 'servant' (cf. Col. 1:23) when he was converted on the Damascus road (vv. 2, 8). Paul's calling to be a missionary to the Gentiles was not of his own doing; rather, it was wholly due to the gracious, sovereign intervention of God. That he who was so conscious of his own unworthiness because he had been an opponent of the Lord Jesus points out this deeply held personal truth in an emphatic way: first, by indicating that he 'was made' a servant of that gospel *by God*,[60] and, secondly, by heaping up expressions for grace (as already noted) and power. The cause of his reception of this commission to proclaim this divine message, which he regarded as the highest honour indeed, was 'the gracious gift which God imparted to me'.[61]

Although Paul does not use the exact phrase 'minister of the gospel' in his earlier letters,[62] he does speak of himself and his colleagues as 'ministers', particularly when he wishes to stress that both they and he are on the same footing as servants through whom God works (notably 1 Cor. 3:5). It is clear in these epistles that such ministers are servants of the word who preach and teach the gospel anyway (cf. 2 Cor. 3:6 with 2:17 and 4:2).[63] In the contexts of Colossians 1:23 and Ephesians 3:7, where 'minister' appears, Paul is making the point that the message, which focusses on the lordship of Christ and reconciliation, and the fulfilling of the salvation-historical plan of God by which Gentiles are incorporated into the body of Christ, is the mighty gospel of which he has been

---

59. S. Kim, *Origin*, 24.

60. If the passive ἐγενήθην is to be pressed; cf. Barth, 339.

61. F. F. Bruce, *An Expanded Paraphrase of the Epistles of Paul* (Exeter: Paternoster, 1965), 273. δωρεά is the '*gift, bounty* of God' (BAGD, 210), and τῆς χάριτος is a genitive of quality or definition.

62. Some interpreters (cf. H. Merklein, *Das kirchliche Amt*, 222-24) have argued that when the title 'minister of the gospel' is here applied to Paul it is the voice of the sub-apostolic age looking back to him as the guarantor of the apostolic office. So a later generation is in these words (at Col. 1:23 and Eph. 3:7) asserting that the Pauline gospel has binding validity because of its apostolic character. But such a reading of the situation fails to come to grips with: (a) the glaring omission of the significant term 'apostle' (ἀπόστολος), which would have uniquely served this supposed intention of the post-Pauline writer, and (b) Paul's use of the term 'ministers' to emphasize that he and his colleagues are servants through whom God works. See the Introduction, 33-37.

63. The διάκονοι ('ministers, servants'), according to E. E. Ellis, 'Paul and his Co-Workers', *Prophecy and Hermeneutic in Early Christianity: New Testament Essays* (Tübingen: J. C. B. Mohr [Paul Siebeck], 1978), 6-10, were a special class of co-workers who were active in preaching and teaching.

privileged to become a servant. He of all people has become a minister of that gospel. And by styling himself in this way he is implying that he is on the same level as his colleagues who are 'ministers'.[64]

In the final phrase of v. 7, *through the working of his power,* Paul makes two additional points that throw further light on his understanding of his calling to the missionary task and its execution. First, the phrase is linked with '[God's grace] given to me'.[65] God's gracious gift to Paul, by which he was called to be a servant, was due to the effective working of divine power.[66] Just as nothing short of God's mighty intervention could transform him from being a persecutor into a Christian, so it took that same almighty and effective working to make him into a 'servant of the gospel'. Secondly, since both 'working' and 'power' in other contexts[67] draw attention to the ongoing mighty work of God, here the apostle is focussing not simply upon God's powerful working in grace to *commission* him. The expression also points to his ever-present consciousness that day by day he experiences 'the operation of his power' in the *fulfilment* of his missionary calling. It was not only in God's initial call but also in the subsequent enabling that he knows of the divine power operating mightily within him. This is the explicit point he makes in the parallel passage (Col. 1:29) and elsewhere in his writings, notably 1 Corinthians 15:10:

> But by the grace of God I am what I am, and his grace to me was not without effect. No, I worked harder than all of them — yet not I, but the grace of God that was with me.

We therefore find in Ephesians 3:2-7 the recurring emphasis that everything Paul has become and achieved in his apostolic mission is 'not his own doing, but the result of God's grace — God's choice of him, God's call to him, God's enabling power'.[68] And in the exercise of his apostleship to the Gentiles 'he gave practical effect to the divine plan made known to him by revelation'.[69]

64. As a term used to describe Paul's function, it 'is not a word which would stress either his importance or personal renown' (Best, 314).

65. Most commentators contend, rightly in our judgment, that the two κατά ('according to')-clauses in the verse are not coordinate.

66. 'The grace experienced by Paul in his ministry flowed out of the mighty power of God' (Lincoln, 182).

67. It has often been noted that God's power is a prominent motif in both Colossians and Ephesians (Col. 1:29; 2:12; Eph. 1:19; 3:7, 16, 20; 6:10) denoting that might which he exercised when he raised Christ from the dead and by which he now works in and through the lives of *his apostle* and people (see on 1:19).

68. Mitton, 124.

69. Bruce, 317.

3. Making Known the Mystery in God's Purposes, 3:8-13

8   As he reflects on his commission to be Christ's missionary to the Gentiles Paul is filled with amazement at the extraordinary privilege that has been given to him.[70] Using a very striking expression in which he neither indulges in hypocrisy nor grovels in self-deprecation,[71] he indicates how deeply conscious he is of his own unworthiness and of Christ's overflowing grace to him: *to me who am less than the least of all God's people has this grace been given*.[72] As if the superlatives 'least' (among the apostles, 1 Cor. 15:9) or 'first and foremost' (of sinners, 1 Tim. 1:15) were insufficient to express his unworthiness, Paul creates a new form of this Greek adjective, that is, a comparative of a superlative ('leaster', 'less than the least').[73] What grounds are there for such self-effacement? Barth rightly points out that the apostle is not just thinking in general terms about the weakness of his flesh or the continued struggle of the 'old man' against the 'new'. He considers lifelong weakness, temptation, and failure to be characteristic of all believers. Rather, he has in view here his violent persecution of the church *of God*[74] (1 Cor. 15:9). His repeated, specific references to his role as a persecutor reveal his consciousness of sin.[75]

But the paragraph is not dominated by the notion of Paul's unworthiness, real though this was. He has experienced the amazing grace of God, and so he goes out of his way to emphasize it. In this instance 'the

70. A new sentence begins here and continues to the end of v. 12. The thought now moves forward from the grace of God embodied in the gospel (v. 2) to the process of preaching that gospel (cf. v. 7). This has three steps 'distinguished from one another in stating those to whom it is offered': the Gentiles (v. 8), all people (v. 9), and the powers (vv. 9, 10); so Best, 316.

71. Stott, 119.

72. Schlier, 152, aptly remarks: 'Preaching to the Gentiles is a privilege which paradoxically is given to the least of all the saints'.

73. Gk. ἐλαχιστότερος. Cf. BDF §§60(2), 61(2); cf. S. E. Porter, *Idioms,* 124; and D. B. Wallace, *Greek Grammar,* 302.

74. τοῦ θεοῦ ('of God') stresses the enormity of the crime: it was *God's* church that Paul sought to destroy.

75. Barth, 340, adds: 'because this awareness has a specific focus, it is distinct from a possibly morbid preoccupation with himself or with sin in general. His self-humiliation is unlike the expression of hidden pride and its concomitant fishing for compliments'. Cf. O. Haas, *Paulus der Missionar. Ziel, Grundsätze und Methoden der Missionstätigkeit des Apostels Paulus nach seinen eigenen Aussagen* (Münsterschwarzach: Vier Türme-Verlag, 1971), 19; and Caird, 66. Some have argued that the phrase 'I am less than the least of all saints' is too exaggerated and artificial a self-denigration to be authentic to Paul. But it is even less likely that a Paulinist, who is thought to have penned these words, would speak of his hero in this fashion! On the other hand, if Barth's suggestion is right, then the apostle's statement is quite understandable. (Note, e.g., the criticisms of Lincoln, 183, by D. B. Wallace, *Greek Grammar,* 302.)

grace given' is that grace which enables him to discharge his missionary commission, although one needs to realize that this 'special' grace is part and parcel of the comprehensive grace by which he became a Christian. Further, God works effectively in Paul's life, for although he is deeply conscious of his own unworthiness, this does not hinder him from assuming his missionary responsibilities in relation to the Gentiles.[76] He sets about fulfilling this task energetically, profoundly aware that God has called him to it.

This grace given to Paul consists in[77] his 'bringing to the Gentiles the good news of Christ's unfathomable wealth'. This impressive rhetorical expression describes an activity of proclamation, the content of which is both glorious and comprehensive. Already in this paragraph it was asserted that 'in Christ Jesus' and through the instrumentality of the *gospel* Gentiles inherit the promises made to Abraham (v. 6). Not surprisingly, the apostle now speaks of his commission in gospel terms by using the cognate verb 'to proclaim the gospel'.

The object of the verb, *the unsearchable riches of Christ*, is rather unusual. Often the verb 'to announce the gospel' is employed specifically with the 'gospel', or some element of it, as its direct object (1 Cor. 15:1; 2 Cor. 11:7; Gal. 1:11, 23; cf. Rom. 10:15). In other instances where no object is expressly mentioned it is clear from the context that the preaching of the gospel is in view (Rom. 1:15; 15:20; 1 Cor. 1:17, etc.).[78] Here in Ephesians 3:8, however, Paul uses rhetorical language to show that his proclamation is about the wealth of divine grace and glory which Christ possesses in himself and which he lavishly gives to others.[79] The adjective qualifying riches, which means 'unfathomable, impossible to compre-

76. Schlier, 152, rightly observes that 'to the Gentiles' picks up the 'on behalf of you Gentiles' of v. 1.

77. So Abbott, 86; Gnilka, 170; and Barth, 340. This is tantamount to saying the same as Schlier, 152 (it is by the grace that he is given that Paul preaches the gospel), and M. N. A. Bockmuehl, *Revelation*, 202-3 (who thinks that grace was given to Paul 'in order that he should preach it to the Gentiles'; cf. also C. C. Caragounis, *Mysterion*, 106).

78. Cf. Best, 318. For further details see J. H. Schütz, *Paul and the Anatomy of Apostolic Authority* (Cambridge: Cambridge University Press, 1975), 39, and P. T. O'Brien, *Gospel and Mission*, 62-65, where it is also shown that the verb εὐαγγελίζομαι ('proclaim the gospel') can cover a broad range of activities, from the initial announcement of the gospel to the building up of believers and grounding them firmly in the faith.

79. Although the genitive τοῦ Χριστοῦ ('of Christ') could be objective, signifying that 'Christ himself constitutes the content of the riches of the gospel' (so Lincoln, 183, 184), it is preferable to regard it as possessive, signifying 'the riches *of Christ*', i.e., those which he has or possesses. At the same time these riches are for others, since they are the subject of the apostolic announcement. The genitive τοῦ Χριστοῦ ('of Christ') at 3:8 functions differently from the other instances in Ephesians where πλοῦτος is followed by an objective genitive of the particular quality, i.e., χάριτος ('grace') or δόξης ('glory'); cf. 1:7, 18; 2:7; 3:16.

241

hend',[80] has already been employed by the apostle in Romans of the deep mysteries in God's plan of salvation by which his purpose is to have mercy on all, both Jew and Gentile: 'how *unsearchable* are his judgments, and his paths beyond tracing out' (Rom. 11:33). In the book of Job (LXX 5:9; 9:10; cf. 34:24, 28) the wonders of God's creation and providence are 'unfathomable'. The riches of Christ are similar. They are too vast to explore completely and too deep to fathom.[81]

If these *unsearchable riches of Christ* are that wealth which he possesses in himself and which he bestows on those who are 'in him', then something of their content has already been mentioned in Paul's exposition of Ephesians 1 and 2, particularly in the introductory eulogy of 1:3-14, where significant elements in God's plan of salvation — which includes Gentiles within the sphere of blessing — are enunciated. Because these amazing riches of God in Christ are true *wealth,* then the gospel Paul proclaims will enrich his hearers immeasurably as they respond. Here the wealth of God has been lavished in a wonderful way. Paul is so convinced of this that he is almost overwhelmed at the great privilege given to him as a missionary of proclaiming God's great kindness in the Lord Jesus Christ.

Somewhat paradoxically the apostle has written, on the one hand, of the mystery of the gospel being *revealed* to him (v. 3) and, on the other, of that message focussing on *the riches of Christ,* which are 'unfathomable'! Christ Jesus had made himself known to Paul on the Damascus road; but the apostle had not *fully comprehended* 'all the treasures of wisdom and knowledge hidden in him' (Col. 2:2-3). He had come to know Christ at his conversion in an intensely personal way and could speak of 'the surpassing greatness of knowing Christ Jesus my Lord' (Phil. 3:8); but the great ambition and goal of his life was to know Christ more and more (Phil. 3:9-10). In the gospel of Christ that *came by revelation* there were vast treasure houses of his riches which had *not* been *explored* and depths which had not been plumbed, either by the apostle himself or any other Christian. His riches were 'infinite'. So in revealing himself God had graciously given himself to men and women, but he is not comprehended by them, nor does he submit himself to humankind's intellectual or technical control. 'Revelation creates rather than annihilates wonder, awe and respect'.[82]

---

80. So Louw and Nida §32.23. ἀνεξιχνίαστος (from ἴχνος, 'footprint, track') does not appear in the New Testament apart from here and in Rom. 11:33.

81. Best, 318: 'Implied in [this word] are both the wonder of God's activity and the inability of the human mind, even after revelation, to deduce and plumb the depths of God'.

82. Barth, 341. Citing E. Gaugler, Barth adds: 'The god who has been comprehended . . . is always an idol'.

9 The grace of God given to Paul consists not only in his *preaching the unsearchable riches of Christ to the Gentiles* (v. 8), but also in his revealing to all how God's 'hidden purpose was to be put into effect' (NEB). The keyword that has to do with God's 'administration or arrangement'[83] is used once again and, as in Colossians 1:25 and Ephesians 3:2, there is a role given to Paul, namely, that of making it known. This activity of enlightening, though certainly related to, is not identical with his preaching the unsearchable riches of Christ to the Gentiles, for v. 9 does not simply repeat what has been said in v. 8.[84]

This verb,[85] which can mean to 'give light to, shed light upon' in the sense of showing up something for what it is (cf. John 1:9), is here employed figuratively denoting to 'bring to light', and so to 'reveal or illuminate', a nuance it has elsewhere in Paul's letters when it points to the present revelation of something that was previously hidden (1 Cor. 4:5; 2 Tim. 1:10).[86] Here Paul's task has both a salvation-historical and a personal dimension to it. Regarding the latter, if the longer text is preferred,[87] then the direct object of this enlightening activity is 'all people', while the temporal and salvation-historical note is struck by the words which qualify the mystery, namely, that it was 'previously hidden from eternity' in God.[88] The content of what is enlightened is *the administration of this mystery*, that is, how God chose to accomplish his purpose.

As Paul fulfilled his commission of preaching the unsearchable riches of Christ to the Gentiles, so through this proclamation of the gospel men and women came into a relationship with God through his Son, the Lord Jesus. They were joined with Christ in his death and resurrection,

83. οἰκονομία refers not to the divine 'plan' but the working out, or putting into effect, of the mystery; see on v. 2.

84. The infinitival expression 'and to enlighten' (καὶ φωτίσαι) is not an expansion or amplification of the infinitive 'to preach [the unsearchable riches]' (εὐαγγελίσασθαι) of v. 8. Mitton, 125, speaks of Paul's proclaiming the gospel in such a way 'that its implications were unmistakably clear, so as *to make all men see* God's unfolding plan' (original emphasis).

85. Gk. φωτίζω.

86. Cf. BAGD, 872-73.

87. The shorter reading (which omits πάντας, 'all') is stating that through the apostle's ministry God's secret is revealed and shines in its own light. The majority text (which includes πάντας, 'all'), on the other hand, emphasizes that the administration of the mystery is made plain to all (not simply Gentiles, as Barth suggests). The shorter reading may have been a scribal error, while the flow of the argument in chap. 3:1-13 is from 'the revealed secret itself to the many beneficiaries of God's grace'; so Barth, 342. Cf. Lincoln, 167, who argues cogently for the inclusion of πάντας, 'all'.

88. ἐν τῷ θεῷ, '[hidden] in God', has a locative sense, and makes the point that the mystery had been secure. Not only had it previously been inaccessible, but also because it had been safely hidden in God certainty 'accompanies its realization' (cf. Lincoln, 185).

and so became fellow-members, along with Jewish Christians, of the same body. In this way the previously hidden mystery (described in v. 6) was being implemented in a wonderful manner: God was putting into effect his age-old plan, something that had not been seen or imagined before, and as the apostle to the Gentiles Paul had the great privilege of revealing this magnificent, divine administration to the eyes of human beings on earth, Jew and Gentile alike *(all)*. Paul's commission, then, contained this second element, not as something additional or unrelated to the proclamation of the gospel but integral to it.

The God in whom this secret had previously been hidden from eternity is the one *who created all things.* The text makes plain that the God who has redeemed his people and reconciled them through Christ's death to himself and to one another is the God who created everything. His 'mystery', though not understood by men and women, had been planned by him, the Creator, from eternity. Before the foundation of the world he chose a people for himself in Christ and predestined them to be his children (Eph. 1:4-5). He had prepared this plan before the creation and put it into operation at the right time. His act of creation did not in any way militate against redemption and reconciliation. Quite the reverse. It subserved their accomplishment, since all alike take place 'according to the purpose of him who works all things according to the counsel of his will' (Eph. 1:11).[89] God has not changed; nor is he abandoning his first creation by forming a new creation in Christ. Salvation and the unity of Jew and Gentile in Christ have always been his purpose (see on 1:9-10); his creation of heaven and earth was an important step in the fulfilment of that plan. And he who *created* all things in the beginning with this goal in mind will consummate his work of *re-creation* on the final day when he brings all things together in unity in his Son, the Lord Jesus (1:10).

10 God's intention was that his many-splendoured wisdom might now be made known through the church to the principalities and powers in the heavenly places. This verse indicates the purpose[90] of Paul's 'preaching' (v. 8) and 'making plain' (v. 9), which together spell out the content of his missionary task.[91] Grace was given to him to announce the

---

89. Bruce 320. Cf. also Best, 321-22.

90. It begins with a ἵνα-clause ('in order that, so that').

91. So C. C. Caragounis, *Mysterion,* 108, and Gnilka, 174, among others. This interpretation is preferable to (1) linking the clause with the preceding words of v. 9 ('God, who is the creator all things'), and understanding it as signifying that God created everything *for the purpose of* showing his wisdom to the angelic hosts through the church. This unnecessarily limits Paul's reference and does not fit the rest of the sentence with its emphasis on his preaching the unsearchable riches of Christ and bringing to light God's ad-

unsearchable riches of Christ (v. 8) and to enlighten all as to how God's previously hidden plan was being put into effect (v. 9); the goal of these activities was that the wisdom of God should be made known. V. 10 thus winds up the preceding paragraph and indicates an important purpose, if not the grand design, of God's salvation-historical plan (cf. RSV).

The manifold wisdom of God, which in the divine purpose was to be made known at the present time,[92] is a unique expression. The compound adjective meaning 'manifold, variegated, very many sided'[93] was poetic in origin, referring to an intricately embroidered pattern of 'many-coloured cloaks' or the manifold hues of 'a garland of flowers'.[94] It is used here in a figurative sense to speak of the *richly diversified nature* of the divine wisdom.[95] This manifold wisdom of God has been in evidence in the earlier chapters of Ephesians, and may be summarized in 1:3-14, commencing with his predestinating wisdom in choosing Jews and Gentiles in Christ from before the foundation of the world (v. 4) up to the final redemption of those who are his possession (v. 14). In our present context, however, this variegated wisdom has particular reference to God's richly diverse ways of working which led to a multiracial, multi-cultural community being united as fellow-members in the body of Christ.[96] In other words, it is integrally related to the mystery: 'the *mysterion* is shaped by God's wisdom, it is a product of it. At the same time God's wisdom is reflected and revealed in the *mysterion*'.[97] Not only is this variegated wisdom *God's;* it is he who discloses it (hence the passive *be made known*) to the authorities and powers in the heavenly places. Paul may be active, as part of his missionary commission, in preaching the unsearchable riches of Christ and revealing to all how God's hidden purpose is being put into effect. But the making known of this variegated wisdom is ultimately due

---

ministration of the mystery. Further, this interpretation is not in line with the flow of the paragraph as a whole (vv. 2-13). It is also to be preferred to (2) tying the clause closely with the reference in v. 9 to the hidden mystery. So GNB, 'God . . . kept his secret hidden through all the past ages, *in order that* at the present time'. Cf. NEB and NIV, which begins a new sentence with v. 10: *His intent was that now.*

92. The νῦν ('now'), which stands in contrast with ἀπὸ τῶν αἰώνων ('for ages past', v. 9), has salvation-historical significance: it is only 'now' that the mysterious plan of God has been disclosed to the spiritual rulers and authorities.

93. Gk. πολυποίκιλος.

94. Euripides, *Iphig. Taur.* 1149, and Eubulus, *Athen.* 15.7.

95. Note the variety of divine wisdom in Wisdom 7:22-23. H. Seesemann, *TDNT* 6:485: 'The wisdom of God has shown itself in Christ to be varied beyond measure and in a way which surpasses all previous knowledge thereof'.

96. For further details as to how wisdom has been interpreted in this passage, see Best, 323.

97. C. C. Caragounis, *Mysterion,* 108.

to God. In a sense this is not surprising. What is amazing, however, is that this enlightening of the principalities and powers in the heavenly places is effected *through the church.*

In the earlier reference within this letter to 'church' (1:22) it was suggested that the term was to be understood metaphorically of a heavenly gathering around Christ in which believers already participate (cf. Heb. 12:22-24). We saw that to speak of 'church' as a gathering taking place in heaven was a figurative way of saying that they now enjoy fellowship with him; they are personally related to Christ and consequently to one another (see on 1:22). Since it was appropriate that this new relationship with the ascended Lord should find concrete expression in believers' regular coming together, that is, 'in church' (cf. Heb. 10:25), then the term here in 3:10 should probably be taken as the heavenly gathering that is assembled around Christ[98] *and* as a local congregation of Christians, in which Jews and Gentiles are fellow-members of the body of Christ. The latter reference to a local gathering as an earthly manifestation of this relationship to Christ makes sense in the immediate context where the manifold wisdom of God is being made known to the spiritual rulers *through the church.* Most interpreters believe that Paul has in mind neither evangelism, social action, nor any other additional activity[99] by God's people. Instead, *through the church* signifies that the very existence[100] of this new multiracial community in which Jews and Gentiles have been brought together in unity in the one body is the manifestation of God's richly diverse wisdom. Its presence is the means by which God himself discloses[101] to the powers his own richly diverse wisdom. Later, the apostle will point out that this precious unity which has been won through Christ's death is nothing short of 'the unity of the Spirit' which they are to be eager and zealous to maintain (4:3).

The *rulers and authorities* before whom 'this object-lesson of divine wisdom is displayed'[102] are *in the heavenly realms* (see on 1:3).[103] These authorities probably include the whole host of heavenly beings, good and

---

98. Cf. Gnilka, 174, who claims that the domain of the church, like that of the principalities and powers, is 'in the heavenlies'.

99. Against W. Wink, *Naming the Powers*, 93, 95-96, who incorrectly claims that the church's task here is 'preaching to the Powers', even though he finds this unintelligible (note the criticisms of Arnold, 63).

100. Cf. C. C. Caragounis, *Mysterion,* 109; Arnold, 63; and note S. E. Porter, *Idioms,* 149, 150.

101. The passive verb *be made known* (γνωρισθῇ) suggests that God himself is the author of the disclosure.

102. F. F. Bruce, *Ephesians,* 64.

103. Note also W. H. Harris, '"The Heavenlies"', 78-79.

bad alike,[104] although the apostle's particular concern is obviously with hostile forces.[105] The fact that evil powers are present in the heavenly realm indicates that heaven, like earth, must participate in Paul's two-age eschatological framework. It, too, is involved in this present evil age, and the powers which reside there have already been defeated through Christ's death and now await their final overthrow. Although Paul does not make explicit the nature of the testimony given to the rulers, it has been inferred that the church 'provides the angelic powers [with] a tangible reminder that their authority has been decisively broken and that all things are to be subject to Christ'.[106] The powers cannot hinder the advance of the gospel to Gentiles or their incorporation, along with Jews, into the body of Christ.

Ephesians 3:9, 10 bears a significant relation to the consummation of the mystery, the bringing together of 'all things' into unity in Christ (1:9, 10). The terms employed in 3:9 for the disclosure of the mystery, namely, 'make known', 'administration', and 'mystery', were all used in the earlier discussion of the mystery at 1:9, 10. There Christ's summing up of all things involved 'the things in heaven' (the chief representatives of which are the powers) and 'the things on earth' (especially the church) coming under Christ's lordship so that these divine purposes might be fulfilled. But with the reconciliation of Jews and Gentiles in the body of Christ and the new creation of the two in one new humanity (2:13-16; 3:3-6), together with the disclosure of this as tangible evidence of the manifold wisdom of God, one difficulty to 'all things' being summed up in Christ was being overcome. The consummation of God's cosmic plan was drawing nearer every day, and this reconciliation was a token that his final purpose in Christ was about to reach its conclusion.[107]

Furthermore, if the very existence of the church is a reminder that the authority of the powers has been decisively broken, and that their final defeat is imminent, then the overcoming of the second obstacle, namely, 'the things in heaven', moves to its completion. Perhaps, as F. F. Bruce suggests, the church appears as 'God's pilot scheme for the recon-

104. Note the Old Testament and apocalyptic background to the presence of hostile beings in heaven (cf. Job 1:6; Dan. 10:13, 21; *1 Enoch* 61:10). According to 1 Pet. 1:12 the foretelling and accomplishment of Christian salvation are said to be 'things into which angels long to look', to which Bruce, 321, adds: 'there is no reason why even the angels of the presence should not learn lessons about the ways of God from the working out of his saving purpose'.

105. Note the many references throughout Ephesians to the evil 'powers', and the detailed treatment by Arnold, passim.

106. A. T. Lincoln, *Paradise*, 155.

107. Note the discussion of C. C. Caragounis, *Mysterion*, 143-46; and Arnold, 68, 69.

ciled universe of the future'. The uniting of 'Jews and Gentiles in Christ was . . . God's masterpiece of reconciliation, and gave promise of a time when not Jews and Gentiles only, but all the mutually hostile elements in creation, would be united in that same Christ'.[108] The church is not only the pattern, but also the means God is using to show his purposes are moving triumphantly to their climax.

Finally, these words of v. 10 in the context of Ephesians would have been of great comfort to the readers. Troubled by the powers, these Christians have been reminded that the presence of the church, the body of Christ, means that the authority of the rulers has been broken, that they cannot hinder the progress of the gospel, and that all things are to be subject to Christ. Such assurances would surely encourage them as they engage in a spiritual warfare and await the final day.[109]

11 God's making known his many-splendoured wisdom through the church to the authorities in the heavenly realms was his intention from all eternity, and he has now accomplished this in Christ Jesus. Just as in the eulogy of 1:3-14 God's choosing men and women in Christ to be his inheritance was in accordance with his eternal plan (1:11), so here also what has been made known through the church to the powers can be traced back to his everlasting purpose.[110] The adjective *eternal* is a rendering of the literal expression 'of the ages'[111] and points to the decision taken by God before all time. What he had planned he has now accomplished in Christ Jesus[112] our Lord, and we await its final outworking. The expression used here, (lit.) 'the eternal purpose which he made', has been understood by many to refer to the original formation of God's plan, that is, his decision taken in eternity. However, on contextual grounds it seems preferable to understand it of the accomplishment of God's purpose (so RSV, NEB, NIV). In the revelation schema of vv. 9 and 10, God's wisdom has been made known through the church to the rulers

---

108. Bruce, 321-22, 262. He adds that there is probably a further implication that the church is to be God's agent for bringing about this ultimate reconciliation (cf. A. T. Lincoln, *Paradise,* 155). If this is so, then Paul himself is indirectly God's 'instrument for the universal reconciliation of the future' (Bruce, 322).

109. Arnold, 64.

110. The same phrase, κατὰ πρόθεσιν ('according to purpose'), appears in both passages. In 3:11 the opening words, κατὰ πρόθεσιν ('according to purpose'), are syntactically connected with v. 10, indicating that God's making known his wisdom through the church was in accordance with his eternal purpose.

111. The expression [πρόθεσιν] τῶν αἰώνων is a Hebraism with the genitive '[purpose] of the ages' functioning as an adjective (cf. 3:21; 1 Tim. 1:17, and note BDF §165[1]).

112. Barth, 347, suggests that 'the name "Jesus" may be added to the titles Messiah and Lord in order to draw attention to the ministry of the incarnate and crucified (cf. 2:13-18) rather than to the function of the preexistent'.

and authorities, while in v. 12 access into God's presence with freedom and confidence has already been won. The mention of Christ's lordship suggests the fulfilment of the divine plan, not simply its formation, while the parallel expression at 1:11 has to do with God's *achieving* 'his purpose'. Other instances of the verb 'do' in Ephesians support the notion of accomplishment here.[113] And because God's overarching purpose has been fulfilled in Christ, its final outworking is certain.

12 After the exposition of God's plan of salvation the consequences for the present situation of believers are drawn out. The readers have already been assured that through Christ Jewish and Gentile believers alike have access 'in one Spirit to the Father' (2:18). Now this assurance is repeated, but with a slightly different nuance: in their union with Christ they presently *have* boldness and confident access to God that cannot be hindered by the hostile powers and authorities.

Once again the centrality of Christ is to the fore: the phrase 'in whom', referring to him, appears at the beginning of the verse, indicating that it is only in their union with him that they have this confident access to God, while the concluding words 'through his [*sc.*, Christ's] faithfulness' focus on his obedience to the Father's will as the means by which this marvellous privilege of coming to the throne of grace is provided.[114] 'As his place in the presence of God is unchallengeable, so is theirs, because they are "in him"'.[115]

The two words 'boldness' and 'access' appear separately in parallel

113. It has been claimed that a stronger verb than ποιέω ('do') was needed to signify the *achievement* of God's purpose. However, ποιοῦντες τὰ θελήματα at 2:3 means 'carrying out' the wishes', while this verb is employed powerfully elsewhere in Ephesians by Paul at 2:14, 15; 3:20. Cf. Meyer, 170, 171; Schnackenburg, 141; and Lincoln, 189.

114. Although the majority interpretation understands διὰ τῆς πίστεως αὐτοῦ of believers' faith in Christ 'by which they appropriate the new situation for themselves' (so, e.g., Lincoln, 190), a good case can be made here (as also in Eph. 2:8) for taking the referent as 'Christ's faithfulness', the objective means by which this boldness to enter God's presence is made possible. The subjective element is expressed here by ἐν πεποιθήσει (which Lincoln acknowledges), and is virtually equivalent to 'in faith' (cf. BAGD, 643). Once again in a disputed passage with διὰ [τῆς] πίστεως, to interpret πίστις of our response effectively duplicates another expression in the passage. For a recent advocacy of this, see I. G. Wallis, *Faith*, 128-34, esp. 131-32, who observes that: (1) διά ('through, by means of') followed by a reference to Christ in the genitive is often used in Ephesians to describe the means by which salvation is secured (1:5, 7; 2:8, 16, 18; 3:6, 16, 17); (2) the correspondence between 3:12 and 2:18 'militates against interpreting διὰ τῆς πίστεως αὐτοῦ as an objective genitive (i.e. faith in him) and favours a reference to Christ's own faith (e.g. ". . . in whom [i.e., Jesus Christ] we have boldness and confidence of access to God through his [i.e., Christ's] faith [in which we share] . . ."'. Note the assessment of Best, 330, who thinks, however, that we do not have enough evidence elsewhere in the letter to be certain.

115. Bruce, 322.

249

statements in the New Testament.[116] Only here are the two found together, and they are further strengthened by the phrase 'with confidence'.
Since these two nouns are governed by the one definite article 'the', they
are probably best regarded as forming one idea (a hendiadys), while the
phrase 'with confidence' qualifies the second noun and strengthens the
notion so that the whole expression signifies 'the boldness of confident
access', or 'the boldness to enter confidently'.[117] Paul has gone out of his
way to make this declaration of assurance as strong as possible for his
readers. They need to know that this privileged and certain access to the
Father is theirs.

'Boldness',[118] which signified 'freedom of speech' in classical Greek,
is occasionally used in the New Testament, including Ephesians, to denote the fearless and open proclamation of the gospel (6:19; cf. v. 20; Acts
4:31). Here the context denotes a freedom of another kind, namely, that of
joyful confidence to enter the presence of God, based on Christ's saving
work. It has to do with the fearless and unrestricted way in which Christians are to draw near to the throne of grace (Heb. 4:16) and by which
they enter the heavenly sanctuary through the blood of Jesus (Heb.
10:19). (On the Old Testament background and the meaning of 'access'
see 2:18.) The additional phrase 'with confidence'[119] focusses on the assurance and certainty with which believers may enter God's presence. A
similar attitude comes to expression almost immediately as Paul bows
his knees to the Father in the prayer of vv. 14-19.

13 The final words of the paragraph are an entreaty to the readers
not to become discouraged because of Paul's sufferings. The inferential
particle *therefore*[120] draws out the implications of the great truths he has
set before them (vv. 2-12). Paul has written about the eternal purposes of
God, the place of his Gentile readers within the divine plan, as well as his
own role in relation to it. God had appointed him to enlighten them
about the mystery, and as a result he undergoes suffering for them. In

---

116. Rom. 5:2; Eph. 2:18; Heb. 3:6; 4:16; 10:19, 35; 1 John 2:28; 3:21; 4:17; 5:14.

117. The Greek expression is προσαγωγὴν ἐν πεποιθήσει. D. B. Wallace, *Greek Grammar*, 286, suggests that in the very close relationship between 'boldness' and 'access', one
refers to 'the internal attitude which corresponds to the external reality'.

118. Gk. παρρησία. See Louw and Nida §25.158; W. C. van Unnik, 'The Christian's
Freedom of Speech in the New Testament', and 'The Semitic Background of ΠΑΡΡΗΣΙΑ
in the New Testament', in *Sparsa Collecta*, pt. 2 (Leiden: Brill, 1980), 269-89, 290-306; S. B.
Marrow, '*Parrhēsia* in the New Testament', *CBQ* 44 (1982), 431-46; and D. E. Fredrickson,
'Παρρησία in the Pauline Epistles', in *Friendship, Flattery, and Frankness of Speech: Studies on
Friendship in the New Testament World*, ed. J. T. Fitzgerald (Brill: Leiden, 1996), 163-83.

119. πεποίθησις ('trust, confidence') is a Pauline word in the New Testament (2 Cor.
1:15; 3:4; 8:22; 10:2; Phil. 3:4). Cf. BAGD, 643.

120. Gk. διό.

view of so momentous a task given to him in his calling, they are entreated[121] not to become disheartened[122] at his sufferings, which he undergoes on their behalf.

Elsewhere Paul refers to his sufferings as integral to his apostolic ministry,[123] and as such they were tied in with the clear proclamation of the gospel.[124] For him the conjunction of affliction with this ministry of the gospel was no new thing; he had been forewarned by Christ at the very beginning when he was called to preach him among the Gentiles (cf. Acts 9:16). Here at v. 13 the mention of Paul's afflictions recalls the opening words of the chapter, 'the prisoner of Christ Jesus' (v. 1). His arrest and subsequent imprisonment appeared to be a real setback to the cause of the gospel and Gentile equality with Jewish believers in the one new people of God. It was understandable that his readers should be dismayed at his being deprived of his freedom to move around for the advance of the gospel and the strengthening of the churches.

The response is clear and positive: using the key term 'affliction,'[125] which has already been employed in Colossians 1:24 for a somewhat different purpose,[126] Paul speaks of his sufferings as being *for you* and *which are your glory*.[127] Although this enigmatic final clause has been taken to mean 'for your honour or prestige' and 'for your benefit', it is better to understand it in the usual sense of glory. Earlier references to the term in the letter denote God's glory (1:6, 12, 14, 17); but this is a glory in which believers participate, both now (see on 1:18) and fully on the last day (2:7; cf. Col. 1:27; 3:4; 2 Thess. 2:14). Paul elsewhere makes clear the organic relationship between suffering and glory (2 Cor. 4:17; Rom. 8:17, 18). Here, too, in Ephesians suffering is the prelude to glory, except that in this case the suffering is Paul's while the glory will be his readers'. On another oc-

---

121. Paul is making a request of his readers, not praying to God. His intercession to God on their behalf does not commence until v. 14.

122. The verb rendered *discouraged* (ἐγκακέω) appears elsewhere in Paul's letters signifying either to lose heart (2 Cor. 4:1, 16) or to grow weary (Gal. 6:9; 2 Thess. 3:13; cf. NRSV). Here the apostle is not asking God to keep him constant. This interpretation is out of character with the confident tone of the passage, not least of all v. 12. Rather, it is the readers who are entreated not to become disheartened.

123. 1 Cor. 4:9-13; 2 Cor. 11:23-33; 12:9, 10; 13:4; and Gal. 6:17.

124. 2 Cor. 4:4-6 with vv. 7-18; 5:18-21 with 6:1-11; cf. 1 Thess. 1:5, 6; 3:3, 4 and Acts 14:22.

125. Gk. θλῖψις.

126. The text in Colossians emphasizes in particular that Paul completes in his flesh 'what is lacking in Christ's afflictions for the sake of his body, the church', whereas Eph. 3:3 makes the statement that the apostle's sufferings are for the readers' glory.

127. The clause, which is explanatory, is intended to motivate the readers to fulfil Paul's entreaty; cf. Meyer, 173.

casion, the apostle can speak of his suffering leading to salvation (2 Cor. 1:6) and life (2 Cor. 4:12) for others; the sense is much the same in this context. Accordingly the apostle's words are similar to Colossians 1:24 after all, where he views himself as contributing to the completion of the messianic woes prior to the consummation in glory.[128] A clear expression of this notion in relation to Paul's ministry appears in 2 Timothy 2:10: 'Therefore I endure everything for the sake of the elect, that they too may obtain the salvation that is in Christ Jesus, with eternal glory'.

The mention of the apostle's afflictions has recalled the opening words of the chapter, 'the prisoner of Christ Jesus', and has prepared the way for his petitionary activity of v. 14. The one who kneels before the Father and offers the following intercession is the same person who has been appointed to declare the mystery to them and who, as a result, undergoes affliction on their behalf. Paul is a prisoner who serves Christ, and what he does is for the benefit of them as Gentiles; indeed, it is for their final glory.

F. Paul's Intercession for Power, Love, and Spiritual Maturity, 3:14-21

> [14]For this reason I kneel before the Father, [15]from whom his whole family in heaven and on earth derives its name. [16]I pray that out of his glorious riches he may strengthen you with power through his Spirit in your inner being, [17]so that Christ may dwell in your hearts through faith. And I pray that you, being rooted and established in love, [18]may have power, together with all the saints, to grasp how wide and long and high and deep is the love of Christ, [19]and to know this love that surpasses knowledge — that you may be filled to the measure of all the fullness of God. [20]Now to him who is able to do immeasurably more than all we ask or imagine, according to his power that is at work within us, [21]to him be glory in the church and in Christ Jesus throughout all generations, for ever and ever! Amen.

The opening words of v. 14, *For this reason,* take up the same expression at v. 1, where Paul was about to lay his concerns for his Gentile readers before God in prayer. However, he broke off almost immediately in order to give an account of his ministry to them and their distinctive place within the mystery of God that had been revealed to him. Now he

128. Note C. C. Caragounis, *Mysterion,* 112, *'will lead to your being glorified';* cf. Schnackenburg, 142; and Lincoln, 191, 192. On the messianic woes in relation to Col. 1:24, see P. T. O'Brien, *Colossians, Philemon,* 75-81.

completes the sentence of v. 1 and reports the content of his intercession for them (vv. 14-19), which has been enriched by all that has been said in the so-called digression of 3:2-13. What Paul does here, namely, intercede for his readers, naturally flows out of his ministry — indeed, it is part of what it means to serve them as Gentiles. Here is a servant of the gospel whose ministry involves a profound commitment to intercession for the ultimate maturity of his readers.

Paul's prayer report of vv. 14-19, which picks up and repeats some of the main themes of 1:15-19, is one long sentence in the original Greek. The opening verses (vv. 14, 15) introduce the prayer and address God as 'Father': he is the one 'from whom every family in heaven and on earth derives its name'. Vv. 16-19 spell out the content of the apostle's intercession.[129] It contains two central petitions (vv. 16-17a, 17b-19a) together with a climactic summarizing request that the readers might be filled with all the fulness of God (v. 19b). The first petition (vv. 16-17a) is for inner strengthening through God's Spirit. This request consists of two parallel infinitival clauses in which the second elaborates or explains the meaning of the first: to be strengthened by the Spirit in the inner being (v. 16b) corresponds to Christ's dwelling in their hearts by faith (v. 17a). The second petition (vv. 17b-19a), which builds upon the first, is essentially a prayer for knowledge of (1) the four dimensions (v. 18b), and (2) the love of Christ (v. 19a). Finally, v. 19b concludes Paul's intercessory prayer: it has been viewed as the third and climactic request, or the summarizing request in which the contents of the two preceding petitions are realized. The apostle desires that they might 'be filled up to all the fulness of God'.

The passage concludes with a single-sentence doxology (vv. 20-21) in which God, in the light of the far-reaching prayer that has been offered (vv. 14-19), is praised as the one 'who can do far more abundantly than all we ask or think'. Glory is ascribed to God in the church and in Christ Jesus for all generations. Doxologies such as this are short, spontaneous ascriptions of praise to God which frequently appear as concluding formulas to prayers, hymnic expressions, and sections of Paul's letters.[130] Their basic structure is threefold: first, the person to whom praise is ascribed is mentioned (e.g., 'to him who is able to do immeasurably more . . .', 3:20). Then follows the word of praise, usually 'glory' (v. 21, or an equivalent), and, finally, the doxology concludes with a temporal description, nor-

---

129. Note the recent detailed analysis of both the intercession (3:14-19) and concluding doxology (vv. 20-21) by Arnold, 85-102.

130. Note the important study of R. Deichgräber, *Gotteshymnus und Christushymnus in der frühen Christenheit* (Göttingen: Vandenhoeck und Ruprecht, 1967), 25-40. Cf. P. T. O'Brien, *DPL*, 69.

mally an eternity formula ('for ever and ever', v. 21). In most cases the doxology is followed by 'Amen'. This doxology forms a fitting conclusion to the petitionary prayer of vv. 14-19 on the one hand, and also to the entire first half of the letter (see the exegesis below).

Both the intercessory prayer and the doxology hark back to earlier themes of the letter. In particular, they contain a number of parallels to the praise and prayer of chapter 1. In a sense, 3:14-21 could be considered a further application of the ideas developed in the earlier prayer:[131] petition is offered to the Father (1:17; 3:14-15); it is for the Spirit (1:17; 3:16); there is a concern for knowledge and fulness (1:18-19; 3:18-19); a linking of knowledge and power (1:19; 3:19); and, finally, praise and glory are offered to God (cf. 1:6, 12, 14; 3:21). At the same time, Paul's intercession and doxology provide a transition from the 'theology' of chapters 1–3 to the 'paraenesis' that follows in chapters 4–6.[132]

1. Prayer for Power, Love, and Maturity, 3:14-19

14 With the opening words *For this reason* Paul takes up and completes the sentence he began in v. 1, and leads into his petitionary prayer as the expression of his earnest concerns for his readers. This intercession for them has been enriched by the 'digression' of vv. 2-13 with its reminders of their place in God's people and the church's role in God's cosmic plan. At the same time, his petitionary prayer is a vital part of his ministry to those for whom his apostolic responsibility has just been so eloquently recounted. *For this reason* points back particularly to the concluding words of chapter 2, where his readers have become part of the new temple in which God dwells by his Spirit (vv. 19-22), but also to 2:1-10, where God's gracious saving work for them was recounted. In his sovereign grace God brought lost Gentiles and Jews into one new humanity, a new community, and he has accomplished this through his Son's reconciling work on the cross. Yet Ephesians 2 is closely linked with the prayer and thanksgiving of 1:15-23, so that this petition in some sense takes up 'the burden of the first prayer by developing and supplementing it'.[133] Accordingly, this intercessory prayer is ultimately grounded in God's declared purpose of creating a new humanity in Christ, which is an essential element in his sovereign design of summing up all things in his Son (1:10).

---

131. So Patzia, 220.

132. Cf. Best, 335.

133. So Arnold, 86. More doubtfully, Bruce, 309, 324, thinks that the prayer of 1:15-19 is 'resumed' at 3:1, 14-19.

The solemn introduction of vv. 14 and 15 gives great weight to the prayer. Two elements make this introduction unusual: first, the reference to bowing the knee, and, secondly, the turning to one who is humbly addressed as *Father* and then identified as the one 'from whom every family in heaven and earth derives its name' (v. 15). The more usual posture in Jewish and early Christian prayer was standing (Mark 11:25; Luke 18:11), although kneeling was not uncommon (1 Kings 8:24; Ezra 9:5; Luke 22:41; Acts 21:5). The latter signified great reverence and submission, especially marking the humble approach of the worshipper who felt his need so keenly that he could not stand upright before God (cf. Ezra 9:5, 15). Here Paul's language suggests that he may be echoing the words of Isaiah 45:23 (cf. Rom. 14:11; Phil. 2:10), where the bowing of the knee was a sign of homage to the universal King. With an acute sense of need and head bowed down to the ground he brings his earnest request to this powerful King. The one to whom he bows in homage is called *Father*,[134] which in the ancient world was not only a term of intimacy but also one that had overtones of dignity and authority. A father not only sought the good of his family but also ruled the clan or family unit.[135] The God whom the apostle approaches in prayer is a powerful and loving heavenly Father. Paul has already asserted that through Christ believers have access 'in one Spirit to the *Father*' (2:18; cf. 3:12); here he boldly and confidently avails himself of this access to make intercession for his readers in their need. Because the Father will surely respond to the petition of even his lowliest servant, as Paul himself was (v. 8), his prayer may confidently be addressed to him.

15 God's universal power over all is enhanced in the address, the Father 'from whom every family in heaven and on earth derives its name'. The word rendered *family* is a play on the preceding 'father'[136] and stands for any group derived from a single ancestor. It was used in the LXX of a family, clan, tribe, or even a nation. Here it is best taken as referring to every family or family grouping.[137] Some interpreters, as well as the NIV with its rendering *from whom his whole family in heaven and on earth derives its name,* make this a reference to the *one* family, that is, the

---

134. Note the other references in Ephesians to 'Father' at 1:2, 3, 17; 2:18; 4:6; 5:20; 6:23.

135. 'When Jews spoke of God as Father, they meant he ruled the world which owed him its obedience' (Turner, 1235).

136. πατριά is a play on πατήρ.

137. Cf. BAGD, 636. The only other New Testament references are in Luke's writings (Luke 2:4; Acts 3:25). Although some have interpreted v. 15 to mean that God is the archetypal father and that all other fatherhood in the universe is derived from his, this is based on a false rendering of πατριά as 'fatherhood'.

church or the people of God, which includes past saints (note the words *in heaven*).[138] But this would require the definite article in the Greek, which is missing. Instead, 'every family' is preferred to 'the whole family'. Every family *in heaven* points to family groupings and classes of angels (see on 1:21),[139] good and rebellious alike, which owe their origin to God, while every family *on earth* speaks of family groupings and so of the basic structures of human relationships which owe their existence to him.

In ancient thought a 'name' was not just a means of distinguishing one person from another; it was particularly the means of revealing the inner being, the true nature of that person (cf. Gen. 25:26; 1 Sam. 25:25). So for God to give creatures a name was not simply to provide them with a label, but signifies his bringing them into existence, exercising dominion over them (cf. Ps. 147:4; Isa. 40:26), and giving each their appropriate role. The verse thus affirms that the Father is the Creator of all living beings (cf. Eph. 3:9; 1 Cor. 8:6; Col. 1:15-18), so that their existence and significance depend on him. His greatness and thus his sovereign power and authority in both heaven and earth are stressed. The readers, then, who fear the threat of hostile powers, would be further reassured that God is indeed able to fulfil the petitions addressed by the apostle on their behalf.[140]

16 At the heart of Paul's first petition (vv. 16-17a) for his readers is a request for power.[141] He has already prayed that they might *know* God's incomparably great might for them as believers (1:18-19a). Now he asks for divine power more directly — that God may *strengthen* them inwardly through his Spirit.[142] If the apostle had urged his Christian readers not to be *discouraged* on account of his sufferings (3:13), then his prayer for them to be strengthened by God's power was in order to meet this need.

The resources available to fulfil this confident request are limitless: they are (lit.) 'according to the riches of his glory', an expression similar to one used in the earlier prayer of 1:18, where the readers, who are God's own inheritance, share in 'the riches of his glory'. That glory is God's ra-

---

138. Caird, 69, understands every family on earth to speak of believing Jews and Gentiles, with every family in heaven as the powers who have been reconciled, while Mitton, 131-32, also limits the description to the sphere of redemption.

139. The rabbis later spoke of 'the family above' when referring to the angels (cf. *b. Sanhedrin* 98b).

140. Arnold, 96.

141. The ἵνα ('that')-clauses in vv. 16 and 18 indicate the content of Paul's prayer, while the ἵνα ('that')-clause of v. 19 is a summarizing request (see below). Cf. Arnold, 86.

142. Literally the petition reads: 'that he may give to you . . . to be strengthened with power' (ἵνα δῷ ὑμῖν . . . δυνάμει κραταιωθῆναι).

diance or splendour, which conveys the ideas of the perfection of his character and activity. His glory is often conjoined with power (Rom. 6:4; Col. 1:11) and parallelled with his goodness (cf. Exod. 33:22 with v. 19). Here this preposition, which Paul often uses in petitions and thanks-givings (Eph. 1:19; Phil. 4:19),[143] draws attention not simply to the idea of source, thereby signifying 'out of the wealth of his glory', but also indicates that his giving corresponds to the inexhaustible riches of that glory. It is on a scale commensurate with his glory: he gives *as lavishly as only he can*. It is not surprising, therefore, that the apostle frequently speaks of 'fulness', 'riches', and 'abundance' in his prayers (Rom. 15:13; 1 Cor. 1:4-5; 2 Thess. 1:11; note also Jas. 1:5). The one to whom he directed his requests gives richly and generously: 'And my God will fully meet every need of yours *in accordance with his riches in glory* in Christ Jesus' (Phil. 4:19). By formulating his prayer along these lines, the apostle assured his readers that the Father was wholly able to meet their needs.

This prayer, like the counterpart of 1:15-23, is loaded with terms for power (vv. 16, 18). God's mighty activity is stressed, first, by means of the relatively rare Greek word rendered 'strengthen',[144] and then by the addition of the words 'with power' (a Semitic manner of expression; cf. 2 Kings 22:33),[145] as Paul petitions God for their inner strengthening. This divine empowering will be effected through God's Spirit,[146] the same Spirit who, according to Paul's prayer of 1:17, imparts wisdom and revelation so that the readers may know God better. The agency of the Spirit in dispensing divine power is in line with other New Testament teaching where the Spirit and power are intimately linked (Acts 1:8; Rom. 1:4; 15:19; 1 Cor. 2:4; 1 Thess. 1:5).

The sphere[147] in which the strengthening is to take place is 'the in-

---

143. κατά ('according to') with the accusative is found in both Old Testament and Pauline prayers, where it points to God's power, grace, or glory as the source of blessing to the recipient (see on 1:19). Note the Psalter (51:1; 109:26; cf. 36:7), which, according to G. Harder, *Paulus und das Gebet* (Gütersloh: Bertelsmann, 1936), 45, seems to have influenced later Jewish prayers, e.g., Prayer of Manasseh 14; Dan. 3:42 (cf. also Phil. 4:19).

144. κραταιόω means 'to become strong, to become powerful' (Louw and Nida §76.10). The passive voice here draws attention to God's activity (as it does at 1 Cor. 16:13; cf. Luke 1:80; 2:40). The verb occurs only on these four occasions in the New Testament. Note Arnold, 87-88.

145. Note the similar expressions in the Qumran writings: 1QH 7:17, 19; 12:35; 1QM 10:5. See Lincoln, 205, who follows K. G. Kuhn.

146. This is rather different from the interpretation of G. D. Fee, *God's Empowering Presence*, 695, who speaks of the Spirit as the 'source' of that empowering.

147. On this view the preposition εἰς in the phrase εἰς τὸν ἔσω ἄνθρωπον is rendered by '*in* the inner person', and thus equivalent to ἐν (cf. BDF §205). Most commentators regard the phrase as denoting the sphere in which the divine strengthening will occur.

ner person', a uniquely Pauline phrase in the New Testament (cf. Rom. 7:22; 2 Cor. 4:16). Some have understood this expression to denote 'the new creation inwardly begotten by the Spirit in those who are united by faith to Christ' (cf. Col. 3:10; Eph. 4:24).[148] However, it is better to understand the inner person as 'the interior of our being . . . the seat of personal consciousness, . . . [and] of our moral being'.[149] It is the focal point at the centre of a person's life where the Spirit does his strengthening and renewing work. Indeed, the inner self stands in need of empowering given our struggle against sin (Rom. 7:22) and the need for daily renewal (2 Cor. 4:6). When the 'outer person' of the believer is wasting away, the 'inner person' is being renewed day by day (2 Cor. 4:16). In the context of both 2 Corinthians 4 (v. 6; 5:12) and the following verse here (v. 17) *heart* is parallel to the 'inner person'.[150]

17a The prayer that the readers may be strengthened inwardly through God's Spirit is explained and amplified by the following clause: 'that Christ might dwell in your hearts through faith'.[151] Several EVV render these words as the purpose (or result) of the preceding (cf. the NIV's *so that*), and give the impression that Paul wants the readers first to be empowered by the Spirit so that subsequently Christ may dwell in their hearts.[152] Although this interpretation is syntactically possible, it is unlikely. The language of the two clauses is parallel, and the experience of the Spirit's strengthening activity is the same as that of Christ's indwelling (cf. 1 Cor. 15:45; 2 Cor. 3:17; Rom. 8:9, 10; Gal. 4:6). *In your hearts* is equivalent to 'in the inner person' of v. 16, while Christ's indwelling defines more precisely the strengthening role of the Spirit in v. 16. His indwelling is not something additional to the strengthening. To be empowered by the Spirit in the inner person means that Christ himself dwells in their hearts.

At first sight it seems strange for Paul to pray that Christ may dwell in the hearts of believers. Did he not already live within them? In answer, it is noted that the focus of this request is not on the initial indwelling of Christ

148. Bruce, 326.

149. G. D. Fee, *God's Empowering Presence*, 695-96.

150. Contrast Eph. 5:19, where 'heart(s)' refers to the whole person (see below).

151. This second infinitival clause, introduced by κατοικῆσαι ('to dwell'), is syntactically parallel to the first clause (κραταιωθῆναι κτλ., 'to be strengthened . . .', v. 16b) and dependent on the verb δῷ ('he may give'). The second clause, however, does not spell out the goal or result of the strengthening; rather, it elaborates and explains the first. So most commentators, including, most recently, Best, 341. ἐν ταῖς καρδίαις ὑμῶν ('in your hearts', v. 17a) is equivalent to εἰς τὸν ἔσω ἄνθρωπον ('in the inner person', v. 16b), while Christ's indwelling parallels the role of the Spirit in v. 16. His indwelling is not something additional to the strengthening, but is a further definition of it.

152. Hoehner views v. 17a as the 'contemplative result' of the infinitive κραται-ωθῆναι ('to be strengthened'). But against this see the preceding note.

but on his continual presence. The verb used in this prayer is a strong one, signifying a permanent indwelling rather than some temporary abode.[153] It has already occurred in Colossians in relation to the fulness of the Godhead permanently abiding in Christ (cf. Col. 1:19; 2:9),[154] while the notion of Christ being 'in you' Gentiles is a prominent thought in this parallel letter (1:27). The sphere of Christ's continuing presence is *your hearts,* which, as we have seen, is equivalent to *your inner being* (v. 16). The 'heart' here, as elsewhere in Ephesians,[155] is employed in its customary Old Testament sense of the centre of one's personality, the thoughts, will, emotions, and whatever else lies at the centre of our being. If Christ has taken up residence in our hearts, he is at the centre of our lives and exercises his rule over all that we are and do.[156] This indwelling is *through faith* — that is, as they trust[157] him he makes their hearts his home. The implication of the apostle's prayer, then, is that the more the Spirit empowers their lives the greater will be their transformation into the likeness of Christ, a point that will be developed throughout the second half of the letter.

17b-18 The function of the following participial clause *you, being rooted and established in love* within Paul's intercession (3:14-19) is not entirely clear. It has been regarded as (1) a subsidiary request flowing from the previous petition for the indwelling of Christ (and the empowering of the Spirit). Within the New Testament participles can express wishes (or exhortations),[158] and in the context of this prayer (3:14-19) 'being rooted' and 'established' are thought to have the force of a prayer-wish.[159] (2) A variation on this is to regard these two coordinated participles, which break the pattern of a finite verb followed by two infinitives (vv. 16-17a, 18-19), as a prayer-wish which spells out the aim of the indwelling/ strengthening. As a result, one of the goals of Christ's indwelling is to establish believers on a firm foundation of love.[160] (3) Our preference is to

---

153. κατοικέω signifies to 'settle down' and is different from παροικέω, to 'sojourn'.

154. Paul usually speaks of the Spirit's indwelling (οἰκέω) believers (Rom. 8:9, 11) or the congregation (1 Cor. 3:16). Earlier in Eph. 2:22 the cognate κατοικητήριον ('dwelling place') refers to the church as God's dwelling place in the Spirit.

155. Chaps. 1:18; 4:18; 5:19; 6:5, 22.

156. So L. Morris, *Expository Thoughts on the Letter to the Ephesians* (Grand Rapids: Baker, 1994), 104.

157. Here faith refers to the human response, rather than to Christ's faith(fulness). Note the discussion at 2:5, 8; 3:12.

158. BDF §468(2).

159. So, e.g., Gnilka, Schnackenburg, Bratcher and Nida, and Lincoln.

160. Cf. Arnold, 98, who acknowledges that the participles ἐρριζωμένοι καὶ τεθε-μελιωμένοι ('rooted and grounded') are syntactically irregular because they are in the nominative case. He thinks that they are best understood in an optative sense as a prayer-wish, rather than as participial imperatives.

interpret the words *you, being rooted and established in love* as expressing the contemplated result of the two previous infinitives, which in turn provides the condition for the next request. Through the strengthening of the inner person by God's Spirit and Christ's indwelling in their hearts, the readers are to be established in love so that they will comprehend the greatness of the love of Christ.[161]

In order to stress the foundational nature of the love that is envisaged, two metaphors, one botanical and the other architectural (which had been tied in closely with 'the faith' at Col. 1:23; 2:7),[162] are closely linked: *rooted and established in love*. The word order of the original[163] stresses love, while the two perfect passive participles depict the notions of progress and the resulting state.[164] Love is the soil in which believers are rooted and will grow, the foundation upon which they are built.[165] Here the *agapē* in view is the love of God revealed in Christ and poured into his people's hearts by the Spirit (cf. Rom. 5:5, 8; 8:35-39). Already in Ephesians God's love has been shown to be the source of our salvation (2:4; cf. 5:2, 25), while later in this prayer Christ's love is specifically mentioned (v. 19). God's love in Christ provides the motivating power that enables believers to love others, and this prayer significantly anticipates the exhortations of the following chapters (cf. 4:2; 5:2). Those who are strengthened by the Spirit and in whom Christ dwells will have their lives rooted and grounded in love.

The second petition (vv. 18b-19a) of the apostle's intercessory prayer is essentially a request for knowledge of (1) the four dimensions ('the breadth and length and depth and height') which have no explicit object (v. 18b), and (2) the love of Christ (v. 19a).[166] This second request presupposes and builds upon the first: Paul desires that, as his readers are strengthened by God's Spirit and indwelt by Christ so that they are rooted and grounded in love, 'they might be empowered to grasp with all the saints what is the breadth and length and depth and height, and to know the love of Christ which surpasses knowledge'.

It is obvious that only God himself can impart this knowledge to Paul's readers: not only is he the one whom the apostle petitions, but also

---

161. Note Meyer, 180-81; and C. C. Caragounis, *Mysterion*, 75; cf. RSV, JB. On this view, ἐν ἀγάπῃ ἐρριζωμένοι καὶ τεθεμελιωμένοι ('rooted and grounded in love') is prefixed to the ἵνα-clause of v. 18, rather than linked with the preceding.

162. On the use of ῥιζόω ('cause to take root') and θεμελιόω ('establish') see P. T. O'Brien, *Colossians, Philemon*, 107, 69-70.

163. With ἐν ἀγάπῃ ('in love') appearing first.

164. S. E. Porter, *Verbal Aspect*, 394.

165. Stott, 135; and Lincoln, 207. (Cf. REB: 'With deep roots and firm foundations'.)

166. Arnold, 89.

the preface to the request ('that you may have power to grasp') implies that divine enabling is essential.[167] The word used is a hapax legomenon that belongs to the vocabulary of power which 'carries the nuance of the ability to attain an objective',[168] while that of knowing, according to Arnold, has been 'employed to emphasize the difficulty of comprehending the vastness and magnitude of the intended object'.[169]

Paul asks first that his readers might comprehend *with all the saints* what is 'the breadth, length, height, and depth' (v. 18b). This request is made without any mention of an object of these four dimensions. Does this formula stand for the dimensions of the cosmos? Or the inexhaustible greatness of some object? And what is the relationship of this formula to the second element of the petition, namely, that the readers might 'know the love of Christ'? The following are the most important scholarly suggestions regarding the background and meaning of this puzzling expression:[170]

(1) *The mighty power of God.* It has long been recognized that the four dimensions (breadth, length, height, and depth) feature frequently in the magical texts and were put to use as spells in relation to light and brightness. Recently, Arnold has argued at length for the relevance of magical practices as a background to the major issues of Ephesians and claimed that the four dimensions are spiritual hypostases or expressions for power. They would convey to the readers 'some notion of the power of God'. Within the prayer of 3:14-19 they function 'as a dynamic, rhetorical expression for the vastness of the power of God'.[171] The absolute use of the terms in a succession such as this does not require an expressed object. Accordingly, the petition of vv. 18-19 is for a knowledge, first, of 'the incredible vastness of the power of God' and, secondly, of 'the love of Christ which surpasses knowledge'. This interpretation, it is claimed, provides a parallel structure to the first two petitions of 3:14-19 (power is coordinated with love in each), and is consistent with the prayer of 1:15-23. Leaving aside the issue of Arnold's overall thesis, which has much to

167. Cf. Arnold, 89-90.

168. Best, 343. ἐξισχύω means to 'be able, be strong enough, be in a position'; so BAGD, 276; Louw and Nida §74.10. The verb appears elsewhere in the Greek Bible only at Ecclesiasticus 7:6.

169. Arnold, 90. καταλαμβάνω (in the middle voice) means to 'grasp, find, understand' at Acts 4:13; 10:34; 25:25; and Eph. 3:18; so BAGD, 413; Louw and Nida §32.18. This verb was employed to describe 'a fight against a strong opponent or sacking an acropolis', where 'strength [was] required to accomplish both tasks' (Arnold, 90; cf. Judg. 9:45; 2 Kings 12:26; and note the close parallel to our expression found in the Greek magical papyri: *PGM* XIII.226).

170. Note the careful evaluation by Lincoln, 208-13, to which I am indebted.

171. Arnold, 90, 95; note his detailed arguments, 93-96.

commend it, two specific difficulties have been raised in relation to the four dimensions being interpreted of the vastness of God's power. First, many of the magical texts (*PGM* IV.960-85) to which he makes reference come from the fourth century A.D. Secondly, if the readers were familiar with these magical traditions so that there was no need to mention a qualifying object, why did not the apostle make it clear that the four dimensions referred to God's power rather than these spiritual hypostases? The original connotations have changed.

(2) *The mystery of salvation.* The language of the four dimensions has been understood as a rhetorical formulation taken over from the Old Testament (and from Stoicism, some claim) which has to do with Christ and the salvation that is found in him. Several writers, such as Schnackenburg, tie this in with the mystery of Ephesians 1 and 3, and interpret the four-dimensional reference of v. 18 in terms of God's great plan of salvation.[172] While it is true that throughout Ephesians Paul has sought to engender in his readers an appreciation of the greatness of the salvation won for them in Christ (note the eulogy of 1:3-14, as well as 2:1-10, 11-22) and a knowledge of the mystery has been mentioned in 3:9, it is difficult to explain Paul's use of width, length, height, and depth here and why he did not make the reference explicit with an additional 'of the mystery' or 'of salvation'.

(3) *The manifold wisdom of God.* The infinite scope of divine wisdom, which is equated with 'the deep things of God', is emphasized in Job 11:8-9, where the four dimensions are actually mentioned:

> '[The mysteries of God] are *higher* than the heavens — what can you
>   do?
> They are *deeper* than the depths of the grave — what can you know?
> Their measure is *longer* than the earth,
>   and *wider* than the sea'. Cf. Sirach 1:3; Job 28:12-14, 21-22.

The purpose of these passages was to focus on the infinite dimensions of divine wisdom, not on the magnitude of the universe. In Ephesians, it is claimed, Paul has in view not the actual dimensions of the cosmos but the metaphorical dimensions of the infinite wisdom of God, which earlier in the chapter he called *manifold* (v. 10). The parallel passage in Colossians, with its reference to Christ 'in whom are hid all the treasures of wisdom and knowledge' (2:2, 3), is adduced in support of the fourfold dimension referring to the infinite wisdom of God, while Romans 11:33-34, which speaks of the incomprehensibility of divine wis-

---

172. Schnackenburg, 151-52; note, with some variations, J. A. Robinson, F. Mussner, E. Percy, and J. Ernst.

dom and uses the dimensional term 'depth', leads on to a doxology, as here in Ephesians.[173] If Paul does understand the wisdom of God as the unexpressed object of the four dimensions, 'width, length, height, and depth', then that infinite wisdom finds its focus in the love of Christ of v. 19a.[174] One difficulty in linking the four dimensions with the wisdom of God is the lack of any direct reference.

(4) *The matchless love of Christ.* The most popular view among commentators has been to understand the object of the four dimensions as the love of Christ, which is explicitly mentioned in the following clause, v. 19a. These dimensions, 'width, length, height, and depth', are regarded as a unity, since they are governed by the one definite article. They are 'a totality which evokes the immensity of a particular object'.[175] On this view, the object of the dimensions is made explicit in the following parallel clause, thereby providing a climactic effect. The conjunction in v. 19a provides a close connection between the two clauses, while the mention of that love as 'surpassing knowledge' functions as an equivalent of the four dimensions which draws attention to its magnitude. Already at Romans 8:35-39 Paul has mentioned two of these dimensions ('height' and 'depth') in close association with the love of Christ. Accordingly, the movement in Paul's prayer is from the idea of being rooted and grounded in love (v. 17b) to the readers' being empowered to grasp the vast dimensions of that love.

Although it is not possible to be certain, on contextual grounds a reference to the love of Christ is preferable.[176] If this is correct, then it is understandable that grasping Christ's all-encompassing love is something shared with other believers, hence the phrase *with all the saints*, which is a reference to Christians (cf. 1:1, 15; 3:8; 6:18), not angels. The knowledge for which the apostle prays is not some esoteric understand-

---

173. Note A. Feuillet, M. Barth, and F. F. Bruce.

174. Cf. Turner, 1236. Even N. A. Dahl, 'Cosmic Dimensions and Religious Knowledge', in *Jesus und Paulus: Festschrift für Werner Georg Kümmel zum 70. Geburtstag*, ed. E. E. Ellis and E. Grässer (Göttingen: Vandenhoeck & Ruprecht, 1975), 57-75, esp. 74-75, who thinks that the four dimensions should retain their cosmic connotations, argues that the expression must be understood as a rhetorical preamble to v. 19: the one thing that matters is to know the vastness of Christ's love.

175. Lincoln, 212. Others who adopt this view include J. Calvin, H. A. W. Meyer, T. K. Abbott, G. B. Caird, C. L. Mitton, A. van Roon, C. C. Caragounis, R. G. Bratcher and E. A. Nida, and Best, in addition to Lincoln himself.

176. This brief survey has not presented all the major contenders in the history of interpretation. Others regard the object of the four dimensions to be the heavenly inheritance (conceived of in terms of a cube, like the heavenly Jerusalem in Rev. 21:16), the cross of Christ embracing the world in all its dimensions, or simply the cosmos. See further Barth, 395-97; and Lincoln, 208-13.

ing for individual initiates but a true insight given by God for the benefit of all believers.

19 As suggested above, the first clause, 'and to know the love of Christ which surpasses knowledge', parallels and advances upon the preceding words of v. 18, 'that you may grasp . . . what is the width, length, height, and depth'. Paul wants the readers to be empowered so as to know the love of Christ which surpasses knowledge. This petition is remarkable, for although the apostle has said much in chapters 1–3 about his readers being in Christ, he assumes that they do not adequately appreciate Christ's love. Also, God's almighty power is needed to grasp its dimensions; hence he prays for *power* to enable them to understand how immense it is.[177] This is not a petition that they may love Christ more, however important this might be; rather, that they might understand Christ's love for them.[178] Further, their grasping this cannot be simply a mental exercise. Clearly, it is personal knowledge, and, although it undoubtedly includes insight into the significance of God's love in the plan of redemption, it cannot be reduced simply to intellectual reflection. Paul wants them to be empowered so as to grasp the dimensions of that love in their own experience.

Paradoxically, the request is that they may know the love of Christ that *surpasses knowledge*. The earlier expression, 'what is the breadth and length and height and depth', focussed on the vast dimensions of Christ's love. Now, by means of a more specific equivalent, its immensity and incomprehensibility are brought to the fore. The wording of this prayer, however, does not suggest any disparagement of knowledge. After all, Paul regarded revealed knowledge as essential for the Christian life (cf. 1:9; 3:3-5, 9; 4:13; 5:17), and he prayed for it in relation to his readers, not least of all twice in this prayer (vv. 18, 19; cf. 1:17, 18). Rather, to speak of Christ's love as 'surpassing knowledge' means that it is so great that one can never know it fully. We can never plumb its depths or comprehend its magnitude. No matter how much we know of the love of Christ, how fully we enter into his love for us, there is always more to know and experience.[179] And the implication, in the light of the following words, is that we cannot be as spiritually mature as we should be unless we are empowered by God to 'grasp the limitless dimensions of the love of Christ'.[180]

---

177. Note especially the treatment of D. A. Carson, *A Call to Spiritual Reformation: Priorities from Paul and His Prayers* (Grand Rapids: Baker, 1992), 191.

178. ἡ ἀγάπη τοῦ Χριστοῦ cannot refer to the readers' love for Christ, but his love for them and others. In fact, the apostle does not specify who is loved, for his emphasis is on Christ as the loving one.

179. Morris, 107.

180. D. A. Carson, *Spiritual Reformation,* 195.

Paul's prayer to the Father reaches its climax in this final, summarizing request.[181] As believers are strengthened inwardly through God's Spirit when Christ dwells in their hearts through faith and they know in a personal way more of the immeasurable love of Christ, so they will be 'filled to the measure of all the *fulness* of God'. (A similar thought is expressed in Ephesians 4:13, where the divinely intended purpose for God's people is their attaining 'to the measure of the stature of the *fulness* of Christ'.) It is God who infills them, as the divine passive of the verb indicates, while his dynamic activity clearly has a movement towards a specific goal in view, namely, all the fulness of God. The genitive 'of God' is subjective and thus refers to God in all his perfection, including his presence, life, and power. That fulness or perfection is the standard or level to which they are to be filled[182] (hence the NIV's *to the measure of all the fullness of God*), and thus it may also imply that they are filled with this fulness.[183]

According to Ephesians 1:23, the church as Christ's body *already* shares in his fulness. Yet Paul now prays that the readers might be filled to the measure of all the plenitude of God. How are we to explain this apparent contradiction? The tension between the 'already' and the 'not yet' is part of the New Testament's, and in particular Paul's, eschatological perspective. Because of their union with the resurrected and exalted Christ in whom the fulness of deity resides, God's people, the church, possess the divine fulness. According to Colossians 1:19; 2:9 the divine fulness is perfectly found in Christ, and from him believers have already come to fulness of life (cf. 2:10). Paul's predominantly Gentile readers have already been united with Christ in his death, resurrection, and exaltation (Eph. 2:5, 6). Yet they are still to walk in newness of life, and need to attain to this fulness (4:13; cf. 5:18). They are to become what they already are. Divine enabling is essential for them (3:19) in the midst of the tension as they live between the two ages,[184] and being filled by the Spirit is an important means in the process (5:18). When the apostle desires that his readers may be strengthened through the Spirit and experience the ef-

181. Note Arnold, 86, 96-97; cf. Lincoln, 197, 214.

182. So, among others, Stott, 138. BAGD, 671, hold that εἰς ('to') denotes the goal.

183. D. B. Wallace, *Greek Grammar*, 375, states: 'The explicit *content* of πληρόω ['fill'] is thus God's fullness' (original emphasis).

184. Arnold, 97, rightly observes that the same eschatological tension is evident in Eph. 2:19-22, where Gentile believers, who already have a privileged position in the building where God dwells, are at the same time growing into a holy temple in the Lord (cf. P. T. O'Brien, 'Entity', 88-119). This tension between the 'already' and the 'not yet' has been removed by A. Lindemann, *Aufhebung*, who interprets the eschatology of Ephesians as fully realized.

fects of Christ's indwelling so that they may be *filled to the measure of all the fullness of God,* he is praying that they may 'be all that God wants them to be', that is, spiritually mature. Since God himself, Christ himself, is the standard, then this means being perfect as he is perfect, being holy as he is holy.[185]

Paul's prayer of Ephesians 3 plays an important role in preparing for the exhortatory material that follows. This intercession has taken up and developed a number of themes in the earlier petition of 1:17-19 (see above). There the apostle had prayed that his readers would come to know the greatness of God's power working on their behalf. Now he intercedes with the Father that they might be strengthened by his power in order to know and experience Christ's love which surpasses knowledge. By this they will come to full spiritual maturity. Paul has laid the foundation for the following paraenesis by stressing that divine empowering is necessary if they are to 'fulfill the primary ethical imperative — manifesting love according to Christ's own example' — encapsulated in the exhortation of 5:2, 'Walk in love, just as Christ loved us and gave himself for us'.[186] The first half of the letter culminates with this petition for an establishment in the love of Christ and an awareness of the magnitude of this love, so that they might become spiritually mature.

2. Doxology to God Who Can Do More Than All We Ask or Imagine, 3:20-21

20 The apostle Paul was accustomed to asking God for extravagant blessings on behalf of his Christian readers (Phil. 1:9; 4:19; Col. 1:9-14; 1 Thess. 3:12; 2 Thess. 1:3; cf. 1 Cor. 1:5). Here he has just petitioned the Father for spiritual blessings of extraordinary value, including the request that they might be filled to the measure of all the fulness of God. Armitage Robinson writes of this petition: 'No prayer that has ever been framed has uttered a bolder request'.[187] Has the apostle, then, 'gone over the top'? No, for it is impossible to ask for too much since the Father's giving exceeds their capacity for asking or even imagining.

Appropriately, the apostle concludes his lengthy petition with a

---

185. D. A. Carson, *Spiritual Reformation,* 195.

186. Arnold, 100. Chapters 4–6 contain a series of instructions to love (4:2, 15, 16; 5:2, 25, 28, 33; 6:24) which are best summed up in the words of 5:2. Note Arnold's insightful discussion (98-100) of the function of Paul's intercession (with its interweaving of the motifs of power and love) in relationship to the following paraenesis in the letter.

187. Robinson, 89, adds that the petition is 'a noble example of παρρησία, of freedom of speech, of that "boldness and access in confidence"' about which Paul has just spoken (cf. Lincoln, 215).

doxology, that is, a short, spontaneous ascription of praise to God as the one who can do *immeasurably more than all we ask or imagine*. The doxology not only follows Paul's petitionary prayer; it is also integrally connected with it: the ascription of power to God in the designation 'to him who is able', the mention of his power at work within the readers (cf. v. 16), and the fact that he can achieve more than they can ask (in prayer), all show plainly that this ascription of praise is closely linked with the preceding intercession.

The first element in New Testament doxologies, namely, the mention of the one to whom glory is given, is the most variable, and here vv. 20 and 21 are no exception. The doxology begins with an ascription of power to God. The literal rendering, 'to him who is able', obscures the link with power[188] in vv. 16 and 20. He is 'the powerful One' (cf. Rom. 16:25; Jude 24, 25), who can accomplish incredibly great deeds on behalf of his people. Perhaps Paul has in mind the Father bringing 'every spiritual blessing in the heavenly places' (1:3) to realization among his Christian readers.[189] Not even the immensity of the request in the preceding verses nor the unfettered ability of the human imagination can provide any limit to God's mighty ability to act. As the readers are drawn in to share his prayer concerns, 'all *we* ask or imagine', the apostle's language is stretched to its limits: he uses a comparison of a rare compound adverb which is best rendered by 'infinitely more than'.[190] There is no limit to what God can do.

In the earlier petition of chapter 1, God's effective power towards believers (1:19) was said to be nothing less than 'the operation of his mighty strength' exerted in the resurrection of Christ (1:20). Now that same power which raised Christ from the dead, enthroned him in the heavenlies, and then raised and enthroned us with him, is at work[191] *within us* to achieve infinitely more than we can ask or imagine. In the doxology Paul thus praises God for the bestowal of strength by his Spirit on his people, and affirms that the full realization of God's gracious purposes for them and in them becomes possible.[192]

188. δυναμένῳ (to 'be able') is cognate with δύναμις ('power').

189. As Arnold, 101, suggests.

190. Gk. ὑπερεκπερισσοῦ. BAGD, 840. It stresses to 'an extraordinary degree, involving a considerable excess over what would be expected' (Louw and Nida §78.34), and has been described as one of Paul's coined 'super-superlatives' (F. F. Bruce, *Ephesians*, 70).

191. Although the verb ἐνεργουμένην ('at work') may be a middle voice here and in Col. 1:29, it is more probably a passive, implying that God is the subject of the action. In the context of Colossians the reference is to the almighty power which God works in Paul. Here in Ephesians God is powerfully at work in believers generally. Note the discussion in P. T. O'Brien, *Colossians, Philemon,* 91, and Arnold, 101, 201.

192. Bruce, 331.

21   The second element of the New Testament doxology[193] is the ascription of 'glory' (or its equivalent — honour, greatness, or power), which properly belongs to God and is, therefore, rightly ascribed to him. In the Old Testament *doxa* was primarily the brightness or radiance of God's presence. To give God glory is not to add something to him; rather, it is an active acknowledgement or extolling of who he is or what he has already done (Ps. 29:2; 96:8). Although many New Testament doxologies contain no verb, the indicative 'is' or 'belongs' is presupposed: the doxology is an affirmation rather than a wish.[194] So, for example, in Galatians 1:5 glory *belongs* to God, for it was in accordance with his will that the 'Lord Jesus Christ . . . gave himself for our sins to set us free from the present evil age'.

Here the wording *to him be glory in the church and in Christ Jesus* is unusual, for this is the only doxology in the New Testament where the term 'church' and the phrase 'in Christ Jesus' appear (though cf. Rom. 16:25-27; Jude 24-25). But both are appropriate in the light of the immediate and wider contexts of chapters 1–3. As the community of the redeemed, both Jews and Gentiles, the church is the masterpiece of God's grace (cf. 2:7). It is the realm of his presence and authority (1:22, 23; 2:22), the instrument through which his wisdom is made known to the spiritual powers in the heavenly realm (3:10). It was earlier suggested that *ekklēsia* ('church') denoted a heavenly gathering in which believers, as members of the body of Christ, now participate (see on 3:10; cf. 2:5, 6). This assembly's consummation will take place on the final day, though its earmarks are presently expressed through local Christian congregations. In the local churches, then, which received this circular letter glory is ascribed to God. Here and now on earth that ascription by believers, who currently enjoy fellowship with Christ in the heavenlies, is only partial. In the final assembly of the redeemed, the new humanity fully composed (2:15), God will be perfectly glorified (cf. 3:13; 5:27).[195]

God's glory *in the church* cannot be separated from his glory *in Christ Jesus*. This expression of incorporation signifies that believers are able to ascribe glory to God because they are 'in Christ Jesus' (see on 1:3). Just as 'every spiritual blessing' is given to us 'in Christ' (1:3), so our acknowledging the Father's glory is wholly dependent on Christ Jesus; it is rendered by those who have been incorporated into him. He is the mediator of God's activity to us, and the mediator of our response of praise to

---

193. After ascribing power to God in v. 20, the introductory element is repeated by means of αὐτῷ ('to him').

194. Cf. BDF §128(5); and P. T. O'Brien, *DPL*, 69.

195. See now W. J. Dumbrell, *The Search for Order: Biblical Eschatology in Focus* (Grand Rapids: Baker, 1994), 266-68.

the Father.[196] Just as our thanksgiving to God can only be given in the name of the Lord Jesus (5:20), so also glory can be ascribed to God only within the realm of Christ Jesus.

This ascription of glory to God will have no end. The present as well as the coming ages, when the incomparable wealth of God's grace continues to be *expressed in his kindness to us in Christ Jesus* (2:7), provides the occasion for endless praise. The third element of Paul's doxologies is the temporal expression: *throughout all generations for ever and ever* is without parallel in the New Testament, though characteristic of the style of Ephesians.[197] Glory is due to God for generations to come and right on throughout all eternity. The more common eternity formula is 'for ever and ever' (cf. Gal. 1:5; 1 Tim. 1:17; 2 Tim. 4:18), which is an emphatic variation of the common LXX expression and means 'for all eternity' in an unlimited sense (cf. Ps. 84:5).

The spontaneous endorsement of the doxology by each congregation, as it was read in their hearing, follows in their *Amen*. Glory does indeed belong to God in the church and in Christ Jesus in history and for all eternity. 'Amen' was the response uttered on solemn occasions in the Old Testament to confirm a curse or adjuration, to accept a blessing, or to associate oneself with a doxology. Each of the doxologies which concludes the first four books of the Psalter (Ps. 41:13; 72:19; 89:52; 106:48) ends with an 'Amen', while prayers and doxologies in the New Testament are strengthened and endorsed by it (Rom. 1:25; Gal. 1:5). The 'Amen' makes it clear that the ascription of praise is not simply a matter of the lips, but is the spontaneous response of the whole congregation. Elsewhere Paul strikingly connects believers' response of 'Amen' to the faithfulness of God, who has said 'Yes' to all his promises in Christ (2 Cor. 1:20). With this loud 'Amen' the first half of the letter is concluded.

The doxology at the end of Paul's prayer concludes the first half of the letter on the same note with which it began in the introductory eulogy (1:3-14), namely, in praise of God for his mighty salvation, initiated in eternity, carried into effect in Christ, and intended to redound to the praise of God's glorious grace for all eternity. Paul wants his readers to have a theological perspective on God's mighty saving purposes. He prays that they might be empowered by Christ through his Spirit, so that

---

196. Schnackenburg, 156; and Lincoln, 217.

197. εἰς πάσας τὰς γενεὰς τοῦ αἰῶνος τῶν αἰώνων (lit. 'to all the generations of the age of the ages'). The inclusion of the term γενεά ('generation') and its combination with the singular and plural forms of αἰών ('age') are unique features. On the variable third element of the doxology see R. Deichgräber, *Gotteshymnus*, 27, 28.

they might walk in love just as Christ loved us and gave himself for us (5:2). The prayer and doxology of chapter 3 function in an important preparatory way for the subsequent admonitions to love in the second half of the letter.

Ephesians 4

III. THE NEW HUMANITY IN EARTHLY LIFE, 4:1–6:20

A. Unity, Diversity, and Maturity within the Body of Christ, 4:1-16

¹As a prisoner for the Lord, then, I urge you to live a life worthy of the calling you have received. ²Be completely humble and gentle; be patient, bearing with one another in love. ³Make every effort to keep the unity of the Spirit through the bond of peace. ⁴There is one body and one Spirit — just as you were called to one hope when you were called — ⁵one Lord, one faith, one baptism; ⁶one God and Father of all, who is over all and through all and in all. ⁷But to each one of us grace has been given as Christ apportioned it. ⁸This is why it says: "When he ascended on high, he led captives in his train and gave gifts to men." ⁹(What does "he ascended" mean except that he also descended to the lower, earthly regions? ¹⁰He who descended is the very one who ascended higher than all the heavens, in order to fill the whole universe.) ¹¹It was he who gave some to be apostles, some to be prophets, some to be evangelists, and some to be pastors and teachers, ¹²to prepare God's people for works of service, so that the body of Christ may be built up ¹³until we all reach unity in the faith and in the knowledge of the Son of God and become mature, attaining to the whole measure of the fullness of Christ. ¹⁴Then we will no longer be infants, tossed back and forth by the waves, and blown here and there by every wind of teaching and by the cunning and craftiness of men in their deceitful scheming. ¹⁵Instead, speaking the truth in love, we will in all things grow up into him who is the Head, that is, Christ. ¹⁶From him the whole body, joined and held together by every supporting ligament, grows and builds itself up in love, as each part does its work.

At the conclusion of his petitionary prayer and doxology, which round out the first three chapters of Ephesians, Paul begins his lengthy paraclesis ('admonition') which extends from 4:1 to 6:20, in other words, almost to the end of the letter. The beginning of the ethical admonition is signalled by the clause beginning with *I urge you*, together with the introductory *therefore* (cf. 1 Thess. 4:1; Rom. 12:1), which follows a fairly fixed pattern, and here serves to mark a transition[1] from the doctrinal material of chapters 1–3 to the practical instruction of chapters 4–6.

In the first half of Ephesians the apostle has unfolded for his readers the eternal plan of God with its goal of summing up all things in Christ. His direct appeal in chapter 4 is based on the foundation of their being reconciled in Christ and made part of God's new humanity. The content of his exhortatory material is regularly informed by what has been written in the earlier eulogy, thanksgiving period, and didactic sections.[2] The readers have been reminded of the high destiny to which God has called them, and now they are shown that the hope of this calling requires them to live lives in keeping with it. 'Behaviour is thus seen in Ephesians as both response to what God has done in Christ, and as the proper accompaniment to the praise of God, the two themes present in chaps. 1–3'.[3]

This is not to suggest, however, that 'theology' and 'ethics' have been placed in two separate, watertight compartments, chapters 1–3 and 4–6 respectively. Already within the first half of the letter, as our exegesis has shown, theology and ethics are closely intertwined: profound attitudinal and behavioural implications were to flow from a right understanding of the apostle's teaching. Furthermore, in chapters 4–6, as in the case of Colossians, Paul frequently combines theological and ethical statements (cf. Col. 3:1–4:6), with the former often providing the bases for the latter (e.g., Eph. 4:4-16, 32; 5:2, 8, 23-32).

---

1. The form usually consists of a verb in the first person singular or plural (παρακαλῶ, 'I urge or exhort'), followed by the conjunction οὖν ('therefore') or an equivalent, the direct object ὑμᾶς ('you'), to which is occasionally connected the vocative ἀδελφοί ('brothers and sisters'), a prepositional phrase commencing with διά ('through') or ἐν ('in'), and the content of the exhortation expressed by an infinitive, an imperative, or a ἵνα ('that') clause (cf. Rom. 12:1; 15:30; 16:17; 1 Cor. 1:10; 4:16; 16:15; 2 Cor. 2:8; 6:1; 10:1; 1 Thess. 4:1, 10; 5:14; Phlm. 8-10). Note the important discussion of C. J. Bjerkelund, *Parakalô*, and the criticisms of Lincoln, 226, 227. Cf. also M. Breeze, 'Hortatory Discourse in Ephesians', *Journal of Translation and Textlinguistics* 5 (1992), 313-47.

2. Note, e.g., the references to the great love of the Father for the Son (1:6) and for believers who are in Christ (1:4; 2:4; 3:17, 19), which occur in chaps. 1–3, followed by the admonitions to love (4:2, 15, 16; 5:2, 25, 28, 33; 6:24). Yet the further point needs to be made that within chaps. 4–6 theological 'indicatives' concerning Christ's love are interwoven with the 'imperatives' (5:2, 25; 6:23).

3. Best, 353.

Verses 1-16 set the stage for what follows in 4:17–6:20, and amplify 'how the exhortation of v. 1 is to work out in the various community and household relationships'.[4] In terms of its structure of thought, the passage falls into two main parts. The first (vv. 1-6) begins with the exhortation to the readers to live worthily of their calling, an exhortation which is based on the first half of the letter and which soon focusses on the appeal to keep the unity of the Spirit (vv. 1-3). V. 1 is the 'topic sentence' for the rest of the epistle, with the subsequent exhortations being an amplification of what is involved in walking worthily of their calling, as they do so in love and maintain the unity of the Spirit. This leads on to a sevenfold assertion of the fundamental realities of the faith, which provide the basis for the preceding admonitions. The essential issues of chapters 1–3, such as the readers' calling, the prayer for love, the people of God as one body in the Spirit, and the trinitarian basis of everything, are picked up in this short paragraph of vv. 1-6.

The beginning of the second half of the section (vv. 7-16) is clearly marked by *but to each one of us* (v. 7), as Paul introduces the note of diversity. This diversity is not at variance with the overarching unity, nor is it at the cost of unity. The purpose of the ascended Christ's giving various gifts to the church, particularly the gifts of apostles, prophets, evangelists, pastors, and teachers, is to build the whole body so as to enable it to attain maturity and unity (v. 13), a unity in which there is an integral role for the individual (v. 16). The various ministries are intended to equip the whole body for 'ministry', so that it might 'grow up' into a healthy (mature) body, with Christ at the head and the whole of it drawing its life from him as it grows into his likeness (vv. 12-16).

1. The Unity of the Church as an Urgent Concern, 4:1-6

This paragraph on the need to maintain unity may be divided into two parts. The first section begins with the 'topic sentence', a general exhortation to the readers to live worthily of their calling (v. 1), and this is grounded *therefore* in the first three chapters of the letter.[5] But what kind of behaviour is appropriate to their calling, and how can it be recognized? The general admonition is amplified in what follows by means of three modifiers that include four graces (humility, gentleness, patience, and loving forbearance), as Paul urges his readers to be eager to maintain the unity of the Spirit (vv. 2-3). The second part (vv. 4-6) consists of a sevenfold confession of the unifying realities of the faith, which provide a

---

4. G. D. Fee, *God's Empowering Presence*, 698.

5. U. Luz, 'Überlegungen zum Epheserbrief', 379-86, believes that the exhortatory material of chaps. 4–6 has the prayers of 1:15-23 and 3:14-21 as its basis.

strong motivation for the appeal for unity. These verses are specifically linked with the first part through the language of calling (v. 1), though now the emphasis is on the one hope which springs from this call (v. 4b).

1 On the basis of God's mighty salvation in Christ, the readers are now admonished to lead lives that are in keeping with their high destiny and calling. Paul introduces the exhortatory section of the letter with the words *I urge you* that are characteristic of his epistles, and marks a transition to a new section. In 1 Thessalonians 4:1 and Romans 12:1, as here, the major paraenesis of the letter begins with this clause.[6] The verb itself covers a broad range of meanings, but here it signifies to 'urge' or 'exhort'.[7] Although Paul expected his churches to accept his authority, he normally requests or exhorts his readers rather than commands them, and his verb reflects this approach.[8] He often associates the term 'brothers' with the phrase (Rom. 12:1; 15:32; 1 Cor. 16:15; 1 Thess. 4:10), but this word is lacking as an address in Ephesians, an omission that is in keeping with the general nature of the letter.

The exhortation comes from one who styles himself 'I, the prisoner in the Lord', which is similar to the earlier self-designation, *I Paul, the prisoner of Christ Jesus* (see on 3:1). Just as the whole of his Christian life is 'in the Lord', so his being a prisoner comes within the same sphere of Christ's lordship. This recurrent prisoner theme appears to have a rhetorical function:[9] Paul's pastoral appeal is underscored by reference to his own costly commitment. He was imprisoned for the sake of those whom he now addresses, and because he was committed to the unity that he now requests of them (see 3:13).

The admonition *to live a life worthy of the calling you have received* arises out of the gracious, saving purpose of God (cf. 2 Cor. 5:20), which has been presented in the first three chapters. This appeal, like other Pauline ethical 'imperatives', is grounded in the 'indicatives' of God's saving work in Christ.[10] It is a comprehensive exhortation (cf. 1 Thess. 2:12; Rom. 12:1; 1 Cor. 10:31; Phil. 1:27; Col. 1:10; 3:17) which covers every aspect of

6. However, against C. J. Bjerkelund, *Parakalô*, 140, etc., the παρακαλῶ-clause does not have simply an epistolary function, but is an expression of the apostolic admonition and is part of the 'specifically Christian paraclesis' (so Schnackenburg, 162).

7. Gk. παρακαλῶ. BAGD, 617; against C. J. Bjerkelund, *Parakalô*, 185-87, who by stressing the friendly elements tones down the exhortatory aspect; so rightly Hoehner; cf. S. R. Llewelyn, *New Documents* 6 (1992), 145-46.

8. Note the discussion of Paul's authority and its exercise (along with further bibliographical details) by L. L. Belleville, 'Authority', *DPL*, 54-59.

9. D. G. Reid, 'Prison, Prisoner', *DPL*, 752-54, and Turner, 1236. (Cf. also Phil. 1:7, 13, 14, 17; Phlm. 1, 9.)

10. Note S. C. Mott, 'Ethics', *DPL*, 269-75, together with further bibliographical details.

the readers' lives and stands as the 'topic' sentence over what follows. The subsequent admonitions throughout the paraenesis amplify what is involved in walking worthily of this calling.

Within Ephesians the apostle has already used the language of 'walking' to describe the readers' former lifestyle in sin and death (2:1-2; cf. v. 3) and then, by contrast, in relation to the good works God has prepared for them to *walk* in (v. 10). Now, at the beginning of the exhortatory material in chapters 4–6, this significant motif appears again, as the readers are admonished to lead a life that is in conformity with the calling they have received, and it continues like a scarlet thread through the next two chapters (4:17; 5:2, 8, 15).

Elsewhere in the Pauline letters 'calling' refers to God's drawing men and women into fellowship with his Son through the preaching of the gospel (1 Cor. 1:9; Rom. 8:30), or into his kingdom and glory (1 Thess. 2:12). Here in Ephesians, by admonishing the readers to live worthily of the calling with which they have been called[11] Paul is reminding them of the prior action of God in their midst. As believers they have already been called into the blessings of salvation (1:3-14) with its wonderful hope (1:18). They have been united with Christ in his resurrection and exaltation so that they now share in his rule over the new creation (1:20-22; 2:6). Both Jews and Gentiles have been reconciled to God by the death of Christ and called into the one new humanity (2:13-16). They have become members of God's household, the new temple in the Lord (2:15, 19, 21), and have freedom of access to the Father by one Spirit (2:18). As those who have been *called* into one body, the church (cf. Col. 3:15), they have a divinely ordained role in God's purposes for the cosmos (Eph. 3:10). But God's gracious calling not only bestows great privileges on them; it also carries with it solemn responsibilities. His election and predestination of them for adoption into his family (1:4, 5), together with his preparing good works beforehand for them to walk in (2:10), do not remove the responsibility of their heeding the apostolic injunction.[12] They are expected to respond to the divine initiatives, and God's calling establishes the norm or criterion[13] to which their conduct should

---

11. In the expression ἀξίως περιπατῆσαι τῆς κλήσεως ἧς ἐκλήθητε ('to lead a life worthily of the calling with which you were called') the relative pronoun ἧς ('with which') has been attracted to the genitive case of the preceding noun, κλήσεως ('calling'). Further, typical of the style of Ephesians the cognate noun and verb of 'calling' (κλῆσις, καλέω) are used together.

12. Cf. Lincoln, 235.

13. This is the significance of ἀξίως ('worthily, in a manner worthy of'). The apostle usually employs ἀξίως in phrases by way of admonition and normally with the verb περιπατέω ('walk, live': 1 Thess. 2:12; Col. 1:10; Eph. 4:1; note, however, Rom. 16:2; cf. 3 John 6).

conform. The subsequent admonitions, which fill out in greater detail their responsibilities, are set within this framework of an appeal that is grounded in the gospel of salvation which they have received.

2 The admonition to live worthily of the divine calling is now more clearly explained as being a life characterized by the graces of humility, gentleness, patience, and loving forbearance, as the readers make every effort to maintain the unity of the Spirit in the bond of peace. Significantly, relationships within the body of Christ, especially conduct characterized by harmony, are the first issue Paul addresses as an essential element in their living consistently with this calling. It is not until v. 17, where the language of 'walking' is deliberately picked up again, that life in Christ is contrasted with that of outsiders.

The exhortation of v. 1 continues not with imperatives but with two prepositional phrases ('with all humility and gentleness, with patience') and two participial clauses which function as imperatives ('bear with one another in love' and 'make every effort to keep the unity'). These admonitions 'lead in an ascending line to the goal to be aimed for — preserving unity' (v. 3).[14]

The three graces 'humility', 'gentleness', and 'patience', together with the notions of 'bearing with one another' and 'love', all appear in the similar positive exhortatory material of Colossians 3:12-15,[15] although in Ephesians they function as the necessary graces without which the aim of the exhortation, namely, to maintain the unity of the body, would not be achieved. In effect, the readers are being urged to cultivate the graces that were seen in perfection in Christ. Most occur in the ninefold list of the fruit of the Spirit in Galatians 5:22-23, and exemplify the reconciliation that has been won for the readers through Christ's death (Eph. 2:14-18).

The first two graces, 'with all humility and gentleness', are closely related: they are joined by the one preposition 'with', while the 'all', which is characteristic of Paul's style in Ephesians, is applied to both nouns and underscores how necessary he considers these ethical qualities to be in the lives of his readers. 'Humility, lowliness', as is well known, occurred in Greek literature generally on only a few occasions, and then usually in the derogatory sense of servility, weakness, or a

---

14. Schnackenburg, 162; cf. G. D. Fee, *God's Empowering Presence*, 699, 700, who claims that grammatically μετὰ πάσης ταπεινοφροσύνης κτλ. ('with all humility, etc.') modifies the main verb, though conceptually it belongs with the final participial clause towards which it is heading.

15. The three graces 'humility, gentleness, patience' are the last three nouns in the list of Colossians 3:12, and appear in the same order. For a discussion of this passage see P. T. O'Brien, *Colossians, Philemon*, 195-206.

shameful lowliness.[16] In the Old Testament, however, the adjective 'lowly or humble' and its cognates occur more than 250 times, often in contexts which speak of the Lord bringing down the proud and arrogant, and exalting the lowly or poor whose trust is in him.[17] In the New Testament the noun signifies the 'lowliness' with which one serves the Lord, as Paul did when his ministry was conducted among the Ephesians 'with great humility' (Acts 20:19),[18] or is submissive to other Christians (Phil. 2:3; Col. 3:12; 1 Pet. 5:5). The pattern or model is Jesus, who invited people to come to him as the one who was 'meek and lowly in heart' (Matt. 11:29). The twin themes of humiliation and exaltation, noted in the Old Testament, come to their clearest expression in the hymn of Philippians 2:6-11, where it is stated that Jesus humbled himself to death on a cross, and God exalted him (v. 9) by bestowing on him the name above all others. Christ's action in humbling himself is the pattern for believers, who in humility are to esteem others better than themselves and to be concerned about others' welfare (v. 4).

'Gentleness' or 'meekness', in its adjectival form, designated the poor and oppressed in the Old Testament,[19] who in their deep need humbly sought help from the Lord. 'Meekness' was one of the marks of Jesus' rule. He fulfilled the role of the messianic king who brought salvation without using force (Matt. 21:5; cf. Zech. 9:9), describing himself as meek and lowly of heart (Matt. 11:29). Paul mentions the 'meekness of Christ' as characteristic of Jesus' behaviour toward human beings during his life on earth, and he exhorts the Corinthians on the basis of this example (2 Cor. 10:1). 'Meekness' is to characterize the lives of Christians in relation to fellow-believers who have sinned (Gal. 6:1, 2, by bearing one another's burdens they 'fulfil the law of Christ'; 2 Tim. 2:25; cf. 1 Cor. 4:21). It is a fruit of the Spirit (Gal. 5:23), standing in lists of graces as a concrete

16. In Epictetus 3.24.56 ταπεινοφροσύνη, which carries the derogatory sense of 'servility', heads a list of qualities which cannot be commended (noted by Best, 362).

17. The prophets express it in warnings of judgment (Amos 2:6, 7; 8:6, 7; cf. Isa. 2:9, 11), the historical books spell it out with reference to events (Judg. 4:23; 1 Sam. 1:11), while the psalmists mention the theme in their prayers (Ps. 10:17, 18; 25:18; 31:7), and in the proverbs of the wisdom literature 'humility' is the fruit of experience and the rule of life (Job 5:11; Prov. 3:34; 11:2), occasionally being parallelled with 'the fear of the LORD' (cf. Prov. 15:33). See further W. Grundmann, *TDNT* 8:1-26; and H.-H. Esser, *NIDNTT* 2:259-64.

18. Exactly the same expression, μετὰ πάσης ταπεινοφροσύνης, 'with all humility', is used by Luke at Acts 20:19 with reference to Paul's ministry in Ephesus. Significantly, the Lord is served (note the verb δουλεύω) with all humility as Paul carries out his ministry among the Ephesians in a lowly and Christlike manner.

19. On 'meekness' in the Old Testament and the Qumran community, see F. Hauck and S. Schulz, *TDNT* 6:645-51; and W. Bauder, *NIDNTT* 2:256-59.

expression of Christian love (cf. 1 Tim. 6:11; 1 Pet. 3:4). This gentleness is not to be confused with weakness (as contemporary Graeco-Roman thought regarded it), but has to do with consideration for others and a willingness to waive one's rights.

The third grace, 'long-suffering', appears in both Old and New Testaments to describe the 'patience' of God with his people (esp. Exod. 34:6).[20] Because of his forbearance with them, they ought to act in a similar manner towards others (cf. the parable of the wicked servant, Matt. 18:23-35; 1 Thess. 5:14). In some contexts, this word can signify 'steadfastness' or 'forbearance', and this is its sense here, given that the following clause, 'bearing with one another in love', amplifies what is meant by it. 'Patience' is that long-suffering which makes allowance for others' shortcomings and endures wrong rather than flying into a rage or desiring vengeance. It is a fruit of the Spirit (Gal. 5:22) and a necessary quality for maintaining right relationships within the body of Christ (cf. 1 Thess. 5:14; 1 Cor. 13:4; 2 Cor. 6:6).

Paul's exhortation continues with the following participles, 'bearing [with one another]' and 'making every effort' (v. 3), each of which functions as an imperative.[21] The first clarifies the meaning of 'patience'. Mutual forbearance is the practical expression of patience.[22] As believers bear with[23] one another's[24] weaknesses and failures (cf. 4:32) in the midst of tensions and conflicts, they show a lifestyle that is consistent with their divine calling. This kind of behaviour can spring only from God's love — a point that is made plain by the additional words *in love*.[25] The apostle has just prayed to God that his readers might be *rooted and established in love* (3:17). Now he addresses his urgent appeal to them to live accordingly.

---

20. Gk. μακροθυμία. 'The LORD, the LORD, a God merciful and gracious, *slow to anger and abounding in steadfast love and faithfulness*' (italics added). Because of God's dealings with his people, this word, which was not very significant in secular Greek, was given a new and unexpectedly profound significance, so that the human attitude of 'long-suffering' is now set in a new light.

21. Cf. BDF §468(2); and S. E. Porter, *Verbal Aspect*, 376, 377.

22. So Abbott, 106; cf. Meyer, 195.

23. ἀνέχομαι here has a linear connotation and means to 'endure, bear with, put up with'; cf. Col. 3:13; 2 Cor. 11:19 (BAGD, 65). The nominative of the participle, ἀνεχόμενοι, is a construction according to sense because the logical subject of ἀξίως περιπατῆσαι ('walk worthily') is ὑμεῖς ('you').

24. ἀλλήλων ('one another'), the genitive case, is used after a verb of emotion; so BDF §176(1); and A. T. Robertson, *Grammar*, 508, who rightly adds that putting up with other members of the congregation(s) is in view.

25. The phrase ἐν ἀγάπῃ ('in love') goes with the preceding clause, not the following, and indicates the basis of the mutual forbearance.

3 The apostle has urged his readers to display humility, gentleness, patience, forbearance, and love since they are necessary to achieve the aim of the exhortation: *Make every effort to keep the unity of the Spirit through the bond of peace.* Without these graces which are essential to their life together, they would have no hope of maintaining the unity of the Spirit, a unity in the body of Christ about which Paul is deeply concerned. This second participial clause ('making every effort . . .') is stylistically parallel to the previous one, and also functions as an imperative.[26]

Paul's appeal is urgent and cannot be easily translated into English. The verb he uses has an element of haste, urgency, or even a sense of crisis to it,[27] and has been rendered by Barth as: 'Yours is the initiative! Do it now!'[28] Further, the exhortation is an unusual one. The church's unity is described as *the unity of the Spirit*,[29] which signifies a unity that God's Spirit creates[30] and therefore not the readers' own achievement, yet they are exhorted urgently to maintain[31] it. God has inaugurated this unity in Christ, through the events described in Ephesians 2:11-22, as a result of which believers, Jew and Gentile together, have access to God 'in one Spirit' (2:18). In the following verses, this unity, which includes Jew-Gentile relations in the body of Christ but is not limited to them,[32] is underscored by a series of acclamations of oneness, which means that it is as 'indestructible as God himself'.[33] Ultimately, the unity and reconciliation that have been won through Christ's death (2:14-18) are part and parcel of God's intention of bringing all things together into unity in Christ (1:9, 10). Since the church has been designed by God to be the masterpiece of his goodness and the pattern on which the reconciled universe of the future will be modelled (see on 2:7), believers are expected to live in a man-

26. The opening participle σπουδάζοντες ('making every effort') parallels ἀνεχόμενοι ('bearing'), while the concluding prepositional phrase with ἐν (ἐν τῷ συνδέσμῳ τῆς εἰρήνης, 'in the bond of peace') is parallel to ἐν ἀγάπῃ ('in love').

27. σπουδάζω means to 'be zealous or eager', 'take pains', 'make every effort' (cf. Gal. 2:10; 1 Thess. 2:17; 2 Tim. 2:15; 4:9, 21; Tit. 3:12; BAGD, 763; Louw and Nida §25.74).

28. So Barth, 428, who comments: 'Not only haste and passion, but a full effort of the whole man is meant, involving his will, sentiment . . . the whole attitude. The imperative mood of the participle . . . excludes passivity, quietism, a wait-and-see attitude'.

29. The term ἑνότης ('unity') appears only here and in v. 13 in the New Testament, although it turns up frequently in Ignatius.

30. The genitive τοῦ πνεύματος ('of the Spirit') is best taken as one of source or origin.

31. The verb τηρεῖν (to 'keep or maintain') indicates that the unity already exists prior to the exhortation. Cf. J. D. G. Dunn, *The Theology of Paul the Apostle* (Grand Rapids/Cambridge: Eerdmans, 1998), 562.

32. Best, 364, rightly notes that it may refer as much to 'Jewish-Jewish and Gentile-Gentile relations as to Jewish-Gentile relations'.

33. Stott, 152.

ner consistent with this divine purpose. To *keep* this unity must mean to maintain it *visibly*. If the unity of the Spirit is real, it must be transparently evident, and believers have a responsibility before God to make sure that this is so. To live in a manner which mars the unity of the Spirit is to do despite to the gracious reconciling work of Christ. It is tantamount to saying that his sacrificial death by which relationships with God and others have been restored, along with the resulting freedom of access to the Father, are of no real consequence to us!

The 'unity of the Spirit' is to be maintained 'in the bond of peace', that is, in the bond which consists of peace.[34] Although the phrase has been understood instrumentally (cf. NIV's *through the bond of peace*), so that peace, which has a bonding effect, is the means by which the addressees will maintain and show forth the unity of the Spirit,[35] it is preferable on grounds of Pauline usage and sequence within this context to regard the phrase as locative, signifying that peace is the bond in which their unity is kept.[36] Accordingly, as the readers heed the apostolic injunction to bend every effort so as to maintain their oneness in the local congregation(s) as well as in their wider relationships with other believers, the peace which Christ has won and which binds Jews and Gentiles together into the one people of God will be increasingly evident in their lives.

4-6 The apostle, however, is not speaking of a unity at any price in which the fundamental truths of the gospel are jettisoned. As a strong motivation for his appeal for unity he presents a series of seven acclamations, each using the word 'one', in which the readers are reminded of the fundamental unities on which the Christian faith and life are based. This theological undergirding begins without any linking conjunction or verb in v. 4 as the apostle moves from exhortation (vv. 1-3) to assertion. The motifs *one body* and *one Spirit* are declaratory, yet they have the force of an appeal.[37] The sevenfold list is basically threefold since three of these unities allude to the three persons of the Trinity, while the remaining four refer to believers' relationship to the Spirit, Son, and Father.

It has been argued that Paul is citing an early Christian confession or creed. This is possible but unlikely. The order (Spirit, Lord, and God) is

---

34. σύνδεσμος ('bond') refers to that which holds something together. It is most natural to understand peace itself as the bond, with τῆς εἰρήνης ('of peace') being a genitive of apposition (so, among others, Meyer, 197; Schlier, 185; and G. D. Fee, *God's Empowering Presence,* 701). In the parallel passage, Col. 3:14, 15, love is the bond that leads to perfection, while Christ's peace rules in believers' hearts.

35. So, among others, Mitton, 139; Schnackenburg, 164, 165; and Lincoln, 237.

36. Meyer, 197, 198; Abbott, 107; and G. D. Fee, *God's Empowering Presence,* 701.

37. Cf. Schnackenburg, 160.

quite different from that of the early confessions (Father, Son, and Spirit), while several clauses point rather to an ad hoc creation. So, for example, the expression 'even as you were called in one hope of your calling' (v. 4) is not the usual credal style, but is characteristic of Paul's own expressions. The most that can legitimately be claimed, then, is that Paul may have utilized some items of credal material[38] as he stresses the need for unity.[39]

The immediate context explains the reason for the Spirit being mentioned before the Father and the Son (cf. 1 Cor. 12:4-6). Paul has just exhorted his readers to 'maintain the unity of the Spirit in the bond of peace'. The theological basis for that exhortation comes from Ephesians 2: through Christ both Jewish and Gentile believers have been reconciled 'in one body' (2:16) and have been granted access to the Father 'in one Spirit' (2:18). The apostle now turns to the fact that there is but *one Spirit*, and only later in the series does he mention *one Lord* and *one God and Father of all*.

The context also explains the order of the first two items, *body* and *Spirit*. The *one body* is mentioned first, for this is the apostle's primary concern in these exhortations. This *body* is the church, Christ's body (1:23), which comprises Jewish and Gentile believers alike. It is the heavenly gathering, assembled around Christ, in which believers now participate. That body of Christ is, by definition, *one*. Each congregation is a local manifestation of this heavenly entity, not a part of it. So although the apostle is writing about the *one body* which is in heaven, all that he says applies also to each local congregation, for it is here that the unity of the body is visible. The *one Spirit* brings unity and cohesion to the body by his indwelling and animating activity (v. 3). 'By the one Spirit we were all baptized into one body' (1 Cor. 12:13; cf. Rom. 8:9). Believers are members of the body by virtue of the work of the Holy Spirit. And as there is only one body, so also there is only one Spirit.

The concluding clause of v. 4, 'just as you were called in the one hope of your calling', is specifically linked to the 'topic' sentence of v. 1, with its general exhortation to the readers to live worthily of their calling,

---

38. L. W. Hurtado, *DPL*, 564, suggests that the term 'credal' is 'perhaps a bit misleading'. The phrases were 'neither intended as full confessions of early Christian beliefs nor were they the result of doctrinal deliberations'. Rather, Hurtado prefers to call them 'acclamations', which, rather narrowly, he thinks originated 'in the setting of corporate worship in Christian circles'.

39. Caird, 72, asserts that the 'modern passion for finding credal and liturgical formulae in the epistles has far outrun the evidence'. He adds that the fact that 'not one of these "formulae" is ever quoted twice in identical words is surely good reason for caution'! But whether Caird's own suggestion, namely, that Paul in each of these passages is 'adapting the Jewish confession, the Shema (Dt. 6:4-9), in the light of Christian faith and experience' is more likely, may be questioned.

and it provides the framework for the rest of the paraenesis in the letter. Although the 'just as'-clause of v. 4 breaks the nicely balanced sequence, it functions as an envelope *(inclusio)* with its mention of calling, as Paul pointedly returns to what was already stated in order to make it more urgent. Now, however, the emphasis is upon the one hope that springs from the call. God's calling finds its origin in the choice of his people in Christ before the world's foundation (Eph. 1:4) and becomes effective in their lives through the preaching of the gospel (Rom. 8:30). When God calls believers into a relationship with himself he calls them to a particular hope (Eph. 1:18)[40] which is sure and certain since it rests on his faithfulness — previously the Gentile readers had been separated from Christ and had no real hope (Eph. 2:12). It is sometimes called 'the hope of the gospel' (Col. 1:23) because it is held out in the saving message of the gospel, and 'the hope of glory' (1:27; Rom. 5:2), the expectation of appearing with Christ in glory when he is revealed (Col. 3:4) and of sharing in his glory. In Ephesians this hope is particularly expressed in terms of God's gracious purpose of summing up and bringing together all things in Christ, both in heaven and on earth (1:9-10). As a foretaste of this grand hope the very existence of the church, a society of pardoned rebels, a multiracial community in which Jews and Gentiles have been brought together in unity in the one body, is the means God uses to manifest his richly diverse wisdom to the principalities and powers in the heavenly realm. Thus, Paul reinforces his admonition by reminding his readers of the hope held out in their calling. A sense of expectancy, therefore, should motivate and unify their actions.

Having begun with a series of unities related to the work of the Holy Spirit, Paul continues without elaboration to the second triad, *one Lord, one faith, one baptism* (v. 5).[41] This may have been a traditional baptismal affirmation, given the mention of baptism as the third member, and because faith in Jesus as the one Lord was usually the focus of baptismal confession (e.g., Acts 2:34-39; 19:5).[42] However, one should not assume that such a confession was confined to this occasion.

40. In the expression 'the hope of *his* [i.e., God's] calling' (ἡ ἐλπὶς τῆς κλήσεως αὐτοῦ, Eph. 1:18), κλῆσις is to be understood comprehensively of God's call within his saving purposes, while at 4:4 'the one hope of *your* calling' (μία ἐλπὶς τῆς κλήσεως ὑμῶν) the attention is more narrowly focussed on the readers who have been called. However, the 'hope' which belongs to the calling is the same.

41. There is a change in the Greek from the masculine to the feminine to the neuter of the numeral one: εἷς-μία-ἕν.

42. Bruce, 336, comments: 'It is not difficult to understand why "one faith" and "one baptism" are attached to the "one Lord": he is the object of his people's faith . . . and it is into him that they have been baptized (Rom. 6:3; Gal. 3:27)'. The confession of Jesus as Lord is linked with belief in his resurrection in Rom. 10:9, 10.

'Lord', which was the title for Yahweh in the Old Testament, was used in acclamation of Jesus by early believers, even before Paul's conversion.[43] 'Lord' is a favourite title for Jesus in the apostle's letters,[44] and Ephesians is no exception. He shares with other Christians the conviction that Jesus is Lord on the basis of his resurrection and exaltation to the place of highest honour (cf. 1 Cor. 8:6; 12:3; Rom. 10:9; 14:8, 9; Phil. 2:9-11). Already in Ephesians, where there are some twenty references to Jesus as *Lord*, the apostle has spoken of the *Lord* Jesus Christ as the one in whom every spiritual blessing comes (1:3; cf. v. 2), as the sphere in which faith is exercised (1:15), and as the one in whom God's new creation, the holy temple, is growing (2:21). God's eternal purpose has been accomplished in Christ Jesus, our *Lord,* while Paul exhorts the readers as one who is a 'prisoner in the *Lord*' (4:1). Jesus is the Lord who fills the universe with his sovereign rule (1:23; cf. 4:10), and who as head has been given to the church (1:23; cf. 4:15, 16).

According to Gordon Fee, after the expression *one Lord* two 'entry' experiences are introduced: *one faith* and *one baptism*.[45] The former is probably objective, as many commentators suppose, referring to the substance of one's faith (Jude 3), their common body of belief. This appears to be the meaning of 'faith' later in the chapter (v. 13). If, as is less likely, *one faith* is subjective, then it denotes the act or attitude of believing in Christ which is common to all members of the one body. Either way, it is true that Christians have *one* faith. In the context of Ephesians, there is not one faith for Jews and another for Gentiles (as Rom. 3:20 makes clear). There can be only

43. The earliest evidence of the pre-Pauline origin of calling on Jesus as Κύριος ('Lord') is the apostle's use, without explanation, of the Aramaic *maranatha* ('Our Lord, come!') at 1 Cor. 16:22, suggesting that (1) he had taken it over unchanged from early Aramaic-speaking Jewish Christians, and (2) the Corinthian Christians understood what was meant by the expression since it had been conveyed to them earlier by Paul.

44. For Paul κύριος ('Lord') in most instances designates Jesus Christ; sometimes Paul refers to God as κύριος in Old Testament citations (e.g., Rom. 4:8). On occasion, 'Lord' is used of the earthly life of Jesus (cf. 1 Cor. 2:9; Gal. 1:19), but normally the title refers to the heavenly, ascended Lord (Eph. 6:9; Col. 4:1) who died (Gal. 6:14; 1 Cor. 11:26), was raised from the dead (1 Cor. 6:14; 2 Cor. 4:14), and will come again (1 Thess. 4:15, 16; 1 Cor. 4:5). He is the Lord who is present among his people. Frequently the word is used to refer to the position of Jesus Christ as the overruling one to whom the believer is subject in a life of obedience, who is the master of the Christian (cf. Col. 3:18–4:1), the source of his new life, and the object of his invocation and praise (Rom. 10:9, 10; 1 Cor. 12:3). Paul expresses the intensely personal relationship when he speaks of 'my Lord' at Phil. 3:8. For further details and bibliography, though without any treatment of Ephesians or other 'Pauline writings widely regarded as pseudepigraphical', see L. W. Hurtado, 'Lord', *DPL,* 560-69.

45. G. D. Fee, *God's Empowering Presence,* 704, who adds that this best explains why Paul makes no mention of the Lord's Supper in this context.

one faith since there is only *one Lord*. Furthermore, there is only *one baptism* because there is one Lord Jesus Christ in whom believers are united, one body into which all Christians are incorporated. Those who have been baptized into Christ have put on Christ (Gal. 3:27). Significantly, baptism and unity are connected in Galatians 3:27, 28, as well as at 1 Corinthians 12:13. The apostle is not making distinctions as to whether it is water baptism or baptism in the Spirit that is in view. The one without the other was an anomaly. However, much of Paul's teaching on baptism elsewhere in his epistles does not make sense unless the notion of spiritual union with Christ, at least, is in view (Rom. 6:3, 4; 1 Cor. 10:2; 12:13; Gal. 3:27; Col. 2:12; though cf. 1 Cor. 1:13-17; 15:29).

Finally, Paul's threefold acclamation reaches its climax as he praises the *one God and Father of all* for his universal rule and presence (v. 6). This acclamation, like that of 1 Corinthians 8:6 (itself a Christian reworking of the Shema of Deut. 6:4), characteristically acclaims the *one God* as *Father*, and then affirms[46] his supreme transcendence *over all* and pervasive imminence, *through all and in all*. But how is the term 'all' to be interpreted: as masculine, so referring to people, or as neuter, denoting 'all things', that is, the universe?[47]

(1) Many interpreters regard the references to 'all' as masculine, thus denoting people, rather than neuter and signifying 'all things'. This is normally taken to denote 'all Christians', which in the context of Ephesians signifies both Jews and Gentiles,[48] not 'all people' indiscriminately.[49] The grounds for this view are threefold: first, in the context of a series of acclamations where the unity of the church is in view, it is claimed that what might have been an original cosmological formula is here related to members of the church. Secondly, in Paul's letters God is the 'Father' of Christ (cf. Eph. 1:3) and of those who are in him, that is, Christians (Rom. 8:15; Gal. 4:6; Eph. 1:2). The exception in Ephesians 3:15, where the vision is broadened to include the whole of creation, does not apply here, it is argued, since the '[Father] *of all*' is picked up in the expression 'each one of us' (v. 7),

46. As in the case of 1 Cor. 8:6, the adjectival clause which follows, ὁ ἐπὶ πάντων καὶ διὰ πάντων καὶ ἐν πᾶσιν ('who is over all and through all and in all'), amplifies the statement about God as Father.

47. The expression 'one God and Father of all' (εἷς θεὸς καὶ πατὴρ πάντων) is related to 'all' in a threefold manner: he is 'over all and through all and in all' (ὁ ἐπὶ πάντων καὶ διὰ πάντων καὶ ἐν πᾶσιν). If the 'all' (πάντων) in the expression 'Father of all' (πατὴρ πάντων) is taken as masculine, then the following three are also masculine; if, however, it is regarded as neuter, the following are understood as neuter.

48. So Bruce, 337, who adds that the people of God are now 'elect from every nation'.

49. However, Bratcher and Nida, 96, 97, understand πάντων of 'all people', i.e., humanity as a whole.

and this can only refer to members of the church. Finally, although some manuscripts read 'in us all' or 'in you all', the additional pronouns, which are generally conceded as a gloss,[50] are nevertheless thought to be correct and recognize that it was only among Christians that God was confidently known as Father. On this interpretation, the apostle is stating that God is transcendent over all his children, that they are the instruments or agents through whom he works, and that they constitute his dwelling place in the Spirit.

(2) However, a cosmic understanding of 'all'[51] makes good sense in this context. First, at significant points in Ephesians where the sovereignty of God and Christ are in view, 'all' denotes the whole universe (1:10, 11, 22, 23; 3:9; cf. 4:10). Secondly, in similar (confessional?) formulae within Paul's letters (1 Cor. 8:6; Rom. 11:36; Col. 1:16) where different prepositions (e.g., 'from', 'into', 'in', 'through') are skilfully linked together in order to qualify God's or Christ's relationship to 'all', the word regularly signifies 'everything', not just persons or even believers. Thirdly, although there are formal affinities between Paul's language and Stoic terminology, notably his use of 'all' and the play on prepositions by which the final unity of all that exists is expressed, the apostle's ideas are very different from Stoic notions. They are, in fact, dependent on Old Testament statements about God, who fills heaven and earth (Jer. 23:24), whose glory fills both temple and land, and whose power given to the Messiah is exercised over the whole of creation, not just believers (cf. Pss. 2, 8).[52]

The real difficulty with this line of interpretation is that the expression 'the Father of all' refers to God as the Father of all creation, whereas Paul usually speaks of him as the Father of Jesus Christ and of those who are in him. However, already in Ephesians 3:14-15 God is 'the Father, from whom every family in heaven and on earth derives its name'. He is the Creator of all living things, so that their existence and significance depend on him. On this interpretation Paul is affirming that God is supremely transcendent 'over everything' and that his immanence is all-pervasive: he works 'through all and in all'. If this latter understanding is correct, then God's universal sovereignty and presence are set forth as the climactic ground for the unity of the Spirit that believers are to maintain. His universal rule is being exercised to fulfil his ultimate purpose of unifying all things in Christ. The unity of the church is the means by which

---

50. One variant reading (cf. D F G K L etc.) has ἡμῶν after πᾶσιν ('all of us'), and this agrees with ἡμῶν ('us') in v. 7, while another reading (preserved in the Textus Receptus) has ὑμῖν ('to you') instead after πᾶσιν ('all of you'). But the shorter reading which omits them both has the strongest textual support: 𝔓[46] ℵ A B C P 082 6, etc.

51. With πᾶς being neuter and signifying 'all things'.

52. Barth, 471; cf. P. T. O'Brien, *Colossians, Philemon,* 47-48, 52.

the manifold wisdom of God is being displayed to the universe. The church is the eschatological outpost, the pilot project of God's purposes, and his people are the expression of this unity that displays to the universe his final goal.

2. Diversity in Unity That Leads to Maturity, 4:7-16

The opening words of v. 7, '*But* to each one of us', which begin a new paragraph on the overall theme of unity, introduce the motif of diversity in Christ's distribution of grace to each individual believer. Vv. 7-16 are a distinct unit within the section as a whole (vv. 1-16), and this is underscored by the presence of 'each one' in both vv. 7 and 16, which forms an envelope within the passage *(inclusio).* We move from the stress on unity (vv. 4-6) to diversity in vv. 7-10, and back again to unity in vv. 11-16.

At first sight it might seem that this diversity is at odds with the overarching unity of which the apostle has just spoken. But the diversity contributes to the unity of the body, since Christ's giving different gifts to each is for the purpose of enriching the whole, so that all are prepared for full maturity when they meet their Lord (v. 13).[53] Christ's giving of gifts (v. 8) is supported by a quotation from Psalm 68:18. In vv. 9 and 10 the words 'he ascended' and 'he descended' from the Psalm are picked up and applied to Christ. The ascent also implied a descent: Christ who ascended is the giver of gifts. Vv. 11-16 then interpret the second line of the Psalm quotation, expanding on the nature (v. 11) and the purpose (vv. 12-16) of the exalted Christ's gifts within the context of the people of God. V. 11 specifies the nature of the gifts in terms of persons who are involved in some form of ministry and proclamation of the word. The function of these ministers towards other believers is expressed (v. 12a), as is the goal for all to aim at, first positively (v. 13) and then negatively (v. 14). Through an additional participial clause (v. 15) Paul speaks of growing into Christ as the head. Finally, v. 16 recalls in summary fashion the previously mentioned purposes of growth and building of the body, processes which have their source in Christ and the active participation of each member of the body.

7 In a paragraph that has expanded on the overall theme of unity, the focus of attention shifts[54] to the issue of diversity in relation to

---

53. Note the similar discussions of the apostle in Rom. 12:3-8 and 1 Cor. 12:4-11, 12-31.

54. The introductory δέ ('but') signals the beginning of a new section with a change of subject. However, δέ ('but') is not here being used as a strong adversative. We move from unity (vv. 4-6) to diversity (vv. 7-10) within the theme of prevailing unity (vv. 11-16); cf. Best, 375.

Christ's distribution of grace. In vv. 4-6 the word 'one' has been used in relation to a sevenfold unity; now it refers to the individuals (*each one of us*) who make up this unity in the body. The appeal to individual believers is thus made a little more emphatic,[55] while the first person plural 'us' shows that Paul himself is included within the process by which the whole church is built into a unity. Within the flow of vv. 7-11 the key theme is that of Christ's giving: 'grace has been given [by him]', it is 'according to the measure of Christ's giving' (v. 7); 'he gave gifts' (v. 8); and 'it was he who gave' (v. 11). Christ sovereignly distributes his gifts to all the members of his body. The recipients are not limited to some special group, such as the ministers of v. 11.[56] *Each one of us* is to be understood comprehensively since it includes Paul and all his readers (it is thus the counterpart to 1 Cor. 12:7, 11). None misses out on Christ's bounty.

Within the unity of the body each member has a distinctive service to render for the effective functioning of the whole. The ability to perform this service is due to the 'grace' given by the ascended Christ to each one. Grace is viewed in terms of its outworking in a variety of ways in the lives of individuals, and thus comes to signify much the same as *charisma* does in the parallel passages in Paul (1 Cor. 12:4; Rom. 12:6). Perhaps the use of *charis* here, rather than *charisma*, is to stress the source of divine grace in providing the gifts. Not all believers, however, have the same abilities or receive the same gift. Grace was distributed in varied measure to each individual, and this is ultimately due to Christ's sovereign distribution.[57] The proportionate allocation of gifts is underscored elsewhere by the apostle: according to 1 Corinthians 12:11 it is the Spirit who 'apportions to each one individually as he wills', while in Romans 12:3 the similar notion of God measuring out different degrees of faith appears. In

---

55. ἑκάστῳ ('to each one') by itself would have conveyed the sense; ἑνί ('to one') strengthens the point.

56. H. Merklein, *Das kirchliche Amt*, 59-62 (cf. Schlier, 191), argues at length that the author identified himself ('each one of *us*') with the ministers named in v. 11. While there is a closely knit structure in vv. 7-11 (so that v. 11 interprets the citation of Ps. 68:18 that supports v. 7), the narrower reference in v. 11 is not intended to limit the 'each one of us' of v. 7 to the ministers. There is a difference of emphasis between v. 7, where Christ's grace is said to be given to *each*, and v. 11, where those named are Christ's gifts to the church. V. 11 is best understood as a particularizing from the argument of the preceding verses. Note the detailed arguments of R. Y. K. Fung, 'Ministry in the New Testament', in *The Church in the Bible and the World*, ed. D. A. Carson (Exeter: Paternoster, 1987), 154-212, 318-42, esp. 321-22; Schnackenburg, 174-75, who reversed his earlier view; Lincoln, 241; and Best, 376-77.

57. The expression κατὰ τὸ μέτρον τῆς δωρεᾶς τοῦ Χριστοῦ may be rendered: 'in proportion to Christ's allotted giving'. Here μέτρον means a '*measure* as the result of measuring'; cf. vv. 13, 16 (so BAGD, 515).

Ephesians 4 this measuring, like the giving in general, is the work of the ascended Christ. So grace was given to the apostle Paul for his ministry to Gentiles (cf. 3:2, 7, 8); now it is said to be given to each individual Christian for the benefit of the whole body.

8 This bestowal of gifts by the ascended Christ is now confirmed by the application of an important Old Testament text — Psalm 68:18. The quotation is introduced by the formula, 'therefore it says' (cf. Eph. 5:14),[58] which probably implies 'Scripture says', although for the apostle 'Scripture says', 'God says', and 'David says' are simply different ways of expressing the same thing:[59] the words quoted are God's and come with his authority.

The NIV renders Psalm 68:18 as follows:

> When you ascended on high,
>> you led captives in your train;
>> you received gifts from men.

In its original context Psalm 68[60] is a call to God to come and rescue his people (vv. 1-3). He is to be praised (vv. 4-6) for his past acts of deliverance and provision for his people. After the exodus he went in triumph before them (v. 7), so that Mount Sinai shook (v. 8) and kings were scattered (vv. 11-14). The Lord desired Mount Zion as his dwelling (v. 16), so he came from Sinai to his holy place (v. 17), and ascended the high mount leading captives in his train. The 'you' in v. 18 refers to God's ascent of Zion, probably in the person of the victorious king (or perhaps in reference to the establishment of the ark, which symbolizes the invisible presence of the God of Israel, on Zion). He led his captives in triumphal procession as they made their way up the temple mount.[61]

Paul applies this picture to Christ's ascension, not because there

---

58. διὸ λέγει ('therefore it says') occurs in Jas. 4:6 (introducing Prov. 3:34). On the use of this formula in Eph. 5:14, see 374.

59. Paul employs λέγει ('he or it says') without a subject when an Old Testament quotation is being introduced (Rom. 9:25; 10:21; 15:10; Gal. 3:16), but also uses the formulae 'Scripture says' (Rom. 4:3; 9:17; 10:11; 11:2; Gal. 4:30; 1 Tim. 5:18), 'God says' (Rom. 9:15; 2 Cor. 6:2, 16), and 'David [or Isaiah, etc.] says' (Rom. 4:7, 8; and 11:9, 10 where Ps. 68 is introduced). See further E. E. Ellis, *Paul's Use of the Old Testament* (Grand Rapids: Eerdmans, 1981), 23, and the older work of B. B. Warfield, *The Inspiration and Authority of the Bible* (Philadelphia: Presbyterian and Reformed, 1948), 299-348.

60. The interpretational difficulties of Ps. 68 in relation to its historical setting, major motifs, and theological purposes have been set forth by R. A. Taylor, 'The Use of Psalm 68:18 in Ephesians 4:8 in Light of Ancient Versions', *BSac* 148 (1991), 319-36, esp. 320-23.

61. For an alternative outline, see T. Moritz, *A Profound Mystery*, 66.

was some vague analogy between the two events, but because he saw in Jesus' exaltation a further fulfilment of this triumph of God. The original wording of the Psalm, which addresses the Lord directly after his triumphant ascent of Mount Zion, 'when you ascended on high,' is understood of Christ's exaltation,[62] an event of momentous theological significance, as Ephesians 1:20-22 makes plain.

It is generally claimed that since Christ's triumphant ascent and the issue of gifts are the apostle's primary concerns here, he does not expand on or develop the notion of Christ's leading a host of prisoners captive. Clinton Arnold, however, claims that vv. 8-10 provide supplementary evidence to Ephesians 1:19-22 in establishing Christ's supremacy over the powers of evil. They are the 'captives' whom Paul had in mind when he applied Psalm 68:18 to Christ's ascension. The text 'underlines the cosmic supremacy of Christ in a fresh way',[63] and this would have brought further comfort to the readers in their spiritual warfare with the hosts of darkness. (For an alternative view regarding the identity of the captives, see [5] below.)

The key clause, *and [he] gave gifts to men*, is a notorious crux. It is vital to the apostle's presentation since the text undergirds (v. 8)[64] his argument in vv. 7-11 about grace being given by Christ. The major difficulty, however, is that both the Hebrew text and the LXX read '[you] received gifts' rather than 'gave gifts',[65] and it appears at first glance that Paul has turned the original meaning of the Psalm on its head.

(1) As a result, some have claimed that the apostle simply misquoted the Old Testament here. He has read into the Psalm an unwarranted theological interpretation and changed the wording from 'you received' to 'you gave' in order to advance his point.[66]

---

62. The change from the second person singular ('you have ascended') to the third person in Ephesians adapts the construction to the contextual argument. The first finite verb 'you ascended' has been changed to a participle (ἀναβάς) so that the following verbs 'he carried off' (ᾐχμαλώτευσεν) and 'he gave' (ἔδωκεν) become the main statements. 'The one who ascends on high has accomplished a sovereign, victorious deed and then distributed gifts in a generous providential way' (Schnackenburg, 177). Paul gives an exposition of the first line in vv. 9, 10 and the second line in v. 11.

63. Arnold, 56-58, esp. 58; cf. D. G. Reid, *DPL*, 754.

64. διό means 'therefore, for this reason' (BAGD, 198).

65. Apart from the change of verbs from the second person singular of the Psalm to the third person of Ephesians (noted above).

66. So J. A. Fitzmyer, 'The Use of Explicit Old Testament Quotations in Qumran Literature and in the New Testament', *NTS* 7 (1960-61), 297-33, esp. 325, asserts: 'Here Paul completely disregards the original context of the Psalm in order to retain the words "he went up" and "he gave"'. Note the critique of this assertion by R. A. Taylor, 'The Use', 324.

(2) Another suggestion is that Paul, like other New Testament writers, cited a portion of the Old Testament from memory and this has led to a minor discrepancy. But this proposal is not convincing since the change under consideration is much too deliberate and striking.

(3) A much more serious attempt to solve the dilemma takes its starting point from a variant form of the Old Testament textual tradition. The Syriac Peshitta rendering of Psalm 68:18 is 'you have *given* gifts', and although there is difference of scholarly opinion as to its value as evidence, it may reflect a textual tradition different from that represented by the MT and the LXX.[67] Furthermore, the paraphrase of Psalm 68:18 in the Aramaic Targum is remarkable, for like the Peshitta it reads 'you gave' rather than 'you received' (as in the MT). It is unlikely that the New Testament wording of the passage has influenced the Targum, and although the Targum on the Psalms is late, it reflects a tradition and text form that are much earlier.[68] M. Wilcox has cautiously concluded that the author of Ephesians 'was here quoting either from, or in the light of, an Old Testament textual tradition resembling that of the Targum, but disagreeing with the tradition preserved in the LXX and MT at this point'.[69]

Accordingly, it has been claimed that Paul has taken over the textual tradition as reflected in the Targum ('you gave'), and employed a common technique of early Jewish hermeneutics, known as *midrash pesher,* in which his exposition of the text in the light of its fulfilment in Christ is integrated into the actual quotation.[70] This procedure, which appears elsewhere in the New Testament's use of the Old, would account for the differences present in Ephesians 4:8.

---

67. Note the evaluation of the issues by R. A. Taylor, 'The Use', 335.

68. This has been examined at length by W. H. Harris, *The Descent of Christ: Ephesians 4:7-11 and Traditional Hebrew Imagery* (Leiden: Brill, 1996), 64-142.

69. M. Wilcox, *The Semitisms of Acts* (Oxford: Clarendon Press, 1965), 25, cited by R. A. Taylor, 'The Use', 24. Note also Wilcox's recent discussion, 'Text Form', in *It Is Written: Scripture Citing Scripture,* ed. D. A. Carson and H. G. M. Williamson (Cambridge: Cambridge University Press, 1988), 193-204, esp. 198-99. R. A. Taylor, 'The Use', 332-35, prefers the view that Paul was familiar with a variant text-form, preserved in the Targum reading (in which there was a transposition of one consonant, which read *ḥālaq* ['share, divide'] instead of *lāqaḥ* ['receive']), and that he chose this in preference to the common text, since it was better suited to his theological argument here.

70. E. E. Ellis, *Paul's Use,* 144, 149. Cf. R. N. Longenecker, *Biblical Exegesis in the Apostolic Period* (Grand Rapids: Eerdmans, 1975), 125; Bruce, 342-43; B. Lindars, *New Testament Apologetic* (London: SCM, 1961), 53; and Lincoln, 242-44. According to R. A. Taylor, 'The Use', 328-29, 333-36, Paul has used this Jewish hermeneutical technique in a restrained manner, choosing the variant text-form of Ps. 68:18 since it was 'particularly well suited to his theological argument in Ephesians 4' (335). For a recent discussion and further bibliographical material see I. H. Marshall, 'An Assessment of Recent Developments', in *It Is Written,* 1-21, esp. 10-15.

The application of Psalm 68:18 to Christ's ascent and subsequent distribution of gifts stands in contrast to the rabbinic tradition as reflected in the Targum which associates Psalm 68:18 with Moses' ascent of Mount Sinai, an ascent that was understood as a going up to heaven to receive the Torah and other heavenly secrets.[71] The 'Moses mysticism' associated with this interpretation of the Psalm was widespread and apparently early, appearing in the rabbinic writings and Philo.[72] If this background is in view, Paul may be deliberately presenting Christ as greater than Moses. He ascended far above all the heavens in order to fill all things (v. 10). His *gift* is not the Torah but grace (v. 7), while his special gifts of ministry are for building up the whole body (vv. 11-16), not heavenly secrets for an elite few. The liturgical custom in synagogues associated Psalm 68 with Pentecost, which was increasingly regarded by Jews as the feast which commemorated the giving of the law to Moses on Mount Sinai. This has suggested to some Christian scholars that Pentecost lies in the background to the apostle's handling of the Psalm here. 'Paul's use of [Psalm 68] . . . in reference to the Christian Pentecost then makes a remarkable analogy. As Moses received the law and gave it to Israel, so Christ received the Spirit and gave him to his people in order to write God's law in their hearts and through the pastors he appointed (v. 11) to teach them the truth'. The idea that 'giving' and 'receiving' belong together is appropriately illustrated in Acts 2:33: 'Exalted to the right hand of God, he has received from the Father the promised Holy Spirit and has poured out what you now see and hear'.[73]

(4) Despite the differences between the verbs 'take' in Psalm 68:18 and 'give' in Ephesians 4:8, there has been a tradition of Christian interpretation which has argued that the notion of 'giving' was also implied in the Old Testament context.[74] The Hebrew verb rendered 'receive', it is suggested, sometimes has the sense of 'to take in order to give' to someone else, or perhaps to 'fetch'. After every conquest in the ancient world there was both a receiving of tribute and a distributing of gifts. The conqueror's spoils were divided, and the booty shared (Gen. 14; Judg. 5:30; 1 Sam. 30:26-31). On this interpretation the renderings in the Psalm and Ephesians 4 are 'only formally but not substantially contra-

---

71. Cf. *Midrash T^ehillîm* on Ps. 68:11 and *'Abot de Rabbi Nathan* 2.2a; note the detailed discussion of W. H. Harris, *The Descent*, 64-142.

72. Cf. *Midrash T^ehillîm* on Ps. 24:1 and 106:2; *b. Sabbat* 88b; see Lincoln, 243.

73. Stott, 157, 158; for further details see Lincoln, 241, 242.

74. Chrysostom saw no real difficulty, hence his oft-quoted comment: 'The one [word] is the same as the other'; to 'receive' is to take for the purpose of giving to another. Cf. R. A. Taylor, 'The Use', 327.

dictory'.[75] While this would neatly solve the problem, it runs up against both linguistic and textual difficulties.[76]

(5) The idea of God's receiving gifts in order to give them back to his people has been presented from a different perspective by G. V. Smith.[77] He claims that Psalm 68 reminisces God's triumphs in the past (vv. 1-19), including the exodus and wilderness period in Israel's history, and his appearance on Mount Sinai where the heavens dropped and the earth trembled (v. 8). The Lord defeated the Canaanites and then chose to set his sanctuary in Zion. Accompanied by myriads of heavenly hosts, he ascends the heights, leads captives captive, and receives gifts among men, even the rebellious, in order that he might dwell among them (v. 18). Smith rejects the notion that the procession of v. 24 is to be understood of a cultic procession of the ark and the people of Israel into the sanctuary. Instead, the reference is to 'the movement and presence of God in past and present history which is revealed in acts of mercy' (vv. 19, 20, 28), judgment (v. 21), and particularly the theophany (vv. 1, 8, 16-18, 35). The final section looks forward to the eschatological time in which God is in his 'temple in Jerusalem and has universal dominion over all kings and kingdoms'.[78]

The military language of Psalm 68:17 and 18 is poetic and not to be taken literally. Its function was to focus on the main point of the Psalm, namely, the entrance of God into his sanctuary in Zion. But first he ascends the mount and takes captives with him (v. 18a). These prisoners are not Gentile foes, but Israelites who were often rebellious (vv. 5-6, 18b). Smith claims that Psalm 68 is itself referring to earlier Scripture; it 'echoes' the language of Numbers 8 and 18, where the Levites are mentioned[79] as being taken by the Lord from among the people of Israel (8:6, 14) since they belong to him in a special way ('the Levites shall be mine', v. 14; cf. 3:45). But having taken them for himself, he then gives them back as gifts to the people so as to serve the congregation. Thus, Numbers 18:6, 'I have *taken* your brothers the Levites from among the people of Israel; to you they are *given*

75. Stott, 157.

76. R. A. Taylor, 'The Use', 327, has shown that in none of the supposed Old Testament parallels (Gen. 15:9; 18:5; Exod. 25:2, etc.) is the Hebrew *lāqaḥ* ('receive') rendered in Greek by some form of δίδωμι ('give'), which might be expected if the original had the nuance of to 'take in order to give'. Further, when the Hebrew verb signifies to 'fetch', it is usually accompanied by a prepositional phrase which is lacking in Ps. 68:18. Finally, if the original had the meaning suggested, does it adequately explain the presence of a variant textual tradition, as witnessed by the Targum (and possibly the Peshitta)?

77. G. V. Smith, 'Paul's Use of Psalm 68:18 in Ephesians 4:8', *JETS* 18 (1975), 181-89.

78. G. V. Smith, 'Paul's Use'; 186.

79. G. V. Smith, 'Paul's Use', 186. Recent research into the conscious embedding of fragments from an earlier text into a later one has been styled 'intertextuality'; see R. B. Hays, *Echoes of Scripture in the Letters of Paul* (New Haven: Yale University Press, 1989).

as a *gift* for the Lord, to do the service of the tabernacle of the congregation'. If Psalm 68 is read in this light, then the captives taken in Yahweh's train as he enters his sanctuary are not his foes, but ministers whom he has taken and then given to his people to serve them on his behalf (cf. Isa. 66:20-21).

Knowing that Psalm 68:18 was itself referring to earlier Scripture (Num. 8, 18) and that the Lord's *receiving gifts,* that is, chosen individuals, from among the people was for the purpose of *giving* them back to his people for ministry, Paul cites the Psalm using the verb 'gave' in an explanatory way, and places the emphasis on the persons given back ('gifts', vv. 8, 11) and the ministries they are to fulfil (vv. 11-16). According to Smith, 'Paul wants his readers to understand that throughout history God has chosen special men as leaders of the community of believers'.[80] The grace given to fulfil these different responsibilities may vary (cf. v. 7). The apostle's exegesis of Psalm 68, then, is not that of *midrash pesher,* 'but a remoulding of the thought of Psalm 68:18 on the basis of the Scriptural commentary in Numbers 8:6-19; 18:6 which the Psalmist used. . . . [T]he controlling factor [is that] of a grammatical-historical understanding of the text'.[81]

None of the above-mentioned suggestions fully solves this difficult crux. Smith's attractive proposal, however, has drawn attention to a number of likely connections between Numbers 8 and 18, Psalm 68, and Ephesians 4. God's action in taking and receiving the Levites as a gift, then giving them back to his people in order to minister to the congregation parallels the ascended Christ's leading captives and giving gifts in Ephesians 4. Whether these links, however, have demonstrated a clear case of intertextuality, recurring typological patterns, or simply parallels is more difficult to ascertain.

9-10   After quoting Psalm 68:18, the apostle expounds its meaning with reference to Christ's ascension and bestowal of gifts on his people. In particular, two verbs are selected from the Psalm, and their meaning and implications are explained: *he ascended* (vv. 9, 10), and *he gave* (v. 11). The first, *he ascended,*[82] which originally applied to God coming from Sinai and majestically ascending Zion (Ps. 68), and was then taken up in

---

80. G. V. Smith, 'Paul's Use', 188.

81. G. V. Smith, 'Paul's Use', 189.

82. The direct quotation is introduced by the neuter article (τό, cf. Mark 9:23; Matt. 19:17, 18). τὸ δὲ ἀνέβη points back to ἀναβάς ('having ascended', v. 8). Paul quotes the underlying meaning (ἀνέβη, 'he ascended') rather than the exact form, probably to make it more noticeably parallel with the following κατέβη ('he descended'); so K. L. McKay, *A New Syntax of the Verb in New Testament Greek: An Aspectual Approach* (New York: Lang, 1994), 98-99. However, D. B. Wallace, *Greek Grammar,* 238, thinks that, although only one word ἀνέβη ('he ascended') from Ps. 68:18 is repeated, 'the idiom suggests that the whole verse is under examination'. Wallace claims that the author is not asking, 'What does he ascended mean?' but, 'What does the quotation from Ps 68:18 mean?'

(later) Judaism as referring to Moses, who climbed the mountain of God (Mount Sinai) to receive the tables of the law, is here applied to Christ's return from earth to the highest heaven, an ascent of great significance which has already been mentioned in 1:20-21. There God was the subject of the actions: he raised Christ from the dead and 'seated him . . . in the heavenly realm'. Here Christ himself is the subject: it is he who *ascended*. There is, however, no final dichotomy between the two.

Verse 9 is usually rendered as a question in EVV (cf. NIV: *What does "he ascended" mean . . . ?*). But the question is rhetorical since it is not seeking to elicit information. Instead, it is calling special attention to the phrase 'he went up', and this is seen to imply that Christ also 'descended'. To what descent, however, does the text refer — a descent into Hades, Christ's descent at his incarnation, or the descent of the exalted Christ in the Spirit?

(1) *A descent into Hades.* Although this interpretation of Christ's descent into the realm of the dead has had a long and considerable influence in the history of the exegesis of Ephesians, it has less support today.[83] The early fathers associated Ephesians 4:9 with 1 Peter 3:19 ('he went and preached to the spirits in prison'), which they interpreted as Christ's 'harrowing of hell'. But there is no obvious reference to Hades or hell here in Ephesians. On the traditional view a descent into Hades is from the earth to the underworld or realm of the dead. Although Romans 10:6, 7 and Philippians 2:8-10 ('under the earth') have been drawn in to support this view, the contrast here in Ephesians 4:9, 10 is between an ascent to heaven and a descent from there. The unusual expression 'the lower parts of the earth' is better interpreted as 'the earth below'[84] than as the abode of the dead. Paul's contrast is 'not between one part of the earth and another, but between the whole earth and heaven',[85] and this

83. This includes E. G. Selwyn (on 1 Peter), F. W. Beare, J. A. Robinson, C. E. Arnold, and A. T. Hanson.

84. In τὰ κατώτερα [μέρη] τῆς γῆς the genitive τῆς γῆς ('of the earth') is a genitive of apposition ('the lower regions, the earth'); so most recent commentators. It has also been pointed out that if Paul had three levels of the universe in mind he might well have used the superlative, 'the lowest parts (κατώτατα) of the earth', for which there was good precedent in the Psalms (63:9; 139:15), rather than the comparative. Further, the cosmology of Ephesians is two-storied: the distinction is regularly drawn between heaven and earth. Finally, Christ's triumph over the powers, according to Ephesians, occurs not in a descent to the underworld, but in the course of his victorious ascent. For further details and bibliography, see Barth, 433-34, and W. H. Harris, "'The Heavenlies'", 80-85. For a different view see W. J. Dumbrell, *Search*, 300.

85. So John Calvin, who adds: It is 'as if he had said, "From that lofty habitation He descended into our deep gulf"'; *The Epistles of Paul the Apostle to the Galatians, Ephesians, Philippians and Colossians*, trans. T. H. L. Parker (Edinburgh: Oliver & Boyd, 1965 = Grand Rapids: Eerdmans, 1972), 176, cited by Bruce, 343.

fits with the twofold cosmology of the letter, where 'all things' is made up of 'heaven and earth'.

(2) *Christ's descent at his incarnation (and death).* The one who ascended and now fills the universe (and who gives different gifts to us) is the same person who first descended in his incarnation and death for us on the cross (cf. Eph. 2:14-17). This sequence parallels the order of Psalm 68, where Yahweh first descended to deliver his people and triumph over his enemies before ascending to his dwelling place. Moreover, this is the same perspective as that of the descending and ascending of the Redeemer of John's Gospel (3:12; 6:62; cf. 6:33, 38, 50-51; 20:17), and as the humiliation and subsequent exaltation of Christ in Philippians 2:6-11. (Paul may therefore have in mind not so much descent and ascent in spatial terms, but humiliation and exaltation as a result of which Christ bestows on the church his gifts in order to bring it to maturity.)[86] Although this reference to Christ's descent at his incarnation and death has been regarded as something of a digression to the apostle's main purpose,[87] it appears to have been made in order to show that the passage from the Psalm had to refer to Christ, since an ascent implies a previous 'descent', and Christ is the only one who descended (from heaven) before ascending.[88]

(3) *The descent of the exalted Christ in the Spirit.* A recent interpretation takes the descent of Christ to be subsequent[89] to his ascent to heaven, and thus referring to his descent in the Spirit at Pentecost. This view, it is claimed, makes more sense in the immediate context, with the result that vv. 9 and 10 do not need to be treated as a parenthesis. Christ's descent in the Spirit fits neatly between the two main foci of the passage, namely, his ascent and his giving of gifts. Paul has already spoken of the Spirit's work in unifying the body (vv. 3, 4); now he makes the important connection with the coming of the Spirit. Such an interpretation is interesting in the light of the Jewish exegetical tradition which applied the going up mentioned in Psalm 68 to Moses: he ascended to receive the law and then descended in order to give it to Israel. So, according to Caird, Psalm 68 is no longer a Jewish Pentecostal psalm relating to Moses but 'a Christian Pen-

---

86. Stott, 159.

87. Many texts and translations (including NIV), place vv. 9, 10 within parentheses to show that the argument moves directly from v. 8 to v. 11.

88. Cf. Bratcher and Nida, 99. Lincoln, 225, however, claims that these verses are 'treated by commentators as a digression with little agreement about their purpose'.

89. Several significant manuscripts insert the word πρῶτον ('first') after κατέβη ('he descended'). This would represent 'an insurmountable difficulty' for view (3) if it was part of the original text. However, the shorter reading is probably genuine. The πρῶτον ('first') appears to have been added by later copyists in order to clarify the meaning (cf. W. H. Harris, '"The Heavenlies"', 82).

tecostal Psalm, celebrating the ascension of Christ and his subsequent descent at Pentecost to bestow spiritual gifts upon the Church'.[90] Although this third option is possible, it runs into the difficulty of the Pentecostal event being thought of as a descent of *Christ*.[91] Further, v. 10 suggests that Christ ascends and fills the universe from heaven (see on 1:23), rather than that he again descends from heaven to bring gifts.

On balance, then, the incarnation provides the most obvious reference for the descent. But it needs to be borne in mind that, although the descent has attracted much discussion, Paul's main focus is on Christ's *ascent* in the context of his giving gifts.

Having descended to the earth below in his incarnation, Christ then ascended *higher than all the heavens.* The 'all' indicates that a number of heavens is in view. Whether three (cf. 2 Cor. 12:2), seven, or more heavens are referred to, Christ has ascended above everything to the place of highest supremacy. This language parallels his exaltation and enthronement 'in the heavenly realms, far above all rule and authority, power and dominion' (1:20-21). In the light of this similar phraseology, and the following purpose clause, 'in order that he might fill the whole universe', which corresponds to the expression in 1:23 (Christ 'fills everything in every way'), 'all the heavens' is best understood as a metaphorical reference to the powers of 1:21 who have been subjugated to him.[92]

The goal of Christ's exaltation to the place of highest supremacy is 'that he might fill all things'. This final clause corresponds to 1:23, 'the fullness of him who fills everything in every way,' where the verb 'fill' signifies to 'control by exercise of sovereignty'. Christ fills the universe, not in some semi-physical sense,[93] but by his mighty rule over all things

90. G. B. Caird, 'The Descent of the Spirit in Ephesians 4:7-11', *SE* 2 (= TU 87; Berlin: Akademie, 1964), 535-45, esp. 541. So also E. D. Roels, *God's Mission: The Epistle to the Ephesians in Mission Perspective* (Franeker: Wever, 1962), 161-63; Lincoln, 246-47; W. H. Harris, *The Descent*, 171-97, and his 'The Ascent and Descent of Christ in Ephesians 4:9-10', *BSac* 151 (1994), 198-214; cf. B. Lindars, *Apologetic,* 51-59.

91. Although Lincoln, 247, seeks to counter this difficulty by claiming that there is a 'virtual interchange' between Christ and the Spirit elsewhere in Ephesians (cf. 1:13 and 4:30; 3:16 with v. 17; and 1:23 with 5:18), his argument is not wholly convincing. For a number of criticisms, see Hoehner.

92. So W. H. Harris, '"The Heavenlies"', 84, who takes τῶν οὐρανῶν ('of the heavens') as 'a metaphor of simple replacement' in which the 'powers' of 1:21 are 'replaced . . . by a reference to the locus of their dwelling'. Lincoln, 248, on the other hand, considers the language of Christ's exaltation to be paradoxical: he is both locally in heaven (1:20; cf. 6:9) and at the same time above the heavens (4:10).

93. This is the line taken by those who claim that the ἵνα-clause 'that he might fill all things' (ἵνα πληρώσῃ τὰ πάντα) is linked with both Christ's descent and ascent. But syntactically the ἵνα-clause is dependent on the ascent alone, and his filling all things has to do with his sovereign rule over everything.

(see on 1:22-23), a notion that is parallelled in the Old Testament where filling the universe, in this sense of exercising sovereign rule, is predicated of God: '"Do I not fill heaven and earth?" says the LORD' (Jer. 23:24). Here the idea is transferred to Christ: he fills the universe through the exercise of his lordship over everything. This entails his functioning as the powerful ruler over the principalities (1:21), and giving grace and strength to his people (4:13, 15-16), through whom he fulfils his purposes.

11 Christ now sets out[94] to accomplish the goal of filling all things by supplying[95] his people with everything necessary to foster the growth and perfection of the body (v. 13). Having achieved dominion over all the powers through his victorious ascent,[96] he sovereignly distributes gifts to the members of his body.[97] The building of the body is inextricably linked with his intention of filling the universe with his rule, since the church is his instrument in carrying out his purposes for the cosmos.[98]

While in 1 Corinthians 12:4-11 the 'varieties of gifts' are the diverse ministries allocated by the Spirit and the ability to exercise them, here the gifts are the persons themselves, 'given' by the ascended Christ to his people to enable them to function and develop as they should.[99] Christ supplies the church with gifted ministers.[100] Four (or five) categories are mentioned: *apostles, prophets, evangelists, pastors and teachers*.[101] The words

94. V. 11 commences another long, intricate sentence which runs through to the end of v. 16.

95. According to D. B. Wallace, *Greek Grammar,* 375, Christ is the one who fills all things, and v. 11 adds 'the specifics of his giving spiritual gifts'.

96. W. H. Harris, '"The Heavenlies"', 84; cf. Arnold, 56, 57.

97. The exalted Christ who fills the universe by his rule is *the one* of whom the Psalm said, 'he gave gifts to men' (note that the αὐτός, 'he', of v. 11 picks up the αὐτός of v. 10).

98. The connection between v. 10c ('that he might fill all things') and v. 11 is more natural than Best, 388, seems to suggest.

99. Bruce, 345. In 1 Cor. 12 Paul spoke not only of the gift of prophecy (v. 10) but also of 'prophets' who had been appointed in the church (v. 28). Similarly, in Rom. 12:6-8 he moves freely from abilities to persons. The fact that the gifts mentioned in Eph. 4 are the gifted persons is not surprising, but simply illustrates 'the close relationship between the individual and the gift one possessed'; so K. S. Hemphill, *Spiritual Gifts: Empowering the New Testament Church* (Nashville: Broadman, 1988), 180.

100. Best, 388, comments: 'The gifts are not gifts made to people but gifts of people, people who have a particular role in the church'. Following Calvin, he adds: 'it may be assumed however that the charisma appropriate to the role which each is to play will have been bestowed'.

101. Paul enumerates and distinguishes his list through the expression τοὺς μέν . . . τοὺς δέ . . . τοὺς δέ. . . . The definite article probably belongs directly with the following nouns, rather than functions as a substantive with the nouns serving as predicates. Accordingly, the rendering '[he gave] the apostles, the prophets, the evangelists, etc.' is preferred to the usual translation, '[he gave] some to be apostles, some to be prophets, some

'he gave gifts to men' are not restricted to these, but they exemplify all the gifts of Christ's victory[102] by which he endows the church. The words which commence the Psalm citation, 'This is why' (v. 8), indicate that *all* the varying graces of v. 7 are gifts from Christ's bounty. These in v. 11 are deliberately emphasized since they provide the church with the teaching of Christ for the edification of the body (v. 12) and for the avoidance of false teaching (v. 14). They enable others to exercise their own respective ministries so that the body is built to maturity, wholeness, and unity. Those listed are ministers of the Word through whom the gospel is revealed, declared, and taught. The return to 'each one' occurs in v. 12 with its reference to 'the saints' who have been equipped by the ministries which the apostle lists here.

The New Testament contains five such lists (Rom. 12:6-8; 1 Cor. 12:8-10, 28-30; Eph. 4:11-12; cf. 1 Pet. 4:10-11) which between them number more than twenty different gifts, some of which are not particularly spectacular (cf. Rom. 12:8). Each list diverges significantly from the others. None is complete, but each is selective and illustrative, with no effort to force the various gifts into a neat scheme. Even together all five do not present a full catalogue of gifts.

The specific mention, first of all, that Christ gave *apostles* and *prophets* corresponds to the earlier references in 2:20 and 3:5 (see the exegesis above) to their *foundational* role as the authoritative recipients and proclaimers of the mystery of Christ (note also their appearance first in Paul's list of 1 Corinthians 12:28). Because of the mention of *evangelists, pastors,* and *teachers,* many modern commentators[103] have concluded that the *apostles* and *prophets* had passed from the scene by the time Ephesians was written and had been replaced by a second generation of ministers. But this conclusion is unnecessary. *Evangelists, pastors,* and *teachers* exercised their ministry during the apostles' time and subsequently, and were no doubt the church workers whom most of the readers had encountered. Many did not know the apostle Paul. It was his fellow-evangelists through whom the gospel was proclaimed outside Ephesus, while to-

---

to be evangelists, etc.' So H. Merklein, *Das kirchliche Amt*, 73-75; Schnackenburg, 180; Lincoln, 249; R. A. Campbell, *The Elders: Seniority within Earliest Christianity* (Edinburgh: T & T Clark, 1994), 109; and E. Best, 'Ministry in Ephesians', in *Essays*, 157-77, esp. 162; cf. BDF §250. Against this S. E. Porter, *Idioms*, 113, suggests that the μέν . . . δέ, when coordinated with the article, causes it to function much like a pronoun, here in a partitive sense: 'he gave some apostles, some prophets, some evangelists, some pastors and teachers'.

102. Turner, 1238.

103. Note, e.g., Schnackenburg, 180-81. E. Best, 'Ministry', 157-58, nuances this somewhat by claiming that the ministry of the apostles and prophets, as 'the foundation of the church' and as 'the recipients of the revelation that the gospel is for Gentiles as well as Jews', belongs to the past, even if the holders of these offices were still alive.

wards the end of his ministry the term 'pastor' or 'shepherd' was used alongside 'overseer' and 'elder' to describe church leaders (cf. Acts 20:17, 28, where 'elders' are 'overseers' who 'pastor' the flock).[104] (Note particularly the example of Epaphras, through whom the congregations at Colossae, Laodicea, and Hierapolis were founded: Col. 1:7-8; 4:12-13.)

Evangelists[105] were engaged in the preaching of the gospel. They are not mentioned elsewhere in the Pauline corpus except at 2 Timothy 4:5, where Timothy is urged to 'do the work of an evangelist'. The only other New Testament occurrence of the noun is in Acts 21:8, where Philip (one of the 'seven' of Acts 6:3-6) is called 'the evangelist'. As proclaimers of the gospel *evangelists* carried on the work of the apostles. While the term probably included itinerant individuals who engaged in primary evangelism, it was not limited to them. The admonition to Timothy to 'do the work of an evangelist' is set within the context of a settled congregation,[106] which presumably meant a ministry to believers and unbelievers alike, while the cognate verb, rendered 'preach the gospel',[107] covers a range of activities from primary evangelism and the planting of churches to the ongoing building of Christians and the establishment of settled congregations (cf. Rom. 1:11-15).[108] Here in Ephesians 4 evangelists are given by the ascended Christ for the purpose of building his body, and this included both intensive and extensive growth.

The term 'pastor' is used only here in the New Testament to refer to a ministry in the church, although the related verb 'to shepherd' appears several times in this sense (Acts 20:28; 1 Pet. 5:2; cf. John 21:16), and the noun 'flock'[109] is used of the church (Acts 20:28-29; 1 Pet. 5:2, 3). *Pastors*, whose functions are similar to those of overseers (cf. Phil. 1:1) and elders (cf. Acts 20:17, with 28; also 14:23; 1 Tim. 4:14; 5:17, 19, etc.), exercise lead-

---

104. So, rightly, Turner, 1238.

105. εὐαγγελιστής is rare in Greek literature (*Inscriptiones Graecae* XII.1.675.6) and may have been a Christian coinage. Cf. U. Becker, *NIDNTT* 2:114; G. Strecker, *EDNT* 2:70; and the discussions of F. S. Spencer, *The Portrait of Philip in Acts: A Study of Roles and Relations* (Sheffield: Academic Press, 1992), 262-69, esp. 263-65; and Best, 'Ministry', 163-66.

106. Although it may be true that Timothy is not instructed in so many words 'to seek the conversion of unbelievers' (so E. Best, 'Ministry', 164), his ministry of preaching and teaching the word (cf. 2 Tim. 4:2) is directed to Christian and non-Christian alike, even when exercised within the congregation (against Best). The gospel addresses both believers and unbelievers. Regarding Paul's concern, expressed in the Pastoral Epistles, that Timothy and other believers, as members of churches, might be wholly committed to the spread of the gospel, see the recent work of P. H. Towner, *1-2 Timothy & Titus* (Downers Grove/Leicester: Inter-Varsity, 1994), 29.

107. Gk. εὐαγγελίζομαι.

108. Note the detailed discussion in P. T. O'Brien, *Gospel and Mission*, 61-64, etc.

109. The terms belong to the ποιμήν word-group.

ership through nurture and care of the congregation. They manage the church (1 Thess. 5:12; Rom. 12:8), and are to be regarded in love 'because of their work'. The imagery of the shepherd, which was applied to God (Gen. 49:24; Ps. 23:1; 80:1; 40:11) to denote the way he cared for and protected his people, as well as to leaders (both good and bad) in Israel (2 Sam. 5:2; Ps. 78:71; Jer. 23:2; Ezek. 34:11), comes to be applied to church leaders as those who carry on Jesus' pastoral ministry. He is the Good Shepherd, who cares for God's flock (John 10:11-18; Matt. 18:12-14; Luke 15:3-7; Heb. 13:20; 1 Pet. 2:25; 5:4). Leaders in the church are exhorted to be 'shepherds of God's flock' (1 Pet. 5:2; Acts 20:28) who pattern their pastoral ministry after Christ's example.

The *pastors* and *teachers* are linked here by a single definite article in the Greek,[110] which suggests a close association of functions between two kinds of ministers who operate within the one congregation (cf. 2:20). Although it has often been held that the two groups are identical (i.e., 'pastors who teach'),[111] it is more likely that the terms describe overlapping functions (cf. 1 Cor. 12:28-29 and Gal. 6:6, where 'teachers' are a distinct group).[112] All pastors teach (since teaching is an essential part of pastoral ministry), but not all teachers are also pastors.[113] The latter exercise their leadership role by feeding God's flock with his word.

Teaching[114] is often an exposition or application of Scripture (Acts 15:35; 18:11, 25; Rom. 2:20, 21; Col. 3:16; Heb. 5:12), or an explanation and reiteration of apostolic injunctions (1 Cor. 4:17; Rom. 16:17; 2 Thess. 2:15; 2 Tim. 2:2; 3:10). In the Pastoral Epistles, teaching appears to be an authoritative function concerned with the faithful transmission of apostolic doctrine or tradition and committed to men specially chosen (e.g., 2 Tim. 1:13-14; 2:1-2; 1 Tim. 3:2; 5:17; Tit. 1:9). Timothy is urged not only to pursue a teaching ministry himself but also to entrust what he has learned to faithful men who will be able to teach others also (1 Tim. 4:13, 16; 2 Tim. 2:2). Teachers did not simply impart information or open up new ways of

110. τοὺς δὲ ποιμένας καὶ διδασκάλους. Note the discussion of shepherds and teachers in E. Best, 'Ministry', 166-70.

111. According to Barth, 438-39, the one ministry was being described, namely, that of 'teaching shepherds'.

112. E. Best, 'Ministry', 167-68, while conceding that two groups may be envisaged, acknowledges that the same people could exercise the different functions of shepherding and teaching from time to time. He adds that we should not think of a rigid separation between them.

113. D. B. Wallace, *Greek Grammar*, 284, argues on syntactical grounds that the ποιμένας ('shepherds') were part of the διδασκάλους ('teachers'). This is 'in keeping with the semantics of the plural noun construction', in which 'the first-subset-of-second category is well-attested'. Calvin, 179, came to a similar exegetical conclusion.

114. Cf. Lincoln, 251-52; and Best, 391-92.

thought. They also urged their hearers to live by what they taught (Eph. 4:20-21). So important is this ministry for building the body of Christ that provision is made for its continuity for succeeding generations.

Ephesians 4 focusses on the exalted Christ's action of giving these 'ministers' to the church. We may assume that they regularly functioned as *apostles, prophets, evangelists,* and the like, and that their ministries were accepted and recognized in the churches. It is appropriate, then, to speak of them as 'officers'. To suggest, as Fee does, that the listing in v. 11 'has to do with *function,* not with office' is to introduce a false antithesis.[115] Arnold's comment is more balanced: 'Christ supplies the church with gifted men; he provides both charisma and office in an inseparable unity'.[116]

12 The purpose of Christ's bestowing these gifts on the church is expressed in three successive prepositional phrases, the precise meaning and construction of which are not entirely clear: 'for the equipment of the saints', 'for the work of ministry', and 'for building the body of Christ'.[117] These phrases have been understood along the following main lines:

(1) Until recently the dominant view has been to take the first phrase, 'for the equipment of the saints', as directly related to the main verb *he gave* (v. 11), and to express the reason for Christ's giving these ministers. Then, in line with the change of preposition,[118] the phrase 'for the work of ministry' has been understood as subordinate to the first, 'for the equipment of the saints', while the next phrase, 'for building the body of Christ', is dependent on the previous phrases together (cf. NIV: *to prepare God's people for works of service, so that the body of Christ may be built up*).[119] On this view, ministers have been given by Christ to equip believ-

---

115. G. D. Fee, *God's Empowering Presence,* 706-7. This view had already been argued by J. D. G. Dunn, *Jesus and the Spirit* (London: SCM, 1975), 254, etc. (who emphatically asserted that 'charisma is always an event, the gracious activity of God through a man' which manifests God's grace and power in a particular instance and only for that instance'), and rejected by M. Turner, 'Spiritual', 31-32, 35; and R. Y. K. Fung, 'Ministry', 162-79. Paul can speak of believers 'having' (Rom. 12:6) differing gifts, and they can be exhorted to use or exercise them in the service of the community (cf. 1 Pet. 4:10). See further in H. Merklein, *Das kirchliche Amt,* 79-80, 348-92; and note the discussion of L. M. White, 'Social Authority in the House Church Setting and Ephesians 4:1-16', *ResQ* 29 (1987), 209-28.

116. Arnold, 159.

117. πρὸς τὸν καταρτισμὸν τῶν ἁγίων; εἰς ἔργον διακονίας; and εἰς οἰκοδομὴν τοῦ σώματος τοῦ Χριστοῦ.

118. From πρός to εἰς (each of which signifies 'to' or 'for').

119. Note Robinson, 99, who writes of the second εἰς-phrase: 'This is the process to the forwarding of which all that has been spoken of is directed'. He was the first in recent times to challenge the older view (see [2]) that Christ had three distinct purposes in mind in giving gifts to his church. Instead, Robinson argues that there were two purposes, one immediate — 'to equip the saints for work in his service' — and the other ultimate — 'for building up the body of Christ'. Robinson has been followed by many commentators.

ers for the exercise of their gifts (v. 7; cf. v. 16) in Christian service, so that by means of *both* the ministers and the common service of believers the body of Christ may be built. This interpretation, it is claimed, does justice to the change of prepositions in the Greek, to the emphasis in v. 11 on Christ's giving of ministers, and to the corresponding part which each believer plays in the growth of Christ's body (v. 16).[120]

(2) This dominant approach, however, has been challenged,[121] and an earlier interpretation, as represented by the AV and the RSV, has been preferred. The three phrases of v. 12 are taken as coordinate and dependent on Christ's giving. The various ministers of v. 11 have been given 'for the equipment of the saints', 'for the work of ministry', and 'for building the body of Christ'. The change of preposition, it is claimed, cannot bear the weight placed on it by the earlier view (and may be simply a stylistic variation), while there are no grammatical or linguistic grounds for making specific links between the first and second phrases. In response to the charge that this represents a 'clerically dominated' interpretation, it is asserted that the active role for all believers is preserved in vv. 7 and 16, while the focus in the context of v. 12 is on the task and function of Christ's specific gifts, that is, the apostles, prophets, and the like, not all the saints. On this view, the term translated as 'preparing,' or 'equipping', is instead taken to signify 'completion', and does not need to be supplemented with an additional phrase such as 'for the work of ministry'. This latter expression is believed to refer to the special ministry of those mentioned in v. 11, not Christian service in general. Those who take this line suspect that the alternative view is motivated by a desire to avoid clericalism and to support a 'democratic' model of the church![122]

The difficulties with the second view are syntactical and contextual. The prepositional change is not finally decisive: syntactically the three phrases could be dependent on the verb 'he gave'. But if there is a movement from the discussion of the work of the ministers (v. 11) to that of all God's people between v. 12a and v. 12bc, as we contend, then the change in preposition confirms that movement, and the mention of 'saints' in v. 12a underscores it. If the three phrases described activities in which

---

120. So R. Y. K. Fung, 'The Nature of the Ministry according to Paul', *EvQ* 54 (1982), 140-41. Along with many others note recently G. D. Fee, *God's Empowering Presence*, 706.

121. Schnackenburg, 182-84; Lincoln, 253-55; T. D. Gordon, '"Equipping" Ministry in Ephesians 4?' *JETS* 37 (1994), 69-78; R. A. Campbell, *The Elders*, 110; and Turner, 1238, who changed his earlier view as expressed in 'Spiritual Gifts', 29.

122. So Lincoln, 253. Cf. R. A. Campbell, *The Elders*, 110: 'The passage needs to be rescued from an anachronistic exegesis according to which its purpose is to teach the "ministry of the laity"'.

ministers alone were engaged, then one might have expected the term 'saints' to appear at the point of change, namely, in v. 12c; instead, it occurs at the conclusion of the first phrase, v. 12a, 'for equipping the *saints*'.[123]

Further, the letter as a whole has emphasized Christ's riches being received by *all* the saints (1:3-19; 3:20), while the immediate context of vv. 7-16 is framed by an insistence at the beginning of the paragraph that each believer was given 'grace' (v. 7), and at its conclusion that the *whole* body is growing from the head as *each part* (v. 16) does its work. If it is only the leaders of v. 11 who perfect the saints, do the work of ministry, and edify the body of Christ, then this is a departure from Paul's usual insistence that every member is equipped for ministry.[124] It is better, therefore, to regard those enumerated in v. 11 as helping and directing other members of the church so that all may carry out their several ministries for the good of the whole. An emphasis on 'word' ministries corresponds with Romans 12:6-8 and the ranking of 1 Corinthians 12:28, while the connection between the 'special' ministers and others enhances our understanding of the relationship between gifted members and gifted leaders.

The meaning of the first phrase, rendered 'to equip God's people' by the NEB, turns on a noun[125] which occurs nowhere else in the New Testament, although the cognate verb is found frequently. The latter has several related meanings, including 'repairing' (Matt. 4:19; Mark 1:19), 'equipping, preparing', 'completing', and 'training, disciplining'.[126] The notion of equipping or preparing, in the sense of making someone adequate or sufficient for something, best suits the context. However, it does require an object: people are prepared for some purpose. That purpose is 'for the work of ministry', an activity of the saints for which the leaders are to prepare and equip them. Christ has given 'special' ministers so that they will 'make God's people fully qualified', thus enabling them to serve their Lord by serving one another.[127] 'Work' describes an ongoing activity (cf. 1 Cor. 15:58; Phil. 2:30; 1 Thess. 1:3; 2 Tim. 4:5) seen in 'service'. In

123. Note Best's arguments, 395-99, esp. 398.
124. K. S. Hemphill, *Spiritual Gifts*, 176-79; cf. M. Turner's earlier handling in 'Spiritual Gifts', 29.
125. Gk. καταρτισμός.
126. So E. Best, 'Ministry', 173, following LSJ. The meaning of 'making complete', especially through restoring and training, is preferred by those who adopt (2). On this view, the ministers given by Christ (v. 11) are the means by which this completion is effected, and they achieve this through their ministries of proclamation, teaching, and leadership. So, e.g., Lincoln, 254.
127. Louw and Nida §75.5; cf. BAGD, 418.

Paul's letters the latter term occasionally refers to the specific ministry of the word (2 Cor. 3:6-8; 4:1; 5:18; 6:3; Rom. 11:13; Col. 4:17); but here it is used more comprehensively for the service of believers generally — as, indeed, it is in the parallel list of 1 Corinthians 12:5 (cf. Rom. 12:7; 1 Cor. 16:15). 'The ministry of the officials does not find its fulfilment in their own existence but only in the activity of preparing others to minister'.[128] The ministry mentioned in v. 11 fulfils an important role in the Lord's purposes: it is pioneering in nature, since it leads the way in serving the Lord's people (i.e., the 'saints'; see on 1:1, 15) and in equipping them for their own ministry. On this interpretation 'for the work of ministry' is subordinate to the first phrase, 'for the equipment of the saints', and refers to the common service of all believers. The 'work of ministry' thus corresponds to 'the grace given to each one of us' (v. 7), which is the subject of the section.

What has been done *for* the saints, by the apostles, prophets, and others preparing them, and *by* the saints through the exercise of their gifts in Christian service, is 'for *building* the body of Christ'.[129] All that has been spoken of in v. 11 and in the first two phrases of v. 12 is directed towards the goal of building the body of Christ, so that together the ministers of v. 11 and 'the saints' serve this divinely appointed goal. To the metaphor of building Paul has joined the idea of growth. Previously he used biological imagery of growth when referring to the building of the temple (cf. 2:21; 4:16); now he employs building imagery in speaking of the church as a body. The key term used in the phrase, 'for *building*[130] the body of Christ', here denotes the activity of building. The cognate verb appears outside the New Testament for the literal building of houses, temples, and other structures, and figuratively for the establishment of individuals or nations.[131] In the LXX this verb is employed in both a literal and a figurative sense of building (cf. 2 Sam. 7:11-13, where both senses are found). According to the prophetic literature of the Old Testament, the restoration of Israel after the judgment of the exile is promised in terms of God building a people for himself (Jer. 24:6;

---

128. E. Best, 'Ministry', 173.

129. Cf. Foulkes, 120.

130. οἰκοδομή can refer to the act of building (Rom. 15:2; 1 Cor. 14:3, 12, 26; 2 Cor. 10:8; 13:10; Eph. 4:16, 29) or to the resulting construction (Matt. 24:1; Mark 13:1, 2, etc.). Louw and Nida §42.34, comment: 'the construction of something, with focus on the event of building up or on the result of such an event'; hence it means 'to build up, to construct, construction'. Here it has the former sense (cf. BAGD, 558-59).

131. P. Vielhauer, *Oikodome: Aufsätze zum Neuen Testament* (Munich: Kaiser, 1979), 4-52; note also the treatment of D. G. Peterson, *Engaging with God: A Biblical Theology of Worship* (Leicester: Apollos, 1992), 206-15, esp. 206.

31:4; 33:7), and this he does by putting his words in the mouths of his prophets (Jer. 1:9-10). Matthew 16:18 ('I will *build* my church, and the gates of Hades will not overcome it') expresses the idea that as the Messiah Jesus is the one who builds or establishes the renewed community of the people of God.

In line with this salvation-historical dimension, Ephesians 4 indicates that the exalted Messiah gives ministries of the word to equip God's people for work in his service so as to build his body.[132] This constructing has both an extensive and an intensive dimension to it. Growth in size is implied in the mention of the gifts of apostles and evangelists (v. 11), while the introduction of the body metaphor implies the notion of development of the church as an organism from within, by means of its own God-given life.[133] Although the expression *may be built up* has sometimes been interpreted individualistically, this is inappropriate, since it regularly has a corporate dimension in the apostle's teaching, and this is clearly its significance in the present context.

13 The final goal to which the process of building the body of Christ is to lead is described in terms of attaining 'to the unity of the faith and of the knowledge of the Son of God, to mature manhood, to the measure of the stature of the fulness of Christ'. Those given by Christ as 'ministers' (v. 11), along with the 'saints' (v. 12), render their service so that God's people might reach this objective, and they are to continue serving *until* it is attained.[134] The verb employed here is used figuratively and means to 'attain or arrive at a particular state', with the focus on the end point.[135] Significantly, Christian growth or progress does not occur in isolation, for Paul's language here envisages God's people *collectively (we all)* as en route to this vital destination.

Three similar expressions, each introduced by the same preposi-

---

132. For a discussion of 'the body of Christ', see on Ephesians 1:23; 2:16; 4:4.

133. The use of οἰκοδομή in 2 Cor. 10:8; 12:19; 13:10 suggests that 'edification involves also a process of teaching and encouragement beyond the initial task of evangelism'. It entails 'founding, maintaining and advancing the congregation' (so D. G. Peterson, *Engaging with God*, 208, following P. Vielhauer, *Oikodome*, 72); note also H. Ridderbos, *Paul: An Outline of His Theology* (Grand Rapids: Eerdmans, 1975), 429-38, where the point is made that edification involves both an increase in numbers and the consolidation of the church as God's eschatological building.

134. The temporal clause introduced by μέχρι ('until') has both a prospective and a final force; so BDF §383(2); and Lincoln, 255.

135. So Louw and Nida §13.16. καταντάω occurs thirteen times in the New Testament, eight of which are in the literal sense of arriving at a place (cf. Acts 16:1; 18:19, 24, etc.). Other instances, including Eph. 4:13, have the figurative meaning to 'reach/attain' to something (Acts 26:7; Phil. 3:11; cf. 1 Cor. 10:11; 14:36); O. Hofius, *EDNT* 2:265; cf. BAGD, 415.

tion,[136] depict the final goal. The first is '[until we attain] to the unity of the faith and of the knowledge of the Son of God'. The unity which has been inaugurated in Christ through the events described in 2:11-22, and which the readers are strongly urged to *maintain* (i.e., 'the unity of the Spirit', v. 3), is here spoken of as a unity to which they are to *attain*. This oneness thus partakes of the tension between the 'already' and the 'not yet': it has been proclaimed as a given fact, but is now presented as the goal of Christian endeavour, a goal which can only be reached by *all* collectively, and will finally occur at Christ's coming, when he brings his people to complete maturity. The eschatological tension is evident in the first element — the unity of the *faith*. This *faith* has already been given (v. 5), yet its oneness is still to be fully appropriated. In the light of the syntactical connection between faith and knowledge,[137] the immediate context with its emphasis on instruction (v. 11), the reference to steadfastness in the face of false teaching (v. 14), and the likelihood that faith in v. 5 refers to that which is believed, it is best understood here in terms of its objective content rather than the readers' activity of believing.[138] The point being made, then, is that God's people are moving towards the goal of appropriating all that is included in the one faith.

Likewise, the eschatological tension between the already and the not yet is present in the second half of this expression, namely, the unity of *the knowledge of the Son of God*. God has already made known to the readers the mystery of his saving purposes in Christ (1:9-10). The apostle has prayed that they might grow in their spiritual understanding and know more of their hope, of God's inheritance, and of his mighty power on their behalf (1:17-19; 3:16-19). Now 'the unity of the knowledge of the Son of God' is the goal to be attained. This *knowledge*, like the preceding *faith*, is probably objective, thus referring to what is known of the Son of God.[139] Although it is

---

136. Gk. εἰς.

137. Both τῆς πίστεως ('of the faith') and τῆς ἐπιγνώσεως ('of the knowledge') are in a genitival relationship with the one noun ἑνότης ('unity'): 'the unity of the faith and [the unity] of the knowledge . . .'.

138. K. S. Hemphill, *Spiritual Gifts,* 186, contends that faith here 'must be given an objective content'. He adds: 'Personal belief in Christ committed a person to the objective truths which they had been taught (Col. 2:6-7; Eph. 4:20-21)'. And knowledge of 'this body of truth which they had been taught in Christ (4:21) would give these early Christians stability against false teaching'. Cf. Caird, 76; and Lincoln, 255. Bruce, 350, however, thinks it 'unlikely that a body of belief is intended'.

139. The expression 'the Son of God' (τοῦ υἱοῦ τοῦ θεοῦ) is the object of the knowledge only, and not also of 'the faith' (τῆς πίστεως) — however true this may be theologically — since the definite article (τῆς) is repeated before 'knowledge' (τῆς ἐπιγνώσεως), thus separating 'the knowledge of the Son of God' from 'of the faith' (τῆς πίστεως); against Meyer, 222.

marvellously variegated, since it concerns the one in whom all the treasures of wisdom and knowledge are hidden (Col. 2:2-3), it ultimately has a unity to it (cf. v. 5). The apostle, then, has in view an ongoing appropriation by believers, in fellowship together, of 'all that is involved in the salvation which centers in Christ',[140] and this goal is to be sought through the proper exercise of gifts.

The second statement which indicates the destination of God's people on the final day is that '[we all attain] to the mature man'.[141] This destination to which all believers are headed is understood as a corporate entity: it is not described in individual terms,[142] but refers to the totality of believers as the body of Christ (cf. v. 12),[143] in an expression that is akin to 'the one new man' of 2:15. The phrase 'mature man' is somewhat unusual since the term for an adult male or full-grown man is used, rather than the generic word for man or human.[144] The adjective has the sense of 'mature' (cf. 1 Cor. 2:6; 14:20; Heb. 5:14) rather than 'perfect', and focusses on the mature adult person in contrast with the infants of v. 14 who are immature and unstable, like a storm-tossed boat blown in all directions by the winds of false teaching.

The full maturity to be attained is more specifically defined by the third expression: it is 'measured by nothing less than the full stature of Christ' (NEB). Although the word rendered 'stature' can signify 'age', and in the light of the contrast between children and adults some have taken the term in this latter sense,[145] the imagery of 'fulness' is more naturally suited to spatial categories so that 'stature' is more appropriate here. The church is already the fulness of Christ (1:23; cf. 4:10). There is thus a realized dimension to its existence. But the future element is still present: the apostle has prayed that the readers might be 'filled up to all the fulness of God' (3:19); now in the immediate context the goal to be reached is mature manhood, and this is defined by the fulness of Christ.

140. Note the discussion in Lincoln, 255-56.

141. Gk. εἰς ἄνδρα τέλειον.

142. As Mitton, 154, thinks. But Paul does not write εἰς ἄνδρας τελείους ('to mature men') because he views the πάντες ('all') as *one* person (cf. Meyer, 223).

143. So most commentators. Barth, 484-96, however, contends that this refers to the Lord Jesus as 'the Perfect Man', whom the church as the Bride of Christ meets at his triumphant appearing. But this suggestion is ruled out by the other two phrases, which are dependent on the verb καταντήσωμεν ('[until] we attain').

144. That is, ἀνήρ rather than ἄνθρωπος. It is unnecessary, with H. Schlier and others, to look for a Gnostic background to the expression ἀνήρ τέλειος ('perfect man'). On the general question of understanding Ephesians in relation to Gnosticism, see Arnold, 7-13.

145. Meyer, 223-24, interprets ἡλικία as 'age', which is then more precisely defined by τοῦ πληρώματος τοῦ Χριστοῦ ('the fulness of Christ') and understood in temporal terms.

The maturity of this growth is measured by nothing less than Christ's full stature. 'The glorified Christ provides the standard at which his people are to aim: the corporate Christ cannot be content to fall short of the perfection of the personal Christ'.[146]

14 The threefold description in v. 13 points to the ultimate destination of God's people on the last day. Now, through a negative contrast, Paul sets forth the more immediate objective that is in line with this final goal and which should take place in the lives of the readers in their current situation. The introductory clause, 'so that we may no longer be children . . .', which is subordinate to v. 13, provides general comments about their present circumstances (cf. 'no longer'), at the same time indicating what should occur if genuine progress is to be made. The exalted Christ has given his gifts to the church so that by building his body immaturity and instability will increasingly be left behind. 'The ministry was given not only to enable the church to grow but also so that it would be able to resist any forces that might corrupt or destroy it'.[147] Paul writes tactfully as he pens these words, since he associates himself with his readers by using the first person plural *we* (cf. Phil. 3:15). He too desires, along with them, to stand firm, not to be tossed to and fro but to speak the truth in love and grow up into Christ, the head (v. 15).

The contrast between 'the mature person' of v. 13 and the 'children' here is pointed. Not only do the latter's ignorance and instability stand over against the knowledge of the *mature* adult (cf. 1 Cor. 2:6; 3:1; Heb. 5:13, 14),[148] but also the use of the plural 'children' (with its implications of individualism) stands in contrast to the *one* 'mature person' who is a corporate unity. The nature of the children's immaturity is graphically pictured in the following clauses and phrases: they are unstable, lacking in direction, vacillating, and open to manipulation. Like small, rudderless boats, they are *tossed back and forth by the waves* and driven this way and that by the prevailing wind.[149] The immediate,

---

146. Bruce, 350-51. 'When the goal is ultimately reached, and the body of Christ has grown up sufficiently to match the Head Himself, then will be seen that full-grown Man which is Christ together with His members. That spectacle will not fully appear until the day when they are glorified together with Him; but the expectation of that day will act as a powerful incentive to spiritual development in the present time'; F. F. Bruce, *Ephesians,* 87-88.

147. Best, 403.

148. Sometimes the term νήπιοι ('infants, small children') can be free from polemical overtones (in Matt. 11:25; 21:16; Luke 10:21 νήπιοι are the 'child-like, innocent' ones, with whom God is pleased; BAGD, 537). But in those passages, as here, where a value judgment is made, the term signifies those who are unstable and immature; cf. Barth, 441-42.

149. The verb κλυδωνιζόμενοι, which derives from κλύδων ('a succession of waves'), signifies 'to be tossed back and forth by the motion of waves' (Louw and Nida §16.12),

though not ultimate, cause[150] of their instability is 'every fresh gust of teaching' (NEB). This teaching, though regarded by some as Christian doctrine that has been 'endangered and perverted by various currents of wind',[151] is really false instruction. The full expression '*every* wind of doctrine' suggests different kinds of teaching (note Col. 2:22) which stand over against the unity of faith and knowledge to which the readers are to attain (v. 13). Accordingly, Paul's reference is best understood, along with most commentators, of the various religious philosophies which threatened to undermine or dilute the apostolic gospel.[152] No specifics are spelled out (though note 5:6-13), suggesting that the apostle has in view ongoing general dangers which were a hindrance to those not firmly grounded in the faith. Unable to come to settled convictions or to evaluate various forms of teaching, they fall an easy prey to every new theological fad.

Behind this dangerous and misleading teaching by which immature believers are tossed to and fro are deceitful people who seek to manipulate them by evil trickery. Paul's language is graphic, if not forthright. The false teaching which causes so much strife is promoted by the *cunning of men*. *Cunning* literally refers to dice-playing and comes to be used metaphorically of a trickery that results from craftiness, while the qualifier *of men* (as in Col. 2:8, 22) depicts it as human — that, and nothing more — and therefore opposed to Christ and his teaching. The second phrase, 'with cunning', intensifies the first. It literally means a 'readiness to do anything'. Although used in the LXX in a good or indifferent sense, its five occurrences in the New Testament have a negative connotation,[153] and here it signifies the malicious deception by which the false teachers seek to lead the unstable astray.

But, in addition to this, the apostle may have had in mind another

---

while περιφερόμενοι means to be 'carried here and there [by the wind]'. These metaphors were natural for ancient peoples, who were afraid of voyaging and of the omnipotence of both wind and waves. Note the vivid description in Ps. 107:23-27 of the impression made by the raging sea on those who were not seafarers. Cf. Barth, 442; and Schnackenburg, 186.

150. The dative παντὶ ἀνέμῳ [τῆς διδασκαλίας] ('by every wind [of doctrine]') is a dative of cause.

151. Schnackenburg, 186; cf. H. Merklein, *Das kirchliche Amt*, 107. This line is taken on the grounds that ἡ διδασκαλία ('the teaching'), with the article, denotes Christian instruction in Rom. 12:7; 15:4, as well as in the Pastoral Epistles, where it is almost a technical term (cf. 1 Tim. 1:10; 4:6, 13, 16; 5:17; 6:1; 2 Tim. 3:16, etc.), while false teaching is often indicated by a plural (Matt. 15:9; Mark 7:7; Col. 2:22; and 1 Tim. 4:1).

152. So Lincoln, 258, in agreement with most exegetes.

153. Gk. πανουργία (Luke 20:23; 1 Cor. 3:19; 2 Cor. 4:2; 11:3; Eph. 4:14); the adjective πανοῦργος (2 Cor. 12:16) has the sense of 'crafty'. Cf. Abbott, 122; and BAGD, 608; against Caird, 77.

source of that seductive 'cunning' which preys on human weakness, namely, the evil one himself. Paul employs the same word with reference to the serpent deceiving Eve 'by his *cunning*' (2 Cor. 11:3), while the synonym, which appears in the next phrase, denotes a 'crafty scheming with the intent to deceive'[154] that describes the intrigues of the devil (Eph. 6:11). Satan's machinations have 'method'; his aim is to *mislead* the immature who are not grounded on apostolic doctrine. If this connection is in view, then behind the false teaching are not simply evil men and women who pursue their unscrupulous goals with a scheming that produces error.[155] There is also a supernatural, evil power who seeks to deceive them with devilish cunning; his 'intrigues' are to be resisted energetically with the aid of God's armour (6:11).

Within the context of vv. 7-16, the dangers presented here only serve to highlight the importance of the ascended Christ giving ministers of his word to his people. They are to be firmly grounded in the apostolic teaching so that they may leave behind all immaturity and instability.

15 As Paul now focusses positively on the ultimate goal towards which he and his readers are moving, he desires that together they may grow up into Christ, who is the head. This growth will occur as they speak the truth in love rather than being misled by the malicious scheming of the false teachers. A sharp contrast, heightened by a chiasmus, is drawn between the final words of v. 14 and this opening clause of v. 15. Over against the 'crafty scheming' stands the expression *in love* (a key phrase in the letter, see below), while *speaking the truth* is set in opposition to the words 'of error'. Thus, *speaking the truth in love* lays out a twofold contrast with the false teachers: the latter were presenting *false* doctrine in a *deceptive* manner, but over against this God's people are to grow through proclaiming the *truth* in *love*.[156]

There is a considerable body of scholarly opinion which contends on both semantic and contextual grounds that the verb rendered to 'speak the truth' really signifies here to '*live out* the truth'.[157] However, in

---

154. According to C. Spicq, *TLNT* 2:462, μεθοδεία, can be defined as 'the well-thought-out, methodical art of leading astray . . . "machinations"'. Note also W. Michaelis, *TDNT* 5:102-3.

155. πλάνη ('error, deceit'), which frequently denotes false teaching (cf. Jude 11; 1 John 4:6; 2 Pet. 2:18; 3:17), stands over against apostolic practice (1 Thess. 2:3) and the truth (cf. 2 Thess. 2:11, 12), as here in v. 15.

156. K. S. Hemphill, *Spiritual Gifts*, 190.

157. Gk. ἀληθεύω. So, among others, J. A. Robinson, F. F. Bruce, C. L. Mitton, J. R. W. Stott, R. G. Bratcher and E. A. Nida, A. G. Patzia, and L. Morris. The phrase is often rendered 'truthing in love', and understood as signifying a 'living out of the truth in a spirit of love' (H. Hübner, *EDNT* 1:58, renders it *'be genuine, upright* [in love]'). Note the detailed discussion in C. Spicq, *TLNT* 1:81-82.

our judgment, there are stronger reasons for thinking that the word here refers to verbal testimony. Occasionally, it meant to 'speak the truth' in secular Greek,[158] and it consistently signified this in the LXX.[159] At Galatians 4:16, the only other instance of the word in the New Testament, Paul refers to 'speaking the truth' of the gospel (cf. Gal. 2:5, 14).[160] The same meaning makes better sense within the immediate context of Ephesians 4,[161] where the ascended Christ gives ministers of the word, and where speaking the truth provides a pointed contrast with the scheming of the false teachers and the dangerous winds of doctrine that were swirling around throughout proconsular Asia. Accordingly, the apostle is not exhorting his readers to truthfulness in general or speaking honestly with one another, however appropriate or important this may be. Rather, he wants all of them to be members of a 'confessing' church, with the content of their testimony to be 'the word of truth', the gospel of their salvation (1:13). This truth, which is guaranteed by God and is depicted as part of his own armour, is the belt which believers are to buckle around their waist as they resist the onslaughts of the evil one (6:14).

As Christians witness to the truth of the gospel they cannot use the same methods as the false teachers or the tempter whose evil activity lies behind them. Instead, they are to set forth this truth *in love*,[162] an expression that rules out all cunning and deception. Love has a prominent place in Ephesians: the first half of the letter (chaps. 1–3) climaxes with a prayer for the readers' establishment in the love of Christ and for a greater awareness on their part of the magnitude of this divine love (3:17, 19). The second half (chaps. 4–6) contains a series of instructions to love, the fulfilment of which is the outworking of the apostle's prayer. These are summarized by the exhortation to 'walk *in love,* just as Christ loved us and gave himself for us' (5:2). Here the key phrase *in love,* which occurs six times in the epistle,[163] begins and ends this paragraph on unity, diversity, and maturity in the body of Christ (4:2, 15, 16). It thus forms an *inclusio* or envelope to the passage (4:1-16). All those who have been

---

158. For details see C. Spicq, *TLNT* 1:81.

159. So Gen. 20:16; 42:16; Prov. 21:3; Isa. 44:26; Sirach 34:4 (against some renderings of C. Spicq, *TLNT* 1:82).

160. J. D. G. Dunn, *The Epistle to the Galatians* (London: Black, 1993), 237.

161. Note particularly Barth, 444; K. S. Hemphill, *Spiritual Gifts,* 190; Schnackenburg, 187; and Lincoln, 259-60; cf. BAGD, 36, and Louw and Nida §33.251.

162. Although it is syntactically possible to link ἐν ἀγάπῃ ('in love') with αὐξήσωμεν ('we will grow'), so that it is parallel with the idea of growing in love in v. 16, it is preferable with most commentators to connect the phrase with 'speaking the truth' which precedes.

163. In no other New Testament writing does this formula occur as often as it does in Ephesians: 1:4; 3:17; 4:2, 15, 16; 5:2.

urged to live a life worthy of their calling (v. 1) are to bear with one another in love (v. 2) and to testify to the truth of the gospel in love (v. 15; see also on v. 16). *In love* describes the sphere of the Christian life and spells out the manner in which the ministry of all is to occur. Its juxtaposition with truth is no accident. The claims of the two should not be held in tension. The truth as proclaimed should not be dissociated from love or promoted at the expense of love, while a life of love should embody the truth of the gospel.

By *speaking the truth in love*, then, we will all *grow up in every way into him who is the Head, that is, Christ.* Although it is grammatically possible to understand the verb 'grow' in a transitive sense ('we may cause the cosmos to grow'),[164] referring to God's people bringing the world to growth and maturity in Christ, both usage and context favour its being taken intransitively to denote the church's growth to maturity. Elsewhere in Ephesians and Colossians this word is used intransitively.[165] But nowhere else in Paul is the cosmos said to grow up into Christ, although growth is certainly envisaged of God's people. Believers are expected to grow in faith (2 Cor. 10:5; 2 Thess. 1:3) and in the knowledge of God (hence the apostle's prayer to this end, Col. 1:10). According to Colossians 2:19, which is akin to Ephesians 4:15, the whole body of Christ, which is totally dependent on the head to nourish and unify it, is said to 'grow with the growth of God'. Here the growth is to be comprehensive: God's people are to grow into Christ 'in every way',[166] that is, in faith, knowledge, unity, and, especially in this context, in love.[167]

This growth of the body has Christ as its goal: he is the one into whom we are to grow. The earlier reference to increase underscored his indispensable position as the foundation stone of the building which grows into a holy temple *in him* (2:21). In the following verse of this paragraph he is the source of the body's expansion (*from him*, 4:16). At v. 15 the stress is on the readers' progress and maturity towards him as the goal. Together believers become more and more like their Lord, so that they are fully and completely incorporated into him. And once more, by using the first person plural (lit. 'in order that *we* might grow') the apostle includes himself among those who are progressing and maturing into him. Already in the letter Christ has been called the *Head* over all things *for* the

---

164. 1 Cor. 3:9; 2 Cor. 9:10.

165. Cf. BDF §101, §309(2); BAGD, 121-22; and Barth, 445. Note the important reference, Eph. 2:21, 'In him the whole structure is joined together and grows (αὔξει) into a holy temple in the Lord'; also 4:16; Col. 1:10; 2:19 (cf. 1:6).

166. The expression 'all things' (τὰ πάντα) is an accusative of respect; cf. BDF §160; and BAGD, 633.

167. Cf. Schnackenburg, 188.

church, which is his body (1:22, 23). Implicit in this was his headship *over* the church. Now this notion is made explicit, for the one who is the goal of believers' growth is identified as Christ, the head of the body, and this means that he rules or governs it.

16 In this concluding verse of the paragraph (vv. 7-16) several prominent ideas of the earlier exposition, such as unity and diversity within the body, together with the body's growth in love, are repeated in summary form. In addition, the metaphor of the body is further developed in relation to 'the supporting ligaments' and 'each part'. Christ is not only the goal of the body's growth (v. 15); as the head who rules over the body he is the ultimate source *(from him)*[168] of its growth, for he supplies all that is necessary for its well-being, including its unity, nourishment, and progress.

Paul's focus is on the growth of the body as a whole,[169] not on the need for individuals to become mature in Christ, however necessary this may be. Both the subject of the sentence, 'the whole body', and the final expression, 'for its own upbuilding in love', clearly affirm this corporate emphasis.[170] Although the distinct contribution of each member to the life and development of the whole is highlighted through the clause *as each part does its work,* the stress still falls on the corporate growth of the body. The notion of believers' unity and their growing together as a collective whole is further accented by the following two verbs. The first, 'joined together', has already been used of the harmonious construction of the church as 'a holy temple in the Lord' (2:21), while the second, 'held together', appears in Colossians, where it refers to the body knit together as a unity by the head alone (Col. 2:19).[171] The two verbs are virtually synonymous and indicate that there is an ongoing,[172] unified growth to

---

168. ἐξ οὗ ('from whom') refers back to Christ (v. 15). The growth mentioned here is 'from Christ as person rather than as head' (which strictly would require ἐξ ἧς: so Best, 410, following E. D. Roels, *God's Mission,* 107-9; cf. G. Howard, 'The Head/Body Metaphors', 354). Even if κεφαλή ('head') was the antecedent, this does not indicate that the term means 'source' (which is to confuse referent with meaning); rather, Christ, as head of the body, exercises his rule over it by leading it and by supplying its needs. G. W. Dawes, *The Body,* 144-47, does not make this distinction clear.

169. E. Best, *One Body,* 150; Barth, 446; and D. G. Peterson, *Engaging with God,* 209.

170. Note C. E. Arnold, 'Jesus Christ', 362.

171. For a discussion of συμβιβάζω ('knit together'), see P. T. O'Brien, *Colossians, Philemon,* 147.

172. The participles συναρμολογούμενον ('being joined together') and συμβιβαζόμενον ('being held together') are both in the present tense. K. S. Hemphill, *Spiritual Gifts,* 191, therefore, speaks of 'the present process of growth'. The passive voice has been interpreted to signify that God (through Christ), or Christ himself, is the one effectively at work in the process of joining and knitting together the body.

the body. It is 'not shapeless', but is 'ordered and united, . . . fitly framed and knit together'.[173]

While the empowering for growth comes from above, members of the body themselves are fully involved in the process. Paul continues the physiological language,[174] using it metaphorically[175] to speak of the divine energy being channelled *by every supporting*[176] *ligament*.[177] The ligaments make contact with other parts of the body and are the channels which extend nourishment from the head.

But to whom do the 'ligaments' refer? To those who are 'special ministers' (cf. v. 11) or all the members of the body? The answer, in part, turns on whether the phrase 'according to the due measure of each individual part' clarifies the preceding expression, *by every supporting ligament*, or makes an additional point with a broader reference to each member of the body. Is 'each ligament' to be identified with 'each individual part'? Or is the latter a broader reference to every member, while the ligaments point to a narrower group? Two main approaches are as follows:

(1) The usual interpretation is to understand 'according to the due measure of each individual part' as a clarification of *by every supporting ligament*, and to identify 'every ligament' with 'each individual part'. Accordingly, these ligaments are taken as representing all the members of the body, not 'special ministers' or officebearers. It is argued that the

173. E. Best, *One Body*, 151.

174. For a recent evaluation of the evidence from ancient medical writings, see C. E. Arnold, 'Jesus Christ', 346-66. He concludes: 'Paul draws on the current physiological understandings of the head in relationship to the body as exhibited in the medical writers to enrich his notion of the church as a corporate body. . . . The medical writers describe the head not only as the ruling part of the body, but also as the supply center of the body' (366). Philo, in particular, reflects this same concept of the head's functions, but develops the metaphorical usage of the imagery in relation to leadership and the head's provision of the animating energy and life (cf. *Quaest. in Gen.* 1.10).

175. The objection of some commentators to the apostle's medical picture, based on the view that the joint itself has no power, misses the point of Paul's metaphorical language. The joint is like a fulcrum through which the empowering of God is magnified and applied (cf. K. S. Hemphill, *Spiritual Gifts*, 191; and C. E. Arnold, 'Jesus Christ', 362).

176. ἐπιχορηγία denotes 'support, aid, or supply' (cf. Phil. 1:19) and is best understood in an active sense. The cognate verb ἐπιχορηγέω (to 'provide, give, support') is found five times in the New Testament (Gal. 3:5; also at 2 Cor. 9:10; Col. 2:19; 2 Pet. 1:5, 11). The word ἐπιχορηγία belongs to several worlds: in marriage contracts, as evidenced in the papri, it connotes the 'provision for a spouse'; in the Athenian drama festivals the 'furnishing of the chorus'; and, in medical terminology, as here (cf. Col. 2:19), the 'ligament which acts as a support'.

177. ἀφή, which means literally a 'joint, or connection', is akin to the verb ἅπτομαι ('touch'); cf. BAGD, 125. Barth, 449, understands the noun to mean 'contact', but this is unlikely in the immediate context or in the Colossians parallel (2:19).

singular 'ligament' together with the addition of 'every' stresses the contribution that each part makes to the whole, while the phrase 'according to the due measure of each individual part', which is unique to Ephesians, also 'highlights the importance of the active contribution of each individual member'.[178] Every member of the body is in view in both expressions, it is claimed, and this is consistent with the mention of joints and ligaments in Colossians 2:19. Accordingly, the spiritual gifts of each believer become the channel for focussing divine power in the life of the church.

(2) The alternative view is that *every supporting ligament* refers to 'particular ministers of the word' rather than ordinary church members. Lincoln, for example, claims that 'what is being highlighted is the role of the ministers in the whole body ruled and nourished by Christ and that, just as in v 11 the giving of Christ was embodied in particular persons, so . . . [in this phrase of] v 16 the growth from Christ is mediated by particular persons'.[179] The broader reference to every member then appears in the following line, 'according to the due measure of each individual part'. In this summarizing picture of v. 16, both gifted ministers and gifted members have a part to play in the body's growth. The former are represented by the ligaments which provide connections between the other parts of the body, while the latter have their distinct role to play in the well-being of the whole.

The second explanation is consistent with the movement of thought within the paragraph (vv. 7-16): first, grace is given to each believer in accordance with Christ's apportioning (v. 7). The focus then narrows to the 'special ministers', whom the ascended Christ gives, together with their functions of ministry (vv. 8-12b), before widening out to the saints who build Christ's body (v. 12c) and 'us all' (v. 13) who reach unity in the faith and the knowledge of the Son of God. In this summarizing sentence of v. 16, the decisive role of Christ is once again asserted (v. 16a), while both special ministers (v. 16b) and all members (v. 16c) have a part to play.[180] The ministers are presented as the means of support or supply for the other parts of the body, and this is consistent with the earlier emphasis in the paragraph on the ministry of God's word and the role of teaching leaders (cf. vv. 8-12b).

The importance of each member's active contribution to the growth of the whole body is asserted in the words *as each part does its work*, which recall the language of v. 7, especially 'each one' (and 'according to mea-

---

178. C. E. Arnold, 'Jesus Christ', 362.
179. Lincoln, 263; cf. Schnackenburg, 173, 189-90.
180. Note especially Schnackenburg, 189-90.

sure').[181] Every member of the body, to whom grace has been given by the ascended Christ (v. 7), receives the necessary enabling power to perform his or her proper function so that the growth of the whole body is in proportion to and adapted to each.[182] God's supernatural empowering has already been mentioned in Ephesians to describe his raising Christ from the dead, and now it is operative in believers (1:19), as well as in the life of Paul as an example (3:7; cf. Col. 1:29). In the light of God's dynamic enabling through Christ believers should eagerly exercise their ministry for the good of the whole. The presence of gifted persons within the body makes us dependent on one another, and as every Christian fully utilizes his or her gifts for the growth of the body, divine fullness will be experienced.

By means of architectural imagery (cf. 2:21-22), the ultimate goal of Christian growth is now reiterated in the final phrase, 'for the purpose of building itself in love'. Clearly the whole body is involved in this process of building, not simply those who are leaders or who have special ministries. '[Of] itself' adds to the previous reference of the church's active participation (though ultimately Christ is the source of growth), while the words *in love,* which begin and end the paragraph (note the discussion at v. 15; cf. v. 2), further underscore Paul's emphasis on *agapē* as the indispensable means of building the body. If it is only *in love* that the body increases, then it is only *in love* that true Christian ministry will contribute to the building of the body. The 'spiritually gifted community is not only distinguished by its full possession of gifts through which divine energy flows, but it is also marked by its divine nature'.[183] Love thus becomes the criterion for an assessment of the church's true growth. Even the fullest demonstration of gifts has no spiritual value if love is lacking (cf. 1 Cor. 13).

Ephesians 4:1-16 stands at the beginning of the explicitly exhortatory half of the letter (chaps. 4–6). It consists of two main sections (vv. 1-6, 7-16), the first of which reminds the readers of their calling into membership of the body of Christ (4:1). The rest of this lengthy paragraph underscores Paul's distinctive concerns for the unity of the church, as he admonishes his readers with the utmost urgency to preserve the oneness given by the

---

181. Ἐνὶ δὲ ἑκάστῳ ἡμῶν ('to each one of us', v. 7) corresponds to ἑνὸς ἑκάστου ('of each one', v. 16), and κατὰ τὸ μέτρον ('according to measure', v. 7) recalls ἐν μέτρῳ ('in measure', v. 16).

182. So Lincoln, 266, who concludes: 'The whole body is to be active in the promoting of its own building up and growth in the quality of its life, as every part of the organism functions in harmony through a process of continual mutual adjustment'.

183. K. S. Hemphill, *Spiritual Gifts,* 192.

Spirit (v. 3; cf. 2:14-18; 3:6), a unity that is organically related to the divine intention of bringing all things together in unity in Christ (1:9, 10). The second section (vv. 7-16) introduces the note of diversity and shows how it contributes to the unity of the body, since Christ's giving different gifts of grace to each is for the purpose of enriching the whole, so that all may be prepared for full maturity when they meet their Lord (v. 13). The whole paragraph, then, is concerned about unity, diversity, and maturity.

This important paragraph focusses very specifically on the church. It is the sphere into which believers have entered by being called by God into a relationship with his Son. A major image for this community is the body (vv. 4, 12, 16), and it is combined with the language of building (vv. 12, 16) and the fulness of Christ (v. 13). Ministries have been given by Christ, particularly ministries of the word, to enable the body of Christ to attain to its ultimate goal, that is, 'the unity of the faith and of the knowledge of the Son of God, to mature manhood, to the measure of the stature of the fulness of Christ' (v. 13). In one sense the body of Christ is already complete: it is a true body, not simply part of one. In another sense that body is said to grow to perfection, a process that will be completed only on the final day. The body metaphor reflects the 'already–not yet' tension of the two ages. It is both complete and yet it grows. It is a heavenly entity and yet it is an earthly reality; and it is both present and future, with a consummation occurring at the parousia.

Although the church is at the forefront of Paul's thinking in this passage, Christology has not collapsed into ecclesiology, as some seem to suggest. The lordship of Christ is clearly evident throughout. He remains the 'one Lord '(v. 5) who as the exalted one gives grace both to individuals (v. 7) and to ministers of the word (v. 11) for the church. The church is his fulness (v. 13) and his body (v. 12). As its head who rules over it Christ is the source and goal of its growth (vv. 15-16).[184]

B. Live according to the New Humanity, Not the Old, 4:17-24

> [17]So I tell you this, and insist on it in the Lord, that you must no longer live as the Gentiles do, in the futility of their thinking. [18]They are darkened in their understanding and separated from the life of God because of the ignorance that is in them due to the hardening of their hearts. [19]Having lost all sensitivity, they have given themselves over to sensuality so as to indulge in every kind of impurity, with a continual lust for more. [20]You,

184. Cf. Lincoln, 268.

*however, did not come to know Christ that way. ²¹Surely you heard of him
and were taught in him in accordance with the truth that is in Jesus. ²²You
were taught, with regard to your former way of life, to put off your old self,
which is being corrupted by its deceitful desires; ²³to be made new in the attitude of your minds; ²⁴and to put on the new self, created to be like God in
true righteousness and holiness.*

Ephesians 4:1-16 has set the stage for the exhortatory material that
follows in 4:17–6:20, and serves as the introductory framework for the
rest of the paraenesis. What follows consists of a series of paragraphs
which spell out in detail how local congregations and Christian households should heed the exhortation of 4:1-3. In his opening injunction Paul
admonishes his readers to *live* worthily of the divine calling they have received (4:1). Significantly, relationships within the body of Christ, especially conduct characterized by harmony, are the first issue the apostle
addresses as an essential element in their living consistently with this
calling (vv. 1-3; note also vv. 4-16). Now in 4:17-24, the first of several major sections which follow, Paul deliberately picks up again the language
of 'walking', and contrasts the readers' lifestyle in Christ with that of outsiders (v. 17).

In this first paragraph (4:17-24), as well as in the subsequent two
sections (4:25–5:2; 5:3-14), there is a discernible 'progression from the
negative depiction of the early Christian environment to a positive description of a Christian existence and life-style'.[185] Vv. 17-24 consist of
two parts: (a) a strong, urgent exhortation not to live as the Gentiles (vv.
17-19). Their pagan lifestyle is painted in dark colours (note the similar
ideas in Rom. 1:21, 24; Col. 3:5-11), beginning with idolatrous thinking,
culpable ignorance of God, and rebellion against him and moving to a
further darkened understanding and downward spiral into sin. Their situation may be summed up in the word 'alienated' (v. 18). (b) In sharp
contrast to this, the kind of lifestyle expected of those who have 'learned
Christ' is set forth (vv. 20-24). He is the pattern of the new creation. Accordingly, Paul's positive expectations are presented in terms of the readers being renewed and putting on the *new person* who is characterized by
righteousness and holiness (note the central motif of the old and the new
person in Col. 3:9-10).

The idea of the people of God 'walking' in ways that are different
from those of the surrounding nations reaches back to the Old Testa-

185. Schnackenburg, 193. Note the examination of Eph. 4:17-21, 22-24; 5:8, 15-18 by
E. Best, 'Two Types of Existence', *Essays*, 139-55, in relation to Christian existence set over
against a non-Christian lifestyle.

ment (particularly the holiness code of Lev. 18:1-5, 24-30; 20:23). The contrast between the 'two ways' of life also has its background in the Old Testament (Ps. 1; Deut. 11:26-28; 30:15-20; Jer. 21:8), and Judaism (*T. Asher* 1.3, 5; 1QS 3, 4), and turns up in Matthew 7:13, 14, *Didache* 1–5, and *Barnabas* 18–20.[186]

This paragraph also reflects features of early Christian teaching on the new life that has come about through conversion (cf. Rom. 6:4; Gal. 6:15; 2 Cor. 5:17; Col. 3:10; Tit. 3:5; 1 Pet. 1:22; 2:2; Jas. 1:18), the need to abandon the old ways of life (Rom. 13:12; Col. 3:8; 1 Pet. 2:1; Jas. 1:21), and the mention of vices and sins to be put away and graces to be put on (Col. 3:5-12).

17 The apostle now turns his attention from relationships within the body of Christ (4:1-16) to his direct exhortation ('therefore'), begun in vv. 1-3. He urges his readers not to fall back into the patterns of thinking and behaviour of their former Gentile way of life, a lifestyle that is subsequently painted in dark colours (vv. 18-19). The language shows that Paul's admonition is both important and urgent, and that it comes with divine authority: *I tell you this, and insist on it in the Lord*. The first verb, 'I say, tell', is strengthened by means of the second, 'I affirm, declare' (cf. 1 Thess. 2:12),[187] which stresses its solemnity and significance, while the additional *in the Lord* points to the source of its authority. Paul does not simply urge his readers on his own initiative. He writes as one who is 'a prisoner in the Lord' (4:1) and whose admonition comes with the full weight of the Lord's authority (cf. 1 Thess. 4:1).

The content[188] of the exhortation is that *you must no longer live as the Gentiles do*. The readers had been unconverted *Gentiles* before they came to know Christ, and even now they can still be addressed as 'you Gentiles' (3:1; cf. 2:11). What is more, they are currently living in a Gentile environment. Although they once *lived* as unconverted pagans (2:1-2), they must now abandon this lifestyle. They have been raised and seated with Christ in the heavenly places (2:6), and have become members of 'the one new man' (2:15). Let them demonstrate a manner of life that conforms to the character of this new man, Jesus Christ himself. God has created them in Christ for the good works which he has already prepared for them; let them now 'walk' in those good works and show that they are truly part of this new creation (2:10).

The following clauses paint the Gentile way of life in the darkest of

---

186. Cf. Hermas, *Mandates* 6.1; Ignatius, *Letter to the Magnesians* 5; *2 Clement* 4 (Lincoln, 272).

187. The Greek verbs are λέγω and μαρτύρομαι respectively.

188. τοῦτο ('this') refers to the content of the following admonition, while the infinitive περιπατεῖν ('walk') and the accusative are used instead of an imperative.

colours. This picture is in line with traditional Jewish apologetic,[189] and Paul's own fuller description of the ethical bankruptcy of contemporary paganism in Romans 1:18-32. The prepositional phrases and various clauses in vv. 17-19 are not intended to provide strict logical connections but present the progress of thought from the Gentiles' inner thinking and disposition to their effects in everyday life.

Paul's Gentile Christian readers should have left behind an existence whose *thinking*, that is, mind-set,[190] was so distorted that it was marked by *futility* and had fallen prey to folly. In the LXX this word[191] denoted the futility of idol-worship as well as the emptiness of human endeavours which sought to bring lasting satisfaction.[192] The word-group in the New Testament can refer to idolatry (cf. Acts 14:15), although here in Ephesians 4:17 the 'futility' of the pagan mind is not restricted to idolatry. Because it lacks a true relationship with God, Gentile thinking suffers from the consequences of having lost touch with reality and is left fumbling with inane trivialities and worthless side issues. Romans 1, which is parallel to Ephesians 4 in its development of the human plight, states that the ungodly who have not recognized or honoured God 'became futile in their thinking, and their senseless minds were darkened' (NRSV). Paul's indictment moves from futility to foolishness to idolatry (vv. 21-23).

18 The desperate condition of Gentiles outside of Christ is now depicted in terms of their being *darkened in their understanding*. It is noteworthy that the apostle goes out of his way to emphasize the perceptive and mental dimension in the human estrangement from God. The Gentiles' mind-set has been drastically affected (v. 17b), their thinking[193] has become darkened so that they are blind to the truth, and their alienation from God is *because of the ignorance within them*. This darkness in their thinking was not some temporary condition; as the emphatic periphrastic expression[194] indicates, the light of their un-

---

189. Wisdom 12–15; 18:10-19; *Epistle of Aristeas* 140, 277.

190. νοῦς has to do with 'the psychological faculty of understanding, reasoning, thinking, and deciding', hence the 'mind' (Louw and Nida §26.14). The apostle is referring, not to 'a defect in the ability of his readers to reason but their "mind-set", the total person viewed under the aspect of thinking' (Best, 417).

191. Gk. ματαιότης, which denoted 'emptiness, futility, purposelessness, transitoriness' (BAGD, 495; Louw and Nida §65.37). Cf. H. Balz, *EDNT* 2:396-97.

192. Isa. 28:29; 30:15; 33:11. Note especially the many references to ματαιότης ('futility') in Ecclesiastes (1:2, 14; 2:1, 11, 15, 17, etc.), which have probably influenced Paul (cf. P. W. Comfort, *DPL*, 321).

193. διάνοια ('thinking, mind') is often interchangeable with καρδία ('heart') and is used in the LXX for the centre of human perception (cf. Gen. 8:21; 17:17; 24:45; 27:41; Exod. 28:3). Cf. Lincoln, 277.

derstanding had gone out so that they were now in a state of being incapable of grasping the truth of God and his gospel. As noted above, this description of the Gentiles' spiritual darkness is akin to the apostle's earlier words in Romans 1:21, 'their foolish hearts were darkened', although here in Ephesians 4, as befits an exhortation, there is greater stress on their own responsibility for their abandonment to sin (see on v. 19).[195] In sharp contrast, Paul's Christian readers, through the enabling power of 'the Spirit of wisdom and revelation' given to them, are able to know God better and to understand the truth of his purposes (Eph. 1:17-18).

Not only are Gentiles darkened in their understanding; they are also *separated from the life of God*,[196] that life which God possesses in himself and bestows on his children. Gentiles who do not belong to Christ are 'dead' through their trespasses and sins (2:1, 5), and have no relationship at all with the living God (2:12). Their state of alienation[197] from his life was *because of the ignorance that is in them*. Paul's view of knowledge and ignorance is largely determined by the Old Testament. To know God means to be in a close personal relationship with him. Knowledge has to do with an obedient and grateful response of the whole person, not simply intellectual assent. Likewise, 'ignorance'[198] is a failure to be grateful and obedient. It describes someone's total stance, and this includes emotions, will, and action, not just one's mental response. Not to know the Lord is to ignore him, to say 'no' to his demands. Such ignorance is culpable. It is not an excuse for sin, though it is often understood this way in contemporary thought. The Gentiles' inability to understand the light of God's truth is no excuse for their broken relationship with him. Indeed, the additional words, '[the ignorance] that is *in them*', show that the re-

---

194. The perfect passive participle ἐσκοτωμένοι ('[they are] darkened'), together with the additional participle ὄντες ('being'), expresses very 'forcibly the persistence of the . . . state of things' (BDF §352). Cf. Col. 1:21.

195. Note Turner, 1239.

196. Schnackenburg, 196, suggests that the two expressions go together because of the coordination of the participles (ἐσκοτωμένοι and ἀπηλλοτριωμένοι) with the one periphrastic particle (ὄντες). For a discussion whether the construction should be taken as a single periphrasis with the first participle being modified by the second (e.g., 'you are darkened in mind, being strangers of the life of God'), or a double periphrasis sharing ὄντες ('you are darkened in mind and are strangers'), see S. E. Porter, *Verbal Aspect*, 475.

197. Note the perfect participle ἀπηλλοτριωμένοι ('alienated', already used at 2:12; cf. Col. 1:21), which focusses on a continuous and persistent separation from God as the source of all life.

198. On ἄγνοια ('ignorance, delusion') and its cognates, see W. Schmithals, *EDNT* 1:21.

sponsibility is not finally due to external factors.[199] The blame falls squarely on their shoulders.

As if to underscore the point, Paul adds that their delusion is 'due to hardness of heart'. This second causal clause is subordinate to the first,[200] rather than coordinate or parallel with it: the Gentiles' culpable ignorance arose out of their obstinate rejection of God's truth. Although the term rendered *hardening* has been interpreted to mean 'blindness'[201] (cf. AV; and note Calvin), in the New Testament it consistently refers to 'stubbornness', and here it signifies that 'pagan immorality is . . . wilful and culpable . . . , the result of their deliberate refusal of the moral light available to them in their own thought and conscience'.[202] And an obstinate rejection of the truth of God is the beginning of the terrible downward path of evil.

19 The recital of the Gentiles' lifestyle concludes with a brief but stark sketch of the moral depravity into which they have sunk. The thought of hardening their hearts (v. 18) continues[203] in the statement that they have 'lost all sensitivity', a vivid classical term[204] which literally could refer to skin that had become callous and no longer felt pain. Here it means to 'lose the capacity to feel shame or embarrassment',[205] while the perfect tense describes a state of affairs that led to (or else accompanied) the loss of all self-control.[206] Because of their lack of moral feeling and discernment there were no restraints to their plunging into all kinds

199. Note Barth, 501; and Schlier, 212.

200. Meyer, 240. The ignorance of the Gentiles is culpable and due to hardness of heart. Cf. Lincoln, 278; against Best, 420, who takes the second phrase ('due to hardness of heart') as parallel to the first ('because of the ignorance that is in them').

201. Most particularly by Robinson, 264-74. Bruce, however, 355, rightly speaks of the Gentiles' hardening as 'the progressive inability of conscience to convict them of wrongdoing'. πώρωσις ('hardening, obstinacy'), which appears often in the Old Testament (Exod. 4:21; 7:3; 9:12; Ps. 95:8; Isa. 6:10; 63:17), frequently has to do with the response of Israel to the gospel (Mark 3:5; John 12:40 [citing Isa. 6:10]; Rom. 11:7, 25; 2 Cor. 3:14). Here in Ephesians, however, the notion of hardening applies more generally to the Gentile world.

202. Houlden, 317. So also Louw and Nida §27.52.

203. The relative pronoun of quality οἵτινες ('being those who') 'may emphasize a characteristic quality' by which the 'preceding statement is confirmed' (so BAGD, 587, and Lincoln, 278), or be a substitute for the simple relative pronoun and continue the earlier thought (cf. Gnilka, 225, who speaks of the human outworking of the hardened heart in concrete terms; and Schnackenburg, 198).

204. Gk. ἀπαλγάω.

205. Louw and Nida §25.197; cf. BAGD, 80. This is the only New Testament use of the verb ἀπαλγέω (cf. Thucydides 2.61; Polybius 1.35.5; 9.40.4), and it appears here in the perfect tense.

206. S. E. Porter, *Verbal Aspect*, 399.

of degrading activities. They abandoned themselves to debauchery, impurity, and covetousness. According to Romans 1, the element of divine retribution is emphasized: God delivered humanity over (vv. 24, 26, 28) to their own desires, especially to unnatural vices (vv. 24-32), because they refused to accept his self-revelation. Here in the paraenetic context of Ephesians the 'handing over' is ascribed to the heathen 'themselves', with their active pursuit of evil brought out in the phrase 'for the practice [of]' (NIV: *so as to indulge*). The two emphases are not contradictory: God gives men and women over to the debased behaviour which they gladly choose. In the human activity the divine judgment takes place, and it is at the same time a self-judgment.[207]

The three evils to which pagans have given themselves, namely, debauchery, impurity, and covetousness, frequently appear in catalogues of vices.[208] 'Debauchery', which according to Galatians 5:19 is one of the works of the flesh, is that vice which 'throws off all restraint and flaunts itself, "unawed by shame or fear," without regard for self respect, for the rights and feelings of others, or for public decency'.[209] The Gentiles have given themselves over to it in order to indulge in every kind of 'impurity'. This term,[210] which has a wide range of meanings and encompasses riotous and excessive living, can refer to unrestrained sexual behaviour. Although the latter may be particularly in view, the reference here cannot be restricted to this, since the text speaks of 'every kind of impurity'. Finally, 'covetousness'[211] appears as the climax of the list (cf. the similar position in Eph. 5:5; and Col. 3:5, where it is emphatically stressed because of its close relationship to idolatry). Although it is possible to understand 'greed' as a third vice, alongside debauchery and impurity, the prepositional expression 'with covetousness' suggests that the indecent conduct already described was practised *with a continual lust for more.* The pagan way of life was characterized by an insatiable desire to participate in more and more forms of immorality. 'Ultimately, it becomes a vicious circle because new perversions must be sought to replace the old'.[212]

207. Schnackenburg, 198.
208. See below for references to each term, and note the wider discussion in P. T. O'Brien, *Colossians, Philemon,* 173-84.
209. Bruce, 356. Gk. ἀσέλγεια; cf. Mark 7:22; Rom. 13:13; 2 Cor. 12:21; 1 Pet. 4:3; 2 Pet. 2:2, 7, 18; Jude 4.
210. Gk. ἀκαθαρσία. Rom. 1:24; 2 Cor. 12:21; Gal. 5:19; Eph. 5:3, 5; Col. 3:5; 1 Thess. 2:3; 4:7.
211. Gk. πλεονεξία. Mark 7:22; Rom. 1:29; 1 Cor. 5:10, 11 (cf. Eph. 5:5); Col. 3:5; 2 Pet. 2:3. Note the discussion in P. T. O'Brien, *Colossians, Philemon,* 182-84.
212. Patzia, 249; cf. Mitton, 161-62.

20-21 In sharp contrast to their former manner of life,[213] the readers are reminded of what they were taught concerning Christ, both in the initial proclamation of the gospel and through subsequent instruction.[214] Over against the hardness, ignorance, and depravity which characterize the pagan world to which they once belonged, Paul sets forth the whole process of Christ-centred teaching. His expressions in vv. 20 and 21 are quite striking, and 'evoke the image of a school'.[215]

The first formulation, 'you did not *learn* Christ that way', is without parallel. The phrase 'to learn a person' appears nowhere else in the Greek Bible, and to date it has not been traced in any prebiblical Greek document. In Colossians, the same verb is used of the readers having 'learned' the 'grace of God' from Epaphras, who had given them systematic instruction in the gospel (Col. 1:7). Here in Ephesians Christ himself is the content of the teaching which the readers learned. Just as he is the subject of the apostolic preaching and teaching (1 Cor. 1:23; 15:12; 2 Cor. 1:19; 4:5; 11:4; Phil. 1:15; cf. Acts 5:42), so he is the one whom the hearers 'learn' and 'receive'. This formulation signifies that when the readers accepted Christ as Lord, they not only welcomed him into their lives but also received traditional instruction about him. Colossians 2:6 and 7 (the nearest parallel to our expression) makes a similar point: 'just as you *received* Christ Jesus as Lord' refers not simply to the Colossians' personal commitment to Christ (though this notion is obviously included); the statement also points to their having *received* him as their tradition (the verb[216] appears in this semitechnical sense). Learning Christ means welcoming him as a living person and being shaped by his teaching. This involves submitting to his rule of righteousness and responding to his summons to standards and values completely different from what they have known.

The following twofold statement in v. 21, 'if indeed you have heard of him and were taught in him', explains more fully what was involved in 'learning Christ'. The first expression, 'you heard of him', draws attention to the initial response to Christ, while the second, 'you were taught in him',

---

213. Best 425, notes that the abrupt beginning of this verse stresses the contrast between Christian and non-Christian existence. The ὑμεῖς ('you') is emphatic (Best adds: 'it is not the basis of everyone's life that has been changed, only that of believers'), while οὐχ οὕτως ('not so') picks up vv. 17-19.

214. The syntax of this sentence (vv. 20-24) is not easy to unravel, although the general sense is reasonably clear. Caird, 80, speaks of it as being 'chaotic, and any translation is bound to be makeshift'! In the opening words, the contrast with the readers' previous Gentile lifestyle begins. On the relationship of the clauses and phrases see below.

215. Barth, 504.

216. Gk. παραλαμβάνω.

picks up the point of ongoing instruction.[217] The introductory 'if indeed' does not express doubt, but implies confidence and certainty (NIV has *surely*), since it confirms the preceding assertion about the readers having so learned Christ that they are no longer in the darkness and ignorance of the Gentiles.[218] Although the first expression has been rendered 'you heard him' and taken to mean that Christ had instructed the readers through the voice of their Christian teachers, the Greek construction suggests that he was the one about whom they had heard.[219] In the proclamation of the gospel they had first learned about Christ (cf. 1:13), and that preaching was reinforced in the systematic instruction they were given,[220] through those especially equipped by the ascended Lord Jesus (4:11; cf. 2:20; 3:5).

In learning Christ the readers had heard of him and been instructed in him *in accordance with the truth that is in Jesus*. This clause qualifies the preceding so that the whole expression corresponds to the first formulation 'you learned Christ' (v. 20). A contrast is set up with the 'not so' of v. 20 and indicates that the truth, as embodied in Jesus, was the norm by which the readers had been instructed in the gospel tradition of Christ, and so was wholly at odds with the Gentile lifestyle depicted in vv. 17-19.[221]

The general sense of the clause 'as the truth is in Jesus' is clear enough, even if some of the details contain difficulties. First, the noun *truth* has no article in the original, but has been rendered as 'the truth', since this makes the most sense in the context.[222] It is not unusual for abstract nouns to appear without the article (e.g., sin, death, and grace),[223]

---

217. Note Meyer, 243; and Abbott, 135.

218. Note the discussion of εἴ γε ('if indeed') at Eph. 3:2.

219. Although there is some variation in the New Testament, after the verb ἀκούω ('hear'), the person about whom one hears is occasionally in the accusative case (as here in Eph. 4:21; cf. 1 Cor. 1:23; 2 Cor. 1:19), while the one whose words are heard stands in the genitive case; so BDF §173(1); cf. BAGD, 31-32.

220. Christ was the focal point of that instruction. In both clauses the reference to 'him' receives the emphasis since it precedes the finite verb: 'about *him* you heard, and in *him* you were taught' (αὐτὸν ἠκούσατε καὶ ἐν αὐτῷ ἐδιδάχθητε). Bruce, 357, suggests that 'to be taught in Christ is to be taught in the context of the Christian fellowship'. Barth, 530, thinks that the words 'in him' describe Christ as 'the foundation upon, the sphere within, or the administration under which teaching and learning have taken place'.

221. Note the discussions of Meyer, 243; and Lincoln, 283.

222. Other interpretations are fraught with considerable difficulties. So Barth's understanding (505, 533-36) of καθώς as an introductory formula to the citation, 'Truth in Jesus!' (which also includes vv. 22-24), raises more problems than it solves, while I. de la Potterie's insistence ('Jésus et la verité d'après Eph 4,21', *AnBib* 18 [1963], 45-57) that because ἀλήθεια is anarthrous it must be in a predicative position (signifying 'as he is truth in Jesus') does not make much sense. The meaning 'as there is truth in Jesus' is clear, but appears to be too indefinite in this context. Note the full discussion of Lincoln, 280-83.

223. χάρις ('grace') is used anarthrously at Eph. 2:5, but with the article at v. 8.

and this is the case with truth in Paul's letters, apparently for a variety of reasons.[224] There is considerable stress on 'the truth' throughout this section of Ephesians. The apostle calls on these Christians to speak the *truth* of the gospel in love, rather than being misled by the malicious scheming of the false teachers, so that they might grow up into Christ as head (vv. 14, 15). Next, reference is made to the new person who is 'created according to God in righteousness and holiness of the *truth*' (v. 24), while the immediate consequence of the new life in Christ is that each one should put away falsehood and speak the *truth* to his neighbour (v. 25; cf. 5:9; 6:14).

A second unusual feature is the use of the name 'Jesus', the only occasion in Ephesians where it occurs by itself (though cf. 'Lord Jesus' in 1:15). The change from the title 'Christ' seems to be deliberate, not because the name 'Jesus' was aimed at Gnostic teaching with its division between the heavenly Christ and the earthly Jesus,[225] but in order to stress that the *historical* Jesus is himself the embodiment of the truth.[226] The apostle reminds his readers that the instruction they had received in the gospel tradition was indeed 'the truth as it is in Jesus'.

22 The content of the Christian instruction they had been given, and which is found in the person of Jesus (v. 21), is now amplified in vv. 22-24 by means of three infinitives: 'to put off' (v. 22), 'to be renewed' (v. 23), and 'to put on' (v. 24). Although these infinitives have been taken as imperatives,[227] as indicating the purpose of the instruction,[228] or as denoting the result[229] of the readers' being taught, it seems best to treat them as epexegetic and therefore as spelling out three fundamental

---

224. Note, e.g., Rom. 2:2; 9:1; 2 Cor. 12:6; Eph. 4:25; 5:9; 6:14; Col. 1:6. Cf. BDF §258; and Lincoln, 281.

225. This line is taken by Schlier and Gnilka, among others. But Gnosticism does not appear to be opposed elsewhere in Ephesians (cf. Arnold, 7-13), while the immediate context of 4:21 is not christological but paraenetic. There is no hint that the Gentile attraction to the immorality described in vv. 17-19 was because of a false Christology.

226. Cf. Best, 429-30. The variation seems to be more than stylistic.

227. Both infinitives and participles can sometimes function as imperatives, particularly in ethical codes (note Rom. 12:9-15). Cf. Barth, 505-6. See the treatment of D. Daube with reference to rabbinic usage, 'Participle and Imperative in 1 Peter', in E. G. Selwyn, *The First Epistle of St Peter* (London: Macmillan, 1947), 467-88, and with reference to Col. 3:9-10, see P. T. O'Brien, *Colossians, Philemon*, 188-92. It has been argued, however, that the presence of ὑμᾶς ('you') with the infinitive ἀποθέσθαι ('put off') rules out this imperatival interpretation.

228. The readers were taught (ἐδιδάχθητε) in order that they might put off (ἀποθέσθαι ὑμᾶς κτλ.) the old person and put on the new.

229. The consequence of their being instructed is that they have put off the old person, are being renewed, and have put on the new. This interpretation is thus regarded as being consistent with the Colossians parallel (3:9-10). But the point being made in Colossians is slightly different (see below).

aspects[230] of the gospel tradition which had been passed on to them. The NIV represents this interpretation by repeating *You were taught* of v. 21, and then continuing, *with regard to your former way of life, to put off . . .* (v. 22); *to be made new . . .* (v. 23); *and to put on . . .* (v. 24). The readers have been instructed that to become believers signifies a fundamental break with the past. At the same time, in this exhortatory context the three infinitives also seem to have an implied imperatival force, not in the sense that the readers are to repeat the event of putting off the old person and putting on the new, but in terms of their continuing to live out the implications of their mighty break with the past.[231]

The picture of putting off and putting on a garment was widespread in the ancient world and was employed in the mystery religions with reference to the act of initiation. The donning of the garment consecrated the initiate so that he or she was filled with the powers of the cosmos and shared in the divine life. In Gnostic texts putting on the garment indicated that the redemption had come, a redemption that would subsequently be perfected. But the background of the expression 'putting off the old man' and 'putting on the new man' was neither Gnosticism nor the mystery religions.[232] In the Old Testament the notion of being clothed with moral and religious qualities is found, examples being strength (Isa. 51:9; 52:1), righteousness (Ps. 132:9; Job 29:14), majesty (Ps. 93:1), honour (Ps. 104:1; Job 40:10), and salvation (2 Chron. 6:41).[233] However, neither the Old Testament nor the extrabiblical Greek writings refer to putting on a 'person'.

The Pauline expression, then, is without exact literal parallel. Romans 13:14 speaks of being clothed with the Lord Jesus Christ, while in Galatians 3:27 putting on Christ is equated with being baptized into Christ. The notion of putting away various sins appears elsewhere in Paul,[234] and Romans 6:6 speaks of the believer's old person being cruci-

230. So several commentators, including Robinson, Houlden, Caird, Bruce, and Lincoln. Meyer, 244-46, Gnilka, 229, and Stott, 179-80, regard the infinitives as explaining the truth that is in Jesus. This makes very little difference to the sense, but syntactically it is more natural to relate them to ἐδιδάχθητε ('you were taught').

231. Note R. A. Wild, '"Be Imitators of God"; Discipleship in the Letter to the Ephesians', in *Discipleship in the New Testament,* ed. F. F. Segovia (Philadelphia: Fortress, 1985), 127-43, esp. 133; Schnackenburg, 199-200; and Lincoln, 285-86.

232. See the discussion in P. T. O'Brien, *Colossians, Philemon,* 188-89.

233. Compare the notion of being clothed with dishonour (Ps. 109:29) and cursing (Ps. 109:18). The rabbinic literature refers to clothing with spiritual and ethical qualities, e.g., the Torah clothes with humility and reverence (Mishnah *'Abot* 6:1; cf. Str-B 2.301, for further references), which are analogous to our expressions (Eph. 4:22, 24; cf. Col. 3:8, 12). Note P. W. van der Horst, 'Observations on a Pauline Expression', *NTS* 19 (1972-73), 181-87.

fied with Christ. In Colossians and Ephesians the clothing imagery is linked directly with 'the old person' and 'the new person' (v. 24). These two expressions do not so much refer to Adam and Christ as the representative heads of the old and new creations as to the individuals who are identified with these orders of existence. The 'old person' here, as in Romans 6:6 and Colossians 3:9, designates the whole personality of a person when he is ruled by sin.[235] In the Romans and Colossians references the definitive break with the old person has been made in the past. Here in Ephesians the readers are taught 'to put him off'. If, as suggested, this epexegetic infinitive has an implied hortatory force, then the tensions between the indicative and the imperative and between the 'already' and the 'not yet' in putting off the old person are emphasized more strongly here.[236] The readers' *former way of life,* which has earlier been characterized as 'the desires of the flesh' (2:3), was earmarked for demolition. It is foolish to let it play any role in their lives. Let them instead live out the implications of that dramatic change which has taken place in them.

The 'old man' stands in stark contrast to the 'new', as the respective appositional clauses clearly show.[237] The former is in the process of being corrupted by deceitful desires, while the latter is created according to God's likeness in true righteousness and holiness (see on v. 24). The verb 'corrupt', which in the active signifies to 'ruin or destroy something', is here used in the passive to refer to the ongoing moral corruption of the 'old person', a process of decay and ruin that finally ends in death (cf. Rom. 8:21; Gal. 6:8).[238] The cause[239] of this ultimate disintegration is the harmful desires which beguile men and women into sin and error. They

234. Rom. 13:12; Col. 3:8 (cf. Heb. 12:1; Jas. 1:21; 1 Pet. 2:1).

235. Cf. E. Larsson, *Christus als Vorbild: Eine Untersuchung zu den paulinischen Tauf- und Eikontexten* (Uppsala: Almqvist and Wiksells, 1962), 197.

236. See above, 29-33.

237. The two clauses which are in apposition to τὸν παλαιὸν ἄνθρωπον ('the old man', v. 22) and τὸν καινὸν ἄνθρωπον ('the new man', v. 24) respectively stand in sharp contrast, and may be set out as follows:

τὸν φθειρόμενον κατὰ τὰς ἐπιθυμίας τῆς ἀπάτης
'who is being corrupted because of deceitful desires',

τὸν κατὰ θεὸν κτισθέντα ἐν δικαιοσύνῃ καὶ ὁσιότητι τῆς ἀληθείας
'who is created according to God's likeness in true righteousness and holiness'.

238. Cf. Louw and Nida §20.39: φθείρω means 'to ruin or destroy something, with the implication of causing something to be corrupt and thus to cease to exist', hence 'to destroy' (1 Cor. 3:17). See also BAGD, 857, who note that the ruin of someone is 'by erroneous teaching or immorality'. Significantly, the issues of right teaching and the contrasting immorality occur in the context.

239. On the preposition κατά with the accusative indicating the ground or basis of something, see 3:3.

have already been called 'the desires of the flesh', characteristics of the old way of life (2:3). Now they are styled the desires 'of deceit'. They are illusory since they have lost touch with reality and lead to the destruction of the old man. As desires which are generated by *deceit,* they stand in opposition to the truth of the gospel which Paul considers to be so essential for the growth of God's people (4:15; cf. vv. 21, 24).

23 Between the contrasting portraits of the old person we put off (v. 22) and the new we put on (v. 24) stands v. 23: [*you were taught*] . . . *to be made new.* The readers had been instructed not only to put off the old man with his deceitful ways and to put on the new; they had also been taught that inward renewal was called for. This notion of renewal is independently stressed here and functions differently from that found in the parallel passage in Colossians 3:10.

To describe the putting off of the old person (v. 22) and putting on of the new (v. 24), Paul uses two aorist infinitives:[240] he depicts each action as a complete or undifferentiated whole.[241] However, when inward renewal is spoken of in v. 23, the *present* infinitive[242] is employed. Paul pictures this renewal as a process. The verb is best taken as a passive (meaning 'to be made new') rather than as a middle,[243] and this suggests that God is the one who effects the ongoing work of renewing his people. At the same time, the implied exhortation (see above) underscores the notion of a continual challenge for the believer. When the readers were instructed in Christ, they were urged to be made new. They are to yield themselves to God and allow themselves to be renewed in their inner person. A similar point is made in Paul's exhortation to the Roman Chris-

---

240. ἀποθέσθαι ('to put off') and ἐνδύσασθαι ('to put on').

241. This is true 'regardless as to how in actual fact the action occurs' (S. E. Porter, *Idioms,* 21).

242. ἀνανεοῦσθαι ('to be made new').

243. The middle does not seem to have the reflexive sense of 'renew oneself' (so BAGD, 58; cf. Louw and Nida §58.72). Although it has been argued that a deliberate distinction is drawn between νέος ('new') and καινός ('new') and their respective cognates, with the former being regarded primarily as a temporal adjective meaning 'young' and the latter having qualitative connotations of newness which supplants the old, the two terms for newness are synonymous, and both can have either qualitative or temporal connotations (cf. R. A. Harrisville, 'The Concept of Newness in the New Testament', *JBL* 74 [1955], 69-79; E. Larsson, *Christus,* 200). So the supposed distinction here (cf. Schnackenburg, 200) between the new person which is καινός, i.e., qualitatively different because it is a divine creation, and the renewal that is expressed by ἀνανεοῦσθαι ('to be made new', a cognate of νέος), and thus refers to a human rejuvenating activity, cannot be sustained. See P. T. O'Brien, *Colossians, Philemon,* 190; Lincoln, 286; and on this and related 'newness' passages note C. B. Hoch, *All Things New: The Significance of Newness for Biblical Theology* (Grand Rapids: Baker, 1995).

tians, where the imperative is in the passive voice: '*Be transformed* by the renewal of your mind' (Rom. 12:2).

According to Ephesians 4:23, the sphere in which the renewal takes place is 'the spirit of your mind', an unusual expression which has no analogy in the rest of ancient Greek literature. Many regard the phrase as a reference to the Holy Spirit and render the verse, 'Be renewed by the Spirit in your mind'.[244] Nowhere else in Ephesians does the term refer to the human spirit, while throughout the letter there is an emphasis on the work of the Holy Spirit in the lives of believers (1:17; 3:16; 4:3; 5:18; 6:18). The larger context of v. 3 (with its reference to keeping the unity of the Spirit) and the more immediate context of v. 24 support this reference to the divine Spirit. Paul's urging his readers to have their minds renewed by the Spirit and to 'put on the new person', it is claimed, are two ways of expressing the same reality, while the role of the 'renewed mind' in Christian ethics (Rom. 12:2) has much the same emphasis.[245] Further, the Holy Spirit is the explicit agent of renewal, according to Titus 3:5.

But against this majority interpretation, the text states 'the spirit *of* your mind', not '*in* your mind', and it is hard to imagine how God's Spirit can be described as belonging to 'your mind'. Had Paul intended to speak of the 'renewal of the mind *by the Spirit*', usage would normally require a different grammatical construction.[246] It is preferable, then, to understand the terms 'spirit' and 'mind' as further examples in Ephesians of the accumulation of synonyms. The sphere of this renewing work, then, is the person's inmost being (cf. 'the inner person' of 3:16), and the implication is that 'the pattern, motivation and direction of our thinking needs to be changed'.[247] Theologically, this inward renewal is the work of the Holy Spirit (Tit. 3:5), progressively transforming believers into the image of Christ 'from one degree of glory to another' (2 Cor. 3:18). It is by the Spirit's power that the inner being is renewed every day (4:16). Further, although this ongoing transformation takes place from within, the men-

244. So, e.g., Schlier, Houlden, Gnilka, Ernst, Schnackenburg, and note G. D. Fee, *God's Empowering Presence*, 710-12.

245. G. D. Fee, *God's Empowering Presence*, 710-11.

246. Such as ἐν πνεύματι τοῦ νοὸς ὑμῶν. G. D. Fee, *God's Empowering Presence*, 711, whose preference is to understand the expression as pointing to the Holy Spirit, reluctantly concedes, on grounds of both grammar and usage, that the phrase is 'a highly peculiar way of speaking about the interior life of the human person'. Fee does claim, however, that while the first referent is the human spirit, we should be prepared to recognize that 'the Holy Spirit is hovering nearby' (712).

247. D. G. Peterson, *Possessed by God: A New Testament Theology of Sanctification and Holiness* (Leicester: Apollos, 1995), 132. Note his treatment of this motif of renewal on 126-32.

tion of righteousness and holiness in the following verse shows that there are consequences for the believer's conduct as well.

The contrast with the preceding section of the paragraph (vv. 17-19) could hardly be sharper. There, the desperate condition of Gentiles outside of Christ is depicted in terms of their being darkened in their understanding so that they are blind to the truth, and their alienation from God is the result of the ignorance within them. In consequence, they abandon themselves to all kinds of degrading activities. Here, the ongoing transformation of the mind leads to just and holy living which reflects the character of God himself (cf. Rom. 12:2). The flow of Paul's argument implies that the human mind, apart from divine renewal, is unable to guide or keep us in a way of life that is pleasing to God. 'If heathen degradation is due to the futility of their minds, then Christian righteousness depends on the constant renewing of our minds'.[248]

24 The third fundamental aspect of the gospel tradition that the readers had been taught (cf. vv. 22-23) was *to put on the new self* which was created to display those ethical qualities, such as righteousness and holiness, that belong to God. Furthermore, this third infinitive, *to put on,* like the previous two, has an implied imperatival force, not in the sense that they were to continue putting on the new man, but that they should conduct their lives in the light of the mighty change God had effected.

In Ephesians the 'new person' has both corporate and individual connotations.[249] The expression has already appeared in 2:15 to refer to the one new humanity comprising Jews and Gentiles who have been united in Christ as the inclusive representative of the new order. Now in v. 24 the corporate entity comes to expression individually. As the old person is under the rule of this present evil age, so the new person is part of the new creation and the life of the age to come. It is God's mighty work, not ours; yet the fact that this new identity is *put on* shows that his new creation is gladly appropriated by the believer. Divine activity and human response are carefully balanced (cf. Phil. 2:12-13),[250] while the concluding phrase, 'in the righteousness and holiness that come from the truth', shows that there are significant ethical implications to this donning of the new person.

Several important features of this new person are drawn to our attention in the adjectival clause which concludes the paragraph (vv. 17-24): '[the new person] is created in God's likeness in the righteousness and holi-

248. Stott, 182.

249. Gk. καινὸς ἄνθρωπος. Cf. Lincoln, 287.

250. Note the discussion of the relationship between divine activity and human response at Philippians 2:12-13 in P. T. O'Brien, *Philippians,* 273-89.

ness which come from the truth'. First, this entity is a new creation effected by God himself: the verb 'create', here used in the passive, refers to the divine creative activity (cf. Eph. 2:10, 'For we are his [i.e., God's] workmanship, *created* in Christ Jesus').[251] By definition the new creation is the work of God himself, and therefore the ethical qualities of righteousness and holiness which explain what is meant by the phrase 'like him' are also thought of preeminently as God's creation. As such, the new person stands in sharp contrast to 'the old humanity' that is perishing (v. 22).

Secondly, God is not only the author of this mighty work; he is also the pattern or model of the new creation. It is made 'in his likeness' (lit. 'in accordance with God'),[252] that is, created 'like him'. It is not surprising, therefore, that the qualities of righteousness and holiness which characterize the new person are predicated of God in both Old and New Testaments. The LXX parallels insist that it is *God* who is truly just and holy; so in Deuteronomy 32:4, he is praised for his greatness:

> He is the Rock, his works are perfect,
> and all his ways are *just*.
> A faithful God who does no wrong,
> *upright* and *just* is he. (Cf. Ps. 145[LXX 144]:17; Rev. 16:5.)[253]

Thirdly, in this exhortatory context 'according to God' probably has a teleological connotation as well.[254] The new person has been created 'like God'; it is therefore *to be like him*. Believers are already, in principle, part of God's new creation (2:10, 15; cf. 2 Cor. 5:17; Gal. 6:15). Their conduct, therefore, needs to be consistent with their new position and status in Christ.[255] They are to be righteous as he is righteous, and holy as he is holy. Together the terms 'holiness' and 'righteousness'[256] (cf. Luke

---

251. Gk. κτίζω. Schnackenburg, 201; and R. A. Wild, '"Be Imitators"', 133, 135.

252. The prepositional phrase κατὰ θεόν designates the relationship of the new humanity to God and may be rendered 'in accordance with God', 'similar to God', or 'Godlike'. 'According to God's will', while true theologically, does not capture sufficiently the nuances of the context; it refers only to a 'voluntaristic relationship' (cf. R. A. Wild, '"Be Imitators"', 142, 135) and is not an appropriate rendering in the light of the concluding prepositional phrase ἐν δικαιοσύνῃ καὶ ὁσιότητι τῆς ἀληθείας ('in the righteousness and holiness which come from the truth').

253. Deut. 9:5 denies that human justice and holiness had anything to do with Israel's reception of its inheritance; rather, it was due to the Lord's love for his people and his keeping the oath he had sworn to the forefathers (7:7-8). Wisdom 9:3 speaks of human government of the world 'in holiness and justice', but does so in the context of stressing that it was God who established this order (9:1-2); so R. A. Wild, '"Be Imitators"', 134.

254. R. A. Wild, '"Be Imitators"', 135.

255. Arnold, 143.

256. As in Eph. 5:9 and 6:14, δικαιοσύνη here signifies an ethical virtue.

1:75) refer to virtuous living as a whole — a meaning which fits the immediate context and is consistent with the linguistic usage in the Graeco-Roman world generally, even if the meaning is slightly different.[257] The paired expression thus explains what it means to be like God. The tension in the paragraph between the old order and the new corresponds to the interplay between the so-called 'indicative' and the 'imperative' found elsewhere in Paul: believers are to become what they are in Christ. The language in this context is somewhat different from the parallel in Colossians 3:10, which alludes to Genesis 1:26 and speaks of the new man being 'renewed in knowledge after the Creator's image'.[258] In Ephesians there is no allusion to the creation of Adam, while the emphasis falls on a life patterned after God's.

Finally, the concluding genitival phrase 'of the truth' is best understood as denoting source or origin. The graces of holiness and righteousness which are to characterize the new person come from 'the truth', which is another way of saying from God himself. He is the truth. These qualities originate in him, are consistent with his character, and are ultimately real. In this sense it may be said that they are '*true* holiness and righteousness'. In the wider context of Ephesians 'the truth' is the truth of the gospel (1:13) which the readers learned when they were instructed in Christ Jesus (see on 4:21). This truth stands over against false teaching and all forms of trickery (v. 14), while the immediate consequence of showing forth these graces which spring from the truth of the gospel is that each believer should put away falsehood and speak the truth to his neighbour (v. 25).

This passage, which has continued the address to the readers begun in 4:1-3, is a piece of direct exhortation spelling out what is inappropriate and appropriate to the believer's calling. Most of these readers had been brought into a living relationship with God from a Gentile and pagan background. The apostle, therefore, has drawn a clear distinction between the way of life which characterized 'the old humanity' and that

---

257. R. A. Wild, '"Be Imitators"', 134-35, 142 nn. 49, 50, has drawn attention to instances in Plato (*Apology* 35D; *Crito* 54B; *Theaetetus* 172B, 176B) and in Philo (*De Sacrificiis Abelis et Caini* 57; *De Specialibus Legibus* 1.304; 2.180; *De Virtutibus* 50), where the two terms together denote virtuous living in general and what it signifies to be like God. He concludes: 'We may also safely assume that a Greco-Roman audience would have understood this phrase as a comprehensive statement encompassing the sum of all virtue and excellence' (135). Wild thinks that Paul's goal in discipleship was 'assimilation to God', following traditional Platonic thought, but it may be questioned whether 'assimilation' is an actual description of Paul's view (see on 5:1).

258. Note the discussion of this phrase in P. T. O'Brien, *Colossians, Philemon*, 191-92. Bruce, 359, thinks that the differences between the two passages are slight. He interprets the phrase 'according to God' as meaning 'in the image of God'.

which marked out 'the new' (4:17-24), and has urged his readers not to go back to the old ways. He has laid the groundwork for the more detailed and specific ethical exhortations which will follow.

C. Specific Exhortations about the Old Life and the New, 4:25–5:2

> ²⁵*Therefore each of you must put off falsehood and speak truthfully to his neighbor, for we are all members of one body.* ²⁶*"In your anger do not sin":* *Do not let the sun go down while you are still angry,* ²⁷*and do not give the devil a foothold.* ²⁸*He who has been stealing must steal no longer, but must work, doing something useful with his own hands, that he may have something to share with those in need.* ²⁹*Do not let any unwholesome talk come out of your mouths, but only what is helpful for building others up according to their needs, that it may benefit those who listen.* ³⁰*And do not grieve the Holy Spirit of God, with whom you were sealed for the day of redemption.* ³¹*Get rid of all bitterness, rage and anger, brawling and slander, along with every form of malice.* ³²*Be kind and compassionate to one another, forgiving each other, just as in Christ God forgave you.* ⁵:¹*Be imitators of God, therefore, as dearly loved children* ²*and live a life of love, just as Christ loved us and gave himself up for us as a fragrant offering and sacrifice to God.*

Paul now proceeds to set forth specific, concrete exhortations which flow directly from the paraenesis of the preceding paragraph with its clear distinction between the old way of life and the new (4:17-24). The movement of thought is from the lofty heights of learning Christ and the new creation to 'the nitty-gritty of Christian behaviour — telling the truth and controlling our anger, honesty at work and kindness of speech, forgiveness, love and sexual control'.[259] Each of the exhortations has to do with personal relationships within the body of Christ (v. 25). In particular, they are intended to foster unity within the people of God, that unity of the Spirit which the readers have been urged zealously and energetically to maintain (v. 3), while 'the evils to be avoided are all destroyers of human harmony'.[260] In vv. 25-31, Paul mentions negative ways of behaving from which the addressees are to refrain. In each example (apart from anger, vv. 26, 27),[261] each negative

---

259. Stott, 184.
260. Houlden, 320.
261. Though note that in vv. 31 and 32 the list of negative features associated with *anger* is replaced by positive qualities necessary for forgiveness; this is then followed by the motivating clause, 'just as God in Christ forgave you'.

prohibition is balanced by a corresponding positive exhortation. The apostle urges his readers not only to give up lying, stealing, and losing their temper; they are also to speak the truth, work hard, and be kind to others. Further, a motivating clause for each command, which is tantamount to a theological reason, is given or implied. The exhortations are wholly positive in 4:32–5:2, where the readers are urged to practise mutual generosity, mercy, and forgiveness. Paul then moves to the central demand for love before concluding the section with a reference to Christ's love as the model: 'just as Christ loved us and gave himself up for us as a fragrant offering and sacrifice to God' (5:2).

Verse 25, with its opening *therefore,* is logically connected with the preceding paragraph as Paul moves from the more general to the more specific exhortations. The verb 'put off' has already been used in v. 22 in relation to laying aside the old person, while the key term 'truth' is picked up from the concluding phrase of v. 24. Although it has been suggested that this unit of paraenesis (from v. 25) ends at 4:32, there are stronger grounds for seeing its conclusion at 5:2.[262] The exhortation to live in love summarizes the preceding specific admonitions, while the motivating clause about Christ's death, which provides the theological basis for the admonition, rounds out the passage in a climactic way.

The epistolary paraenesis of 4:25–5:2 contains a series of exhortatory sentences which provide rules for conduct in daily life. These ethical sentences, which frequently appear in Hellenistic philosophers and had been adopted by Hellenistic Judaism, make use of a common form in paraenesis, namely, the catalogue of vices and virtues.[263] Within the New Testament these catalogues function in apologetic and exhortatory contexts (Rom. 1:29-31; 1 Cor. 5:10-11; Gal. 5:19-23, etc.), and are sometimes part of the exhortation itself (Eph. 4:31-32; cf. Phil. 4:8). There are differences of opinion as to the ultimate origin of these lists of virtues and vices, and suggested sources include the Old Testament, the 'two ways' pattern of Judaism, the Qumran literature, Stoicism, and popular Graeco-Roman philosophy.

---

262. The reasons for taking the break at chap. 5:2 (rather than at 4:32) are as follows: (1) The γίνεσθε οὖν ('be [imitators] then', 5:1) picks up the γίνεσθε [δέ] ('be [kind]') of chap. 4:32. God's pardoning love, mentioned in chap. 4:32, becomes the model for the behaviour of Christians to one another. Chap. 5:1 picks up the preceding rather than introduces a new theme. (2) The passage ends on a positive note, with the exhortation to 'walk in love' (5:2) rounding out the preceding specific admonitions. (3) Chap. 5:3 turns to a fresh area of moral instruction, namely, the sexual sphere, which was not mentioned in chap. 4:25-32. πορνεία δέ ('But fornication') then commences a new paragraph. Note the detailed discussion in Schnackenburg, 204; cf. Lincoln, 294, and now Best, 443.

263. Note the discussion and bibliography in Lincoln, 294-97, and C. G. Kruse, 'Virtues and Vices', *DPL,* 962-63.

More significant is the use to which these ethical lists have been put in Ephesians. While commentators have rightly noted the similarity of this list with that in Colossians 3:8-14,[264] here in Ephesians 4:25–5:2 Paul fills out his exhortation by explicit reference to the Old Testament (vv. 25, 26),[265] as well as by language and allusion which recall the earlier Scriptures (v. 30; 5:2).[266] Within the christological and eschatological dimensions of Paul's gospel the vices are regarded as the outworkings of the 'old person', while the virtues or graces are produced in the 'new person', and these reflect the character of Christ. As we have seen, the preceding context of 4:17-24 lays out the theological and ethical basis. The vices mentioned are those which disrupt the unity of God's people, a crucial issue within the context of 4:1-16, while the virtues enhance the life of the community. Occasionally the apostle emphasizes theological expressions which he has used earlier in the letter; so the motivating clause in v. 25, 'because we are members of one another', refers to the 'body language' of vv. 12 and 16, while the mention of God's Holy Spirit, 'in whom you were sealed for the day of redemption' (v. 30), picks up the important reference to the Spirit in 1:13-14.

Although it is going too far to suggest that the sins or virtues listed have little or nothing to do with the contexts in which they appear, the general applicability of this type of paraenetic material means that one should not simply read off specific and detailed problems in every community being addressed — for example, that vv. 25 and 28 indicate that Paul knew there were thieves and liars in these churches who needed to be confronted. The issues addressed, namely, speaking the truth, dealing with anger, hard work, edifying speech, kindness, and love all show, as 4:1-16 has made plain, that Paul is concerned that God's people may demonstrate unity in love in a practical way.[267]

25 The consequences[268] for those who have been created in God's likeness are now spelled out as Paul presents a series of specific exhortations aimed at fostering behaviour appropriate to the 'new person'. There are conscious links with the preceding paragraph: the verb 'put off' has already been used in v. 22 with reference to laying aside the old person, while the key notion of 'truth' is picked up from the concluding phrase of v. 24 (cf. vv. 15, 21). The readers had been taught to put aside the 'old person' which was being corrupted by deceitful desires (v. 22). Let them now

---

264. See P. T. O'Brien, *Colossians, Philemon,* 179-81, 186-204.

265. Zech. 8:16; Ps. 4:4.

266. Isa. 63:10; Ps. 40:5 (LXX 39:6); Exod. 29:18; Ezek. 20:41. On the significance of the use of the Old Testament in Ephesians, see the work of T. Moritz, *A Profound Mystery.*

267. Lincoln, 299.

268. διό is a strong inferential conjunction meaning 'therefore, for this reason'.

'put off'[269] all falsehood,[270] which characterized their old manner of life with its harmful and deceitful ways.

But it is not enough to give up lying. Let each[271] of the readers speak the *truth* to his or her neighbours. Paul balances his negative prohibition with a corresponding positive command. They have put on 'the new person' which has been created in God's likeness. Accordingly, *the truth*, which comes from God himself (v. 24) and is found in Jesus (v. 21), should be the distinguishing mark of their speech.

The exhortation *each of you must . . . speak truthfully to his neighbour* is cited from Zechariah 8:16, picking up the keywords 'truth' and 'neighbour' from this Old Testament text.[272] It has been suggested that, by quoting this verse from Zechariah, Paul may have hoped to add the weight of Old Testament teaching to his own ethical admonitions. His intention was to show, it is claimed, that his own moral teaching was in line with Old Testament ethics, so that his Gentile readers would know that 'the exhortation to speak the truth to one's neighbour would have been seen as primarily general Christian ethical teaching'.[273] This suggestion is probably correct.

But there are also profound salvation-historical and typological connections between Zechariah 8 and Ephesians 4, and the communities addressed in each. 'Speak the truth to each other' is the first of a series of admonitions ('These are the things you are to do', v. 16) in the exhortatory section (vv. 16-19) of Zechariah 8, which follows immediately upon the divine promises regarding the new Jerusalem (vv. 1-15). The imperative of v. 16 is directed to the remnant of God's people. They will inhabit Zion, which

269. The verb ἀποθέμενοι ('putting off'), which echoes its use in v. 22, is once again employed figuratively, this time with τὸ ψεῦδος ('falsehood') as its direct object. The participle is best understood in an imperatival sense ('put off falsehood'), rather than as referring back to the life-changing event God had effected ('after putting aside falsehood'); note, however, the different emphasis in Col. 3:9. See the arguments of Schnackenburg, 206; and Lincoln, 300.

270. 'Falsehood' (τὸ ψεῦδος) brings to mind the deceitful (ἀπάτη) desires in their former manner of life. The abstract noun τὸ ψεῦδος has been taken by some to describe not falsehood in the abstract, but 'the lie', and it has been suggested that Paul is here referring to 'the great lie of idolatry' (cf. Rom. 1:25). Paul's readers had renounced the supreme falsehood of paganism and were now being urged to forsake all lesser lies and speak the truth (cf. Stott, 184-85). But the singular τὸ ψεῦδος is used collectively for 'lies', or the practice and habit of lying, while the parallel passage tells against this interpretation (Col. 3:8-9).

271. The adjective ἕκαστος, together with the second person plural λαλεῖτε ('each one of you must speak'), reinforces the idea of their individual responsibility to speak the truth.

272. Eph. 4:25 closely follows the LXX. The only variation is the use of the preposition μετά ('with') in Ephesians rather than the πρός ('to') of the LXX.

273. So T. Moritz, *A Profound Mystery*, 88-89, esp. 89.

will be called 'the City of *Truth*'[274] because of the indwelling presence of Yahweh (v. 3).[275] His people will be characterized by truth, righteousness, and holiness, and thus the *neighbour*, who is a member of this community, may expect to be dealt with truthfully. Ephesians 4:25 picks up this first exhortation and addresses it to the new community in Christ, the 'new man', that is created to be like God in 'righteousness and holiness of the truth'. Within this new society one's *neighbour* is a fellow-believer, who has a right to the truth. What is predicated of the eschatological future of God's people in terms of new Jerusalem language in the Old Testament passage is picked up by Paul in relation to the 'new person', God's new community in Christ, upon whom the ends of the ages have come. The salvation-historical and typological connections between the two communities, and thus the accompanying practical exhortations, are patent.[276]

In Ephesians the exhortation to tell the truth is undergirded by an appeal to the fact that we are members of one another (cf. Rom. 12:5). The idea of the church as Christ's body has already been mentioned in the letter (1:23; cf. 2:16; 4:4, 12), and the mutual dependence of members of the body was taken up specifically at 4:15 and 16 (although the terms 'members' and 'body' are not specifically linked until 5:30). The means by which this body is built, according to 4:15, is speaking the truth of the gospel in love. Here at 4:25, the apostle's point is that, in the body which is a model of harmonious relationships, there is no place for anything other than the truth. We are 'no longer alienated, independent beings, but people who now belong together in unity with others whom we must not rob of the truth according to which they will decide and act'.[277]

---

274. There are six references to 'truth' (*'emeth*) in the prophecy of Zechariah. Apart from the admonition to God's people in 7:9 to practise 'true justice' (lit. 'justice of truth'), all the instances of 'truth' appear in chap. 8 (vv. 3, 8, 15, 16, and 19). In Ephesians, six of the seven references to the ἀλήθεια ('truth') word-group appear in the paraenesis of chaps. 4–6, four of them in this chapter (vv. 15, 21, 24, 25; cf. 5:9; 6:14).

275. The new Jerusalem is to be the centre of divine revelation to which the nations will come in pilgrimage (vv. 20-23), in fulfilment of the expectations of Isa. 2:2-4. As God's people heed the admonitions of vv. 16-19, their integrity will reflect the divine presence. The Gentiles' reaction in the new age will be to repeat the old confession made by the Philistine Abimelech to Abraham, 'God is with you' (Gen. 21:22). The divine presence among the Lord's renewed people is recognized by the Gentiles who come in pilgrimage to Zion.

276. T. Y. Neufeld, *Put On the Armour of God: The Divine Warrior from Isaiah to Ephesians* (Sheffield: Academic Press, 1997), 133-34, has noted a number of these important connections between Zech. 8 and Eph. 4, and asserts: 'It is difficult to resist the conclusion that the brief citation of Zech. 8.16 in Eph. 4.25 is but the tip of the iceberg in terms of the role Zech. 8 plays in the thought of the author of Ephesians'.

277. Turner, 1240. This motivation for telling the truth, in the light of the above comments, may be 'more theological or christological' than Best, 448, thinks.

26-27 In God's new society believers are not to sin by indulging in anger, for this is a serious obstacle to harmonious relationships within the body. Unlike the other exhortations in this paraenetic material of 4:25–5:2, this second topic sentence begins with a positive admonition (though note its significance below), follows with a negative exhortation ('Do not sin'), and then gives the reason for dealing with anger promptly (v. 27).

Again the Old Testament Scriptures are cited, this time Psalm 4:4.[278] Here, too, the Old Testament context is important for understanding its use in Ephesians. The Psalmist has been accused, quite unjustly, of some crime or sin, and though he knows he is innocent, the reproach of this hangs heavily upon him. But God replaces the anger which resulted from the lies of others (v. 2), giving him instead a heart full of joy and peace (vv. 7-8). So he admonishes his hearers, as he further consoles and strengthens himself, not to sin in their anger.[279] What Paul then urges of the 'new man' (Eph. 4:24) has already been foreshadowed by the Psalmist's own experience (Ps. 4:7-8).

The two imperatives in the sentence, 'be angry and do not sin', have puzzled commentators. Some have contended, on the grounds that the Hebrew idiom in Psalm 4:5 allows for it, that the first imperative functions as a conditional or a concessional clause ('if [or although] you do get angry, make sure you do not sin').[280] Accordingly, the exhortation permits and restricts anger, rather than actually commanding it. The English equivalent is *in your anger do not sin.* It is possible, however, that the sentence should be understood as a normal variation within the commanding use of the imperative, even if the resulting translation is not significantly different: 'be angry ['if you are angry'], and don't sin'.[281] Since *anger* is not explicitly called 'sin', it has been suggested that the reference here is to righteous indignation, while the *anger* of v. 31 which is to be put away is evidently unrighteous anger. There is a proper place for righ-

---

278. ὀργίζεσθε καὶ μὴ ἁμαρτάνετε is an exact quotation of the LXX (Ps. 4:5).

279. According to T. Moritz, *A Profound Mystery,* 89-90, the admonition in Ephesians is parallel to this. Note the discussion of Ps. 4 in P. C. Craigie, *Psalms 1–50* (Waco, TX: Word, 1983), 77-83.

280. K. L. McKay, *A New Syntax,* 81, observes that such commands, positive and negative, may be used to express a hypothetical case or an assumption. Cf. S. E. Porter, *Verbal Aspect,* 352-53, and *Idioms,* 226. See also Schnackenburg, 207; Lincoln, 301; and T. Moritz, *A Profound Mystery,* 89-90. Note John 2:19.

281. D. B. Wallace, 'Ὀργίζεσθε in Ephesians 4:26: Command or Condition?' *Criswell Theological Review* 3 (1989), 353-72; and *Greek Grammar,* 491-92. Wallace adds: 'In Eph 4:26 Paul is placing a moral obligation on believers to be angry as the occasion requires' ('Ephesians 4:26', 372). He thinks that this must be in relation to church discipline, but there is no evidence that this issue is under consideration here (note Best's criticisms, 449).

teous anger, but also the 'subtle temptation to regard my anger as righteous indignation and other people's anger as sheer bad temper'.[282] If ours is not free from injured pride, malice, or a spirit of revenge, it has degenerated into sin. The warning of James 1:19-20 makes the same point: 'Everyone should be . . . slow to become angry, for human anger does not bring about the righteous life that God desires'.

In order to prevent anger from degenerating into sin a strict time limit is to be put on it: 'Do not let the sun go down on your anger'. The particular term for 'anger' occurs only here in the New Testament. Elsewhere it usually signifies an active 'provocation' to anger, that is, the source of anger rather than its result.[283] Apparently this saying was proverbial. Plutarch mentions that if ever the Pythagoreans were led by anger into recrimination, they were never to let the sun go down before they joined hands, embraced one another, and were reconciled.[284] Similar texts appear in the Qumran literature.[285] Sunset was regarded as a time limit for a range of activities, for example, the paying of a poor man his wages lest by failing to do so one would be guilty of sinning (Deut. 24:15).[286] In the apostle's admonition this expression with its reference to sunset is used as a warning against brooding in anger or nursing it. It is to be dealt with promptly, with reconciliation being effected as quickly as possible.

The third exhortation in relation to anger, *do not give the devil a foothold* (v. 27), provides the motivation[287] for dealing with anger promptly. If it is prolonged, Satan can use it for his own ends, exploiting the strains that develop within the Christian community. The word rendered *foothold* literally means 'place', but it can signify 'possibility, opportunity, or chance' (cf. Acts 25:16). Accordingly, the verse may be translated, 'Do not give the devil a chance to exert his influence'.[288] In

---

282. Bruce, 361.

283. Gk. παροργισμός. So D. B. Wallace, *Greek Grammar*, 491; instances are 2 Kings 23:26; also 1 Kings 15:30; 2 Kings 19:3; Neh. 9:18, Ps. Sol. 8:8-9; the only exception is Jer. 21:5.

284. Plutarch, *Moralia* 488c.

285. CD 7.2, 3; 9.6; 1QS 5.26–6.1.

286. T. Moritz, *A Profound Mystery*, 90, thinks that this saying found its inspiration, to some extent, from Ps. 4:5b ('when you are in your beds, search your hearts and be silent'), and that Ephesians spells out the concept implied in the Psalm in terms borrowed from Deut. 24:15. Accordingly, two Old Testament texts have been strung together like pearls in Eph. 4:26.

287. The negative disjunctive particle μηδέ continues the preceding negation, 'do not [μή] let the sun go down on your anger' (v. 26), and may be rendered as 'and do not [give the devil . . .]'. Cf. BDF §445.

288. BAGD, 823.

Romans 12:19 Paul uses the term in a similar way when he states, 'Do not take revenge, my friends, but leave *room* [lit. give a place or chance] for God's wrath'. The apostle does not explain what kind of 'foothold' the devil can gain in the life of the believer,[289] although it is noteworthy that Satan is not credited with producing the anger. The source apparently is to be found in the person himself or herself. Anger can give the devil an opportunity to cause strife within the life of the individual and the community.[290] Such discord is to be avoided by managing the anger properly and speedily.

Paul uses the designation 'devil' only in Ephesians and the Pastoral Epistles.[291] Elsewhere in the Pauline corpus he is always referred to as 'Satan' (as also in 1 Tim. 1:20; 5:15).[292] But no conclusions ought to be drawn from this regarding the authorship of Ephesians. References to Satan are infrequent anyway, although the designation does turn up in the Pastorals. The word is often used in the LXX (including Zechariah, which Paul has just cited in v. 25), and is appropriate in the present context to refer to a slanderer who seizes an opportunity afforded by the festering of anger to cause division within the body.

Believers have been raised with Christ and seated with him in the heavenlies (2:6). Nevertheless, they are engaged in a spiritual warfare against the principalities and powers in this heavenly realm. They are to put on the full armour of God so as to stand against the devil's schemes (6:10-20, esp. v. 11). Ephesians 4:26-27 provides an example of how this spiritual warfare is to be fought. The struggle takes place in the moral sphere, that is, within the hearts and lives of believers. Through uncontrolled anger Satan is able to gain a foothold in the Christian's life. But anger may not be the only means the devil can use to achieve his own wicked ends. Within the exhortatory context of vv. 25-31 there are prohibitions against lying (v. 25), stealing (v. 28), and 'unwholesome talk' (v. 29). The temptation to do any of these, or, for that matter, to behave in a manner that is characteristic of the 'old person' (v. 22), is presumably the occasion of a spiritual battle which the devil is able to exploit to his own advantage.[293] Believers need to withstand every temptation so that the influence of the evil one may be re-

289. But it does not signify, as Robinson, 112, claimed, an 'opportunity for the entry of an evil spirit'.

290. Cf. S. H. T. Page, *Powers*, 188-89.

291. Gk. διάβολος, Eph. 4:27; 6:11; 1 Tim. 3:6, 7, 11; 2 Tim. 2:26; 3:3; Tit. 2:3.

292. Rom. 16:20; 1 Cor. 5:5; 7:5; 2 Cor. 2:11; 11:14; 12:7; 1 Thess. 2:18; 2 Thess. 2:9; 1 Tim. 1:20; 5:15.

293. 'Spiritual victories and defeats are the results of the ways in which everyday temptations are handled' (S. H. T. Page, *Powers*, 189).

sisted. For Paul there can be no middle ground or nominal Christian-ity.[294]

28 The third topic which illustrates the change from the old way of life to the new (vv. 22-24) is that of believers working hard, rather than stealing, so that they will have something to share with those in need. Following the pattern of v. 25, there is first a negative injunction, then a positive exhortation, followed by a motivation for the latter.

The present participle has been taken to refer to an action preceding the main verb which has durative force, and rendered 'he who used to steal'.[295] But the participle does not denote time and should be understood as equivalent to a substantive, 'the thief'.[296] Theft was considered a cardinal sin in the Old Testament (Exod. 20:15; Deut. 5:19; Isa. 1:29; Jer. 7:9), and a violation of social behaviour (Lev. 19:11). The commandment, 'You shall not steal', is repeated in New Testament summaries of the Decalogue (Mark 10:19 and parallels; Rom. 13:9).

Some have argued that stealing is mentioned here in Ephesians simply because it was a traditional topic in paraenetic material.[297] But it is likely that this exhortation informs us about the kind of people who became Christians in the first century, not least in Asia Minor, and indicates 'how difficult they found it to break away from the ethical norms of the society from which they had been converted'.[298] Ernest Best suggests that while it is possible that Paul had slaves in mind (cf. Phlm. 18 in relation to Onesimus),[299] they were not in a position to steal as a common practice, nor could they give it up so as to devote their labour to earning and contributing to the welfare of the community.[300] Accordingly, he thinks that day labourers or skilled tradesmen whose work was seasonal are probably in view. When they were out of work there was no welfare system to assist them, and many would be forced to steal in order to maintain themselves and their families.

If stealing had been part of the way of life of some Christians before their conversion, they are to practise it *no longer.* It is inconsistent with

---

294. So rightly C. E. Arnold, *Powers of Darkness,* 128-29. Note also the insightful discussion of S. H. T. Page, *Powers,* 188-89.

295. BDF §339(3); C. F. D. Moule, *Idiom Book,* 206; and K. L. McKay, *A New Syntax,* 80.

296. A. T. Robertson, *Grammar,* 892, 1116; S. E. Porter, *Verbal Aspect,* 379; and E. Best, 'Ephesians 4:28: Thieves in the Church', *Essays,* 182.

297. So Lincoln, 303. Cf. Schnackenburg, 208. Elsewhere Paul includes thieves along with other wrongdoers as those who cannot 'inherit the kingdom of God' (1 Cor. 6:10).

298. E. Best, 'Thieves', 181.

299. For a discussion of this see P. T. O'Brien, *Colossians, Philemon,* 299-300.

300. E. Best, 'Thieves', 182-83.

their having put on the 'new person' whose lifestyle is characterized by righteousness and holiness (v. 24). Instead,[301] stealing is to be replaced with hard work. The ingenuity and effort devoted to theft are now to be given to honest labour.[302] Work was highly valued in the Old Testament and Judaism (Exod. 20:9; Ps. 104:23; Prov. 6:6; 28:19; Sir. 7:15), as well as in the Graeco-Roman world generally (Epictetus, *Dissertations* 1.16.16-17; 3.26.6-7; Dio Chrysostom, *Orations* 7.112, 124-25). Paul supported his missionary activity through his work as an artisan, making tents from leather, and he exhorted his congregations to work with their hands as well (1 Thess. 4:11, 12; 2 Thess. 3:6-12).[303]

The term for work found here denotes labour to the point of weariness. (Together with its cognate noun, it described work in general, especially manual labour [2 Cor. 6:5; 11:27], as well as Christian work in and for the community.)[304] What may have been obtained previously with little effort is now to be achieved through diligent toil. The participial expression of manner which follows indicates how the thief is to labour, namely, by *doing something useful with his own hands*. This language does not suggest that only manual labour is recommended. Rather, 'working with one's hands' emphasizes hard work for gain as opposed to what was obtained by theft. Instead of using their hands to steal, believers are to put them to good use through hard work. The 'good' that is in view, as in Galatians 6:10 and elsewhere, denotes what is beneficial to others.[305] Already in Ephesians believers have been described as God's workmanship who have been created 'for *good* works' (2:10). In the present context, working hard with one's hands is viewed as doing what is good and, in the light of the motivation which follows, points to the means of sharing[306] with the needy.

---

301. The sharp contrast with the preceding negative is marked by μᾶλλον δέ ('but rather').

302. E. Best, 'Thieves', 183.

303. On the subject of work in the Old Testament, Judaism, and the New Testament, see G. Agrell, *Work, Toil and Sustenance* (Verbum: Hakan Ohlssons, 1976), 126-32, and for insights into Paul's attitudes to work note R. F. Hock, *The Social Context of Paul's Ministry* (Philadelphia: Fortress, 1980).

304. Both the noun κόπος and verb κοπιάω were used of Paul's apostolic ministry (1 Cor. 4:12; 15:10; Gal. 4:11; Phil. 2:16, etc.), as well as the toil of other Christians (1 Cor. 3:8; 15:58; 16:16; 1 Thess. 5:12).

305. 2 Cor. 9:8; Col. 1:10; 1 Thess. 5:15; 2 Thess. 2:17; 1 Tim. 6:18. Note the discussions of 'the good' in E. Best, 'Thieves', 185-86; and Hoehner.

306. The verb μεταδίδωμι ('to give part of, give a share'; cf. Rom. 1:11; 12:8; 1 Thess. 2:8) here indicates that the hard worker will have something to share with others. His industrious effort will obviously result in benefit to himself, but the particular point here is that he is to *share* the good that he has gained with others in need.

Exhortations to care for the poor and needy (cf. Rom. 12:13, 'Contribute to the needs of the saints') reflect the emphasis on the sharing of goods among the early Jerusalem Christians (Acts 2:45; 4:32–5:11; 6:1-7), which led to the collection made among the Gentile churches for them (Rom. 15:26-27; 2 Cor. 8–9; Gal. 2:10). Generosity, particularly to fellow-believers,[307] was to be part and parcel of the Christian lifestyle (Luke 6:29-36; 2 Cor. 8:1-15; 9:6-12), but 'when it is practiced by a former thief it stands in total contrast to his previous course of life'.[308]

29 The fourth sentence returns to the topic of speech (cf. v. 25), this time, however, in terms of 'good' and evil rather than 'truth' and 'falsehood'. The links between v. 28 and this verse are made through the catchwords 'good' and 'need'. In the preceding admonition the contrast between good and evil was associated with action; here it is linked with speech, with the mouth rather than with the hands. And in both the well-being of others is the goal of the apostle's exhortations. Believers are to achieve what is good with their mouths as well as with their hands, and this good is described in terms of what is beneficial to others.[309]

Christians should keep their lips free not only from lying (v. 25) but also from unwholesome language of any kind. Paul's exhortation is comprehensive: it is directed to all his readers[310] who have put on the 'new man', and stresses that *no* word they utter should be harmful.[311] The adjective is used elsewhere in the New Testament in the literal sense of 'decayed' trees which produce 'rotten' fruit (Matt. 7:17-18), and in relation to 'rotten' fish (Matt. 12:33-34). Here the word is employed figuratively to denote language that is 'harmful' or 'unwholesome'.[312] What is prohibited, then, is harmful speech of any kind (cf. Col. 3:8; Eph. 5:4), whether it be abusive language, vulgar speech, or slander and contemptuous talk.

307. This is not to suggest that believers should not help the needy among non-Christians. Elsewhere Paul urges his readers to 'do good to all people'. But they do have a special responsibility to 'those of the household of faith' (Gal. 6:10), and in the context of Eph. 4:25 the neighbour to whom one has a particular commitment is the fellow-believer. Paul's reason is '*because* we are all members of one another'.

308. Bruce, 362. Lincoln, 304, aptly remarks: 'The thief is to become a philanthropist, as the illegal taking of the old way of life is replaced by the generous giving of the new'.

309. Lincoln, 306.

310. The singular for mouth (στόμα) is a Semitic distributive singular relating to each member of the group. All are to heed the apostolic command.

311. The πᾶς ('every, each') before an anarthrous substantive, λόγος ('word'), indicates that Paul wishes to stress that 'every word' is to be wholesome, not simply some important words (cf. BDF §275[3]; BAGD, 631).

312. So Louw and Nida §20.14, who add that σαπρός stands in contrast to ἀγαθός. The latter means 'good' in the sense of 'building up what is necessary', and thus 'helpful'. By contrast, σαπρός means 'harmful' or 'unwholesome'. BAGD, 742, has 'evil'.

Lips given to this kind of utterance not only defile the speaker (Matt. 15:11) but are also destructive of communal life. Our Lord had already warned that people would have to render account on the final day for every careless word they speak (Matt. 12:36).

By contrast, the Christian's words should be well chosen so that they may edify others and have a beneficial effect on them. Having spelled out the negative admonition, Paul now follows with the positive counterpart:[313] 'but whatever is good for building others as the need arises'.[314] The conversation of Christians should be wholesome and beneficial (v. 28) so that it edifies others, rather than harming or destroying them. We are to use our special gift of speech in this constructive way whenever the need arises (cf. v. 16). The motivating purpose of this positive exhortation is that 'it might give grace to those who hear'. Having put on the 'new man', we will want to develop new standards of conversation so that our words will be a blessing,[315] perhaps even the means by which God's *grace* comes to those who hear.

30 After the fourth exhortation a further prohibition follows in which the readers are urged to do nothing to distress the Holy Spirit of God. The coordinating conjunction 'and' links this exhortation to the negative imperative of v. 29, so that the two clauses can be rendered: 'let no unwholesome word come from your mouths . . . *and* do not grieve the Holy Spirit of God'. This latter prohibition serves as a motivation for the preceding advice about speech and parallels the motivating element of v. 27, *do not give the devil a foothold*, which also took the form of a prohibition. The Spirit, who is the divine agent of reconciliation and unity in the body (2:18, 22; 4:3-4), is especially grieved when unwholesome speech is uttered by members against one another.

At the same time, this admonition not to grieve the Spirit, which is of central importance to the whole paragraph (4:25–5:2), provides a fur-

313. Syntactically, the second clause contains no exhortatory verb, though it is implied from the preceding. The literal rendering of ἀλλὰ εἴ τις ἀγαθὸς πρὸς οἰκοδομὴν τῆς χρείας is 'but if there is any good [word] for the building of the need'. The conditional particle with the indefinite pronoun εἴ τις is virtually equivalent to the indefinite relative pronoun ὅστις and can be rendered as 'whatever, everything that' (A. T. Robertson, *Grammar*, 956; and BAGD, 220).

314. The phrase 'of need' (τῆς χρείας) could be a genitive of quality, signifying 'the needed upbuilding', or an objective genitive ('for the building of what is needed or lacking'), which is very similar in meaning (cf. BAGD, 885).

315. The expression χάριν διδόναι means 'to confer a benefit, do a favour'. It is just possible that the notion of divine 'grace' is in view, although the parallel in Col. 4:6 is unlikely to be a reference to God's grace. There ἐν χάριτι means 'gracious', or 'charming'. Hoehner thinks that the Ephesians context emphasizes the notion of 'enablement', so that the words spoken are to enable 'the believers to fill up . . . [any] lack or need among them'.

ther motivation for the earlier warnings, not simply that of v. 29.[316] It 'occurs as a balanced response to the first set of exhortations that conclude, "neither give room to the devil"'. The Spirit, who plays a leading role in assuring the readers of Christ's victory over the powers, is appropriately set over against the devil in this important exhortatory material.[317] Accordingly, the Spirit is grieved when God's people continue in any of the sins that divide and destroy the unity of the body.

As elsewhere in Ephesians, Paul's words 'echo' the language of an Old Testament text, in this case Isaiah 63:10,[318] and once again an understanding of the scriptural context is important for interpreting the Ephesians passage. After depicting the messianic judgment and the victory of the anointed conqueror (Isa. 63:1-6), the prophet is stirred to eloquent intercession as he focusses on God's past goodness and the present desperate situation of his people. As the prophet reviews God's gracious actions, he begins with the exodus and recounts how Yahweh brought his people Israel into a covenant relationship with himself (v. 8). In language which directly recalls Exodus 33:12-14, v. 9 states that it was the 'presence' of God himself, not simply an angel or a messenger, which saved his people in the wilderness.[319] Israel, for its part, 'rebelled and grieved

---

316. Barth, 547-49, contends that the short negative imperative 'do not grieve (μὴ λυπεῖτε) the Holy Spirit of God' resembles the Ten Commandments in form. Unlike the other prohibitions in vv. 17-24, this one has no complementary positive command, and this suggests that v. 30, which speaks of a sin against God, stands somewhat independently, and provides an effective motivation for the paragraph as a whole. The loose connective καί ('and') at the beginning of the prohibition suggests that it is related to the preceding verses, particularly v. 29 (so Schnackenburg, 209, among others).

317. So G. D. Fee, *God's Empowering Presence*, 713, who adds that the exhortations in vv. 25-32 not only offer specific examples of the two ways of walking but also indicate their respective sources: 'the sins that divide and thereby destroy the unity of the body come directly from Satan; to continue in any of them is to grieve the Spirit, who has "sealed them for the day of redemption"'.

318. Paul's Greek is καὶ μὴ λυπεῖτε τὸ πνεῦμα τὸ ἅγιον τοῦ θεοῦ ('do not grieve the Holy Spirit of God'), while the LXX of Isa. 63:10 has καὶ παρώξυναν τὸ πνεῦμα τὸ ἅγιον αὐτοῦ ('and they vexed his holy spirit'). Paul uses the verb λυπεῖτε (which is closer to the original Hebrew and corresponds to the usual LXX rendering of this Hebrew verb), turning the indicative statement of Isaiah into an imperative (for reasons see below). Cf. T. Moritz, *A Profound Mystery*, 92. Best, 457, is much more cautious, unnecessarily so in our judgment, about the dependence of Eph. 4:30 on Isa. 63:10. See the comments below regarding the intertextual relations between Exod. 33 and Isa. 63 and what we judge to be significant salvation-historical and, ultimately, theological connections between this New Testament text and its Old Testament antecedents.

319. The words 'so he became their Saviour' (Isa. 63:8) seem to hark back to Exod. 14:30, where the verb 'to save' is used comprehensively of 'the Red Sea event [which] completed and sealed the whole enterprise as a work of salvation'; J. A. Motyer, *The Prophecy of Isaiah* (Leicester: Inter-Varsity, 1993), 513.

his Holy Spirit' (v. 10). Nevertheless, the Lord placed his Holy Spirit in the midst of his people to deliver them and give them rest (v. 14).

The 'presence' of God is interpreted in the Isaianic passage in terms of the 'Holy Spirit' (vv. 10, 11). Although the Exodus narrative makes it plain that Yahweh himself led his people through the desert and gave them rest (note esp. Exod. 33:14, 'My presence will go with you, and I will give you rest'), v. 14 of Isaiah 63 unequivocally asserts that it was 'the Spirit of the LORD' who gave them rest. The conclusion in the following line, 'this is how *you* guided your people', underscores this equation of God's presence with his Holy Spirit.[320]

The links between the two biblical passages are so significant as to suggest a typological correspondence between the two events in the history of God's covenant people. In Isaiah 63, which looks back to the exodus, Yahweh is presented as the Saviour of Israel, who *redeemed* his people from Egypt, brought them into a covenant relationship with himself, led them by his own personal presence (i.e., his Holy Spirit) through the wilderness, and gave them rest. For its part, Israel the covenant people had rebelled against its Lord 'and grieved his Holy Spirit' (v. 10). In Ephesians Paul addresses the new covenant community, 'the one new man' (2:15) comprising Jews and Gentiles who have been *redeemed* (1:7) and reconciled to God through the cross of Christ (2:14-18). They have become a holy temple in the Lord, the place where *God himself* dwells by his Spirit (2:21, 22). Using the language of Isaiah 63:10, Paul issues a warning to this new community not to grieve the Holy Spirit of God, 'as Israel had done' in the wilderness (cf. 1 Cor. 10:1-11), the more so since they have been sealed by that same Holy Spirit until the day of *redemption* (4:30).[321] The change from the

320. Commenting on Isaiah 63, J. Wright, 'Spirit and Wilderness: The Interplay of Two Motifs within the Hebrew Bible as a Background to Mark 1:2-13', in *Perspectives on Language and Text: Festschrift for F. I. Andersen,* ed. E. W. Conrad and E. G. Newing (Winona Lake, IN: Eisenbrauns, 1987), 269-98, esp. 289, states: 'The spirit in this chapter is not the spirit of the special endowment as of the leaders of old, but is the very presence of God himself manifested in power and in operation'. Note the discussion of G. D. Fee, *God's Empowering Presence,* 713-14.

321. In the preceding verse, Isa. 63:9, the prophet refers back to the Exodus event when he speaks of Yahweh acting 'in love and mercy' to redeem his people (and this is parallel to 'the angel of his presence [i.e., his Holy Spirit] saved them'), and as he looks forward to a new Exodus of Israel from exile. Isaiah's use of Exodus typology to depict Israel's future redemption from exile in a new Exodus has recently been shown to provide an important pattern for the substructure of Mark's Gospel and an understanding of Jesus' mission in Luke. Note R. E. Watts, *Isaiah's New Exodus and Mark* (Tübingen: J. C. B. Mohr [Paul Siebeck], 1997), and M. Turner, *Power from on High: The Spirit in Israel's Restoration and Witness in Luke-Acts* (Sheffield: Academic Press, 1996), 247-66, etc., respectively. The parallels here in Eph. 4 suggest that Paul also was aware of this new Exodus focus in relation to his Gentile Christian readers.

indicative ('they [Israel] grieved his Holy Spirit') to the imperative ('do not grieve the Holy Spirit of God') is deliberate and makes eminent sense in this exhortatory context. Paul picks up the Isaianic text in a chapter that highlights the work of God's Spirit (= God's personal presence; Isa. 63:10, 11, 14) in relation to the major salvation-historical event of the Old Testament, namely, the exodus. As he handles this scriptural passage, the apostle is obviously not engaging in some kind of atomistic exegesis, as he is often charged. Rather, he reads the Old Testament text with an understanding of its immediate context, its place in the flow of salvation history, and, apparently, within a pattern of new Exodus typology. Paul interprets the passage according to its plain sense, applying it to the new covenant community upon whom the ends of the ages have come (cf. 1 Cor. 10:11).

The exalted title used in Paul's exhortation, that his readers should not cause grief or distress to God's Spirit, echoes the language of Isaiah. *The Holy Spirit of God,* which is a rich expression not usually found elsewhere (cf. 1 Thess. 4:8), emphatically underscores the identity of the one who may be offended, and thus the seriousness of causing him distress. He is the 'Spirit' who is characterized by holiness, and therefore sensitive to anything unholy. And he is none other than the Spirit *of God,* who is at work in those who have been *created to be like God* in the *righteousness and holiness* that come from the truth (v. 24). Paul understands the Spirit in fully personal terms, since only persons can be grieved or feel pain and distress.[322] His injunction is striking, for it refers not to a direct attack on the Spirit but to believers engaging in sinful activities mentioned in the previous verses (especially harmful speech) which destroy relationships within the body and so mar the Spirit's work in building Christ's people (cf. 2:22; 4:3, 4). Anything incompatible with the unity or purity of the church is inconsistent with the Spirit's own nature and therefore grieves him.[323]

The following clause, 'by whom[324] you were sealed until [or for][325] the day of redemption', furnishes the motivation for Paul's exhortation. By sealing believers with his Spirit, whether Gentile or Jewish, God has

322. The verb λυπέω has the basic idea of grief or sorrow, and occurs frequently in the LXX (cf. Gen. 45:5; 2 Sam. 19:2), as well as some fifteen times in Paul (cf. 2 Cor. 2:2-5; 7:8-11), out of a total twenty-six New Testament occurrences. Here the verb signifies 'to cause someone to be sad, sorrowful or distressed'; cf. Louw and Nida §25.75.

323. Stott, 189.

324. The ἐν ᾧ could refer to the sphere in which believers are sealed ('in whom'), but probably denotes the instrument with which they were sealed ('by whom').

325. The preposition εἰς may signify purpose, i.e., 'for [the day of redemption]' (Lincoln, 307), or it may indicate time, 'until or with a view to the day of redemption' (Hoehner). Bruce, 360, 363, understands the sealing with the Spirit as *'against* the day of redemption'.

stamped them with his own character and guaranteed to protect them (see on 1:13) until he takes final possession of them on 'the day of redemption'. How ungrateful would they be if they now behave in a manner which grieves the very Spirit by whom they have been marked as God's own.

The 'day of redemption', which is unique to Ephesians, refers to the final day of salvation and judgment, that is, the goal of history. Elsewhere in Paul it is called 'the day of the Lord' (1 Thess. 5:2; 2 Thess. 2:2; 1 Cor. 1:8; 5:5; 2 Cor. 1:14), or 'the day of Christ' (Phil. 1:6, 10; 2:16). Believers have already experienced a present redemption which includes the forgiveness of sins (1:7); but one element of that redemption is yet to be realized.[326] On the final day God will 'redeem' his own possession, and the guarantee he has given of this is his sealing of them with the Spirit. The mention of a future redemption is consistent with other references to the future in Ephesians (cf. 1:10, 14; 2:7; 5:5, 27; 6:8, 13), and shows that Paul did not envisage salvation as being fully or completely realized. There is a fulfilment yet to come, and believers eagerly await it. For the moment, however, the apostle's gaze is on the presence of the Spirit in their midst. They are to live out the future in the here and now until that 'day' of redemption arrives, and this reminder that the Holy Spirit is God's own seal should be an incentive to holy living and speaking.

31-32 The sixth sentence returns to the topic of the second — anger (v. 26).[327] Once again the threefold pattern observed in this paragraph appears: first, there is a negative exhortation (a call to remove anger and related vices, v. 31), which is then balanced by a corresponding positive admonition to practise mutual generosity, mercy, and forgiveness (v. 32). Finally, a motivating clause ('just as God in Christ forgave you'), which is tantamount to a theological reason, rounds out the topic.

As is fitting for those who have stripped off what belongs to the old man (4:22, 25), anger in all its forms and the vices associated with it are to be removed[328] totally from the readers. Paul's list appears to be climactic, progressing from an inner resentful attitude, through its indignant outburst and seething rage, to public shouting and abusive language or cursing.[329] Although v. 26 recognizes that in exceptional circumstances one

---

326. According to Rom. 8:23, believers have the firstfruits of the Spirit and eagerly await the redemption of their bodies.

327. Although two of the expressions (κραυγή, 'shouting', and βλασφημία, 'slander') have to do with anger expressed in speech, the topic in vv. 31 and 32 is not unworthy speech as such but the anger and vices associated with it (against Bruce, 364).

328. The passive voice of the verb αἴρω ('carry off, take away, remove') is not a divine passive, which would indicate that the activity was God's (against Barth), but appears to be a stylistic device, similar to the English expression 'this must be removed'.

329. So Barth, Stott, Schnackenburg, and Lincoln, among others.

may be angry without sinning, so great are the dangers of this passion that on all other occasions it is to be rooted out comprehensively. The language is emphatic: the introductory adjective 'all' signifies 'every form [of anger]', five different aspects of rage are specified, and there is a generalizing addition 'all malice'. These features show that human wrath and the vices associated with it are to be rejected completely.

The first to be removed is 'resentment, or bitterness'.[330] This is followed by *rage and anger*, two terms that are often used synonymously (cf. Col. 3:8). If any distinction is intended here, then the first signifies an indignant outburst of rage while the second points to a steady festering or seething of anger. Both are destructive of harmony within the body of Christ and must be put away. The fourth term[331] is used of the sound of a loud scream or shout. It can denote a shout of joy (Luke 1:42), a cry of weeping (Rev. 21:4), or the shouting of people back and forth in a quarrel (Acts 23:9). A lack of restraint is in view here, hence the rendering *brawling*. The final word in this list of five vices is 'blasphemy', which was used in nonbiblical Greek of profane or abusive speech. In both Old and New Testaments the term most frequently referred to 'speech against God', and therefore was rendered 'blasphemy'.[332] Against others it has the sense of defamation and covers any type of vilifying, either by lies or gossip. In the present context it may be rendered 'abusive language' or 'cursing'.

The rhetorical effect of this accumulation of terms for anger is powerful, and together with the summarizing phrase, 'along with all malice', indicates that anger in all its forms, together with every form of malice[333] associated with it,[334] is to be removed completely from them.

---

330. πικρία denotes 'a state of sharp, intense resentment or hate'; so Louw and Nida §79.40. Aristotle described it as 'the attitude that creates a lasting wrath, hard to reconcile, and sustaining anger for a long time' (*Ethica Nicomachea* 4.5.1126A; quoted by Barth, 521; cf. Acts 8:23; Rom. 3:14; Heb. 12:15).

331. Gk. κραυγή.

332. Gk. βλασφημία. In the Old Testament, even when the object of the attack was human, it was usually in some sense God's representative (so 2 Kings 6:22; 19:4; Isa. 52:5; Ezek. 35:12, 13). In the New Testament 'blasphemy' was directed immediately against God (Rev. 13:6; 16:11, 21), against his name (Rom. 2:24; 1 Tim. 6:1; Rev. 16:9), against his word (Tit. 2:5), against Moses and God, and so against the bearer of the revelation in the law (Acts 6:11).

333. κακία is a general term ranging from 'trouble' (with no moral implications, Matt. 6:34) to a definitely culpable attitude of 'wickedness'. It might denote a single iniquity such as the grasping desire of Simon Magus (Acts 8:22) or be used more generally for the evil men and women do to each other. In this context it signifies 'malice, ill will' (BAGD, 397), as in other lists (Rom. 1:29; Col. 3:8; Tit. 3:3; 1 Pet. 2:1).

334. On the listing of vices associated with anger, see Philo, *De Ebrietate* 223, and among the Stoics note Chrysippus, *frag.* 395, and Seneca, *De Ira* 1.4 (so Lincoln, 309).

In contrast to practising these vices which destroy the unity of the Christian community, the readers are urged to 'be kind to one another, compassionate, and forgiving each other'. This list of three graces is shorter than its parallel in Colossians 3:12-13, which mentions five. According to the Old Testament, *kindness* is a quality which God himself demonstrates concretely, to all men and women as his creatures, but especially to his covenant people.[335] The prophets speak of the amazing kindness of God in the face of Israel's sin (Jer. 33[LXX 40]:11; cf. 24:2, 3, 5). (Is the conjunction of kindness and forgiveness in Paul's exhortation significant here?) Elsewhere the apostle repeatedly mentions the incomprehensible kindness of God, demonstrated in his gracious attitude and acts towards sinners (see on Eph. 2:7; cf. Rom. 11:22; Tit. 3:4). As a response to his merciful kindness those who have put on the new man are to be kind to others in the Christian community. This does not come naturally and cannot be produced from one's innate resources; it is a fruit of the Spirit (Gal. 5:22). Nevertheless, like the other graces it is urged on those who have been taught the truth that is in Jesus (Eph. 4:21). Next, the readers are encouraged to be tenderhearted or *compassionate*. 'Compassion' is regularly used in the New Testament of God or Christ to speak of their unbounded mercy to sinners (Matt. 9:36; 14:14; 18:27; Luke 1:78; 7:13; 10:33; 15:20).[336] The Ephesians are to be tenderhearted, which will mean being sympathetic to the needs of their brothers and sisters in Christ.

Finally, they are to forgive[337] each other.[338] The motivation for this response is of the highest order: 'just as God in Christ forgave you'. This statement is part of the New Testament's 'conformity' pattern,[339] in which God or Christ's saving activity, especially Christ's sacrifice on the cross, is set forth as a paradigm of the lifestyle to which believers are to

335. His mercy and readiness to help are essential themes of the Psalms (e.g., Ps. 25[24]:7; 31[30]:19; 65[64]:11).

336. It has been suggested that the frequent use of the σπλάγχνον word-group in the *Testaments of the Twelve Patriarchs* to speak of the the merciful love of God prepares the way for the New Testament usage (e.g., *T. Levi* 4:4; *T. Naphtali* 4:5; *T. Zebulun* 8:1, 2).

337. χαρίζομαι, which can mean to 'give freely or graciously as a favour', has the specific nuance here of 'forgiving'. It is not the common word for remission or forgiveness (which is ἀφίημι), but one of rich content which emphasizes the gracious nature of the pardon (cf. Jesus' parable of the two debtors, Luke 7:42). The aspect which the present tense χαριζόμενοι (note the contrast with the following aorist indicative, ἐχαρίσατο) may suggest is that this forgiveness is to be unceasing, even unwearying (cf. Matt. 18:22).

338. The reflexive pronoun ἑαυτοῖς ('to yourselves') functions like the reciprocal pronoun εἰς ἀλλήλους ('to one another'), which has already been used with χρηστοί ('kind'; cf. 5:19). The change is simply stylistic (cf. Col. 3:13; note BDF §287), but both pronouns indicate that other members of the congregation(s) are in view.

339. Note especially the seminal work of N. A. Dahl, 'Form-Critical Observations', 34-35, who has been followed by many commentators.

'conform'. The introductory 'just as also' has both comparative and causal force (cf. 5:2, 25, 29): what God has done 'in Christ'[340] for believers, which has been so fully set forth in chapters 1–3, provides both the paradigm of and the grounds for their behaviour. Here God's forgiveness of them is the model of their forgiveness of one another. In Colossians 3:13 the nuance is slightly different ('because the Lord [i.e., Christ] has forgiven you, so should you also forgive one another'), but the fundamental point is the same. They are to forgive each other, and that forgiveness is to be worked out in their ongoing relationships.

5:1-2 This concluding sentence, with its positive exhortations, *Be imitators of God* and *live a life of love,* summarizes the preceding admonitions (4:25-32) and, together with the motivating clause, *Christ loved us and gave himself up for us,* rounds out the whole paragraph on a positive note.[341] The introductory 'therefore', with the repetition of 'become [imitators]', draws out the consequences of the preceding exhortation. The readers are urged to imitate their heavenly Father by showing the same generous forgiveness to others as he has shown to them.[342] The designation of them *as dearly loved children* is not simply a comparison between father and children, but signifies the basis on which this demand to be imitators is made.[343] They have been adopted into God's family (cf. 1:5), and are his beloved children. His love has now been poured into their hearts by the Holy Spirit (cf. Rom. 5:5). Since they have richly experienced that love, they should be imitators of him and reproduce the family likeness.

Elsewhere in his letters Paul uses the language of imitation[344] when he enjoins believers in his churches to be imitators of him as he is of Christ (1 Cor. 4:16; 10:31–11:1; Phil. 3:17; 1 Thess. 1:6; 2 Thess. 3:7, 9). On occasion, the apostle urged his churches to imitate other congregations (cf. 1 Thess. 2:14). Following the example of the Lord Jesus, who humbled himself to death, Paul made himself a slave in his relationships with others (cf. 1 Cor. 9:19). He lived in conformity with this dominical model and

---

340. The rendering 'through Christ', which interprets the phrase ἐν Χριστῷ as instrumental, does not capture the full range of Paul's meaning. Christ is the sphere in whom God has achieved his people's forgiveness. In Christ he has given them redemption (1:7), just as it is in him that God was 'reconciling the world to himself' (2 Cor. 5:19). Further, the phrase should not be translated 'in your union with Christ', since the word order is against it. ἐν Χριστῷ is linked with ὁ θεός ('God'), not ὑμῖν ('to you').

341. See n. 262 for the reasons for understanding chap. 5:1-2 as the conclusion of the preceding paragraph rather than the beginning of a new section. For a different view note Hoehner and the discussion of Barth, 555.

342. Bruce, 367.

343. Schnackenburg, 212; cf. R. A. Wild, '"Be Imitators of God"', 143 n. 60.

344. The μιμητής word-group.

sought to show a truly Christian lifestyle.[345] Only here in Ephesians, however, does he enjoin believers to be 'imitators of God'. In fact, there is no other explicit reference in either Old or New Testament to imitating God, although the notion of following the Lord wholeheartedly turns up in the Old Testament (e.g., Num. 14:24; 32:11, 12; Josh. 14:8, 9, 14; 1 Sam. 12:14),[346] and the exhortation to be holy because the Lord is holy appears regularly in the Holiness Code (cf. Lev. 19:2). Jesus taught his disciples that if they love their enemies and do good to them, they will be 'sons of the Most High'. He urged them: 'Be merciful, just as your Father is merciful' (Luke 6:35-36; cf. Matt. 5:44-48). God's kindness and mercy are to be the model of their conduct.

The concept of being imitators of God is found in Hellenistic Judaism, particularly in Philo.[347] He cites Plato and urges his readers to flee from earth to heaven. This flight meant to become like God, and it involved becoming holy, just, and wise,[348] which is similar to the present context where the new person is 'created in God's likeness in righteousness and holiness' (4:24). Philo illustrates from Moses that a person should imitate God as much as possible,[349] since there is no greater good. One does this by showing kindness and forgiveness,[350] motifs which appear in a similar cluster here in Ephesians 4:32–5:2. Paul may have been aware of this tradition of imitating God in Hellenistic Judaism in the first century. In the present context of Ephesians a new relationship in God's family serves as the basis of the appeal to imitate God, and this relationship is finally based on God's saving work in Christ, as v. 2 shows.

It is 'impossible to imitate God in everything'.[351] Paul's exhortation to 'walk in love' (v. 2) explains more specifically[352] what is involved in being such imitators. The two statements parallel each other, for to imitate God is to walk in love. For the third time in the second half of the letter

---

345. On the issue of Paul as a model, its purposes, and whether exhortations to follow his example were consistent with Christian humility, see P. T. O'Brien, *Gospel and Mission,* 83-107; and A. D. Clarke, '"Be Imitators of Me": Paul's Model of Leadership', *TynBul* 49 (1998), 329-60, together with the relevant secondary literature.

346. Note the further examples in Barth, 556.

347. According to R. A. Wild, '"Be Imitators"', 128-33, whose study is followed by many recent commentators, several of Philo's exegetical treatises reveal significant points of comparison with Eph. 5:1.

348. Philo, *De Fuga et Inventione* 63, citing Plato's *Theaetetus* 176A-B.

349. Philo, *De Virtutibus* 168.

350. Philo, *De Specialibus Legibus* 4.73, 187-188.

351. Best, 466, who adds: 'Since human beings are part of his creation they can create neither him nor one another'.

352. The καί ('and, that is') is an epexegetical conjunction giving a further specification of the injunction of v. 1; cf. BDF §442(9). Cf. A. T. Lincoln, in *Theology,* 119.

(chaps. 4–6) the readers are instructed as to how they should 'live' as Christians. In the comprehensive exhortation of Ephesians 4:1, which covers every aspect of their lives and stands as the 'topic' sentence to what follows, Paul urges them to *walk* worthily of the calling they have received. At 4:17, they are to *walk* in holiness and not as the Gentiles live. Now they are urged to *live a life of love,* which means that their thinking, attitudes, and behaviour are to be characterized by this grace of Christ. (Two further references to the right kind of walk will appear in the subsequent paraenesis: 5:8, 15.) The second half of Ephesians (chaps. 4–6) contains a series of instructions to love (4:2, 15, 16; 5:2, 25, 28, 33; 6:24; see on 4:15), the fulfilment of which is the outworking of the apostle's prayer (3:17, 19). These are now summarized succinctly by this exhortation of v. 2. Consequently, 5:1, 2 not only round out the admonitions of 4:25-32 on a positive note but also indicate what it means to imitate God. The pivotal reference to 'walking in love' also encapsulates the instructions to love in this second half of the letter.

The model and ground[353] for their living *a life of love* is Christ's love and sacrificial offering of himself. Once again a 'conformity' pattern is used, though this time in relation to Christ's saving activity, whereas in 4:32 it was of God's action in forgiving us. Here for the first time in Ephesians the love of Christ is mentioned. Previously, it was the Father's love (2:4) which was set forth as the motivation for our salvation. But the two are not at variance, as the dual reference in 4:32 shows: 'God in Christ forgave you'. By living a life of love the readers will imitate God; yet that life of love is modelled on Christ's love so signally demonstrated in the cross. Hence the imitation of God is ultimately the imitation of Christ.[354] Costly, sacrificial love, then, is to characterize believers in their relationships with one another.

In an earlier letter Paul wrote of his personal indebtedness to 'the Son of God, who loved *me* and gave himself for *me*' (Gal. 2:20). According to the present context this is true for every believer: 'Christ loved *us* and gave himself for *us*'. The change from the second person plural ('you'), speaking of his readers, to the first person plurals ('us'), which apply to Paul and other Christians, is deliberate. Later when he wishes to affirm Christ's love for the church collectively he states that Christ loved it and gave himself up for it (Eph. 5:25). How Christ loved us is amplified in the following clause, which speaks of his sacrificial death on the cross: he *gave himself up for us as a fragrant offering and sacrifice to God.* The verb

353. Again the introductory καθὼς καί ('just as also') has both a comparative and a causal force (see on 4:32).
354. Cf. Lincoln, 311.

'gave over', together with the reflexive pronoun 'himself', indicates that Christ took the initiative in handing himself over to death. He went to the cross as the willing victim,[355] and this he did on behalf of believers ('for us'), language which at least indicates representation, even substitution (cf. Gal. 3:13; 2 Cor. 5:14, 21).

The sacrificial nature of Christ's death is made explicit in the appositional phrase *as a fragrant offering and sacrifice to God*. The two terms 'offering and sacrifice', which are probably a hendiadys and appear in Psalm 40:6 (LXX 39:7),[356] include all kinds of sacrifices, both grain and animal. The words *to God* are best connected to the preceding nouns ('as an offering and sacrifice to God'),[357] while the final phrase, 'for a fragrant aroma', which was used in the Old Testament of all the main types of sacrifice in the levitical ritual,[358] indicates what is well pleasing to God. Paul is here capturing this Old Testament sense of a sacrifice that is truly acceptable to God. Christ willingly offered himself as a sacrifice to the Father, and this was fully pleasing to him.

The apostle's point is plain. Christ's handing himself over to death for his people was the supreme demonstration of his love for them. Because he is both the ground and model of their love, costly, sacrificial love is to be the distinguishing mark of their lives.[359] To serve others in this way is not only to please God; it is also to imitate both God and Christ.

Paul has depicted in the strongest possible terms the contrast between the readers' previous way of life in the society of his day and their present existence in Christ. The standards presented in this passage are very different from the lifestyle of the surrounding world. This is not to say

355. There may be a deliberate contrast being drawn between Christ's action in giving himself over to death (παρέδωκεν ἑαυτόν) and that of the Gentiles who '*gave themselves over* to immorality' (ἑαυτοὺς παρέδωκαν, 4:19).

356. προσφορὰ καὶ θυσία. On the two terms see W. Schenk, *EDNT* 3:178, and H. Thyen, *EDNT* 2:161-63. Ps. 40:6 is cited by the writer of Hebrews (10:5), who consistently speaks of the work of Christ in terms of sacrifice. Paul does so occasionally: Rom. 3:25, as a 'means of atonement'; 8:3, as a sin-offering; and 1 Cor. 5:7, as a passover lamb who has been sacrificed.

357. This is more natural than linking the phrase with the preceding verb παρέδωκεν ('he gave'), which is too distant, or connecting it to the following phrase εἰς ὀσμὴν εὐωδίας ('for a fragrant aroma'), since one would expect τῷ θεῷ ('to God') to follow εἰς ὀσμὴν εὐωδίας (as it does in almost every instance in the Old Testament). Note the discussion by Hoehner.

358. It was applied to the burnt-offering (Lev. 1:9), the meal-offering (Lev. 2:2), the peace-offering (Lev. 3:5), and the sin-offering (Lev. 4:31).

359. Significantly, Paul writes of the Philippians' sacrificial love for him in terms of Christ's sacrifice, 'a fragrant offering, an acceptable sacrifice which is pleasing to God' (4:18); see P. T. O'Brien, *Philippians*, 540-42.

that some moralists would have disagreed with the apostle's assessment and given contrary advice. Some would have concurred with him at a number of points. Virtue and vice lists, and negative and positive injunctions of a kind similar to Paul's can be found in the Graeco-Roman and Hellenistic-Jewish literature of the day. But it is 'the framework of motivations supplied by his gospel' that makes his 'ethical teaching coherent and distinctly Christian'.[360] Particularly significant is the motivation not to grieve the Holy Spirit of God by whom they were sealed until the day of redemption (v. 30). God has stamped the readers with his own character and guaranteed to protect them until the final day. How ungrateful they would be if they now behaved in a manner which grieved the very Spirit by whom God had marked them as his own. Further, they are to forgive others just as God in Christ forgave them (v. 32), and they are to be imitators of God by walking in love. The model and ground for such a life of love is Christ's love so signally demonstrated in the cross. Ultimately, then, to imitate God is to imitate Christ, and costly, sacrificial love is to characterize believers in their relationships with one another.

360. Lincoln, 315.

Ephesians 5

D. From Darkness to Light, 5:3-14

> ^{3}But among you there must not be even a hint of sexual immorality, or of any kind of impurity, or of greed, because these are improper for God's holy people. ^{4}Nor should there be obscenity, foolish talk or coarse joking, which are out of place, but rather thanksgiving. ^{5}For of this you can be sure: No immoral, impure or greedy person — such a man is an idolater — has any inheritance in the kingdom of Christ and of God. ^{6}Let no one deceive you with empty words, for because of such things God's wrath comes on those who are disobedient. ^{7}Therefore do not be partners with them. ^{8}For you were once darkness, but now you are light in the Lord. Live as children of light ^{9}(for the fruit of the light consists in all goodness, righteousness and truth) ^{10}and find out what pleases the Lord. ^{11}Have nothing to do with the fruitless deeds of darkness, but rather expose them. ^{12}For it is shameful even to mention what the disobedient do in secret. ^{13}But everything exposed by the light becomes visible, ^{14}for it is light that makes everything visible. This is why it is said:
>
> > "Wake up, O sleeper,
> > rise from the dead,
> > and Christ will shine on you."

The specific exhortations in the previous paragraph (4:25–5:2) focussed on the differences between the old life and the new, particularly in relation to speech and conduct. The apostle ended this section on a positive note with his admonition to love as Christ had loved us and given himself up for us (5:2). In the present paragraph (vv. 3-14), the contrast is between believers and sinful outsiders (as in 4:17-21), and is presented in terms of the imagery of light and darkness (vv. 8-14). The key verb 'walk, live', which is a catchword in each section of the paraenesis (from 4:1), appears again at v. 8 in the exhortation, '*Live* as children of light'.

Once again Paul makes use of a common exhortatory form, that is, catalogues of vices (vv. 3-5) and virtues (v. 9; see on 4:25–5:2),[1] as well as another example of the 'once–now' contrast schema which has already featured prominently in chap. 2 (vv. 1-10, 11-22). There is also a citation introduced by the expression 'wherefore it says' (v. 14b), which appears at Ephesians 4:8 together with a scriptural quotation. The three-line piece here in 5:14b, which summons the sleeper to wake up and to rise from the dead, with the promise that 'Christ will shine upon you', has generally been taken as a citation of an early Christian hymn or hymnic fragment that was familiar to the readers. However, the dependence on the Old Testament context of Isaiah is considerably stronger than most commentators allow, while its meaning (whether a hymnic piece or not) must be determined within the movement of the paragraph (see the exegesis below).

The passage falls into two parts: the first, vv. 3-7, which begins on a negative note, admonishes believers to have nothing to do with the sexual vices and greed of the Gentile world. It concludes with two warnings about the serious consequences of indulging in sexual immorality, namely, exclusion from the divine kingdom and experiencing God's wrath (vv. 5, 6). The second part, vv. 8-14, which is connected with the first by v. 7, presents a sustained contrast between light and darkness. A list of virtues (v. 9) and the quotation of a (possible hymnic) fragment (v. 14) are employed, as Paul reminds his readers of the change that has taken place in their lives. Once they belonged to the dominion of darkness. Now through their relationship to their Lord they are members of the realm of light. Let them then live as children of light (vv. 8b-10). This will mean that the fruit of the light will be produced in their lives (v. 9), that they will discover what pleases their Lord (v. 10), and that they will no longer participate in the fruitless deeds of darkness (v. 11). The conclusion (v. 14b) sums up the call to leave behind the realm of darkness and death.

1. Abstain from Immorality and Greed, 5:3-7

3 Paul begins a fresh series of warnings against behaviour that is completely alien to a Christian lifestyle, returning to the contrast between the Christian community and outsiders found in the earlier exhortatory

---

1. Although as Best, 478, notes, the three vices of v. 4 are *hapax legomena* in the New Testament and do not occur regularly outside it in vice catalogues.

material of 4:17-24. Sexual sins dominate as he turns from the theme of self-sacrificial love (5:2) to its opposite, self-indulgent sensuality, from behaviour that imitates God and walks in love to a manner of life that is diametrically opposed. The sins of sexual immorality and greed are particularly in view later in the paragraph when mention is made of 'the deeds of darkness' and 'what is done in secret' (vv. 11, 12). Two of the three vices listed here, 'impurity' and 'covetousness', have already appeared in the triad of 4:19 (see the discussion there). As in the fivefold parallel catalogue of Colossians 3:5, 'sexual immorality' is mentioned first. It heads the list of works of the flesh (Gal. 5:19) from which believers are to abstain (1 Thess. 4:13) or which they are to shun (1 Cor. 6:18), and, as here, the apostle regularly brings to the attention of his Gentile readers the incompatibility of sexual immorality and the kingdom of God (1 Cor. 6:9; cf. 5:9-11; Col. 3:5). The term denotes any kind of illegitimate sexual intercourse, especially adultery and sexual relations with prostitutes.[2] One who surrenders to sexual immorality indicates ultimately that he or she has broken from God. In contrast to the loose living that prevailed in the Hellenistic world, New Testament (and in particular Pauline) teaching required unconditional obedience to the prohibition against 'fornication' (note Paul's warnings to the Corinthians: 1 Cor. 5:1; 6:12-20; 7:2; 10:8; 2 Cor. 12:21).

Although the second vice here in Ephesians, 'impurity', can signify unrestrained sexual behaviour and is sometimes combined with 'sexual immorality' (1 Thess. 4:3, 7; Gal. 5:19; 2 Cor. 12:21), the expression 'every kind of' points not only to sexual impurity but to much more besides (see on 4:19). It, too, is a work of the flesh (Gal. 5:19), and is incompatible with life in the Spirit (1 Thess. 4:7, 8). The presence of these two vices points to the immoral state of the pre-Christian life, to the behaviour of the person whose actions are determined by his or her commitment to natural lusts. It was all too easy for Gentile converts to slip back into preconversion ways — hence the admonition.

At Colossians 3:5 'greed' appears as the final vice in a fivefold list, and was especially accented as a gross sin. There the apostle begins with the outward manifestations of sin ('sexual immorality') and moves to the

---

2. The πορνεία word-group was employed in the LXX (rendering the Hebrew *zānâh*) to denote unchastity, harlotry, prostitution, and fornication (Gen. 34:31; 38:15; Lev. 19:29; Deut. 22:21). In later rabbinic literature the noun was understood to include not only prostitution and any kind of extramarital sexual intercourse, but also all marriages between relatives forbidden by rabbinic law (cf. Str-B 2.729-30). Incest (*T. Reuben* 1:6; *T. Judah* 13:6; cf. Lev. 18:6-18) and all kinds of unnatural sexual intercourse (e.g., *T. Benjamin* 9:1) were regarded as fornication (πορνεία). Note the discussion between B. Malina, 'Does *Porneia* Mean Fornication?' *NovT* 14 (1972), 10-17, and J. Jensen, 'Does *Porneia* Mean Fornication? A Critique of Bruce Malina', *NovT* 20 (1978), 161-84.

inward cravings of the heart ('ruthless greed'), from fornication to covet-ousness. Here in Ephesians, greed occurs at the end of a (threefold list). It is distinguished from the two preceding vices by the disjunctive particle 'or', as Paul moves from the acts of immorality and uncleanness to their inner spring — 'greed', that insatiable desire to have more, even the coveting of someone else's body for selfish gratification.

All these forms of sexual immorality and greed are so serious that they must not even be mentioned among God's people. The negative disjunctive particle, which is best rendered 'not even', together with the repetition in v. 12, 'it is shameful even to mention the things done by them in secret', indicates that believers should not only shun these sins but also avoid thinking and talking about them. Clearly, such vices will be mentioned in lists as here, but they are not to become the subject of Christians' conversation. Thinking and talking about sexual sins 'creates an atmosphere in which they are tolerated and which can . . . even promote their practice'.[3] The motivation for the avoidance of such conversation is what is fitting[4] for 'saints' (cf. 1:1). The absence of the definite article before this noun accents the qualitative note, namely, their holiness as God's people. They are reminded that he has called them to be holy and blameless before him (1:4). It is *appropriate* that their lifestyle be consistent with this holy calling (1 Thess. 4:3-7).

4 The warning of v. 3 about avoiding sexual sins is here continued in the triad of terms that refer to sinful speech: *obscenity, foolish talk,* and *coarse joking* about sex are to be avoided as entirely inappropriate among those who are saints. Over against these and the preceding vices of v. 3, however, stands thanksgiving, the fundamental Christian response of gratitude, expressed by those who have experienced God's grace in Christ (cf. 1:3-14).

Each of the words used for sinful speech, *obscenity, foolish talk,* and *coarse joking,* appears only here in the New Testament. The first is best understood concretely in the present context as signifying disgraceful speech,[5] and in the light of the preceding sexual sins is rendered *obscenity.*

---

3. Lincoln, 322.

4. The verb πρέπει ('fitting, proper, right') appears as a motivation at 1 Tim. 2:10; Tit. 2:1, while a similar motive, ἀνῆκεν ('fitting, proper') is used here in v. 4; cf. Louw and Nida §66.1. The appeal to what was fitting was a Stoic criterion for behaviour, but Paul does not use it in the Stoic manner to speak of conduct that is in accord with nature (cf. E. Best, *Ephesians* [Sheffield: Academic Press, 1993], 80).

5. αἰσχρότης points generally to 'indecent behavior; ugliness, or wickedness'; so BAGD, 25; and Louw and Nida §88.149. The Colossians parallel (αἰσχρολογία, 3:8), however, suggests that Paul has this more specific connotation in view here in Eph. 5:4. Hoehner thinks that αἰσχρότης signifies 'shame' in a general sense, in relation to both con-

The second term means 'foolish or silly talk'. The third word in the triad was used in classical Greek in the good sense of 'wittiness' or that sense of wit which was regarded as essential to good social converse. Even in early times, however, the term could have negative connotations, perhaps 'buffoonery or some kind of inhumane or degrading jesting'. P. W. van der Horst thinks that the context of Ephesians 5:4 suggests the meaning of *coarse joking* that has suggestive overtones and double entendres.[6] All three terms refer to a dirty mind expressing itself in vulgar conversation. This kind of language must be avoided as utterly inappropriate among those whom God has set apart as holy.

In striking contrast[7] to all forms of sexual immorality and obscene language, *thanksgiving*, the distinctive mark of Christian speech, is enjoined on the readers. Some writers have suggested that noble talk or truthful speaking would have been a more appropriate antithesis here. But thanksgiving stands over against the six preceding vices of vv. 3 and 4, not simply the vulgarity and obscene speech of v. 4, and it indicates a fundamentally different attitude: 'Whereas sexual impurity and covetousness both express self-centred acquisitiveness, thanksgiving is the exact opposite, and so the antidote required; it is the recognition of God's generosity'.[8] Thanksgiving is almost a synonym for the Christian life. It is the response of gratitude to God's saving activity in creation and redemption, and thus a recognition that he is the ultimate source of every blessing. All people, as God's creatures, ought to render thanksgiving and glory to him, but fail to do so (Rom. 1:21; cf. the 'ungrateful' of 2 Tim. 3:2, which describes humanity in the last days). Christians, because of the grace given to them in Christ Jesus (cf. 1:3-14, 15-23), are to live out their lives with joyful thanksgiving. It should be the accompaniment of every activity, being the appropriate response of those who have been filled by God's Spirit (Eph. 5:18-20).[9] Here in v. 4 thanksgiving reflects a Christian attitude to sex that is antithetical to a pagan attitude with its immorality and vulgarity.

5 Two severe warnings follow. They serve to underline the preced-

---

duct and speech, and therefore it serves as a transition for the next terms, which focus on sinful speech.

6. P. W. van der Horst, 'Is Wittiness Un-Christian? A Note on εὐτραπελία in Eph. v.4', in *Miscellanea Neotestamentica*, vol. 2, ed. T. Baard, A. F. J. Klijn, and W. C. van Unnik (Leiden: Brill, 1978), 163-77, esp. 175, who is followed by Lincoln, 323. Aristotle, who regarded εὐτραπελία ('wittiness') as a virtue (*Ethica Eudemia* 3.7.1234a.4-23), was also aware that the term had negative connotations (*Ethica Eudemia* 4.8.1128a.14-15).

7. Note the strong adversative ἀλλὰ μᾶλλον, rendered *but rather*.

8. Houlden, 324, whose words are often quoted.

9. P. T. O'Brien, 'Thanksgiving', in *Pauline Studies*, 62-63.

ing admonitions of vv. 3 and 4, and are intended to motivate the Christians solemnly to heed them (note the introductory 'for'). These warnings spell out the dire consequences for those who are immoral or sexually covetous: the first (v. 5) speaks with certainty of exclusion from the kingdom of Christ and of God, the second (v. 6) of the experience of the wrath of God.

The opening words of the Greek are an unusual periphrastic construction,[10] though the general sense is clear enough. They may be taken as an imperative and rendered, 'Be sure of this' (NRSV; lit. 'know, knowing'), or as an indicative and interpreted as an affirmation, *For of this you can be sure* (lit. 'you know, knowing'). Either way Paul is drawing attention to a certainty:[11] persistent sinners are excluded from God's kingdom. In v. 3 he had denounced the sins of *sexual immorality, impurity,* and *greed.* Now he returns to them, censuring those who habitually practise them.[12] As in Colossians 3:5, the danger of covetousness is emphatically stressed: here the person who practices unrestrained sexual greed is an idolater.[13] The sins of covetousness and idolatry stood together in Jewish exhorta-

10. ἴστε γινώσκοντες ('[you] know, knowing'). ἴστε is a present indicative or imperative of the verb οἶδα ('know') — normally a periphrasis has the verb 'to be' — while γινώσκοντες is a present participle of another verb γινώσκω, which means 'I know'. It has been thought that this is a Hebraism of an infinitive absolute construction which reinforces the idea of the verb, but here the two words for 'know' are not the same. Others, recognizing that it may not be a Hebraism, nevertheless think of it like the infinitive absolute and take the ἴστε as an imperative ('be very sure of this'). S. E. Porter, 'Ἴστε γινώσκοντες in Ephesians 5,5: Does Chiasm Solve the Problem?' *ZNW* 81 (1990), 270-76, regards it as an indicative and suggests that the periphrastic phrase should be understood as a component of a chiastic structure in vv. 3-5. But there are elements of the chiasm that do not fall easily into place. See also his *Verbal Aspect,* 286, 362, 465; note further BAGD, 556; and BDF §353(6); §422.

11. The demonstrative pronoun τοῦτο ('this') refers to the content which follows, ὅτι πᾶς πόρνος κτλ. ('that every immoral person . . .').

12. The three nouns used refer quite specifically to the persons who commit the acts described in v. 3: πόρνος ('immoral'), ἀκάθαρτος ('impure'), and πλεονέκτης ('greedy') are cognate with the words of v. 3 and in the same order. The Semitic πᾶς . . . οὐκ ('everyone . . . not') construction is again used to negate the verb (cf. A. T. Robertson, *Grammar,* 753), while πᾶς before an anarthrous noun means 'everyone' (BDF §275[3]). Accordingly, Paul is stating that 'no one' in any of these three classes has an inheritance in God's kingdom.

13. πλεονέκτης ὅ ἐστιν εἰδωλολάτρης ('covetous person who is an idolater'). The neuter relative pronoun ὅ is probably the original reading (rather than the masculine ὅς, 'who') since it has stronger manuscript support and, as the more difficult reading, might have been changed by early scribes to the masculine. The neuter relative pronoun picks up the whole idea or general notion of covetousness (A. T. Robertson, *Grammar,* 713; BDF §132[2]) but still should be rendered by 'who'. The singular relative refers simply to the 'covetous person', not to all the members of the triad ('immoral', 'impure', and 'covetous').

tions and were condemned as part of the horrors of paganism;[14] in particular, fornication and sexual lust were linked with idolatry.[15] Along with greed for riches and power, sexual lust is an idolatrous obsession; it places self-gratification or another person at the centre of one's existence, and thus is the worship of the creature rather than the Creator (Rom. 1:25).

It is certain that persistent sinners like the *immoral, impure,* and *greedy* have no part or lot in God's heavenly kingdom. Believers have already been assured that they have a secure hope of inheriting the glorious life to come (see on 1:14, 18 above). But they are here warned not to live like unbelievers, for they are not going to inherit the kingdom of Christ and of God. Those who have given themselves over to immorality, impurity, and greed, even if they call themselves Christian, show that they are excluded from eternal life. The apostle is not asserting that the believer who ever falls into these sins is automatically excluded from God's kingdom. Rather, what is envisaged here is the person who has given himself or herself up without shame or repentance to this way of life.[16]

Paul finds it necessary to warn his converts repeatedly about this. He reminds the Corinthians that *the wicked will not inherit the kingdom of God,* and then proceeds to describe this unrighteous behaviour in the list of ten vices that follow (1 Cor. 6:9-10; cf. Gal. 5:21). Some of the Corinthians have lived like this in the past. But they have been washed, sanctified, and justified (v. 11). The fact, however, that they still need to be warned against such vices even after their conversion shows how strong was the temptation, in a pagan environment, to go back to the old ways.[17]

The apostle's language here about not sharing in the heavenly inheritance is rather striking: first, unlike the earlier instances in his paraenesis where the verb 'to inherit' appears in the future tense ('*will* not inherit . . .', 1 Cor. 6:9, 10; Gal. 5:21), Ephesians uses the present: the immoral person '*has* no inheritance'. It is possible, with Porter, to regard this as a 'future-referring present',[18] so indicating that evildoers will not have any future lot in the divine kingdom. But it is better to understand the

---

14. According to *T. Judah* 19:1, greed seizes control of a person, leads him away from God, and holds him captive in idolatry. Elsewhere in Jewish thought 'greed' is soundly condemned (by Philo, *De Specialibus Legibus* 1.23-27; cf. G. Delling, *TDNT* 6:270; for rabbinic examples see Str-B 3.606, 607; and note the negative judgment on possessions in relation to covetousness in the Qumran writings: 1QpHab 6:1; 8:11, 12; 1QS 10:19; 11:2, etc.).

15. Wisdom 14:12; *T. Reuben* 4:6; *T. Judah* 23:1.

16. Stott, 197.

17. Bruce, 371.

18. S. E. Porter, *Verbal Aspect,* 230-32.

present tense, 'has [no inheritance]',[19] as signifying a process, without reference to past, present, or future: no immoral person has any part in the divine kingdom.

This aspectual interpretation is confirmed by the double expression *the kingdom of Christ and of God*, which is unique to the New Testament (cf. Rev. 11:15). There is a tendency in Paul's letters to distinguish two phases of the heavenly kingdom, reserving the expression 'the kingdom of God' for its future and eternal aspect (1 Cor. 6:9, 10; 15:50; Gal. 5:21),[20] while 'the kingdom of Christ' denotes the present phase of God's rule (1 Cor. 15:24; Col. 1:13; cf. also Eph. 2:6; 2 Tim. 4:1, 18), which is destined to merge with the future. So in 1 Corinthians 15:24 Christ, after reigning until all things are put under his feet, delivers up the kingdom to God the Father. Thus, the double formulation *the kingdom of Christ and of God* signifies the divine kingdom in both its present and future aspects, from which those who have given themselves over to immorality, impurity, and greed are excluded. One and the same kingdom belongs to and is ruled by Christ and God.[21] Let the readers, then, heed Paul's exhortations. Those in slavery to their sexual appetites are surely excluded from the rule of Christ and God.

6 It is all too easy for believers to be influenced by the surrounding world and to succumb to its ways of thinking and behaving. The result is that what is acceptable to the culture of the day becomes acceptable in the church. This is particularly true in contemporary Western society in the area of sexual morality.

Paul now underscores his first warning (v. 5) with a second as he urges his readers to heed the admonitions to avoid sexual immorality and obscene speech (vv. 3, 4). They should not be misled by *anyone* who encourages sexual permissiveness, thinking that such activities are a matter of indifference. Arguments of this kind are 'empty' and devoid of the truth (cf. Col. 2:4, 8) because they do not reckon with God's holy judgment on sin. The identity of those who might try to lead them astray is not specifically indicated.[22] They may be members of the Christian community (perhaps with libertine or gnosticizing tendencies) who do not take sin seriously. But the context, with its references to 'the sons of dis-

---

19. οὐκ ἔχει, which grammaticalizes the imperfective aspect.

20. Other instances of 'the kingdom of God' (e.g., Rom. 14:17; 1 Cor. 4:20; Col. 4:11; 1 Thess. 2:12; 2 Thess. 1:5) are more general in their reference.

21. Note the discussion of the grammatical issues relating to this phrase in M. J. Harris, *Jesus as God: The New Testament Use of* Theos *in Reference to Jesus* (Grand Rapids: Baker, 1992), 261-63.

22. The verb ἀπατάω signifies to 'deceive, mislead' (cf. 1 Tim. 2:14; Jas. 1:26) and is akin to the cognate noun ἀπάτη ('deception, deceitfulness'), which has already appeared in Eph. 4:22.

obedience', 'partakers with them' (v. 7), and 'you were once darkness' (v. 8), may point to unbelieving Gentiles who tried to justify their vices as matters of indifference.[23] This suggestion has the merit of maintaining the 'insider/outsider' contrast that runs through the passage. Whatever the source of the temptation, though, the readers are not to be led astray.

The powerful reason for not being deceived by such hollow arguments is that 'on account of these things', that is, the vices denounced in vv. 3-5, God's holy and righteous anger against sin is coming on the disobedient.[24] As in 2:2, the forceful expression 'sons of disobedience' points not to those who commit the occasional act of disobedience but to men and women whose lives are characterized by disobedience. They do not submit to God's authority; instead, they prefer to rule their own lives and go their own way. The present tense *(comes)* has been understood to indicate that even now such sinners experience something of the divine wrath. Others suggest that the present tense of this verb often has a future nuance, thereby indicating that the divine wrath will be manifest on the last day, or else it occurs in both present and future. However, the present tense probably depicts the action taking place as a process: *those who are disobedient* experience the divine wrath (cf. Rom. 1:18-32), whether in this age or in its full manifestation at the end.

7   Since the consequences of living an immoral life are so serious, the readers are strongly urged not to become partners with disobedient Gentiles in their sinful behaviour. Although the words *with them* may be taken to refer to the vices previously described (vv. 3-5), it is preferable to understand the antecedent as the persons themselves, namely, 'the sons of disobedience'.[25] But Paul is not prohibiting all contact or association with such people, as the NRSV ('do not be associated with them'; cf. RSV) seems to imply.[26] If this is what the apostle means, then they would need to go out of the world altogether (note his argument in 1 Cor. 5:10)! Rather, the term *partners,* which appears in the New Testament only here and at 3:6, is used to signify 'one who shares in a possession or a relationship'.[27] Accordingly, the readers are to make sure that they do not share

23. Note esp. Meyer, 269, who thinks that unbelieving Gentiles may have tried to entice Christians back to their old Gentile way of life. Cf. also Schnackenburg, 220; and Lincoln, 325. Barth, 567; and Best, 484, on the other hand, think that it is erring church members who are in view.

24. For a discussion of the 'wrath' of God and the 'sons of disobedience', see on 2:2, 3.

25. So Meyer, 270; Bruce, 372; and Schnackenburg, 221, among others.

26. The Qumran writings urged the members of its community to practise a radical separation, particularly from other Jewish groups (1QS 1:4, 5; 5:10, 11; CD 6:14, 15).

27. Louw and Nida §57.8.

with disobedient Gentiles in their immorality and thus escape the judgment that rightly falls with it (cf. 2 Cor. 6:14–7:1). Those who participate with Jewish believers in the promise of Christ Jesus through the gospel (3:6) cannot be partners with pagans in their sins. The two forms of participation are mutually exclusive.

2. Once Darkness, But Now Light, 5:8-14

8 The positive reason for believers not to be involved with the disobedient in their immoral conduct is not, in this case, the future judgment of God (as in v. 6), but the mighty change that occurred in their lives when they were converted. This whole paragraph, commencing with v. 8, plays on the rich symbolism of light and darkness, and again Paul introduces the 'once–now' contrast schema (see on 2:1-10, 11-22) to focus attention on the transfer of dominions experienced by believers. Once they belonged to the rule of darkness (cf. Col. 1:13), but now because of their new relationship with their Lord they are identified with the realm of light. How contradictory it would be, then, for them to become involved with the immorality of the past. If they are *light,* then let them behave as *children of light,* and this will mean living by values that are diametrically opposed to those of their surrounding society.

Already the difference between believers and non-Christians has been depicted in terms of the 'old person' and the 'new' (Eph. 4:22, 24). Now that distinction is made through the imagery of darkness and light: unbelievers are darkness, Christians are light.[28] This symbolism of light and darkness was popular in ancient religions generally, and appears regularly in the Old Testament,[29] the Qumran literature,[30] and elsewhere in the New Testament, especially the Johannine material.[31] In Ephesians darkness represents ignorance, error, and evil (cf. 4:18), and in particular comes to signify immorality as the way of life of those who are separated

28. The imagery of darkness and light is used elsewhere in connection with conversion: Acts 26:18; Col. 1:12, 13; 1 Pet. 2:9; note also Heb. 6:4; 10:32. Cf. Philo, *De Virtutibus* 179.

29. Light stands for life and salvation, whose source is God (Ps. 27:1; Isa. 9:2; 10:17; 42:6, 16; 49:6; 60:1).

30. The symbolism of light and darkness in the Qumran material often signifies the two ways of life in relation to God. This is especially evident in the War Scroll (1QM 1:1-16; 3:6, 9; 13:16; 14:17) and in the Rule of Discipline (1QS 1:9, 10; 3:13, 19-21, 24, 25); so K. G. Kuhn, 'The Epistle to the Ephesians', 122-24, who is followed by many recent commentators.

31. John 1:4, 5, 7-9; 3:19-21; 8:12; 9:5, etc.; 1 John 1:5; 2:8. In Paul it appears at Rom. 13:12, 13; 2 Cor. 4:4, 6; 6:14; Col. 1:12, 13; 1 Thess. 5:5; 1 Tim. 6:16; 2 Tim. 1:10. For further details see G. L. Borchert, *DPL*, 555-57.

from God. Light, on the other hand, stands for truth, knowledge (cf. 1:18), and now holiness, all of which come from God.

Surprisingly, the readers are not presented simply as having been in the realm of darkness and being now in the sphere of light, although this would have been true enough (cf. John 8:12; 1 Pet. 2:9; 1 John 1:5-7; 2:9). It is not their environment or the surroundings in which they and the rest of humanity live that is in view. Rather, they themselves were once *darkness*, but now they are *light in the Lord*. Those ruled by the dominion of *darkness* or of *light* represent that dominion in their own persons. So when they were converted, it was their lives, not their surroundings, that were changed from darkness to light. This radical transformation had taken place *in the Lord*.[32] He is the one who has made the decisive difference, and it is through their union with him that they have entered a new dominion and become *light*.

The implications of this change are now put positively. Their behaviour must conform to their new identity. Paul moves from the 'indicative' of what they are in the Lord to the 'imperative' of how they should live. Since the readers are now *light*,[33] then they are to walk as *children of light*, that is, their lives are to be characterized by light. What this involves is indicated in the verses that follow. Once again the key verb 'walk', which has appeared at significant points in the paraenesis of the letter (see on 4:1, 17; 5:2, 15; cf. 2:2, 10), is used.

9 In a brief aside[34] Paul explains first what it means to live as children of light by referring to three Christian graces: *goodness, righteousness and truth*. These are depicted as 'the fruit of light', and stand in stark contrast to the 'unfruitful works of darkness' (v. 11).[35] In addition to its literal

---

32. The antithetic parallelism of the first two lines shows that the words in the second line, ἐν κυρίῳ ('in the Lord'), are without parallel in the first, and make the decisive difference. With darkness there is no qualifier, but with light there is the additional phrase ἐν κυρίῳ:

ἦτε γάρ ποτε σκότος,
νῦν δὲ φῶς ἐν κυρίῳ.

'For you were once darkness,
but now [you are] light *in the Lord*'.

33. Again the realized eschatological note is struck in the letter: believers are even now *light in the Lord*. But as elsewhere in the Pauline corpus the present responsibilities that flow from the readers being in him are considerable.

34. Verse 9 is rightly rendered by the NIV (cf. RSV) as a parenthesis. δοκιμάζοντες ('examining') introduces a participial clause that further defines what it means to walk as children of light (v. 8).

35. Literally, 'the fruit of light *consists in* all goodness, righteousness and truth'. There is no verb in the sentence, and one needs to be supplied; together with the follow-

meaning of 'fruit' or 'produce', the term is employed in a figurative sense to denote the result, outcome, or profit of an action.[36] So the apostle can use the term metaphorically of the good results he looked for from his ministry (Rom. 1:13). Here it signifies the ethical outcome of light, which is viewed as a divine power. Light has marked effects on those who receive it. It manifests itself in the graces of goodness, righteousness, and truth, and these reflect the character of God himself (see on 4:24). In this sense, then, the fruit of light is very close in meaning to the 'fruit of the Spirit'[37] (Gal. 5:22; cf. the 'fruit of righteousness', Phil. 1:11).

The three characteristics which briefly depict what the new life is like remind the reader of points already covered, especially in 4:20–5:2. The first, rendered 'goodness', has a range of meanings as wide as its cognate adjective 'good', though it can have the nuance of 'generosity', as in the Old Testament, where it sometimes refers to the Lord's goodness.[38] According to Ephesians, God has created his people in Christ Jesus for the purpose of *good* works (2:10). Similarly, Paul prays that the Colossians may 'bear fruit in every *good* work' (Col. 1:10). The 'new person' of Ephesians has been created to display those ethical qualities that belong to God himself, such as *righteousness* and holiness, which have their origin in his *truth* (4:24). As a result, the new person speaks the *truth* in love (4:15, 25), since he or she has found the *truth* in Jesus (4:21).

Goodness, righteousness and truth, as the fruit of light, are supernatural characteristics, the result of God's creative activity. Yet within the flow of Paul's paraenesis, especially the imperative *Live as children of light*

---

ing prepositional phrase ἐν πάσῃ ἀγαθωσύνῃ κτλ. ('in all goodness, etc.'), it signifies 'consists in' or 'is characterized by [all goodness]'. The fruit of light expresses itself in the sphere of goodness, righteousness, and truth. Cf. Hoehner.

36. Louw and Nida §42.13 regard this as a figurative extension of the literal meaning of καρπός, 'fruit', the natural result of what has been done — 'deed, activity, result of deeds'. On Paul's use of καρπός, see P. T. O'Brien, *Philippians,* 80-81.

37. Several manuscripts (including 𝔓[46] D[2] Ψ 88 104) read 'the fruit of the Spirit' (πνεύματος), rather than 'the fruit of light' (φωτός). The latter, however, is the better-attested reading, with both widespread and early manuscript support (including 𝔓[49] ℵ A B D* a number of minuscules, as well as important versions and Fathers) in both the Alexandrian and Western textual traditions. Further, 'the fruit of light' (φωτός) fits the context better, while the reading πνεύματος ('of the Spirit') has probably come into the tradition from Gal. 5:22.

38. ἀγαθωσύνη, which does not occur in classical Greek, appears some fourteen times in the LXX and covers a wide semantic range, including beneficence someone has shown (Judg. 8:35; 2 Chron. 24:16), kind generosity (in this case the Lord's, Neh. 9:25, 35), moral goodness (Ps. 52:3), together with well-being and happiness (Eccl. 4:8; 5:10, etc.). Louw and Nida §57.109 render the word 'generosity'; it refers to 'the act of generous giving, with the implication of its relationship to goodness'. Note the discussions in C. Spicq, *TLNT* 1:3-4, and Hoehner.

(v. 8), the readers themselves are expected to demonstrate these Christian graces. Once again in this letter, divine activity and human response are carefully balanced (cf. Phil. 2:12-13, and see on 4:24). The trilogy is reminiscent of the statement in Micah 6:8 that God requires human beings to act justly, to love mercy, and to walk humbly with him.[39]

10 After the brief parenthesis of v. 9, Paul spells out the manner in which he wants his readers to *live as children of light*, that is, as those who 'discern what is pleasing to the Lord'.[40] The verb rendered 'discern' can mean to 'put to the test, examine', or it can refer to the result of the examination and so signify to 'accept as proved, approved'.[41] In this context it has the former sense of examining and evaluating issues[42] in order to determine the right course of action, here described as 'pleasing the Lord' (cf. Col. 1:10).[43]

This word-group plays an important role in the apostle's ethical teaching. Particularly close to our text is Romans 12:2, where the Christians in Rome are urged to be transformed by the renewing of their minds so that they may be able to *test* and *approve* the good, pleasing, and perfect will of God. In his prayer report of Philippians 1:10 Paul prays that believers' love may increase in knowledge so that they may be able to *choose* the really important issues in their lives, while in 1 Thessalonians 5:21 the readers are taught to *test* everything and hold fast to what is good.

The Jew who knew God's will was to 'approve' what was essential on the basis of the law (Rom. 2:18).[44] Christians, however, have 'learned Christ'. They have responded to the gospel and received further instruction about him (4:20, 21) from those specially equipped by the ascended Lord Jesus (4:11; cf. 2:20; 3:5). Thus, their lives are shaped *in accordance*

---

39. The list of three also has parallels in 2 Chron. 21:30 and the Qumran literature (1QS 1:5; 8:2), although these graces are not described as 'fruit' in any of these references.

40. The main theme is now resumed, with the participle δοκιμάζοντες ('examining, discerning') dependent on the imperative περιπατεῖτε ('live, walk').

41. Gk. δοκιμάζω. BAGD, 202; cf. Louw and Nida §27.45. Other instances of the former sense are 1 Cor. 11:28; 2 Cor. 13:5; Gal. 6:4; 1 Thess. 2:4; 5:21; 1 Tim. 3:10, while examples of δοκιμάζω pointing to the result of the examination and so signifying to 'accept as proved, approved' are 1 Cor. 16:3; 2 Cor. 8:22; Phil. 1:10. Hoehner understands the verb here in the sense of 'approving'.

42. C. Spicq, *TLNT* 1:356, thinks that δοκιμάζω signifies here in Eph. 5:10, as on other occasions in Paul, to '"discern" what is important to do, the best course to follow, the decision to make, and especially to discern what is pleasing to the Lord'.

43. In both texts *Lord* refers to the Lord Jesus rather than to God.

44. Which is in line with the Rule of Discipline at Qumran, where returning to every commandment of the law of Moses is the means by which one seeks God's will (1QS 5:9).

with the truth that is in Jesus (4:21). This Christ-centred instruction, which focusses on the truth of the gospel, is the yardstick by which believers are to discern in specific situations what pleases their Lord. Those who belong to the light are to live as children of light: as members of Christ they are to grow corporately and individually, and their overarching goal is to please him in all circumstances (cf. Rom. 12:2; 14:18; 2 Cor. 5:9; Phil. 4:18; Col. 3:20).

11 Walking as children of light (v. 8) not only entails the fruit of light being produced in their lives (v. 9); it also excludes participation in the unfruitful works of darkness. Because light and darkness are incompatible, it is completely inappropriate to live in the light (with its resulting *goodness, righteousness and truth*) and then to adopt the *lifestyle* of those who are still in darkness. The readers have already been urged to live as children of light (v. 8); now they are admonished not to participate in the unfruitful works of darkness.[45] Earlier they had been warned not to be partners with disobedient Gentiles (v. 7), and this was understood, not as prohibiting all contact or association with them, but of believers not taking part in their immorality. V. 11 now makes this explicit with its mention of not participating[46] in their evil deeds.

The sharp dichotomy between light and darkness, which began in v. 8, thus continues: light yields the fruit of *goodness, righteousness and truth,* but darkness produces only 'works' (like the 'works of the flesh', Gal. 5:19) which are useless, unproductive, and sterile (Matt. 13:22; Mark 4:19; Tit. 3:14; 2 Pet. 1:8; Jude 12).[47] These works cannot please the Lord (contrast v. 10). Their source is *darkness,* and they bear the marks of this realm,[48] that is, the dominion of death. Further, the people themselves who carry out these actions can be described as *darkness* (note that believers, in their former condition, were called 'darkness', but now they are 'light', v. 8): their works reveal their true condition and show that they embody this realm in their own persons.

The negative admonition not to participate in the fruitless deeds of darkness is now balanced by its positive counterpart: instead, believers

---

45. The positive exhortation τέκνα φωτὸς περιπατεῖτε ('walk as children of light') continues with the negative καὶ μὴ συγκοινωνεῖτε κτλ. ('and do not participate in [the unfruitful works] . . .').

46. The synonymous verb συγκοινωνέω ('to participate with, to be in partnership with, to associate with'; Louw and Nida §34.4) is used at Phil. 4:14 of the Philippians' sympathetic participation with Paul in his affliction, while at Rev. 18:4 the saints are warned to come out of fallen city, Babylon, lest they *share* in her sins.

47. See C. Spicq, *TLNT* 1:56-57.

48. The genitive σκότους ('of darkness') is both a genitive of source and a characterizing genitive.

are to *expose them*. Since the object of this reproving activity, both here and in v. 13,[49] is 'the unfruitful *works*' rather than the persons themselves, it is preferable to understand the verb in the sense of 'bringing to light or exposing' these deeds,[50] rather than convincing or convicting those[51] engaged in such activities. Both the flow of the argument and the context of darkness suggest that the fruitless deeds which are exposed are the sins of unbelievers. The conduct of the children of light will shine as a beacon to others, revealing evil deeds for what they are. To interpret the verb along these lines of exposing sin for what it is does not imply that Christians should remain silent or fail to speak out against evil. But the particular point being made here is that of living a godly lifestyle and showing evil to be evil.

12 A further reason is now given for both the positive and negative aspects of the exhortation in v. 11: the readers are to have nothing to do with the fruitless deeds of darkness; instead, they are to expose them *'because* it is shameful even to mention what is done by them in secret'.[52]

The earlier expression, 'the fruitless deeds of darkness' (v. 11), is a general one and could include sins done openly as well as those committed secretly. Such a description focusses on their evil character — they belong to the realm of darkness — and the fact that they are utterly futile. These 'works' are the sexual vices (perhaps even perversions) mentioned in v. 3, not immoral pagan religious rites, as some have suggested. They are now described as 'the things done in secret': those who commit them (i.e., the 'disobedient' of vv. 6, 7) do not want their sins to be brought out into the open (cf. John 3:20). But their dark deeds are so abhorrent, Paul asserts, that it is 'shameful even to mention' them, much less to do

---

49. Where ἐλέγχω appears again. The object is implied, from the first clause, in v. 11 and is explicit in v. 13: *'all things* (τὰ δὲ πάντα ἐλεγχόμενα) are exposed [by the light]'.

50. So BAGD, 249. Against T. Engberg-Pedersen, 'Ephesians 5,12-13: ἐλέγχειν and Conversion in the New Testament', *ZNW* 80 (1989), 89-110, who has argued that the root meaning of the verb ἐλέγχειν is that of confronting somebody or something with the aim of showing him or it to be at fault. He claims that in Ephesians believers are enjoined not only to have nothing to do with the works of darkness, but also to confront them by verbal reproof in order to show their falsity. But, in this context, it is the deeds themselves which are to be confronted, and this occurs through their being *exposed* to a godly lifestyle. F. Porsch, *EDNT* 1:428, aptly comments: 'the exhortation encourages Christians to *expose* "the unfruitful works of darkness," so that their true (dark) character might come to light'.

51. Whether understood of fellow-believers being corrected or rebuked when they fall into sin (so Gnilka, 255-56; and E. Best, *Ephesians* [1993], 52, 82), or unbelievers being urged to be converted (so K. G. Kuhn, 'The Epistle to the Ephesians', 124-31).

52. Cf. Lincoln, 330.

them.[53] He utterly repudiates these sexual sins, but desires to convey their seriousness without mentioning the details of the depravity. Paul and his readers knew what they were, and he will not dignify them by naming them. Instead, he wants the light of the gospel to shine through the readers' lives and expose these deeds for what they are.

13-14a The meaning of these verses is not entirely clear, and this has given rise to a variety of interpretations. The flow of the argument is from the exposure of the deeds of darkness (v. 11), through their illumination by the light (v. 13), to a focus on the light itself (v. 14). It appears, then, that the process by which darkness is transformed into light is being described.

Believers used to be darkness, but now they have become light in the Lord (v. 8). By their righteous lifestyle they are to show up the 'works of darkness' for what they are (v. 11). What happens when this exposure occurs is now explained: 'Everything is illumined[54] by the light'.[55] 'Everything' refers not to all things generally, but to all that is done in secret, that is, the hidden sexual sins about which he has been speaking (v. 12). Darkness hides the ugly realities of evil, but the light makes them visible. Evil is then seen for what it is without any possibility of concealment.

But the light has positive effects as well as negative ones. Within the movement of the argument the further explanation of v. 14a, *'for* everything that is illumined is light', suggests this. Admittedly, Paul's language is compressed, but the logic appears to be that the light not only exposes; it also transforms (cf. 2 Cor. 4:6). The disclosure of people's sins effected through believers' lives enables men and women to see the nature of their deeds. Some abandon the darkness of sin and respond to the light so that they become light themselves. This understanding is confirmed by v. 8, which speaks of the transformation that had taken place in

53. The καί before λέγειν is to be understood ascensively: it is shameful *'even* to mention', let alone to do the things in secret. The tacit contrast is with ποιεῖν ('to do'). Cf. Meyer, 273.

54. The finite verb φανεροῦται (as well as the participle φανερούμενον in v. 14a) is best understood as a passive ('made visible, illumined'), rather than a middle voice with an active sense; so BAGD, 852-53, and most commentators.

55. The prepositional phrase ὑπὸ τοῦ φωτός ('by the light') could be taken with either ἐλεγχόμενα ('exposed') or φανεροῦται ('is illumined'). The difference in meaning is slight, but the phrase is probably better taken with the latter: light is not explicitly mentioned with the exposure in v. 11, and on this interpretation v. 13 is read consistently with it. Light is now appropriately linked with the illumination. Also, prepositional phrases in Ephesians tend to precede the finite verb or participle which they qualify rather than to follow it (cf. 1:4). So reading ὑπὸ τοῦ φωτός with φανεροῦται ('illumined by the light') is preferable. Cf. Meyer, 275-76; Schnackenburg, 226; Lincoln, 330-31; and T. Moritz, *A Profound Mystery,* 113; against Hoehner; Snodgrass, 273; and many EVV, including NIV and NRSV.

the readers' experience, and by the confession of v. 14b. Furthermore, it is in line with John 3:19-21, which refers, on the one hand, to the failure of a person in darkness to come to the light, lest his or her deeds be exposed, and, on the other hand, of the person who does the truth and comes to the light in order that his or her deeds might be revealed for what they are. J. B. Phillips's oft-quoted rendering brings the force of v. 14a out well: 'It is even possible (after all, it happened to you!) for light to turn the thing it shines upon into light also'. The light thus has a twofold effect on the prevailing darkness: it makes visible and transforms.

A number of other interpretations, however, understand the light as shining on believers rather than transforming those outside of Christ:[56]

(1) Schnackenburg, for example, thinks that the parenthesis of v. 14a is simply 'a general statement which illustrates the function of light', and reiterates the point of v. 8, namely, that believers have become light in the Lord.[57]

(2) Hoehner, for his part, claims that the context is about the restoration of believers. They have become copartners in the works of unbelievers. When their deeds are exposed and shown to be the unfruitful works of darkness, 'the believer, with the aid of the Spirit, will change to the fruit of light, namely, goodness, righteousness, and reality (v. 9)'.[58]

(3) Moritz rejects the suggestion that the shameful things are themselves being turned into light by the process of illumination.[59] When an object is exposed to the light it does not become light. It simply reflects the light as long as it remains in the light's sphere of influence.[60] Accordingly, he understands Christ's illuminating activity to refer to the Christian. As the shameful things are being exposed by believers, they are shone upon Christ himself, who is the light, and so revealed himself. The one 'who is illumined by the true light in this way', that is, the believer, will continue to be shone upon by Christ, and so 'equipped to expose further shameful things'.[61] The intention of the passage, which explains the

---

56. Note the recent discussions of Schnackenburg, 227; Lincoln, 330-31; T. Moritz, *A Profound Mystery*, 113-15; and Hoehner.

57. Schnackenburg, 227.

58. Hoehner. Similarly E. Best, *Ephesians* (1993), 52, claims that it is 'the reproof of one member of the community who has sinned by another' that is in mind; in this way hidden sin is brought to light. Best then argues that the following hymn (v. 14b) supports this interpretation (but see below).

59. He argues that the introductory γάρ ('for') does not explain the previous statement 'everything exposed becomes illumined by the light', and must be understood as consecutive since it makes an additional point (T. Moritz, *A Profound Mystery*, 114-15). But this is doubtful.

60. T. Moritz, *A Profound Mystery*, 113-14.

61. T. Moritz, *A Profound Mystery*, 114.

presence of the early Christian hymn (v. 14b), is 'to remind the readers that the past is best left behind and that they must continue to expose themselves to the light of Christ'.[62]

Several of these arguments, particularly those of Moritz, have considerable force. But, for the reasons given, we believe that the passage is describing the process by which darkness is transformed into light. The function of the light is twofold: it exposes the sins of unbelievers, and transforms them so that they enter the realm of light (cf. Col. 1:13).

14b The exhortatory material of vv. 8-14 is now brought to its climax with a quotation, introduced by the same formula as the citation from Psalm 68:18 in Ephesians 4:8: 'this is why it says'. Although this introductory formula suggests that the quotation stems directly from the Old Testament[63] and the substance of the citation is scriptural, the words do not correspond precisely to the biblical text. As a result, there has been considerable debate regarding the source of the quotation, as well as its underlying ideas, with Old Testament texts such as Isaiah 26:19 ('You who dwell in the dust, awake and shout for joy!'), 60:1 ('Arise, shine; for your light has come, and the glory of the LORD has risen upon you'), and Jonah 1:6 ('How can you sleep? Arise, call upon your god!') being suggested, along with other material from, for example, the mystery religions and Gnostic thought. Most recent scholars reject the notion that v. 14b is an altered quotation from the Old Testament,[64] and prefer to understand it as a fragment of an early Christian hymn that was originally associated with baptism. The readers would be reminded of the summons to awake and of the promise they received at their baptism. As a result, they are now urged to live in the light of that life-changing experience.

However, several caveats to the current scholarly view need to be entered before we can satisfactorily nail down the meaning and function of this hymnic piece within the flow of vv. 8-14. As T. Moritz has claimed, the issues seem to be more nuanced than the scholarly consensus allows.[65] First, the links with and dependence on the Old Testament context of Isaiah are stronger than most recent writers concede. Given the other connections between Ephesians and Isaiah that have al-

---

62. T. Moritz, *A Profound Mystery,* 115.

63. The origin of quotations in 1 Cor. 1:31; 2:9; 3:19b; 9:10; 15:33; 2 Cor. 4:6; 1 Tim. 5:18b. 2 Tim. 2:19b is not entirely clear, even though an introductory formula appears; cf. T. Moritz, *A Profound Mystery,* 97.

64. Neither the mystery religions nor Gnostic sources provide an appropriate background for understanding either the imagery or the main elements of the citation.

65. T. Moritz, *A Profound Mystery,* 97-116.

ready been noted,[66] it is necessary to examine Isaiah 26:19 and 60:1, 2 within the wider theological and salvation-historical context of this Old Testament prophecy. Secondly, whatever the original setting of this three-line hymn (whether baptismal or not), the argument of Ephesians 5:8-14 has to do with believers' behaviour and the possible effects of this on those who live in darkness. The hymnic piece must be interpreted within the flow of these verses, not in some supposed 'earlier life'.

(1) Although Ephesians 5:14b does not correspond precisely to any Old Testament text, or apparently to a combination of such texts, it nevertheless has structural, linguistic, and conceptual connections with Isaiah 26:19 and 60:1-2.[67] According to Moritz, this three-line early Christian hymn was influenced by these Old Testament passages. The following points are noted:

(a) The rhythmic pattern of Isaiah 26:19 is close to that of Ephesians 5:14b, while there are significant verbal connections between the two texts.[68] Both verses use 'rise' and 'wake', as well as the term 'the dead'.[69] The address in Ephesians to the 'sleeper', which is a euphemism for death (see below), corresponds to the mention of 'those in the tombs' (Isa. 26:19). The Isaiah text appears in a narrative, and so the verbs are in the indicative mood. Ephesians, on the other hand, uses imperatives rather than indicatives. This does not indicate a lack of connection between the two texts; it only shows that Paul has adapted the narrative material to a new exhortatory setting.[70]

(b) There are substantial links between the Ephesians context and Isaiah 60:1-2.[71] The light-darkness motif which dominates the opening verses of this Old Testament passage provides a natural point of connection with Ephesians 5:8-14. In the third line of the hymn, the original 'Lord' has understandably been changed to 'Christ', while the more powerful and intense verb 'shine'[72] turns up in place of the more common word-group meaning to 'appear'.[73] This New Testament hapax was used in the LXX to describe the shining of the sun (Job 31:26) and the moon (Job 25:5), and it conveys the idea of a dominating, transforming light in

66. Note the links between Eph. 2:13, 17 and Isa. 57:19; Eph. 4:30 and Isa. 63:10; Eph. 6:14, 15, 17 and Isa. 59:17; cf. 11:5; 52:7. Cf. P. Qualls and J. D. W. Watts, 'Isaiah in Ephesians', *RevExp* 93 (1996), 249-59.

67. So T. Moritz, *A Profound Mystery*, 100-105, to whose discussion I am indebted.

68. T. Moritz, *A Profound Mystery*, 101-2.

69. ἔγειρε, ἀνάστα, and οἱ νεκροί.

70. Note the similar changes in mood from their respective Old Testament texts in Eph. 4:8, 30.

71. T. Moritz, *A Profound Mystery*, 102-4.

72. Gk. ἐπιφαύσκω.

73. Gk. φαίνω.

the midst of darkness. The final line of the hymn, then, with this strong verb 'shine', summarizes these opening, programmatic verses of Isaiah 60 with their reference to the glory of the Lord rising over Zion like the sun and effecting the transformation of the Lord's people. This wider Old Testament context is important for helping us determine the function of the hymnic piece within Ephesians 5:8-14.

(c) The textual differences between Ephesians 5:14b and Isaiah 26:19; 60:1, 2, on the one hand, and the linguistic and conceptual connections between the Old Testament material and the Ephesians reference, on the other, are best accounted for if one assumes that an early Christian hymn (or a creation of Paul himself) has been based on these two Old Testament passages.[74] Perhaps, too, the call to awake in Ephesians 5:14b is consistent with and was inspired by similar calls in the prophecy of Isaiah (52:1, 'Awake, awake! O Zion'; cf. 51:9, 17; 60:1, 2).

(2) The dominant scholarly view claims that the original setting of the Ephesians hymn was a baptismal one. This alleged background then determines the function of the text in Ephesians: it reminds the readers of the summons and promise they received at their baptism. But serious questions have been raised as to whether this was, in fact, the original setting. Even if it could be shown to be the case, the text must still be interpreted within its immediate context, and it is better to speak in terms of conversion rather than baptism.[75]

The conjunction 'therefore' is linked with v. 14a,[76] as well as v. 8, where the imagery of light and darkness began. The readers ought to know that whatever is revealed or lit up by the light becomes part of the realm of light, because they themselves had experienced the light in this way when they were converted (cf. v. 8). V. 14b seems to function as an *inclusio* in relation to v. 8: 'you were once darkness, but now you are light in the Lord', thereby underscoring the movement in the paragraph from darkness to light.

The imperatives address the non-Christian, as a *sleeper*, to *wake up* and *rise from the dead*. This is preferable to taking the expression to refer to disobedient or wayward Christians, whose deeds or lives are being exposed by other Christians. Sleep was sometimes used as an image of physical death (cf. Job 14:12),[77] although in this context, sleep, death, and darkness are striking figures which describe the condition of the individual apart from Christ, who is in a state of spiritual death that has been

---

74. T. Moritz, *A Profound Mystery*, 104-5.
75. So, rightly, T. Moritz, *A Profound Mystery*, 108-9.
76. The introductory διό is best understood in a causal sense, 'therefore' (Lincoln), rather than as denoting consequence, 'so then' (T. Moritz).
77. Louw and Nida §23.104. Note also *Psalms of Solomon* 16:1-4.

brought about through sins (cf. Eph. 2:1, 5).[78] Sleep is also the situation of forgetfulness and drunkenness which is part and parcel of the sinful world of darkness (1 Thess. 5:5-8; Rom. 13:11-14). The call to *wake up and rise from the dead* refers to the fundamental turnaround at conversion, and involves being brought out of darkness into the light of Christ. The connection between Christ and the light shining has already been made in relation to the language of Isaiah. Christ is the dominating transforming light, who in line with Old Testament imagery has shone upon his people and saved them: 'make your face shine upon us that we may be saved' (Ps. 80:3, 7, 19; cf. Deut. 33:2; Ps. 50:2).[79]

By citing these words, either an early Christian hymn or his own composition, based on the Old Testament, Paul reminds the readers of their conversion: they had been summoned by God's call to awaken from their sleep of spiritual death and to turn from the old life. They had responded to this summons, and the mighty light of Christ shone upon them and saved them (cf. 2:5, 8). Let them now live out the ethical implications of this wonderful change (v. 15), the implications of which Paul will spell out in the following verses. At the same time, the readers are reminded that Christ's light which had transformed their darkness was able to change the lives of others also.

Once again Paul draws a sharp distinction between the life and behaviour of those who are God's holy people (v. 3) and the surrounding society. The dominant imagery throughout the passage is that of light and darkness; there is no middle ground or shades of grey. The apostle wants his Christian readers to realize that they are to live by values that are diametrically opposed to the standards of their contemporary world, values that include sexual purity and wholesome speech. Instead of being corrupted by the surrounding darkness, believers are to exercise their influence on it. Paul adopts no defeatist attitude towards the society around him. Christ is the light who has summoned the readers to wake up and rise from the dead. He has shone upon them so that they have become light in the Lord. As children of light their lives are to shine as a beacon, exposing the darkness around for what it really is. Some who sit in darkness may be attracted to the light and even choose to enter it.

---

78. This is confirmed by the second line of the hymn, which directly refers to death ('arise from *the dead*') and explains the significance of sleep in line 1 ('Awake, O sleeper'). For further bibliographical references, see Best, 498.

79. Elsewhere in the New Testament Christ is presented as a shining light: Luke 2:32; John 1:4, 5, 9; 3:19-21; 8:12; 9:5; 12:46; Rev. 1:16. Cf. Lincoln, 332.

E. Be Careful How You Live: Generally and within the Christian Household, 5:15–6:9

In the three preceding paragraphs (4:17-24; 4:25–5:2; 5:3-14) Paul has used the language of 'walking' (4:17; 5:2, 8) to depict the contrast between the readers' lifestyle in Christ and that of outsiders. Now, in the following section of the letter (5:15–6:9), the same verb appears for the last time as the apostle urges his readers to be careful how they *walk*. This is amplified in terms of general Christian living (5:18-21) and three basic relationships within the believing household: wives and husbands (5:22-33), children and parents (6:1-4), and slaves and masters (6:5-9).

For the sake of convenience, we shall look at each section separately. Thematically and structurally, however, 5:15–6:9 form a well-knit unit. The instructions in the household code of 5:22–6:9 follow directly from the admonition of 5:21 ('Submit to one another in the fear of Christ'), which itself is a significant outworking of the exhortation to be filled by the Spirit (v. 18). There is an evident movement within the whole unit, and no sharp division should be made between each of the paragraphs.

The passage begins (5:15) with the final occurrence of the key verb 'walk', which has already been employed some four times in chapters 4–6 to spell out the ethical implications of the eternal plan of God which, among other things, involves the readers' being reconciled in Christ and made part of God's new humanity (chaps. 1–3). The 'topic sentence' in which this key verb occurs, *I urge you to live a life worthy of the calling you have received* (4:1), introduces the paraenetic material and is grounded in ('therefore') these first three chapters of the letter. At 4:17 the readers are urged to *walk* in holiness, and not to fall back into the patterns of thinking and behaviour of their former Gentile way of life. At 5:2 the admonition to *walk* in love explains what is involved in being imitators of God, while at v. 8 those who were once darkness but have now become light in the Lord are to *behave* as children of light, that is, they are to live by values that are opposed to those of the surrounding society. The final instance of this key paraenetic verb 'walk' occurs in the admonition to the readers to be very careful how they *live* (v. 15). This will involve them in being wise (v. 15), in understanding what the Lord's will is (v. 17), and in being filled by the Spirit (v. 18) — the last of which results in the readers speaking to each other in psalms, singing to the Lord, giving thanks to God, and submitting to one another (vv. 19-21).

1. Be Careful, Then, How You Live, 5:15-21

¹⁵Be very careful, then, how you live — not as unwise but as wise, ¹⁶making the most of every opportunity, because the days are evil. ¹⁷Therefore do not be foolish, but understand what the Lord's will is. ¹⁸Do not get drunk on wine, which leads to debauchery. Instead, be filled with the Spirit. ¹⁹Speak to one another with psalms, hymns and spiritual songs. Sing and make music in your heart to the Lord, ²⁰always giving thanks to God the Father for everything, in the name of our Lord Jesus Christ. ²¹Submit to one another out of reverence for Christ.

Ephesians 5:15-21 has been aptly called a 'summary climax'[80] of the paraenesis in chapters 4–6. At the beginning of this paragraph the key verb 'live', which Paul has used to define the Christian ethic, appears once more. The passage further explains what it means to *live a life worthily of the calling you have received* (4:1), the opening admonition and 'topic sentence' of the lengthy exhortatory material that extends from 4:1 to 6:9.

Although v. 15 begins the next major unit in the structure of the letter (5:15–6:9), the paragraph it introduces (5:15-21) has links with what precedes as well as with what follows. *Living* as wise people (v. 15) is akin to *living* a life of love (v. 2) or *walking* as children of light (v. 8). As those upon whom God has lavished his grace and *wisdom* (1:8; cf. v. 17), they are now urged to live consistently with this, namely, as those who are *wise* (5:15). Such a lifestyle stands in contrast to that of the *unwise,* pagan Gentiles whose *thinking* is futile and *understanding* is darkened (4:17, 18). The importance of *thanksgiving* was underscored in the previous paragraph (5:4; cf. also 1:16). There the giving of thanks was to characterize the readers' speech. Now in v. 20 this fundamental Christian response of gratitude for all that God has done is to be offered regularly to him in the name of the Lord Jesus Christ and as the proper response of those who are filled by the Spirit. Finally, the striking exhortation to 'be filled by the Spirit' (v. 18) is connected with and builds upon the earlier references in the letter to the Holy Spirit's work in the lives of believers (1:3, 13, 14, 17; 2:18, 22; 3:16; 4:30; cf. 6:17, 18). It is this exhortation about the Spirit that sets the direction for the rest of the paragraph (vv. 19-21), for what is involved in being filled by the Spirit is explained in the four clauses introduced by the participles 'speaking', v. 19; 'singing', v. 19; 'giving thanks', v. 20; and 'submitting', v. 21.[81]

---

80. Snodgrass, 286.
81. On the relationship between the imperatives of v. 18 ('Do not get drunk' and 'be filled by the Spirit') and the following five participles, see on vv. 18-21.

This exhortatory material of vv. 15-21 continues the contrast between the behaviour of the people of God and that of unbelievers. In the previous section (vv. 3-14), Paul had presented this contrast in terms of light and darkness, as he focussed on issues of sexual morality. Now, in vv. 15-21 the paraenetic thrust is more general (although some interpret the exhortations more particularly in relation to the community's corporate worship), and the contrasting patterns of behaviour are presented in terms of wisdom and folly. The first exhortation, *Be very careful, then, how you live* (v. 15), which stands like a heading, is explained by three antitheses, 'not . . . but', in the following clauses: (1) not as unwise, but as wise (v. 15b); (2) not foolish, but understanding the Lord's will (v. 17); (3) not drunk with wine, but filled by the Spirit (v. 18).[82]

15 As we have seen, Paul again uses the key verb 'walk' in order to draw out the implications of what it is to *live a life worthily of the calling you have received* (4:1), as he admonishes his readers to take great care in the conduct of their Christian lives. Literally the text reads 'watch carefully, then, how you walk'. The adverb rendered 'carefully' signifies something done accurately, precisely, or after close attention has been given. Together with the imperative 'watch',[83] it indicates that this admonition regarding godly behaviour is both important and urgent.

How one should walk is then explained by the first of three contrasts, *not as unwise, but as wise*. Although these adjectives have not appeared earlier in Ephesians, wisdom language has already turned up on three significant occasions in the letter. Wisdom language often needs definition from its context, and these earlier instances provide us with some clues as to how we should understand 'wise' and 'unwise' in this passage. According to 1:8, 9 it was God's intention that believers should understand his saving plan. He therefore lavished his grace upon us 'in

---

82. The three contrasts of vv. 15, 17 and 18, which amplify the meaning of the general admonition in v. 15a, βλέπετε οὖν ἀκριβῶς πῶς περιπατεῖτε ('Be very careful, then, how you live'), are parallel, as their form with μή . . . ἀλλά ('not . . . but') shows:

μὴ ὡς ἄσοφοι	ἀλλ' ὡς σοφοί . . .
'Not as unwise,	but as wise . . .' (v. 15b),

μὴ γίνεσθε ἄφρονες,	ἀλλὰ συνίετε τί τὸ θέλημα τοῦ κυρίου
'don't be foolish,	but understand what the will of the Lord is' (v. 17).

μὴ μεθύσκεσθε οἴνῳ . . . ἀλλὰ πληροῦσθε ἐν πνεύματι
'Do not get drunk with wine . . . , but be filled with the Spirit' (v. 18).

83. Although some texts read πῶς ἀκριβῶς, so associating 'carefully' with 'walking' rather than 'watching', the external evidence favours ἀκριβῶς πῶς, with the adverb modifying the watching (note the discussion of B. M. Metzger, *Textual Commentary*, 608; Schnackenburg, 234; Lincoln, 337; and Best, 503; against Hoehner).

all *wisdom* and insight' by making known to us the divine mystery, the content of which is his consummate purpose to sum up all things in Christ. In the following intercessory prayer (1:17-19) the apostle prayed that God, who had given his Spirit to the readers at their conversion, might impart this same Spirit of *wisdom* and revelation for them to understand more fully his mystery and to live in the light of it. The mystery had already been made known in Christ (1:9-10), but the readers needed to grasp its full significance. The third reference is to the manifold *wisdom* of God (3:10) which had to do with his richly diverse ways of working that led to a multiracial, multicultural community being united as fellow-members of the body of Christ (3:10). That divine wisdom is integrally related to the mystery. The latter is shaped by the divine wisdom; at the same time it is reflected and revealed in the mystery.

So wisdom and mystery go together. Truly to understand the mystery is to be *wise*, and commits believers to bringing their lifestyle into conformity with God's wonderful plan of saving men and women in Christ. To be *wise* is to grasp the significance of the Lord's will, as the parallel contrast in v. 17 makes clear ('do not be foolish, but understand what the Lord's *will* is'), which is another way of referring to his saving plan. All of this necessarily involves the *wise* person in walking worthily of the Lord (cf. Col. 1:9-10). But the *unwise* live as those who despise or have no true understanding of God's gracious purposes.[84]

The contrast between wisdom and folly, the wise and the foolish, has its roots in the wisdom traditions of the Old Testament, not least in relation to the 'two ways' teaching of Proverbs (4:10-14; 9; 10:8, 14; cf. Ps. 1, etc.), which is reflected in the later Qumran literature.[85] According to the Proverbs, the way of wisdom that members of the covenant community are to walk requires insight and understanding into God's will. This involves not simply an intellectual knowledge (though it is included), but also a skill in living, an ethical walk. To be wise in this sense is to demonstrate a perception and understanding that works itself out in practice (cf. Prov. 1:1-7). Ultimately, however, this wisdom of the Old Testament is for the covenant community and is therefore set within the context of God's redemptive plan for his people. Those who know his saving purposes should behave in a holy way as the people of God.

It has sometimes been claimed that the interests of Ephesians, here and elsewhere, are narrower than those of Colossians (cf. 4:5), where spe-

---

84. They have no insight into 'the true nature of things' (Hoehner).

85. K. G. Kuhn, 'The Epistle to the Ephesians', 125-26, draws attention to 1QS 4:24 as a close parallel to this use of 'wise' and 'unwise': the sons of light walk in wisdom, while the sons of darkness walk in foolishness.

cific reference is made to believers' behaviour in relation to outsiders. Ernest Best, for example, contends: 'Ephesians gives no advice on how to live in relation to the world outside the church'.[86] But Paul's purpose in this passage has a slightly different focus; it is more distinctly nuanced than Best implies. By using wisdom language the apostle presents the broad sweep of God's redemptive plan, the mystery, for he wants to expand the readers' horizons and encourage them to live in the light of God's declared intentions for the universe. This will have ramifications for all their relationships, with fellow believers in addition to those outside God's people, as the following verse makes clear. Both this text and other passages (see, e.g., on 6:15, 17, 19-20) cast serious doubt on Best's contention that the interests of the author of the letter are 'inward' rather than 'outward'.

16 Those who are *wise* will have a right attitude to time. An expression, 'you are buying time', similar to the one used here *(making the most of every opportunity)*, appears in Daniel 2:8[87] in relation to the Chaldeans who were unable to tell Nebuchadnezzar his dream, and so attempted to gain time before their death. If the meaning is the same in Ephesians, the force would be that believers are living in the last days, and so they should try to gain time in order to walk in a manner that pleases the Lord. The verb 'redeem' is drawn from the commercial language of the marketplace, and its prefix denotes an intensive activity, a buying which exhausts the possibilities available. It seems better, then, to understand the expression as metaphorical, signifying to 'make the most of the time'.[88] Believers will act wisely by snapping up every opportunity that comes.[89]

The reason for taking full advantage of every occasion is that *the days are evil*. Although this temporal expression has been understood simply as a general description of the presence of evil in the world which has now become 'widespread and arrogantly powerful',[90] Paul's language,

---

86. E. Best, *Ephesians* (1993), 82.

87. καιρὸν ὑμεῖς ἐξαγοράζετε (LXX).

88. See R. M. Pope, 'Studies in Pauline Vocabulary: Redeeming the Time', *ExpTim* 22 (1910-11), 552-54; and F. Büchsel, *TDNT* 1:124-28. Cf. Louw and Nida §65.42, (an idiom, literally 'to buy out the time') to take full advantage of any opportunity — 'to make good use of every opportunity, to take advantage of every chance'. The middle voice signifies a personal interest of the subject; so A. T. Robertson, *Grammar,* 810; cf. D. B. Wallace, *Greek Grammar,* 421.

89. The participial clause ἐξαγοραζόμενοι τὸν καιρόν specifies the means or manner by which the command for the readers to be wise is to be carried out, i.e., by *making the most of every opportunity.*

90. Mitton, 188; cf. Snodgrass, 288, and E. Best, *Ephesians* (1993), 52. A. Lindemann, *Die Aufhebung,* 232-34, argues that because the present time is evil, the wise person does

given his eschatological perspective, suggests an additional nuance. In continuity with Old Testament and Jewish apocalyptic thought, the apostle distinguishes two ages, 'the present age' and 'the coming age',[91] which is the time of salvation. The former was called 'this present *evil* age' (Gal. 1:4; cf. Rom. 8:18). In apocalyptic literature evil was understood to characterize the last days generally;[92] this age was dominated by rulers or demonic powers which were doomed to pass away (1 Cor. 2:6, 7). The notion that 'the days are evil' appears to be similar to the idea of 'this present evil age' in Galatians 1:4 (cf. 'the *evil* day', Eph. 6:13).[93] These 'evil' days are under the control of the prince of the power of the air (Eph. 2:2), who is opposed to God and his purposes. He exercises effective and compelling authority over men and women outside of Christ, keeping them in terrible bondage (2:1-3). But the Ephesian Christians have already participated in the world to come, the powers of the new age have broken in upon them, and they have become 'light in the Lord' (5:8). Although they live in the midst of these evil days as they await their final redemption, they are neither to avoid them nor to fear them. Rather, they are to live wisely, taking advantage of every opportunity in this fallen world to conduct themselves in a manner that is pleasing to God. How this is done is amplified in the following verses.

17 The general exhortation of v. 15, which urges the Christian readers to be very careful how they live, is further explained by this second contrast:[94] they are admonished not to be foolish but to understand what the Lord's will is. Although this exhortation is parallel to v. 15b *(not as unwise but as wise)*, it is not simply a restatement of the former: there is a development of thought in v. 17 and a slightly different focus on the Lord's will.

The adjective *foolish*, like the references to wisdom and folly in v. 15, has its roots in the wisdom traditions of the Old Testament. It describes

---

not have to show it any respect, but can exploit it to the full. Lindemann's particular exegesis, however, as well as his desire to abrogate temporal categories from Ephesians, has not commended itself to scholars. Here the text asserts that one is to take advantage of the opportunity, not disregard it, because the days are evil.

91. A key statement in Jewish apocalyptic literature about the division of time into two aeons is 4 Ezra 7:50, 'The Most High made not one age but two'.

92. *T. Dan* 5:4; *T. Zebulun* 9:5, 6; 2 Tim. 3:1; 2 Pet. 3:3.

93. So Arnold, 113. Following G. Harder (*TDNT* 6:554; cf. BAGD, 271, and R. Dabelstein, *EDNT* 2:1), Arnold understands the eschatological associations of the expression 'the days are evil' to indicate that Paul stresses the note of 'urgency in view of an implicit speedy end (i.e. parousia)'. It is doubtful, however, whether this nuance has compelling support from the immediate context (note the cautions of Lincoln, 342, and Hoehner).

94. On the three contrasts in vv. 15, 17, and 18, see above.

the 'fool' (Prov. 10:18, 23) who is careless (Prov. 14:26; 21:20), lacks understanding (Prov. 17:18), and despises wisdom (Prov. 1:22). He refuses to acknowledge dependence on God, and acts foolishly and presumptuously. This person lacks discernment in practical living.[95] Believers are to be very careful how they live, and *therefore*[96] they should not return to the *senseless* ways of the past (Eph. 4:18). In sharp contrast and as a corrective to being foolish,[97] they are urged to understand the Lord's will.

The 'will of God', which is clearly a Pauline phrase,[98] turns up in important contexts of Ephesians. In the first half of the letter (chaps. 1–3) it is used broadly of God's saving plan, various facets of which are described in different contexts. At 1:9-10 God's will is identified with the *mystery*,[99] which is a comprehensive concept, the content of which is his intention to bring all things together into unity in Christ. God, who works out everything in conformity with the purpose of *his will* (1:11), predestined men and women for adoption as his sons and daughters (1:5). Similarly, it was through the will of God, that is, in line with his gracious redemptive plan, that Paul was called to be an apostle of Christ Jesus (1:1; cf. v. 11).

Significantly, in the latter half of Ephesians (chaps. 4–6) the two references to the divine will (5:17; 6:6) appear in exhortatory contexts where the stress falls upon believers' responsibility to work out that will day by day. With broad brush strokes the apostle has painted the will of God on a large canvas in the first three chapters of Ephesians; now in the latter half of the epistle he moves to the fine details of the divine masterpiece. According to 6:6 God's will is that which is *done* from the heart by slaves when, as bondservants of Christ who serve their Lord wholeheartedly, they obey their masters. (Cf. Col. 4:12, where God's will appears in the context of an intercessory prayer for believers to stand firm and be perfect in the light of the final day.)

95. Louw and Nida §32.52 comment that ἄφρων involves 'not employing one's understanding, particularly in practical matters', and they render it as 'foolish, senseless, unwise'. Cf. D. Zeller, *EDNT* 1:184-85.

96. Hoehner thinks that διὰ τοῦτο ('on account of this') draws the foregoing discussion of vv. 15 and 16 to a conclusion. It is better, however, to regard v. 17 with its introductory διὰ τοῦτο ('on account of this') as providing a further exhortation based on v. 15: because it is necessary to walk ἀκριβῶς ('carefully'), 'therefore . . .' Cf. Abbott, 160.

97. As already indicated, ἀλλά ('but') functions as a strong adversative. It is also likely that the clause which it introduces, with its focus on understanding the content (τί) of the Lord's will, provides the counter or corrective to being foolish. Note the similar function of the ἀλλά in Phil. 4:6.

98. Rom. 1:10; 2:18; 12:2; 15:32; 1 Cor. 1:1; Gal. 1:4; 1 Thess. 4:3; 5:18; 2 Tim. 1:1.

99. It has already been claimed (see on 1:9) that the genitive '[the mystery] *of his will*' (τοῦ θελήματος αὐτοῦ) is one of apposition, and should be rendered, 'the mystery, namely, which he [God] willed'.

Turning to the phrase 'the *Lord's* will' at 5:17, several important features are to be noted:

(a) Believers are exhorted to *understand* the divine will, even though God has already made it known (1:9). The apostle is not suggesting that the readers have no insight into this will. Rather, in a *paraenetic context* he is admonishing them to appropriate it more fully for themselves. God has revealed to them the mystery of his will in the Lord Jesus Christ. Let them lay hold of it and understand its implications for their day-to-day living. An imperative following an indicative which states what God has already done is characteristically Pauline. Further, it is another example of the interplay between the divine action and the human (cf. Phil. 2:12-13, where the Philippian Christians are urged: 'work out your salvation with fear and trembling' *because* 'the One who works mightily in you is God, who produces in you both the determination to work and the power to carry it out — all in accordance with his good pleasure').

(b) The verb used here signifies to 'understand, comprehend, gain insight into something',[100] while the content to be grasped[101] is the divine will. Both the immediate and wider contexts of v. 17 make it plain that the apostle does not have in mind simply an intellectual understanding of the Lord's will. The cognitive dimension is clearly included, but in true Hebraic fashion the believers' understanding of God's gracious saving plan is to lead to right conduct.[102] In fact, living in a godly and blameless fashion is an essential element of the will of God since this was the goal of the readers' election in Christ (1:4, 5). Because the divine plan has to do with the summing up of all things in him (1:9, 10) and the formation of a people in the Creator's image who bear the family likeness (cf. 4:24), wise and careful behaviour is part and parcel of the divine will.

(c) Somewhat unusually, Paul speaks of the *Lord's* will rather than God's,[103] which is his customary expression (note the parallel Rom. 12:2). Although some take *Lord* to be a reference to God,[104] elsewhere in Ephesians it refers to Christ, and it should be so understood here. The difference may not be particularly significant. However, there is a christo-

---

100. Gk. συνίημι. BAGD, 790; cf. Louw and Nida §32.26.

101. The verb συνίετε ('understand') is followed by τί τὸ θέλημα τοῦ κυρίου, an accusative of content signifying 'what the Lord's will is'.

102. Bruce, 379, aptly remarks: 'The doing of his will is not a matter of irrational impulse but of intelligent reflection *and action*' (emphasis added).

103. A number of manuscripts, including A 81 365 (and several of the versions), read τοῦ θεοῦ ('[the will] of God'), thereby bringing the text into line with the usual Pauline expression. However, the more difficult reading, τοῦ κυρίου ('of the Lord'), is clearly original.

104. So, most recently, Hoehner.

logical focus within the preceding paragraph (vv. 8-14), and a flow of thought that begins with the mention of believers now becoming light in the *Lord* (v. 8) moves to their finding out what pleases the *Lord* (v. 10) and climaxes with a statement about *Christ* shining upon them (v. 14). References to the 'Lord' and 'Christ' are bracketed as a rhetorical device to frame the paragraph, which then leads into the final exhortatory section of the letter (5:15–6:9). Furthermore, a christological focus is consistent with the apostle's earlier statement that these believers have already 'learned Christ', and that their lives were shaped *in accordance with the truth that is in Jesus* (4:20, 21). Christ-centred instruction, with its focus on the truth of the gospel, enables them to discern in specific situations what *pleases the Lord* (v. 10). Let them now reflect upon what the will of the Lord Jesus Christ entails and act upon it.

In our contemporary context, the 'Lord's will' is frequently understood by Christians to refer to matters of personal guidance, and thus to God's immediate plans for their future. But the divine will in the Pauline letters, particularly in Ephesians, has a different focus, without neglecting the personal dimension. The 'will of God' is closely related to, even identified with, God's gracious saving plan and, as a significant element of this, the formation of a people into the likeness of Christ who will be pure and blameless on the final day. These priorities are presupposed in the apostolic injunction of v. 17. The contemporary preoccupation with personal guidance is wrongly directed if it is not understood first of all within this framework of God's gracious saving purposes for his world. Personalised concerns about 'guidance' may, in fact, be evidence of a *folly* which stands in contrast to, and needs to be corrected by, a true understanding of the Lord's will.

18-21 The third contrast, which further amplifies what it means for the Christian readers to live carefully and wisely (v. 15), is provided by the twofold exhortation of v. 18, which begins with the prohibition against getting drunk and concludes with the positive admonition, 'Be filled by the Spirit'. It is the latter which is particularly emphasized and which sets the direction for the rest of the passage. Paul's primary concern is to urge his readers to live by the Spirit continually. This exhortation plays a key role within the paraenetic material in Ephesians 4–6. It brings to a conclusion the long series of exhortations that began in 4:17, and leads into the participles that deal with Christian relationships generally (vv. 19-21) and those within the Christian household more specifically (5:22–6:9).

Although the point is often missed in the English translations, verses 18-21 form one long sentence, with five participles modifying the imperative 'be filled by the Spirit': 'speaking [to one another]' (v. 19a), 'singing' (v. 19b), 'making music' (v. 19b), 'giving thanks' (v. 20), and 'submitting [to one another]' (v. 21).[105] The basic structure of the sentence is as follows:

Do not get drunk on wine, . . .
But be filled   by the Spirit,
    speaking *to one another*
        with psalms, hymns and spiritual songs,
    singing and making music with your hearts *to the Lord,*
    giving thanks *to God*
        for all things
        in the name of our Lord Jesus Christ,
    submitting yourselves *to one another*
        in the fear of Christ,
        wives to husbands . . .[106]

Although these participles have been understood as imperatival (particularly the last one, 'submit [yourselves to one another]', v. 21), it is better to regard them as dependent participles[107] of result[108] which describe the

105. The NIV, e.g., hides the structure of the Greek. It uses five sentences with six commands and one participle to translate the one sentence (vv. 18-21): the commands are 'do not get drunk', 'be filled' (v. 18); 'speak', 'sing', 'make music' (v. 19), and 'submit' (v. 21), while the one participle is 'giving thanks' (v. 20).

106. Cf. G. D. Fee, *God's Empowering Presence,* 719.

107. The reasons are as follows: (1) The imperatival participle is less frequent in the New Testament than some have contended. Note the recent discussion by D. B. Wallace, *Greek Grammar,* 650-52 (cf. 613 for further bibliographical details); contra BDF §468(2). (2) The semantic and stylistic situation of Eph. 5:18-21 is different from that of other instances of the imperatival participle. In this paragraph all five participles are anarthrous and follow the main verb, πληροῦσθε ('be filled'). Stylistically, Ephesians has other examples of dependent participles, the most obvious example of which is 1:3-14, where several are strung together. (3) The asyndeton at v. 22, together with the lack of an imperative ὑποτάσσεσθε ('submit'), has led texts (e.g., NA[27]) and translations (e.g., RSV, NRSV, NIV), as well as commentators, to view ὑποτασσόμενοι ('submitting') as having been borrowed from v. 21 and to be taken as an imperative. But in spite of the distance from v. 18, ὑποτασσόμενοι ('submitting') is best read with the four preceding participles — there are no indicators in the Greek that it should be taken otherwise. The asyndeton at the beginning of the household tables in v. 22 is unusual for Ephesians: this passage on the household is the only major section in the body of the letter which commences without a conjunction. It suggests that 5:22–6:9 is not a separate unit but is more closely connected with the preceding than many have supposed. So D. B. Wallace, *Greek Grammar,* 651 (cf. 639, 644-45, 659), who adds that it is as though the instruction in vv. 18-21 is 'ringing in the ears' of the hearers as they turn to the section on the extended family. Cf. G. D. Fee, *God's Empowering Presence,* 719; and Snodgrass, 286-87.

108. This conclusion fits the context better than the suggestion that these are participles of means, manner, or attendant circumstances. Note the discussion of D. B. Wal-

overflow or outworking of the Spirit's filling believers. Spirit-filled Christians are people whose lives are characterized by singing, thanksgiving, and mutual submission.

V. 21 is a hinge verse which leads into the household codes of 5:22–6:9. Many commentators link it with what follows, so that the paragraph runs from 5:21 to 6:9. But this structure obscures the fact that all *five* participles (including 'submitting' of v. 21) modify the imperative 'be filled [by the Spirit]', and that the 'house codes' which follow in 5:22–6:9 are *'explicit instances of submission within the body of Christ'*.[109] On the other hand, to commence a separate paragraph at v. 22 destroys the relationship to the theme of submission in v. 21,[110] while the English translations (cf. NIV) which commence a fresh paragraph in v. 21 lose 'the focus on submission as an essential mark of being filled with God's Spirit'.[111] Thematically and structurally 5:15–6:9 forms a well-knit unit.

18 The opening prohibition, 'Do not get drunk with wine', is rather surprising, and one wonders how much the readers would have been prepared for it. The more specific nature of the admonition, the wording of which corresponds with the LXX of Proverbs 23:31 (see below), introduces a change from the preceding general exhortations. Is there some particular reason for this prohibition, or is it part of the more general exhortatory material which also acts as a foil to the positive exhortation to be filled by the Spirit? The following suggestions merit consideration:

(1) Some have alleged that Paul was aware of misconduct among Christians in Asia Minor, similar to the supposed (though unlikely) drunkenness at the Lord's table in Corinth (1 Cor. 11:21). There is, however, no evidence to support this. Further, one would have expected the apostle to be more specific in his criticism had drunkenness been the particular problem within their congregational meetings.[112]

---

lace, *Greek Grammar,* 639, 644-45. Recently Lincoln, 345; G. D. Fee, *God's Empowering Presence,* 721; and Snodgrass, 287 (cf. Schnackenburg, 233), have taken the participles as describing the beneficial results of being filled by the Spirit.

109. Snodgrass, 286 (his emphasis).

110. Note the repetition of the word 'fear' in vv. 21 and 33; the term functions as a rhetorical device bracketing the section (vv. 21-33) together as a unit as the apostle returns to the same theme with which he began.

111. Snodgrass, 287.

112. P. W. Gosnell, 'Ephesians 5:18-20 and Mealtime Propriety', *TynBul* 44 (1993), 363-71, suggests a background in Graeco-Roman mealtime practices, where solemn meals were followed by serious discussion, even of a religious kind. Discussion would be hindered if the participants were drunk. Gosnell thinks that the statements of Eph. 5:18-20 may reflect the author's assumption that the readers frequently gathered in a mealtime context.

(2) Others understand Paul's prohibition to be directed against pagan mystery cult celebrations, especially the cult of Dionysius, the god of wine, in which the Gentile Christian readers may have previously participated. A major feature of this worship was the holding of orgies that included heavy intoxication with wine. The purpose was to cause Dionysius to enter and fill the worshipper's body so that he or she would comply with the deity's will. Interpreting the prohibition of v. 18 against this background is obviously attractive: Being filled by the Spirit is to be substituted for getting drunk with wine, speaking in psalms and singing in one's heart to the Lord stand in sharp contrast to the 'raving of drunken worshippers singing praises to Dionysius',[113] while Christian behaviour in marriage, which is expounded in vv. 21-33, must take the place of sexual debauchery in the name of Dionysius. The real difficulty, however, with this interpretation is the lack of clear evidence. Although such cults were widespread, there is nothing to suggest that they had a continuing influence in the churches of Asia Minor.

(3) From 4:17 on Paul has drawn a sharp contrast between behaviour which characterizes the unbelieving world and that of God's people. In 4:17-24 the pagan lifestyle is painted in dark colours and the readers are urged not to go back to these old ways. Instead, as men and women who have 'learned Christ' (v. 20), they are to live according to the 'new man'. The antithesis between the two 'ways' continues first in the concrete exhortations of the following paraenesis (4:25–5:2), then in terms of the light-darkness contrast at 5:8-14, with its particular mention of their having become 'light in the Lord' (v. 8), and finally with reference to wisdom and folly in the material immediately preceding (vv. 15-17). The rejection of drunkenness at v. 18 (with its contrasting exhortation to be filled by the Spirit) is a continuation of this same antithesis, for drunkenness is depicted in the Pauline paraenesis as epitomizing the ways of darkness (1 Thess. 5:6-8; Rom. 13:12, 13).[114] It leads to[115] dissipation, that is, to sexual excess and debauchery,[116] for those who are drunk give way

---

113. C. Rogers, 'The Dionysian Background of Ephesians 5:18', *BSac* 136 (1979), 249-57, esp. 257, who is followed, among others, by T. Moritz, *A Profound Mystery*, 94-95.

114. Note the other New Testament references to this vice: Matt. 24:49; Luke 12:45; 1 Cor. 5:11; 6:10; 1 Tim. 3:8; Tit. 2:3; 1 Pet. 4:3.

115. ἐν ᾧ ἐστιν ἀσωτία means 'in which is excess'. The relative prepositional phrase ἐν ᾧ ('in which') picks up the previous clause μὴ μεθύσκεσθε οἴνῳ ('don't get drunk with wine'), not simply the noun οἴνῳ ('with wine'): it is *in the drunkenness caused by wine* that there is excess or recklessness.

116. ἀσωτία (which, according to Louw and Nida §88.96, signifies behaviour which shows lack of concern or thought for the consequences of an action — 'senseless deeds, reckless deeds, recklessness') is condemned in Tit. 1:6 (children of elders must not be guilty of 'debauchery'), and 1 Pet. 4:4 (where it is associated with drunkenness, and pre-

to dissolute and reckless deeds. Drunkenness lay at the centre of the destructive and unacceptable lifestyle that belonged to the readers' past, and was not consistent with membership in the new people of God. The apostle's prohibition, then, is part of more general exhortatory material, and is not as abrupt or sharply different from the preceding admonitions as might first appear.[117] Further, Paul's use of an Old Testament wisdom text (Prov. 23:31), which appears within a paragraph (vv. 29-35) that rejects drunkenness as inappropriate for those who belong to the Lord's covenant people,[118] makes sense within the immediate flow of the paraenesis where the readers are being urged to walk *wisely* (Eph. 5:15-18).[119]

(4) The prohibition, 'do not get drunk with wine', serves as a foil to its positive counterpart, 'be filled by the Spirit', which is the apostle's special concern. While the warning never[120] to get drunk is a timely one, it is the latter admonition which receives the emphasis, and the results of this infilling are amplified in the participial clauses which follow (see above). The readers have already been told that they have been 'sealed' by the Holy Spirit, and that they must not 'grieve' him (1:13;

---

viously characterized the lives of those converted from paganism). At Luke 15:13 the corresponding adverb (ἀσώτως) describes the 'riotous living' by which the prodigal son wasted his inheritance.

117. Cf. G. D. Fee, *God's Empowering Presence*, 720, following Schnackenburg, 236; and Lincoln, 345-46. A. W. D. Hui, 'The Concept of the Holy Spirit in Ephesians and Its Relation to the Pneumatologies of Luke and Paul' (Ph.D. thesis, University of Aberdeen, 1992), 311, rightly thinks that 5:15-21 'contrasts two completely different lifestyles. The Spirit-filled life of the believer stands in opposition to the licentious life of the drunkard'.

118. The wording of this prohibition against drunkenness coincides fully with the LXX A text of Proverbs 23:31 (μὴ μεθύσκεσθε οἴνῳ). Some contend that its use in Ephesians is indirect, having been mediated through Jewish ethical traditions. Attention is often drawn to the *Testaments of the Twelve Patriarchs* (esp. *T. Judah* 14:1; cf. *T. Issachar* 7:2-3; *T. Judah* 11:2; 12:3; 13:6; 16:1), since warnings against drunkenness are there, as in Ephesians, linked with warnings against debauchery (cf. Gnilka, 269; Lincoln, 340, and note the discussion of T. Moritz, *A Profound Mystery*, 94). While the mediation of this text through Jewish ethical traditions is possible, it may be more complicated than is necessary, given the way that the Old Testament is handled elsewhere in Ephesians.

119. A. J. Köstenberger, 'What Does It Mean to Be Filled with the Spirit? A Biblical Investigation', *JETS* 40 (1997), 232, correctly notes that being drunk with wine is parallelled with foolishness (v. 15).

120. The exhortation in the present tense, μὴ μεθύσκεσθε ('do not get drunk'), does not signify that the Ephesians had been getting drunk and that Paul was urging them to stop. Rather, it has the sense of prohibiting a course of action, viewed as an ongoing process. Note the discussion of D. B. Wallace, *Greek Grammar*, 714-17, following the groundbreaking work of K. L. McKay, 'Aspect in Imperatival Constructions in New Testament Greek', *NovT* 27 (1985), 201-26; cf. A. T. Robertson, *Grammar*, 854, 890; C. F. D. Moule, *Idiom Book*, 21; S. E. Porter, *Verbal Aspect*, 357; and *Idioms*, 54.

4:30). Now they are bidden to be filled by the Spirit, and this is consonant with their living as children of light (v. 8) and walking wisely
(v. 15).

The wording of Paul's imperative is unusual, since it is unparal-
lelled elsewhere in the Bible. Rather than admonish his Christian readers
to 'be full of the Spirit', which might be a closer counterpart to being full
of wine, the apostle urges them to 'be filled continually[121] by the Spirit'.
The usual rendering of this exhortation is 'be filled *with* the Spirit', which
is rather ambiguous, since 'with' may be understood instrumentally (and
therefore equivalent to 'by'),[122] or, in line with the dominant view, it may
be taken to refer to the Holy Spirit as the content with which believers are
filled. Some interpreters, following the lead of J. Armitage Robinson,
think that the original signifies both (1) *by* the Spirit that believers are to
be filled, *and* (2) *with* the Spirit as the content of the fulness.[123] But the latter raises important syntactical difficulties. There are no other examples
in the Greek Bible of this verb to 'fill' followed by this prepositional
phrase to indicate content.[124] The flow of the argument does not demand
such an interpretation (in fact, the reverse is true), while understanding
en pneumati as an instrumental dative,[125] indicating the *means* by which

121. The present imperative πληροῦσθε ('be filled') suggests that the Spirit's infilling is to be continual.

122. Hoehner argues for an instrumental understanding of ἐν πνεύματι, but translates the exhortation: 'Be filled *with* the Spirit' (emphasis added).

123. Robinson, 203-4, contends that the preposition ἐν signifies instrumentality (or
agency; cf. 1 Cor. 12:3, 13; Rom. 15:16), so that the clause is rendered: 'Let your fulness be
that which comes through the Holy Spirit'. But he concludes that while 'Be filled with the
Spirit' is 'not strictly accurate, [it] suffices to bring out the general sense of the passage'.
Note also Bruce, 379-80; Snodgrass, 290; Lincoln, 344, who states: 'Believers are to be
filled by the Spirit and thus also filled with the Spirit'; and G. D. Fee, *God's Empowering
Presence*, 721, who thinks that ἐν πνεύματι indicates the 'means' by which believers are
filled. However, he then claims that it is 'but a short step' to seeing the Spirit as the 'substance' with which one is filled. Cf. A. J. Köstenberger, 'Filled', 231.

124. That is, the preposition ἐν ('in, with, by') with the dative case (as ἐν πνεύματι
here). Abbott, 161, comments that 'the use of ἐν with πληρόω to express the content with
which a thing is filled would be quite unexampled'. Normally verbs of filling are followed by a genitive case to indicate the content with which one is filled (cf. Phil. 1:11).
There are three possible instances of πληρόω ('fill') taking a dative of content (Rom. 1:29;
2 Cor. 7:4; Luke 2:40), but no clear examples with the preposition ἐν plus the dative case.

125. The instrumental use of ἐν πνεύματι ('by the spirit/Spirit') is consistent with
other references in Paul (1 Cor. 12:3, 13; Rom. 15:16), while in the present context the notion of the Spirit as the instrument in sealing believers appears; at 4:30 the Holy Spirit of
God is the one 'by whom' (ἐν ᾧ) they were sealed. See C. F. D. Moule, *Idiom Book*, 76, 77;
D. B. Wallace, *Greek Grammar*, 93, 94, 170-71, 375; and Hoehner. Although some exegetes
acknowledge that ἐν πνεύματι could denote the sphere of the Spirit (= 'in the Spirit'), most
prefer the instrumental sense; note Hoehner's discussion.

believers are filled (i.e., by the Holy Spirit),[126] is preferable syntactically and makes better sense.

On this interpretation, the content of the filling is not specifically mentioned. However, the earlier uses of the 'fulness' language in Ephesians are determinative for understanding what that fulness is here at 5:18. According to 1:23 the church as Christ's body already shares *his* fulness. (At Col. 1:19; 2:9, the divine fulness is perfectly found in Christ, and from him believers have already come to fulness of life, 2:10.) In the 'hinge' prayer of 3:19, which introduces the latter half of Ephesians, the apostle's climactic petition is that his Christian readers will 'be filled to all the fulness of God',[127] a reference not simply to the Father but to the triune God who is the content of this fulness. According to 4:10 the ascended Christ is the agent who fills all things, and this he does by giving ministers to his people (4:11). The final goal to which the body of Christ is moving is mature manhood, and this is defined in terms of the *fulness* of Christ (4:13).

In the light of these earlier instances of the 'fulness' language, then, we conclude that the *content* with which believers have been (or are being) filled is the fulness of (the triune) God or of Christ. No other text in Ephesians (or elsewhere in Paul) *focusses* specifically on the Holy Spirit as the *content* of this fulness. It is better, then, to understand 5:18 in terms of the Spirit's mediating the fulness of God and Christ to believers.[128] In other words, Paul's readers are to be transformed by the Spirit into the likeness of God and Christ, ideas which are entirely consistent with the earlier exhortations of 4:32–5:2. Significantly, as we have seen, it is only in this passage of Ephesians that believers are urged to be imitators of God (5:1). To be admonished, 'Be filled by the Spirit', then, means that Paul's readers are urged to let the Spirit change them more and more into the image of God and Christ, a notion which is consistent with Pauline theology elsewhere. This explanation accords well with the parallel passage in Colossians, 'Let the word of Christ dwell in you richly as you teach and admonish one another in all wisdom by means of Spirit-inspired psalms, hymns and songs, singing

126. Earlier commentators understood this difficult expression to mean, 'be filled in one's own spirit' (note, e.g., Abbott, 161-62). But this view has not convinced later scholars on the grounds that it is not consistent with Pauline usage generally, the context of the letter as a whole (where, apart from 2:2, all twelve other instances of πνεῦμα refer to the Holy Spirit), or the immediate context.

127. Gk. πληρωθῆτε εἰς πᾶν τὸ πλήρωμα τοῦ θεοῦ.

128. Lincoln, 344. D. B. Wallace, *Greek Grammar*, 375, on the grounds that Christ is the agent of the filling in 4:10, claims that in 5:18: 'Believers are to be filled *by* Christ *by means of* the Spirit *with* the content of the fullness of God'.

thankfully to God with your whole being' (Col. 3:16). It also synchro-
nizes with the preceding context of Ephesians 5:15-17, where believers
are urged to walk wisely (v. 15) and to understand what the Lord's (i.e.,
Christ's) will is.

It is obvious from these references to the fulness terminology in
Ephesians that the exhortation to be filled by the Spirit is part of the eschatological tension between the 'already' and the 'not yet'.[129] The church
as Christ's body *already* shares his fulness (1:23). Yet Paul's petition for his
readers (3:14-19), which is based on God's mighty salvation effected in
the Lord Jesus and described in the first three chapters of Ephesians, is
that they might be filled to all the fulness of God (v. 19). Paul's intercession presupposes that the readers have *not yet* been filled: God begins to
answer this petition in the here and now, and he will consummate his
work on the final day when the readers are filled with *all* his fulness. Similarly, the body of Christ has *not yet* reached mature manhood; it is moving towards the fulness of Christ (4:13). And in the process the Holy
Spirit is powerfully at work transforming believers both individually and
corporately into the likeness of Christ.

Further, although there is a strong emphasis on God's activity in
bringing his people to fulness, this transforming work is not done apart
from their personal involvement. Once again, the interplay between the
divine and the human emerges. The petition of 3:19, which anticipates
this exhortation, is addressed to 'the Father', and this, together with the
passive 'that you may be filled', makes it clear that God is the one who accomplishes this total infilling.[130] According to 4:10, Christ fills all things
and gives special ministers to his people, which lead ultimately to his
body reaching fulness. In 5:18 it is 'by the Spirit' that God's people are
filled. At the same time believers, both individually and corporately, are
to be wholly and utterly involved in this process of infilling. All are actively engaged in building Christ's body so that it reaches mature manhood, that is, his fulness (4:12-13). All are urged to be imitators of God,
and this involves walking in love after the pattern of Christ's love (5:1, 2).
Believers are the recipients of the exhortation at 5:18, for, although we do
not fill ourselves, we are to be receptive to the Spirit's transforming work,
making us into the likeness (i.e., fulness) of God and Christ. We are to be
subject to the Spirit's control (cf. 1:17; 3:16), which is tantamount to let-
ting Christ's word rule in our lives (Col. 3:16), so that we may walk

---

129. Surprisingly, for all that is said about the emphasis on realized eschatology in
Ephesians, the majority of the 'fulness/filled' references are part of the eschatological
'not yet'.

130. Cf. A. J. Köstenberger, 'Filled', 232.

wisely (Eph. 5:15)[131] and understand more fully the Lord's will (v. 17). The goal is to attain to what in principle we already have in Christ — fulness and spiritual maturity.

19 If drunkenness leads to dissolute behaviour, then Spirit-filled Christians whose lives are characterized by singing, thanksgiving, and submission present a very different picture. These divinely inspired expressions of joy and gratitude are reminiscent of the opening doxology (1:3-14), where Christians are encouraged to praise the God and Father of our Lord Jesus Christ for having blessed us with every spiritual blessing in Christ (v. 3). Now, those who are being filled by God's Spirit are able to join the apostle in offering appropriate praise to the triune God for all that he has done in Christ.

Of the five participles (vv. 19-21) that follow the exhortation to be filled by the Spirit, and which describe the results of that infilling,[132] the first three have to do with singing: 'speaking [with psalms, hymns, and songs]', 'singing', and 'making music' (v. 19). The verse may be structured as follows:

Speaking to one another in Spirit-inspired psalms, hymns and songs singing songs and making music with your heart to the Lord.[133]

Given the frequent repetition of keywords, cognate terms, and synonymous expressions in Ephesians, the parallelism of this verse suggests that the two halves should be taken closely together. 'Speaking in psalms and songs' is the same as 'singing songs and making music', a point which is underscored by means of the chiastic relationship between the nouns 'psalm' and 'song' of the first clause and the verbal forms of the *same* words in the second. Accordingly, the apostle is not referring to two separate responses of speaking in songs (v. 19a) and singing (v. 19b), but is describing the same activity from different perspectives. Each clause, then, has its own particular focus and emphasis:

(1) The first has a horizontal and corporate dimension with its reference to believers addressing one another, presumably in formal worship but also on other occasions,[134] in Spirit-inspired psalms, hymns, and

131. A. W. D. Hui, 'The Concept', 306-7, observes that in Ephesians the Spirit, who is active in the believer's ethical life (3:16), imparts 'wisdom and revelation' to God's people (see on 1:17).

132. Note the discussion above.

133. λαλοῦντες ἑαυτοῖς [ἐν] ψαλμοῖς καὶ ὕμνοις καὶ ᾠδαῖς πνευματικαῖς
ᾄδοντες καὶ ψάλλοντες τῇ καρδίᾳ ὑμῶν τῷ κυρίῳ.

134. Many recent scholars assume that the speaking in Spirit-inspired songs takes place in public 'worship'. While this is no doubt included, the text does not suggest such a restriction. Presumably believers filled by the Spirit could edify one another by singing in informal contexts as well.

songs (v. 19a). This is akin to Colossians 3:16, which may be based on Ephesians 5:19, where members of the Colossian congregation are to teach and admonish one another in psalms and hymns. In Ephesians the more general verb 'speak' replaces the specific 'teach and admonish' (of Col. 3:16), but the sense appears to be the same:[135] the apostle has in view mutual instruction, edification, and exhortation which take place in a range of songs prompted by the Spirit.[136] That such hymns can be described as 'spiritual' says nothing about their spontaneity; instead, the focus is on the source of their inspiration, namely, the Holy Spirit. And the fact that believers address one another[137] in these psalms and songs shows that Paul has intelligible communication in view, not meditation, unknown speech, or glossolalia.

It is not possible to distinguish sharply between the three terms, 'psalms', 'hymns', and 'songs'. They are the most common words used in the LXX for religious songs,[138] and occur interchangeably in the titles of the psalms. The first, 'psalm',[139] is employed by Luke of the Old Testament psalms,[140] though it came to be used more generally of a song of praise (1 Cor. 14:26; Col. 3:16) of which the Old Testament psalms were probably regarded as spiritual prototypes. The second term, 'hymn',[141] denotes any 'festive hymn of praise' (Isa. 42:10; cf. Acts 16:25; Heb. 2:12). In its two New Testament occurrences it refers to an expression of praise to God or Christ (Col. 3:16 and here). The third word, 'song',[142] is used in the New Testament of the song in which God's acts are praised and glorified (cf. Rev. 5:9; 14:3; 15:3). Although firm distinctions cannot be drawn between the terms, nor can an exact classification of New Testament hymns[143] be made on the basis of the different words, taken together

135. So several recent exegetes, including Lincoln, 345; M. Hengel, 'Hymns and Christology', in *Between Jesus and Paul* (London: SCM, 1983), 79; and Hoehner; cf. G. D. Fee, *God's Empowering Presence*, 722.

136. While the adjective πνευματικαῖς ('prompted by the Spirit'), consistent with Greek usage, agrees grammatically with the last term ᾠδαῖς ('songs'), it refers to all three nouns. So most exegetes; against G. D. Fee, *God's Empowering Presence*, 653-54.

137. As in 4:32 the reflexive pronoun ἑαυτοῖς ('to yourselves') functions as the reciprocal pronoun ἀλλήλων ('to one another'); cf. A. T. Robertson, *Grammar*, 690; and Best, 511.

138. M. Hengel, 'Hymns and Christology', 80.

139. Gk. ψαλμός. BAGD, 891; Louw and Nida §33.112; and H. Balz, *EDNT* 3:495-96.

140. Luke 20:42; 24:44; Acts 1:20; 13:33.

141. Gk. ὕμνος. BAGD, 836; Louw and Nida §33.114; and M. Rutenfranz, *EDNT* 3:392-93.

142. Gk. ᾠδή. BAGD, 895; Louw and Nida §33.110; and W. Radl, *EDNT* 3:505-6.

143. New Testament scholarship has claimed that Phil. 2:6-11; Col. 1:15-20; 1 Tim. 3:16, etc., may provide examples of early Christian hymnody. M. Hengel, 'Hymns and Christology', 81, following R. Deichgräber, suggests that in early Christian worship there

'psalms', 'hymns', and 'songs' describe 'the full range of singing which the Spirit prompts'.[144] Through these songs members of the community who are continually filled by the Spirit will instruct, edify, and exhort one another.

(2) The focus of the second clause is singing with one's whole being to the *Lord* Jesus. The two participles, 'singing songs' and 'making music', should be considered as one unit, since they are conjoined by 'and', and together, rather than separately, they are followed by the one qualifying expression: *in your heart to the Lord*. Both verbs, 'sing' and 'make music',[145] pick up their cognate nouns from the previous clause. The additional words 'with your heart' do not specify an inward disposition (NIV: *in your heart*), as though the apostle is referring to silent worship in contrast to 'with your voices'. Rather, *heart* here signifies the whole of one's being. The entire person should be filled with songs of praise, thereby expressing the reality of life in the Spirit.

In the Colossians parallel the singing is addressed to God (Col. 3:16). Here in Ephesians praise is offered *to the Lord*, which, in the light of this chapter (vv. 8, 10, 17, 20) as well as the rest of the letter, refers to 'Christ'.[146] Hymns in the book of Revelation are addressed both to God and to Christ (5:9, 13; 7:10; 12:10), and a regular feature of other so-called hymns of the New Testament (e.g., Phil. 2:6-11; Col. 1:15-20; 1 Tim. 3:16) is their focus on Jesus as Lord, the Son through whom God has brought his eschatological salvation. Pliny's famous letter to Trajan, which described Christians as meeting early to sing antiphonally a hymn to Christ as to God, is often cited as evidence of songs directed to Christ (*Epistles* 10.96.7).

(3) In the light of this exegesis, then, v. 19 describes the singing of psalms, hymns, and songs by those who are Spirit-filled from different, though closely related, perspectives. The two clauses of v. 19 refer not to two separate responses or activities, but to one and the same action, each with a slightly different focus. To start with, the 'audiences' are distinct. According to v. 19a, believers speak in psalms, hymns, and songs *to one another*, reminding each other of what God has done in the Lord Jesus

---

is more evidence of hymns to Christ than of hymns to God. For further discussion and bibliographical details see R. P. Martin, *DPL*, 419-23.

144. E. Lohse, *Colossians and Philemon* (Philadelphia: Fortress, 1971), 151; cf. M. Hengel, 'Hymns and Christology', 80.

145. For the view that ψάλλω means to make music by singing, without any suggestion of musical accompaniment, see BAGD, 891; and Hoehner.

146. M. Hengel, 'Hymns and Christology', 81, comments that 'to the Lord . . . must certainly be given a christological interpretation'. Cf. Gnilka, 271; Schnackenburg, 237-38; and J. Adai, *Der Heilige Geist*, 229, 449.

Christ. A further distinction is the purpose of this singing, namely, to instruct and edify members of the body. In a sense, this singing has a horizontal and corporate focus to it. In v. 19b, the singing and making music are directed *to the Lord* Jesus. This activity thus has a vertical focus and a personal dimension, for believers praise the Lord Jesus 'with their whole being'. It is in and through singing and making music, by which other members of the body are instructed and edified, that praise is offered to the Lord Jesus. The same singing has a twofold function and purpose.[147]

20 Christians filled by the Spirit will not only sing hymns to Christ but also offer regular thanksgiving to God the Father in the Son's name for the riches which have been lavished upon them. The introductory participle, 'giving thanks', is the fourth in a series of five (cf. vv. 19, 21) which describe the results of the Spirit's filling believers. This participle has four modifiers that draw attention to significant features of the giving of thanks. As a result the comprehensive nature of thanksgiving in the Christian life is especially emphasized (see on 5:4).[148]

The verse may be structured as follows:

'Giving thanks constantly
for everything
in the name of our Lord Jesus Christ
to God the Father'.

First, attention is drawn to the frequency of their thanksgiving: it is to be offered 'regularly' or 'constantly' (rather than 'always' or 'continually'), for this is what the adverb[149] signifies (see on 1:16). God's people, both corporately and individually, are to have a thankful attitude of mind and heart which comes to expression regularly in thanksgiving and praise. Gratitude to God, which permeates their whole being, will be obvious as they express their praise of him constantly.[150]

---

147. G. D. Fee, *God's Empowering Presence,* 722, correctly observes that 'singing of all kinds . . . functions *both* to instruct the believing community *and* to praise and adore God' (emphasis added). Cf. Snodgrass, 291: 'The purpose of singing is both praise to God and instruction of believers'.

148. On the subject of thanksgiving, see on 1:16; 5:4; and for bibliographical details, note P. T. O'Brien, *DPL,* 68-71.

149. Although the context of vv. 18-20 suggests that believers are to sing and make music to the Lord repeatedly, the adverb πάντοτε specifically modifies εὐχαριστέω (cf. Meyer, 288), suggesting that thanksgiving, like prayer, is not only a constant activity of the Christian life, but is almost synonymous with being a Christian.

150. Our English word 'thank' means to express gratitude to a person because of personal benefits received, and can therefore be rather self-centred; thanksgiving for the apostle, however, approximated what we normally understand by 'praise'.

Secondly, there are good grounds for such Spirit-inspired thanksgiving. We are to give thanks to God *for everything*,[151] an expression which is to be taken comprehensively. 'The innumerable benefits which we receive from God yield fresh cause of joy and thanksgiving'.[152] Also, believers are to be thankful during times of trial and suffering as we endure them patiently, not because we have lost all feelings of moral sensitivity or because we can no longer distinguish between good and evil. Rather, we humbly and gratefully submit to his sovereignty, knowing that he works *in everything* for the good of those who love him, who have been called according to his purpose (Rom. 8:28). This is not to claim that God is the author of evil or that we are praising him for what he abominates.[153] But we recognize that he uses even the suffering which comes upon us to produce character, perseverance, and hope (Rom. 5:3-5). And a life filled with thanksgiving will find spontaneous expression in psalms, hymns, and songs.

Thirdly, Christians direct their thanks to the ultimate source and goal of all things, *God the Father*,[154] and we do this *in the name of our Lord Jesus Christ*. In the Colossians parallel the whole of life is to be lived under the authority of the Lord Jesus and in grateful allegiance to him. Every activity is to be done in his name and accompanied by the giving of thanks to God the Father through him (Col. 3:17). Although Ephesians 5:20 is the only reference in the New Testament to thanks being offered in Jesus' name, elsewhere it is said to be 'through him' (in addition to Col. 3:17, note Rom. 1:8; cf. 1 Cor. 15:57), which means that thanksgiving could now be addressed to God through him as the mediator who had opened the way to the Father's presence. 'Name' in these passages refers to all that a person stands for and what he has accomplished.[155] Accordingly, Christians filled by the Holy Spirit give thanks to God the Father on the basis of who Jesus is and what he has accomplished for his people by his death and resurrection. The 'unconscious' trinitarian focus of the passage is very powerful indeed.

21 Finally, believers whose lives have been filled by God's Spirit

---

151. ὑπὲρ πάντων could be rendered 'for all people' (taking πάντων as masculine); however, both the immediate context and the parallel passage in Col. 3:17 suggest that the phrase is neuter, meaning 'for all things'.

152. Calvin, 204.

153. Note the discussion of this issue by Stott, 207.

154. This is an example which fits the Granville Sharp rule where there is an articular personal noun τῷ θεῷ ('God') followed by καί ('and'), together with an anarthrous noun in the same case that describes the first noun, πατρί ('Father'). For a detailed discussion see D. B. Wallace, *Greek Grammar*, 270-90; and note Hoehner.

155. Snodgrass, 291. On the significance of the 'name' in a variety of New Testament contexts, see H. Bietenhard, *TDNT* 5:270-81, and *NIDNTT* 2:652-55.

will be marked by submission within divinely ordered relationships. As we have seen, v. 21 is a hinge verse: the verb 'submitting' is the fifth and final participle that is dependent on the imperative 'be filled' (v. 18), and it concludes the list of responses that should characterize the Spirit-filled living of those in Christ (vv. 18-21). At the same time, v. 21 introduces a new topic of 'submission', which is then developed throughout the household table (5:22–6:9), particularly in 5:22-33, which presents the longest statement in the New Testament on the relationship of husbands and wives.

The key verb used here means literally to 'arrange under'.[156] It regularly functioned to describe the submission of someone in an ordered array to another person who was above the first in some way, for example, the submission of soldiers in an army to those of superior rank. The term appears some twenty-three times in the Pauline corpus[157] and has to do with order. Markus Barth[158] discerns two groups of statements: (a) when the active 'subordinate' is used (or the so-called divine passive), the power to subject belongs to God alone (1 Cor. 15:24-28; Rom. 8:20; Eph. 1:21, 22; Phil. 3:21);[159] (b) the apostle uses middle indicatives, participles, or imperatives of the verb to describe the subordination of Christ to God, members of the congregation to one another, to believers with prophetic gifts, or to wives, children, and slaves (1 Cor. 15:28; 14:32; Col. 3:18; as well as Eph. 5:21, 22, etc.).[160] In the forty or so New Testament occurrences the verb carries an overtone of authority and subjection or submission to it.[161]

---

156. ὑποτάσσω, which appeared in Greek literature relatively late, meant in the active voice to 'place under', 'subordinate', and in the middle to 'order oneself under' a leader (cf. Josephus, *Jewish War* 2:566, 578; 5:309), to 'subject oneself' out of fear, or to 'submit oneself voluntarily' (cf. Col. 3:18). In the LXX the word was not very common, but was employed in the active voice with the meaning to 'place under', 'subordinate', especially of God, who makes other creatures subject to humans (Ps. 8:6), the people subject to David (143:2), the people to the nations (17:48), and the nations to the Israelites (46:4). The middle voice of the verb denotes to 'subject oneself', 'acquiesce in', and to 'acknowledge someone's dominion or power', such as Yahweh's and his people's (1 Chron. 22:18). It came to mean to 'surrender to God' (Ps. 36:7; 61:2, 6) and to 'humble oneself before him' (2 Macc. 9:12). For details see G. Delling, *TDNT* 8:40. Cf. Louw and Nida §36.18, and C. Spicq, *TLNT* 3:424, 425.

157. The cognate τάγμα, 'order', 'division', and διαταγή, 'ordinance', 'direction', appear once each, τάξις, 'order', twice, and ὑποταγή, 'subjection', 'subordination', four times.

158. Barth, 709-15; cf. G. Delling, *TDNT* 8:41-45.

159. Cf. Rom. 13:1; Heb. 2:8; 1 Pet. 3:22; Luke 10:17, 20.

160. However, G. W. Dawes, *The Body,* 207-12, interprets these instances of ὑποτάσσομαι as passives rather than examples of the middle voice, which describe a variety of relationships where believers are urged to 'be subordinate'.

161. So recently G. W. Dawes, *The Body,* 207-12; and A. Perriman, *Speaking of Women: Interpreting Paul* (Leicester: Apollos, 1998), 52-53. The claim of C. C. Kroeger, 'The

The meaning of this verse, however, is disputed for several reasons: first, is this submission to be understood as 'mutual'? Secondly, how does the content of v. 21 relate to the household table (5:22–6:9) with which it is closely linked (see above)? The following are the main lines of interpretation (although there are several intermediate positions) in response to these questions:

(1) A widely held view is that v. 21 states a general principle of *mutual* submission by all Spirit-filled Christians to others in the body of Christ. In the subsequent verses of the household table, where the roles of husbands and wives, parents and children, and masters and slaves are set forth, the focus is on specific kinds of mutual submission in the light of this general principle. The following arguments are advanced in support of this interpretation:

(a) Although the verb is a strong word meaning 'subject' or 'subordinate' (in the active voice), here in v. 21 Paul employs the middle voice to signify a voluntary submission or subordination, and this means to act in a loving, considerate, self-giving way towards one another. Such a voluntary yielding to the needs of others is an example of that self-sacrificing love which is to characterize the Christian community.[162] It is urged elsewhere in the New Testament (cf. Phil. 2:3),[163] not least in Ephesians itself, where 'bearing with one another in love' is necessary for 'making every effort to maintain the unity of the Spirit' (4:2, 3). Further, this is the pattern of Christ's love for the church which is held out for husbands to follow in 5:25-31.

(b) This view, it is claimed, does justice to the reciprocal pronoun '[submitting] to one another'). Gilbert Bilezikian, for example, recognizes that the natural meaning of the verb 'submit', wherever it appears in the

Classical Concept of *Head* as "Source"', in *Equal to Serve*, ed. G. G. Hull (London: Scripture Union, 1987), 267-83, esp. 281, that ὑποτάσσειν can have the sense of 'to attach one thing to another or to identify one person or thing with another' is rightly rejected by Dawes (210) as being 'quite without parallel in the New Testament'. Such a rendering falls outside the semantic range of the word.

162. Lincoln, 365, admits that 'only here in the Pauline corpus is the actual verb "to submit" employed for mutual relationships among believers'. Elsewhere the notion is used only for the attitude of specific groups, e.g., women, children, or slaves or the attitude of believers to the state. View (2), mentioned below, gets round the problem Lincoln recognizes.

163. According to G. Delling, *TDNT* 8:45, this general rule of 'mutual submission demands readiness to renounce one's own will for the sake of others, i.e., ἀγάπη, and to give precedence to others'. Both Delling and E. Kamlah, "Ὑποτάσσεσθαι in den neutestamentlichen Haustafeln', in *Verborum Veritas: Festschrift für G. Stählin zum 70. Geburtstag*, ed. O. Bocher and K. Haacker (Wuppertal: Brockhaus, 1970), 237-43, hold that being subordinate (ὑποτάσσομαι) bears a close semantic relationship to Christian humility (ταπεινοφροσύνη), which appears in Phil. 2:3.

New Testament, is 'to make oneself subordinate to the authority of a higher power . . . to yield to rulership'. However, the addition of the reciprocal pronoun *to each other* in here in 5:21 'changes its meaning entirely. . . . By definition, mutual submission rules out hierarchical differences'. He rejects any thought of obedience to authority in vv. 21-24, claiming instead that it is appropriate to speak of 'mutual subjection' and this 'suggests horizontal lines of interaction among equals'.[164] For Bilezikian, then, the presence of the reciprocal pronoun 'to one another' is decisive. As a result, v. 21 controls our understanding of 5:22–6:9. Mutual submission requires that all Christians, regardless of status, function, sex, or rank, are to serve one another in love (Gal. 5:13). All become subordinate to one another, and 'there remains no justification for distinctions among them of ruler and subordinate'. Bilezikian concludes that 'mutual subjection as defined on the basis of Ephesians 5:18-21 refers to relationships of reciprocal servanthood under the sole lordship of Christ'. This 'reciprocity of such relationships renders hierarchical distinctions irrelevant within the Christian communities of church and family'.[165] Accordingly, wives are to submit to husbands and husbands are to submit to wives, in exactly the same way.

(2) A different interpretation recognizes that v. 21 is a general heading urging Spirit-filled believers to be submissive or subordinate.[166] The particular ways in which Christians are to submit to others are then specified in the household table for wives, children, and servants. It is not mutual submission that is in view, as the first interpretation claims, but submission to appropriate authorities. The following reasons are advanced in favour of this:

(a) The primary argument concerns the meaning of the verb rendered 'submit'. As already indicated, the term regularly functions to describe the submission of someone in an ordered array to another who was above the first, that is, in authority over that person.[167] Further, none of

---

164. G. Bilezikian, *Beyond Sex Roles* (Grand Rapids: Baker, [2]1985), 154; cf. C. S. Keener, *Paul, Women and Wives: Marriage and Women's Ministry in the Letters of Paul* (Peabody, MA: Hendrickson, 1992), 168-72.

165. G. Bilezikian, *Beyond Sex Roles*, 156. Note also C. S. Keener, *DPL*, 583-92, esp. 588. The majority cited in the bibliography (592), with some variations, support the notion of 'mutual submission' (view [1]).

166. Most advocates of this view regard ὑποτάσσομαι as a middle voice rather than a passive. Though see nn. 156, 160.

167. Elsewhere in the New Testament the verb is used of the submission of Jesus to his parents (Luke 2:51); of demons being subject to the disciples (Luke 10:17, 20 — it certainly cannot mean to 'act in a thoughtful or considerate way'); of citizens being subject to governing authorities (Rom. 13:1; Tit. 3:1; 1 Pet. 2:13); of the universe being subject to Christ (1 Cor. 15:27; Eph. 1:22); of unseen powers being subject to Christ (1 Pet. 3:22); of Christ being subject to God the Father (1 Cor. 15:28); of church members being subject to

the relationships where this verb appears is reversed: husbands are not told to be subject to their wives, nor parents to children, nor the government to citizens, nor disciples to demons. The word does not describe a 'symmetrical' relationship since it always has to do with an ordered relationship in which one person is 'over' and another 'under'. In this sense the term is not mutual in its force. V. 21 'does not focus specifically on the relationship of husbands and wives'. Within the flow of the argument this issue is not taken up specifically until vv. 22-24. But even at this point v. 21 is not calling 'for [the] mutual submission of all Christians to each other'.[168] This is to misunderstand the semantic range of the term. Instead, believers are urged to be submissive to those who are are in authority over them. If the apostle's argument had taken a different turn,[169] this presumably might include church members submitting to their leaders (1 Cor. 16:15-16; 1 Pet. 5:5), citizens being subject to governing authorities (Rom. 13:1; Tit. 3:1; 1 Pet. 2:13), or the church being subject to Christ (Eph. 5:24). Furthermore, in its other New Testament instances the semantic range of our verb does not include acting in a thoughtful or considerate way, or showing mutual courtesy, deference, or respect. The term, then, should not be assigned a meaning that is outside its semantic range, especially when its usual meaning makes good sense in this context. We are not suggesting that acting in a loving, considerate, self-giving way is absent from the household table; only that words other than 'submit, be subordinate or submission' are used to describe this loving service (cf. vv. 25, 28, 29).[170]

---

their leaders (1 Cor. 16:15-16; 1 Pet. 5:5); of the church being subject to Christ (Eph. 5:24); of servants being subject to their masters (Tit. 2:9; 1 Pet. 2:18); of Christians being subject to God (Heb. 12:9; Jas. 4:7); and of wives being subject to their husbands (Col. 3:18; Tit. 2:5; 1 Pet. 3:5; cf. Eph. 5:22, 24). For full details see W. Grudem, in *Recovering Biblical Manhood and Womanhood: A Response to Evangelical Feminism,* ed. J. Piper and W. Grudem (Wheaton: Crossway, 1991), 493.

168. Against B. Witherington, *Women in the Earliest Churches* (Cambridge: Cambridge University Press, 1988), 56, who thinks that because v. 21 does not address the relationship of husbands and wives — which is not taken up until vv. 22-24 — Paul's admonition here is addressed generally to all Christians, urging them to be *mutually submissive to each other.* Similarly, G. W. Dawes, *The Body,* 216, claims that 'all believers are to "be subordinate" to one another in v 21', but 'in v 22 this subordination is asked only of wives'. Neither Witherington nor Dawes has grasped the point that ὑποτάσσομαι is dealing with submission within ordered relationships. It is for this reason that Dawes' criticisms of Piper and Grudem are wide of the mark, and one reason why there is a dichotomy, if not an intolerable tension, in his own conclusions (cf. 232-35).

169. Though in fact it leads directly onto v. 22, as we have demonstrated below.

170. Accordingly, the claim (see n. 163) that showing 'humility' (ταπεινοφροσύνη; Phil. 2:3; Eph. 4:2) and 'bearing with one another in love' (ἀνεχόμενοι ἀλλήλων ἐν ἀγάπῃ; Eph. 4:2) are semantic equivalents of 'being subordinate' (ὑποτάσσομαι), is incorrect.

(b) The pronoun 'one another' is not always fully reciprocal. Although advocates of the mutual submission interpretation assume that the relationships expressed by the Greek pronoun are always symmetrical (and so must mean 'everyone to everyone'), this depends entirely on the context. On occasion, the pronoun does have a fully reciprocal significance (Eph. 4:25; cf. John 13:34, 35; 15:12, 17; Rom. 1:12). But in other contexts a symmetrical relationship cannot be in view. For example, Revelation 6:4, 'so that men should slay *one another*', cannot mean that each killed the other at precisely the same time as he or she was killed.[171] Likewise, Galatians 6:2, 'Bear *one another's* burdens', does not signify that '*everyone* should exchange burdens with *everyone* else', but that '*some* who are more able should help bear the burdens of *others* who are less able' (cf. also 1 Cor. 11:33; Luke 2:15; 21:1; 24:32).[172] In the present context, then, given that 'submit' is one-directional in its reference to submission to authority, and that the pronoun does not always indicate a symmetrical relationship, it is preferable to understand the clause 'submitting to one another' to refer to submission to appropriate authorities, not mutual submission.[173]

(c) The flow of the argument. V. 21, 'being submissive to one another in the fear of Christ', is a programmatic statement which introduces the topic of 'submission', and this is developed in the household table of 5:22–6:9. The verse is tightly linked with what immediately follows: there is no verb in v. 22, and so 'submitting' must be understood from v. 21 for its meaning and sense. The idea of 'submission' is unpacked in v. 22 without the verb being repeated. It is as though the apostle is saying: 'Submit to one another, and what I mean is, wives submit to your husbands, children to your parents, and slaves to your masters'. To interpret v. 21 by ab-

---

171. The natural meaning is 'so that some would kill others'. To suggest that ἀλλήλους is fully reciprocal does not make sense.

172. Note the discussion of W. Grudem, in *Recovering Biblical Manhood and Womanhood*, 493-94.

173. This is the line taken by J. B. Hurley, *Man and Woman in Biblical Perspective: A Study in Role Relationships and Authority* (Leicester: Inter-Varsity, 1981), 140-44; S. B. Clark, *Man and Woman in Christ: An Examination of the Roles of Men and Women in Light of Scripture and the Social Sciences* (Ann Arbor: Servant, 1980), 74-76; and W. Grudem, in *Recovering Biblical Manhood and Womanhood*, 493-94. Against G. Bilezikian, *Beyond Sex Roles*, 154, the addition of the reciprocal pronoun ἀλλήλοις ('to each other') does not change the meaning of the verb ὑποτάσσομαι at all. G. W. Dawes, *The Body*, 214, criticizes Piper and Grudem (and by implication others) for not demonstrating from the context that ἀλλήλοις is being used in a restricted sense, and therefore not fully reciprocal. But Dawes has not realized that the semantic range of ὑποτάσσομαι ('be subordinate'), which is in use *in the context*, has to do with a hierarchical order in relationships, and thus ἀλλήλοις must be taken in this nonsymmetrical way.

stracting it from the context not only misunderstands how the verb 'submit' would be grasped by a first-century reader but also fails to see the natural flow of the apostle's argument.[174] What submitting to one another means is spelled out in the household table, with its ordered array in society. And submitting to one another is a significant outworking of being filled by the Spirit.

To conclude. On grounds of semantics, syntax, and the flow of Paul's argument we prefer the latter interpretation. The apostle is not speaking of *mutual* submission in the sense of a reciprocal subordination, but submission to those who are in authority over them.

If this subordination is the result of the Spirit's infilling believers, then its motivation is 'the fear of Christ'.[175] Although many modern translations tone down the term to 'reverence' or 'respect' (cf. RSV, NEB, JB, NIV, NRSV), these renderings are too soft to catch the nuance intended. 'Fear' is still the best translation. Although it does not convey the idea of 'terror' or 'intimidation' for those who are in Christ, it signifies a sense of awe in the presence of one who is Lord and coming Judge.[176] The motive of the fear of God is prominent in the Old Testament, especially as the appropriate response to his mighty acts. It is significant in the laws of the Old Testament (Lev. 19:14, 32; Deut. 13:11, 17:13) as well as in Old Testament piety generally (Ps. 103:11, 13, 17; Prov. 1:7; 23:17), and leads to obedience to his will.[177] On four other occasions in the New Testament the term 'fear' is followed by a noun (an objective genitive) which refers to one of the persons of the Godhead. This is the only instance of the fear of *Christ* being mentioned. Elsewhere reference is made to 'the fear of the Lord' (Acts 9:31; 2 Cor 5:11) and 'the fear of God' (Rom. 3:18; 2 Cor. 7:1).

174. Because J. P. Sampley, *'And the Two Shall Become One Flesh': A Study of Traditions in Eph 5:21-33* (Cambridge: Cambridge University Press, 1971), 116, 117, regards this submission as mutual, he runs into difficulties integrating v. 21 ('a general admonition calling for the submission of each one to the other') with the following household code. The latter reflected a viewpoint with which the author did not entirely agree. To solve the difficulty Sampley treats v. 21 'as the author's critique of the basic stance of the Haustafel form wherein one group is ordered to be submissive to another group vested with authority over it'! Lincoln, 366, rightly asks: 'if he disagreed with it, why would the writer have made such extended use of it as is made in this letter?' Unfortunately, Lincoln's own solution, which fails to understand ὑποτάσσομαι in terms of submission to appropriate authority, is unsatisfactory.

175. Gk. φόβος Χριστοῦ. The motive of 'fear' turns up seven times in the household tables in addition to this reference: Eph. 5:33; 6:5; Col. 3:22; 1 Pet. 2:17, 18; 3:2, 6. The repetition of the term 'fear' at Eph. 5:33 serves to bracket vv. 21-33 together as a unit: Paul returns to the same theme with which he began.

176. Note the discussions of this phrase by Barth, 662-668, and J. P. Sampley, *'And the Two'*, 117-21.

177. H. R. Balz, *TDNT* 9:189-219; and Lincoln, 366.

The three Pauline texts are in the context of judgment, and thus point to the believer's godly fear in view of the final day. As Ernst Käsemann aptly notes: 'The fear of the Lord is no empty rhetorical phrase here'.[178] In the light of Christ's power and holiness believers will be subordinate to those who are in authority over them.

2. Relationships within the Christian Household, 5:22–6:9[179]

This lengthy section in Ephesians (along with its parallel, Col. 3:18–4:1)[180] contains a series of admonitions addressed successively to wives and husbands, children and fathers, slaves and masters. The paragraph is introduced without any connecting particle[181] so that it may have originally been an independent unit, but if so it has been significantly incorporated into the paraenesis of the letter. Further, the passage on husbands and wives (5:22-33) is creatively related to the larger vision of the church as the bride/body of Christ; Paul draws together both theological and ethical concerns in relation to God's purpose of bringing all things together in unity in Christ (1:9, 10). Martin Luther called this scheme a *Haustafel*, which means 'a list of rules for the household', but it is usually translated into English as 'house-table'. The rules formulated to govern behaviour patterns within the Christian household have also been called 'station codes', since each member is addressed according to their role and position within the household (wives/husbands, children/parents, slaves/masters). Each is named (e.g., 'wives'), a command is given (in the imperative mood, e.g., 'Be subject to your husbands') and a motivating statement for the behaviour is supplied ('For the husband is head of the wife', v. 23).

There has been considerable scholarly discussion about the origin and source of the New Testament household codes: whether they derived from Stoic moral philosophy, were a distinctively Christian creation, or were mediated to early Christianity from Hellenistic Judaism.[182] More re-

178. So E. Käsemann, cited by Hoehner.

179. For references to the vast and increasing secondary literature on the subject, see Lincoln, 355-65; E. Best, 'Haustafel', 146-60; his commentary, esp. 519-20; and Hoehner's introduction to 5:22–6:9 of his commentary.

180. Parallels are found in 1 Tim. 2:8-15; 6:1-10; Tit. 2:1-10; 1 Pet. 2:18–3:7; and in the writings of the Apostolic Fathers (*Didache* 4:9-11; *Barnabas* 19:5-7; *1 Clement* 1:3; 21:6-9; Ignatius, *Polycarp* 4:1–6:2; Polycarp, *Philippians* 4:2–6:1), although in these passages there is an absence of the reciprocal obligations which are a distinctive mark of the 'house-tables', and they do not arise out of a household situation.

181. Although the verb 'submit' carries over from v. 21, with the imperative understood instead of the participle (see the exegesis below).

182. For a brief survey, see P. T. O'Brien, *Colossians, Philemon*, 214-18. The earlier consensus regarding the New Testament household codes as mediated to early Chris-

cently, however, these household codes have been understood against the background of household management in the Graeco-Roman world, which was an important area of debate.[183] The discussion treated husband-wife, parent-child, and master-slave relationships in connection with matters of authority and subordination, and understood the household as intimately related to the wider issue of the state.[184] In the Graeco-Roman world the household was viewed as the foundation of the state. Proper management of the household, then, was a vital social and political concern. The main lines of the discussion on household management, which were set by Aristotle,[185] continued through to the first century A.D., with the Peripatetics, Dio Chrysostom, Seneca, and many others comparing it with the various management forms of the political state.[186] Jewish writers such as Philo and Josephus also adopted Aristotle's outline of household management concepts, particularly that of subordination, in relation to the proper conduct of husband–wife, parents–children, and master–servants.[187]

Although the Graeco-Roman notion of household management has significant points of contact with the New Testament household codes, there are also important differences. The New Testament does not compare the household with a political entity such as a city or nation, in the way Aristotle and others do. The New Testament treatment of household regulations (e.g., Eph. 5:22–6:9; Col. 3:18–4:1; 1 Pet. 2:18–3:7; 1 Tim. 2:8-15; 6:1-10; Tit. 2:1-10) makes no mention of the state (though cf. 1 Pet. 2:13-17), while Paul's discussion of the state (Rom. 13) does not refer to the household. Other differences have been noted, not least the basis or model of the codes: in Hellenism the model was political, but in Ephesians and Colossians, for example, the model and motivating force is Christ himself. In these two household tables wives, children, and slaves are addressed equally with husbands, fathers, and masters. Although this is not totally new, there are no extant examples which are as thoroughgoing as Colossians 3:18–4:1 and Ephesians 5:22–6:9 in this emphasis on reciprocal obligations. Slaves are to be treated well, not simply because they might be more productive, as Aristotle suggested, but because

---

tianity from Hellenistic Judaism was based on the work of J. E. Crouch, *The Origin and Intention of the Colossian Haustafel* (Göttingen: Vandenhoeck & Ruprecht, 1972).

183. Note the detailed bibliography in Hoehner.

184. Cf. Lincoln, 357-58.

185. Cf. Aristotle, *Politica* 1.1253b, 1259a.

186. The Stoic philosopher Areius Didymus (e.g., monarchic, aristocratic, or democratic). Cf. D. L. Balch, *Let Wives Be Submissive: The Domestic Code in 1 Peter* (Chico, CA: Scholars Press, 1981), 33-49.

187. Philo, *Hypothetica* 7.3; Josephus, *Against Apion* 2.24 §199.

there is one who is Lord of both slave and master, and each is accountable to him (6:9).

There is little agreement, then, on the source of the New Testament household codes.[188] Even Andrew Lincoln admits that although discussions about household arrangement in the contemporary Graeco-Roman world may have influenced Christians to take up this topic, there is no single model on which the Christian codes are directly dependent.[189] Ernest Best suggests that the 'question as to the origin of the form may not be all that important'![190] There is, however, other traditional material, notably Genesis 2:24 (also Lev. 19:18; Exod. 20:12; Ezek. 16:1-14), which undergirds and provides the theological grounding of 5:22-33 (cf. 6:1-2).

It was natural that in any given society there would be specific rules for the order of life, whether political, domestic, social, or religious. It might be expected that because believers are part of a society they, too, would need a code of conduct. The household table of Ephesians addresses this with its Christian ethic.[191] This leads on to the question of purpose: Why were the household tables included in New Testament letters, and particularly in Ephesians? In general terms, it has been claimed that despite their conversion to a new religion, Christian wives and slaves should still be subordinate and so silence the criticisms of outsiders (cf. 1 Peter).[192] Given the important emphasis on the household in the Graeco-Roman world, relationships within the Christian home were bound to have an effect on the surrounding society. Specifically in Ephesians, while there is no mention of relationships with outsiders in the household table itself, Paul ties in appropriate behaviour with believers' wise conduct in the world, which involves them in making the most of every opportunity and understanding the Lord's will in the present (see the exegesis of 5:15-17).

The early Christian household codes were, if anything, socially conservative, and show that believers were not about to overthrow the social order. They were patriarchal, or at least hierarchical,[193] in a world where the subordination of wives to husbands, children to parents, and slaves to

---

188. P. H. Towner, *DPL*, 418-19. Note the discussion of Hoehner.

189. Lincoln, 360.

190. Best, 521.

191. J. M. G. Barclay, 'The Family as the Bearer of Religion in Judaism and Early Christianity', in *Constructing Early Christian Families: Family as Social Reality and Metaphor*, ed. H. Moxnes (London/New York: Routledge, 1997), 66-80, esp. 76-78; and S. C. Barton, 'Living as Families in the Light of the New Testament', *Int* 52 (1998), 130-44, esp. 141.

192. So D. L. Balch, *Let Wives Be Submissive*, 81-116.

193. See the discussion at the end of this section regarding the idea that the household table of Ephesians reflects a patriarchal or hierarchical pattern.

masters was the overriding norm.[194] But to suggest that the tables were simply conformist is misleading, for 'within the hierarchical social order they uphold they were radical and profoundly liberating'.[195] As we have seen, wives, children, and slaves are addressed equally with husbands, fathers, and masters (5:22; cf. 6:1, 5, 9). They have their own calling before the Lord, which is as responsible, honourable, and important as that of husband, parent, and master.[196] The Lord to whom everything is to be done is impartial, and slaves and masters, for example, are equally responsible. Those in authority have different roles with greater responsibility, but they are not *better* roles. The value, dignity, or worth of the members of the Christian household in a subordinate position is no less than that of those in authority. Rather than being at variance with Galatians 3:28 and Colossians 3:11, the tables confirm them. Furthermore, and most significantly, Ephesians provides a radical Christian understanding of marriage, as a 'one flesh' relationship which mirrors Christ's marriage to his bride, the church (2:14-18; 4:1-16), and ultimately points to the bringing of all things together in unity (1:9-10; see below).

Finally, however, the hierarchical pattern of the household table reflects not simply a patriarchal model but one which is creational (note Paul's use of Gen. 2:24), and in the light of his statements in vv. 25-33, it is entirely consistent with Christ's redemptive role for his people. (Indeed, one might fairly argue from elsewhere in Paul and the rest of the New Testament that there was a 'trinitarian' pattern which lay at the heart of this 'mystery'.) A truly Christian marriage will mirror the relationship between Christ and his church. The two are closely intertwined. Further, this 'mirroring' will involve both the husband *loving* his wife as Christ loves the church, and the wife gladly *submitting* to her husband as the church is to be subordinate to Christ. The two elements, love and submission, are nonnegotiables within the relationship. Theologically, we are not free to retain a supposedly exalted view of Christian marriage with its loving service, commitment, trust, and growth, on the one hand, and to jettison hierarchical patterns of submission or subordination, on the other, because they are expressions of an outmoded first-century worldview that are unacceptable in our contemporary situation.

In this household table Paul deals with concrete human relations within the ancient 'house' or 'household', not with abstract ordinances. Its form is identical to the one in Colossians 3:18–4:1, and is similar to that

194. D. C. Verner, *The Household of God: The Social World of the Pastoral Epistles* (Chico, CA: Scholars Press, 1983), 27-81.

195. Turner, 1241.

196. Turner, 1241.

in 1 Peter 2:18–3:7. The first of the three pairs in the table to be addressed are wives and husbands. This lengthy section, which is the longest statement in the New Testament on the relationship of husbands and wives, comprises twelve verses (vv. 22-33). The second pair concerning children and parents consists of only four verses (6:1-4), while the third, relating to slaves and masters, is treated in five verses (6:5-9). Of the lengthy section devoted to wives and husbands, forty words are addressed to wives and 115 to husbands.

In line with the programmatic statement of v. 21 which introduces the topic of 'submission', the three paragraphs of the household table which follow are given as examples of Christian submission. The subordinate member is mentioned first and is exhorted to 'be subject' or to 'obey'. Wives, children, and slaves are addressed equally with their husbands, fathers, and masters. They, too, are ethically responsible partners who are expected to do 'what is right' (6:1), 'as to the Lord' (5:22; cf. 6:5), just as the husband, the father, and the free man. But the exhortations to subordination do not stand alone; the second member of each pair is immediately addressed and reminded of his responsibilities. The twin admonitions stand together, and the first ought not to be interpreted apart from the second. Each member of the family or household stands in his or her place within the created order (at 1 Cor. 11:9 Paul expressly mentions the creation ordinances) and has certain responsibilities.

a. Wives and Husbands:
Christ and the Church, 5:22-33

[22]Wives, submit to your husbands as to the Lord. [23]For the husband is the head of the wife as Christ is the head of the church, his body, of which he is the Savior. [24]Now as the church submits to Christ, so also wives should submit to their husbands in everything. [25]Husbands, love your wives, just as Christ loved the church and gave himself up for her [26]to make her holy, cleansing her by the washing with water through the word, [27]and to present her to himself as a radiant church, without stain or wrinkle or any other blemish, but holy and blameless. [28]In this same way, husbands ought to love their wives as their own bodies. He who loves his wife loves himself. [29]After all, no one ever hated his own body, but he feeds and cares for it, just as Christ does the church — [30]for we are members of his body. [31]"For this reason a man will leave his father and mother and be united to his wife, and the two will become one flesh." [32]This is a profound mystery — but I am talking about Christ and the church. [33]However, each one of you also must love his wife as he loves himself, and the wife must respect her husband.

Apart from the hinge statement of v. 21, in which believers are to submit to one another in the fear of Christ, and which is unpacked in the household table of 5:33–6:9 (see above), this exhortatory material of 5:21-33 falls into three main sections. The first, vv. 22-24, urges wives to be subordinate to their husbands as to the Lord. V. 22 provides the initial exhortation, and this is grounded in the husband's headship over his wife, which is like Christ's headship over the church (v. 23). In v. 24 the admonition is repeated and reinforced by the additional words, 'in everything'. This time the sequence of the sentence is reversed so that the analogy of the church being subject to Christ precedes the exhortation to wives to be subordinate.

The second section, which is the longest in the household table, is the exhortation to husbands in 5:25-32. This comprises two parts, the first (vv. 25-27) in which husbands are admonished to love their wives as Christ loved the church, and the second (vv. 28-32) where the exhortation to love their wives is repeated, but this time grounded in the person's love for himself and Christ's love for the church. Elements of the first and second sections (vv. 22-24 and vv. 25-28a) are structured in a similar way. First, a command is given (to 'wives' [v. 22] and 'husbands' [v. 25], respectively). Then Christ's relationship to the church is presented as the model to emulate ('as . . . Christ' [v. 24]; 'just as Christ' [v. 25]). Finally, the command is reiterated ('so also wives . . .' [v. 24]; 'in this same way . . .' [v. 28]). The significant variation is that Paul fills out in greater detail Christ's relationship to the church in the second section (i.e., with reference to husbands) than he does in the first. Finally, in v. 33 the discussion is rounded off with two summarizing exhortations in which the duties and responsibilities of husbands and wives are briefly restated.[197]

The question has been raised as to why Paul has placed such a heavy emphasis on the marriage relationship here in the Ephesians household table.[198] As with the rest of the letter, so here we have few specifics to go on regarding the life-setting of the readers. Perhaps some married members of the churches addressed were not living out the distinctives of their faith in their marriages, but were behaving like their non-Christian neighbours. More specifically it has been suggested that sexual immorality was a real threat (cf. 4:19; 5:3-6, 12, 18), and so Paul wants to stress the special status of Christian marriage in God's purposes in order to combat this danger. On the other hand, ascetic tendencies had

197. On the interrelation of Christ and the church with marriage, see the exegesis and concluding remarks.
198. Note the summary treatment and suggestions of Lincoln, 364-65.

to be combatted in Colossians 2:16-23, and this may have been a danger in western Asia Minor to which Paul's circular letter was sent. But finally, there may have been no specific difficulties in this area that caused him to expand on Christian marriage here. In the light of God's intention to sum up all things in Christ (1:9-10), and this includes the unity of his people within that eschatological vision, the harmony of the Christian family is an essential element of this oneness, and Paul expands on the vital unity of husband and wife within the divine purposes. The 'marriage relationship is transparent to God's purposes on a larger scale . . . no other relationship within the family so fully mirrors God's purposes in the universe'.[199]

22 Within the marriage relationship wives[200] are addressed first, and they are urged to be subordinate to their[201] husbands as to the Lord. Although the verse does not contain any verb, 'submit' carries over from v. 21, with the imperative being understood instead of the participle.[202] The notion of submission in the preceding verse is now unpacked without repeating the verb.[203] As we have already seen, the keyword rendered 'submit' has to do with the subordination of someone in an ordered array to another who is above the first, that is, in authority over that person. At the heart of this submission is the notion of 'order'. God has established certain leadership and authority roles within the family, and submission is a humble recognition of that divine ordering. The apostle is not urging every woman to submit to every man, but wives to their husbands. The use of the middle voice of this verb (cf. Col. 3:18) emphasizes the voluntary character of the submission. Paul's admonition to wives is an appeal to free and responsible persons which can only be heeded voluntarily, never by the elimination

199. J. P. Sampley, *'And the Two'*, 149, cited by Lincoln, 365.

200. Here the nominative case with the article (αἱ γυναῖκες), rather than the vocative, is used in address (cf. BDF §147[3]). It is 'wives' who are in view, not women generally.

201. Although the adjective ἴδιος originally signified what was 'one's own', by New Testament times it differed little from a reflexive or possessive pronoun. In this context it is rendered *'their* husbands' (so BAGD, 369; Bruce, 384; Schnackenburg, 246; and Best, 532).

202. The verb 'submit' does not appear in the best Greek text, so that the verse is dependent for its sense on the participle of v. 21. This is the reading of 𝔓⁴⁶ B Clement Origen and several Greek mss. according to Jerome. Other textual traditions supply some form of ὑποτάσσειν ('submit') before or after τοῖς ἰδίοις ἀνδράσιν ('their husbands'), such as ὑποτάσσεσθε ('be subject') or ὑποτασσέσθωσαν ('let them be subject'). Most editors argue for the omission of the verb because it is the shorter reading and it is likely that later scribes included the verb for the sake of clarity. For a detailed discussion see B. M. Metzger, *Textual Commentary*, 608-9.

203. D. B. Wallace, *Greek Grammar*, 659.

411

or breaking of the human will, much less by means of a servile submissiveness.[204]

The idea of subordination to authority in general, as well as in the family, is out of favour in a world which prizes permissiveness and freedom. Christians are often affected by these attitudes. Subordination smacks of exploitation and oppression that are deeply resented. But authority is not synonymous with tyranny, and the submission to which the apostle refers does not imply inferiority. Wives and husbands (as well as children and parents, servants and masters) have different God-appointed roles, but all have equal dignity because they have been made in the divine image and in Christ have put on the new person who is created to be like God (4:24).[205] Having described the single new humanity which God is creating in his Son, with its focus on the oneness in Christ of all, especially Jew and Gentile (cf. Col. 3:11; Gal. 3:28), the apostle 'does not now [in this household table] destroy his own thesis by erecting new barriers of sex, age and rank in God's new society in which they have been abolished'.[206] That the verb 'submit, be subordinate' can be used of Christ's submission to the authority of the Father (1 Cor. 15:28) shows that it can denote a functional subordination without implying inferiority, or less honour and glory.[207]

The motivation for the wife to be subject to her husband is spelled out in the final phrase, *as to the Lord*.[208] The general admonition of v. 21 to be submissive in 'the fear of Christ' finds concrete expression for the wife in the marriage situation: as she is subordinate to her husband, so in that very action she is submitting to the Lord. Her voluntary response is not called for because of her role in society, nor is it to be understood as separate from her submission to Christ. Rather, it is part and parcel of the way that she serves the Lord Jesus (cf. Col. 3:23 of servants who engage in wholehearted work for their masters and in that very action serve their heavenly Lord).

23 The reason for the wife's submission to her husband is now ex-

---

204. Cf. Barth, 609. M. J. Harris, *Colossians and Philemon* (Grand Rapids: Eerdmans, 1991), 178, comments: 'It is a case of voluntary submission in recognition of the God-appointed leadership of the husband and the divinely ordained hierarchical order in creation (cf. 1 Cor. 11:3-9)'.

205. 'Equality of *worth* is not identity of *role*', J. H. Yoder, cited by Stott, 218.

206. Stott, 217. Note his timely discussion of v. 22 in the light of contemporary attitudes (215-20).

207. Against the view of G. Bilezikian, 'Hermeneutical Bungee-Jumping: Subordination in the Godhead', *JETS* 40 (1997), 57-68.

208. 'Lord' (κύριος) is not a reference to her husband, as some have claimed. The plural 'to their lords' (τοῖς κυρίοις) would have been written to correspond to 'to their husbands' (τοῖς ἰδίοις ἀνδράσιν).

pressed through the causal clause: 'for the husband is head of the wife as Christ also is head of the church'. On two earlier occasions in Ephesians the key term 'head' has been used, both with reference to Christ (1:22; 4:15). Now, for the first time, the husband's headship is stated as a fact, and made the basis of his wife's submission. The origin of this headship is not elaborated here, although in the fuller treatments of 1 Corinthians 11:3-12 and 1 Timothy 2:11-13 it is grounded in the order of creation, especially the narrative of Genesis 2 (cf. 1 Cor. 11:8, 9).

In each of the earlier instances of this term in Ephesians it signifies 'head' as 'ruler' or 'authority',[209] rather than 'source',[210] or one who is 'prominent, preeminent'.[211] At 1:22 'head' expresses the idea of Christ's supremacy and authority over the cosmos, especially the evil powers, which he exercises on behalf of the church (cf. Col. 1:18; 2:10). His rule over his people is described at 4:15, and this headship is expressed in his care and nourishment, as well as in his leadership of them in the fulfilment of the divine purposes.[212] Here the headship of the husband, in the light of the usage at 1:22, the general context of the authority structure of the Graeco-Roman household,[213] and the submission of the wife to her husband within marriage in vv. 22-24,[214]

209. So W. Grudem, 'Does *kephalē* ('head') Mean "Source" or "Authority Over" in Greek Literature? A Survey of 2,336 Examples', *TrinJ* 6 (1985), 38-59; and 'The Meaning of Κεφαλή ('Head'): A Response to Recent Studies', *TrinJ* 11 (1990), 3-72. Note the summary of the debate by J. A. Fitzmyer, 'Kephalē in 1 Corinthians 11:3', *Int* 47 (1993), 52-59; see also the detailed discussion of G. W. Dawes, *The Body*, 122-49, who concludes that κεφαλή is used as a metaphor indicating 'authority over'. Only in this verse in Ephesians, however, does the term have 'two distinct referents', namely, Christ and the husband.

210. Advocates of the meaning 'source' include S. Bedale, 'The Meaning of κεφαλή in the Pauline Epistles', *JTS* 5 (1954), 211-15; G. D. Fee, *1 Corinthians*, 502-5; C. C. Kroeger, '*Head*', 267-83; and *DPL*, 375-77.

211. A. Perriman, *Speaking of Women*, 13-33, who rejects both 'source, origin' and 'leadership, authority over' as meanings for κεφαλή, argues in favour of the term signifying 'prominence' or 'pre-eminence'. He acknowledges that this may 'also entail authority and leadership', but 'it is a mistake to include this as part of the common denotation of the term' (31; cf. Hoehner). This interpretation, however, runs into difficulties with the expression 'Christ is head of the church' (Paul is saying more than that Christ is pre-eminent in relation to the church, though this is true), while his exegesis of vv. 23-24 (55-57) is not convincing. The ἀλλά ('but') in v. 24 does not signify a change of emphasis from headship (v. 23), which only has to do with prominence and preeminence, to subordination with its notions of authority over others. Instead, the adversative ἀλλά ('but') provides a contrast with the preceding clause, 'he himself is the Saviour of the body' (v. 23c), which is not true of the husband's relationship to his wife (see on v. 24).

212. C. E. Arnold, 'Jesus Christ', 365.

213. For recent discussions of authority structures in the Graeco-Roman family see Lincoln, 357-59; and Hoehner.

214. Cf. Lincoln, 369.

refers to his having authority over his wife; thus he is her leader or ruler.[215]

The mere presence of the terms 'head' and 'submission' in this context does not of itself 'establish stereotypes of masculine and feminine behaviour'.[216] Different cultures may assign different roles for men and women, husbands and wives. What is important here is that the nature of the husband's headship in God's new society is explained in relation to Christ's headship. The husband is head of the wife *as also*[217] Christ is head of the church. 'Although [Paul] . . . grounds the fact of the husband's headship in creation, he defines it in relation to the headship of Christ the redeemer'.[218] Christ's headship over the church is expressed by his loving it and giving his life for it, as vv. 25-27 so clearly show. This will have profound implications for the husband's behaviour as head of his wife (v. 28).

The additional words, 'he himself is the Saviour of the body', at first sight appear rather surprising and have caused exegetes to question whether they refer to the husband's role as his wife's protector or are part of the Christ-church/husband-wife analogy, thereby signifying that as Christ is the Saviour of the body, so also the husband is in some sense the saviour of his wife. While the term 'saviour' could possibly be taken in a general sense of protector or provider of the wife's welfare, so that the analogy of Christ's relationship to the church can be paralleled in the husband's 'saving' his wife, both syntax and usage are against it.

Instead, the clause is specifically focussed on Christ, not the husband: the personal pronoun 'he *himself*' is emphatic by its presence and position, and clearly refers to Christ. Nowhere in the context is the wife

215. Note the discussion of the lexical semantics of this, together with several criticisms of the view that 'head' means 'source', in P. Cotterell and M. Turner, *Linguistics and Biblical Interpretation* (London: SPCK, 1989), 141-45. They conclude that 'head' carries the sense of 'master' or 'lord'.

216. Stott, 225.

217. ὡς καί has comparative force, 'as also'. Cf. BAGD, 897; and Hoehner.

218. Stott, 225. Contra Schnackenburg, 246, who acknowledges that Paul argues from creation in 1 Cor. 11, but considers this argument 'no longer convincing to us'. It loses its status in the light of Christ's headship, expressed in Eph. 5:23b. But if we assume that the 'author' of Ephesians is reflecting a view similar to that expressed in 1 Cor. 11, why should the words 'as Christ is head of the church' overthrow the husband's headship? It is better to speak of the latter being defined or explicated in the light of Christ's headship. K. H. Fleckenstein, *Ordnet euch einander unter in der Furcht Christi: Die Eheperikope in Eph 5,21-33: Geschichte der Interpretation, Analyse und Aktualisierung des Textes* (Würzburg: Echter, 1994), 216, understands the role of the husband as 'head of the wife' to be derived from 'the patriarchal structure of the ancient family', but does not tie it to creation.

regarded as the husband's body as the church is Christ's body.[219] Further, the term 'saviour', which turns up twenty-four times in the New Testament, always refers to Jesus or God, but never to human beings.[220] To interpret the words, then, of Christ[221] fits appropriately within the flow of the apostle's argument. Paul has been urging wives to be submissive to their husbands. The reason for this turns on the headship of the husband, which is parallel to Christ's headship or rule over the church. Paul then adds that the person who is head of the church is none other than the one who is the Saviour of the body. His saving activity, especially his sacrificial death (2:14-18; cf. 5:2), was for the deliverance of men and women in dire spiritual peril (2:1-10).

Later in the paragraph the apostle will urge husbands as heads of their wives to serve them in love. Their pattern is the Lord Jesus, whose headship was demonstrated in his loving the church and giving himself up for it, in order to present it faultless to himself (vv. 25-27).

24 The church's submission to Christ is now presented as the model of the wife's submission to her husband. The exhortation to wives in v. 22 is repeated and reinforced with the addition of the words 'in everything'. Here, however, the sequence of v. 22 is reversed. The analogy of the church being subject to Christ is mentioned before the admonition that *wives should submit to their husbands in everything*.

Although the NIV's introductory *now* does not indicate it, the verse begins with the adversative conjunction 'but', which provides a contrast with the preceding clause, 'he himself is the Saviour of the body' (v. 23c).[222] This is not true of the husband's relationship to his wife. Al-

---

219. The husband and the wife are 'one flesh' (5:31), and husbands are to love their wives 'as their own bodies', but this is a reference to the husbands' bodies, not the wives'.

220. Of Jesus: Luke 2:11; John 4:42; Acts 5:31; 13:23; Phil. 3:20; 2 Tim. 1:10, etc. Of God: Luke 1:47; 1 Tim. 1:1; 2:3; 4:10, etc.

221. The suggestions that 1 Cor. 7:16 (with its reference to the believing spouse being the instrument of the unbelieving spouse's salvation) and Tobit 6:18 (where Tobias marries his cousin Sarah to save her) provide significant parallels to the husband being the saviour of his wife have been shown to be unconvincing by Lincoln, 370, and Hoehner. Note the discussion in G. W. Dawes, *The Body*, 150.

222. So the majority of commentators, including Calvin, Alford, Meyer, Abbott, M. Barth, Sampley, Schnackenburg, Lincoln, and Hoehner. This is better than regarding the ἀλλά as having resumptive ('consequently'; so Robinson, 124, 205; and Bruce, 385) or consecutive force (S. F. Miletic, *"One Flesh": Eph. 5.22-24, 5.31: Marriage and the New Creation* [Rome: Pontifical Biblical Institute, 1988], 102-3). The variations in the English versions ('therefore': AV; 'but': RV, ASV, NASB, NEB; 'and': TEV, JB, NJB; 'now': NIV; or the conjunction was left untranslated: RSV, NRSV) indicate something of the difficulties translators have had in understanding the force of the conjunction (so Hoehner).

though he has responsibility for her welfare, he is not her saviour (see on v. 23). So by means of the adversative 'but' (= 'notwithstanding this difference')[223] Paul makes the distinction between Christ and the husband, before comparing the church's submission to Christ with the wife's submission to her husband.[224] By using the same verb 'submit' (a middle voice in the original) the apostle stresses the willing character of the church's submission to Christ, and thus underscores what has already been asserted in v. 22 about the free and voluntary nature of the wife's subordination to her husband.

But what is involved in the church's submission to Christ, and what light does this throw on the wife's submission to her husband? The church's relationship to Christ is the focus of attention in several passages within Ephesians, and these spell out important facets of its submission to its Lord. God has graciously placed everything under Christ's feet and caused him to be head over all for the benefit of the church. The church gladly submits to his beneficent rule (1:22). Christ is the vital cornerstone on whom God's building is constructed. As this new community looks to Christ it grows and progresses to its ultimate goal of holiness (2:20, 21). Christ indwells the hearts of his people, establishing them so that they may be able to comprehend the greatness of his love (3:17, 19). The church receives Christ's gift of grace (4:7), and the ministers he gives for the purpose of enriching the whole body (4:11, 12). The church thus grows towards its head, the ultimate goal of which is the whole measure of Christ's fulness (v. 13), and it receives from him all that is necessary for this growth (vv. 15, 16). In submitting to its Lord, God's people had 'learned Christ': they welcomed him as a living person and were shaped by his teaching (v. 20). This involved submitting to his rule of righteousness and living by standards and values completely different from what they had known. The church is to imitate Christ's sacrificial love (5:2). It seeks to please its Lord (5:10) by living in goodness, holiness, and truth and by understanding his will (5:17). His people sing praises to him (5:19), and live in godly fear and awe of him (5:21). Accordingly, the church's submission to Christ means 'looking to its head for his beneficial rule, living by his norms, experiencing his presence and love, receiving from him gifts that will enable growth to maturity, and responding to him in gratitude and

---

223. Cf. Abbott, 166.

224. The comparative particle ὡς ('as') begins the comparison, and this is balanced by the adverbial particle οὕτως ('so') and the conjunction καί ('and') which introduce the second clause. Wives (αἱ γυναῖκες) are the subject of the admonition, and the present middle imperative ὑποτασσέσθωσαν ('let them be subordinate') needs to be supplied (A. T. Robertson, *Greek Grammar*, 394).

awe'.[225] It is these attitudes that the wife is urged to develop as she submits to her husband.

The additional element which reinforces this exhortation (cf. v. 22) is the concluding phrase, 'in everything'. In the Colossians household table the similar expression 'in everything' is used of the *obedience* of children to parents (Col. 3:20), and of slaves to masters (Col. 3:22; cf. Tit. 3:9). Although this phrase has raised modern questions about the *limitations* of a wife's submission to her husband (arising out of the contemporary desire to control the scope of someone's authority, specifying what decisions a person in authority can make),[226] 'in everything' indicates that the wife is to be subordinate to her husband *in every area of life.* In this sense it is all-encompassing, and is not, as some have suggested, restricted to sexual matters or some other special sphere of their relationship. 'No part of her life should be outside of her relationship to her husband and outside of subordination to him'.[227] Just as the church is to submit to Christ in everything, so in every sphere wives are expected to submit to their husbands. The motivation for doing this is a true and godly reverence for Christ (5:21; cf. v. 33).

Furthermore, the exhortation to be subordinate 'in everything' should be read within the flow of the argument in the chapter. By God's design husband and wife are 'one flesh' (v. 31; Gen. 2:24), and the divine intention is that they should 'function together under one head, not as two autonomous individuals living together'.[228] This subordination of wife to husband 'has a practical aspect in that it creates a greater effectiveness in their working together as one'.[229] And it anticipates God's ultimate intention of bringing back all things into unity in Christ (1:10; see below).

The question, then, as to whether the wife is to submit to her husband regardless of what he commands is not addressed. But the words

225. Lincoln, 372. Cf. S. F. Miletic, *"One Flesh",* 43, who aptly comments that 'the Christ/church relationship provides direction ("to the Lord"), perception (husband as "head" as Christ is "head") and example (church as paradigm) for the wife's act of subordination'.

226. Rightly noted by S. B. Clark, *Man and Woman,* 83.

227. S. B. Clark, *Man and Woman,* 83. If 'in everything' refers to every sphere of the husband-wife relationship, then it confuses the issue to speak of 'complete obedience' or 'full and complete subordination' (as Lincoln, 373, does).

228. G. W. Knight, 'Husbands and Wives as Analogues of Christ and the Church: Ephesians 5:21-33 and Colossians 3:18-19', in *Recovering Biblical Manhood and Womanhood: A Response to Evangelical Feminism,* ed. J. Piper and W. Grudem (Wheaton, IL: Crossway, 1991), 170. He adds that the wife's 'submission is coextensive with all aspects of their relationship'.

229. S. B. Clark, *Man and Woman,* 81.

'in everything', however they are interpreted, are not intended to reverse the instructions and exhortations already laid upon *all* believers in the paraenesis of Ephesians 4–6. This admonition to wives in the household table cannot be interpreted as a kind of grid through which all the earlier exhortations are filtered in the interests of serving the husband's authority.[230] Further, it goes without saying that wives are not to be subordinate in matters that are sinful or contrary to God's commands (cf. Acts 5:29).

There is no suggestion that this exhortation to be submissive is intended to stifle the wife's thinking or acting. She should not act unilaterally, but rather submit willingly to her husband's leadership. 'Just as the church should willingly submit to Christ in all things and, if it does so, will not find that stifling, demeaning, or stultifying of growth and freedom, so also wives should willingly submit to their husbands in all things and, if they do so, will not find that stifling, demeaning, or stultifying'.[231] As with the other admonitions in the household table, God sets forth these instructions for our good.

Accordingly, the wife's submission to her husband is *not conditional* on his loving her after the pattern of Christ's love or showing his unceasing care for her. Later the apostle will make it clear that husbands are not to rule their wives insensitively (vv. 25-27). Those in authority should not 'lord it over' those who are led (2 Cor. 1:24). But the wife's response of submission, which is not an unthinking obedience to his leadership, is to be rendered gladly, irrespective of whether the husband will heed the injunctions explicitly addressed to him or not. Contrary to much contemporary Western thinking, there is no suggestion that wives are to be submissive to their husbands only if their husbands are loving. We have already seen that the church's submission to Christ leads to blessing, growth, and unity for God's people. Similarly, the wife's submission to her husband, as she seeks to honour the Lord Jesus Christ, will *ultimately* lead to divine blessing for herself and others.

25 The wife's subordination to her husband has its counterpart in the husband's duty to love his wife.[232] This exhortation to husbands begins the second main section of the household table (vv. 25-32).[233] It is by

230. Barth, 620-21, points out that 'in everything' cannot mean mere blind obedience, especially when it would mean acting contrary to God's commands. On the other hand, it is inappropriate to 'compil[e] a short or long list of exemptions to prove that "in everything" actually means "not in everything"' (621)!

231. G. W. Knight, 'Husbands and Wives', 170.

232. This does not mean, as Snodgrass, 296, claims, that: 'In the final analysis submission and *agape* love are synonymous'. See above on 5:21, 22.

233. Exhortations to husbands to love their wives occur only infrequently outside the New Testament (see Pseudo-Phocylides 195-97; and in the rabbinic tradition *b. Yeba-*

far the longest and consists of two parts: in the first (vv. 25-27), husbands are urged to love their wives as Christ loved the church, while in the second (vv. 28-32) the admonition is repeated and again grounded in Christ's love for the church as well as in the husband's love for himself.

Although the husband's headship (v. 23) was mentioned in the section addressed to his wife (vv. 22-24), Paul does not here, or elsewhere for that matter, exhort husbands to rule over their wives. They are nowhere told, 'Exercise your headship'! Instead, they are urged repeatedly to love their wives (vv. 25, 28, and 33). This will involve each husband showing unceasing care and loving service for his wife's entire well-being. Elsewhere in both Old and New Testaments the command to love demands the total response of those addressed (cf. Lev. 19:18; Matt. 5:43; 19:19). Here, too, husbands are to respond wholeheartedly to the apostolic injunction. Their love, as a result, will involve an act of the will, and is not simply an emotional or physical response. Earlier in Ephesians *love* is seen as a grace that all believers are to show in their relationships with others (1:4; 3:17; 4:2, 15, 16; 5:2). Now it is required of husbands in relation to their wives.

The model and ground[234] of the husband's love for his wife are Christ's love for the church. The character and description of that love are amplified in the following clause, *and gave himself up for her*.[235] Again the verb 'gave over', together with the reflexive pronoun 'himself', stresses the fact that Christ took the initiative in handing himself over to death (5:1, 2). He went to the cross as the willing victim, and this action on behalf of his people was the supreme demonstration of his love for them. Such self-sacrificing love provided the earlier warrant for calling *all believers* to serve one another in love as they imitate God (vv. 1, 2).[236] Now it

---

mot 62b; cf. Lincoln, 374), while the ἀγάπη word-group does not appear in any extrabiblical Hellenistic rules for the household; so W. Schrage, 'Zur Ethik der neutestamentlichen Haustafeln', *NTS* 21 (1974-75), 1-22, esp. 12, 13.

234. As in 4:32 and 5:2 καθὼς καί ('just as also') has both comparative and causal force. It is part of the New Testament's 'conformity' pattern in which God or Christ's saving activity, especially Christ's sacrifice on the cross, is presented as a model of the lifestyle to which believers are to 'conform' (see on 4:32).

235. Stott, 227, notes that Paul uses five verbs to indicate 'the unfolding stages of Christ's commitment to his bride, the church', namely, 'loved', 'gave himself', 'sanctify', 'cleansed', and 'present'. These, he claims, 'trace Christ's care for his church from a past to a future eternity'. The words *Christ loved the church*, 'preceding as they do his self-sacrifice on her behalf, seem to look back to his eternal pre-existence in which he set his love upon his people'. Although this last point is quite acceptable theologically, it is better, in the light of the apostle's usage elsewhere, to understand καὶ ἑαυτὸν παρέδωκεν ὑπὲρ αὐτῆς ('and gave himself up for her') as epexegetical of ἠγάπησεν τὴν ἐκκλησίαν ('[Christ] loved the church'). Both expressions refer to the cross.

236. Note the earlier references in Ephesians to Christ's death and its significance: 1:7; 2:15, 16; 5:1, 2.

furnishes the basis[237] for the exhortation to husbands to sacrifice their own interests for the welfare of their wives. Their love, which is modelled on Christ's love for the church, means they will be willing to make even the ultimate sacrifice of life itself.

In the Old Testament the image of marriage was often used to depict the covenant relationship between Yahweh and his people, Israel.[238] Jesus took over this teaching and boldly referred to himself as the Bridegroom (Mark 2:18-20; cf. John 3:29). He presented 'himself in the role of Yahweh in the divine marriage with the covenanted people'.[239] Paul expands on the image in 2 Corinthians 11:1-3 and here in Ephesians 5, and focuses particularly on 'the sacrificial steadfastness of the heavenly Bridegroom's covenant-love for his bride'.[240] It is this sacrificial love which husbands are to imitate.

If they heed this apostolic injunction, husbands will not behave in an overbearing manner. All areas of married life will be characterized by this self-giving love and forgiveness. The original order of the Creator, which was troubled by the rule of sin and self-centredness, and which ended in the tyranny of eros and the slavery of sex, can be lived in love and forgiveness.

26 If Christ's love for the church is to be the model for husbands in its self-sacrifice, then it is also to be their pattern in relation to its goal (vv. 26-27). Accordingly, Paul proceeds to spell out the goal of Christ's sacrificial love for the church by means of three purpose clauses: that he might 'sanctify her' (v. 26), 'present her to himself' in splendour (v. 27a), and enable her to be 'holy and blameless' (v. 27c). As indicated above, the imagery from the Old Testament about God's relationship to Israel stands behind this use of the marriage analogy. In particular, the background to Ephesians 5:26-27 is probably Ezekiel 16:1-14, which describes God as caring for, washing, marrying, and adorning his people with splendour.[241]

---

237. At 5:2 the object of Christ's loving and giving himself up is 'us'; here in v. 25 the words are repeated, except that the object is 'the church'. Cf. Bruce, 386, 387; and K. H. Fleckenstein, *Die Eheperikope*, 187. The difference, however, does not necessarily mean that a sharp distinction is being made between 'us' as individuals and the church as a corporate whole.

238. Isa. 54:5-8; Jer. 2:1-3; 31:31-32; Ezek. 23; Hos. 1–3. For further details see R. C. Ortlund, *Whoredom: God's Unfaithful Wife in Biblical Theology* (Leicester: Apollos, 1996), the focal point of which is 'God's marital love and . . . his people's presently harlotrous but ultimately faithful response' (176).

239. R. C. Ortlund, *Whoredom*, 139. He adds that 'the Old Testament expectation of the marriage of Yahweh with his people, to be restored and enjoyed for ever, comes into the framework of New Testament theology through the teaching of Jesus himself'.

240. Stott, 227; cf. Bruce, 386.

241. Note, most recently, Snodgrass, 297-98; cf. T. Moritz, *A Profound Mystery*, 150-51.

The first of the three purpose clauses states that Christ gave himself up for the church in order to 'sanctify her'. The basic idea of this verb 'sanctify or make holy' is that of setting someone apart to God for his service. Christians are described as those who are 'sanctified in Christ Jesus' (1 Cor. 1:2), whom God has set apart for himself in the name of the Lord Jesus Christ (1 Cor. 6:11). In an expression which is without parallel in Paul's letters, v. 26 stresses the corporate dimension by asserting that it is the *church* (note the emphatic position of 'it') which is sanctified through Christ's death. Some understand the verb here (and the language of sanctification generally) as describing a *process* of moral renewal and change,[242] which is preceded by an initial cleansing from sin.[243] But the verb refers to the church being brought into 'an exclusive and dedicated relationship with God, as the holy people of the New Covenant' (cf. 1 Cor. 1:2; 6:11),[244] not to an ongoing process of sanctification, while the participial clause, 'cleansing it by washing . . .', is probably best explained along other lines (see below). Through his sacrificial death Christ claimed the church as his own to be his holy people (cf. v. 27). 'Christ died to devote the church to himself in an exclusive and permanent relationship analogous to marriage'.[245] There are two elements: a separation from all that is unclean and evil, and a consecration to God and his will.

Closely related to Christ's sanctifying work is his 'cleansing' the church 'by the washing of water through the word'. This cleansing, expressed through an aorist participle, has often been taken as describing an action antecedent to that of the main verb and rendered 'having cleansed'.[246] On this view, the cleansing of the church is thought to precede her sanctification or consecration (which, as we have seen, has been viewed as a process). Other versions and commentators understand the action of the participle to be coincident with that of the verb 'sanctify',

242. Note, e.g., Stott, 228; Hoehner.

243. The aorist participle καθαρίσας ('having cleansed') is taken to be antecedent to the action of 'sanctifying'.

244. D. G. Peterson, *Possessed by God*, 136. Against 'the common assumption that the New Testament views sanctification as primarily a process', he argues that its 'emphasis falls upon sanctification as a definitive event'. Both Schnackenburg, 249, and Snodgrass, 298, understand 'sanctify' in Eph. 5:26 as a comprehensive expression for Christ's work of salvation.

245. D. G. Peterson, *Possessed by God*, 53. This notion of setting apart as one's own is precisely what one does in marriage, and thus fits the imagery of Ezekiel 16. Whether Paul also had in mind the special meaning of *qādash* in rabbinic literature, 'to separate out for oneself' in the sense of marriage (as J. P. Sampley, 'And the Two', 42-43, thinks), is doubtful. Note the criticisms of Bruce, 387; Lincoln, 375; and Hoehner.

246. So RV, ASV, RSV, NRSV; cf. Meyer, 294; and Stott, 227.

and prefer the translation 'cleansing'.[247] Abbott argues that the cleansing occurred at the same time as the sanctification but logically preceded it.[248] However, in the light of recent studies on verbal aspect, neither the main verb 'make holy', which is an aorist subjunctive, nor the aorist participle 'cleansed' is temporally based. Because the participle here follows the main verb, it is likely that the cleansing is coincidental with the making holy.[249] The two aorists view each action as a complete whole (not as completed), and any temporal reference must be determined from the context. It is best, then, to understand the participle as denoting the means by which the action of the main verb was accomplished. Christ died for the church 'to make her holy by cleansing her' (NRSV). Cleansing points to the removal of sin, while sanctification focusses on being set apart to God. To use systematic theological categories, it is positional or definitive sanctification that is in view here, not progressive sanctification.

This cleansing was effected 'by the washing of water through the word' (cf. Tit. 3:5). Many commentators assume that 'the washing' refers to baptism.[250] But references to washing or water do not necessarily point to baptism, and the only specific mention of this motif in the entire letter is at 4:5, where it is listed in a sevenfold confession but is not specially emphasized. Instead, when Paul speaks of 'washing', his focus, as in 1 Corinthians 6:11, is on the spiritual cleansing accomplished by Christ rather than on baptism. Nowhere else in the New Testament is the *church* baptized![251]

Further, v. 26 is more likely to have been influenced by the marital imagery in Ezekiel 16:8-14 and the prenuptial bath in the Jewish marital customs than by baptismal considerations. Accordingly, the language of 'the washing with water' may well have a secondary reference to the bridal bath.[252] When Yahweh entered his marriage covenant with Jerusa-

---

247. AV, NEB, JB, NIV, NJB; cf. many recent commentators, including Barth, 626; Schnackenburg, 249; Lincoln, 375; and note Snodgrass, 298.

248. Abbott, 168. Following this, Hoehner recently suggested that the participle denotes the means, manner, or cause (!) of the sanctification, and the expression is best rendered, 'in order that he might sanctify her, having cleansed her'.

249. S. E. Porter's researches have indicated that aorist participles following the main verb in the Pauline corpus (there are 42 out of a total 120) show 'a definite tendency toward coincidental action'; *Verbal Aspect*, 384 (Eph. 5:26 is cited as an example).

250. The definite article '*the* washing' (τῷ λουτρῷ) has been taken to refer to a specific event, and it is claimed that the readers would probably think of their experience of baptism.

251. So Snodgrass, 298.

252. Recent commentators, including Bruce, Lincoln, and Hoehner (cf. T. Moritz), support the allusion to the bridal bath.

lem, he bathed her with water, washed off the blood from her (v. 9), anointed her with oil, and clothed her with magnificent garments, making her so beautiful that she was fit to be a queen. Christ's death on behalf of the church was to make her holy by cleansing her with the washing of water, and this is analogous to the bridal bath.

The final phrase 'through the word' is closely linked by most commentators to the immediately preceding expression, 'the washing of water', and understood as accompanying the baptism. It is thus rendered 'with the word', and interpreted either as the baptismal confession of faith or as the baptismal formula pronounced over the candidate. The latter, it is claimed, would have included a reference to the name of Christ (cf. Acts 2:38), and so to what he had achieved on behalf of believers. But we have already raised serious doubts about any reference to baptism in v. 26, while the term 'word' is used nowhere else in the New Testament in connection with baptism. A better interpretation is to join the phrase 'through the word' with the 'cleansing', and to understand it as signifying 'through the word of the gospel'. This is precisely how this particular term 'word' is employed elsewhere in Ephesians, namely, as the preached word of the gospel which the Spirit uses as his sword (6:17; cf. Rom. 10:8, 17; Heb. 6:5; 1 Pet. 1:25). Moreover, it is consistent with every instance of the term in Paul (except 2 Cor. 13:1), where it denotes words that come from God or Christ. In the present context, the apostle asserts that the church is made pure by a spiritual cleansing ('by the washing of water'), and this is accomplished through the purifying word of the gospel — a notion that is akin to our Lord's words about his disciples being *cleansed* and *sanctified* through the word which he had spoken (John 15:3; 17:7).[253] This word is not something additional to the spiritual cleansing effected 'by the washing of water', but as the gracious word of the gospel it is the means by which it is accomplished. In the present context this is a word of love by which 'the Bridegroom binds himself to his "bride", and brings the church to himself in love'.[254]

Christ gave himself to the church to make her holy by cleansing her. This cleansing was effected by a spiritual washing brought about through Christ's gracious word in the gospel. His love for the church is the model for husbands in its purpose and goal, as well as in its self-sacrifice (v. 25). In the light of Christ's complete giving of himself to make the church

253. Many understand the phrase ἐν ῥήματι ('through the word') to be an accompaniment of the cleansing. The cleansing is effected instrumentally through the washing of the water, and this is accompanied by the preached word of Christ; Hoehner; cf. Lincoln, 376. Calvin, 206-7, takes 'the washing with water' as a reference to baptism, and 'the word' as the promise which explains the meaning of the sacramental sign.

254. D. G. Peterson, *Possessed by God*, 53, following Barth, 691.

holy and cleanse her, husbands should be utterly committed to the total well-being, especially the spiritual welfare, of their wives.

27 The goal of Christ's sanctifying and purifying work, and thus the ultimate purpose of his sacrificial love for the church (v. 26), is 'to present her to himself in splendour, without spot or wrinkle or any other blemish . . . so that she might be holy and blameless'. Just as in v. 26 Christ is the one who makes the church holy, so here also he is the subject who presents the church in all its splendour. In Colossians the general notion of presenting believers holy and blameless appears without any specific reference to marriage (1:22), while according to 2 Corinthians 11:2 Paul's role, as the friend of the bridegroom, is to present the Corinthians as a pure virgin to Christ. Here in Ephesians, however, by adding the personal pronoun '[he] himself', together with the reflexive pronoun 'to himself', Paul goes out of his way to emphasize that it is Christ who will present the church to himself — not the friend of the bridegroom, nor the bride herself. He has done everything necessary to achieve this goal.

This presentation of the church as his bride will be 'in all its splendour',[255] an expression which probably reflects the imagery of Ezekiel 16:10-14, where Yahweh clothes his bride in magnificent apparel and jewelry, so that her beauty is 'perfect because of my splendor that I had bestowed on you, says the Lord GOD' (v. 14; NRSV).[256] Paul does not say when this will happen, but it seems likely that he has in mind the parousia, for it is then that the glorified church will be with Christ forevermore, and will be seen to be 'glorious'.[257] The reasons for taking this line are as follows:

(a) It is better to understand 'glorious' of the eschatological radiance and brightness of God's presence on the final day, than the glory in which the church currently participates. This glory is the radiance of God, the shining forth and manifestation of his presence. The immediately following statements in v. 27, which depict the church as 'free from spot, wrinkle or anything of the sort', amplify and explain what is meant by 'glorious', and, in the light of the following purpose clause (that the church

---

255. ἔνδοξος ('distinguished; glorious, splendid') is used of the fine clothing one would find in the courts of kings (Luke 7:25), of the 'glorious' things that Jesus did (13:17), and of the 'glorious' opinion the Corinthians had of themselves, in contrast to the apostles (1 Cor. 4:10); cf. BAGD, 263; and Louw and Nida, §79.19.

256. Cf. Lincoln, 377. For a recent exposition of Ezek. 16 see R. C. Ortlund, *Whoredom*, 101-17.

257. Those who hold that Christ's presentation of the church occurs during this present age include Schnackenburg, Lincoln, Best, and Snodgrass, while those who favour a parousia reference include Calvin, Meyer, J. P. Sampley, Stott, Bruce, Morris, and Hoehner.

'might be *holy* and *blameless*'), are best taken as referring to the spiritual and ethical perfection on the last day. The glory is 'the perfection of character with which the Lord has endowed her'.[258]

(b) The verb to 'present' appears in Pauline contexts where it can only refer to the final day (2 Cor. 4:14; cf. Rom. 14:10; 1 Cor. 8:8).[259] This is particularly the case when the verb is used, as in Colossians 1:22, 28, where the same ('holy', 'blameless') or similar terms ('irreproachable', 'perfect') focus on the occasion of the great assize. Believers will be presented perfect in Christ at the parousia.

(c) The closest conceptual parallel to our text appears in 2 Corinthians 11:2, where Paul speaks of his presentation of the congregation at Corinth as a 'pure virgin' to Christ. This is best understood as occurring at the end of the world (2 Cor. 11:2),[260] and is thus akin to Revelation 21:9-11, where in an obvious parousia reference 'the bride' of Christ will be presented to him, 'having the glory of God'.

(d) Finally, it is inappropriate to claim that, because the eschatological emphasis in Ephesians is on the 'now' rather than the 'not yet', v. 27 must be read the same way, thereby providing further evidence that this epistle is not from the hand of Paul. Ephesians, like the generally accepted Pauline epistles, contains future eschatological statements as well as realized ones (see on 29-33).

What is meant by the church being 'glorious' is now described in physical terms. Using the image of a lovely young woman, Paul states that she will be *without stain or wrinkle or any other blemish.* Not even the smallest spot or pucker that spoils the smoothness of the skin will mar the unsurpassed beauty of Christ's bride when he presents her to himself. Hers will be a splendour that is exquisite, unsurpassed, matchless. For the present the church on earth is 'often in rags and tatters, stained and ugly, despised and rejected'.[261] Christ's people may rightly be accused of many shortcomings and failures. But God's gracious intention is that the church should be *holy and blameless,* language which speaks of a beauty which is moral and spiritual. Both words have already appeared in Ephesians: the purpose of God's election of believers from before the foundation of the world is that they should be *holy and blameless* before him (1:4). They have also been used in Colossians of the eschatological presentation

---

258. Bruce, 389.

259. The verb παραστῆσαι ('to present') was often employed in legal language with the meaning 'to bring another before the court'. Some take 1 Cor. 8:8 and 2 Cor. 4:14 in this way (cf. Rom. 14:10; 2 Tim. 2:15).

260. Cf. P. Barnett, *The Second Epistle to the Corinthians* (Grand Rapids/Cambridge: Eerdmans, 1997), 499. Cf. Bruce, 389.

261. Stott, 228.

of believers before God at the parousia (Col. 1:22). Holiness and blamelessness will characterize Christ's bride, the church, on that glorious day.

28 Husbands have already been exhorted to love their wives (v. 25a). The warrant and example for this admonition are Christ's sacrificial love for the church (vv. 25b-27). Now the concluding application *(in this same way)*[262] is drawn from Christ's love as husbands are urged again to love their wives. The main point of vv. 25-27 is driven home as Paul reinforces his assertion with a verb that stresses obligation: 'husbands *ought* to love their wives'.

They are to love them *as their own bodies*, a statement that is rather surprising and has been regarded as: (1) a descent from the lofty heights of Christ's love to the rather low standard of self-love; (2) too demeaning and degrading since the wife is viewed simply as her husband's body,[263] or (3) at best a commonplace that is rather pragmatic in its self-interested approach.[264] But the issue is more nuanced than these comments suggest. The statement applies the second great commandment, 'You shall love your neighbour as yourself' (Lev. 19:18), in a direct way to the love which the husband should have for his nearest and dearest neighbour, namely, his wife.[265] In support of this, Bruce points out that 'neighbour' (in its Hebrew feminine form) is used repeatedly 'by the lover in the Song of Songs when addressing his beloved or speaking about her to others' (Song 1:9, 15; 2:2, 10, 13; 4:1, 7; 5:2; 6:4).[266] Both Leviticus and Ephesians assume that

262. It is possible that οὕτως ('so, in the same manner') looks forward to the following ὡς ('as'), with the resulting translation: 'so also husbands ought to love their wives as their own bodies' (cf. v. 33); note Bruce, 391; and Schnackenburg, 252. But, on balance, it is better to understand οὕτως καί ('so also') functioning as a conclusion to what began with καθὼς καί ('just as also') in v. 25. The appropriate rendering would then be: 'just as also Christ loved the church . . . so also ought husbands to love their wives'. This stylistic construction is similar to v. 24 ('as [ὡς] the church submits to Christ, so also [οὕτως καί] wives . . .'), and is not uncommon elsewhere in Paul (Rom. 5:12 with v. 18; 5:19, 21; 6:4). Cf. J. P. Sampley, *'And the Two'*, 141; Barth, 630; Lincoln, 378; and B. Witherington, *Women*, 59. See the full discussion by Hoehner, including his treatment of the text-critical question.

263. So, e.g., Meyer, Abbott, and Barth. In order to get round the difficulty, the Greek ὡς τὰ ἑαυτῶν σώματα is taken to mean 'as *being* their own bodies'. But the next sentence, 'he who loves his wife loves himself' (v. 28b), endorses the obvious meaning, while v. 33 suggests that ὡς ἑαυτόν ('as himself') is equivalent to ὡς τὰ ἑαυτῶν σώματα ('as their own bodies'). See, among others, Lincoln, 378.

264. Note E. Best, *Ephesians* (1993), 79.

265. So J. P. Sampley, *'And the Two'*, 32-23, 139-42; Bruce, 391; G. W. Knight, 'Husbands and Wives', 172, 173; Morris, 186; and Snodgrass, 297. Lincoln, 378, 379, thinks that the language of Lev. 19:18 is reflected in v. 33, but is not necessary for the flow of the argument in v. 28 (cf. T. Moritz, *A Profound Mystery*, 149, and Hoehner).

266. Bruce, 391.

a person will look after his or her own interests and welfare. Similarly, in the 'golden rule' Jesus urged his hearers to treat others as they themselves like to be treated (Matt. 7:12).

The expression 'as their own bodies' instead of 'as themselves' (the equivalent in the Leviticus text) is presumably due to the influence of Genesis 2:24, which is cited in v. 31. This Old Testament Scripture declares that in marriage husband and wife are 'one flesh'. In the context of Ephesians 5 'flesh' and 'body' are equivalent (note the shift to 'flesh' in v. 29a). Husband and wife, then, are regarded as one person, a single entity. Accordingly, the husband's obligation to love his wife as his own body is not simply a matter of loving someone else just like he loves himself. It is, in fact, to love himself.[267] Finally, the idea of husbands loving their wives as their own bodies reflects the model of Christ, whose love for the church can be seen as love for his own body (cf. vv. 23, 30).

29 As he continues to urge husbands to love their wives, the apostle supports and develops his statement that whoever loves his wife loves himself: 'after all,[268] no one ever hates[269] his own flesh, but instead nourishes and cherishes it'. It is natural for people to regard their own bodies as important. Although some eccentrics have engaged in self-mutilation, and ascetics have sometimes regarded it as meritorious to make their bodies uncomfortable, people generally do not act in this way.

On the contrary, each person, and Paul has the husband particularly in view, does everything possible to take care of his body (lit. 'flesh').[270] He 'nourishes' and 'cherishes' it, terms full of affection which are drawn from the language of the nursery and are the very reverse of hating one's body. 'Nourish' appears later in the household table in relation to fathers 'bringing up' their children (6:4), while 'cherish' appears in 1 Thessalonians 2:7 with reference to Paul caring for the Thessalonians as a

---

267. Though note the discussion of G. W. Dawes, *The Body*, 153-54.

268. The γάρ functions as an emphatic particle ('indeed, to be sure'); note Rom. 2:25; so J. P. Sampley, *'And the Two'*, 143; cf. BAGD, 152. The point is further strengthened with the particle ποτε ('ever').

269. The aorist tense here (ἐμίσησεν) has been regarded as 'gnomic' or timeless since it expresses a general truth, in this case a proverbial saying, with no particular time reference. So K. L. McKay, *A New Syntax*, 47; cf. S. E. Porter, *Idioms*, 38, who comments: 'One of the ways in which language users refer to events is to see them not simply as confined to one temporal sphere (past, present or future) but as occurring over time and perhaps as representative of the kind of thing which regularly occurs, especially in nature'.

270. What is referred to as 'bodies' (σώματα) in v. 28a becomes 'himself' (ἑαυτόν) in v. 28c, and is changed to 'flesh' (σάρξ) in v. 29a. 'Flesh' (σάρξ) is used interchangeably here with 'body' (σῶμα) and therefore without any negative connotation. Most interpreters agree that the movement to 'flesh' here anticipates the quotation of Gen. 2:24 in v. 31: 'and the two shall become *one flesh*' (εἰς σάρκα μίαν).

427

nurse cares for her children. Both words do, however, appear within a papyrus in reverse order to describe the husband's duties according to a marriage contract: he is to 'cherish and nourish and clothe her'.[271] Within the flow of Ephesians 5 there is an inner appropriateness in the husband tenderly cherishing and nurturing his wife since they have in fact become 'one flesh' (v. 31).

But it is the powerful example[272] of Christ that is again invoked. For all its imperfections Christ nurtures and tenderly cares for his body, the church. He is both its Head and Saviour (1:22-23; 4:15; 5:23). He gave himself up for the church in order to sanctify it (5:25, 26), and he constantly provides for its nourishment and growth (4:11-16).[273] Let each husband, then, follow Christ's example and be wholehearted in loving and tenderly caring for his wife.

30 In a magnificent supporting statement[274] Paul underlines the fact that both he and his readers are so intimately joined to Christ that they have become part of him. What has been said in the preceding argument about Christ's care for the church applies to them all. They (and we) have been incorporated into Christ and are the very members of his body, whom he nourishes and cherishes. 'The "body" is not a vague ecclesiological concept for Paul; rather, it is a term that expresses the solidarity of believers with Christ'.[275] Indeed, so intensely personal is this truth that Paul interrupts his style and changes to the first person singular 'we', thereby including himself within the sphere of blessing. He, like them, is a member of Christ's body and knows what it is to be cared for and nurtured by him. Earlier in Ephesians it was stated that Christians are members of one another, and this provided the theological motivation for telling the truth (4:25); now it is affirmed that *we are members of his body*.[276]

Further, within the flow of the paragraph, the relationship between Christ and his church is presented not simply as the ideal model for a husband and wife in their marriage. It is also the reality in which they and other Christians are included.[277] Husbands and wives, like other believers,

271. For details see Gnilka, 285; Schnackenburg, 253; and Lincoln, 379-80.

272. Again in Ephesians a comparison with Christ is introduced by καθὼς καί ('just as also'). See on 4:32.

273. Arnold, 127, thinks that an element in this 'nourishing' is the provision of divine empowering for believers to enable them to engage in spiritual warfare.

274. T. Moritz, *A Profound Mystery,* 134, discusses at some length the connection between vv. 29 and 30, and thinks that the causal force of ὅτι should probably not be pressed. He prefers the rendering 'after all' to 'because'.

275. Snodgrass, 299.

276. Cf. Robinson, 208, who states that the 'relation of the parts to the whole is here emphasised, as is the relation of the parts of the whole to one another in iv 25'.

277. Schnackenburg, 253.

are profoundly indebted to Christ because they know what it is to be loved and cherished by him day by day. This text serves to remind 'husbands and wives of that which they have in common, as "members" of the body of Christ'.[278] Let the husband, then, who understands Christ's tender affection and nurture follow this example in his love for his wife.[279]

31-32 Paul has invoked the example of the Lord Jesus Christ nourishing and caring for his church as he urges husbands again to love their wives (vv. 28-29; cf. vv. 25-27). He reminds his readers that they have been recipients of Christ's tender care. After all, they are intimately joined to their Lord and have become part of him (v. 30). Now as the apostle moves to the climax of the paragraph, he cites the text that has provided the substructure of his thought throughout, namely, Genesis 2:24, the most fundamental statement in the Old Testament concerning God's plan for marriage.[280] Within its original context the narrator of Genesis 2 describes how woman was taken from the side of man to be his companion. He then adds: 'This is why a man will leave his father and mother and be joined to his wife, and the two will become one flesh'.

This key Old Testament text, cited from the Septuagint,[281] has been on view from v. 28 on: the term 'flesh' (which appears in Gen. 2:24) has been used interchangeably at v. 29 with 'body' in v. 28. The quotation appears without an introductory formula, and its opening phrase, *for this reason*, has been interpreted as linking vv. 22-30, 25-30, or 29-30 to the Genesis text. In our judgment the immediate antecedent of Genesis 2:24 is v. 30, 'because we are members of his body'. The absence of an introductory formula is that the opening words, *for this reason*, dovetail neatly and logically into Paul's argument.[282] Paul was perfectly aware of the literal

278. G. W. Dawes, *The Body*, 156.

279. The phrase 'of his body' was later amplified by the addition in some manuscripts of 'flesh of his flesh, bone of his bone', which is self-evidently derived from Gen. 2:23. See the textual note in Lincoln, 351.

280. Foulkes, 161.

281. The wording differs only slightly from the LXX: ἀντὶ τούτου ('because of this') replaces ἕνεκεν τούτου ('for the sake of this, for this reason'), and the possessive pronoun αὐτοῦ ('his') is omitted after πατέρα ('father') and μητέρα ('mother'). None of these matters is material to the sense of the whole (though see the following note).

282. See also Eph. 4:25-26 and 6:2, where Old Testament quotations blend seamlessly into their new literary context, and do not have the kind of introductory formula that appears in Eph. 4:8 and 5:14. Cf. R. C. Ortlund, *Whoredom*, 153. T. Moritz, *A Profound Mystery*, 135, on the other hand, thinks that the change from the LXX text to ἀντὶ τούτου ('because of this') is deliberate and results in a smoother transition from v. 30 to v. 31. His suggestion, however, that vv. 30-32 function as 'an explanatory digression, not as the syntactical climax' of the whole paragraph (135-36) is incorrect. These verses are far more significant to Paul's argument than Moritz allows, and highlight the importance of the Christ-church relationship (the significance of which Moritz consistently downplays). See below.

meaning of this Old Testament text, but now he states that it is referring to the union of Christ and his church, and so provides warrant for the assertion that believers are members of Christ's body. Because of the particular focus on the spiritual marriage between Christ and the church, it is only the latter part of the quote, 'and the two shall become one flesh', that serves Paul's purpose.[283]

The apostle then comments that 'this mystery is great' (v. 32),[284] that is, it is significant and profound. Several distinct though related questions must be addressed before we can understand the meaning of this notorious crux: First, what is meant by the expression 'this mystery', and is it consistent with other instances of the term in Ephesians? Secondly, to what does '*this* mystery' refer? And, thirdly, what is being said about it in this context?

In answer to these questions there is a range of varying interpretations. The following are the more important ones:

(1) 'Mystery' refers to *the marriage relationship*.

The view that 'this mystery' is a reference to the marriage relationship has taken two main forms. First, Roman Catholic theologians, within the context of their 'sacramental' theology, have regarded it as speaking of human marriage. The Vulgate rendered the Greek word as 'sacramentum', and Catholic dogma holds that the institution of marriage conveys grace.

Secondly, and more generally, some exegetes claim that the paragraph is about the Christian husband and wife living out the Pauline vision of marriage (vv. 22-30) because Genesis 2:24 shows that such a relationship is true to the 'one flesh' meaning of marriage. On this view, the flow of Paul's argument in vv. 22-30 has been about human marriage. The relationship between Christ and the church is incidental to this thrust, and any parallels with the relationship between husbands and wives are merely illustrative. The earlier Christology functions only in a supplementary way since it is incidental to Paul's pastoral admonition.[285]

---

283. So most commentators. It is not suggested that each part of the quotation applies to Christ and the church, so any allegorizing about Christ leaving his heavenly Father and mother in order to cleave to the church is fundamentally incorrect (cf. Lincoln, 380).

284. It is better to regard μέγα as a predicate adjective, 'this mystery is great' (RV, ASV, NASB), with the τοῦτο ('this') modifying μυστήριον ('mystery'), than as an attributive adjective, 'this is a great mystery' (AV, NEB, NIV, NRSV). The former expresses 'the magnitude, importance, or profundity of the mystery' (Hoehner), while the latter conveys the idea to the modern reader that the μυστήριον is mysterious or difficult to understand, a notion which is inappropriate here.

285. In general terms, the recent exegetical work of T. Moritz, *A Profound Mystery*, 117-52, falls into this category. The relationship between Christ and the church is incidental to the main thrust of the passage, which is fundamentally about human marriage.

But there are difficulties with this view which limits the 'mystery' to the relation of husband and wife: first, the term in Ephesians usually connotes a truth that was previously hidden and has now been revealed. This is hardly true of marriage itself, even as a sacrament.[286] Further, the citation of Genesis 2:24, on this interpretation, does not adequately explain the meaning of v. 30, 'for we are members of his body'. Structurally, Paul's argument from vv. 22 (or 25) to 31 is not limited to the relation of husband and wife. Indeed, one wonders whether it was necessary for Paul's argument to introduce the Christ/church parallels with Christian marriage at all.[287] Although v. 32 is a difficult crux, its mention of the mystery's greatness suggests that there is a further and more profound dimension to the apostle's citation of the Genesis text. Finally, this approach does not correctly identify the content and referent of 'mystery', while nothing in marriage itself as an institution 'mystically' dispenses divine grace.[288]

(2) The 'mystery' is *the union of Christ and the church.*

The second main interpretation takes 'mystery' in Ephesians 5:32 as a direct reference to the union of Christ and his church. It is claimed, over against the first view, that in Ephesians Paul highlights the motif of the church as the body of Christ. It is more consistent, then, within the argument of the epistle to understand 'mystery' as a reference to this larger theme. This approach, it is argued, also fits with other uses of the term in Ephesians. Within the structure of 5:22-33 there is a shift in emphasis (esp. in vv. 28a-32) to the church as the body of Christ, while the immediate antecedent of the Genesis 2:24 quotation is the clause 'for we are members of his body' (v. 30). Further, the demonstrative pronoun in the expression '*this* mystery' probably points to 'a certain aspect of the marital union', that is, 'the two shall become one flesh', which ties in with the Christ-church relationship.[289] Finally, Paul's assertion at the end of v. 32,

286. Note the criticisms of A. J. Köstenberger, 'The Mystery of Christ and the Church: Head and Body, "One Flesh"', *TrinJ* 12 (1991), 79-94, esp. 86-87.

287. So R. C. Ortlund, *Whoredom,* 154. Unfortunately, this is a major difficulty with T. Moritz's detailed treatment of the passage (*A Profound Mystery,* 117-52). Although he has provided readers with many insightful comments, and concedes that the author's 'understanding of Gen 2.24 is typological in that it regards marriage before the Christ event as a prefiguring of Christ-centred marriage', he (1) effectively treats the relationship between Christ and the church as incidental to the main point of the paragraph, (2) considers vv. 30-32 to be a digression rather than the high point, and (3) excludes the possibility that Yahweh (or Christ) has entered into a marriage relationship with his people.

288. A. J. Köstenberger, 'The Mystery', 87. Note also the criticisms of Barth, 747-49.

289. So J. P. Sampley, *'And the Two',* 86, who admits that τοῦτο ('this') could refer to any part of the section beginning with v. 21; cf. A. J. Köstenberger, 'The Mystery', 87.

'but I speak with reference to Christ and the church', comes by way of contrast[290] and indicates that he is no longer dealing with the physical union of husband and wife but is making clear that the mystery is the union of Christ and the church.

While this interpretation contains many insights which we shall build on, its real drawback is that it fails to take into account the correspondence between marriage and the Christ-church relationship throughout the paragraph, a drawback which the following interpretation seeks to overcome.

(3) The mystery refers to the relationship between *Christ and the church as a typology of marriage.* In support of this view it is recognized that:

(a) Genesis 2:24 has undergirded the paragraph from v. 28 on, and has been applied to human marriage. As noted above, in v. 29 the term 'flesh', drawn from this Old Testament text, was used synonymously with the word 'body' (v. 28). At a fundamental level wives are their husbands' bodies because Genesis 2:24 declares that marriage makes husband and wife one 'flesh'. Paul was perfectly aware of the literal meaning of this passage and has employed it accordingly.[291]

(b) The quotation from Genesis 2:24 refers directly to the union of Christ and his church. The immediate antecedent of the citation, as we have suggested, is v. 30. This Pauline affirmation, 'we are members of his body', and the Pentateuchal statement, 'the two shall become one flesh', 'spring to life as a breathtaking juxtaposition', as Raymond Ortlund puts it.[292]

(c) The Genesis text, then, affirms that marriage makes husband

---

290. ἐγὼ δὲ λέγω ('But I speak') has been taken to indicate: (1) a change of subject matter from human marriage to the relationship between Christ and the church (so A. J. Köstenberger, 'The Mystery', 87), (2) that this particular interpretation of Genesis 2:24 as referring to the union between Christ and the church is his own (Lincoln, 382; though note the criticisms of T. Moritz, *A Profound Mystery,* 143), or (3) that the apostle is saying something about himself, his agenda. ἐγὼ δὲ λέγω ('but I speak') appears elsewhere in Matt. 5, where six times (vv. 22, 28, 32, 34, 39, 44) Jesus gave his interpretation of the Mosaic law in contrast to the generally accepted view. Cf. Lincoln, 382, and Hoehner. See below, n. 302.

291. Snodgrass, 299, states: the 'relevance of Genesis 2:24 to the relation of husband and wife is assumed'. In 1 Cor. 6:16 Paul uses this text of the 'one-flesh union' that is created through the most casual intercourse with a prostitute; cf. B. Witherington, *Women,* 60.

292. R. C. Ortlund, *Whoredom,* 156. In his discussion of 'this mystery', G. W. Dawes, *The Body,* 178-85, rightly recognizes that the expression 'one flesh' (v. 31) has a double referent, i.e., 'the union of Church and Christ described in words drawn from the bodily union of husband and wife'. He calls this 'an implicit metaphorical identification', but stops short of referring to the former as a typology of marriage, which is to be understood along salvation-historical lines.

and wife one body; it also explicates the union between Christ and the church.[293] The parallels between the two are central to the apostle's argument,[294] and their relationship is best understood in terms of typology. 'The first Adam's love for his wife as *one flesh* with himself and the last Adam's love for his own bride, his body, are . . . the typology [that] serves Paul's pastoral purpose of providing a model for Christian marriage which is grounded in primeval human origins and reflective of ultimate divine reality'.[295] Theologically, Paul's argument does not move from human marriage to Christ and his church;[296] rather, Christ and the church in a loving relationship is the paradigm for the Christian husband and wife.

(d) On this view v. 32 is a summarizing affirmation: 'this mystery' does not simply refer to the immediately preceding words of v. 30,[297] but to the line of thought running through the passage, that is, 'Christ and the church reflected in the dynamic interplay of a truly Christian marriage'.[298] 'Mystery' is thus used consistently with other instances in Ephesians. Elsewhere it points to the once-hidden plan of God which has now been revealed in Jesus Christ. Different aspects of the mystery can be highlighted in any one context; there are not many mysteries but several

293. A. T. Lincoln, in *Theology*, 123, 'Through his citation and interpretation of Gen. 2.24 in 5.31, 32 the writer stresses both the union of Christ and the Church and marital unity'.

294. Lincoln, 382, helpfully observes that 'Christ had already been seen in Adamic terms in Eph 1:22 . . . and so a text that refers to Adam's bodily union can now be claimed for Christ's union with the Church'. Cf. Turner, 1242.

295. R. C. Ortlund, *Whoredom*, 156.

296. As R. A. Batey, *New Testament Nuptial Imagery* (Leiden: Brill, 1971), 30, thinks: 'The author sees in the "one flesh" concept where husband and wife become one body a key for understanding the unity maintained by Christ and his Body, the church'. Note the criticisms of R. C. Ortlund, *Whoredom*, 157-58.

297. It is unlikely that 'this mystery' is a reference back to the quotation of Gen. 2:24. Nor should we take the expression to be pointing to a deeper meaning of this Scripture (cf. G. Bornkamm, R. E. Brown, M. Barth, F. F. Bruce, etc.), what M. N. A. Bockmuehl (*Revelation*, 204) calls 'an *exegetical* mystery: a deeper (in this case either allegorical or prophetic) meaning of a Scriptural text which has been elicited by means of some form of inspired exegesis'. This sense of 'mystery' is not parallelled elsewhere in Ephesians, or the rest of the New Testament for that matter, although it is found at Qumran (note the criticisms of Lincoln, 381). For Bockmuehl 'this mystery' is 'the deeper meaning of Gen 2:24 [which] points typologically to Christ and the church' (204). In our view, the mystery has to do with the interplay of human marriage and the divine marriage between Christ and his people. We agree with G. W. Dawes, *The Body*, 179-80, that μυστήριον ('mystery') here does not signify a 'hidden meaning of a scriptural passage'; but his conclusion that there 'is no indication that the author wants to draw attention to its scriptural origin' is unnecessary (see below).

298. R. C. Ortlund, *Whoredom*, 157.

aspects of the one mystery.[299] In Ephesians 3, for example, the particular emphasis is on Jews and Gentiles being brought together in the one body of Christ. Here at 5:32[300] there is the same salvation-historical perspective moving from creation to new creation and a focus on the gospel mystery of Christ and the church. 'Both the OT passage and the marriage relationship of which it speaks are connected with the mystery, but their connection is that they point to the secret that has now been revealed, that of the relationship between Christ and the Church'.[301] The mystery is not any particular marriage or marriage itself; it is the union of Christ and the church which is reflected in a truly Christian marriage. Such a mystery is indeed 'profound'.

(e) In his final comment, 'but I speak with reference to Christ and the church' (v. 32b), the apostle is in effect saying that 'Human marriage claims his personal attention primarily because it speaks of Christ and the church'.[302] He is telling us something about himself, his agenda. Just as his responsibility before God is to proclaim the mystery of the gospel which speaks of Gentiles being incorporated into the body of Christ along with Jews (3:2-9), so, too, he is aware of the burden of declaring this mystery of Christ and the church.

(f) A Christian marriage, as envisaged in this paragraph, is 'to reveal the mystery of Christ loving his responsive church. Such a marriage bears living witness to the meaning of "two becoming one"'. It reproduces in miniature the beauty shared between the Bridegroom and the Bride. And through it all, the mystery of the gospel is unveiled.[303] Further, within the wider context of Ephesians as a whole the union between Christian husband and wife which is part of the unity between Christ and the church is thus a pledge of God's purposes of unity for the cosmos.[304]

Of the three views examined above, the last makes best sense of vv. 22-33, particularly the quotation from Genesis 2:24 in v. 31. This approach does not treat the Christ-church relationship as incidental to the household discourse (as does view [1]). It also avoids the pitfall of understand-

---

299. C. C. Caragounis, *Mysterion,* 136-46, esp. 143.

300. Although C. C. Caragounis, *Mysterion,* 59, takes this differently, regarding it as 'a special use of the term verging more on the incomprehensibility of the union of the Church with Christ'.

301. Lincoln, 381.

302. R. C. Ortlund, *Whoredom,* 158. See also n. 290 on the significance of the expression ἐγὼ δὲ λέγω ('but I speak').

303. R. C. Ortlund, *Whoredom,* 157, 158. G. W. Knight, 'Husbands and Wives', 176, aptly comments: 'Paul saw that *when God designed the original marriage He already had Christ and the church in mind.* This is one of God's great purposes in marriage: to picture the relationship between Christ and His redeemed people forever!' (original emphasis).

304. A. T. Lincoln, in *Theology,* 123.

ing the whole passage in terms of the Christ-church relationship so that human marriage functions as a secondary theme (cf. interpretation [2]).

This particular view of marriage has its antecedents in the Old Testament, where marriage is used typologically of the relationship between God and his covenant people. In the earlier Testament the image of marriage was often used to depict the covenant relationship between Yahweh and his people, Israel (Isa. 54:5-8; Jer. 2:1-3; 31:31-32; Ezek. 23; Hos. 1–3). Jesus took over this teaching and boldly referred to himself as the Bridegroom (Mark 2:18-20; cf. John 3:29). He presented 'himself in the role of Yahweh in the divine marriage with the covenanted people'.[305] Paul expands on the image in 2 Corinthians 11:1-3 and here in Ephesians 5, and focuses particularly on 'the sacrificial steadfastness of the heavenly Bridegroom's covenant-love for his bride'.[306] At one level, then, Paul's teaching on marriage is grounded in the Old Testament, while at another level the church's marriage to Christ is prefigured in Adam and Eve.

33 Paul now rounds off his discussion with two summarizing exhortations in which the duties and responsibilities of husbands and wives are briefly restated. The opening conjunction, which is elsewhere used as an adversative 'however' or 'but', can also conclude a discussion and emphasize what is important. This is its significance here, so it is better to render the word by 'in any case', or 'now'.[307]

In the preceding verses the apostle has set forth a high view of marriage. The relationship between Christ and the church has momentous consequences for Christian husbands and wives in their relationships. The Christ-church parallel is not simply an illustration for marriage; it is 'the generating theological centre of . . . [Paul's] entire presentation'.[308] At the same time, this profound theology is intended to serve practical ends. Husband and wife need to grasp clearly the implications of the Christ-church relationship for their marriage. Accordingly, both are addressed, though now in reverse order. Having focussed on the responsibilities of husbands in vv. 25-32, Paul exhorts them[309] first. The admonition is indi-

---

305. R. C. Ortlund, *Whoredom*, 139. He adds that 'the Old Testament expectation of the marriage of Yahweh with his people, to be restored and enjoyed for ever, comes into the framework of New Testament theology through the teaching of Jesus himself'.

306. Stott, 227; cf. Bruce, 386.

307. πλήν functions in a similar way at Phil. 3:16; 4:14; and 1 Cor. 11:11. It is used adversatively at Matt. 11:22, 24; Luke 22:22, etc. Note BAGD, 669; BDF §449(2); A. T. Robertson, *Grammar,* 1187; and most recent commentators. Cf. also M. E. Thrall, *Particles,* 21.

308. R. C. Ortlund, *Whoredom,* 156.

309. καὶ ὑμεῖς ('you also'), which is slightly emphatic, signifies 'you Christian husbands as well as the Heavenly Bridegroom' (Morris, 188).

vidualized: 'let each one of you[310] so love his wife as himself'. Every husband in the congregations that received this circular letter, not simply the leaders, is addressed directly and personally. None is exempt from giving himself to his wife in loving service so that she might become what God intends for her.

This injunction picks up the earlier admonition that husbands ought to love their wives as their own bodies (v. 28), and also incorporates the exhortation of v. 25 that they should love them as Christ loved the church. Furthermore, since vv. 31 and 32 show that Christ's love for the church involves its becoming one body with him so that he loves the church *as himself*, Paul can conclude by calling upon the husband to love his wife as himself.[311] As in v. 28 (see above), the language echoes the second great commandment, 'You shall love your neighbour as yourself' (Lev. 19:18), and it is applied in a direct way to the love which a husband should have for his nearest and dearest neighbour, namely, his wife. This exhortation does not involve a further command to love oneself; it is assumed that love of self is present in each one of us (see on v. 29). The apostle, then, summarizes what he has already urged in vv. 25-29. Here, however, the injunction is particularized for each individual.

The wording to the wife, as in the case of her husband, is also different from the earlier admonition (v. 22). She, too, is addressed in the singular,[312] and this emphasizes her individual responsibility to heed the apostle's exhortation. Rather than the customary imperative, a different construction is used, but it still has an imperatival force and may be rendered 'let the wife fear her husband'.[313] In place of the earlier exhortation to submit to her husband (v. 22), she is here called upon to 'fear' him. The verb 'to fear' is akin to the noun which appears at the beginning of the household table (v. 21). Paul ends this lengthy paragraph of marriage paraenesis with an *inclusio* or envelope: the fear of Christ provided the motivation to be subordinate in the opening appeal of v. 21. Thus, vv. 21

310. The distributive phrase οἱ καθ' ἕνα ἕκαστος ('each one of you') individualizes the ὑμεῖς ('you'), while the imperative ἀγαπάτω ('let him love') is also singular. Cf. Hoehner.

311. Lincoln, 384.

312. In the New Testament household codes this is the only verse in which members are addressed in the singular.

313. The construction is ἵνα plus the subjunctive (ἵνα φοβῆται). This is best understood, not as denoting purpose or result, but as one of the few examples of an imperatival ἵνα in the New Testament (Mark 5:23; 2 Cor. 8:7; Gal. 2:10). The parallel with the imperative ἀγαπάτω in the first half of the verse indicates the independent force of the ἵνα-clause, and the subjunctive φοβῆται is the main verb. So, among more recent grammarians, C. F. D. Moule, *Idiom Book*, 144-45; K. L. McKay, *A New Syntax*, 82; S. E. Porter, *Idioms*, 223-24; and D. B. Wallace, *Greek Grammar*, 476-77.

and 33 are the frame for this important passage. Here, too, 'fear' is a better rendering than 'reverence' or 'respect'. But it is no slavish fear that is in view. Rather, the wife's fear of her husband, which reflects the fear of believers who are subordinate to those in authority over them (v. 21), recognizes his God-given position as head.[314] Hers is the answer of a free and responsible person (note the middle voice of the verb 'fear'), which is neither conditional nor due to her husband's merits or performance. Her response reflects not only what she does but also her attitude in doing it.

In line with his programmatic statement of v. 21 with its call for submission within divinely ordered relationships, Paul first turns to his exhortatory material on marriage and urges wives, as responsible moral agents, voluntarily to subordinate themselves to their husbands in everything. This submission is called for, not because it was conventional for wives in Graeco-Roman society, but because it was part and parcel of the way in which they were to serve their Lord (v. 22). The husband has authority over his wife just as Christ is head of the church, and the latter's submission to Christ is the model for her submission to her husband (vv. 23-24). The next, and major, part of Paul's marriage paraenesis is devoted to the role of husbands, in two stages (vv. 25-27, 28-32). In both sections husbands are exhorted to love their wives in the way that Christ loves the church. His authority is exercised in loving, self-giving sacrifice for the church; let theirs be the same for their wives. Christ's voluntary giving of himself in death for his people furnishes the basis for husbands to sacrifice their own interests for the welfare of others (v. 25), and it also provides their pattern for its goal in relation to their wives' welfare (vv. 26-27). In the second section, Paul stresses the obligation that husbands have to love their wives as their own bodies; after all, husband and wife are one person, so for the husband to love his wife is in fact to love himself. This reflects the model of Christ, whose love for the church can be seen as love for his own body (vv. 23, 30). The body of Christ of which they are members is also nourished and cherished by Christ, since he lovingly provides for its growth and sanctifies and cleanses it. As he draws the threads of the exhortation together Paul moves to the climax of the paragraph and cites the text that has provided the substructure of his thought throughout, namely, Genesis 2:24, and asserts that this Old Testament text is referring to the union of Christ and his church and so provides the warrant for asserting that believers are members of Christ's body. The Genesis text affirms that marriage makes husband and wife one body; it

314. B. Witherington, *Women*, 61, who follows E. Kähler; and G. W. Knight, 'Husbands and Wives', 175.

also explicates the union between Christ and the church. In a summarizing affirmation, Paul states that the union of Christ and the church which is reflected in a truly Christian marriage is 'a profound mystery'. Such a marriage bears living witness to the meaning of 'two becoming one', and within the wider context of Ephesians as a whole the union between Christian husbands and wives which is part of the unity between Christ and the church is thus a pledge of God's purposes of unity for the cosmos. In v. 33, at the conclusion of this section of exhortatory material, Paul rounds off his discussion with two summarizing exhortations in which the duties and responsibilities of husbands and wives are briefly restated.

In this distinctive teaching on Christian marriage, Paul has not only combined the theological and ethical concerns of the letter as a whole,[315] as he presents the typological relationship between Christ and the church and Christian husbands and wives. He also develops what he had written earlier in the epistle about Christ's relationship to the church, that is, as head he loves and gives himself for believers, brings the church into being through his saving death, nourishes and cherishes the church, sanctifies her, and is concerned for his bride's glory and purity (v. 27). His relationship to the church can now be described as a spiritual marriage union. Indeed, it was God's intention from the beginning when he instituted marriage to picture the relationship between Christ and his redeemed people.

315. Lincoln, 388.

Ephesians 6

b. Children and Parents, 6:1-4

¹Children, obey your parents in the Lord, for this is right. ²"Honor your father and mother" — which is the first commandment with a promise — ³"that it may go well with you and that you may enjoy long life on the earth." ⁴Fathers, do not exasperate your children; instead, bring them up in the training and instruction of the Lord.

Following the exhortations to wives and husbands, Paul now lays out the reciprocal duties of children and parents. This set of instructions in vv. 1-4, like the following set addressed to slaves and masters (vv. 5-9), is considerably shorter in form than the exhortatory material on marriage (5:22-33). Structurally, the opening admonitions addressed to 'children' (6:1) and 'slaves' (6:5) to 'obey', like the exhortation to wives voluntarily to 'submit' to their husbands (v. 22), are specific examples of the submission within divinely ordered relationships that is called for in the programmatic statement of v. 21, 'Submit to one another in the fear of Christ'. And this submission (which is expressed by the fifth result participle that is dependent on the imperative 'be filled', v. 18) concludes the list of responses that should characterize the Spirit-filled living of those in Christ (vv. 18-21). Christian children and slaves who heed this apostolic exhortation to obey, and wives who voluntarily submit to their husbands (v. 22), show that they are receptive to the Spirit's work of transforming them into the likeness of God and Christ. They demonstrate that they understand the Lord's will (v. 17), and provide concrete examples of a wise and godly lifestyle (v. 15).

In vv. 1-9, as Snodgrass has acutely observed, 'Paul applies his ethic

439

described in 4:25–5:21 to the household relations'.[1] So in v. 1 'right' picks up what is 'proper' (5:3), 'fitting' (5:4), or characterized by 'righteousness' (5:9), while at 6:4 Paul's exhortation to fathers not to 'exasperate' their children echoes his earlier concern about 'anger' in 4:26-27, 31.[2] The positive exhortation to bring up children in the training and admonition of the Lord recalls the earlier emphasis on learning the tradition of Christian teaching (4:20-21). In the instructions addressed to slaves and masters the key term 'good' appears (6:8), as in the earlier paragraph (4:28, 29), while the notion of a future judgment which has been mentioned with great solemnity at 5:5-6 becomes the motivation for slaves and masters to behave in a right manner (6:8, 9).

The structure of the two paragraphs (6:1-4, 5-9), which has close parallels with Colossians 3:20–4:1, is straightforward. As in the earlier part of the household code, the instructions to children and parents (vv. 1-4) are similarly presented. First, there is the address to the subordinate group, here the 'children',[3] which is then followed by an imperative 'obey your parents in the Lord' (v. 1). The motivation or warrant for this follows, 'for this is right' (v. 1b). Paul then cites the Old Testament (Exod. 20:4-6): this provides additional warrant for his injunction (vv. 2-3) and contains a further exhortation to the children. To this is added two further motivating clauses, 'that it may go well with you and that you may live long on the earth'. In the appeal to parents, 'fathers' are specifically addressed in a brief exhortation, which contains both negative ('do not make your children angry') and positive elements ('but bring them up in the training and admonition of the Lord', v. 4).

1 Paul passes from the reciprocal duties of wives and husbands to those of children and parents (vv. 1-4), and then to those of slaves and masters (vv. 5-9). It is obvious from these exhortations that the apostle thinks of local congregations as consisting of whole families who come together not only to praise God but also to hear his word addressed to them. As the household tables are read out, children, too, would learn of their own Christian duties as well as those of other family members.

The term 'children'[4] primarily denotes relationship rather than age, and could on occasion include adult sons and daughters, who were expected to honour their parents, especially fathers, who could maintain authority in the family even until death. Here the text has in view chil-

---

1. Snodgrass, 320.

2. παροργίζω ('exasperate') is cognate with ὀργή ('anger', v. 31), παροργισμός ('anger', v. 26), and ὀργίζομαι ('be angry', v. 26).

3. Again the nominative case with the definite article (τὰ τέκνα) is used for the vocative; cf. 5:22, 25; 6:4, 5, 9.

4. Gk. τέκνα.

dren who are in the process of learning and growing up (cf. v. 4). Presumably they were old enough to understand their relationship to their Lord and the commitments that followed from it. Although children's duty to obey their parents was taken for granted in the ancient world, disobedience to parents, according to the apostle, was indicative of Gentile depravity (Rom. 1:30), or a sign of the evil of the last days (2 Tim. 3:2).

Children are here addressed as responsible members of the congregations. They are to 'obey' both parents (though the corresponding exhortation in v. 4 is addressed to fathers only), and this is a further example of the submission within divinely ordered relationships that is expected in God's new society (v. 21). This injunction to children, like that to slaves, is put rather more strongly than the one to wives (note the discussion of 'submit' at vv. 22, 24): the verb is an active imperative of 'obey' and denotes absolute obedience. In Paul the term (and its cognate noun 'obedience') usually had reference to one's submission to Christ, the gospel, and apostolic teaching.[5] The obedience of Christian children to their parents is all of a piece with their submission to Christ: the additional motivating phrase, 'in the Lord',[6] is virtually synonymous with 'as to the Lord' or 'as to Christ' (cf. 5:22; 6:5)[7] and indicates that their obedience is part of their Christian discipleship. It is not rendered simply because of their parents' greater authority or status.

As with the wife's submission, so here Paul builds his instruction on a carefully laid foundation. In addition to his appeal to Christian commitment ('in the Lord'), the apostle provides several further grounds for Christian children obeying their parents. The first motivation[8] is that such obedience is 'right'. This expression[9] has generally been taken to signify that Paul is appealing to a general sense of what was fitting and right (cf. Phil. 4:8; Col. 4:1), to which he then links the Old Testament quo-

---

5. ὑπακούω ('obey'): Rom. 6:17; 10:16; Phil. 2:12; 2 Thess. 1:8; 3:14; cf. Matt. 8:27; Mark 1:27; 4:41; Heb. 5:9; 11:8. ὑπακοή ('obedience'): Rom. 1:5; 5:19; 6:16; 15:18; 16:19, 26; 2 Cor. 10:5, 6.

6. Although it has been thought that the phrase ἐν κυρίῳ ('in the Lord') was added by later scribes to conform to Eph. 5:22 and 6:5, or to assimilate to the wording of Col. 3:20, neither of these explanations is convincing. The external evidence for the longer reading is early, widespread, and strong (including 𝔓⁴⁶ ℵ A D¹ 33 1739 1881 vg sy co and the majority text). Accordingly, the reading with ἐν κυρίῳ ('in the Lord') is preferred as the original. Note the recent discussions in B. M. Metzger, *Textual Commentary,* 609; T. Moritz, *A Profound Mystery,* 153; and Hoehner.

7. The injunction does not mean that children are to obey only those parents who are 'in the Lord', i.e., Christian parents. The prepositional phrase is best connected with the verb. Children are to be obedient in the Lord (cf. Col. 3:20).

8. Expressed by means of γάρ ('for').

9. τοῦτο γάρ ἐστιν δίκαιον ('for this is right').

tation. According to Graeco-Roman ethics generally, obeying one's parents was the right and proper thing to do.[10] Indeed, most civilizations have regarded the recognition of parental authority as necessary to a stable society. However, it has recently been suggested that Ephesians may be combining, rather than distinguishing, 'what is *right* and and what is *demanded by the Law*'.[11] It may be better, therefore, to understand the clause 'for this is right' as an introduction to the Old Testament commandment (which follows in vv. 2, 3), rather than as a separate reason for the exhortation to obey one's parents.

2-3   Paul cites the fifth commandment of the Decalogue, 'Honour your father and mother', to support his exhortation to children to obey their parents. He quotes from the LXX of Exodus 20:12,[12] but, after citing these opening words, adds that this is the first commandment in the law that has a promise attached to it.

The prominent position in the Decalogue of the command to honour one's parents and the importance given to it elsewhere in the Old Testament[13] show that true obedience to this injunction arises out of

10. Note the survey of the relevant Graeco-Roman texts in Lincoln, 398-402. The Stoics, e.g., believed a son's obedience to his parents was self-evident. It was required by reason and part of 'the nature of things'.

11. T. Moritz, *A Profound Mystery,* 171-74, esp. 171. He argues that: (1) only four verses earlier (Eph. 5:31) a Pentateuchal quotation was introduced into the letter by means of a γάρ-construction; (2) the Old Testament itself regularly connects what is δίκαιος ('right') with keeping the law (cf. Ps. 37:28-31, 34; Prov. 28:1-12, etc.); and (3) the author of Ephesians is elsewhere at pains to link the ethical continuity between the people of God in the old covenant and those in the new (cf. Eph. 4:25-32). A similar connection between what is 'right' and the commandment was made by earlier writers; cf. Calvin, 212; Meyer, 313-14; Robinson, 127; and G. Schrenk, *TDNT* 2:188.

12. Scholars have differed as to which version of the fifth commandment is quoted, Exod. 20:12 or Deut. 5:16. Eph. 6:2, 3 is closer to the LXX of Exod. 20:12 (even though the Massoretic text of this verse omits the clause 'that it may go well with you') than it is to Deut. 5:16. Apart from his omission of the final words, 'the good [land] which the Lord your God is giving you', by which he 'universalizes' the promise, Paul makes only minor changes to the text. See the discussions in Lincoln, 396-97; T. Moritz, *A Profound Mystery,* 154-55; and Hoehner.

13. Within the Ten Commandments, and even within the whole Pentateuch, the command to honour one's parents has pride of place among the 'horizontal' commandments. It 'provides a hinge between the first four commandments to do with God's holiness and the remaining commandments in that the parents to be honoured stand in the place of God and mediate his will to the entire household' (T. Moritz, *A Profound Mystery,* 158). Elsewhere in the Old Testament such honouring of parents is mandated, while disobedience to or rebellion against parents is tantamount to disrespect for Yahweh. It is put on a par with treason and idol-worship. See, e.g., Exod. 21:15, 17; Lev. 19:3; 20:9; Deut. 21:18-21; 27:16. The importance of the parent-child relationship is so great that this imagery is applied to the relationship between Yahweh and his people (Deut. 1:31; 8:2-5; Prov. 3:11-12).

and reflects one's relationship with Yahweh. The exhortation to *honour* one's parents is a broad one and is parallelled by the expression to 'fear' one's mother and father (Lev. 19:3), a verb that is often reserved for the right response to God (Lev. 19:14, 32; Deut. 4:10, etc.). According to the Old Testament, honouring one's parents meant obeying them, while to dishonour them was disobedience. Both parents, not simply fathers, are to be honoured, according to this commandment. For children living at home ('being brought up', Eph. 6:4), this signified obedience to father and mother, while for adult children who had left home it involved not only a respectful attitude but also caring for them in their old age.[14] Significantly, in the context of Ephesians children's obedience to parents is part of their Christian commitment 'in the Lord'. It is an example of submission that arises out of a godly *fear* of Christ (5:21), and this submission is a distinguishing mark of those who are filled by God's Spirit (5:18).

But in what sense is Exodus 20:12 the first commandment with a promise? It has been claimed that the second commandment, which speaks of not making and worshipping idols (Exod. 20:4-6), includes a promise about God showing mercy to those who love him and keep his commandments. Accordingly, the exhortation to honour one's parents has been taken as the first with a promise in relation to other humans (if not the first absolutely: so Gnilka), or that it is 'first' in terms of its importance or difficulty (Schlier). But, strictly speaking, the statement in v. 6 that God shows his mercy to thousands who love him is not a promise attaching to the second commandment but a description of Yahweh's character: on the one hand, he is a jealous God who punishes disobedience (v. 5), and, on the other, he shows mercy to thousands of generations (v. 6). It is appropriate, therefore, to regard Exodus 20:12 as the first commandment with a promise attached to it. If it is objected that it is the only one within the Decalogue, then this is because Paul regards the ten words of Exodus 20:1-17 as the beginning of many commandments in the Torah.[15]

The commandment to honour one's parents appears on five other occasions in the New Testament,[16] but only here in Ephesians 6 is the attached promise also cited. In its original context of Exodus 20, the promise given to obedient children referred to a long and good life in

---

14. This is a concern expressed in both the Old Testament (esp. in Proverbs) and Judaism: T. Moritz, *A Profound Mystery*, 159-63, has drawn attention to this in the writings of Philo, Josephus, 4 Maccabees, and some of the rabbis.

15. So Lincoln, 404; T. Moritz, *A Profound Mystery*, 156; and Hoehner (for a full discussion), following earlier commentators.

16. Matt. 15:4; 19:19; Mark 7:10; 10:19; Luke 18:20.

the land (of Israel) which God was giving to his people. Significantly, when Paul 'reapplies' the commandment to his Christian readers, he omits any reference to the land of Israel and 'universalizes' the promise: 'that it may go well with you and that you may enjoy long life on the earth'.[17] Philo, too, whose writings provide close parallels to the New Testament household codes, omitted any mention of the land, but he spiritualized the reward and understood 'long life' in terms of immortality.[18] This meaning, however, is not intended in Ephesians,[19] and it is better to treat the words as speaking of this present earthly life.[20] Just as in the Old Testament children who honoured or obeyed their parents were blessed with the promise of a full life, so, too, in the age of the new covenant this general principle holds true for obedient Christian children. That there were exceptions in both Testaments[21] does not overthrow this divine promise, any more than our Lord's assurance of answered prayer, 'Ask and it shall be given you, seek and you shall find, knock and it shall be opened to you' (Matt. 7:7), is negated by lack of faith, an unwillingness to forgive, or the treating of prayer as an experiment. For the Christian son or daughter the promise attached to this commandment, which is transformed as it is taken up into 'the law of Christ',[22] is no longer limited geographically. Obedient sons and daughters are assured that it will go well with them and that they will enjoy long life on earth, wherever they may live.

To take this promise simply in a communal sense, indicating that a society where the elderly are cared for by their children is a stable one, is a 'modern reinterpretation', as Lincoln rightly observes. On the other hand, it is both unnecessary and incorrect to assert with Lincoln that these words could only have been penned by a Jewish Christian follower

17. By omitting the clause, 'which the LORD your God gives you' (LXX of Exod. 20:12), and universalizing the promise, Paul intends that it should have ongoing force for the readers of his letter. It is not simply to stress the importance of the commandment that the promise has been included (so rightly Lincoln, 405, against Schnackenburg, 261).

18. Philo, *De Specialibus Legibus* 2.262. Philo also spiritualized the expression, that 'it may be well with you', and understood it to refer to 'virtue'.

19. Although some commentators have taken Paul's words to point to the heavenly inheritance of 1:14; 3:6 (e.g., Schlier, 282).

20. The adjective μακροχρόνιος in the expression μακροχρόνιος ἐπὶ τῆς γῆς ('long life on the earth') denotes a 'long time' (BAGD, 488; Louw and Nida, §67.89), but not one of immortal duration. Furthermore, the apostle could easily have omitted the prepositional phrase ἐπὶ τῆς γῆς ('on the earth'), as he did with the words immediately following, if he had wished to focus on eternal life.

21. Caused during times of war, plagues, or disease, while disobedient children on occasion lived well and had a long life.

22. On the important but complex question of the relationship between the Torah and the law of Christ, see the discussion on 2:15.

of Paul since the idea of 'a longer period of the church's existence on earth' was alien to the apostle, who expected an imminent parousia.[23]

4 If Christian children are exhorted to render obedience to their parents, then the latter, especially fathers, are enjoined not to provoke their children to anger. Instead, they are to bring up their sons and daughters in the training and instruction of the Lord. Each group in the family, not just the subordinate ones, has obligations.[24] While children are to obey both parents (v. 1), fathers have a special responsibility towards them and are specifically addressed here.[25] In contemporary society the Roman *patria potestas*, that is, the authority of the head of the house, gave the father unlimited power over his children, and this law exercised a considerable degree of influence in the Hellenistic culture generally.[26] In Hellenistic Judaism severe punishment could be meted out to disobedient children.[27] This is not to suggest, however, that the Roman period evidences no examples of tender love in the home. But for all that, the relationship 'in the Lord' was new, and in this household table (cf. Col. 3:21) fathers are told nothing about their power of disposal over their children. Instead, their duties are spelled out.

Negatively, Paul exhorts fathers not to 'provoke their children to anger'.[28] In the earlier paraenesis the apostle had expressed his concern about anger among God's people (4:26-27, 31), urging his readers to deal with it promptly. If anger is prolonged, Satan can use it for his own ends, exploit-

23. Lincoln, 405, 406. Paul, along with the other apostles, hoped that the parousia would occur in his lifetime. But he assumed that various events had to happen before the day of the Lord would come (cf. 2 Thess. 2:5). Further, the New Testament idea of the imminency of the parousia had to do not so much with its nearness as that it could occur at any time, and therefore men and women needed to be ready for it. Note the discussion in H. Ridderbos, *Paul*, 487-92, cited approvingly by J. D. G. Dunn, *Theology*, 313.

24. The link between the two exhortations is made by the καί ('and') at the beginning of v. 4, καὶ οἱ πατέρες ('and fathers').

25. οἱ πατέρες can denote 'parents' in general (Heb. 11:23; cf. BAGD, 635), but there is a change of wording in v. 4 (from γονεῖς, 'parents', in v. 1), suggesting that οἱ πατέρες means 'fathers', while there is no mention of mothers after the explicit reference to them in the commandment of v. 2. Further, in the ancient world, in both Graeco-Roman and Jewish writings, fathers were responsible for the education of their children.

26. G. Schrenk, *TDNT* 5:950, 951.

27. Philo's demand for severity on the part of parents has been attributed to this influence: Philo, *Hypothetica* 7.2; *De Specialibus Legibus* 2.32; cf. Josephus, *Against Apion* 2.206, 217; *Antiquities* 4.264; note J. E. Crouch, *Origin*, 114-16.

28. The verb παροργίζω ('to cause to be provoked, to make angry'; Louw and Nida §88.177) occurs only here and at Rom. 10:19 (in relation to God making Israel angry), although the cognate noun παροργισμός ('anger') has appeared in the earlier paraenesis of Eph. 4:26. The present prohibition (μὴ παροργίζετε, 'do not provoke to anger') has the force of a general precept. This kind of prohibition makes no comment as to whether the action is going on or not (cf. D. B. Wallace, *Greek Grammar*, 724-25).

6:4

ing the strains that develop within the Christian community. Now specifically within the family, fathers are urged to avoid those attitudes, words, and actions which would provoke their children to anger (has the 'your' been inserted to remind fathers that the children belong to them?). Effectively, the apostle is ruling out 'excessively severe discipline, unreasonably harsh demands, abuse of authority, arbitrariness, unfairness, constant nagging and condemnation, subjecting a child to humiliation, and all forms of gross insensitivity to a child's needs and sensibilities'.[29] Behind this curbing of a father's authority is the clear recognition that children, while they are expected to obey their parents in the Lord, are persons in their own right who are not to be manipulated, exploited, or crushed.[30]

The apostle, however, does not stop with his negative instruction to fathers. Instead,[31] he complements it by positively urging them to bring up their children 'in the training and admonition of the Lord'. The verb 'nourish', which has already been used at 5:29 in relation to Christ's nourishing the church, is here employed rather more generally of rearing or bringing up children to maturity.[32] The two nouns 'training' and 'admonition' have sometimes been taken as expressing one concept.[33] Although often used together, the words probably have slightly different nuances here. The first word-group could refer to education or training in a comprehensive sense (Acts 7:22; 22:3; 2 Tim. 3:16; Tit. 2:12), or the more specific nuance of discipline or chastisement (1 Cor. 11:32; 2 Cor. 6:9; Heb. 12:5, 7, 8, 11). Here in Ephesians 6:4 the general sense appears to be in view, with the second term (1 Cor. 10:11; Tit. 3:10) pointing to 'the more specific aspect of this training that takes place through verbal admonition or correction'.[34]

This training and admonition which fathers are to give is further described as 'of the Lord'. The phrase could be understood as a subjective genitive, indicating that behind those who teach and discipline their children stands the Lord himself. Ultimately, the concern of parents is not simply that their sons and daughters will be obedient to their authority, but that through this godly training and admonition their children will come to know and obey the Lord himself. Theologically, this interpreta-

---

29. Lincoln, 406.
30. Stott, 246.
31. Note the strong adversative ἀλλά ('but'). Rather than provide the motive, as in Col. 3:21 ('lest they become discouraged'), Paul sets forth his positive exhortation.
32. Louw and Nida §35.51. Often this is done by 'providing for physical and psychological needs'.
33. So recently Snodgrass, 322. The two Greek words are παιδεία and νουθεσία respectively.
34. Lincoln, 407, following Gnilka, 298; and Schnackenburg, 263; cf. Hoehner.

tion makes good sense, and it is consistent with the Old Testament reference, 'the discipline of the LORD' (Prov. 3:11). But if 'training' is to be understood more broadly, then 'of the Lord' is probably a genitive of quality, indicating that the training and instruction is in the sphere of the Lord or has him as its reference point. In other words, it is truly Christian instruction. This interpretation fits with the earlier mention of learning Christ and being taught in him (4:20-21). Accordingly, learning Christ and being instructed in the truth that is in Jesus occur not only within the Christian community as a whole, but also and particularly within the family, coming from fathers whose lives are being shaped by this Christ-centred apostolic tradition.

In contrast to the norms of the day, Paul wants Christian fathers to be gentle, patient educators of their children, whose chief 'weapon' is Christian instruction focussed on loyalty to Christ as Lord. Christian fathers were to be different from those of their surrounding society. Presumably, when these words from the household table were read to them, they had already heard and remembered what Paul had written earlier in the letter, namely, that their fatherhood was derived from the 'one God and Father of us all' (3:14-15; 4:6), and that God's mighty work of reconciliation in his Son had been effected in order to form 'one multinational, multicultural family of God'. Let them as human fathers, then, 'care for their families as God the Father cares for his'.[35]

c. Slaves and Masters, 6:5-9

[5]Slaves, obey your earthly masters with respect and fear, and with sincerity of heart, just as you would obey Christ. [6]Obey them not only to win their favor when their eye is on you, but like slaves of Christ, doing the will of God from your heart. [7]Serve wholeheartedly, as if you were serving the Lord, not men, [8]because you know that the Lord will reward everyone for whatever good he does, whether he is slave or free. [9]And masters, treat your slaves in the same way. Do not threaten them, since you know that he who is both their Master and yours is in heaven, and there is no favoritism with him.

The third pairing in the household code is that of slaves and masters. Paul presents the reciprocal duties of each group. This set of instructions, like that addressed to children and parents (vv. 1-4), is shorter than the exhortatory material on marriage. The opening admonition, addressed to 'slaves' to 'obey' (v. 5), is a further example of submission

---

35. Stott, 245.

within the divinely ordered relationships that is called for in the programmatic statement, 'Submit to one another in the fear of Christ' (5:21). And this submission is part of the instruction about wise living (cf. 5:15-20), as well as a consequence of being filled by the Spirit (5:18).

The structure of 6:5-9 is similar to that of the earlier sections of the code, and it has close parallels to Colossians 3:22–4:1. The most variation occurs in the section where the imperative is amplified. The subordinate group, the slaves, is again addressed first (v. 5a). Then follows a fourfold description of the service to be rendered by them, each with an 'as' phrase: 'with fear and trembling in sincerity . . . *as* to Christ' (v. 5b), 'not serving the eye, *as* pleasing men' (v. 6a), '*as* slaves of Christ, doing the will of God . . .' (v. 6b), and 'wholeheartedly, *as* serving the Lord . . .' (v. 7). The motivation is introduced by 'knowing that' the Lord will judge everyone according to their works (v. 8). The instruction to masters is much shorter than that to slaves: after the customary address they are admonished to 'do the same' to their slaves. This is amplified by the clause 'abandoning the use of threats' (v. 9b), and the motivation is again introduced by 'knowing that' they share a common master in heaven who shows no favouritism (v. 9b).

In the list of household rules here and in Colossians (3:22-25) the admonitions to slaves are more extensive than those to masters, and they have special encouragements attaching to them. This may reflect the social structure of these churches (in the household tables of 1 Pet. 2:18–3:7 the admonitions to slaves have no correlative instructions to masters). In both Ephesians and Colossians the apostle is making no social comment on a prevailing custom. He is addressing himself to Christian readers. The issue was not that of an acceptance of an institution sanctioned by law and part of the fabric of Graeco-Roman society; nor was it a question of how to react to a demand for its abolition. Rather, it concerned the tension between the freedom given in Christ (cf. Col. 3:11) and the 'slavery' in which Christian slaves are to continue to serve their earthly masters (cf. 1 Cor. 7:21-24).

Even those commentators who have asserted most forcefully that Paul took over and Christianized material from Hellenism or Hellenistic Judaism in the household tables concede that these injunctions have been newly formulated as specifically Christian instruction.[36]

5 As in the two previous sections of the household table the subordinate group is addressed first. What is remarkable here is that Paul directly exhorts slaves in a manner that is unprecedented, for in traditional

---

36. So, e.g., Dibelius-Greeven, 47, state: 'The whole section [Col. 3:22-25, relating to slaves] — in contrast to the preceding — has been formed out of original Christian ideas' (cited by J. E. Crouch, *Origin*, 116-17).

discussions of household management the focus of attention was on how a master should rule his slaves. In the Pauline tables slaves, like wives and children, are treated as ethically responsible persons (cf. Col. 3:22-25). They are as much members of the Christian congregations to which this circular letter was sent as their masters. Furthermore, this section addressed to slaves makes specific what the apostle has already urged of all Christians, namely, that they are to please the Lord, do his will, and be submissive (5:10, 17, 21).[37]

Slaves are exhorted to *obey* their *earthly masters*. There is a deliberate wordplay on the Greek *kyrios* ('master, lord'), which is usually rendered 'Lord' with reference to Christ (v. 4) or God. The adjective *earthly* is not to be understood negatively or disparagingly; rather, it shows that these masters are lords within an earthly realm,[38] within the sphere of human relations, in contrast to the Lord, who is in heaven (v. 9). Ultimately, Christian *slaves* belong to the one Lord, Jesus Christ (v. 6), and their obedience to their earthly masters is all of a piece with their serving him (vv. 7, 8).

Yet for all that, their service to these masters is to be wholehearted and genuine. Positively, it is to be 'with fear and trembling, in singleness of heart, as you would obey Christ'. The motif of 'fear' has already appeared in the household table, serving as an envelope to frame the marriage paraenesis in 5:21, 33.[39] Here the twofold expression 'with fear and trembling',[40] which appears on occasion in the LXX almost as a stereotyped expression, usually refers to the fear of humans in the presence of God and his mighty acts.[41] Paul is the only New Testament writer to use this expression (1 Cor. 2:3; 2 Cor. 7:15; Phil. 2:12), and on each of these oc-

37. Snodgrass, 323.

38. κατὰ σάρκα means literally '[masters] according to the flesh', and stands in contrast to ἐν οὐρανοῖς ('in heaven', v. 9), which is predicated of that other Master, the Lord Jesus — hence the rendering 'earthly' (according to Bruce, 293, κατὰ σάρκα has particular reference to this present world-order).

39. Note also the references to the 'fear' of slaves, 1 Pet. 2:18; of wives, 3:2; and of citizens in relation to the state, Rom. 13:7.

40. μετὰ φόβου καὶ τρόμου ('with fear and trembling') indicates the manner in which slaves are to obey their masters.

41. So in the Song of Moses (Exod. 15:16) 'terror and dread' will grip the Canaanites as they learn of the Lord's mighty acts on behalf of his people Israel to deliver them out of Egypt and settle them in the land of their inheritance. At Isa. 19:16 'fear and trembling' describes the future reaction of the Egyptians to the hand of the Lord raised against them in judgment, while in Ps. 2:11 the appropriate response of the rebellious nations and rulers of the earth to the Lord's decisive action of installing his Son and of warning them of imminent destruction is to serve him 'with fear' and to 'rejoice with trembling'. Gen. 9:2 appears to be an exception, for the expression describes the fearful attitude of the animal creation to Noah and his sons. However, even here the dread is prompted by God's decree and results from his mighty interventions. For further details, see P. T. O'Brien, *Philippians*, 282-84.

casions, consistent with LXX usage, the phrase has to do with an attitude of due reverence and awe in the presence of God, a godly fear of the believer in view of the final day (see also on 5:21, 33). It is not the slavish terror of the unbeliever; nor is it an attitude oriented solely to humans.[42] Ephesians 6:5 urges slaves to obey their masters; that obedience should be rendered with reverence and awe in the presence of God and Christ (note the following phrase, [lit.] 'as to Christ', and Col. 3:22),[43] a godly fear in view of the final day (as the two earlier references indicate).

In the contemporary world masters controlled their slaves through fear, since it was believed that fear produced greater loyalty.[44] The perspective of Christian slaves, however, has changed. They have been delivered from the bondage of human intimidation, and now are 'enslaved' to the Lord Jesus Christ. Their service to their masters, then, is to be rendered out of reverence and awe for him. It will also be characterized by integrity and singleness of purpose — what is here called *sincerity of heart*. As the inner centre which determines attitudes and actions, the *heart* is marked by sincerity and purity of motive.[45] The Christian slave will not be guided by false, ulterior motives but will serve his or her master conscientiously and with sincerity. This kind of inner commitment can occur only as slaves recognize that in serving their masters they are rendering obedience to their heavenly Lord, Christ. The performance of their earthly tasks is related to his rule over their lives. Ultimately, then, the distinction between the sacred and the secular breaks down. Any and every task, however menial, falls within the sphere of his lordship and is done in order to please him. Their work is done 'as to Christ', their obedience is rendered 'as slaves of Christ' (v. 6), their wholehearted service is performed 'as to the Lord' (v. 7), because they know that they will be rewarded 'by the Lord' (v. 8) for every good that is done. These instructions provide a specific application of the apostle's comprehensive exhortation of Colossians 3:17, 'Whatever you do, in word or deed, do everything in the name of the Lord Jesus, giving thanks to God the Father through him'.

42. P. T. O'Brien, *Philippians*, 283-84.

43. Note especially Caird, 90; against Lincoln, 420.

44. K. R. Bradley, *Slaves and Masters in the Roman Empire: A Study in Social Control* (Oxford: Oxford University Press, 1987), 113-37. For further bibliographical details, see A. A. Rupprecht, *DPL*, 883; Best, 571; Hoehner; and M. J. Harris, *Slave of Christ* (Leicester: Apollos, forthcoming).

45. καρδία is 'the causative source of a person's psychological life in its various aspects, but with special emphasis upon thoughts' (so Louw and Nida §26.3), and comes to be rendered 'heart, inner self, mind'. ἐν ἁπλότητι τῆς καρδίας, 'with singleness of heart' (BAGD, 86), denotes the innermost part of a person as simple and sincere (cf. 1 Chron. 29:17; Wisdom 1:1; *T. Reuben* 4:1; *T. Simeon* 4:5; *T. Levi* 13:1; 2 Cor. 11:3; Col. 3:22). Cf. Louw and Nida §88.44.

6   The call for slaves to obey their masters with integrity is further elaborated, first negatively, 'not with eye-service as men-pleasers', then positively, 'but as slaves of Christ, doing the will of God wholeheartedly'. The term rendered 'eye-service', which is not attested before the Pauline writings (cf. Col. 3:22) and may have been coined by the apostle, signified that service performed only to attract attention, and which was not for its own sake or to please God or one's own conscience.[46] Those who act in such a way are 'men-pleasers' who seek to curry favour with their masters rather than please God.[47] Christian slaves, however, are enjoined not to obey their masters in this fashion.

Instead, they are to serve in the light of their ultimate allegiance to Christ, recognizing that they are his slaves who do the will of God gladly and wholeheartedly. For the second time in as many verses the christological motivation for their behaviour is to the fore. Twice more their relationship to Jesus' lordship will feature prominently in the apostle's appeal (vv. 7, 8). Those who are servants of their earthly masters are here designated 'slaves of Christ', a privileged designation. The manner in which their household service is rendered is described in terms of 'their doing the will of God from the heart'. The divine will has already been understood in terms of God's gracious saving plan in which it is his intention to sum up all things in Christ (1:5, 9, 11). In the latter half of Ephesians the divine will (5:17; 6:6) turns up in exhortatory contexts where the stress falls upon believers' responsibility to work out that will day by day (see on 5:17). Here God's will is to be performed by 'slaves of Christ' within the everyday life of the household. They are to serve their masters 'wholeheartedly' (lit. 'from the soul'), an expression which is virtually synonymous with 'sincerity of heart' in v. 5. It emphasizes an inner motivation that is unreserved and stands in direct contrast to the 'eye-service' of those who 'men-pleasers'.

7   Paul reiterates several of his earlier points (in vv. 5, 6)[48] as he urges Christian slaves to obey their masters: they are to do so wholeheartedly and enthusiastically, showing that ultimately they are serving

---

46. ὀφθαλμοδουλία means 'eye-service, to serve in order to call attention to oneself' (so Louw and Nida §35.29; cf. BAGD, 599). Note Theodoret's comment on Eph. 6:6, 7, cited by E. Lohse, *Colossians and Philemon*, 160: 'He calls eyeservice that type of service which does not issue from a sincere heart, but is content in mere external appearance'.

47. The only other occurrences of this word (ἀνθρωπάρεσκοι) before the New Testament are Ps. 53:5[LXX 52:6]; *Psalms of Solomon* 4:7, 8, 19. Louw and Nida §215.98 suggest that the term pertains to 'causing people to be pleased, with the implication of being in contrast to God or at the sacrifice of some principle'. The word may sometimes be rendered 'those who are just trying to make people like them'.

48. By means of the participial clause μετ' εὐνοίας δουλεύοντες ('serving wholeheartedly').

not human lords but their one Lord who is in heaven. The term which specifies the manner in which they are to serve appears only here in the New Testament and signifies 'zeal, eagerness, wholeheartedness'.[49] Clearly their enthusiastic service will benefit their masters. But the slaves are reminded of a significant reason or motivation for their conduct:[50] they are serving the Lord and not simply humans.[51] As they engage in wholehearted work for their masters, so in that very action they honour and glorify their heavenly Lord.

8 Finally, the apostle's admonition to obedience with its related appeals is grounded in the knowledge that slaves will be rewarded by their heavenly Lord at the final judgment for the good that they do.[52] Once again in exhortatory material within Ephesians the future perspective, in this case the last day, provides a motivation for appropriate living in the present (cf. 5:5, 6). The use of the verb 'knowing' suggests that the apostle is recalling a pattern of teaching familiar to Christians and to which he can now appeal.

The content of what they have been taught is that their heavenly Lord will reward them for the good that each one does. No doubt many slaves had performed good deeds that were not noticed by their masters and so not appropriately rewarded by them.[53] As a result, Christian slaves, like others, might have gone out of their way to ensure that any service they performed caught their masters' attention. But they did not need to respond in this way. Nothing escapes their heavenly Master's gaze. However they may be treated by their earthly 'lords', they still have *a* Lord[54] who at

49. Louw and Nida §25.72.

50. ὡς ('as') often appears with a participle to indicate the reason or motivation for something happening; but the New Testament, like classical Greek, in abbreviated expressions will omit the participle when it is clear from the context what is meant: e.g., 2 Thess. 2:2; see A. T. Robertson, *Grammar*, 1140; BDF §425(4).

51. Note the contrast between τῷ κυρίῳ ('Lord') and οὐκ ἀνθρώποις ('not humans').

52. So Lincoln, 422, 425; and Hoehner, who claims that the participle εἰδότες ('knowing') is causal and dependent on the main verb ὑπακούετε ('obey'). The parallel εἰδότες ('knowing') in v. 9 is similar. Cf. Snodgrass, 324, who speaks of the '*primary* motivation for this ethic . . . [being] the final judgment' (emphasis added).

53. In some contemporary discussions of household management it was recommended that slaves be motivated by various rewards such as food, clothing, and other benefits (Xenophon, *Oeconomicus* 13.9-12; see Lincoln, 422). Some masters had even promised slaves their freedom but had not delivered on these promises (Tacitus, *Annals* 14.42).

54. παρὰ κυρίου (lit. 'from a Lord'). In relation to the parallel passage in Col. 3:22, J. B. Lightfoot, *Saint Paul's Epistles to the Colossians and to Philemon* (London: Macmillan, 1890), 226, claimed that the absence of the definite article in the phrase ἀπὸ κυρίου ('from a Lord') was remarkable, and he tried to catch the significance of this omission as follows: 'However you may be treated by your earthly masters, you still have *a* Master . . .'.

the end of the day can be trusted to reward[55] them. He notices the good deeds of *each and every one* of them — note the stress on 'each one' — so that none will miss out on being rewarded for *any* good[56] that has been done. There is no promise here of an immediate reward or manumission from slavery; rather, the assurance that when they, along with all other believers, stand before the judgment seat of Christ, they will be rewarded for the good deeds they have done (2 Cor. 5:10).

Consistent with the rest of the New Testament (indeed, the whole Bible), Paul assumes that judgment is according to works (cf. Rom. 2:6). There is clearly a connection between good deeds and reward, although the content of the reward is not spelled out here. In Colossians 3:24, the parallel passage, the reward is identified with the eternal inheritance that has been prepared for believers (cf. Col. 1:5, 12, 27; 3:1-4).[57] Further, the focus of Colossians 3:24-25 is negative, with the passage functioning as a threat: 'for the wrongdoer will be paid back for the wrong he has done'. In Ephesians, where the motif of inheritance has figured rather prominently (1:14, 18; 5:5), it is not identified with the reward as in Colossians. On the other hand, the thrust in Ephesians is positive as the apostle seeks to encourage slaves within the Christian household.

Not only slaves but also freedpersons and masters will stand before Christ at the judgment and receive recompense for the deeds they have done. The additional words, 'whether slave or free', show that all will be similarly rewarded. Social status at this point is immaterial, and none will receive special treatment or favouritism, for all are judged by the same criterion — that of works (cf. Rom. 2:6). Whatever right and proper distinctions were maintained between slaves and masters, or any other groupings within the Christian household, in the light of the coming judgment ultimately all differences are unimportant (cf. Gal. 3:28; Col. 3:11; and 1 Cor. 12:13).

9 Consistent with the pattern in this household table Paul now addresses those in authority, in this case masters, and exhorts them in their responsibilities to their slaves. Once again each group within the house-

---

55. The verb κομίζομαι, which can signify 'to get back, recover' (Matt. 25:27; Heb. 11:19), frequently means 'receive, obtain' (2 Cor. 5:10; Col. 3:25; Heb. 10:36; 11:13, 39; 1 Pet. 1:9; 5:4; 2 Pet. 2:13). It is the latter meaning which best suits this context, hence the translation 'receive recompense' (BAGD, 442-43; Louw and Nida §57.126, 136).

56. The expression τι ἀγαθόν ('any good') is comprehensive. The τοῦτο ('this') refers back to τι ἀγαθόν ('any good') and is in an emphatic position: it is 'this' good that will be noticed and rewarded.

57. In using apparently mercenary terms such as 'reward' and 'punishment' in Col. 3:24, the apostle is speaking of our relationship with God: reward is here described in terms of an inheritance that relates to life in the presence of God, while punishment is deprivation of his fellowship and exclusion from his presence.

hold has obligations, not just the subordinate members. Here the connection between the exhortation to slaves and that to masters is explicitly made,[58] since Paul intends to underscore the reciprocal, though not symmetrical,[59] relationships between the two groups.

In what is a shocking exhortation to slave owners in the first-century Graeco-Roman world, the apostle admonishes masters: *treat your slaves in the same way.* According to a proverbial statement known to Seneca, 'all slaves are enemies', while many masters were tyrants and abusive.[60] In order to deal with their slaves, owners were known to threaten beatings, sexual harassment, or selling male slaves away from the households with the result that they would be parted forever from their loved ones.[61] Paul's cryptic exhortation is outrageous. It does not mean, however, that masters are to serve their slaves, as Chrysostom thought.[62] Nor does it refer simply to their doing good, as in v. 8. More likely it points to their *attitudes and actions,* which, like those of slaves, are to be *governed* by their relationship to their heavenly Lord.[63] An outcome of this will be that masters will abandon the use of threats against[64] their slaves. This is not to suggest that slaves could not be warned of punishment if they did wrong. Rather, the clause rejects all forms of manipulating, demeaning, or terrifying slaves by threats.[65] In the immediate context, slaves have already been instructed to show respect, sincerity of heart, and goodwill; now masters are urged to treat them in a similar manner.

The warrant for Paul's appeals to masters is twofold, as once again he reminds his readers of a pattern of teaching familiar to them and to

---

58. First, the concluding words of v. 8, which speak of the Lord rewarding each one who does good, εἴτε δοῦλος εἴτε ἐλεύθερος ('whether slave or free'), provide a transition to the advice given to masters in v. 9. Then, as in v. 4, the address to masters is linked by καί ('and', v. 9) to that of slaves. Finally, masters are called to adopt a similar attitude, which is to be expressed in appropriate actions, to their slaves: τὰ αὐτὰ ποιεῖτε πρὸς αὐτούς ('do the same things to them').

59. Although masters are urged to 'do the same to them', i.e., to have corresponding attitudes and actions to those required of slaves, they are *not* admonished to 'obey' (v. 5) or 'serve' (v. 7) their slaves.

60. Seneca, *Epistulae Morales* 47.5.

61. T. Wiedemann, *Greek and Roman Slavery* (London: Croom Helm, 1981), 27.

62. Chrysostom thought the exhortation referred to δουλεύοντες ('serving as slaves'); *Homily* 22; 6:9 (Migne, *Patrologia Graeca* 62:157), cited by Hoehner.

63. Lincoln, 423, 425.

64. The participial clause ἀνιέντες τὴν ἀπειλήν ('abandoning the use of threats') amplifies the preceding τὰ αὐτὰ ποιεῖτε πρὸς αὐτούς ('do the same thing to them'). Here the verb ἀφίημι, when used with ἀπειλή ('threat[s]'; Louw and Nida §33.291) means to 'give up, cease, stop' (BAGD, 69; Louw and Nida §68.43).

65. Cf. Lincoln, 425.

which he can appeal.[66] Masters are motivated to treat their slaves *in the same way* because: (1) both the slaves' Master and their own Master is in heaven, and both are accountable to him. Christian slaves have already been exhorted to render service to their earthly masters as to the Lord Jesus. Now Christian masters are reminded that they, too, are slaves, indeed *fellow*-slaves of the same Lord as their own servants. Masters, too, will render an account on the final day to this heavenly Lord for all that they have done, not least as to how they have treated their slaves (cf. Col. 4:1).

(2) The Lord to whom slaves and masters are accountable is completely impartial. At the judgment bar[67] of God there is no 'partiality'[68] or 'bias' with him. The higher social status that masters have gives them no advantage whatever. He does not allow himself to be influenced by appearances. No 'special deals' can be made with him. Let masters, then, treat their slaves in the light of the fact that they are fellow-servants of this heavenly Lord.

As in the earlier sections of the household table (5:22–6:4), which calls for submission by believers within divinely ordered relationships (5:21) and is evidence of their being filled by God's Spirit (v. 18) and walking in wisdom (v. 15), so here in the last paragraph (6:5-9) the subordinate group is addressed first. In an unprecedented fashion, slaves are treated as ethically responsible persons (cf. Col. 3:22-25) who like their masters are members of the body of Christ. They are urged to obey them, recognizing that in serving their earthly masters they are in fact rendering service to their heavenly Lord. Ultimately, however, their responsibility is to him. Accordingly, they are to see themselves as Christ's slaves

66. The participle εἰδότες ('knowing') is causal and dependent on the main verb ποιεῖτε ('do'); note the similar construction in v. 8. The content of what they had been taught and which should now motivate Christian masters to heed the apostolic appeals is expressed by the two clauses following εἰδότες ὅτι ('knowing that'): (1) καὶ αὐτῶν καὶ ὑμῶν ὁ κύριος κτλ. ('he who is both their Master and yours . . .'), and (2) καὶ προσωπολημψία οὐκ ἔστιν κτλ. ('there is no favouritism . . .').

67. Although W. Schrage, 'Zur Ethik', 9-10, thinks that this does not refer to the future judgment of the coming Lord, the context of v. 8, which speaks of receiving recompense in the future, strongly suggests that the judgment of v. 9 is set within the same time frame. In the Old Testament impartiality in judgment is attributed to God; here and in Col. 3:25 this is predicated of Christ as Lord.

68. προσωπολημψία ('partiality'), while occurring first in the New Testament (cf. Rom. 2:11; Eph. 6:9; Col. 3:25; Jas. 2:1), may already have been in use in Hellenistic Judaism. It was formed from the Hebraism meaning 'to raise the face', an expression that is found frequently in the Old Testament to denote respect of persons: Lev. 19:15; Deut. 1:27; 16:19; cf. E. Lohse, *TDNT* 6:779-80. The word group signified making 'unjust distinctions between people by treating one person better than another', hence 'to show favoritism, to be partial, partiality'; so Louw and Nida §88.238.

whose aim is to please him by doing God's will wholeheatedly and unreservedly. Their service is to be enthusiastic and genuine, and without that superficial working, so prevalent in the contemporary world, that was designed to attract their masters' attention and curry favour with them. The good that they render will be recompensed, not by earthly masters with human praise, material benefits, or even manumission,[69] but by the Master who will reward them at the final judgment. In a surprising exhortation to slave owners Paul admonishes them to treat their slaves in the same way — in other words, their attitudes and actions, like those of their slaves, are to be determined by their relationship to the same heavenly Lord.

Paul's admonitions remain general. Clearly, attitudes and motivation are important. What does stand out, however, in this section of the household table as being highly significant (apart from the fact that slaves are addressed as responsible believers), are the references to Christ as Lord (note the Colossians parallel).[70] These slaves are 'slaves of Christ', who are to obey him as Lord (vv. 5, 7). Their service is rendered ultimately to him who knows both the work that they do and their motivation in doing it. They are to do the will of God from the heart (v. 6), seeking to please their Lord, for they know that he will reward them on the final day for all the good that they have done (v. 8). Similarly, masters are responsible to one who is not only their heavenly Lord but also the Lord and Master of their slaves. All are ultimately accountable to him. He dwells in heaven where God is, and shows no favouritism, but he will reward godly and obedient masters on the final day for the good they have done to their slaves (vv. 8, 9). Christ's lordship over the lives of both slaves and masters has the effect of changing the dynamic of the relationship between them and lifting their mutual attitudes and behaviour to a new plane.

F. Spiritual Warfare, 6:10-20

> [10]*Finally, be strong in the Lord and in his mighty power.* [11]*Put on the full armor of God so that you can take your stand against the devil's schemes.* [12]*For our struggle is not against flesh and blood, but against the rulers, against the authorities, against the powers of this dark world and against the spiritual forces of evil in the heavenly realms.* [13]*Therefore put on the full armor of God, so that when the day of evil comes, you may be able to stand your ground, and after you have done everything, to stand.*

69. Cf. Lincoln, 425.
70. Cf. P. T. O'Brien, *Colossians, Philemon,* 219.

14Stand firm then, with the belt of truth buckled around your waist, with the breastplate of righteousness in place, 15and with your feet fitted with the readiness that comes from the gospel of peace. 16In addition to all this, take up the shield of faith, with which you can extinguish all the flaming arrows of the evil one. 17Take the helmet of salvation and the sword of the Spirit, which is the word of God. 18And pray in the Spirit on all occasions with all kinds of prayers and requests. With this in mind, be alert and always keep on praying for all the saints. 19Pray also for me, that whenever I open my mouth, words may be given me so that I will fearlessly make known the mystery of the gospel, 20for which I am an ambassador in chains. Pray that I may declare it fearlessly, as I should.

This final section of the exhortatory material of Ephesians, in which the readers are urged to be strong in the Lord and to put on God's mighty armour as they engage in a spiritual warfare with the powers of evil, occupies a highly significant place in the epistle. The paragraph not only ends the paraenetic material begun in 4:1, but it also serves as the climax of the letter as a whole,[71] bringing it to a conclusion. The paragraph is neither 'an irrelevant appendix' to Ephesians nor 'a parenthetical aside' within it but a crucial element to which the rest of the epistle has been pointing.[72]

Here the apostle looks at the Christian's responsibility of living in the world from a broader, that is, cosmic perspective. The moral issues with which he deals are not simply matters of personal preference, as many within our contemporary and postmodern world contend. On the contrary, they are essential elements in a larger struggle between the forces of good and evil.[73] Throughout this paragraph on spiritual warfare Paul's sustained imagery is drawn from the prophecy of Isaiah, which describes the armour of Yahweh and his Messiah (11:4-5; 59:17; cf. 49:2; 52:7). The Isaianic references depict the Lord of hosts as a warrior dressed for battle as he goes forth to vindicate his people. The 'full armour of God' which the readers are urged to put on as they engage in a deadly spiritual warfare (v. 11) is Yahweh's own armour, which he and his Messiah have worn and which is now provided for his people as they engage in battle (see the following exegesis).

71. So, most recently, Snodgrass, 334-35; T. Moritz, *A Profound Mystery,* 181-83; and T. Y. Neufeld, *Put On the Armour of God,* 110-11.

72. So Arnold, 103, 105. G. D. Fee, *God's Empowering Presence,* 723, even suggests that in 'this final section of the letter we also most likely are coming to Paul's primary concern for his recipients'. His placing this material 'in the emphatic final position suggests that he has been intentionally building the letter toward this climax right along'.

73. S. H. T. Page, *Powers,* 248.

From 4:1 on the readers have been urged to 'live' worthily of the high calling which they have received from God. Five times in the paraenetic material of chapters 4–6 the key verb *peripateō* ('walk, live') has been used to point to the new and distinctive lifestyle the readers are now to adopt (4:1, 17; 5:2, 8, 15). The last of these focusses on Spirit-filled Christians *living* wisely in their relationships within the family (5:21–6:9). Now the paraenesis is drawn to a conclusion as Paul sets forth an effective summary, reinforces his earlier exhortations,[74] and challenges his readers to action. Paul uses battle imagery as he calls them to stand firm in the midst of the spiritual warfare that is already in progress.

At the same time, a number of concerns within the whole letter are brought back to the readers' attention in an emphatic way. The recapitulation of various issues, themes, and terminology from the earlier sections of the letter is very impressive, as several recent writers have shown.[75] For example, the imperative to be strong in the Lord (6:10) brings to mind God's power, which was manifested in Christ's resurrection and exaltation, and is now available to believers (1:19-20). The imperative regarding divine empowering also has links with believers' strengthening through the Spirit (3:16) and the praise that God's power is at work among them (3:20). Often the connections between motifs in Ephesians 1–3 and 6:10-20 highlight the tension between what has already been achieved in Christ, so that believers now experience the life of the 'new age', and this present evil age where the powers are active and in which believers now live. Christ has 'already' triumphed over the powers (1:21; 3:10). But they still exist, and are active in the disobedient (2:2). Through their prince they seek to gain a base of operations against believers (4:27). These evil supernatural forces listed in 6:12 are the principalities and authorities that have been mentioned in 1:21 and 3:10; the sphere in which they function is the heavenly realm (6:12; 3:10), and the present age over which they hold sway is described in terms of darkness (6:12) or evil days (5:16). Christ's triumph over the powers has 'already' occurred (1:21), so believers no longer live in fear of them. But the fruits

---

74. R. A. Wild, 'The Warrior and the Prisoner: Some Reflections on Ephesians 6:10-20', *CBQ* 46 (1984), 284-98, esp. 298, observed that the five imperatives in this concluding paragraph, in effect, reiterate the thirty-one imperatives of 4:1–6:9. Note also S. H. T. Page, *Powers*, 247.

75. See the discussions of Arnold, 103-22; Lincoln, 432-41; and T. Moritz, *A Profound Mystery*, 181-83; cf. Snodgrass, 334-36. Moritz, who has drawn attention to a wide range of connections between all six chapters of the letter and 6:10-20, notes the cluster of important theological terms (truth, righteousness, faith, word, and Spirit) which link 1:13 with 6:14-17 (where the Old Testament weapon imagery appears). He concludes that 6:10-20 'should be interpreted with the entire epistle in view' (182).

of that victory have 'not yet' been fully realized, so Christians must be aware of the conflict and be equipped with divine power to stand against them.[76]

The realities closely connected with the pieces of armour in 6:14-17 have already featured prominently in the earlier chapters of the epistle. So truth (1:13; 4:15, 21, 24, 25; 5:9), righteousness (4:24; 5:9), peace (1:2; esp. 2:14-18; 4:3; cf. 6:23), the gospel (1:13; 3:6; cf. 2:17; 3:8) or word of God (1:13; 5:26), salvation (1:13; 2:5, 8; 5:23), and faith (1:1, 13, 15, 19; 2:8; 3:12, 17; 4:5, 13) are important theological themes which are recapitulated in relation to the weaponry believers are to employ in their spiritual warfare. In addition, the summons to prayer in 6:16-18 picks up terminology already used earlier in the letter: 1:16; 'all the saints' (3:18); the 'mystery' (1:9; 3:3, 4, 9; 5:32), 'boldness' (3:12), and Paul's imprisonment (3:1; 4:1).[77]

Several recent writers have noticed the number of terminological and conceptual links between the paragraph on spiritual warfare and the introductory eulogy and thanksgiving paragraph (with its thanksgiving and intercession) in chapter 1. There are conceptual and thematic links between the beginning and end of the letter,[78] between what God has been praised and petitioned for (1:3-14, 16-23) and what is to be preserved by Christians against evil spiritual forces led by the evil one.

What, then, are we to make of the interconnections between Ephesians 6:10-20 and the earlier paraenesis (4:1–6:9) together with chapters 1–6 overall? Rhetorical criticism in recent New Testament studies has identified this highly charged paragraph as the *peroratio*, the final section of a speech that sought to sum up the main themes and to arouse the audience to action.[79] But there are insurmountable difficulties with this rhetorical-critical approach to classifying Paul's letters,[80] even if there are functional correspondences between parts of an oration and those of an epistle. The purpose of this significant passage is 'to expand and reinforce, to recapitulate and arouse to action',[81] although it is inappropriate to classify it in rhetorical categories as a *peroratio*. Any good writing aims

76. Note especially the treatment of Lincoln, 438-39; cf. G. D. Fee, *God's Empowering Presence*, 724.

77. Lincoln, 439. See also T. Moritz, *A Profound Mystery*, 182, and the exegesis below.

78. This feature has been noted in several of Paul's letters. Cf., e.g., the obvious connections between the introductory thanksgiving of Phil. 1:3-11 and 4:10-20, in which the two paragraphs form an *inclusio* to the whole letter (P. T. O'Brien, *Philippians*, 513-14).

79. So A. T. Lincoln, '"Stand, Therefore . . .": Ephesians 6:10-20 as *Peroratio*', *BibInt* 3 (1995), 99-114; cf. T. Y. Neufeld, *Put On the Armour of God*, 110-11; C. B. Kittredge, *Community and Authority*, 144-45. Note the criticisms of this in relation to v. 19.

80. See the Introduction, 'Ephesians and Rhetoric', 73-82.

81. Snodgrass, 335.

at concluding with a clinching argument that seeks to motivate the readers, and Ephesians does this powerfully.

The paragraph falls into three sections: (a) vv. 10-13 admonish the readers to be strong in the Lord and to put on the armour of God in their warfare against evil supernatural powers. (b) In vv. 14-17 the imperative, *Stand firm,* is followed by a listing of the pieces of armour to be put on. (c) Finally, vv. 18-20 focus on the need for constant prayer and watchfulness for all believers, and especially for the apostle himself in prison, that he might fearlessly proclaim the mystery.

1. Be Strong in the Lord, 6:10-13

10 Having concluded his instructions to the various groups within the Christian household (5:21–6:9), Paul now addresses *all* his readers and exhorts them to be strong in the Lord and in his mighty power. The reason is that they are engaged in an ongoing spiritual battle with the powers of darkness, as the following verses show. The transition from the household table to this concluding section of exhortatory material (6:10-20) is made through 'finally,'[82] which introduces v. 10. This opening exhortation introduces the theme and sets the tone for the rest of the passage.

The first imperative, 'be strong', is best understood as a passive,[83] meaning 'be made strong, be strengthened'.[84] This fits with the corre-

---

82. τοῦ λοιποῦ often has temporal force ('from now on, in the future'; cf. Gal. 6:17), and some interpreters opt for this meaning here on the grounds that it is strength for a future conflict that is in view. But the context makes it clear that the battle is taking place now and that divine strength is needed in the present (against T. Y. Neufeld, *Put On the Armour of God,* 109-10, whose arguments for the temporal, 'henceforth', are unconvincing). τοῦ λοιποῦ is synonymous with the more frequent accusative τὸ λοιπόν ('finally') and indicates that 6:10-20 is the last in a chain of exhortations. Cf. BAGD, 480.

83. Gk. ἐνδυναμοῦσθε. Rather than a middle voice, as Bruce, 403; S. E. Porter, *Verbal Aspect,* 359; and T. Y. Neufeld, *Put On the Armour of God,* 112, interpret it. In favour of the passive, see BAGD, 263; Lincoln, 441; and Hoehner, among others. Cf. the same construction in 2 Tim. 2:1, 'take strength (ἐνδυναμοῦ) from the grace of God which is ours in Christ Jesus'.

84. The plural imperative ἐνδυναμοῦσθε ('be made strong') has been taken by T. Y. Neufeld, *Put On the Armour of God,* 111, as addressed to the community corporately. He comments: the 'whole community is called to be empowered', adding that this exhortation 'should not be understood, as it usually is, in individualistic terms'. But Neufeld has presented a false dichotomy. The plural here (as often elsewhere in Ephesians) signifies *common* action: believers *both* individually *and* corporately are to heed the apostolic injunction. As they engage in a deadly spiritual warfare with the powers of evil they are not only to be empowered themselves so as to stand firm; they are also to encourage their fellow-believers to do likewise, so that *together as one* they will resist the devil.

sponding passive in the prayer of 3:16, 'that you may *be strengthened* with power through his Spirit', and indicates that believers do not empower themselves, even if they are to heed the apostolic injunction and lay hold of the divine resources available to them. Rather, their strengthening comes from an external source, which the following phrase indicates is *the Lord* Jesus. He is the person with whom believers have been brought into union (cf. 2:21; 4:1, 17; 5:8; 6:1, 21), and thus the sphere in whom they now live their Christian lives and from whom they derive their strength. They no longer fall under the tyranny of the prince of the power of the air (2:2), but have come under Christ's loving rule and headship. For this reason they can be urged to 'be strengthened in him': he supplies all they need in their spiritual warfare.

The call to be 'strong' in the midst of a battle has a number of Old Testament precedents, the most notable of which is Joshua, who was urged to 'be strong and of good courage' (Josh. 1:6, 7, 9; cf. Deut. 31:6, 7, 23). In a critical situation David, too, 'found strength *in the* LORD' (1 Sam. 30:6), while later God says of his people gathered home from exile, 'I will make them strong *in the* LORD' (Zech. 10:12).[85] The latter examples mention explicitly that the external source of this empowering is 'the Lord', and in Ephesians this refers to the Lord *Jesus*.

The source of this strengthening is described more specifically as *in his mighty power*.[86] This dynamic phrase[87] has already been used in relation to God's all-powerful strength which raised Christ from the dead and exalted him to the place of honour, far above all rule and authority (1:19-20). The apostle prayed that his readers might understand and experience the extraordinary power of God working on their behalf (1:19). Now he calls upon them to appropriate this might, which in the case of Jesus had already proven itself sufficient to overcome powerful, diabolical opposition.

11 Paul now explains why believers need to be strong in the Lord, and how his mighty power is to be appropriated: they are engaged in a

---

85. Bruce, 403.

86. The καί ('and') in the expression καὶ ἐν τῷ κράτει τῆς ἰσχύος αὐτοῦ ('and in his mighty power') is epexegetical, explaining what it means to be strengthened in the Lord.

87. It is a genitive construction at 1:19 (the full phrase is κατὰ τὴν ἐνέργειαν τοῦ κράτους τῆς ἰσχύος αὐτοῦ, 'according to the working of *his mighty strength*') and a prepositional phrase with ἐν plus the dative at 6:10. Arnold, 108, following R. A. Wild, 'The Warrior', 287, suggests that the author may have been thinking of Isa. 40:26 as he penned Eph. 6:10, since the terms κράτος and ἰσχύος are linked in this Old Testament passage, and he is significantly indebted to Isaiah for many of his terms and metaphors, not least with reference to the divine armour (see below).

deadly spiritual warfare on the side of God against the devil, and if they are to prevail they must put on God's full armour.

Syntactically,[88] the imperative *put on the full armour of God*[89] explains how the admonition of v. 10, *Be strong in the Lord,* is to be carried out.[90] It is only by donning the divine panoply that believers can be properly equipped against the devil's attacks. This exhortation to put on God's armour recalls the earlier instruction about 'putting on the new self', which was *created to be like God in true righteousness and holiness* (4:24). This connection fits the flow of the letter's argument: from 4:25 on in the paraenetic material Paul has elaborated on what is involved in putting off the old humanity. Now, by detailing the armour to be worn, he is developing the idea of putting on the new.[91] Essentially, then, to 'put on the new self' is the same as donning the armour of God.

The expression 'full armour' referred to 'a complete set of instruments used in defensive or offensive warfare'[92] which was worn by a heavily armed foot soldier. Although not all the weapons are mentioned in the subsequent verses, the emphasis here is on donning the 'whole armour' in order to be protected fully in this spiritual warfare. Paul is fond of the simpler term 'weapons' (Rom. 6:13; 13:12; 2 Cor. 6:7; 10:4). His use of the fuller expression here rendered 'whole armour' may be 'explained as a collective for representing the substantial number of arms listed in the context', and as highlighting 'the danger and seriousness of the threat facing the readers and therefore more strongly emphasiz[ing] the importance of total dependence on God's strength'.[93]

88. Although there is no conjunction linking v. 11 with v. 10, the juxtaposition of the two synonymous verbs ἐνδυναμοῦσθε and ἐνδύσασθε, which mean 'put on', shows that the second explicates the first (cf. v. 13). Further, the might of the Lord (v. 10) is parallel with the armour of God (v. 11). So most writers, including Arnold, 109; and T. Y. Neufeld, *Put On the Armour of God,* 118.

89. S. E. Porter, *Verbal Aspect,* 359, helpfully notes that the first exhortation of the paragraph, ἐνδυναμοῦσθε (v. 10), is a present imperative *(Be strong in the Lord).* Paul then specifies what this entails by a series of aorists: two imperatives, ἐνδύσασθε ('put on') the armour of God (v. 11) and ἀναλάβετε ('take up') the armour of God (v. 13), which are followed by four aorist participles: the belt of truth περιζωσάμενοι ('fastened', v. 14), the breastplate of righteousness ἐνδυσάμενοι ('put on', v. 14), your feet ὑποδησάμενοι ('fitted') with readiness (v. 15), and ἀναλαβόντες ('taking up') the shield of faith, and finally an aorist imperative, δέξασθε ('receive') the helmet of salvation (v. 17).

90. The aorist imperative does not of itself suggest urgency, as Hoehner thinks. See the previous note.

91. So Lincoln, 442; cf. Snodgrass, 338.

92. Gk. πανοπλία. Louw and Nida §6.30 note that usually the 'emphasis [is] upon defensive armament, including helmet, shield, breastplate'.

93. Arnold, 118.

The 'armour *of God*' can be understood as the armour that God supplies,[94] his own armour which he wears, or even the armour that is God himself. The context clearly implies the first, namely, that God provides this weaponry for believers. At the same time, in the light of the description of the armour of Yahweh and his Messiah in Isaiah 11:5; 52:7; 57:19, which stands at the centre of Paul's sustained imagery throughout the passage (esp. vv. 14-17), it is important to recognize that the armour given to believers is God's own.[95] The Isaianic references depict the Lord of hosts as a warrior fighting with his own armour in order to vindicate his people. (See the detailed discussion of the armour in the light of its Old Testament background at vv. 14-17.) Further, some of the weapons believers are to don, namely, truth, righteousness, and salvation, suggest that we put on God himself, or at least his characteristics, and this idea is close in meaning to the distinctive exhortation of Ephesians 5:1, 'Be imitators of God'. Accordingly, we can conclude that 'in the end all the armor language is a way to talk about identification with God and his purposes'.[96]

The goal for which the readers are clothed with the divine armour is so that *(pros)* they 'might be able to stand against the schemes of the devil'. Four times over (vv. 11, 13 [twice], and 14) the apostle uses the language of standing, standing firm, or withstanding (various forms of the verb[97] to describe the readers' overall objective in this spiritual warfare).[98] The first reference to 'standing' involves resisting or holding their position against the devil's 'insidious wiles' (see on v. 14) so that they do not surrender to his evil opposition but prevail against it. This term invariably carries a bad sense, and here the plural suggests attacks that are constantly repeated or of incalculable variety. The varied nature of the diabolic attack is brought out again in v. 16, albeit in slightly different language: the 'evil one' launches his 'flaming arrows' against the saints. These differing expressions suggest not only inner temptations to evil but also 'every kind of attack and assault of the "evil one"'.[99]

According to 4:27, Satan tries to gain a foothold and exert his influ-

---

94. Hoehner, e.g., following Gnilka, 305, and others, takes τοῦ θεοῦ ('of God') as a genitive of origin.

95. So many recent writers, including T. Y. Neufeld, *Put On the Armour of God*, 118.

96. Snodgrass, 339.

97. Various forms of the verb ἵστημι. The NIV renderings are as follows: στῆναι ('stand against', v. 11), ἀντιστῆναι ('stand your ground'), στῆναι ('stand', v. 13), and στῆτε ('stand firm', v. 14).

98. T. Y. Neufeld, *Put On the Armour of God*, 120: 'The struggle is initially characterized as resistance to . . . the strategies and tactics of the enemy'.

99. Schlier, 297, cited by Arnold, 118.

ence over the lives of Christians through uncontrolled anger (v. 26) as well as[100] falsehood (4:25), stealing (v. 28), unwholesome talk (v. 29), indeed any conduct that is characteristic of the 'old way of life' (v. 22).[101] Further, the evil one is committed to hindering the progress of the gospel and the fulfilment of the divine plan of summing up all things in Christ (1:10). He will attempt by his 'insidious wiles' to turn believers aside from pursuing the cause of Christ and achieving this goal.

Snodgrass's comment is worth quoting in full:

> Mention of the "schemes" of the devil reminds us of the trickery and subterfuge by which evil and temptation present themselves in our lives. Evil rarely looks evil until it accomplishes its goal; it gains entrance by appearing attractive, desirable, and perfectly legitimate. It is a baited and camouflaged trap.[102]

The apostle's intention, however, in urging his readers to put on God's armour is that they might prevail against the stratagems and tactics of this enemy. Paul wants to see Christians strong, stable, and robust (cf. 4:14-16) so that they remain firm against the devil's wiles. The notion of doing battle with Satan and the powers of darkness 'may seem a frightening prospect', and indeed to take on such formidable foes simply with 'one's own resources would be to court disaster'. Believers would be fatally unprotected and exposed. But this paragraph 'does not foster an attitude of fear. The entire passage is suffused with a spirit of confidence and hope and the reader is left, not with a feeling of despair, but with the sense that Satan can be defeated'.[103]

The fundamental reason for this confidence (though not presumption) is that the decisive victory over the powers has already been won by God in Christ (1:19-22; cf. 4:8). Not only has the authority of the powers been broken, but also their final defeat is imminent, and the very existence of the church, comprising Jews and Gentiles reconciled through the death of Christ to God and to one another in the same body, is evidence that the purposes of God are moving triumphantly to their climax (3:10). The powers cannot finally hinder the progress of the gospel, and all things will ultimately be subject to Christ. It is because of God's victory in

---

100. Within the flow of the exhortatory context of vv. 25-31 the prohibitions against a range of sins suggest that the devil is able to exploit any of these (not simply anger) to his own advantage. See the exegesis of 4:27.

101. R. A. Wild, 'The Warrior', 248, makes the point that since chap. 6:10-18 appears as the climax of the paraenesis in Ephesians, it is natural to understand it as a reinforcement of the earlier ethical exhortations (cf. S. H. T. Page, *Powers*, 247).

102. Snodgrass, 339.

103. S. H. T. Page, *Powers*, 187; cf. Stott, 266.

his Son that believers are in the battle at all.[104] We are not urged to win the victory; rather, to withstand the devil's insidious wiles and to stand firm, a posture that will involve both defensive and offensive positions (see below). Believers live in the overlap of the ages, between the 'already' and the 'not yet'. Christ is already seated in the heavenly places far above every rule and authority; God has placed all things under his feet (1:21, 22), and we have been raised and made to sit with him (2:5, 6). But Christians need to appropriate what has been won for them, and in the present context this means putting on the armour of God and standing firm in the midst of the battle.

12 Paul explains further why believers need God's mighty armour if they are going to stand firm. It is *because* the battle being waged is not against human foes but against evil spiritual powers of great authority (v. 12).[105] The supernatural, powerful, and cunning nature of the opposition makes the use of God's armour absolutely necessary.

The word used to describe this struggle is a term found nowhere else in the Greek Bible, but which was commonly used for the sport of wrestling in the first century.[106] One might have expected the more regular words for a battle or struggle[107] to appear. But the popularity of wrestling in the games of western Asia Minor may account for the use of the word here, and particularly if it was intended to 'heighten the closeness of the struggle with the powers of evil'.[108] In contrast to flesh-and-blood wrestling with which his readers would have been familiar, the apostle asserts that 'the true struggle of believers is a spiritual power encounter

104. Lincoln, 442-43.

105. Rather than function as the central element of vv. 12-20 (as R. A. Wild, 'The Warrior', 286-88, claims), v. 12 informs us of the nature of the enemy (Arnold, 105, 202; Lincoln, 431; and Snodgrass, 337), and so explains the exhortation to put on the armour of God in order to stand.

106. Gk. πάλη. Wrestling was a popular event in the games held in Asia Minor, especially at Ephesus, Smyrna, and Pergamum, but also in Olympia, Greece. So Arnold, 116, 117, who cites an inscription which honours one 'Alexandros . . . who won the wrestling (πάλη) at the Isthmian games, the common games of Asia at Ephesus . . . and very many other games'; H. Engelmann, D. Knibbe, and R. Merkelbach, *Die Inschriften von Ephesos* (Bonn: Rudolph Habelt, 1984), no. 1123 (Arnold's translation). For further references, see Arnold, 117.

107. For example, μαχή ('struggle, fight'; 2 Cor. 7:5; 2 Tim. 2:23; Tit. 3:9; cf. Jas. 4:1); στρατεία ('warfare, battle'; 2 Cor. 10:4; 1 Tim. 1:18); or even ἀγών ('struggle, fight'; Phil. 1:30; Col. 2:1, etc.).

108. C. E. Arnold, *Powers of Darkness*, 153. M. E. Gudorf, 'The Use of πάλη in Ephesians 6:12', *JBL* 117 (1998), 334, claims that by using this term and thus drawing on the figure of a fully armed soldier who was also an accomplished wrestler, the author helps press upon the reader's mind 'that the battle being described here is one in which close-quarter struggling is involved'.

which requires spiritual weaponry'.[109] This athletic term could be transferred to military contexts and stand for any battle or contest,[110] and this seems to be its force here.[111] In this close struggle, hand-to-hand combat is in view, not the firing of computer-guided missiles from a distance! Further, by speaking of the battle as *our* struggle, Paul identifies with his readers (and, by implication, all Christians) in this spiritual conflict.

In a contrasting statement the apostle declares that this spiritual warfare is not against human opposition (lit. 'blood and flesh'; cf. Heb. 2:14), that is, humanity in its weakness and frailty (Matt. 16:17; 1 Cor. 15:50; Gal. 1:16), but against far more deadly foes that can be resisted only through divine empowering. The apostle's antithesis is not absolute, however, since he does not deny that believers may be tempted or deceived by other human beings, perhaps even by fellow Christians. The readers have already been warned about being misled by deceitful persons who seek to manipulate them through evil trickery (4:14). Furthermore, believers, who need to be careful not to fall into the sins mentioned in 4:25-31, may themselves be the objects of bitterness, rage, anger, brawling, and the like. From one perspective, then, their spiritual battle is against human adversaries, against 'flesh and blood'. But Paul's cogent point here is that the Christian life as a whole is a profound spiritual warfare of cosmic proportions in which the *ultimate* opposition to the advance of the gospel and moral integrity springs from evil, supernatural powers under the control of the god of this world (see below).

At v. 11 the 'devil' ('the evil one', v. 16) is the opponent of believers. Here in v. 12, the only place in the Pauline corpus, the enemies against whom Christians must contend in this spiritual warfare are a plurality of powers: *our struggle is . . . against the rulers, against the authorities, against the powers of this dark world and against the spiritual forces of evil in the heavenly realms.*[112] The first two terms, 'rulers and authorities', have already

109. Arnold, 117.

110. Cf. Philo, *De Abrahamo* 243; 2 Macc. 10:28; 14:18; 15:9.

111. As Hoehner comments: 'Certainly a wrestler would not need the pieces of armour described in verses 14-17'! For the different, but unlikely, suggestion that the first-century referent may be fighting in the arena, see T. Moritz, *A Profound Mystery*, 207-12.

112. The series of four prepositional phrases, without conjunctions, is a powerful rhetorical device that gives considerable prominence to those against whom believers are struggling. The phrases may be laid out as follows:

πρὸς τὰς ἀρχάς,	'against the principalities,
πρὸς τὰς ἐξουσίας,	'against the authorities,
πρὸς τοὺς κοσμοκράτορας	'against the world rulers
τοῦ σκότους τούτου,	of this darkness,
πρὸς τὰ πνευματικὰ τῆς πονηρίας	'against the spiritual hosts of evil
ἐν τοῖς ἐπουρανίοις.	in the heavenly realms'.

been mentioned (see on 1:21; 3:10) as those over whom Christ rules, both in this age and that to come. The third designation, 'the world-rulers of this darkness', does not appear in the LXX or elsewhere in the New Testament. The term 'world-rulers' appears in the second century A.D. in astrological and magical traditions in relation to the planets and their influence in human affairs, and to gods such as Sarapis and Hermes.[113] Clinton Arnold, who interprets the expression against a magical background in Ephesus and suggests that it might have referred to deities such as Artemis, has claimed that to speak of evil spirit powers as 'world-rulers' is akin to Paul's notion that pagan gods are closely connected with demonic forces (1 Cor. 10:20).[114] The qualifying phrase *of this dark world* indicates that these potentates belong to this present evil age of darkness,[115] a darkness from which believers have been delivered through Christ (5:8, 11; cf. Col. 1:13). The final description, 'the spiritual hosts of evil', does not point to a separate category of cosmic powers but is a comprehensive term covering all classes of hostile spirits,[116] while the additional phrase *in the heavenly realms* indicates their locality. These potentates are not earthly figures but supernatural beings whose essential character is wickedness. Although they are powerful, and are described as *in the heavenly realms,* this ought not to frighten believers: we have been given every spiritual gift in Christ in the heavenly places (1:3), made alive and seated with him in this domain (2:6), so that our struggle is against *subjected* powers. They may rule the realm of darkness and evil, but Christians have been transferred out of this realm (5:8, 16; cf. Col. 1:13).

This fourfold description is not intended to indicate that four (or seven if we include those mentioned in 1:21) categories of demonic spirits

113. κοσμοκράτορες ('world rulers') describes the sun and other planets in later Mandaean Gnosticism (cf. *Ginza* 99.15-32; 104.5, 6, etc.). Note Lincoln, 444. On the use of the term in the magical papyri with reference to deities claiming to possess cosmic power, see Arnold, 65-68. 'World rulers' refers to evil spirit powers in the second century A.D.; so in the *Testament of Solomon* 18:2 (cf. 8:2), the demons introduce themselves to Solomon as 'the world rulers of the darkness of this age' (the author's language may have been influenced by Ephesians).

114. Arnold, 67, 69; note also Lincoln, 444.

115. This statement serves to indicate 'the terrifying power of their influence and comprehensiveness of their plans, and thus to emphasise the seriousness of the situation'; so W. Michaelis, *TDNT* 3:914.

116. While some translators have suggested that the adjective πνευματικά should be considered as an alternative to τὸ πνεῦμα ('the Spirit') and rendered 'the things relating to the spirit', i.e., spiritual forces or elements (so NASB, NIV, NRSV), it is probably better to regard it as an alternative to τὰ πνεύματα ('the spirits'); it thus designates spiritual armies or hosts (RV, RSV, JB). This fits the present context and meanings of the other three nouns, ἀρχαί ('rulers'), ἐξουσίαι ('authorities'), and κοσμοκράτορες ('world-rulers'), which indicate specific spiritual beings (cf. Hoehner).

exist. The different terms point to the same reality, and any attempts to rank them is pure speculation.[117] The relationship of these powers to the devil is not specifically spelled out, but the context closely allies them with him: they belong to 'this darkness' and are called 'spiritual forces of evil'. They are under the power of the evil one and form a united front. In fact, v. 12 may be an expansion of the reference to the 'devil's schemes' in v. 11.[118] These spiritual authorities are not represented as acting independently of the devil, but as his agents they share with him common objectives and strategies. Certainly, Paul does not present a different strategy for resisting the powers in contrast to how they would resist the devil.[119] The assumption is that they have 'a common nature, objective, and method of attack, which necessitates the believer to depend on the power of God to resist them'.[120]

The devil and his minions are able to rule the lives of men and women who belong to his 'tyranny of darkness' (Col. 1:13) — they are called 'children of disobedience' at Ephesians 2:2 — and the powers exploit culture and social systems in their attempts to wreck the creative and saving work of God. The first-century readers of the letter, and we ourselves, need to understand the spiritual dimension of this struggle, the supernatural, evil nature of the opposition, and the necessity of putting on divine armour for the battle. If we think that the Christian life is simply a matter of human effort or exertion, then we have misread the nature of the campaign and will not be able to resist the evil one's fiery darts.

Our exegesis has led to the conclusion that these powers of evil are personal, demonic intelligences. Considerable scholarly attention, however, which has been devoted to determining the identity of the powers in Pauline and general New Testament teaching, has reached different

---

117. S. H. T. Page, *Powers,* 250. The different combinations of terms in the various lists of the powers (cf. Col. 1:16; Eph. 1:21; 6:12) show that Paul, like other New Testament writers, was not interested in speculating about various angelic orders or rankings. The point of Col. 1:16 is that the invisible forces in this world, whatever their station or rank, are no match for Christ. C. E. Arnold, *3 Crucial Questions about Spiritual Warfare* (Grand Rapids: Baker, 1997), 39, observes that even if the four terms used in v. 12 imply a hierarchy within the demonic realm, we have no means of discerning the various ranks. Further, although these 'terms appear to come from a large reservoir of terminology used in the first century when people spoke of demonic spirits', they do not give us any insight into the demonic realm.

118. S. H. T. Page, *Powers,* 247; and Snodgrass, 341.

119. 'Nothing in the context of Ephesians 6:12 suggests that the methods used by the powers to attack believers are any different from those employed by the devil himself' (S. H. T. Page, *Powers,* 247).

120. Arnold, 119.

conclusions. Of particular note since the Second World War has been that interpretation of the powers which identifies them with structures of thought (tradition, convention, law, authority, and religion) and impersonal social forces that determine human existence.[121] Although the case for this recent interpretation (or some variation of it) has been strongly and enthusiastically presented, a notable example of which is Walter Wink,[122] it fails to do justice to the historical context of the New Testament in which belief in the spiritual realm was widespread, it does not adequately account for explicit statements about these powers in Paul and other New Testament writers, and it is seriously flawed both theologically and hermeneutically.[123]

To reject the *identification* of the powers with human traditions and sociopolitical structures, however, is not to deny that these supernatural intelligences work through such agencies; after all, the New Testament speaks of the whole world lying in the power of the evil one. Satan and his hosts exist for the purpose of bringing their evil and destructive influences to bear on the world and humanity at every level.[124] The evil one works through the events of history, including a visit hindered by him (1 Thess. 2:18), the circumstances surrounding Job's life (Job 1–2), the casting of believers into prison (Rev. 2:10), the inherent distresses of life (cf. Rom. 8:38), and illness which is occasionally due to their demonic activity (Matt. 9:32; 12:22; Luke 9:42), while Christian teachers and their instruction are the subject of attack and distortion by the principalities and powers (cf. 2 Cor. 11:13-15). Heresy is assigned to their activity (1 Tim. 4:1; cf. 1 John 4:1), while according to Colossians 2:20-21 the elemental spirits of the universe made use of the legal demands of the false teacher(s) in order to bring Christians into bondage. Social, political, judicial, and economic structures can be used by Satan and his evil authorities to serve their malevolent ends. The last and greatest enemy to which humanity is exposed by Satan and his lieutenants is death. Men and women, 'through fear of death are in lifelong bondage to him who has the power over death, that is, the devil' (Heb. 2:14). 'Death is, accordingly, the supreme

121. For surveys of the modern discussion and interactions with the hermeneutical issues involved, together with the relevant bibliographies, see P. T. O'Brien, 'Principalities and Powers', 110-50; Stott, 267-75; Arnold, 42-51; *Powers of Darkness*, 167-93; *DPL*, 723-25; D. G. Reid, *DPL*, 746-52; and, more recently, T. Y. Neufeld, *Put On the Armour of God*, 121-24; and G. R. Smillie, 'A Mystery', 204-7.

122. In his trilogy *Naming the Powers, Unmasking the Powers: The Invisible Forces That Determine Human Existence* (Philadelphia: Fortress, 1986), and *Engaging the Powers: Discernment and Resistance in a World of Domination* (Minneapolis: Fortress, 1992).

123. See my arguments in 'Principalities and Powers', 110-50, as well as the other interactions mentioned above.

124. For fuller details see S. H. T. Page, *Powers*.

focus of these enemy forces. They smell of death. They revel in it. They spread it'.[125]

The apostles' clarion call, then, in Ephesians 6 to believers is to recognize the nature and dimension of the spiritual conflict in which we are engaged, and to appropriate God's armour in order to resist vigorously the onslaughts of the evil one (cf. Jas. 4:7). Many contemporary Christians seem to be unaware that there is a war in progress, or if they are, they consider it to be fought at a purely human level, and therefore earthly resources will be entirely adequate for conducting the campaigns. V. 12 warns us that we are engaged in a deadly warfare against the god of this world and his minions, and that our struggle is *not* against flesh and blood, that is, other people, but against spiritual forces of evil headed up by Satan himself. God's own armour has been forged and furnished by him for our use so that we may obey his injunction to stand firm. Only spiritual weapons are of value in this deadly struggle. Hence the apostle will repeat his urgent call to put on this divine armour.

13 The warrant for putting on the whole armour of God has been given in vv. 11 ('so that you can take your stand against the devil's schemes') and 12 (because our battle is against evil spiritual powers of great authority). This warrant now serves as the basis ('therefore') for repeating the imperative of v. 11 in a different form, *put on the full armour of God* (v. 13).[126] Once again the purpose is that the readers might be able to *stand*. Here in v. 13, two forms of the verb are repeated for emphasis: 'in order that you may be able to *withstand*[127] and . . . to *stand*'. The admonition to acquire divine strengthening is not an end in itself: God's almighty power is required for a specific purpose, namely, that believers, both individually and together as a unity, might stand against the powers of darkness and successfully resist them. The three exhortations of vv. 10, 11, and 13, which are similar in meaning and stress the need for divine empowering, at the same time remind the readers that the devil can be resisted since God has provided all the necessary resources for the battle.

125. M. Green, *I Believe in Satan's Downfall* (London/Grand Rapids: Hodder & Stoughton/Eerdmans, 1981), 90.

126. ἐνδύσασθε ('put on') is used in v. 11, while ἀναλάβετε ('put on') appears in v. 13. The expression 'the armour of God' (τὴν πανοπλίαν τοῦ θεοῦ) is identical in the two verses.

127. ἀντιστῆναι (from ἀνθίστημι), which has the basic idea to 'stand against, oppose, resist' (BAGD, 67; Louw and Nida §39.18), was used in military contexts in both classical literature and the LXX (see BDB, 426, 764 for references). It occurs with the New Testament meaning to speak of opposing an idea or message (Luke 21:15; Acts 6:10; 2 Tim. 4:15), or a person in confrontation (Acts 13:8; Gal. 2:11; 2 Tim. 3:8). The verb is also used of resisting an evil person (Matt. 5:39), the devil (Jas. 4:7; 1 Pet. 5:9), or God and his will (Rom. 9:19; 13:2).

The time when believers are to withstand the devil and his hosts is 'on the evil day'. This phrase occurs nowhere else in Paul, although the parallel expression, 'the present evil age', is mentioned in Galatians 1:4, and the plural 'because the *days* are evil' has already appeared in Ephesians as the reason for believers to make the most of every opportunity in the present (5:16). The exact phrase, 'the evil day', turns up in three prophetic passages of the Old Testament (Jer. 17:17, 18; Obad. 13; cf. Dan. 12:1),[128] and has an apocalyptic ring to it with its end-time connotations. In continuity with Old Testament and Jewish apocalyptic thought, the apostle distinguished two ages: 'the present age', which is characterized by evil and dominated by rulers or demonic powers which were doomed to pass away (1 Cor. 2:6, 7); and 'the coming age', which is the time of salvation (note the discussion on Eph. 5:16).

Exegetes have understood the phrase 'the evil day' as: (1) synonymous with the 'evil days' of Ephesians 5:16 and thus referring to the whole of this present age between the two comings of Jesus (Masson, Lindemann); (2) a single day of special tribulation just prior to the parousia when satanic opposition reaches its climax (Meyer, Dibelius, Schlier); (3) pointing to critical times in believers' lives when demonic hostility is at its worst (Hendriksen, Mitton); (4) a combination of the first and second views which understands the present age as the evil day that will climax in a final outbreak of evil in the future (Gnilka, Barth, Schnackenburg, Lincoln);[129] or (5) a combination of the first and third views, in which the present age refers to the present 'evil days' (5:16), while the singular evil *day* points to specific times of satanic attack that come with extraordinary force and when the temptation to yield is particularly strong (Bruce, Arnold, Hoehner).[130] In the final view, which we prefer, the apostle is not only speaking of this present time between the two comings of Jesus, but is also alerting believers to the dangers of the devil's schemes on critical occasions in this present evil age. There may appear to be times of reprieve for Christians, but they must not be lulled into a false sense of security, thinking that the

128. Dan. 12:1 speaks of ἡ ἡμέρα θλίψεως ('the day of tribulation') before a time of deliverance, and this becomes an important theme in apocalyptic Judaism (cf. *Apocalypse of Abraham* 29:2, 8ff., 13; 30:4; *2 Apocalypse of Baruch* 48:31; *Jubilees* 23:16-21; *T. Dan* 5:4ff.; note also 1QM 15:1-2; 16:3; 18:10, 12). For further details see Arnold, 204.

129. Lincoln, 445-46, argues that the two perspectives of the present and future overlap. The readers are already in the evil days, and yet these necessarily climax in a final, evil day when resistance using the armour of God is particularly necessary. Cf. T. Moritz, *A Profound Mystery,* 196-97.

130. The definiteness given to the day by the article (ἐν τῇ ἡμέρᾳ τῇ πονηρᾷ) marks it out in some sense as a critical day, a time of peculiar trial or peril (so Hoehner; cf. G. Harder, *TDNT* 6:554). Note the discussion of the time of the battle in Arnold, 113-15.

battle is over or that it is not especially difficult. They must always be prepared and put on the full armour of God, for the devil will attack when least expected.

Finally, it is crucial that when believers have done everything they stand firm. The Roman centurion, according to Polybius, was to be the kind of person who could be relied upon, when under pressure, to stand fast and not to give way.[131] The same determination is necessary in the spiritual warfare. When they have done everything,[132] that is, made all the necessary preparations for the battle and are fully armed, Christians are to stand firm against the onslaughts of the evil powers. Some have taken the clause to mean 'having subdued or overcome all, they are to stand firm': the victory has been accomplished and believers are now able to stand.[133] But in all twenty-one of its occurrences in the New Testament this verb means to 'achieve, accomplish, do', and this makes good sense here.[134] The devil and his angels are strong but not omnipotent. After the Christian is strengthened in the Lord by putting on the full armour of God, then he or she is able to stand fast against the evil powers.

2. Stand Firm and Put On God's Armour, 6:14-17

14 When believers have made all the necessary preparations for the battle with the appropriate goal in mind, then[135] they are to 'stand firm'. This exhortation, which has been mentioned three times before (vv. 11, 13 [twice]), is repeated, but this time it is expressed as an imperative.[136] It is the chief admonition of the passage, and in the light of the battle imagery used throughout points to the stance of a soldier in combat, one who resolutely opposes the enemy. Clearly for Paul the idea of

131. Polybius, *History* 6.24; cited by Bruce, 406.
132. Gk. κατεργάζομαι.
133. Meyer, 331-32; Mitton, 223; and, most recently, T. Y. Neufeld, *Put On the Armour of God*, 128-31.
134. BAGD, 421; Louw and Nida §42.17. Further, the flow of the argument in the paragraph indicates standing before the foe, not standing victorious. Secondly, vv. 14-17 are introduced by the inferential conjunction 'therefore' (οὖν), which explains that believers stand, having put on the various pieces of armour. Finally, the imperative 'stand' in v. 14 is unusual if the battle has already been won (note Hoehner).
135. This is the inference (οὖν) to be drawn.
136. The three previous occurrences of this key verb have been in purpose clauses: v. 11, πρὸς τὸ δύνασθαι ὑμᾶς στῆναι ('in order that you may be able to stand'); v. 13, ἵνα δυνηθῆτε ἀντιστῆναι . . . καὶ . . . στῆναι ('in order that you may be able to withstand . . . and . . . to stand').

believers standing firm in their Christian lives is vital. It is an emphasis that is prominent elsewhere in the apostle's letters.[137]

Following this brief exhortation, the panoply of God which was announced in v. 11 (cf. v. 13) is described in some detail, each piece of armour being identified with some divine virtue or gift. In discussing these individual weapons Paul illustrates his main point about being equipped with God's full armour. He also shows what it means to have made all the necessary preparations for the battle. The four participles which follow the imperative 'stand', namely, '*having fastened* the belt of truth', '*having put* on the breastplate of righteousness' (v. 14), '*having fitted* your feet' (v. 15), and '*having taken up* the shield of faith' (v. 16), spell out the actions believers need to have taken if they are to stand firm.[138] Given the context, these participles could also be taken as having an implied imperatival force.

For their first piece of armour, the readers are urged to fasten 'the belt of truth around your waist'. For a Roman soldier this belt probably refers to the leather apron which hung under the armour and protected the thighs, rather than the sword belt or the protective girdle worn over the armour.[139] The idea of fastening clothing securely around one's waist signifies preparation for vigorous activity (Luke 12:35, 37; 17:8), in this case, readiness for battle.[140] The apostle's language clearly alludes to the LXX of Isaiah 11, which declares of the Messiah: 'With righteousness shall he be girded around his waist, and with truth bound around his sides' (vv. 4-5). Within its Old Testament context the rule of God's Anointed One in the divine kingdom will be characterized by righteousness and truth. The armour which the Messiah wears in battle is now provided for his people as they engage in spiritual warfare. 'Truth', which occupies a prominent place in Ephesians, refers to the truth of God (4:24; 5:9) re-

---

137. It turns up frequently as an imperative in paraenetic sections of Paul's letters, where he exhorts his Christian readers to be steadfast (2 Thess. 2:15), 'in the faith' (1 Cor. 6:13), 'in the Lord' (Phil. 4:1), in the freedom Christ has won (Gal. 5:1), or 'in one spirit' (Phil. 1:27). Note also Rom. 5:2; 11:20; 1 Cor. 10:12; 15:1; 16:13; 2 Cor. 1:24; Col. 4:12; and 1 Thess. 3:8.

138. Cf. Lincoln, 431, 447. D. B. Wallace, *Greek Grammar*, 629, categorizes the participle περιζωσάμενοι ('having fastened'), and by implication the following three, as participles of means. This participle is often used with 'vague, general, abstract, or metaphorical finite verbs' and indicates how the action of a main verb is accomplished. Cf. Matt. 27:4. The verb comes first and is general in its lexical range.

139. A. Oepke, *TDNT* 5:303, 307.

140. So Louw and Nida §77.5. The 'loins' can be a metaphor for strength, and 'girding oneself' is used in the Old Testament as a symbol of displaying power and courage: Yahweh girds himself with might (Ps. 65:6) and binds up the Psalmist with strength for battle (Ps. 18:32, 39).

vealed in the gospel (1:13; 4:15, 21, 24), which has its outworking in the lives of believers who are members of the new humanity (4:25; 5:9).[141] Here in Ephesians 6 both aspects of truth belong together.[142] As believers buckle on this piece of the Messiah's armour, they will be strengthened by God's truth revealed in the gospel, as a consequence of which they will display the characteristics of the Anointed One in their attitudes, language, and behaviour. In this way they resist the devil, giving him no opportunity to gain an advantage over them (4:27).

Next, Christians need to have put on 'the breastplate of righteousness' if they are to stand firm against the forces of darkness. For the Roman soldier, the breastplate was 'a piece of armor covering the chest to protect it against blows and arrows'.[143] Paul's language here is drawn from Isaiah 59:17 (cf. Wisdom 5:18; at Isa. 11:5, righteousness is the Messiah's girdle), where Yahweh puts on 'the breastplate of righteousness' as he comes to deliver his people and to punish the nation's enemies. According to Ephesians 6 believers need to be armed with God's own righteousness if they are to be protected against the blows and arrows of their spiritual enemies. Some exegetes understand this righteousness to refer to God's justifying, forensic righteousness which results in a right standing before him (cf. Rom. 3:21-26);[144] on this view, God's sovereign verdict of acquittal through Christ's death provides the basis for believers standing firm in their spiritual struggle. Many recent commentators, however, in the light of earlier instances of 'righteousness' in Ephesians (4:24; 5:9), regard it as ethical righteousness.[145] If the expression is to be understood in the light of its Old Testament context where righteousness is parallel to salvation,[146] then to speak of donning God's own righteousness or appropriating his salvation is in effect to urge the readers once more to put on the 'new man' of 4:24, who is cre-

141. T. Y. Neufeld, *Put On the Armour of God,* 134, suggests that the presence of this prominent motif 'truth' in 6:14 functions 'as a recapitulation of a note sounded repeatedly in Ephesians'.

142. T. Moritz, *A Profound Mystery,* 202, however, thinks that it is the objective 'truth' of the gospel that is in view here.

143. Gk. θωράξ. Louw and Nida §6.39.

144. So Barth, 796-97; A. Oepke, *TDNT* 5:310; and, most recently, T. Moritz, *A Profound Mystery,* 203, who stresses the primacy of 'righteousness' as a gift, though he does acknowledge that there is an ethical dimension as well.

145. Not only Calvin and Meyer in earlier times but also more recently Schnackenburg, Bruce, Lincoln, and Snodgrass. Cf. 1 Thess. 5:8, where 'faith and love' are the Christian's breastplate.

146. Note the discussion of v. 17 within its Isaianic context: B. G. Webb, *The Message of Isaiah: On Eagles' Wings* (Leicester: Inter-Varsity, 1996), 229. He understands righteousness to signify God's faithfulness to his covenant promises as shown in his saving acts.

ated to be like God in righteousness and holiness.[147] By putting on God's righteousness believers are committed to being imitators of him (5:1) and acting righteously in all their dealings.

15 The Christian also needs to be outfitted with proper footwear in order to be ready for battle. The Roman soldier frequently wore *caliga*, a half-boot, which was not strictly a weapon but part of his equipment that was used especially in long marches.[148] Paul does not refer directly to believers' footwear here; instead, he employs an unusual expression that speaks of 'having [their] feet fitted[149] with the readiness of the gospel of peace'.

The language has obviously been borrowed from Isaiah 52:7, 'How beautiful upon the mountains are the feet of him who brings good tidings, who publishes peace' — words which, in a shortened form, are applied by the apostle to those sent to preach the Christian gospel (Rom. 10:15). In its original context of Isaiah 52 the picture is painted of a lone messenger whose beautiful feet are drumming across the mountaintops with all the swiftness of a gazelle (Song 2:17; 8:14), bringing good news to Jerusalem. As he comes within earshot of the city he shouts 'peace', 'good tidings', 'salvation', 'Your God reigns' (essentially the same message of consolation as in Isa. 40:9-11).

Here in Ephesians 6:15 the wording of Isaiah has been adapted to fit the syntactical pattern of the sentence:[150] the readers have been exhorted to 'stand firm' (v. 14), and, if they are to be equipped properly with God's armour, one of the actions they need to have taken (note the other three in vv. 14, 16) is to have their feet fitted with 'readiness'. However, the meaning of this metaphorical expression and its significance within the flow of vv. 10-20 are disputed. The following issues need to be addressed:

(1) The *meaning* of the term rendered 'readiness' (NIV). This word appears nowhere else in the New Testament (although the cognate verb

---

147. This is, in effect, to put on Christ (Rom. 13:14); see on Eph. 4:24.

148. A typical soldier might journey for miles as his army advanced to the battlefront (Xerxes led his armies all the way from Persia in an attempt to conquer Greece! Xenophon, *Anabasis* 4.5.14).

149. ὑποδέομαι has to do with putting on and wearing footwear, such as shoes, boots, or sandals, and comes to mean 'to put on, to tie on, to wear (footwear)'; so Louw and Nida §49.17. The verb is akin to ὑποδήματα ('sandals, shoes'), which could be used of military sandals.

150. In vv. 14-16, the imperative στῆτε ('stand') is followed by four aorist participles + a weapon/part of the body + a virtue/gift. In v. 15 this structure is maintained with ὑποδησάμενοι ('having put on') + τοὺς πόδας ('the feet') + ἐν ἑτοιμασίᾳ ('with the readiness, preparation'), although the pattern is expanded by reference to τοῦ εὐαγγελίου τῆς εἰρήνης ('the gospel of peace'), which is in a genitival relationship to ἑτοιμασία ('the readiness'), and ultimately derives from Isaiah (cf. T. Moritz, *A Profound Mystery*, 193).

turns up often enough),[151] and it is not used in Isaiah 52:7. It does occur, however, a dozen times in the LXX, where it often has connotations of a prepared or solid foundation.[152] Accordingly, some understand it here to signify a 'firm footing' or 'steadfastness', and connect it with the overall exhortation to 'stand'.[153] But elsewhere the term does not mean 'firm footing', and readiness, preparedness, or preparation, which is the more usual sense, fits this context.[154] The language is used metaphorically to signify that those who are properly equipped with God's armour have their feet fitted, prepared, and ready in their spiritual warfare.

(2) The *function* of the *genitival expression*, 'of the gospel'. Is the readiness of which the apostle speaks that which is bestowed by the gospel (a genitive of origin, or, perhaps, a subjective genitive), or is it a willingness to share and announce the message of peace (an objective genitive) that is in view? Scholars are divided on the question.

(a) In favour of the former, it is claimed that Paul is referring to the readiness or preparation that comes from God's powerful message of peace,[155] a readiness that enables Christians to heed the repeated injunction to 'stand firm'. This is usually taken to mean adopting a defensive posture, of holding fast to the position that has already been won, of remaining steadfast against the powers of darkness, and resisting temptation.[156] However, this still begs the question whether Paul's language implies that believers are to adopt *only* a defensive stance. Certainly they are to appropriate and preserve the gospel of peace, to withstand every temptation in the ethical sphere, and to resist the diverse influences of the evil one. But standing firm can also involve carrying the attack into enemy territory, of plundering Satan's kingdom by announcing the promise of divine rescue to captives in the realm of darkness.[157] Consistent with his use of military imagery elsewhere, Paul speaks of the weapons he uses in his warfare as being divinely powerful to demolish strongholds,

---

151. It appears forty times in the New Testament, but only three of these are in the Pauline corpus: 1 Cor. 2:9; 2 Tim. 2:21; and Phlm. 22.

152. It is used for a stand or base: Ezra 2:68; 3:3; Zech. 5:11; cf. Robinson, 215.

153. Cf. T. Moritz, *A Profound Mystery*, 203, who takes it as meaning 'firmness'.

154. Ps. 9:17 (LXX 9:38); Wisdom 13:12; *Epistle of Aristeas* 182; Josephus, *Antiquities* 10.1.2 etc.; Lincoln, 449.

155. τοῦ εὐαγγελίου is understood as a genitive of origin.

156. The imagery of footwear, it is claimed, is appropriate to this meaning. The only offensive weapon referred to in the paragraph is 'the sword of the Spirit' (v. 17). But C. E. Arnold, *Powers of Darkness*, 157, contends that being furnished with good footwear enabled a soldier to take an offensive position in battle. He might journey for miles as his army advanced to the battlefront and then pursued the enemy.

157. Note C. E. Arnold's strong advocacy of the view that Christians are to adopt an offensive position as well as a defensive one (*Powers of Darkness*, 156-58).

to overthrow arguments and every pretension that sets itself up against the knowledge of God (2 Cor. 10:4). This undoubtedly involves carrying the attack into enemy territory, which is clearly to adopt an offensive stance.

(b) The alternative is to interpret '[the readiness] *of the gospel'* as an objective genitive, signifying a willingness to share or announce the gospel of peace. The reasons for adopting this line are as follows: first, the noun 'signifies a state of being ready for action — "readiness to, being ready to"', and the phrase is rendered 'in readiness (to proclaim) the good news of peace'.[158] On this view, gospel in the original is a noun of agency signifying 'to proclaim or share the gospel [of peace]', a force which it has in more than half of its sixty other occurrences in Paul. Secondly, the context of Isaiah 52:7 favours this interpretation: the messenger whose beautiful feet glide over the mountaintops is ready[159] to announce good tidings to Zion.[160] Thirdly, the echoes of this Old Testament text earlier in Ephesians, namely at 2:17, draw attention to Christ, the herald of good tidings, who on the basis of his peacemaking work on the cross comes and announces peace to Jews and Gentiles alike. The focus is upon the proclamation of the gospel of peace to those for whom this reconciliation has been won. Finally, the parallel passage (Col. 4:6) stresses the note of the gracious speech of believers to outsiders.

(c) If the words 'of the gospel' are taken as a genitive of origin, that is, view (a), then Paul's expression points to a readiness that derives from the good news of peace which has been appropriated by believers. Because this mighty announcement of reconciliation has become powerful in their lives,[161] they will not only resist the evil influences of the powers and withstand temptation, but they also carry the attack into enemy territory by sharing and proclaiming this good news with others. If the alternative interpretation (b) is followed, then 'the readiness of the gospel' focusses on the sharing of the gospel of peace by those who have already appropriated it. The net difference between the two interpretations of the

158. Louw and Nida §77.1; cf. Robinson, 215; Bruce, 408; W. Radl, *EDNT* 2:68, thinks that the phrase signifies *'readiness* [to battle] for the gospel'; Morris, 206, 'The whole expression points to being fully prepared to preach the gospel'; and Arnold, 111; also his *Powers of Darkness*, 157.

159. Even though the term ἑτοιμασία ('readiness') does not appear in the text of Isaiah 52:7, the notion of the messenger's preparedness to announce the good tidings to Zion is obvious.

160. Cf. Robinson, 215; who is followed by Bruce, 408; note also Stott, 280.

161. Paul often goes out of his way to speak of the gospel being powerful, even explosive (cf. Rom. 1:16; Phil. 2:16), so to speak of it purely in defensive terms is probably a contradiction. On the meaning of Phil. 2:16, in relation to this, see P. T. O'Brien, *Gospel and Mission*, 118-19.

genitive 'of the gospel' is not great, especially if the dynamic dimension to the gospel is recognized.

Because all engaged in the spiritual warfare are urged to have their feet fitted with this preparation of the gospel, then what is predicated of the royal messenger in Isaiah 52:7, and the Messiah himself in Ephesians 2:17, is now stated with reference to all believers.

(3) The *significance* of 'the gospel *of peace*'. The apostle's description of the footwear with which Christians are to be fitted as 'the gospel of peace' is highly expressive, given the Old Testament context of Isaiah 52 and the earlier mention of 'peace' in the foundational passage of Ephesians 2:11-22. As the messenger of Isaiah who brings consolation to Jerusalem (cf. Isa. 40:9-11) comes within earshot of the city, the first word that he cries out is 'Peace!' (52:7).[162] This is followed by the synonymous 'good tidings' and 'salvation', the content of which is then amplified by: 'Your God reigns'. Yahweh's glorious return to Zion (v. 9), which is the ground of his people's bursting into songs of joy, is explained in terms of his acting mightily on behalf of his people (he has 'comforted his people' and 'redeemed Jerusalem', v. 9), and this, in the light of Isaiah 49:3, leads to blessing for the world (he has bared his arm 'in the sight of all the nations', so that 'all the ends of the earth will see the salvation of our God', v. 10).[163] The peace which Yahweh's messenger brings deals with both vertical and horizontal relationships. This is precisely the focus of Ephesians 2:14-18, where God's Messiah by his death makes peace: he destroys the alienation between Jew and Gentile, creates in himself one new humanity out of the two, and in this body reconciles them both to God (vv. 15-16).

We have already observed that the armour being worn by believers is that of Yahweh or his Messiah. Most of the weapons listed in Ephesians 6 have their counterpart in Yahweh's armour of Isaiah 59:17 and that of his Messiah in 11:4-5. An exception to this is the footwear mentioned in Ephesians 6:15. But having one's feet 'fitted with the preparation of the gospel of peace' is more closely linked with the Messiah than has often been thought, especially if the connections between Isaiah 52:7, Ephesians 2:14-18, and Ephesians 6:15 are clearly recognized. Yahweh's messenger announces the good news of peace to his people, Jerusalem. According to Ephesians 2:17, which takes up the language of this Old

---

162. The LXX has πόδες εὐαγγελιζομένου ἀκοὴν εἰρήνης ('the feet of the one who announces a message of peace').

163. Although it is possible, with C. Westermann, to interpret Yahweh's mighty action as done for Israel (v. 9) in the sight of all the nations (v. 10), it seems preferable to interpret the latter as signifying that the nations will 'see' in the sense of participate in Yahweh's salvation; so J. A. Motyer, *Isaiah*, 420.

Testament passage, Christ, who is the embodiment of peace (v. 14), has made peace through his death, and announced this good news far and wide, to Jew and Gentile alike. Those who have appropriated that peace for themselves have their feet fitted with this 'readiness', a preparedness to announce the gospel of peace. Paradoxically, they are prepared to announce the gospel of peace as they engage in a spiritual warfare![164]

16 In addition to[165] the pieces of armour that believers need to *wear*,[166] they are to *take up* the 'shield of faith', for by it[167] they will be fully protected against every kind of assault rained upon them by the evil one. The shield referred to is not the small round one which left most of the body unprotected, but the large shield[168] carried by Roman soldiers, which covered the whole person. In the Old Testament the shield was used as an image of God's protection of his people (Gen. 15:1; Ps. 5:12; 18:2, 30, 35; 28:7, etc.).[169] He is 'a shield to those who take refuge in him' (Prov. 30:5). Here the shield which believers are to take up is 'the shield *of faith*'; the genitive is best understood as one of apposition,[170] meaning that faith itself is the shield. 'Faith' has appeared at key points throughout Ephesians (1:13, 15, 19; 2:8; 3:12, 17; 4:5, 13; 6:23), particularly as the means of acquiring divine strength (1:19; 3:16-17). Although it is possible to interpret faith here as God's or Christ's faith[fulness], it is preferable to understand it of believers laying hold of God's resources, especially his power, in the midst of the evil one's attacks.[171] To *take* the shield of faith,

164. Snodgrass, 342, thinks that the 'readiness' in view pertains to all of life, not simply to a willingness to share the gospel.

165. The fourth clause with an aorist participle (ἀναλαβόντες, 'having taken up') is introduced by ἐν πᾶσιν which could mean 'in all circumstances' but is best understood as 'besides all these' (cf. NIV). It does not signify 'above all' (AV), as if it were the most important of all weapons.

166. The three participles περιζωσάμενοι ('fastened', v. 14), ἐνδυσάμενοι ('put on', v. 14), and ὑποδησάμενοι ('fitted', v. 15) all refer to items of armour fastened to the body or feet of believers. Now they are to have 'taken up' (ἀναλαβόντες) the shield of faith (cf. Hoehner). The fourth clause with an aorist participle is introduced by 'besides all these'.

167. An additional relative clause ἐν ᾧ δυνήσεσθε κτλ. ('by which you are able . . .') explains that this shield enables believers to extinguish the burning arrows of the evil one.

168. That is, Gk. θυρεός, which is the *scutum*; it measured four feet by two and a half feet and was shaped like a door (cf. θύρα). It was usually made of wood and covered with canvas and calf skin; it was reinforced with metal at the top and bottom (note Polybius's description, 6.23.2-6).

169. In Ps. 35:2 (LXX 34:2) God is called upon as divine warrior to take up weapon and shield (θυρεός) to intervene on behalf of his afflicted one; cf. T. Y. Neufeld, *Put On the Armour of God*, 140.

170. Best, 601; and Hoehner.

171. So most recent commentators. T. Moritz, *A Profound Mystery*, 204, however, thinks that the reference is to both Christ's faithfulness and the human response of faith.

then, is to appropriate the promises of God on our behalf, confident that he will protect us in the midst of the battle. According to 1 Peter 5:8-9, firm faith, described as 'a flint-like resolution', is called for in resisting the devil.[172]

By responding in this way believers 'will be able[173] to extinguish all the burning arrows of the evil one'. The large shield used by Roman soldiers was specially designed to quench dangerous missiles, particularly arrows that were dipped in pitch and lit before being fired. These flaming missiles often inflicted deadly wounds, or caused havoc among soldiers, unless the shields had been soaked with water and were able to quench them.[174] Here the burning arrows[175] depict, in highly metaphorical language, every kind of attack launched by the devil and his hosts against the people of God. They are as wide-ranging as the 'insidious wiles' (v. 11) that promote them, and include not only every kind of temptation to ungodly behaviour (cf. 4:26-27), doubt, and despair, but also external assaults, such as persecution or false teaching.[176] Paul's expression conveys the sense of extreme danger. The forces of 'the evil one'[177] are incredibly powerful, and left to our own devices we would certainly fail. But these flaming arrows cannot harm those whose trust and confidence are 'in the Lord and in his mighty power' (v. 10). They are able to resist and overcome these satanic attacks.

17 The last two pieces of armour to be received[178] are the helmet of salvation and the sword of the Spirit, which is identified as the word of God. The helmet used by the Roman soldier was made of bronze and had

---

172. Bruce, 408, citing Selwyn. Cf. 1QH 2.25-26, 29.

173. The future δυνήσεσθε ('you will be able') is a logical future, indicating the result of taking up the shield, and does not indicate that the conflict itself lies in the future (against T. Y. Neufeld, *Put On the Armour of God*, 110).

174. Note Livy's graphic account of how these arrows caused panic and tempted soldiers to throw down their burning shields, thus making them vulnerable to the spears of their enemies (*History* 21.8).

175. βέλος, which appears only here in the New Testament, signifies 'a missile, including arrows (propelled by a bow) or darts (hurled by hand)'; so Louw and Nida §6.36.

176. Cf. S. H. T. Page, *Powers*, 188. Meyer, 337-38, rightly notes that the expression 'flaming arrows' 'present[s] in strong colours the *hostile and destructive* character of the Satanic assaults' (original emphasis).

177. The genitive τοῦ πονηροῦ ('of the evil one') may be possessive ('the evil one's flaming arrows') or a genitive of source ('the flaming arrows from the evil one'). This title for the devil (cf. v. 11) appears nowhere else in the Pauline corpus (though cf. 2 Thess. 3:3), but it does occur in Matt. 13:19; John 17:15; 1 John 2:13, 14; 5:18, 19.

178. This is expressed through a new imperative, δέξασθε ('receive'), which is parallel to the preceding participles (vv. 14-16) and linked with them by καί ('and'); against Hoehner, who makes δέξασθε ('receive') parallel to the imperative στῆτε ('stand') in v. 14 (see also on v. 11).

cheek pieces so as to give protection to the head. Here Paul's language is once again drawn from Isaiah 59, where Yahweh the victorious warrior wears 'the helmet of salvation' (v. 17) as he saves his people and judges their enemies.[179] Now, according to Ephesians, he gives his helmet to believers for their protection. This helmet is salvation itself (the genitive is one of apposition: 'the helmet *which is* salvation'),[180] and believers are urged to lay hold of it as they engage in the spiritual warfare.

Earlier in the letter, salvation language was used to summarize what God has *already* accomplished[181] for believers: his making them alive with Christ, raising them up, and seating them with him in the heavenly places (2:5, 6) are comprehensively described as his having saved them by grace (vv. 5, 8). The present aspect of salvation is emphatically stressed:[182] God has rescued them from death, wrath, and bondage, and transferred them into a new dominion where Christ rules. The position of power and authority with Christ to which they have been raised is greater 'than that possessed by their mighty supernatural enemies'.[183] As they appropriate this salvation more fully and live in the light of their status in Christ, they have every reason to be confident of the outcome of the battle.

The final piece of equipment in the believers' armour which Paul urges them to grasp is 'the sword of the Spirit'. They must not only withstand the devil's fiery missiles; they must also take the offensive against the powers of darkness. The term used[184] refers to the short-handled sword, which was an important offensive weapon in close combat. In the expression 'the sword of the Spirit', the former is not identified with the Spirit (i.e., a genitive of apposition);[185] rather, 'of the Spirit' is probably a

179. This passage (according to the LXX) states: 'He [Yahweh] put on righteousness as a breastplate, and he placed a helmet of salvation (περικεφαλαίαν σωτηρίου) upon his head, and he put on a cloak of vengeance and a covering'.

180. Note also 'the breastplate *of righteousness*' (v. 14) and 'the shield of *faith*' (v. 16), where in each case the former element represents the latter.

181. In 1 Thess. 5:8 'the hope of salvation' serves as a helmet, for in that letter salvation is something which believers are 'destined . . . to obtain . . . through our Lord Jesus Christ' — at his second coming.

182. This is not to suggest, however, that salvation is wholly realized. Paul speaks also of a coming age, a future consummation (1:10), as well as a forthcoming 'day of redemption' (4:30). Cf. Arnold, 149.

183. Arnold, 111.

184. Cf. Rom. 8:34; 13:4. μάχαιρα was 'a relatively short sword (or even dagger) used for cutting and stabbing', and was distinct from ρομφαία, 'a large, broad sword used for both cutting and piercing' (Louw and Nida § 6.33). For a detailed discussion see Hoehner.

185. As in the case of the weapons mentioned earlier: the breastplate *of righteousness*, the shield *of faith*, or the helmet *of salvation*.

genitive of source, indicating that the Spirit makes the sword powerful and effective,[186] giving to it its cutting edge (cf. Heb. 4:12). This sword of the Spirit is identified with 'the word of God',[187] a term which in Paul often signifies the gospel. However, he normally uses *logos* ('word') instead of *rhēma,* which appears here. The two terms are often interchangeable, but the latter tends to emphasize the word as spoken or proclaimed (as in 5:26).[188] If this distinction holds here, then Paul is referring to the gospel (cf. Rom. 10:17), but stressing the actual speaking forth of the message, which is given its penetration and power by the Spirit.[189]

Reference has already been made to Isaiah 11:5 at v. 14 in connection with the girdle of truth. Paul again appears to be drawing on the imagery of Isaiah 11, which refers to the Spirit of the Lord resting on the Messiah, who will smite the earth with the word of his mouth and destroy the wicked with the breath[190] of his lips (v. 4). The Isaiah passage is referring to the future smiting of the nations by the Messiah as depicted in Revelation 19:15. Here in Ephesians it is the ongoing warfare with evil powers in the heavenlies that is in view,[191] and once again a weapon carried by the Messiah into battle is available for Christians to use. In their warfare with the powers of darkness, they are to take hold of the word of God, the gospel (cf. 1:13; 6:15), and to proclaim it in the power of the Spirit. This sword is to be used both for self-defence — 'the gospel empowered by the Spirit is the means by which the well-armed Christian is protected'[192] — and when believers 'go on the attack and make new conquests in God's cause'.[193] What is in view here is not some ad hoc word addressed to Satan, as though what we speak against him will defeat him. Rather, it is the faithful speaking forth of the gospel in the realm of darkness, so that men and women held by Satan might hear this liberating and life-giving word and be freed from his grasp.[194]

186. Cf. Schnackenburg, 279; Lincoln, 451; and G. D. Fee, *God's Empowering Presence,* 728. It is not a genitive of origin, meaning that the sword came from the Spirit.

187. In the following clause the neuter relative pronoun ὅ ('which') refers back to the whole phrase 'the sword of the Spirit' (not simply to 'the Spirit').

188. Though contrast Louw and Nida §33.98, who suggest that ῥῆμα has to do with what 'has been stated or said, with primary focus upon the content of the communication'; hence it means 'word, saying, message, statement, question'.

189. So G. D. Fee, *God's Empowering Presence,* 728-29; Barth, 771; and Lincoln, 451. For a discussion of other options, see Best, 603-4.

190. This is ῥῆμα again.

191. In 2 Thess. 2:8, where Paul takes up Isa. 11:4, the Lord Jesus will slay the lawless one with the breath of his mouth.

192. Snodgrass, 344.

193. Mitton, 227.

194. Note Gordon Fee's perceptive comments on this point, against the background of the fascination of some contemporary Christians with words addressed to the devil which will defeat him (G. D. Fee, *God's Empowering Presence,* 729).

3. Watch and Pray, 6:18-20

This third section of the paragraph on spiritual warfare focusses on the need for constant prayer and watchfulness for all believers, and especially for the apostle himself in prison, that he might fearlessly proclaim the mystery (vv. 18-20).

18 Prayer is given greater prominence within the context of the battle with the powers of darkness than any of the weapons listed in vv. 14-17. This is evident because, first, v. 18 is closely related to what has preceded through two participles[195] which stress the need for continual 'praying' in the Spirit and for 'keeping alert' with perseverance and petition. These participles are best connected with the main exhortation, 'stand' (v. 14),[196] rather than with the imperative 'receive' (v. 17),[197] and underscore the point that standing firm and praying belong together. Secondly, prayer itself is not identified with any weapon.[198] The military metaphors are limited to vv. 14-17, while calling on God for strengthening is the way believers stand firm and appropriate the divine armour. Thirdly, Paul elaborates on the theme of prayer by using cognate words and synonyms[199] to describe the activity, and underscores its importance by employing the word 'all' four times in v. 18: believers are urged to pray at *all* times, with *all* prayer and supplication, with *all* perseverance, and they are to make supplication for *all* the saints. Finally, this emphasis on prayer is extended further in v. 19, where the apostle requests interces-

---

195. The NIV starts a new imperative with v. 18 and a new paragraph at v. 19, while the NRSV begins both a new imperative and paragraph with v. 18. As a result the sequence of thought is lost, while it is questionable whether the participles προσευχόμενοι ('praying') and ἀγρυπνοῦντες ('keeping alert') are to be interpreted as imperatives. Cf. Snodgrass, 344; against J. Adai, *Geist*, 234, who thinks that vv. 18-20 form 'an independent section'. Our separation of vv. 18-20 from the preceding is for the sake of convenience, not because we think that, on structural or exegetical grounds, a wedge should be driven between the two sections.

196. So Bruce, 411; Arnold, 106, 112; Lincoln, 451; and Best, 604.

197. Grammatically these two participles might be connected with the nearer imperative δέξασθε ('take, receive', v. 17; so Snodgrass, 344, among others). However, this would suggest that Paul is urging his readers to offer continuing prayer and to be alert only in relation to their taking up the helmet and the sword. Within the flow of the whole paragraph and in the light of the prominence given to the main imperative στῆτε ('stand') of v. 14, it is better to connect the participles with the latter.

198. Against W. Wink, *Naming*, 88; and G. D. Fee, *God's Empowering Presence*, 730, who does admit, however, that prayer is not associated 'with armor as such'. Best, 604, observes that if either prayer or vigilance were a weapon, 'they would have a spiritual activity attached to them as do the other pieces of armour . . . or be themselves qualifications of pieces of physical armour'.

199. διὰ πάσης προσευχῆς καὶ δεήσεως προσευχόμενοι . . . ἐν πάσῃ [προσκαρτερήσει καὶ] δεήσει ('with every prayer and petition, praying . . . in all [perseverance] and *petition*').

sion for himself that he might effectively use the spiritual weapon of the sword of the Spirit, that is, the gospel. Paul wants his readers to understand that prayer is 'foundational for the deployment of all the other weapons',[200] and is therefore crucial if they are to stand firm in their spiritual struggle. He has already shown his concern for them by praying that they might know the greatness of God's power (1:15-23), and be strengthened by it so as to grasp the dimensions of Christ's love for them and be filled with all the fulness of God (3:14-21). The apostle wants them to realize that a life of dependence on God in prayer is essential if they are to engage successfully in their warfare with the powers of darkness.

In the first clause the readers are encouraged to stand firm, 'praying with[201] every kind of prayer and petition'. The first noun, rendered 'prayer', though used on occasion of prayer in general, regularly occurs in both Old and New Testaments to signify petition.[202] In Paul it often has the meaning of 'petition' for others, that is, intercession.[203] The second word, 'petition or supplication', which originally denoted a 'lack' or 'need' and then an 'entreaty', came to be used exclusively in the New Testament of a 'prayer' addressed to God, especially a 'petition' or 'supplication'.[204] Here the word is used synonymously with the first. The two elements are then taken up separately: first, *praying* at all times in the Spirit', and then 'to this end, keeping alert in all perseverance and *petition* for all the saints'. The effect of this accumulation of terms for petitionary prayer (a verb and two synonymous nouns; cf. Phil. 4:6)[205] is to underscore emphatically the importance in the Christian's warfare of believing and expectant prayer.

Believers are to pray continually[206] because their struggle with the powers of darkness is never ending. And their prayers are to be 'in or by the Spirit', that is, inspired and guided by the same Holy Spirit through

200. Arnold, 112.

201. The preposition διά ('with') is used to indicate the accompanying circumstances; so C. F. D. Moule, *Idiom Book,* 57; BDF §223(3); and Best, 605.

202. Gk. προσευχή. 1 Sam. 7:27; cf. v. 29; 2 Kings 19:4; 20:5; Ps. 4:1; 6:9, etc.; Mark 9:29; Acts 10:31; 12:5. Note BAGD, 713; H. Greeven, *TDNT* 2:807-8; G. P. Wiles, *Prayers,* 19.

203. Rom. 1:10; 15:30; Eph. 1:16; Col. 4:2, 12; 1 Thess. 1:2; Phlm. 4, 22.

204. Gk. δέησις. Rom. 10:1; 2 Cor. 1:11; 9:14; Phil. 1:4; 4:6; 1 Tim. 2:1; 5:5; 2 Tim. 1:3. Also Luke 1:13; 2:37; 5:33; Heb. 5:7; Jas. 5:16; 1 Pet. 3:12; see BAGD, 171-72.

205. See P. T. O'Brien, *Philippians,* 491-93.

206. ἐν παντὶ καιρῷ is lit. 'at every opportunity'. The need for prayer 'at all times' is mentioned frequently in Paul's letters, although a variety of expressions is used, e.g., προσκαρτερέω, 'continue, persist in', Rom. 12:12; Col. 4:2; cf. Acts 2:42, 46; 6:4; οὐ παυόμεθα, 'without ceasing', Eph. 1:16; Col. 1:9; νυκτὸς καὶ ἡμέρας, (lit.) 'night and day', 1 Thess. 3:10; 2 Tim. 1:4; ἀδιαλείπτως, 'unceasingly', Rom. 1:9; 1 Thess. 1:2; 2:13; 5:17; cf. ἀδιαλείπτον, 'unceasing', 2 Tim. 1:3.

whom they have confident access to the Father (2:18). As those who have been built into God's dwelling place in the Spirit (2:22) and who are being filled by the Spirit (5:18), they are to pray to the Father, prompted and guided by the Spirit. This is not a reference to praying in tongues, since not all Christians are expected to engage in such prayer, but has to do with specific requests offered through the Spirit by every believer involved in the spiritual warfare.[207] Even when we do not know *what* to pray as we ought, the Spirit comes to our assistance and intercedes for us with unspoken groanings that are perfectly in line with the will of God (lit. 'according to God', Rom. 8:26-27).

To be committed to this kind of prayer[208] believers need to stay alert. Such vigilance is to be accompanied by perseverance and prayer for all the saints.[209] The exhortation to 'watch and pray' was part of early Christian tradition which derives from the teaching of Jesus, who encouraged his disciples to be vigilant in the light of temptation (Mark 14:38) and in view of his unexpected return (Luke 21:34-36; Mark 13:32-37). Here Paul is not simply describing believers' general stance of being watchful and prayerful at all times. Nor is he speaking of attention and engagement in prayer as opposed to humdrum and lethargic praying. Instead, the term used here, 'be alert, vigilant',[210] together with its synonym, 'stay awake, be watchful', was employed regularly in catechetical contexts of the children of light being awake and renouncing the spiritual sleep of the darkness of this age, with their minds directed towards Christ's coming and the consummation of the hope.[211] The concept of wakefulness had an eschatological character to it, and it seems reasonable to assume that the apostle is here encouraging his readers to be alert in expectation of the Lord's coming (cf. 1 Cor. 16:22; Rev. 22:20). Perseverance and prayer are linked elsewhere in the New Testament (Rom. 12:12; Col. 4:2; cf. Acts 1:14; 2:42; 6:4). Here believers are to persevere so as to overcome fatigue and discouragement, and not to fall into spiritual sleep or complacency.

They are to intercede 'for all the saints', that is, for those with

207. Against G. D. Fee, *God's Empowering Presence*, 730-31, who draws in Rom. 8:26-27 in partial support. For a critique of the view that this refers to praying in tongues, see P. T. O'Brien, 'Romans 8:26, 27: A Revolutionary Approach to Prayer?' *RTR* 46 (1987), 65-73, esp. 70-71.

208. εἰς αὐτό ('to this end, for this purpose') indicates that the purpose of keeping alert is to pray continually.

209. The phrase ἐν πάσῃ προσκαρτερήσει καὶ δεήσει περὶ πάντων τῶν ἁγίων ('with all perseverance and petition for all the saints') expresses accompanying circumstances.

210. Cf. Louw and Nida §27.57.

211. E. Lövestam, *Spiritual Wakefulness in the New Testament* (Lund: Gleerup, 1963), 64-77, esp. 75-77.

whom they have been joined in the new community of God's people (cf. 1:15; 2:14-18; 3:8). The spiritual warfare about which the apostle has been speaking is one in which all believers, both individually and corporately, are engaged; they need the intercession of fellow Christians if they are to stand firm in the thick of battle. The fourfold 'all' in this verse, pray at *all* times, with *all* prayer and supplication, with *all* perseverance, and make supplication for *all* the saints, underscores in a most emphatic way the significance which the apostle gave to such mutual intercession.

19 In addition to encouraging his readers to offer petitions for all God's people, Paul specially requests them to intercede for himself.[212] He desires that, in the midst of his imprisonment, he may be given utterance to proclaim the mystery of the gospel boldly and clearly. He was aware that divine resources were needed in the spiritual warfare for this ministry that sought to rescue men and women from the devil's control.

At the end of his letters, Paul often asks for prayer for himself and his colleagues, particularly in relation to their ministry of the gospel (Rom. 15:30-32; 2 Cor. 1:11; Col. 4:3, 4; 1 Thess. 5:25; 2 Thess. 3:1, 2; cf. Phil. 1:19). Here the language is similar to that of Colossians 4:3-4, although the differences probably reflect the varying historical circumstances of the two letters (see below).[213] Petitionary prayer is now requested for Paul's ministry of 'making known' the mystery of the gospel. God has graciously 'made known' to all believers the mystery of his will, particularly his intention to sum up all things in Christ (1:9-10). This mystery was also 'disclosed' by revelation to the apostle, and his task is now to enlighten all about it (3:3-6, 9). Central to this mystery is the reconciliation of Jews and Gentiles in the one body of Christ (Eph. 1–3), a feature that appears to be significant for the specific circumstances apparently alluded to in v. 20 (see below).

If the apostle's own grasp of the mystery is due to God's grace (3:2,

---

212. The conjunction καί ('and') makes the ὑπὲρ ἐμοῦ ('for me') coordinate with the immediately preceding prepositional phrase περὶ πάντων τῶν ἁγίων ('for all the saints') and probably has adjunctive force, 'and pray *particularly for me*'; so G. R. Smillie, 'Mystery', 199-222, esp. 208.

213. The suggestion that the pseudonymous author of Ephesians adapted material from Col. 4:3-4 because the request is specifically for Paul's needs is unconvincing and a very serious weakness to the theory of pseudonymity. Lincoln's attempt ('Stand, therefore', 108) to explain the author's impersonation of Paul in order to enliven the *peroratio*, on the basis of remarks by Quintilian, a first-century rhetorician, is a misappropriation. 'Quintilian was not referring to pseudonymity, but to the use of dialogue by which the readers or hearers knew the words of someone else were presented, as the examples he gives show' (Snodgrass, 345; see Quintilian, *Institutes* 9.2.29-37). Either Paul requests prayer for himself, or someone seeks to mislead the readers into thinking that he does.

7, 8), it is no less true that he needs divine assistance in its proclamation. So he asks his Christian readers to pray 'that a word may be given to me when I open my mouth'.[214] The passive 'may be given' indicates that this 'word' will be graciously provided by God (hence the petition is addressed to him), while the term here means 'utterance', that is, the right word for him to speak when he opens his mouth to declare the mystery of the gospel. Paul is not suggesting that the substance of the mystery was still a puzzle to him, still less that he was seeking some fresh revelation. Earlier in Ephesians he spelled out the content of this mystery which had been revealed to him (1:9, 17-23; 3:3-10).[215] Rather, like every nervous preacher, he desires 'the liberty of the Spirit to express it freely, clearly, and boldly'.[216] The expression 'to open the mouth' appears in contexts of solemnity where a grave or important utterance from God is about to be made (note esp. Ps. 78:2; Matt. 5:2; Acts 8:35; 18:14).[217] This request would have particular point if Paul was in detention in Rome awaiting his appearance before the supreme tribunal and might have the opportunity of bearing witness before Caesar himself (see below).

The result[218] of God's giving the apostle the 'right word' to speak is that he will make known the mystery of the gospel 'freely'.[219] This term (see on 3:12) denotes the freedom to speak without restraint, that is, clearly or boldly. There is some difference of opinion whether Paul is referring to 'boldness' or 'clarity' here and in v. 20, where the cognate verb appears. A good case can be made, on semantic and contextual grounds, for both meanings. As a result, some render the expression with two words, 'boldly and clearly',[220] although the English 'with freedom' or

214. The Colossians parallel ἵνα ὁ θεὸς ἀνοίξῃ ἡμῖν θύραν τοῦ λόγου ('that God may open for us a door for the word') is not exactly equivalent to Eph. 6:19. First, the Colossians reference is to Paul and his co-workers, but it is only the apostle who is in view in Eph. 6:19 ('*my* mouth'). Secondly, in Col. 4:3 the petition is that a door for the gospel message may be opened, and in this case it is the dynamic character of the word that is particularly the focus (1 Cor. 16:9; 2 Cor. 2:12). In Ephesians, however, 'to open the mouth' has to do with speaking freely, clearly, and boldly.

215. Further, the apostle is not implying that 'a particular supernatural utterance be placed in his mouth' (Jer. 1:9; Ezek. 2, 3); cf. G. R. Smillie, 'Mystery', 215.

216. G. R. Smillie, 'Mystery', 215.

217. Although it is possible to take this expression as referring to God opening Paul's mouth, it is better, with the majority of commentators, to understand it of Paul opening his mouth, at which time God will give him the appropriate word to speak.

218. So A. T. Robertson, *Grammar*, 1090; and D. B. Wallace, *Greek Grammar*, 594.

219. The adverbial phrase 'with freedom' describes the manner in which Paul will make known the mystery.

220. Lincoln, 429, has 'boldly and openly' at vv. 19 and 20. W. C. van Unnik, 'The Christian's Freedom of Speech', 466-88, has shown that, in contexts of fierce opposition and danger to his life when Paul proclaimed the gospel to Jews, the term παρρησία should

'freely' captures the two nuances of the Greek word. Perhaps it is in anticipation of facing the imperial tribune that Paul wants to present the mystery of the gospel with courage and clarity. The genitive 'of the gospel' may be subjective, meaning that the gospel announces the mystery; that is, the word of the gospel proclaims the mystery which is the body of Christ, comprised of Jews and Gentiles united in him (Eph. 2, 3). It is more likely, however, that 'of the gospel' is an epexegetic genitive,[221] signifying that the mystery is the gospel (cf. Col. 4:3). Certainly, as Raymond Brown points out, the two are 'only different aspects of the same basic reality'. He adds: 'The mystery in itself signifies the hidden nature of the divine plan; the gospel is the external manifestation of that plan to the people affected by it'.[222] Colossians and Ephesians show clearly that this gospel is for everyone. It has been revealed openly, and it is to be proclaimed openly.

20 Paul has become an ambassador for the mystery of the gospel.[223] In his earlier letters he had written of himself[224] as Christ's ambassador through whom God announced his message of reconciliation (2 Cor. 5:20; cf. Phlm. 9).[225] Now, in the context of his prayer request, this lofty term for an accredited representative is used again. He is an ambassador on behalf of God, who has entrusted him with a commission to make known the mystery to the Gentiles (3:2, 7, 8). His task is to proclaim to them the unsearchable riches of Christ and to make plain to everyone the administration of this mystery (vv. 8, 9).

However, what is ironic, if not contradictory, is Paul's self-description as an ambassador *in chains*. The notion of a prisoner functioning in such a role during this period is apparently 'without precedent and contradicts the status, honour and prestige characteristic of ambassa-

---

be rendered as 'courage' (Acts 9:27, 28-29; 13:46; 19:8, etc.). At the same time, παρρησία is often paired with an antonym, 'obscurely' or enigmatically', and should therefore be rendered 'plainly' or 'clearly'. Cf. 1 Thess. 2:2, where both aspects seem to be in view. See the discussion of G. R. Smillie, 'Mystery', 214-16, who finally prefers the rendering 'clearly'.

221. M. Bockmuehl, *Revelation and Mystery,* 205, among others.

222. R. E. Brown, *Semitic Background,* 64, cited by G. R. Smillie, 'Mystery', 213.

223. Syntactically, the antecedent of οὗ ('of which') could be τὸ μυστήριον τοῦ εὐαγγελίου ('the mystery of the gospel'), τὸ μυστήριον ('the mystery'), or τὸ εὐαγγέλιον ('the gospel'). However, the difference in meaning is not great, particularly if the words τοῦ εὐαγγελίου ('of the gospel') are epexegetical of τὸ μυστήριον ('the mystery') (see on v. 19).

224. For a recent exposition of the view that Paul is referring to himself as an apostle when he uses the plural, '*we* are Christ's ambassadors' (2 Cor. 5:20), see P. Barnett, *2 Corinthians,* 319-21.

225. Note the full discussion of the exegetical and theological issues in A. Bash, *Ambassadors for Christ: An Exploration of Ambassadorial Language in the New Testament* (Tübingen: J. C. B. Mohr [Paul Siebeck], 1997), 87-119.

dors'. Indeed, '[t]he imprisonment of an ambassador would have been regarded as a serious insult both to the Sender and to the ambassador'.[226] But Paul's chains refer not only to his imprisonment; they also testify symbolically to his calling. His chains indicate that he is under obligation and are therefore his credentials as an ambassador.[227] If the historical context is that of his appeal to Caesar, then his imprisonment in Rome serves to open the door for him to address the emperor or his prefect. What he would have little hope of achieving otherwise, Paul might do as an accused prisoner, that is, as 'an ambassador in chains'.

This may help to explain Paul's surprising response to his circumstances. Instead of expressing feelings of self-pity or resentment, or of requesting prayer for his release from prison, he revels in his mission. Paul did not hide, apologize for, or defend the fact of his imprisonment. His sufferings were not to be a source of disappointment for his predominantly Gentile readers; rather, these afflictions were for their glory and led on to his intercessory prayer for them (3:13, 14).[228]

Paul's ministry to them was a gift of God's grace (Eph. 3:7), and his desire to speak with boldness and clarity, which he mentions again[229] (cf. v. 19), is appropriate for one who is an ambassador.[230] His life was wholly under God's control and direction, even to the extent of his imprisonment as Christ's accredited representative. Divine necessity is laid upon him to proclaim the gospel (1 Cor. 9:16-17). Let him announce the mystery of the gospel freely and boldly, for that is how he ought to make it known.[231]

What was the result? If 2 Timothy 4:17 is recounting the hearing of his appeal, then, although no one came to support the apostle, the answer to the prayer requested here was: 'the Lord stood at my side and gave me

226. So A. Bash, *Ambassadors,* 132.

227. G. R. Smillie, 'Mystery', 211, 212, following M. N. A. Bockmuehl, *Revelation and Mystery,* 192, 205. Note also Phil. 1:7, 8, 12; Phlm. 9, 13; Eph. 3:1; 4:1; 2 Tim. 2:9; and Acts 28:20.

228. A. Bash, *Ambassadors,* 132. Bash rightly observes that at Eph. 4:1 Paul emphasized his imprisonment 'as if it validated the basis of his paraenetic appeal'. On the issue of honour and shame in relation to imprisonment in the first century, see B. Rapske, *Paul in Roman Custody, Vol. 3: The Book of Acts in Its First Century Setting,* ed. B. W. Winter (Grand Rapids/Carlisle: Eerdmans/Paternoster, 1994), 288-98.

229. This second ἵνα-clause, ἵνα ἐν αὐτῷ παρρησιάσωμαι κτλ. ('that I may speak of it boldly and openly . . .'), is probably coordinate with the first in v. 19 and mentions a further content of the prayer request. See Best, 609; and Hoehner.

230. A. Bash, *Ambassadors,* 131.

231. The compulsion implied by δεῖ ('it is necessary') is that of divine appointment, while ὡς probably expresses manner ('in the way I ought to speak') rather than cause ('because I must speak it'). Cf. M. J. Harris, *Colossians and Philemon,* 195, and many others.

strength, so that through me the message might be fully proclaimed and all the Gentiles might hear it'.

In his concluding appeal of 6:10-20, which catches up many of the theological and ethical concerns of the letter, Paul describes in cosmic terms believers' responsibilities as they live in the world. Using the sustained imagery of a spiritual battle, he depicts the Christian life as a struggle against supernatural evil forces. Believers are urged to recognize the nature and dimension of the conflict and stand firm against the devil and his hosts who are arrayed against them (vv. 11, 13, 14). Although Christ has already defeated these foes (1:20-23), they continue to exist and are still active in attempting to separate his followers from him. In order to be strong against this supernatural, cunning, and powerful opposition believers need divine protection and equipping. Paul lists some of the specific pieces of armour they need to put on (vv. 14-17) if they are to stand firm against the powers. These weapons include the belt of truth, the breastplate of righteousness, having feet fitted with a preparedness to announce the gospel of peace, and the shield of faith, by which they will be fully protected against every kind of assault rained upon them by the evil one. Further, believers are to lay hold of the helmet of salvation, by which they are protected against evil attack, and the sword of the Spirit, which is the word of God, in other words, the gospel as proclaimed and made powerful by the Spirit. The third section of the letter's final exhortation (vv. 18-20) makes it clear that appropriating God's armour in order to stand firm in the battle requires a life that is dependent on God in prayer. Only then will they remain alert and keep at bay spiritual sleep and complacency. Their prayer will also include offering petitions on behalf of all believers, and especially the apostle himself, that in the midst of his imprisonment he may be given utterance to proclaim the mystery of the gospel boldly and clearly. This passage with its call to stand firm forms an appropriate conclusion not only to the ethical admonitions of Paul's paraenesis but also to the letter as a whole.

IV. LETTER CLOSING, 6:21-24

> [21]*Tychicus, the dear brother and faithful servant in the Lord, will tell you everything, so that you also may know how I am and what I am doing.* [22]*I am sending him to you for this very purpose, that you may know how we are, and that he may encourage you.* [23]*Peace to the brothers, and love*

with faith from God the Father and the Lord Jesus Christ. ²⁴*Grace to all who love our Lord Jesus Christ with an undying love.*

Paul has asked his Christian readers to pray for his bold proclamation of the gospel, and then reminded them of his situation in prison. He now mentions in his conclusion that he is sending Tychicus to provide them with further information about his welfare and circumstances. This letter closing is made up of two sections: first, the commendation of Tychicus and the explanation of his task as an apostolic emissary (vv. 21-22); and, secondly, the peace wish and final benediction (vv. 23-24).

Verses 21 and 22 provide the longest example of exact correspondence of wording between Colossians and Ephesians: thirty-two words in the original are in verbatim agreement, except for the addition of *what I am doing* in Ephesians 6:21 as well as *and fellow servant* in Colossians 4:7. It looks as though the author of the second document copied from the first. Many have claimed that the author of Ephesians used Colossians, but as Ernest Best points out, if he has used Colossians previously in such a way as to suggest that he was not copying from it, why does he now at this point turn to do just that? The additions and omission cancel each other out, so that it is as likely that the author of Colossians used Ephesians as the reverse. Although it is not his preference, Best concedes that it 'is also possible that the two letters had a common author who simply repeated in the second more or less what he had written in the first'.[232] This would, of course, imply that the two letters were written at about the same time and that the author had a good memory, or that he still had the first letter while penning the second. If, as we have argued, Paul was the author of both epistles, it is possible that Tychicus took both with him when he went to Asia Minor.

21-22 Tychicus will be Paul's messenger to inform[233] the congregations about his personal situation.[234] The expression 'you also' may well refer to letters sent to other recipients, such as Colossians, which were also delivered by Tychicus.[235] At this time he may well have been the apostle's

---

232. Best, 613. See his detailed arguments in 'Who Used Whom?' 72-96, and note our discussion in the introduction.

233. γνωρίζω ('make known'), which has already been used of God's making known the mystery (Eph. 1:9; 3:3, 5, 10; cf. 6:19), is here employed in a secular sense (1 Cor. 12:3; 15:1), as it is on occasion in the LXX: 1 Kings 1:27; Neh. 8:12; Prov. 9:9.

234. τὰ κατ᾽ ἐμέ ('my circumstances') was a common expression to describe the situation of a person, e.g., Herodotus 7.148; 1 Esdras 9:17; Tobit 10:9; 2 Maccabees 3:40; Acts 24:22; 25:14; and especially Phil. 1:12.

235. The exact sense is not entirely clear. καὶ ὑμεῖς could mean: so that 'you for your part' may know my affairs, as I for my part have heard about you (cf. Eph. 1:15); so Robinson, 217. Abbott, 190 (cf. Barth, 809), suggests that the reference is general, describ-

special envoy to the churches of provincial Asia which had been established during Paul's Ephesians ministry. In Acts 20:4 he is mentioned as a native of the province of Asia who was with Paul in Greece and journeyed with him to Troas at the end of the third missionary journey. He accompanied the apostle to Jerusalem when the latter took the collection from the Gentile churches to their needy Jewish brethren in Jerusalem. According to 2 Timothy 4:12 Paul sent him on some undesignated mission to Ephesus, while later he planned to send either him or Artemas to Crete to take Titus's place (Tit. 1:12). Along with several others he appears to have been closely associated with Paul during the latter stages of his ministry, and is likely to have been known to the recipients of the letter.

Tychicus is commended as *the dear brother and faithful servant in the Lord* (cf. Col. 4:7). In this context the term *brother* means not so much 'fellow-Christian' (though Tychicus was obviously this, and the term has this meaning in v. 21) as 'co-worker' or 'helper'.[236] The full expression underscores the close collegial relationship he had with Paul and his proven track record of ministry in the cause of Christ. Such qualifications were important for the task entrusted to him, namely, to convey news of Paul to the readers and to strengthen and encourage them in a ministry that was consistent with the apostle's concerns expressed in the letter.

Paul is sending Tychicus with his letter: in the original the verb is to be understood as an epistolary aorist, that is, it views the action from the standpoint of the recipients as they read the letter, and so should be translated *I am sending;*[237] the RSV rendering 'I have sent' could be interpreted to mean Tychicus had been despatched before Paul wrote the letter. The Greek expression is like a covering note to a letter in which the bearer is mentioned.

23 Authors in the ancient world usually concluded their letters with a wish for the welfare of their readers. Paul turned this wish into a benediction type of prayer.[238] The words 'peace' and 'grace' begin vv. 23 and 24 respectively. Both are found in the salutation of the letter (1:2), but are repeated in the last two verses of this epistle in reverse order. On seven other occasions Paul uses the exact wording of 1:2;[239] but here he deviates from it.[240]

---

ing believers who do not know Paul personally. The intent would be that they 'also' may learn about his circumstances, just as others who do know about his situation.

236. E. E. Ellis, in *Prophecy,* 3-22.

237. So most commentators; cf. also D. B. Wallace, *Greek Grammar,* 563.

238. See J. A. D. Weima, *Neglected Endings,* and 'The Pauline Letter Closings: Analysis and Hermeneutical Significance', *BBR* 5 (1995), 177-98.

239. Rom. 1:7; 1 Cor. 1:3; 2 Cor. 1:2; Gal. 1:3; Phil. 1:2; 2 Thess. 1:2; Phlm. 3.

240. It is unlikely that a pseudonymous author would have departed from the usual Pauline style here.

'Peace' is here given a prominent position, whether this is due to the fact that it is one of the leading themes in the letter (cf. 2:14-18; 6:15), or because it is an important term used in benedictions (Rom. 15:33; 2 Thess. 3:16), or because it occurs frequently near the end of letters (Gal. 6:16; 1 Pet. 5:14; 3 John 15). Certainly its emphatic position here is in accordance with the theology of Ephesians, where peace is closely related to reconciliation in 2:14-18, and virtually equivalent to salvation (cf. 2:5-8). Paul desires peace for the 'brothers (and sisters)', using the third person, rather than 'to you', which is his normal style in addressing his readers. In a circular letter this familial term in the third person applies to members of various churches, whether Jewish Christians or Gentile. Earlier in Ephesians Paul and his readers were called 'members of one another' (4:25), and spoken of as belonging to the same household (2:19). But this is the first time 'brothers [and sisters]' appears. The apostle, then, reminds his readers of the peace of God which is theirs, and he desires that it may flow through them to others.

Paul also desires that 'love with faith' may be conferred on the readers. Love is mentioned in final blessings of Paul's letters, and can refer to the love of God (as in 2 Cor. 13:14) or Paul's own love (as in 1 Cor. 16:24). Here it refers to the former, since it is parallelled with 'peace' and 'grace' (v. 24). The expression 'with faith' signifies not that a priority is given to faith, but that love is accompanied by faith.[241] Its present connection with love takes up Paul's thanksgiving in 1:15 (cf. 3:17), where he expresses his pleasure at news of the readers' faith and their love shown to all the saints. Here, then, at the end of the letter he 'prays that these same qualities may continue to characterize them'. As grace and peace in the introductory benediction (1:2) derive from the twin divine source, so here 'peace and love with faith' have their origin in and flow from *God the Father and the Lord Jesus Christ*.

24 'Grace be with you' is Paul's basic benediction at the end of a letter, although here it would strike the readers as particularly appropriate, given the earlier stress on all that the readers (together with all other Christians) had received through the undeserved favour of God and Christ (cf. 1:6, 7; 2:5, 7, 8; 4:7). While Paul's usual benediction is generally expanded in various forms, here the wording is different: instead of the second person plural, it is cast in the third person: *all who love our Lord Jesus Christ* (cf. 'to the brothers', v. 23). J. Armitage Robinson suggests that this was 'in harmony with the circular nature of this

---

241. The preposition μετά ('with') signifies association, suggesting that there is a close connection between the two nouns, perhaps with an emphasis on love. Cf. BAGD, 509; against Barth, 811.

epistle', but if so, its circular nature has not prevented the use of the second person in vv. 21-22.[242] Paul's wish-prayer of v. 23 has spoken of love coming from God and Christ, while here the benediction is for grace on all who respond in love for Christ. Andrew Lincoln observes: 'Elsewhere the letter has referred to God's love for believers (cf. 2:4) and Christ's love for them (cf. 3:19; 5:2, 25), to believers' love for one another (cf. 1:15; 4:2), to believing husbands' love for their wives (cf. 5:25, 28, 33), and to believers' love in general (cf. 1:4; 3:17; 4:15, 16; 5:2; 6:23), but this is the only place where their love for Christ is made explicit'. He then acutely adds: 'In this way, the letter closes with a stress on believers' personal relationship and commitment to Christ'.[243] The readers, and by implication all believers, need to be aware not only of the objective blessings of the mighty salvation that have been won for us by God in Christ, but also that we have responded in the appropriate way. Further, although our acknowledgement might properly be cast in terms of a response to the Pauline gospel or the apostolic teaching, here it is to the Lord Jesus Christ, who loved us and gave himself for us, that we gladly bow the knee in submission.

Paul's final phrase, rendered *with undying love,* which is a closing rhetorical flourish to the letter, is not entirely clear in its meaning. The noun refers to 'immortality, incorruption', which elsewhere in Paul characterizes the life of the resurrection (1 Cor. 15:42, 50, 52-54; Rom. 2:7; 1 Tim. 1:10).[244] But to what is the phrase connected? Some translators suggest that it should be linked with the immediately preceding words 'our Lord Jesus Christ', who is thus described as being 'in immortality' (cf. 1 Tim. 1:17; Jas. 2:1). But this is doubtful since the word 'immortality' is not used elsewhere in a local sense. Others link the phrase with 'all who love', so that Paul's wish-prayer is that grace may be given to *all who love our Lord Jesus Christ with an undying love.*[245] Immortality belongs to the life of the age to come; believers already participate in it, and so does their love which belongs to that age. While this interpretation is possible, it is preferable to regard immortality as more directly linked with God or one of his blessings rather than the quality of believers' love. Accordingly, 'with immortality' is best taken with the preceding noun 'grace', even though it is somewhat separated from it syntactically. The preposition 'with' is often used to connect two nouns in this way in Ephesians (2:7;

---

242. See Bruce, 415.

243. Lincoln, 466, to whose exposition I am indebted.

244. Cf. Wisdom 2:23; 6:18, 19; 4 Maccabees 9:22; 17:12.

245. ἐν ἀφθαρσίᾳ ('with immortality') is thus an adverbial phrase modifying the participle ἀγαπώντων ('those who love'). Similarly RSV, ASV, NAB, NIV, GNB, and NRSV. Note also Abbott, 191; Robinson, 138, 220; and Hoehner.

3:12; 6:2).[246] So grace and immortality, which are blessings of the new age, are what Paul wants to be given in greater measure to his readers. The two blessings are not unrelated: grace, which has appeared often in Ephesians, is imperishable, not subject to corruption, while immortality flows out of God's grace shown in the present but also in the coming ages (cf. 2:7).

Paul concludes his letter with two important elements: the commendation of Tychicus, whom he is sending to his readers so as to provide further information about his circumstances (vv. 21, 22), and the wish for peace and benediction of grace. Consistent with the letter as a whole (chaps. 1–3 and 4–6), vv. 23 and 24 focus, first, on God's gracious gifts which have been bestowed on believers in the Lord Jesus Christ; and, secondly, on the glad response of love that they are to make to Christ.

---

246. Those who take the preposition ἐν ('in, with') in this comitative sense include Bruce, 416; Schnackenburg, 291; and Lincoln, 466-68. Note NEB and JB.

Index of Subjects

Abolition (of the law), 196-99
Abraham, 98-99, 176, 232, 234, 236, 241, 338
Access, 208, 249-50
Administration, God's, 227, 243-44
Adoption, 102-3
Age, ages (including the 'present' and 'coming' ages), 31, 143, 158-59, 173, 248, 269, 382-83
All things, 30, 33, 58-60, 63, 92, 108-15, 145, 244, 284-85, 397-98
'Already–not yet' antithesis, 151, 179, 265, 306, 317, 393, 425, 458-59, 465
Ambassador, 488-89
Anger, 339-41, 349-50, 445-46
Apostles, 36, 83-84, 213-16, 233-34, 297-98
Armour of God, weapons, 456-90
Artemis, 54
Awake, 374-77

Baptism, 120, 282-84, 374-76, 422-23
Berakah, blessing, eulogy, 88-123, 125
Blameless, 100-101, 360, 385-86, 424-26
Boasting, 175-78
Body, 64-65, 147-48, 201-2, 235-36, 245-46, 280-81, 286-88, 301-5, 338, 414-15, 426-33
Boldness, 249-50, 486-89
Bride, bridegroom, 420, 422-26, 433-35
Brother, 491-92

Building, 28, 212-13, 216, 218-19, 301-5, 316, 345

Calling, 134-35, 273-76, 281-82
Child, children, 308, 352, 367-70, 439-47
Christ (Jesus), 24, 27-28, 130, 175, 187-88, 191-210, 216-19, 229-32, 241-43, 258, 286-90, 296-98, 301, 305-8, 312-13, 324-26, 373-74, 375-77, 386, 392, 404-5, 409-38, 441, 447-53, 455-58, 463, 473-74, 477-79, 482; ascent, 286, 288-89, 291, 293-94, 296; death of, 21-23, 106, 183-84, 190, 196-204, 207, 352, 354-55, 419-23, 437; descent, 286, 294-96; exaltation (of Christ and believers), 21-23, 138-52, 170-71, 465; fulness of, 149-52, 305-8; in Christ, 59, 92, 97-118, 139-40, 178-79, 188, 190, 234-37, 249-50, 268-69; Lord, 21, 61, 280-84, 319, 367, 396-98, 412, 441, 445-51, 455-56, 460-72; love of, 23, 263-66, 352-54, 409-10, 418-29; resurrection (of Christ and of believers), 62, 138-40, 154, 167, 170-71
Church, churches, 25-29, 53, 63-64, 146-47, 245-48, 268, 409-38
Circumcised, uncircumcised, 186-87
Citizenship (of Israel), 188-89, 210-11
Cleanse, cleansing, 421-23
Commandments, 196-99, 442-44
Conduct. *See* Walk, live, life-style
'Conformity' pattern, 351-52, 354

INDEX OF SUBJECTS

Conversion, 376-77
Cornerstone, 216-18
Covenant, covenants, 189-90
Creation, new, 28, 173-81, 199-200, 244, 331-32, 336

Darkness, 320-21, 357-58, 366-67, 370-78, 458, 467-68
Day, days, 382-83, 471-72
Dead, death, 155-58, 321, 375-77, 469-70
Debauchery, 389-90
Desire, evil, 162, 328-29
Devil, Satan, prince of the power of the air, 159-61, 310, 340-41, 383, 462-64, 466-82
Disobedient, 160-61, 364-66
Diversity, 286-87
Dividing wall, 195
Doxology, 253-54, 266-70
Drunkenness, 388-90
Dwell, dwelling, 218-21, 258-60

Earth, things on, 60, 112-13, 247, 256
Election, 98-103
Enmity, hostility, 193, 204-5
Enthronement. See Christ (Jesus): exaltation (of Christ and believers)
Ephesus, 5, 54-55, 84-87
Ephesians, Letter to: as circular letter, 47; authorship, 4-47; central message, 58-65; contents, 66-68; destination, 47-49, 56-57; ecclesiology, 25-29; genre, as a letter, 68-73; genre, as rhetoric, 73-82; language, 5-8; life-setting, 49-51; literary relationship with Colossians, 8-21; provenance, 57-58; pseudonymity, 8, 37-45; purpose, 51-57; readers, 49-51, 57, 84-87; rhetoric, rhetorical analysis, 73-82; style, 5-8
Eschatology, future, 29-33, 113-15, 143, 169-70, 201, 424-25, 485; realized, 29-33, 143, 169-70, 201, 425
'Established', 259-60
Evangelists, 297-99
Exhortation, exhortatory material, 64, 67, 271-74, 317-19, 334-36, 357-58, 378-80, 383-88, 405-11, 439-40, 447-48, 456-60
Eye-service, 448, 451

Faith, 127-28, 174-77, 249, 259, 282-84, 305-6, 479-80
Falsehood, 337
Family, 212, 255-56
Far. See Near and far
Favouritism, 455
Fear, 404-5, 412, 436-37, 449-50
Fill, fulness, 32, 149-52, 265-66, 296-97, 305-8, 386-94
Flesh, 162, 186
Foolish talk, 360-61
Foreigner, 210-11
Forgiveness, 106, 351-52
Foundation, 212-17
Freely, with freedom, 249-50, 486-88
Fulfilment, 113-14
Futility, 320

Gave, gift, 145, 286-93, 297-98, 301
Gentiles, 27-28, 36, 50, 52, 63-64, 92, 109, 115-18, 156, 182-221, 223-28, 230, 232-38, 252-53, 319-25, 389
Gentleness, meekness, 276-77
Glory, glorious, 92, 135-36, 251-52, 256-57, 268-69, 424-25
God, 89-92, 184, 190, 280-82, 292-93, 392, 456-63; as Father, 89, 94, 130-31, 209-10, 255, 281, 284-85, 397-98, 447; glory of, 92, 104, 118, 123, 130-31; goodness (kindness) of, 164; like God (of new creation), 331-33; love of, 163, 164-66; mercy of, 163, 164-66, 172, 443; presence of, 346-47; right hand of, 141
God's saving plan. See Summing up
Goodness. See Kindness, goodness
Gospel, 118-19, 134, 206, 230-32, 236, 241-43, 324, 423, 464, 475-79, 482, 486-88
Grace, 87-88, 104, 164, 168, 172, 174-76, 224-28, 237-41, 243-45, 286-88, 492-94
Greed, 323, 362-63
Greetings, 83-88
Growth, 297, 310, 312-17
Guarantee, 120-21

Hands, made with, 186-87
Hardening, 32
Head, headship, of Christ, 27, 65, 145-

48, 312-13, 410, 413-18, 428; of husbands, 65, 410, 413-19
Heart, 133-34, 258-59, 396-97, 450-51
Heaven, heavenly realm, 54, 60, 96-97, 112-13, 141, 211, 246-47, 256, 296, 466-67
Holy, holiness, sanctify, 100-101, 233, 331-33, 420-26
Honour, 442-43
Hope, 134-35, 189-90, 281-82
Household, household table, 17, 65, 210-12, 378, 399-456
Humanity, the new and the old, 28, 62, 64, 199-200, 209, 305-7, 317-34, 338
Humility, 276-77
Husbands, 405-38
Hymns. *See* Songs, singing

Ignorance, 320-21
Imitators (of God or Christ), 331-33, 352-54, 392
Immorality, 358-60, 362-64, 370-72
Immortality, 494-95
Impurity, every kind of, 323
Inheritance, 115-23, 135-36, 234-35, 362-64
Intercession. *See* Prayer, intercession
Israel, 183-91, 203, 232, 346-47, 420

Jerusalem, Zion, 220-21, 337-38, 478
Jews, 27-28, 52, 63-64, 115-18, 182-221, 248
Justification, 23-24, 169, 174

Kindness, goodness, 351, 367-69
Kingdom, of Christ and of God, 362-64
Knowledge, 107-11, 128-38, 256, 260-64, 305-7, 321

Law, Torah, 24, 176, 196-99, 291, 442-44
Learn, 324-25
Life, long, 443-44
Ligament, 314-15
Light, 357-58, 366-78
Long-suffering, patience, 278
Love, 23, 101, 127-28, 259-60, 263-66, 278, 310-13, 316, 352-54, 410, 418-29, 493-94

Magic, magical background, 53, 137-38, 141-42, 158, 160, 261-62, 467
Malice, 54, 350
Marriage, 32, 65, 409-38
Masters, 447-56
Mind, 330-31. *See also* Understanding, mind
Minister, ministry, 238, 301-4, 315-16
Moses, 291
Mystery, 35, 36, 59, 108-14, 223-52, 262, 381-82, 430-35, 438

Name, 256, 398
Near and far, 183, 190-91, 205, 207-8, 212
Neighbour, 337-38
Nourish (and cherish), 427-29, 446

Obey, obedience, 441-51
'One flesh', 417, 427-34, 438
'Once–now' antithesis, 157-58, 183-84, 190, 231-32, 358

Paraenesis. *See* Exhortation, exhortatory material
Parents, 439-47
Pastors, 297-300
Paul, 4-5, 33-71, 83; apostle (to the Gentiles), commission, 34-36, 83-84, 223-28, 238-39, 243-44, 248; picture of, 33-71; unworthiness, 240-41
Peace, 87-88, 192-94, 200, 204-8, 279-80, 475-79, 492-93
Pleasing the Lord, 369-70
Possession, treasured, 121-22
Power, 55, 131, 136-41, 239, 252-66, 456-90
Prayer, intercession, 123-26, 128-38, 225, 252-66, 483-88
Predicament of humanity outside of Christ, 61-62, 155-64
Principalities and powers, 22, 33, 54, 61-62, 138, 142-46, 160, 244-48, 289, 456-90
Prison, prisoner, 224, 274, 488-91
Promise, 189, 235-36, 442-44
Prophets, 36, 213-16, 233-34, 297-98
Proselytes, 191
Psalms. *See* Songs, singing
Pseudepigrapha, 38, 40-41, 44

Put on, put off, of a garment, 326-29, 331, 334-37

Reconcile, reconciliation, 19-20, 22-23, 61, 63, 115-17, 192-93, 199-205, 207-9
Redemption, redeem, 105-8, 121-23, 347-49, 382
Remember, memory, 185-87
Renewed, be, 326, 329-31
Revelation, reveal, 131-32, 228-34, 241-43
Reward, 452-53
Rhetoric, rhetorical analysis. *See* Ephesians: rhetoric, rhetorical analysis
Riches, wealth, 107, 135, 165, 172, 241-43, 256-57
Right, fitting, 441-42
Righteousness, 331-33, 367-69, 474-75

Saints, holy ones, 87, 128, 211, 233, 261, 263-64, 301-4
Satan. *See* Devil, Satan, prince of the power of the air
Save, salvation, 23-24, 30-31, 66, 118-19, 168-70, 173-81, 262, 480-81
Saviour, 414-15
Schemes, wiles (of the devil), 463-65, 470, 480
Seal, 120
Separation, 321
Servant, service. *See* Minister, ministry
Sins and transgressions, 155-58, 166, 339-40
Slaves, 447-56
Songs, singing, 386-87, 394-97
Speech, 344-45, 360-61, 486-88
Spirit, Holy, 92, 95-96, 117-21, 219, 257-60, 276, 279-81, 295, 345-49, 386-400, 480-85
Spiritual blessing, 93-98
Spiritual warfare, struggle, 33, 341, 456-90
Splendour, 424
Stand, stand firm, withstand, 463-65, 468-84

Steal, 342-43
Stewardship, 223-52
Strengthen, be strong, 256-57, 460-62, 464
Struggle. *See* Spiritual warfare, struggle
Submission, 387, 398-404, 407-9, 437
Subordination. *See* Submission
Sufferings, 250-52
Summing up, 30, 33, 58-60, 63, 92, 108-15, 200-201, 228, 247-49, 254

Teachers, teaching, 297-301, 309, 324-26
Temple, 28, 212, 218-21
Thanksgiving, 94, 123-28, 361, 386-87, 397-98
Training, 445-47
Truth, 118, 310-12, 322, 325-26, 333-38, 367-69, 473-74
'Two ways', 335, 381, 389
Tychicus, 491-92
Typology, 293, 337-38, 347-48, 432-35, 438

Uncircumcised. *See* Circumcised, uncircumcised
Understanding, mind, 320-21, 330-31
Unity, 194, 273-87, 305-7, 316-17

Vices and virtues, lists of, 335-36, 360

Walk, live, life-style, 65, 154-55, 157-59, 180-81, 273-76, 318-19, 352-56, 367-71, 377-80
Watch, be alert, 483-85
Weapons. *See* Armour of God, weapons
Will of God or Christ, 103, 108-10, 383-86, 451
Wisdom, 107, 131, 244-46, 262-63, 380-82
Wives, 405-38
Word, 118-19, 421-23, 482, 486-88
Workmanship, God's, 178-79
Work, works, 24, 174-81, 319, 342-43, 370-73
Wrath, of God, 162-63, 364-65

Index of Authors

Abbott, T. K., 8, 95, 174, 181, 229, 241, 263, 278, 280, 309, 325, 384, 391, 392, 415, 416, 422, 426, 491, 494
Adai, J., 95, 96, 119, 396, 483
Agrell, G., 343
Alford, H., 415
Allan, J. A., 97, 170
Allen, T. G., 125, 143, 154, 170
Andersen, F. I., 165
Anderson, R. D., 76
Arnold, C. E., 9, 14, 22, 24, 27, 30, 31, 33, 47, 48, 51, 52, 54, 55, 56, 61, 70, 86, 93, 114, 120, 135, 137, 138, 141, 142, 144, 146, 148, 149, 151, 159, 160, 161, 163, 164, 169, 171, 176, 202, 246, 247, 248, 253, 254, 256, 257, 259, 260, 261, 265, 266, 267, 289, 294, 297, 301, 307, 313, 314, 315, 326, 332, 342, 383, 413, 428, 457, 458, 461, 462, 463, 465, 466, 467, 468, 469, 471, 476, 477, 481, 483, 484
Aune, D. E., 69, 70, 215

Baard, T., 361
Bahnsen, G. L., 24, 198
Bailey, K. E., 184
Balch, D. L., 406, 407
Balz, H. R., 37, 41, 320, 395, 404
Banks, R. J., 106, 146
Barclay, J. M. G., 407
Barnett, P., 83, 84, 425
Barrett, C. K., 33, 83

Barth, M., 29, 99, 103, 114, 148, 150, 158, 167, 175, 182, 192, 198, 199, 200, 203, 232, 235, 238, 240, 241, 242, 243, 248, 263, 279, 285, 294, 300, 307, 308, 309, 311, 312, 313, 314, 322, 324, 325, 326, 346, 349, 350, 352, 353, 365, 399, 404, 412, 415, 418, 422, 423, 426, 431, 433, 471, 474, 482, 491, 493
Barton, S. C., 407
Bash, A., 488, 489
Batey, R. A., 433
Bauder, W., 277
Baumgarten, J., 180
Baur, F. C., 4
Beare, F. W., 15, 136, 294
Becker, V., 299
Bedale, S., 413
Behm, J., 106
Belleville, L. L., 274
Benoit, P., 148
Berger, K., 168
Bergmeier, R., 157
Best, E., 4, 8, 11, 14, 15, 16, 17, 18, 19, 20, 22, 29, 32, 34, 44, 47, 49, 51, 52, 53, 55, 68, 71, 72, 83, 84, 90, 93, 95, 97, 98, 99, 102, 104, 107, 125, 129, 134, 137, 139, 145, 146, 149, 157, 165, 174, 182, 184, 187, 189, 192, 194, 197, 201, 204, 208, 213, 217, 228, 230, 232, 239, 240, 241, 242, 244, 245, 249, 254, 258, 261, 263, 272, 277, 279, 286, 287, 297, 298, 299, 300, 303, 304, 308, 313, 314,

501

318, 320, 322, 324, 326, 335, 338, 339, 342, 343, 346, 353, 358, 360, 365, 371, 373, 377, 380, 382, 395, 405, 407, 411, 424, 426, 450, 479, 482, 483, 484, 489, 491
Betz, H. D., 73, 74, 77
Bietenhard, H., 398
Bilezikian, G., 400, 401, 403, 412
Billington, A., 56
Bjerkelund, C. J., 71, 272, 274
Blocher, H., 163
Bocher, O., 400
Bockmuehl, M. N. A., 19, 109, 229, 232, 241, 433, 488, 489
Boer, M. C. de, 33
Borchert, H., 366
Bornkamm, G., 109, 433
Bradley, K. R., 450
Bratcher, R. G., 102, 136, 162, 259, 263, 284, 295, 310
Breeze, M., 272
Brown, R. E., 1, 47, 51, 109, 236, 433, 488
Bruce, F. F., 1, 19, 27, 35, 36, 63, 66, 71, 85, 100, 101, 107, 114, 116, 118, 119, 122, 123, 132, 133, 135, 136, 141, 145, 148, 158, 162, 163, 168, 172, 173, 179, 185, 186, 189, 191, 196, 197, 198, 210, 211, 213, 226, 227, 228, 230, 232, 234, 235, 237, 238, 239, 244, 246, 247, 248, 249, 254, 258, 263, 267, 282, 284, 290, 294, 297, 306, 308, 310, 322, 323, 325, 327, 333, 340, 344, 348, 349, 352, 363, 365, 385, 391, 411, 415, 420, 421, 422, 424, 425, 426, 433, 435, 449, 460, 461, 471, 472, 474, 477, 480, 483, 494, 495
Büchsel, F., 105, 382
Bultmann, R., 52, 177
Buttrick, G. A., 15

Caird, G. B., 67, 102, 105, 116, 128, 160, 175, 186, 188, 202, 211, 212, 229, 230, 232, 234, 240, 256, 263, 281, 296, 306, 309, 324, 327, 450
Calvin, J., 1, 175, 263, 294, 297, 300, 322, 398, 415, 423, 424, 442, 474
Campbell, R. A., 298, 302
Caragounis, C. C., 19, 52, 58, 60, 92, 94, 97, 98, 102, 107, 108, 109, 110, 112,

135, 136, 225, 228, 229, 231, 232, 241, 244, 245, 246, 247, 252, 260, 263, 434
Carr, W., 144
Carson, D. A., 4, 43, 44, 47, 51, 85, 144, 199, 215, 216, 264, 266, 287, 290, 329
Chadwick, H., 25, 53
Chae, D. J.-S., 35
Clark, K. W., 137
Clark, S. B., 403, 417
Clarke, A. D., 58, 353
Clarke, K. D., 19, 20, 201
Comfort, P. W., 320
Conrad, E. W., 347
Conzelmann, H., 31
Cotterell, P., 414
Coutts, J., 10
Craigie, P. C., 339
Cross, F. L., 116
Crouch, J. E., 406, 445, 448

Dabelstein, R., 383
Dahl, N. A., 52, 231, 235, 263, 351
Daube, D., 326
Davids, P. H., 37
Dawes, G. W., 111, 146, 147, 149, 150, 152, 194, 313, 399, 400, 402, 403, 413, 415, 427, 429, 432, 433
de Halleux, A., 139
de la Potterie, I., 325
Deichgräber, R., 90, 125, 253, 269, 395
Delling, G., 172, 363, 399, 400
Descamps, A., 139
Dibelius, M., 471
Donelson, L. R., 37, 40
Doty, W. G., 70
Duff, J., 37, 40, 43, 44
Dumbrell, W. J., 268, 294
Dunn, J. D. G., 37, 38, 119, 120, 148, 184, 200, 231, 279, 301, 311, 445

Ellis, E. E., 37, 39, 41, 43, 45, 238, 263, 288, 290, 492
Engberg-Pedersen, T., 371
Engelmann, H., 465
Ernst, J., 9, 116, 117, 150, 262, 330
Esser, H.-H., 277

Faust, E., 198, 206
Fee, G. D., 32, 91, 93, 95, 116, 119, 120, 121, 132, 156, 160, 208, 209, 210, 220,

232, 233, 234, 257, 258, 273, 276, 280, 283, 301, 302, 330, 346, 347, 387, 388, 390, 391, 395, 397, 413, 457, 459, 482, 483, 485
Feuillet, A., 263
Fischer, K. M., 52, 53, 207
Fitzer, G., 120
Fitzgerald, J. T., 250
Fitzmyer, J. A., 139, 289, 413
Fleckenstein, K. H., 414, 420
Fong, B. W., 204
Forbes, C., 215
Foulkes, F., 304, 429
Fredrickson, D. E., 250
Friedrich, J., 121, 174
Fung, R. Y. K., 202, 287, 301, 302

Gaugler, E., 242
Gese, M., 140, 141
Giavini, 184
Gnilka, J., 27, 34, 73, 102, 136, 156, 158, 160, 170, 241, 244, 246, 259, 322, 326, 327, 330, 371, 390, 396, 428, 443, 446, 463, 471
Goodspeed, E. J., 47
Gordon, T. D., 302
Gosnell, P. W., 388
Grässer, E., 263
Green, J. B., 27
Green, M., 470
Greeven, H., 484
Grudem, W., 214, 215, 402, 403, 413, 417
Grundmann, W., 277
Gudorf, M. E., 465
Gundry, R. H., 147
Guthrie, D., 42

Haacker, K., 400
Haas, O., 240
Hagner, D. A., 127, 134
Hanson, A. T., 294
Harder, G., 257, 383, 471
Harris, M. J., 127, 134, 140, 141, 364, 412, 450, 489
Harris, W. H., 97, 139, 171, 246, 290, 291, 294, 295, 296, 297
Harrisville, R. A., 329
Hauck, F., 277
Hay, D. M., 140
Hays, R. B., 292

Hemphill, K. S., 297, 303, 306, 310, 311, 313, 314, 316
Hendriksen, W., 471
Hendrix, H., 72
Hengel, M., 75, 395, 396
Hester, J. D., 121
Hill, D., 106, 214
Hoch, C. B., 329
Hock, R. F., 343
Hodge, C., 175
Hoehner, H. W., 6, 7, 9, 11, 41, 42, 48, 51, 56, 71, 72, 86, 90, 102, 107, 119, 141, 146, 176, 189, 191, 197, 203, 204, 208, 211, 258, 274, 296, 343, 345, 348, 352, 355, 360, 368, 369, 372, 373, 380, 381, 383, 284, 385, 391, 395, 396, 398, 405, 406, 407, 413, 414, 415, 421, 422, 423, 424, 426, 430, 432, 436, 441, 442, 443, 446, 450, 452, 454, 460, 462, 463, 466, 467, 471, 472, 479, 480, 481, 489, 494
Hofius, O., 305
Holtzmann, H. J., 14
Horsley, G. H. R., 137
Houlden, J. L., 322, 327, 330, 334, 361
Howard, G., 146, 151, 313
Hübner, H., 196, 310
Hui, A. W. D., 390, 394
Hull, G. G., 400
Hurley, J. B., 403
Hurtado, L. W., 281, 283

Jeal, R. R., 80
Jensen, J., 359
Jervis, L. A., 231
Judge, E. A., 27

Kähler, E., 437
Kaiser, W., 198
Kamlah, E., 400
Käsemann, E., 25, 52, 72, 405
Keck, L. E., 25
Keener, C. S., 401
Kennedy, G. A., 68, 73, 74, 77
Kern, P. H., 79, 81
Kertelge, K., 34
Kim, S., 228, 230, 237, 238
Kirby, J. C., 15, 52, 184
Kitchen, M., 111, 197
Kittel G., 197

Kittredge, C. B., 69, 81, 459
Klein, W. W., 99
Klijn, A. F. J., 361
Knibbe, D., 465
Knight, G. W., 417, 418, 426, 434, 437
Köstenberger, A. J., 390, 391, 393, 431, 432
Kroeger, C. C., 399, 413
Kruse, C. G., 335
Kuhli, H., 113
Kuhn, K. G., 7, 90, 230, 257, 366, 371, 381
Kümmel, W. G., 21, 71, 85

Lane, T., 56
Larsson, E., 328, 329
Lattke, M., 162
Lemmer, H. R., 30, 95
Lightfoot, J. B., 121, 148, 151, 452
Lincoln, A. T., 6, 7, 8, 9, 11, 12, 13, 14, 15, 16, 19, 20, 21, 23, 25, 28, 29, 31, 34, 39, 40, 45, 46, 47, 49, 53, 55, 56, 59, 60, 61, 63, 66, 69, 71, 72, 73, 80, 81, 84, 86, 87, 91, 92, 97, 98, 100, 101, 106, 107, 111, 112, 113, 114, 116, 117, 118, 119, 122, 125, 126, 127, 133, 135, 136, 137, 139, 140, 144, 145, 147, 149, 150, 152, 155, 156, 159, 160, 162, 166, 169, 171, 174, 176, 179, 181, 183, 188, 189, 190, 191, 192, 194, 197, 201, 202, 203, 204, 205, 206, 207, 208, 209, 211, 213, 217, 220, 228, 229, 230, 233, 239, 240, 241, 243, 247, 248, 249, 252, 257, 259, 260, 261, 263, 265, 266, 269, 272, 275, 280, 287, 290, 291, 295, 296, 298, 300, 302, 303, 305, 306, 307, 309, 311, 315, 316, 317, 319, 320, 322, 325, 326, 327, 329, 331, 335, 336, 337, 339, 342, 344, 348, 349, 350, 353, 354, 356, 360, 361, 365, 371, 372, 373, 376, 377, 380, 383, 388, 390, 391, 392, 395, 400, 404, 405, 406, 407, 410, 411, 413, 415, 417, 419, 421, 422, 423, 424, 426, 428, 429, 430, 432, 433, 434, 436, 438, 442, 443, 444, 445, 446, 450, 452, 454, 456, 458, 459, 460, 462, 465, 467, 471, 473, 474, 476, 482, 483, 486, 487, 494, 495
Lindars, B., 197, 290, 296
Lindemann, A., 8, 30, 31, 53, 114, 167,

169, 170, 180, 185, 188, 265, 382, 383, 471
Llewelyn, S. R., 274
Lohse, E., 186, 396, 451, 455
Lona, H. E., 30, 31, 54, 169, 173
Longenecker, R. N., 35, 75, 290
Louw, J. P., 23, 95, 100, 102, 103, 104, 118, 140, 146, 157, 161, 165, 172, 178, 195, 211, 221, 234, 235, 242, 250, 257, 261, 267, 279, 303, 304, 305, 308, 311, 320, 322, 328, 329, 344, 348, 350, 360, 365, 368, 369, 370, 376, 382, 384, 385, 389, 395, 399, 424, 444, 445, 446, 450, 451, 452, 453, 454, 455, 462, 470, 472, 473, 474, 475, 477, 480, 481, 482, 485
Lövestam, E., 485
Luter, A. B., 168
Luther, M., 405
Luz, U., 24, 34, 52, 174, 273
Lyall, F., 102

MacDonald, M. Y., 34
Maclean, J. B., 111
Malherbe, A. J., 77
Malina, B., 359
Marrow, S. B., 250
Marshall, I. H., 24, 106, 122, 174, 177, 213, 290
Martin, R. P., 37, 52, 192, 396
Martyn, J. L., 25
Masson, C., 90, 471
McKay, K. L., 293, 339, 342, 390, 427, 436
McKelvey, R. J., 212, 213, 216, 217, 219, 221
Meade, D. G., 37, 39, 41, 42, 44, 45
Merkel, H., 202
Merkelbach, R., 465
Merklein, H., 11, 12, 13, 17, 18, 31, 33, 34, 160, 188, 202, 206, 217, 221, 224, 228, 229, 230, 231, 233, 235, 237, 238, 287, 298, 301, 309
Metzger, B. M., 86, 120, 127, 380, 411, 441
Meyer, H. A. W., 133, 135, 157, 162, 174, 186, 190, 197, 204, 213, 218, 229, 249, 251, 260, 263, 278, 280, 306, 307, 322, 325, 327, 365, 372, 397, 415, 421, 424, 426, 442, 471, 472, 474, 480
Michaelis, W., 310, 467

Michel, O., 213, 227
Miletic, S. F., 415, 417
Mitton, C. L., 6, 8, 11, 13, 14, 16, 20, 35, 38, 207, 218, 228, 236, 237, 239, 243, 256, 263, 280, 307, 310, 323, 382, 471, 472, 482
Moo, D. J., 4, 24, 43, 44, 47, 51, 85, 198, 199
Moritz, T., 28, 58, 92, 111, 116, 140, 192, 207, 288, 336, 337, 339, 340, 346, 372, 373, 374, 375, 376, 389, 390, 420, 422, 426, 428, 429, 430, 431, 432, 441, 442, 443, 457, 458, 459, 466, 471, 474, 475, 476, 479
Morris, L., 4, 43, 44, 47, 51, 85, 106, 259, 264, 310, 424, 426, 435, 477
Mott, S. C., 274
Motyer, J. A., 346, 478
Moule, C. F. D., 84, 98, 133, 237, 342, 390, 391, 436, 484
Mouton, E., 68, 69, 81
Moxnes, H., 407
Müller, P. G., 12, 34
Murphy-O'Connor, J., 7
Mussner, F., 145, 177, 262

Neufeld, T. Y., 338, 457, 459, 460, 462, 463, 469, 472, 474, 479, 480
Newing, E. G., 347
Newman, C. C., 99
Nida, E. A., 23, 95, 100, 102, 103, 104, 118, 136, 140, 146, 157, 161, 162, 165, 172, 178, 195, 211, 221, 234, 235, 242, 250, 257, 259, 261, 263, 267, 279, 284, 295, 303, 304, 305, 308, 310, 311, 320, 322, 328, 329, 344, 348, 350, 360, 365, 368, 369, 370, 376, 382, 384, 385, 389, 395, 399, 424, 444, 445, 446, 450, 451, 452, 453, 454, 455, 462, 470, 472, 473, 474, 475, 477, 480, 481, 482, 485
Nock, A. D., 158
Norden, E., 52, 90

O'Brien, P. T., 7, 15, 26, 35, 48, 57, 69, 71, 89, 93, 96, 117, 119, 124, 127, 144, 146, 155, 161, 165, 171, 173, 175, 187, 206, 220, 227, 236, 241, 252, 253, 260, 265, 267, 268, 276, 285, 299, 313, 323, 326, 327, 329, 331, 333, 336, 342, 353, 355, 361, 368, 397, 405, 449, 450, 456, 459, 469, 477, 484, 485
Oepke, A., 473, 474
Olbricht, T. H., 68, 75
Ortlund, R. C., 420, 424, 429, 431, 432, 433, 434, 435

Page, S. H. T., 142, 159, 160, 341, 342, 457, 458, 464, 468, 469, 480
Paige, T., 37, 148
Patzia, A. G., 37, 38, 65, 174, 254, 310, 323
Peake, A. S., 1
Percy, E., 262
Perriman, A., 148, 399, 413
Peterson, D. G., 165, 304, 305, 313, 330, 421, 423
Phillips, J. B., 373
Piper, J., 402, 403, 417
Pöhlmann, W., 174
Pokorný, P., 52
Polhill, J. B., 11
Pope, R. M., 382
Porsch, F., 371
Porter, S. E., 19, 20, 37, 39, 40, 41, 42, 68, 73, 74, 75, 76, 77, 78, 79, 81, 108, 117, 119, 169, 179, 192, 193, 197, 201, 204, 205, 229, 240, 246, 260, 278, 298, 321, 322, 329, 339, 342, 362, 363, 390, 422, 427, 436, 460, 462

Qualls, P., 375

Radl, W., 181, 395, 477
Rapske, B., 489
Reed, J. T., 68, 70, 73, 76, 77, 78, 81
Reid, D. G., 61, 195, 274, 289, 469
Reumann, J., 227, 228
Reynier, C., 237
Richardson, P., 231
Ridderbos, H., 305, 445
Robeck, C. M., 215
Roberts, J. H., 46
Robertson, A. T., 118, 213, 231, 278, 342, 345, 362, 382, 390, 395, 416, 435, 452, 487
Robinson, J. A., 1, 53, 113, 115, 133, 161, 175, 196, 197, 204, 219, 262, 266, 294, 301, 310, 322, 327, 341, 391, 415, 428, 442, 476, 477, 491, 494

Roels, E. D., 296, 313
Roetzel, C. J., 197
Rogers, C., 389
Rupprecht, A. A., 450
Rutenfranz, M., 395

Sampley, J. P., 57, 404, 411, 415, 421, 424, 426, 427, 431
Sand, A., 121
Sanders, J. T., 90, 125
Sandnes, K. O., 207, 213, 214, 216, 233
Sasse, H., 158
Schenk, W., 96, 355
Schlier, H., 52, 72, 95, 136, 158, 160, 195, 197, 228, 231, 232, 235, 240, 241, 280, 307, 322, 326, 330, 443, 444, 463, 471
Schmid, J., 9
Schmithals, W., 52, 321
Schnackenburg, R., 1, 2, 8, 21, 53, 72, 93, 94, 96, 103, 107, 114, 122, 135, 136, 154, 156, 158, 160, 166, 167, 170, 172, 185, 189, 192, 196, 200, 202, 207, 213, 218, 230, 231, 232, 233, 249, 252, 259, 262, 269, 274, 276, 280, 287, 289, 298, 302, 309, 311, 312, 315, 318, 321, 322, 323, 327, 329, 330, 332, 335, 337, 339, 342, 346, 349, 352, 365, 372, 373, 380, 388, 390, 396, 411, 414, 415, 421, 422, 424, 426, 428, 444, 446, 471, 474, 482, 495
Schrage, W., 419, 455
Schreiner, T. R., 176, 198
Schrenk, G., 442, 445
Schubert, P., 15, 71, 124
Schulz, S., 277
Schütz, J. H., 241
Schweizer, E., 167, 235
Scott, J. M., 102
Seesemann, H., 245
Segovia, F. F., 327
Seifrid, M. A., 98, 167
Selwyn, E. G., 294, 326, 480
Silva, M., 134
Simpson, E. K., 175
Smillie, G. R., 17, 469, 486, 487, 488, 489
Smith, D. C., 206
Smith, G. V., 292, 293
Snodgrass, K., 1, 2, 3, 9, 24, 28, 34, 49, 56, 57, 99, 182, 183, 233, 372, 379, 382, 387, 388, 391, 397, 398, 418, 420, 421,

422, 424, 426, 428, 432, 439, 440, 446, 449, 452, 457, 458, 459, 462, 463, 464, 465, 468, 474, 479, 482, 483, 486
Spencer, F. S., 299
Speyer, W., 37, 39
Spicq, C., 310, 311, 368, 369, 370, 399
Stählin, G., 163
Stamps, D. L., 77
Staudinger, F., 165
Steinmetz, F.-J., 30, 231
Stenger, W., 12, 34
Stott, J. R. W., 91, 100, 102, 130, 135, 144, 156, 159, 170, 187, 205, 212, 228, 236, 240, 260, 265, 279, 291, 292, 295, 310, 327, 331, 334, 337, 348, 349, 363, 398, 412, 414, 419, 420, 421, 424, 425, 435, 446, 447, 464, 469, 477
Stowers, S. K., 69
Strack, H., and P. Billerbeck, 327, 359, 363
Strecker, G., 299
Strelan, R., 55
Strickland, W., 24, 198
Stuhlmacher, P., 119, 174, 192, 194, 202, 207

Tachau, P., 31, 157, 231
Tannehill, R. C., 166
Taylor, R. A., 288, 289, 290, 291, 292
Thompson, B. P., 93
Thomson, I. H., 93, 116, 184, 192
Thrall, M. E., 210, 226, 435
Thyen, H., 355
Tombs, D., 77
Towner, P. H., 212, 299, 407
Turner, M., 27, 36, 56, 57, 58, 62, 64, 65, 111, 114, 182, 202, 216, 218, 220, 233, 255, 263, 274, 298, 299, 301, 302, 303, 321, 338, 347, 408, 414, 433

van der Horst, P. W., 327, 361
van Roon, A., 7, 10, 14, 86, 263
van Unnik, W. C., 250, 361, 487
Verner, D. C., 408
Vielhauer, P., 304, 305
Volf, M., 147

Wallace, D. B., 84, 102, 106, 108, 160, 168, 169, 189, 213, 215, 240, 250, 265, 293, 297, 300, 339, 340, 382, 387, 387,

390, 391, 392, 398, 411, 436, 445, 473, 487, 492
Wallis, I. G., 175, 249
Warfield, B. B., 288
Watts, J. D. W., 375
Watts, R. E., 347
Webb, B. G., 474
Weber, B., 170
Wedderburn, A. J. M., 8
Weima, J. A. D., 69, 73, 74, 76, 77, 80, 492
Wessels, G. F., 30
Westermann, C., 89, 478
White, J. L., 70
White, L. M., 301
Wiedemann, T., 454
Wiederkehr, D., 134
Wilcox, M., 290
Wild, R. A., 327, 332, 333, 352, 353, 458, 461, 464, 465

Wiles, G. P., 129, 484
Wilkins, M. H., 37, 148
Williamson, H. G. M., 290
Wilson, R. A., 116
Wink, W., 144, 246, 469, 483
Winter, B., 58, 76, 489
Witherington, B., 402, 426, 432, 437
Wolter, M., 208
Wright, J., 347
Wright, N. T., 184

Yates, R., 149
Yoder, J. H., 412

Zeller, D., 384
Zmijewski, J., 177
Zuntz, G., 85

Index of Scripture References

OLD TESTAMENT

Genesis

1:1	60, 112
1:26	333
1:26-28	145
2	413, 429
2:23	429
2:24	407, 408, 417, 427, 429-34, 437
8:21	320
9:2	449
9:26	94
12:1-3	99, 184
12:1-4	189
12:2-3	234
12:15	159
12:30	98
13:14-18	189
14	291
14:20	89, 94
15:1	479
15:1-21	189
15:7-21	189
15:9	292
17	186
17:1-21	189
17:17	320
18:5	292
20:16	311
21:12	98
21:22	338

24:27	89
24:45	320
25:26	256
26:2-5	189
27:41	320
28:13-15	189
34:31	359
38:15	359
38:17-20	121
42:16	311
45:5	349
49:24	300

Exodus

4:21	322
4:22	102
7:3	322
9:12	322
14:30	346
15:6	141
15:16	449
16:10	104
18:5	191
19:5	122
19:6	87
20	443
20:1-17	443
20:4-6	440, 443
20:5	443
20:5-6	165
20:6	443
20:9	343

20:12	407, 442, 443, 444
20:15	342
21:8	105
21:15	442
21:17	442
24:1-8	189
25:2	292
28:3	320
29:18	336
29:37-38	101
31:3	108
33	346
33:12-14	346
33:14	347
33:19	257
33:22	257
34:6	165, 278
34:6-7	165
35:31	108
35:35	108

Leviticus

1:3	209
1:9	355
2:2	355
3:3	209
3:5	355
4:14	209
4:31	355
11:44	87
18:1-5	319

18:6-18	359
18:24-30	319
19:2	87, 353
19:3	442, 443
19:11	342
19:14	404, 443
19:15	455
19:18	407, 419, 426, 436
19:29	359
19:32	404, 443
20:9	442
20:23	319
25:48	105
26:1	186
26:30	186

Numbers

2:3	159
2:5	159
2:7	159
3:45	292
8	292, 293
8:6	292
8:6-19	293
8:14	292
14:18-19	165
14:21	131
14:24	353
15:39	162
18	292, 293
18:6	292, 293
32:11	353
32:12	353

Deuteronomy

1:27	455
1:31	442
4:10	443
4:19	142
4:20	115, 135
5:15	185
5:16	442
5:19	342
6:4	284
6:4-9	281
7:6-8	99
7:7-8	332
7:8	106
7:9-10	165

8:2-5	442
9:5	332
9:26	106, 135
9:29	115, 135
10:16	187
10:21	177
11:26-28	319
13:5	106
13:11	404
14:2	99, 122
15:15	185
16:12	185
16:19	455
17:13	404
21:18-21	442
22:21	359
24:15	340
24:18	185
24:22	185
26:18	122
27:16	442
28:1-14	95
28:13	146
28:49	191
29:22	191
30:6	187
30:15-20	319
31:6	461
31:7	461
31:23	461
32:4	332
32:8-9	115, 116
32:15	105
32:43	232
33:2	377
33:2-3	136
33:5	105
33:12	105
33:26	105
34:9	108

Joshua

1:6	461
1:7	461
1:9	461
14:8	353
14:9	353
14:14	353

Judges

4:23	277
5:30	291
8:3	159
8:35	368
9:45	261
10:18	146
11:11	146

1 Samuel

1:11	277
7:27	484
7:29	484
12:14	353
25:25	256
30:6	461
30:26-31	291
31:4	186

2 Samuel

1:20	186
5:2	300
7	189
7:5-11	212
7:11-13	304
7:12-17	189
12:5	162
19:2	348
21:3	135
22:44	146
23:5	189

1 Kings

1:27	491
1:48	94
2:19	141
5:21	89
8:10-11	104
8:13	221
8:15	89
8:24	255
8:39	221
8:41-43	209
8:41	191
8:43	221
8:49	221
8:51	115, 135
8:53	135
8:56	89
15:30	340

20:11	177	14:12	376	31:7	277	
22:19	141	15:15	211	31:19	351	
		25:5	375	31:21	94	
2 Kings		28:12-14	262	33:12	115, 135	
6:22	350	28:21-22	262	35:2	479	
12:26	261	29:14	327	36:7	257, 399	
17:16	142	31:26	375	37:28-31	442	
19:3	340	34:24	242	37:34	442	
19:4	350, 484	34:28	242	40:5	336	
20:5	484	38:6	217	40:6	355	
21:3	142	40:10	327	40:11	300	
21:5	142			41:13	69, 89, 94, 269	
22:33	257	**Psalms**		44:3	141	
23:4-5	142	1	319, 381	46:4	399	
23:26	340	2	285	50:2	377	
25:17	217	2:11	449	50:12	149	
		4	339	51:1	257	
1 Chronicles		4:1	484	52:1	177	
16:32	149	4:2	339	52:3	368	
17:21	106	4:4	4, 336, 339, 340	53:5	451	
22:12	108	4:7-8	339	61:2	399	
22:18	399	5:12	479	61:6	399	
29:17	450	6:9	484	63:9	294	
		8	140, 146, 285	65:6	473	
2 Chronicles		8:6	22, 140, 144, 399	65:11	351	
2:11	89	10:17	277, 476	66:20	89	
2:12	89, 94	10:18	277	68	61, 288, 291-93,	
6:41	327	13:3	133		295	
21:30	369	15:2	101	68:1	292	
24:16	368	17:48	399	68:1-3	288	
		18:2	479	68:1-19	292	
Ezra		18:23	101	68:4-6	288	
2:68	475	18:30	479	68:5-6	292	
3:3	475	18:32	473	68:7	288	
9:5	255	18:35	479	68:8	288, 292	
9:15	255	18:39	473	68:11-14	288	
		18:49	232	68:16	288	
Nehemiah		19:8	133	68:16-18	292	
8:12	491	20:6	141	68:17	288, 292	
9:18	340	23:1	300	68:18	61, 286, 287,	
9:25	368	24:1	149		288-93, 374	
9:35	368	24:7	131	68:19	292	
		24:10	131	68:20	292	
Job		25:7	351	68:21	292	
1–2	469	25:18	277	68:24	292	
1:6	160, 247	27:1	366	68:28	292	
5:9	242	28:7	479	68:35	292	
5:11	277	28:9	135	71:20	111	
9:10	242	29:2	268	72:8	94	
11:8-9	262	29:3	131	72:18	94	

72:18-19	69	132:11-12	189	**Song of Songs**	
72:19	131, 269	139:15	294	1:9	426
72:19-20	89	142:5	178	1:15	426
78:2	487	143:2	399	2:2	426
78:62	135	145:17	332	2:10	426
78:71	135, 300	147:4	256	2:13	426
80:1	300	148:14	191	2:17	475
80:3	377			4:1	426
80:7	377	**Proverbs**		4:7	426
80:18	141	1:1-7	381	5:2	426
80:19	377	1:2	108	6:4	426
84:5	269	1:7	404	8:14	475
89:3	189	1:22	384		
89:5	211	3:11	447	**Isaiah**	
89:6	136	3:11-12	442	1–39	42
89:8	136	3:19	108	1:2	102
89:11	149	3:34	277, 288	1:29	342
89:13	141	4:10-14	381	2:1-5	220
89:27-37	189	6:6	343	2:2-4	338
89:49	189	8:1	108	2:4	213
89:52	269	9	381	2:9	277
91:4	178	9:9	491	2:11	277
93:1	327	10:8	381	2:18	186
94:4	177	10:14	381	5:1	105
95:8	322	10:18	384	5:7	105
96:8	268	10:23	384	5:26	191
96:11	149	11:2	277	6:1	149
98:7	149	14:26	384	6:3	131
101:5	134	15:33	277	6:10	322
103:8	165	17:18	384	7:8	146
103:11	404	21:3	311	7:9	146
103:13	404	21:20	384	9:2	366
103:15	134	23:17	404	9:6	194
103:17	404	23:29-35	390	10:17	366
104:1	327	23:31	388, 390	11	473, 482
104:23	343	25:14	177	11:2	132
106:5	135	27:1	177	11:4	482
106:40	115, 135	28:1-12	442	11:4-5	457, 473, 478
106:48	69, 269	28:19	343	11:5	375, 463, 474,
107:23-27	309	30:5	479		482
109:18	327			11:9	186
109:26	257	**Ecclesiastes**		11:10	232
109:29	327	1:2	320	16:12	186
110	140, 142	1:14	320	19:16	449
110:1	22, 140, 144	2:1	320	19:25	135
110:4	140	2:11	320	26:19	374, 375, 376
117:1	232	2:15	320	28:16	217
118:22	217	2:17	320	28:29	320
119:43	119	4:8	368	30:15	320
132:9	327	5:10	368	33:11	320

40–55	42	65:17	179	16:9	423
40:9-11	475, 478	66:18-19	131	16:10-14	424
40:26	256, 461	66:18-20	220	16:14	424
41:10	141	66:20-21	293	19:7	149
42:6	366	66:22	179	20:41	336
42:10	395			23	420, 435
42:16	366	**Jeremiah**		30:12	149
43:20-21	123	1:9	487	34:11	300
44:2	105	1:9-10	305	35:12	350
44:26	311	2:1-3	420, 435	35:13	350
45:23	255	4:4	187	36:23-36	189
47:6	135	5:15	191	43:5	149
48:13	141	7:9	342	44:4	149
49:2	457	8:16	149		
49:3	478	9:23-24	177	**Daniel**	
49:5	184	10:12	108	1:4	230
49:6	184, 366	10:16	135	1:17	230
51:9	327, 376	11:15	105	2:8	382
51:17	376	12:7	105	2:18	109
52	475, 478	17:17	471	2:19	109
52:1	327, 376	17:18	471	2:21	108, 113
52:5	350	21:5	340	2:27	109
52:7	205-7, 375, 457,	21:8	319	2:28-29	109
	463, 475-78	22:24	141	3:42	257
52:8	206	23:2	300	4:37	113
52:9	206, 478	23:24	149, 285, 297	8:13	136
52:10	478	24:2	351	9:7	212
52:13–53:12	207	24:3	351	9:13	230
54:5-8	420, 435	24:5	351	9:23	230
56–66	42	24:6	304	10:1	230
56:6-8	209	31:4	305	10:11	230
57:19	190, 192, 205-8,	31:31-32	420, 435	10:13	142, 160, 247
	212, 375, 463	31:31-34	189	10:20	142
59	481	32:38-40	189	10:21	160, 247
59:17	375, 457, 474,	33:7	305	12:1	471
	478, 481	33:11	351		
60	376	47:2	149	**Hosea**	
60:1	366, 374, 375,	51:19	135	1–3	420, 435
	376	51:26	217	11:1	102
60:1-2	375				
60:2	375, 376	**Ezekiel**		**Amos**	
63	346, 347	2	487	2:6	277
63:1-6	346	3	487	2:7	277
63:8	346	9:4-6	120	8:6	277
63:9	346, 347	9:27	159	8:7	277
63:10	336, 346, 347,	10:3-4	104		
	348, 375	12:19	149		
63:11	347, 348	16	421, 424	**Obadiah**	
63:14	347, 348	16:1-14	407, 420	13	471
63:17	135, 322	16:8-14	422		

Jonah

1:6	374
4:2	165

Micah

4:1-5	220
4:3	213
5:5	194
6:8	369
7:8	165

Haggai

2:7	149

Zechariah

5:11	475
7:9	338
8	337, 338
8:1-15	337
8:3	338
8:8	338
8:15	338
8:16	16, 336, 337, 338
8:16-19	337-38
8:19	338
8:20-23	209, 338
9:9	277
10:12	461

Malachi

3:17	122

NEW TESTAMENT

Matthew

2:3	218
3:15	218
4:19	303
5:2	487
5:7	165
5:16	180
5:22	432
5:28	432
5:32	432
5:34	432
5:39	432, 470
5:43	419
5:44	432
5:44-48	353

6:15	157
6:34	350
7:7	444
7:12	427
7:13	319
7:14	319
7:17-18	344
8:27	441
9:32	469
9:34	159
9:36	351
10:2-4	84
11:22	435
11:24	435
11:25	132, 308
11:27	132
11:29	277
12:22	469
12:24	159
12:33-34	344
12:36	345
13:19	480
13:22	370
13:35	100
14:14	351
15:4	443
15:9	309
15:11	345
15:22	165
16:17	132, 466
16:18	305
16:27	6
17:15	165
18:12-14	300
18:22	351
18:23-35	278
18:27	351
18:33	165
18:35	96
19:17	293
19:18	293
19:19	419, 443
21:5	277
21:16	308
24:1	304
24:49	389
25:27	453
25:34	100
25:35	210
25:38	210

25:43-44	210
26:64	140
27:4	473
27:7	210
27:18	166

Mark

1:1	43
1:4	106
1:11	105
1:19	303
1:27	441
2:18-20	420, 435
3:5	322
3:16-19	84
3:22	159
4:19	370
4:41	441
5:19	165
5:23	436
7:7	309
7:10	443
7:22	323
9:7	105
9:23	293
9:29	484
10:19	342, 443
10:47	165
10:48	165
11:25	255
12:6	105
12:36	140
13:1	304
13:2	304
13:32-37	485
14:38	485
14:58	186, 187
14:61	93
14:62	140

Luke

1:13	484
1:28	104
1:42	350
1:47	415
1:68	93
1:75	333
1:78	166, 351
1:79	193
1:80	257

2:1	197	**John**		1:22-23	84
2:4	255	1:4	366, 377	2	215
2:11	415	1:5	366, 377	2:1	156
2:14	193	1:7-9	366	2:4	215
2:15	403	1:9	243, 377	2:6	215
2:32	377	1:13	6	2:17	215
2:37	484	2:19	339	2:18	215
2:40	257, 391	3:12	96, 295	2:24-36	22
2:51	401	3:19-21	366, 373, 377	2:32-33	141
5:33	484	3:20	371	2:33	120, 291
6:13-16	84	3:29	420, 435	2:33-35	140
6:29-36	344	3:35	105	2:34-39	282
6:35-36	353	4:42	415	2:36	218
7:13	351	5:20	105	2:37	118
7:25	424	6:33	295	2:38	107, 423
7:42	351	6:37	194	2:39	191
9:35	99	6:38	295	2:42	484, 485
9:42	469	6:39	194	2:45	344
10:17	399, 401	6:50-51	295	2:46	484
10:20	399, 401	6:62	295	3:15-16	22
10:21	308	7:13	166	3:21	22
10:33	351	8:12	366, 367, 377	3:25	255
11:15	159	9:5	366, 377	3:26	22
11:50	100	10:11-18	300	4:13	261
12:35	473	12:31	159	4:28	102
12:37	473	12:40	322	4:31	250
12:45	389	12:46	377	4:32–5:11	344
12:47	229	13:34	403	4:33	84
13:17	424	13:35	403	5:29	418
15:3-7	300	14:27	193, 207	5:31	107, 140, 415
15:13	390	14:30	159	5:42	324
15:20	351	15:3	423	6:1-7	344
16:2	227	15:12	403	6:3-6	299
17:8	473	15:17	403	6:4	484, 485
17:13	165	16:11	159	6:7	156
18:11	255	17:2	194	6:10	470
18:20	443	17:7	423	6:11	350
19:42	193	17:15	480	7:2	6, 131
20:13	105	17:23	105	7:6	211
20:23	309	17:24	100	7:22	446
20:41-44	140	17:26	105	7:26	193
20:42	395	20:17	295	7:29	211
21:1	403	21:16	299	7:48	186
21:15	470			7:55-56	140
21:34-36	485	**Acts**		8:22	350
22:22	435	1:8	257	8:23	350
22:41	255	1:13	84	8:35	487
23:35	99	1:14	485	9:4	148
24:32	403	1:15	156	9:16	251
24:44	395	1:20	395	9:27	488

9:28-29	488	20:24	168, 228	1:25	93, 94, 269, 337,
9:31	404	20:28	299, 300		363
9:36	180	20:28-29	299	1:26	323
10	117	20:31	48, 49	1:28	323
10:31	484	21:5	255	1:29	323, 350, 391
10:34	261	21:8	299	1:29-31	335
10:36	193	21:17-36	226	1:30	441
10:43	107	22:3	75, 446	2:2	326
11	117	22:7	148	2:4	172
12:5	484	22:21	191	2:5	132
13:7	118	22:28	58, 111	2:6	453
13:8	470	23:6	22	2:7	494
13:23	415	23:9	350	2:8	161
13:33	395	24:14-15	22	2:11	455
13:38	107	24:22	491	2:18	369, 384
13:44	118	25:14	491	2:20	300
13:46	488	25:16	340	2:21	300
14:4	84	25:25	261	2:24	350
14:14	84	26:7	305	2:25	427
14:15	320	26:12-18	36, 234	2:28	187
14:15-17	76	26:14	148	2:29	187
14:17	134	26:18	107, 366	3	176
14:22	251	26:23	22	3:2	187, 188
14:23	299	28:20	489	3:3	197
15:1	156			3:9	161, 203
15:35	300	**Romans**		3:14	350
16:1	305	1	320, 323	3:18	404
16:4	197	1:1	35, 84, 87	3:19	203
16:25	395	1:2	232	3:20	176, 203, 283
17:7	197	1:4	139, 257	3:21	232
17:18	210	1:5	35, 84, 441	3:21-26	7, 168, 177, 474
17:21	210	1:7	48, 87, 492	3:22	175
17:22-31	76	1:8	89, 398	3:22-25	79
17:24	186	1:8-10	124	3:23-24	168
17:30	157	1:9	129, 484	3:24	105, 168, 174
18:11	300	1:10	129, 384, 484	3:24-25	106
18:14	487	1:11	343	3:25	106, 355
18:18-21	5	1:11-15	299	3:25-26	174
18:19	305	1:12	403	3:26	175
18:24	305	1:13	368	3:27	177
18:25	300	1:15	241	3:28	176
19:1–20:1	5	1:16	78, 119, 174, 477	3:30	174
19:2	119	1:18-32	320, 365	3:31	23, 24
19:5	282	1:18–3:20	161, 163	4	176
19:8	48, 488	1:19-21	161	4:1-5	176
19:10	48, 118	1:20	178	4:1-8	178
20:4	492	1:21	318, 321, 361	4:2	176
20:16-38	5	1:21-23	320	4:3	288
20:17	299	1:24	134, 318, 323	4:4	168
20:19	277	1:24-32	323	4:4-5	176

4:5-8	106	
4:6	176	
4:7	288	
4:8	283, 288	
4:16	234	
4:18	135	
4:25	157	
5:1	193, 209	
5:1-5	128	
5:1-11	193	
5:2	135, 168, 209, 250, 282, 473	
5:3-5	398	
5:5	135, 166, 260, 352	
5:8	140, 166, 168, 201, 260	
5:8-11	157, 158	
5:9-10	169	
5:9-11	178	
5:10	19, 201	
5:11	201	
5:12	106, 163, 426	
5:12-21	148	
5:15	107, 168	
5:15-17	176	
5:16-20	157	
5:18	163, 210, 426	
5:19	426, 441	
5:20	107	
5:21	426	
6:3	282, 284	
6:3-4	171	
6:4	6, 131, 157, 170, 257, 284, 319, 426	
6:5	170	
6:5-8	170	
6:6	328	
6:8	170	
6:9	170	
6:11	170	
6:13	170, 462	
6:16	441	
6:17	441	
6:23	176	
7:2	24	
7:3	210	
7:5	158	
7:5-6	157	
7:6	24, 415	

7:7-25	203	
7:22	258	
7:25	210	
8:3	106, 355	
8:4	157	
8:8	162	
8:9	258, 259, 281	
8:10	258	
8:11	167, 259	
8:12	210	
8:15	209, 284	
8:15-16	103	
8:16	209	
8:17	235, 251	
8:18	251, 383	
8:18-30	169	
8:19	132	
8:20	399	
8:21	328	
8:23	103, 105, 121, 349	
8:24	169	
8:24-25	135	
8:26-27	485	
8:28	398	
8:29	100, 102, 103	
8:29-30	99, 100	
8:30	102, 134, 275, 282	
8:34	22, 140, 141, 481	
8:35-39	260, 263	
8:38	54, 142, 469	
8:38-39	7, 161	
8:39	166	
9–11	45	
9	187	
9:1	326	
9:2	134	
9:4	103, 187, 188, 189	
9:5	93, 94, 187, 188	
9:11-12	177	
9:12	176	
9:15	165, 288	
9:16	165, 210	
9:17	288	
9:18	165, 210	
9:19	470	
9:23	110, 181	
9:25	105, 288	

9:26	103	
9:30–10:4	203	
9:32	176	
10:1	103, 484	
10:4	24	
10:6	294	
10:7	294	
10:8	423	
10:9	282, 283	
10:9-10	174	
10:10	282, 283	
10:11	288	
10:14-17	118	
10:15	241, 475	
10:16	441	
10:17	423, 482	
10:19	445	
10:21	288	
11:2	288	
11:6	176, 177	
11:7	322	
11:9	288	
11:10	288	
11:11-12	157	
11:12	149	
11:13	84, 304	
11:15	157, 201	
11:20	473	
11:22	172, 351	
11:25	109, 149, 237, 322	
11:26	218	
11:30-32	157, 165	
11:33	242	
11:33-34	262	
11:33-39	7	
11:36	285	
12:1	67, 272, 274	
12:2	330, 331, 369, 370, 384, 385	
12:3	287	
12:3-8	286	
12:4	27	
12:4-5	148	
12:5	27, 338	
12:6	287, 301	
12:6-8	297, 298, 303	
12:7	304, 309	
12:8	298, 300, 343	
12:9-15	326	

12:12	135, 484, 485	16:7	214	3:1	156, 308
12:13	344	16:17	272, 300	3:5	238
12:19	341	16:19	441	3:6	219
13	406	16:20	6, 193, 341	3:7	219
13:1	399, 401, 402	16:25	109, 229, 267	3:8	343
13:2	470	16:25-26	109, 214	3:9	312
13:3	180	16:25-27	231, 268	3:9-17	28, 213
13:4	481	16:26	35, 36, 110, 232,	3:11	25, 213, 217
13:7	449		233, 441	3:15	169
13:9	111, 342			3:16	259
13:10	149	**1 Corinthians**		3:16-17	219
13:11	156, 169	1:1	83, 84, 87, 384	3:17	328
13:11-14	377	1:2	26, 48, 87, 421	3:19	309, 374
13:12	319, 328, 366,	1:3	87, 492	4:1	109, 110, 113, 227
	389, 462	1:4	89, 128	4:2	227
13:13	323, 366, 389	1:4-5	257	4:5	243, 283
13:14	16, 327, 475	1:4-8	7	4:6	84
14:8	283	1:4-9	69, 124	4:9	84
14:9	156, 283	1:5	266	4:9-13	251
14:10	425	1:6	98	4:10	424
14:11	255	1:7	132	4:12	343
14:12	210	1:8	101, 349	4:16	272, 352
14:15	157	1:9	275	4:17	300
14:17	364	1:10	272	4:20	364
14:18	370	1:13-17	284	4:21	277
14:19	210	1:17	241	5:1	359
15–16	5	1:18	169	5:5	6, 169, 341, 349
15:2	304	1:23	324, 325	5:7	355
15:4	130, 309	1:26-29	7	5:9-11	359
15:5	130	1:27	194	5:10	323, 365
15:8-12	232	1:28	194, 197	5:10-11	17, 335
15:10	288	1:30	105, 194	5:11	323, 389
15:13	257	1:31	178, 374	6:9	359, 363, 364
15:14-32	226	2:1	109, 110, 156	6:9-10	17, 363
15:16	391	2:1-2	76	6:9-11	157
15:18	35, 441	2:3	449	6:10	342, 363, 364,
15:19	257	2:4	257		389
15:20	241	2:6	307, 308, 383,	6:11	363, 421, 422
15:25	211		471	6:12-20	359
15:26	211	2:6-8	54	6:13	473
15:26-27	344	2:6-9	7	6:14	131, 139, 140,
15:29	149	2:6-10	231		283
15:30	272, 484	2:6-16	132, 214	6:16	432
15:30-32	486	2:7	102, 109, 110,	6:18	359
15:31	211		383, 471	6:20	106
15:32	274, 384	2:8	131	7	32, 65
15:33	193, 493	2:9	283, 374, 476	7:2	359
16	232	2:10	109, 132	7:5	6, 341
16:2	275	2:13	214	7:11	201
16:5	146	3	28, 213	7:16	415

7:19	186, 198	12:8-11	7	15:42	494
7:21-24	448	12:10	297	15:43	140
7:23	106	12:11	287	15:45	258
7:25	165	12:12-27	146, 148	15:45-49	148
7:29-31	32	12:12-31	286	15:47-49	171
7:31	30	12:13	200, 281, 284,	15:48	96
8:5	190		391, 453	15:49	96
8:6	190, 256, 283,	12:21	27, 146	15:50	364, 466, 494
	284, 285	12:28	214, 297, 298,	15:51	237
8:8	425		303	15:52-54	494
9:5-7	84	12:28-29	300	15:52-55	135
9:6	214	12:28-30	298	15:57	398
9:10	374	13	2, 316	15:58	303, 343
9:16-17	489	13:2	109	16:1	211
9:17	113, 227	13:4	278	16:3	369
9:19	352	13:7	135	16:9	487
9:21	199	13:11	196	16:13	257, 473
10:1-11	347	14	215	16:15	272, 274, 304
10:2	284	14:2	109	16:15-16	402
10:8	359	14:3	304	16:16	343
10:11	305, 348, 446	14:5	76	16:19	48
10:12	473	14:12	304	16:22	283, 485
10:19-21	54	14:20	307	16:23	168
10:20	467	14:23	48	16:23-24	43
10:26	149	14:26	304, 395	16:24	493
10:31	274	14:29	215, 216		
10:31–11:1	352	14:30	215	**2 Corinthians**	
10:32	195	14:32	399	1	15, 89, 130
11	414	14:33	193	1:1	43, 83, 84, 87
11:3	146	14:36	215, 305	1:2	87, 492
11:3-9	412	14:37-38	215	1:3	89, 94, 95, 130,
11:3-12	413	15	36		131
11:8	413	15:1	110, 241, 473, 491	1:3-4	15, 89, 93
11:9	409, 413	15:2	169, 174	1:6	252
11:11	435	15:3-28	22	1:11	484, 486
11:21	388	15:7	84, 214	1:14	349
11:26	283	15:8-10	36	1:15	250
11:28	369	15:9	240	1:19	324, 325
11:32	446	15:10	239, 343	1:20	269
11:33	403	15:12	324	1:22	120, 121
12–14	216	15:22	98, 148, 167	1:24	418, 473
12	297	15:24	142, 364	2:2-5	348
12:3	110, 283, 391, 491	15:24-26	54	2:4	134
12:3-11	95	15:24-28	399	2:8	272
12:4	287	15:25	141	2:11	6, 341
12:4-6	281	15:27	145, 401	2:12	487
12:4-11	286, 297	15:28	399, 401, 412	2:15	169, 473
12:5	304	15:29	284	2:17	238
12:7	287	15:33	374	3:4	250
12:8-10	298	15:40	96	3:6	238

3:6-8	304	6:18	103	13:1	423
3:6-15	196	7:1	404	13:4	251
3:7	196	7:4	391	13:5	369
3:7-11	203	7:5	465	13:10	304, 305
3:7–4:6	35	7:8-11	348	13:11	43
3:11	196	7:15	449	13:14	43, 493
3:13	196	8–9	344		
3:14	196, 322	8:1	110	**Galatians**	
3:15	78	8:1-15	344	1	15, 228, 230
3:17	258	8:4	211	1:1	84
3:18	330	8:7	436	1:2	146
4:1	165, 251, 304	8:9	168	1:3	492
4:2	118, 157, 238, 309	8:22	250, 369	1:4	159, 383, 384,
4:4	131, 159, 366	8:22-23	84, 214		471
4:4-6	251	9:1	211	1:5	268, 269
4:5	324	9:6-12	344	1:8	78
4:6	131, 133, 134,	9:7	134	1:11	110, 241
	258, 366, 372, 374	9:8	180, 343	1:11-12	36, 228, 234
4:7-18	251	9:10	219, 312, 314	1:12	132, 229, 230
4:12	252	9:12	211	1:15-16	36, 226, 229, 230,
4:14	170, 283, 425	9:14	484		234
4:16	251, 258	10–12	36	1:15-17	35, 228
4:17	251	10:1	76, 226, 272, 277	1:16	132, 466
5:1	187	10:2	250	1:19	84, 214, 283
5:1-5	21	10:4	462, 465, 477	1:23	157, 241
5:3	226	10:5	312, 441	2:5	118, 311
5:9	370	10:6	441	2:7-9	214
5:10	180, 229, 453	10:8	304, 305	2:10	279, 344, 436
5:11	404	10:10	76	2:11	470
5:12	258	11:1-3	420, 435	2:14	118, 229, 311
5:14	355	11:2	424, 425	2:15	162, 175
5:17	179, 319, 332	11:3	309, 310, 450	2:16	174, 175, 176
5:18	201, 304	11:4	324	2:20	175, 354
5:18-20	19, 20, 201, 207	11:6	76	3	99
5:18-21	251	11:7	241	3:2	176, 235
5:19	201, 352	11:13-15	469	3:4	226
5:20	201, 274, 488	11:14	6, 341	3:5	176, 235, 314
5:21	355	11:19	278	3:6-29	235
6:1	272	11:23-33	251	3:8	232
6:1-11	251	11:27	343	3:9	189
6:2	169, 288	11:31	93, 94	3:10	176
6:3	304	12:2	296	3:10-22	203
6:5	343	12:2-3	171	3:13	106, 117, 355
6:6	278	12:6	326	3:14	96, 99, 117, 119,
6:7	6, 462	12:7	6, 341		120, 235
6:9	446	12:9	251	3:16	99, 288
6:14	366	12:10	251	3:16-22	189
6:14–7:1	366	12:16	309	3:17	197
6:15	87	12:19	305	3:22	175, 194
6:16	219, 288	12:21	323, 359	3:25	24

3:26	103, 175	6:15	178, 200, 319,	1:3-19	70, 303
3:27	16, 282, 284, 327		332	1:3-23	70
3:28	200, 284, 408,	6:16	493	1:3–3:21	66, 71, 88, 125
	412, 453	6:17	251, 460	1:4	6, 12, 19, 49, 87,
4:3	54	6:18	43		89, 90, 91, 92, 96,
4:3-7	157				98-101, 102, 103,
4:4	103, 113, 149	**Ephesians**			104, 108, 115,
4:5	103, 106	1	15, 71, 124, 130,		116, 134, 179,
4:6	209, 258, 284		131, 229, 242,		181, 233, 245,
4:8	190		254, 262, 267, 459		272, 275, 282,
4:8-10	157	1–3	3, 8, 63, 66, 80,		311, 360, 372,
4:9	54		126, 254, 264,		385, 419, 425,
4:11	343		268, 272, 273,		453, 494
4:16	311		311, 352, 378,	1:4-5	95, 244
4:21-31	78		384, 458, 486, 495	1:4-6	98-99
4:24	76	1–6	459	1:4-10	91
4:26	171, 211	1:1	4, 5, 43, 47, 48,	1:4-14	92, 95, 96
4:30	288		50, 51, 69, 83-87,	1:5	7, 49, 50, 66, 84,
5:1	473		103, 128, 136,		89, 90, 91, 92, 96,
5:2	226		214, 233, 263,		98, 99, 102-3,
5:5	135		304, 360, 384, 459		104, 105, 108,
5:5-6	128	1:1-2	9, 16, 66, 69, 83-		110, 115, 116,
5:6	180, 186		88		117, 121, 181,
5:7	118	1:1-23	80, 154		212, 249, 275,
5:8	76	1:2	69, 87-88, 91,		352, 384, 385, 451
5:11	186		255, 283, 284,	1:5-6	94
5:13	401		459, 492, 493	1:6	7, 12, 50, 88, 89,
5:14	199	1:3	3, 6, 26, 29, 31,		90, 91, 92, 95, 96,
5:16	157, 162		49, 60, 62, 87, 89,		99, 103, 104-5,
5:19	323, 359, 370		90, 91, 93, 93-98,		107, 123, 166,
5:19-23	335		99, 103, 104, 112,		172, 251, 254,
5:20	162		115, 125, 130,		272, 493
5:21	363, 364		141, 147, 187,	1:6-7	168
5:22	193, 278, 351,		246, 255, 267,	1:6-8	168
	368		268, 283, 284,	1:7	6, 7, 9, 12, 19, 21,
5:22-23	276		379, 394, 467		22, 50, 66, 88, 89,
5:23	277	1:3-4	98		90, 92, 96, 98, 99,
5:24	162	1:3-7	59, 111		103, 104, 105,
5:25	157	1:3-10	93, 116		106, 122, 168,
6:1	186, 277	1:3-11	7		191, 204, 241,
6:2	277, 403	1:3-14	6, 7, 9, 12, 15, 58,		249, 347, 349,
6:4	369		62, 66, 70, 72, 88-		352, 419, 493
6:6	300		126, 129, 134,	1:7-8	105-8
6:8	328		137, 152, 154,	1:7-9	60, 104, 114
6:9	251		156, 168, 169,	1:8	7, 12, 19, 50, 89,
6:10	180, 210, 212,		172, 182, 185,		90, 91, 92, 96, 99,
	343, 344		192, 236, 242,		107, 108, 379, 380
6:13	177		245, 248, 262,	1:8-9	131, 132
6:14	283		269, 275, 360,	1:9	6, 19, 58, 59, 63,
			361, 387, 394, 459		84, 89, 90, 91, 92,

93, 95, 96, 98, 99, 103, 107, 108-11, 112, 113, 115, 125, 131, 132, 183, 225, 228, 230, 232, 247, 264, 279, 317, 380, 384, 385, 405, 451, 459, 487, 491

1:9-10   35, 45, 55, 57, 58, 60, 62, 91, 98, 108-15, 132, 179, 200, 229, 237, 244, 282, 306, 381, 384, 408, 411, 486

1:10   12, 13, 19, 30, 33, 58, 59, 60, 63, 89, 90, 92-93, 108, 111-15, 135, 144, 145, 149, 183, 201, 225, 227, 228, 244, 247, 254, 279, 285, 317, 349, 385, 405, 464, 481

1:11   84, 90, 91, 92, 96, 98, 99, 102, 115-17, 121, 124, 135, 139, 161, 181, 244, 248, 249, 285, 384, 451

1:11-12   91, 98, 115-18

1:11-14   50, 58, 89, 91, 92, 110, 115-23, 203

1:12   90, 91, 92, 96, 99, 103, 104, 116, 122-23, 124, 128, 135, 172, 181, 211, 251, 254

1:13   5, 6, 12, 30, 33, 44, 49, 50, 90, 93, 99, 115, 117, 118-20, 125, 127, 132, 189, 205, 235, 236, 296, 311, 325, 333, 349, 379, 390, 458, 459, 474, 479, 482

1:13-14   91, 96, 98, 124, 156, 168, 184, 336

1:14   30, 33, 89, 90, 91, 92, 96, 99, 101, 103, 104, 105, 115, 117, 118, 120-23, 127, 135, 143, 172, 235, 245, 251, 254, 349, 363, 379, 444, 453

1:15   4, 5, 48, 49, 50, 86, 101, 124, 127, 136, 204, 233, 263, 283, 304, 326, 459, 479, 486, 491, 493, 494

1:15-16   18, 66, 71, 89, 124, 126-29, 152

1:15-19   15, 70, 124, 139, 253, 254

1:15-23   6, 7, 9, 66, 90, 123-52, 183, 192, 254, 257, 261, 273, 361, 484

1:16   4, 5, 48, 128-29, 379, 397, 459, 484

1:16-19   124, 126-38, 152

1:16-23   459

1:17   6, 18, 94, 107, 124, 125, 126, 129-33, 145, 229, 251, 254, 255, 257, 264, 330, 379, 393, 394

1:17-18   7, 321

1:17-19   3, 67, 125, 129, 131, 132, 137, 153, 266, 306, 381

1:17-23   487

1:18   7, 12, 19, 29, 30, 33, 50, 107, 121, 125, 128, 133-36, 151, 211, 233, 241, 251, 256, 259, 264, 275, 282, 363, 367, 453

1:18-19   126, 133, 254, 256

1:19   7, 12, 66, 71, 126,

136-38, 139, 145, 151, 152, 154, 166, 178, 239, 254, 257, 267, 316, 459, 461, 479

1:19-20   172, 458, 461

1:19-22   54, 61, 171, 288, 464

1:20   6, 12, 22, 60, 96, 97, 112, 113, 114, 139-41, 144, 145, 154, 161, 166, 167, 170, 171, 267

1:20-21   29, 62, 88, 139, 154, 167, 294, 296

1:20-22   31, 33, 115, 145, 161, 275, 289

1:20-23   57, 66, 124, 125, 126, 136, 138-52, 153, 217, 490

1:21   22, 31, 33, 54, 114, 141-44, 151, 154, 158, 159, 169, 171, 173, 256, 296, 297, 399, 458, 465, 467, 468

1:22   25, 26, 50, 60, 61, 114, 126, 139, 144-47, 149, 150, 151, 152, 246, 268, 285, 313, 399, 401, 413, 416, 433, 465

1:22-23   26, 71, 139, 145, 152, 157, 297, 428

1:23   7, 25, 50, 114, 144, 145, 146, 147-52, 202, 265, 268, 281, 283, 285, 296, 305, 307, 313, 338, 392, 393

2   2, 24, 31, 62, 71, 153, 155, 165, 174, 188, 189, 199, 200, 203, 212, 221, 229, 242, 254, 281, 488

2:1   7, 70, 106, 107,

	154, 155, 156-57, 158, 161, 162, 165, 166, 167, 179, 184, 203, 321, 377		164, 165, 166-69, 172, 173, 174, 259, 265, 268, 321, 325, 377, 459, 465, 481, 493	2:11-13	155, 183, 184, 185-91, 192, 194, 202, 203, 210
2:1-2	31, 155, 156, 171, 275, 319	2:5-6	26, 50, 62, 141, 147, 158	2:11-18	62, 225
2:1-3	50, 61, 62, 114, 119, 153, 154, 155-64, 167, 173, 177, 203, 210, 383	2:5-7	154	2:11-19	212
		2:5-8	493	2:11-21	71
		2:6	6, 21, 22, 24, 30, 33, 54, 60, 62, 87, 96, 97, 112, 139, 140, 141, 154, 155, 159, 167, 169, 170-72, 179, 211, 217, 265, 268, 275, 319, 341, 364, 465, 467, 481	2:11-22	10, 28, 29, 32, 52, 60, 64, 66, 113, 154, 155, 156, 182-221, 224, 225, 226, 229, 262, 279, 306, 358, 366, 478
2:1-7	2, 6, 7, 90, 154, 167				
2:1-10	10, 11, 66, 71, 153-81, 183, 184, 185, 190, 192, 221, 254, 262, 358, 366, 415			2:11–3:21	185
				2:12	6, 50, 122, 135, 157, 184, 185, 187-90, 191, 202, 210, 218, 220, 224, 235, 282, 321
2:1-22	154	2:7	7, 33, 88, 107, 137, 143, 154, 155, 159, 164, 168, 169, 172-73, 174, 179, 241, 251, 268, 269, 279, 349, 351, 493, 494, 495		
2:1–3:13	71			2:13	22, 184, 187, 188, 190-91, 192, 193, 196, 202, 204, 205, 207, 212, 375
2:1–3:21	81				
2:2	97, 103, 113, 144, 154, 155, 156, 157-61, 162, 163, 165, 166, 171, 179, 181, 203, 365, 367, 383, 392, 458, 461, 468			2:13-16	63, 247, 275
		2:7-9	168	2:13-18	248
		2:8	24, 30, 31, 50, 87-88, 103, 104, 119, 154, 155, 158, 164, 168, 169, 172, 174-76, 178, 249, 259, 325, 377, 459, 479, 481, 493	2:14	88, 162, 191, 192, 193, 194, 198, 200, 202, 204, 209, 212, 249
2:2-3	61			2:14-15	193-201
2:3	6, 93, 103, 155, 155, 156, 157, 158, 161-64, 165, 172, 203, 205, 249, 275, 328, 329, 365			2:14-16	23, 50, 204, 206, 207, 229
		2:8-10	23, 154, 158, 168, 173-81	2:14-17	204, 295
		2:9	24, 169, 175, 176-78, 179, 180	2:14-18	7, 22, 45, 50, 115, 182, 184, 185, 191-210, 221, 276, 279, 317, 347, 408, 415, 459, 478, 486, 493
2:4	50, 101, 154, 155, 156, 158, 163, 164-66, 172, 173, 190, 260, 272, 354, 494				
		2:10	50, 154, 157, 158, 171, 178-81, 199, 204, 275, 319, 332, 343, 367, 368	2:15	22, 23, 24, 63, 88, 169, 176, 178, 184, 192, 193, 194, 196-201, 202, 204, 224, 249, 268, 275, 307, 319, 331, 332, 347, 419, 444
2:4-6	1, 31, 219, 220				
2:4-7	31, 61, 62, 114, 139, 153, 154, 164-73	2:10-22	57		
		2:11	24, 28, 50, 156, 162, 184, 185-87, 190, 191, 202, 218, 220, 221, 224, 319	2:15-16	478
2:4-8	7			2:16	20, 21, 22, 50, 60, 103, 113, 192,
2:4-10	30	2:11-12	28, 185		
2:5	9, 21, 22, 24, 29-31, 33, 50, 87, 88, 104, 119, 139, 154, 155, 156,				

	193, 194, 196,	3:1-9	214		240-42, 243, 244,
	199, 201-5, 208,	3:1-13	6, 11, 12, 16, 34,		245, 255, 263,
	209, 210, 218,		36, 67, 84, 221,		288, 459, 486,
	224, 235, 249,		223-52		487, 488
	281, 305, 338, 419	3:2	5, 9, 13, 48, 51,	3:8-9	110
2:16-18	194, 236		88, 104, 113, 145,	3:8-12	225, 228
2:17	88, 184, 191, 192,		168, 224, 226-28,	3:8-13	240-52
	193, 205-8, 212,		237, 238, 240,	3:9	9, 13, 19, 63, 110,
	375, 459, 477, 478		243, 288, 325,		113, 178, 225,
2:18	50, 64, 94, 103,		486, 488		227, 228, 232,
	191, 192, 193,	3:2-7	225, 226-39		240, 243-44, 245,
	194, 202, 208-10,	3:2-9	35, 434		247, 248, 256,
	212, 213, 218,	3:2-12	225, 250		262, 264, 285,
	220, 224, 236,	3:2-13	7, 71, 90, 110,		459, 486, 488
	249, 250, 255,		229, 245, 253, 254	3:9-10	63
	275, 279, 281,	3:3	19, 51, 109, 110,	3:10	6, 25, 26, 27, 50,
	345, 379, 485		132, 228-29, 230,		60, 64, 96, 97,
2:19	28, 50, 136, 183,		242, 251, 328,		103, 110, 112,
	184, 210-12, 220,		459, 491		132, 141, 142,
	221, 224, 233,	3:3-4	43, 110, 214		144, 146-47, 160,
	234, 275, 493	3:3-5	264		171, 173, 201,
2:19-22	1, 50, 183, 184,	3:3-6	63, 237, 247, 486		209, 237, 240,
	191, 192, 210-21,	3:3-7	35		244-48, 262, 268,
	224, 225, 234,	3:3-10	487		275, 381, 458,
	235, 254, 265	3:4	19, 34, 36, 110,		464, 467, 491
2:20	25, 28, 36, 84,		229-31, 233, 234,	3:11	248-49
	212-18, 224, 233,		237, 459	3:12	50, 94, 103, 175,
	298, 300, 325,	3:4-8	225		209, 224, 240,
	369, 416	3:4-11	218		249-50, 251, 255,
2:20-22	195, 212-13	3:5	25, 34, 36, 109,		259, 459, 479,
2:21	218-20, 221, 234,		110, 132, 209,		487, 495
	259, 275, 283,		214, 216, 218,	3:13	50, 51, 67, 224,
	304, 312, 313,		224, 231-34, 298,		225, 250-52, 256,
	347, 416, 461		325, 369, 491		268, 274, 489
2:21-22	218, 316	3:6	13, 50, 57, 103,	3:14	212, 223, 225,
2:22	209, 218, 220-		156, 184, 191,		251, 252, 253,
	221, 234, 268,		224, 225, 230,		254-55, 489
	345, 347, 348,		234-37, 241, 244,	3:14-15	130, 254, 285,
	379, 485		249, 317, 365,		447
3	62, 66, 221, 228,		444, 459	3:14-19	7, 66, 67, 71, 72,
	230, 231, 237,	3:7	7, 51, 88, 137,		90, 125, 130, 138,
	262, 266, 270,		145, 226, 228,		221, 224, 225,
	434, 488		237-39, 240, 288,		250, 253, 254-66,
3:1	4, 5, 24, 28, 43,		487, 488, 489		393
	50, 51, 66, 67, 71,	3:7-8	104, 168	3:14-21	10, 11, 12, 252-
	138, 223, 224,	3:8	7, 34, 35, 36, 51,		70, 273, 484
	225-26, 241, 251,		88, 107, 110, 136,	3:15	60, 112, 144, 212,
	252, 253, 254,		145, 206, 207,		253, 255-56, 284
	274, 319, 459, 489		224, 225, 226,	3:16	7, 103, 107, 137,
3:1-6	213		233, 237, 238,		145, 239, 241,

	249, 253, 254, 256-58, 259, 267, 296, 330, 379, 393, 394, 458, 461		136, 157, 166, 171, 181, 273, 274-76, 281, 283, 312, 316, 318, 319, 354, 358, 367, 378, 379, 380, 457, 458, 459, 461, 489	4:7-16	17-18, 64, 273, 286-317
3:16-17	253, 256, 259, 479			4:8	61, 144, 145, 286, 287, 288-93, 295, 298, 358, 374, 375, 429, 464
3:16-19	253, 306			4:8-10	61, 217, 289
3:17	101, 103, 249, 253, 258, 263, 272, 278, 296, 311, 354, 416, 419, 459, 479, 493, 494	4:1-3	23, 72, 273, 280, 318, 319, 333	4:8-12	315
		4:1-6	7, 90, 273-86, 316	4:9	60, 112, 286, 289, 293, 294, 295
		4:1-16	10, 12, 50, 67, 72, 271-316, 318, 319, 336, 408	4:9-10	293-97
		4:1–5:20	12, 17, 18	4:10	60, 97, 112, 141, 151, 193, 283, 285, 286, 289, 291, 293-97, 307, 392, 393
3:17-18	259-64	4:1–6:9	67, 81, 379, 458, 459		
3:17-19	253	4:1–6:20	71, 72, 93, 271, 272	4:10-20	459
3:18	50, 128, 233, 253, 256, 257, 260-64, 459	4:2	64, 101, 260, 266, 272, 276-78, 311, 312, 316, 354, 400, 402, 419, 494	4:11	84, 145, 193, 207, 214, 215, 286, 287, 289, 291, 293, 295, 297-301, 302, 303, 304, 305, 306, 314, 317, 325, 369, 392, 416
3:18-19	65, 254, 259, 260, 261	4:2-3	273		
3:19	3, 32, 33, 101, 133, 137, 149, 150, 151, 253, 254, 256, 260, 263, 264-66, 272, 307, 311, 354, 392, 393, 416, 494	4:2-5	128	4:11-12	298
		4:3	3, 64, 88, 193, 246, 276, 278, 279-80, 281, 295, 306, 317, 330, 334, 348, 400, 459	4:11-13	1
				4:11-16	7, 90, 286, 291, 293, 428
3:20	137, 239, 249, 253, 266-67, 268, 303, 458	4:3-4	345	4:12	7, 33, 202, 219, 233, 286, 298, 301-5, 307, 315, 317, 336, 338, 416
		4:4	25, 29, 50, 134, 202, 210, 274, 281-82, 295, 305, 317, 338, 348		
3:20-21	66, 67, 71, 138, 253, 266-70			4:12-13	393
3:21	25, 26, 50, 136, 146, 248, 253, 254, 267, 268-70	4:4-6	3, 29, 64, 70, 273, 280-86, 287	4:12-16	273, 286
		4:4-16	272, 318	4:13	32, 33, 94, 103, 149, 150, 151, 200, 264, 265, 273, 279, 283, 286, 287, 297, 305-8, 309, 315, 317, 392, 393, 416, 459, 479
4	67, 181, 272, 288, 291, 293, 297, 299, 301, 305, 311, 320, 321, 337, 338, 347	4:5	52, 120, 282, 306, 307, 317, 422, 459, 479		
		4:6	212, 255, 284, 447		
4–6	2, 3, 52, 64, 65, 66, 67, 72, 80, 220, 224, 254, 266, 272-73, 275, 311, 316, 338, 354, 378, 379, 384, 386, 418, 458, 495	4:7	88, 145, 273, 284, 285, 286-88, 291, 293, 298, 302, 303, 304, 315, 316, 317, 416, 493	4:14	286, 298, 306, 307, 308-10, 326, 333, 466
		4:7-10	286	4:14-16	464
4:1	3, 4, 5, 43, 51, 64, 67, 70, 71, 72,	4:7-11	287, 288	4:15	10, 44, 101, 147, 219, 266, 272, 283, 286, 308,

310-13, 316, 326,
329, 336, 338,
354, 368, 413,
416, 419, 428,
459, 474, 494

4:15-16   13, 19, 151, 297,
317

4:16   9, 10, 50, 101,
148, 202, 219,
266, 272, 273,
283, 286, 287,
302, 303, 304,
311, 312, 313-17,
330, 336, 338,
345, 354, 416,
419, 494

4:17   50, 67, 72, 171,
181, 275, 276,
318, 319-20, 354,
367, 378, 379,
386, 389, 458, 461

4:17-19   318, 320, 324,
325, 326, 331

4:17-21   68, 318, 358

4:17-24   64, 67, 317-34,
336, 346, 359,
378, 389

4:17-32   32

4:17–5:2   64

4:17–5:20   10, 12

4:17–6:20   67, 72, 180,
273, 318

4:18   134, 157, 188,
259, 318, 320-22,
366, 379, 384

4:18-19   319

4:19   321, 322-23, 355,
359, 410

4:20   6, 324, 325, 369,
386, 389, 416

4:20-21   301, 306, 324-26,
440, 447

4:20-24   318, 324

4:20–5:2   368

4:21   5, 44, 48, 226,
306, 324-27, 329,
333, 336, 337,
338, 351, 368,
369, 370, 386,
459, 474

4:22   326-29, 332, 335,
336, 337, 341,
349, 364, 366, 464

4:22-23   331

4:22-24   16, 318, 325, 326,
342

4:23   16, 326, 327, 329-
31

4:23-26   1

4:24   32, 44, 178, 200,
258, 326, 327,
328, 329, 330,
331-34, 335, 336,
337, 338, 339,
343, 348, 353,
366, 368, 369,
385, 412, 459,
462, 473, 474, 475

4:25   16, 18, 44, 326,
333, 334, 335,
336-38, 341, 342,
344, 349, 368,
403, 428, 459,
462, 464, 474, 493

4:25-26   64, 429

4:25-31   334, 341, 464,
466

4:25-32   335, 346, 352,
354, 442

4:25–5:2   67, 318, 334-56,
357, 358, 378, 389

4:25–5:21   440

4:26   4, 334, 336, 339,
340, 349, 440,
445, 464

4:26-27   339-42, 440, 445,
480

4:27   6, 144, 145, 159,
161, 334, 339,
340, 341, 345,
458, 463-64, 474

4:28   336, 341, 342-44,
345, 440, 464

4:29   88, 145, 219, 304,
341, 344-45, 346,
440, 464

4:30   30, 33, 50, 93,
101, 105, 120,
121, 122, 143,
236, 296, 336,

345-49, 356, 375,
379, 391, 481

4:31   334, 339, 349,
440, 445

4:31-32   335, 349-52

4:32   9, 23, 50, 272,
278, 334, 335,
349, 354, 356,
395, 419, 428

4:32–5:1   353

4:32–5:2   2, 68, 335, 392

5   181, 420, 427,
428, 435

5:1   50, 64, 333, 335,
353, 354, 392,
393, 419, 463, 475

5:1-2   2, 23, 140, 352-56

5:2   21, 22, 23, 50, 67,
72, 101, 157, 166,
171, 181, 204,
260, 266, 270,
272, 275, 311,
335, 336, 352,
353, 354, 357,
359, 367, 378,
379, 393, 415,
416, 419, 420,
458, 494

5:3   16, 50, 233, 323,
335, 358-60, 361,
362, 364, 371,
377, 440

5:3-5   358, 362, 365,
366

5:3-6   410

5:3-7   358-66

5:3-14   65, 68, 318, 357-
78, 380

5:4   344, 358, 360-61,
362, 364, 379,
397, 440

5:5   16, 30, 33, 143,
235, 323, 349,
358, 361-64, 452,
453

5:5-6   9, 440

5:6   30, 33, 163, 358,
362, 364-65, 366,
371, 452

5:6-13   309

5:7	358, 365-66, 370, 371		380, 383, 386, 387, 388-94, 399, 410, 439, 443, 448, 455, 485	5:22–6:20	32
5:8	2, 50, 67, 72, 134, 171, 181, 272, 275, 318, 354, 358, 365, 366-67, 369, 370, 372, 373, 376, 378, 379, 383, 386, 389, 391, 396, 458, 461, 467	5:18-20	17, 361, 388, 397	5:23	25, 50, 119, 147, 193, 202, 405, 410, 412-15, 416, 419, 427, 428, 437, 459
		5:18-21	65, 378, 379, 386-88, 399, 401, 439	5:23-24	26, 146, 413, 437
				5:23-32	272
		5:19	18, 68, 148, 258, 259, 351, 379, 386, 387, 394-97, 416	5:24	25, 402, 410, 413, 415-18, 426, 441
5:8-10	358			5:25	21, 22, 23, 25, 32, 50, 101, 166, 204, 260, 266, 272, 352, 354, 402, 410, 418-20, 423, 426, 428, 436, 437, 440, 494
5:8-14	10, 32, 68, 358, 365, 366-77, 386, 389	5:19-20	9		
		5:19-21	378, 379, 386, 394		
5:9	44, 326, 332, 338, 358, 367-69, 370, 373, 440, 459, 473, 474	5:20	3, 68, 255, 269, 379, 386, 387, 396, 397-98		
		5:21	17, 68, 145, 378, 379, 387, 388, 397, 398-405, 409, 410, 411, 412, 416, 417, 418, 431, 435, 436, 437, 439, 441, 443, 448, 449, 450, 455	5:25-27	65, 410, 414, 415, 418, 419, 426, 429, 437
5:10	358, 369-70, 386, 396, 416, 449			5:25-28	32, 410
5:11	358, 359, 367, 370-71, 372, 467			5:25-29	436
				5:25-30	429
5:12	359, 360, 371-72, 410			5:25-31	400, 431
				5:25-32	410, 418, 435, 442
5:13	371, 372				
5:13-14	372-77			5:25-33	408
5:14	68, 70, 288, 358, 372-77, 386, 429	5:21-24	401	5:26	25, 87, 420-24, 428, 459, 482
		5:21-33	3, 30, 45, 146, 388, 389, 404, 410	5:26-27	420, 437
5:15	67, 72, 108, 157, 171, 181, 275, 354, 367, 377, 378, 379, 380-82, 383, 384, 386, 391, 393, 394, 439, 455, 458	5:21–6:9	12, 17, 29, 70, 388, 458, 460	5:27	25, 26, 30, 32, 33, 50, 87, 101, 136, 143, 146, 193, 268, 349, 420, 421, 424-26, 438
		5:22	387, 388, 399, 402, 403, 408, 409, 410, 411-12, 415, 416, 417, 418, 436, 437, 439, 440, 441	5:28	101, 266, 272, 354, 402, 410, 414, 419, 426-27, 429, 432, 436, 494
5:15-17	389, 393, 407				
5:15-18	32, 318, 390				
5:15-20	65, 448	5:22-24	402, 410, 413, 419	5:28-29	429
5:15-21	379-405	5:22-30	429, 430	5:28-32	410, 419, 431, 437
5:15–6:9	68, 378-456	5:22-31	431		
5:16	114, 382-83, 384, 458, 471	5:22-32	10	5:29	25, 26, 50, 146, 162, 352, 402, 427-28, 429, 432, 436, 446
		5:22-33	65, 68, 378, 399, 405, 407, 409-38, 439		
5:17	68, 264, 378, 380, 381, 383-86, 394, 396, 416, 439, 449, 451			5:29-30	429
		5:22–6:4	455	5:30	4, 202, 338, 427, 428-29, 431, 432, 433, 437
5:18	65, 68, 93, 151, 209, 265, 296, 330, 378, 379,	5:22–6:9	10, 65, 378, 386, 387, 388, 399, 401, 403, 405-56		

5:30-32	429, 431		460-61, 462, 470,	6:18-20	10, 12, 17, 460,
5:31	162, 415, 417,		480		483-90
	427, 428, 429,	6:10-12	136	6:19	17, 110, 129, 132,
	432, 433, 434,	6:10-13	460-72		145, 250, 459,
	436, 442	6:10-17	10, 17		483, 486-88, 489,
5:31-32	429-35	6:10-18	120, 464		491
5:32	25, 26, 50, 110,	6:10-20	22, 33, 53, 54, 61,	6:19-20	4, 17, 43, 48, 382
	146, 430, 431,		62, 68, 72, 81,	6:20	43, 51, 67, 129,
	433, 434, 436, 459		161, 171, 341,		250, 486, 487,
5:33	101, 266, 272,		456-90		488-90
	354, 388, 404,	6:11	6, 61, 144, 159,	6:21	51, 110, 461, 491,
	410, 417, 419,		310, 341, 457,		492, 495
	426, 435-38, 449,		461-65, 466, 468,	6:21-22	8, 10, 12, 17, 43,
	450, 494		470, 472, 473,		49, 51, 70, 85,
5:33–6:9	410		480, 490		491-92, 494
6	443, 470, 474,	6:11-12	172	6:21-24	66, 69, 490-95
	478	6:11-17	4	6:22	51, 259, 491-92,
6:1	408, 409, 439,	6:12	6, 60, 96, 97, 112,		495
	440-42, 445, 461		141, 142, 143,	6:23	50, 88, 101, 255,
6:1-2	407		144, 160, 162,		272, 459, 479,
6:1-4	9, 68, 378, 409,		458, 465-70		491, 492-93, 494,
	439-47	6:12-20	465		495
6:1-9	439	6:13	62, 114, 143, 349,	6:23-24	10, 43, 491
6:2	176, 199, 429,		383, 387, 462,	6:24	50, 101, 128, 266,
	442, 445, 495		463, 470-72, 473,		272, 354, 492,
6:2-3	440, 442-45		490		493-95
6:3	60, 112, 442	6:14	44, 62, 311, 326,		
6:4	427, 440, 441,		332, 338, 375,	**Philippians**	
	443, 445-47, 449,		462, 463, 472-75,	1:1	87, 299
	454		479, 480, 481,	1:2	87, 492
6:5	17, 162, 259, 404,		482, 483, 490	1:3	89
	408, 409, 439,	6:14-16	475, 480	1:3-8	7
	440, 441, 447,	6:14-17	458, 459, 460,	1:3-11	69, 124, 459
	448-50, 451, 454,		463, 466, 472-82,	1:4	128, 129, 484
	456		483, 490	1:6	180, 349
6:5-9	9, 68, 378, 409,	6:14-20	7, 90	1:7	98, 274, 489
	439, 440, 447-56	6:15	88, 193, 375, 382,	1:8	489
6:6	384, 448, 449,		462, 473, 475-79,	1:9	129, 133, 266
	450, 451, 456		482, 493	1:9-10	101, 102
6:7	448, 449, 450,	6:16	144, 159, 463,	1:10	349, 369
	451-52, 454, 456		466, 473, 475,	1:11	368, 391
6:8	32, 33, 143, 349,		479-80, 481	1:12	489, 491
	440, 448, 449,	6:16-18	459	1:12-14	36
	450, 451, 452-53,	6:17	375, 379, 382,	1:12-17	226
	454, 455, 456		423, 462, 476,	1:13	274
6:9	60, 112, 141, 283,		480-82, 483	1:14	274
	296, 407, 408,	6:18	50, 128, 129, 209,	1:15	103, 166, 324
	440, 448, 449,		233, 263, 330,	1:17	274
	452, 453-56		379, 483-86, 490	1:19	314, 486
6:10	7, 137, 239, 458,			1:27	211, 274, 473

1:27–2:11	7	1:1-2	9, 16	1:24	26, 36, 146, 152,		
1:28	169	1:3	18, 89, 127, 128,		224, 225, 251, 252		
1:29	175		129	1:24-28	224		
1:30	465	1:3-14	9, 69, 124	1:24-29	12, 16		
2:3	277, 400, 402	1:4	18, 102, 125, 127,	1:24–2:3	10		
2:4	277		128	1:25	9, 13, 113, 145,		
2:6-11	142, 277, 295,	1:5	6, 12, 118, 119,		224, 227, 243		
	395, 396		134, 135, 453	1:25-27	225, 229, 231		
2:8-10	294	1:6	312, 326	1:26	9, 36, 224, 233,		
2:9	277	1:7	87, 324		234		
2:9-11	22, 283	1:7-8	299	1:26-27	109, 110, 233, 237		
2:10	54, 96, 255	1:8	102	1:27	12, 13, 19, 107,		
2:11	6	1:9	12, 18, 107, 108,		110, 135, 190,		
2:12	169, 181, 441,		129, 132, 229, 484		194, 224, 230,		
	449	1:9-10	133, 381		237, 251, 259,		
2:12-13	331, 369, 385	1:9-14	266		282, 453		
2:13	181	1:10	132, 180, 274,	1:27–2:10	12		
2:15	101		275, 312, 343,	1:28	108, 224, 225,		
2:16	118, 343, 349, 477		368, 369		425		
2:25	84, 214	1:11	137, 257	1:29	137, 239, 267,		
2:27	166	1:12	116, 135, 366, 453		316		
2:30	303	1:13	12, 104, 160-61,	1:29–3:10	11		
3:2	187		364, 366, 374,	2	15		
3:3	177, 178, 187		467, 468	2:1	465		
3:4	250	1:13-14	11	2:2	110, 133, 229, 262		
3:5	186	1:14	9, 12, 18, 19, 105	2:2-3	107, 242, 307		
3:8	242, 283	1:15-16	100	2:3	108, 133, 262		
3:9	175	1:15-18	256	2:4	364		
3:9-10	242	1:15-20	9, 15, 146, 395,	2:4–3:4	10		
3:10	139		396	2:6	324		
3:11	170, 305	1:16	54, 100, 142, 144,	2:6-7	306		
3:15	308		285, 468	2:7	25, 28, 260, 324		
3:16	435	1:18	12, 26, 146, 147,	2:8	54, 309, 364		
3:17	157, 352		152, 413	2:9	149, 150, 259,		
3:20	171, 211, 220, 415	1:19	149, 150, 259,		265, 392		
3:21	137, 140, 145,		265, 392	2:10	142, 144, 146,		
	399	1:19-20	57		150, 151, 265,		
4:1	473	1:20	12, 18, 19, 20, 21,		392, 413		
4:6	384, 484		61, 193, 201	2:11	185, 187		
4:8	335, 441	1:20-22	61, 114, 201	2:11-12	171		
4:9	193	1:21	158, 188, 321	2:12	12, 137, 139, 170,		
4:10-20	459	1:21-23	10		239, 284		
4:14	370, 435	1:22	12, 19, 20, 100,	2:12-13	167		
4:18	355, 370		101, 196, 201,	2:13	9, 157, 167, 185		
4:19	137, 257, 266		424, 425, 426	2:13-15	167		
4:20	6	1:22-23	157	2:14	197		
		1:23	135, 224, 226,	2:14-15	161		
Colossians			238, 260, 282	2:15	54, 61, 114, 142,		
1	232, 237	1:23-28	11		144, 145		
1:1	83, 84			2:16	143		

2:16-23	411
2:18	143, 144
2:19	9, 10, 12, 18, 147, 148, 312, 313, 314, 315
2:20	54, 156, 171, 197
2:20-21	469
2:21	143
2:22	309
2:23	108
3:1	140, 141, 170, 171
3:1-3	171
3:1-4	135, 141, 220, 453
3:1-17	12, 17, 18
3:1–4:6	272
3:3	171
3:4	135, 194, 251, 282
3:5	16, 163, 323, 359, 362
3:5-6	9
3:5-11	318
3:5-12	319
3:5-17	10, 12
3:5–4:6	220
3:6	163
3:7	157
3:8	319, 327-28, 344, 350, 360
3:8-9	337
3:8-10	16
3:8-12	16
3:8-14	336
3:9	16, 328, 337
3:9-10	318, 326
3:10	133, 258, 319, 329, 333
3:11	200, 408, 412, 448, 453
3:12	16, 105, 276, 277, 327
3:12-13	351
3:12-15	12, 276
3:13	9, 278, 351, 352
3:14	280
3:15	275, 280
3:16	18, 19, 108, 118,

	193, 300, 393, 395, 396
3:16-17	9
3:17	274, 398, 450
3:18	399, 402, 411
3:18–4:1	10, 12, 17, 283, 405, 406, 408
3:20	370, 417, 441
3:20-21	9
3:20–4:1	440
3:21	445, 446
3:22	17, 404, 417, 450, 451, 452
3:22-25	448, 449, 455
3:22–4:1	9, 448
3:23	412
3:24	453
3:24-25	453
3:25	453, 455
4:1	283, 441, 455
4:2	484, 485
4:2-4	10, 12, 17
4:3	17, 110, 487, 488
4:3-4	486
4:4	17
4:5	381
4:5-6	10
4:6	345, 477
4:7	69, 87, 491, 492
4:7-8	8, 12, 17
4:7-9	10, 49, 57
4:8	69
4:9	87
4:10-17	10
4:11	364
4:12	384, 473, 484
4:12-13	299
4:15	25, 146
4:16	41, 86
4:17	304
4:18	10

1 Thessalonians

1:1	146
1:2	128, 129, 484
1:2-5	7
1:2–3:13	69, 71
1:3	128, 303
1:4	100, 105
1:5	251, 257

1:6	251, 352
1:8	118
1:10	169
2:2	488
2:3	310, 323
2:4	369
2:7	427
2:8	343
2:12	274, 275, 319, 364
2:13	100, 118, 484
2:14	352
2:16	174
2:17	279
2:18	6, 226, 341, 469
3:3	251
3:4	251
3:8	473
3:10	129, 484
3:12	266
3:12-13	101, 102
4:1	67, 71, 272, 274, 319
4:3	359, 384
4:3-7	360
4:5	190
4:7	323, 359
4:8	348, 359
4:10	272, 274
4:11	343
4:12	343
4:13	190, 359
4:15	283
4:16	283
5:2	349
5:5	366
5:5-8	377
5:6	210
5:6-8	389
5:8	16, 135, 169, 474, 481
5:9	122, 169
5:12	300, 343
5:14	272, 278
5:15	180, 343
5:17	484
5:18	384
5:20	215
5:21	369
5:25	486

2 Thessalonians

1:1	146
1:2	87, 492
1:2-12	69
1:3	128, 266, 312
1:3-10	7
1:4	146
1:5	364
1:8	441
1:11	129, 257
2:1-2	43
2:2	349, 452
2:5	445
2:8	161, 196, 482
2:9	6, 341
2:11	310
2:12	310
2:13	105, 128
2:13-14	69, 169, 181
2:14	122, 146, 236, 251
2:15	210, 300, 463
2:17	180, 343
3:1	118, 486
3:2	486
3:3	480
3:6-12	343
3:7	352
3:9	352
3:13	251
3:14	441
3:16	193, 493
3:17	43

1 Timothy

1:1	84, 194, 415
1:10	309, 494
1:13	157, 165
1:15	240
1:16	165
1:17	248, 269, 494
1:18	465
1:20	341
2:1	484
2:3	415
2:8-15	405, 406
2:10	180, 360
2:11-13	413
2:14	364
3:2	300

3:6	341
3:7	341
3:8	389
3:10	369
3:11	341
3:15	212
3:16	231, 395, 396
4:1	309, 469
4:6	309
4:10	87, 415
4:12	87
4:13	300, 309
4:14	299
4:16	300, 309
5:5	484
5:10	180
5:15	341
5:16	87
5:17	299, 300, 309
5:18	288, 374
5:19	299
5:25	180
6:1	309, 350
6:1-10	405, 406
6:2	87
6:11	278
6:16	366
6:18	180, 343

2 Timothy

1:1	84, 384
1:3	129, 484
1:4	484
1:8	226
1:9	100
1:9-11	231
1:10	196, 243, 366, 415
1:13-14	300
2:1	460
2:1-2	300
2:2	300
2:9	489
2:10	252
2:15	6, 279, 425
2:19	374
2:20	212
2:21	180, 212, 476
2:23	465
2:25	277

2:26	341
3:1	383
3:2	361, 441
3:3	341
3:8	470
3:10	300
3:16	309, 446
3:17	180
4:1	364
4:2	299
4:5	299, 303
4:9	279
4:12	492
4:15	470
4:17	489
4:18	96, 269, 364
4:21	279

Titus

1:1	84
1:2	135
1:2-3	231
1:5	225
1:6	87, 389
1:9	300
1:12	492
1:16	180
2:1	360
2:1-10	405, 406
2:3	341, 389
2:5	350, 402
2:7	180
2:9	402
2:12	446
2:14	106, 180
3:1	180, 401, 402
3:3	350
3:4	172, 351
3:5	180, 319, 330, 422
3:7	135
3:8	180
3:9	417, 465
3:10	446
3:12	279
3:14	370

Philemon

1	226, 274
2	25, 146

3	87, 492	10:22	209	1:25	423
4	128, 129, 484	10:24	180	2:1	319, 328, 350
4-6	124	10:25	27, 147, 246	2:2	319
4-7	69	10:32	366	2:5	220
5	128	10:35	250	2:9	122, 366, 367
6	133	10:36	453	2:10	158
8-10	272	11:8	441	2:11	211
9	226, 274, 488, 489	11:13	210, 453	2:13	401, 402
11	157	11:16	96	2:13-17	406
13	489	11:19	453	2:17	404
18	342	11:23	445	2:18–3:7	405, 406, 409, 448
19	226	11:39	453	2:18	402, 404, 449
22	476, 484	12:1	328	2:25	158, 300
		12:2	22, 140	3:2	404, 449
Hebrews		12:5	446	3:4	278
1:3	22, 140, 151	12:7	446	3:5	402
1:13	22, 140	12:8	446	3:6	404
2:6-9	145	12:9	402	3:12	484
2:8	145, 399	12:11	446	3:19	294
2:10	181	12:14	101	3:21-22	141
2:12	395	12:15	350	3:22	22, 140, 142, 399, 401
2:14	196, 466, 469	12:22	96, 209, 211		
2:14-15	161	12:22-24	147, 246	4:3	323, 389
3–4	199	12:26	158	4:4	389
3:1	96	13:9	210	4:10	301
3:6	250	13:20	300	4:10-11	298
4:3	100			4:11	94
4:12	482	**James**		5:2	299, 300
4:16	209, 250	1:5	257	5:3	299
5:7	484	1:18	319	5:4	300, 453
5:9	441	1:19-20	340	5:5	277, 402
5:12	300	1:21	319, 328	5:8-9	161, 480
5:13	308	1:26	364	5:9	470, 480
5:14	307, 308	2:1	131, 455, 494	5:14	493
6:1	100	2:8-12	199		
6:4	96, 366	3:15	163	**2 Peter**	
6:5	423	3:18	193	1:5	314
7:25	141, 209	4:1	465	1:8	370
8:1	22, 58, 111, 140	4:6	288	1:11	314
8:5	96	4:7	402, 470	2:2	323
9:11	186	5:16	484	2:3	323
9:14	101			2:7	323
9:23	96	**1 Peter**		2:13	453
9:24	186	1:3	89, 93, 94, 95	2:18	310, 323
9:26	100	1:3-5	89, 93	3:3	383
10:5	355	1:9	453	3:17	310
10:12	22, 140	1:12	247		
10:12-13	141	1:19	101	**1 John**	
10:19	250	1:20	100, 231	1:5	366
		1:22	319		

1:5-7	367	**Jude**		13:6	350
2:8	366	3	283	13:8	100
2:9	367	4	323	14:3	395
2:13	480	11	310	15:3	395
2:14	480	12	370	16:5	332
2:15-17	163	24	101, 267	16:9	350
2:28	250	24-25	268	16:11	350
3:7-10	163	25	267	16:21	350
3:21	250			17:8	100
4:1	469	**Revelation**		18:4	370
4:6	310	1–3	58	19:15	482
4:17	250	1:5	106	20:3	61
5:4	194	1:16	377	21:4	350
5:14	250	2:10	469	21:9-11	425
5:18	480	3:21	22, 140, 141	21:16	263
5:19	480	4:10	141	22:20	485
		5:9	395, 396		
		5:13	396		
		6:4	403		
3 John		7:10	396		
6	275	11:15	364		
15	493	12:10	396		

Index of Extrabiblical Literature

JEWISH LITERATURE

Old Testament Apocrypha and Pseudepigrapha

Apocalypse of Abraham
29:2   471
29:8ff.   471
29:13   471
30:4   471

2 Apocalypse of Baruch
48:31   471
78:2   87

1 Enoch
22:14   131
25:3   131
25:7   131
61:10   247

2 Enoch
20-22   142

Epistle of Aristeas
139   196
140   320
182   476
277   320

1 Esdras
9:17   491

4 Ezra
7:50   383

Jubilees
23:16-21   471

2 Maccabees
1:10-13   124
3:40   491
5:2   160
9:12   399
10:28   466
14:18   466
15:9   466

3 Maccabees
1:3   197

4 Maccabees
9:22   494
10:2   197
17:12   494

Prayer of Manasseh
14   257

Psalms of Solomon
4:7   451
4:8   451
4:19   451
8:8-9   340
16:1-4   376

Sirach
1:3   262
7:15   343
34:4   311

Testament of Asher
1:3   319
1:5   319

Testament of Benjamin
3:4   160
9:1   359

Testament of Dan
5:4   383
5:4ff.   471

Testament of Issachar
7:2-3   390

Testament of Judah
11:2   390
12:3   390

13:6	359, 390	**Dead Sea Scrolls**		3:21		157
14:1	390			3:24		366
16:1	390	**CD**		3:25		366
19:1	363	3:12	159	4		319
23:1	363	3:15	103	4:3-4		108
		6:14	365	4:18		113
Testament of Levi		6:15	365	4:24		381
3:4	141	7:2	340	5:9		369
4:4	351	7:3	340	5:10	157, 365	
13:1	450	9:6	340	5:11		365
				5.26–6.1		340
Testament of Naphtali		**1QH**		8:2		369
4:5	351	2:25-26	480	9:18		230
		2:29	480	9:24		157
Testament of Reuben		5:20	89	10:19		363
1:6	359	7:17	257	11:2		363
4:1	450	7:19	257	11:5-8		110
4:6	363	11:15	89	11:7-8		136
		12:20	230	11:7	211, 220	
		12:35	257	11:8	211, 220	
Testament of Simeon						
4:5	450	**1QpHab**		**1QSb**		
		6:1	363	5:25		108
Testament of Solomon		8:11	363			
8:2	467	8:12	363			
18:2	467			**Rabbinic Literature**		
		1QM				
Testament of Zebulun		1:1-16	366	*m. 'Abot*		
8:1	351	3:6	366	1:1		196
8:2	351	3:9	366	6:1		327
9:5	383	10:5	257			
9:6	383	12:8	131	*'Abot de Rabbi Nathan*		
		13:16	366	2.2a		291
Tobit		14:14	113			
6:18	415	14:17	366	*m. Berakot*		
10:9	491	15:1-2	471	6:1		94
		16:3	471			
Wisdom		18:10	471	*m. Kelim*		
1:1	450	18:12	471	1:6-9		195
2:23	494	19:1	131			
5:18	474			*Midrash Tehillim*		
6:18	494	**1QS**		Ps 24:1		291
6:19	494	1:4	365	Ps 68:11		291
7:22-23	245	1:5	365, 369	Ps 106:2		291
9:1-2	332	1:8	157			
9:3	332	1:9	366	*Numbers Rabbah*		
12–15	320	1:10	366	8		207
13:12	476	3	319			
14:12	363	3:13	366	*b. Sabbat*		
18:10-19	320	3:19-21	366	88b		291

b. Sanhedrin
98b   256

b. Yebamot
62b   418

Philo

De Abrahamo
243   466

De Ebrietate
223   350

De Fuga et Inventione
63   353

De Gigantibus
6   160

Hypothetica
7.2   445
7.3   406

Quaest. in Gen.
1.10   314

De Sacrificiis Abelis et Caini
57   333

De Somniis
1.134-35   160
1.141   160

De Specialibus Legibus
1.23-27   363
1.304   333
2.180   333
2.262   444
2.32   445
4.73   353
4.187-88   353

De Virtutibus
50   333
168   353
179   366

Josephus

Against Apion
2.206   445
2.217   445
2.24§199   406

Antiquities
4.264   445
10.1.2   476

Jewish War
2:566   399
2:578   399
5.194   195
5:309   399

EARLY CHRISTIAN

Barnabas
3:6   105
4:3   105
4:8   105
18–20   319
19:5-7   405

Chrysostom
Homily 22
6:9   454

Clement of Alexandria
Stromateis
6.5.41.6   195

1 Clement
1:3   405
21:6-9   405

2 Clement
4   319

Epistle to Diognetus
1   195

Eusebius
Ecclesiastical History
3.25.4-7   41
6.12.3   41

Didache
1-5   319
4:9-11   405

Hermas
Mandates
6.1   319

Ignatius
Letter to the Magnesians
5   319

Letter to Polycarp
4:1–6:2   405

Letter to the Smyrnaeans   105

Irenaeus
1.8.5   4
5.2.3   4
8.1   4
14.3   4
24.4   4

Polycarp
Philippians
4:2–6:1   405

Tertullian
Adversus Marcionem
5.17   4

GRAECO-ROMAN

Aristotle
Ethica Eudemia
3.7.1234a.4-23   361
4.8.1128a.14-15   361

Ethica Nicomachea
4.5.1126A   350

Politica
1.1253b   406
1.1259a   406

Chrysippus
frag. 395   350

Dio Chrysostom
Orations
7.112   343
7.124-25   343

Epictetus
3.24.56   277

Dissertations
1.16.16-17   343
3.26.6-7   343

Eubulus
Athen.
15.7   245

Euripides
1149   245

Herodotus
7.148   491

Livy
History
21.8   480

Plato
Apology
35D   333

Crito
54B   333

Theaetetus
172B   333
172A-B   353
176B   333

Plutarch
Moralia
488c   340

Polybius
1.35.5   322
6.24   472
6.23.2-6   479
9.40.4   322

Pseudo-Phocylides
195-97   418

Quintilian
Institutes
9.2.29-37   486

Seneca
De Ira
1.4   350

Epistulae Morales
47.5   454

Tacitus
Annals
14.42   452

Thucydides
History
2.61   322

Xenophon
Anabasis
4.5.14   475

Cyropaedia
1.3.8   209
7.5.45   209

Oeconomicus
13.9-12   452

Papyri

Papyri Graecae Magicae
I.97-194   160
IV.569   141
IV.960-85   262
IV.2699   160
XII.256   141
XII.284   137
XIII.226   261
CI.39   160